IN
NAPOLEON'S
SHADOW

IN NAPOLEON'S SHADOW

The Memoirs of Louis-Joseph Marchand,
Valet and Friend of the Emperor 1811–1821

including the original notes of
JEAN BOURGUIGNON
Académie Des Beaux Arts
and
HENRY LACHOUQUE

Preface by JEAN TULARD
Member of the Institute of France,
Professor at the Sorbonne

Greenhill
Books

Greenhill Books

In Napoleon's Shadow

First published in the United States in 1998 by
Proctor Jones Publishing Company

First published in Great Britain in 2018 by Greenhill Books
c/o Pen & Sword Books Ltd,
47 Church Street, Barnsley,
South Yorkshire, S70 2AS
www.greenhillbooks.com
contact@greenhillbooks.com

Copyright © Atelier Associates, a California limited partnership, 1998

ISBN: 978-1-78438-289-6

The right of PROCTOR PATTERSON JONES to be identified as the
author of this work has been asserted by them in accordance with the
Copyright, Designs and Patents Act 1988.

A CIP catalogue record for this book is available from the British Library.

Printed and bound by CPI Group (UK) Ltd, Croydon, CR0 4YY

DEDICATION

*This book is dedicated to the establishment
of a better understanding of Napoleon Bonaparte,
Educator,
Statesman, Public Administrator,
Political and Military Leader*

*For their encouragement of my work,
it is further dedicated to:*

*Dr. Donald D. Horward, Director,
The Institute on Napoleon and The French Revolution,
Florida State University*

*Colonel John R. Elting (USA-Retired),
Associate Professor,
Department of Military Art and Engineering,
U. S. Military Academy at West Point*

*and to my esteemed friend,
John Joseph Piel, M.D.*

TABLE OF CONTENTS

Avant Propos

Proctor Jones

After having spent three years putting together *Napoleon: An Intimate Account of the Years of Supremacy 1800-1814*, (ISBN 0-679-41458), I began reading about what happened after 1814. I discovered some truly exciting things, amongst which was the introduction to a young man named Louis-Joseph Marchand who started to work in the entourage of the Emperor in 1811.

Eventually, Marchand became first valet to the Emperor. He kept detailed notes of his time in the presence of Napoleon until the day of the Emperor's death. The Marchand Memoirs, for many years having been kept in private hands, at last in 1952 saw the light of day in published form in French. I was able to secure the first English language rights to this work. We have reproduced it in English exactly as it was published under the direction of Jean Bourguignon of the Académie Des Beaux Arts.

Jean Tulard recognizes this work as the last of the significant Napoleonic manuscripts to be translated into English. A valet's task does not, under circumstances of his employment, sign his labors as worthy of attention. However, the fascinating chronology of the lives of these two men makes what he has to say most interesting, even to the amateur.

Marchand does not try to write history. He writes an engaging reminiscence of experience in the Imperial presence. A gifted man of intelligence, he was without personal or material ambition. Although Napoleon respected Marchand, he, of course, did not know what a magnificent memoir Marchand would produce depicting what happened after 1811—the Russian campaign, the campaigns of Germany and France, Elba, the Hundred Days, culminating in Waterloo and Saint Helena.

It is all laid out in clear and orderly fashion, practically day by day. Rich though it is as a daily record, it also preserves the stories Napoleon recounted of past events.

This work is important to English-speaking people who unfortunately, in the main, know this Emperor only as a warrior. As his story unfolds, we find an administrative genius, a warm personality, a true and inspired civil servant, a gallant lover, a man married to the idea of protecting the garden of his beloved France.

Asked to give in a sentence the greatest of his accomplishments, it can be said that he finished off feudalism in Europe and returned the land to the people. He encouraged all religions and he discouraged religious efforts to interfere with the government. His very being threatened the tottering autocratic thrones of Russia, Prussia, and Austria. His interest in the East threatened the trade lanes of the English. Great leader that he was, he could not fend off the combined force of these governments, and eventually he was overrun.

The remarkable narrative presented in Marchand's memoirs takes the reader from the apex of Napoleon's accomplishments through the miseries of defeat, imprisonment, and death.

Seldom is greatness accompanied to the grave by such a friend. How fortunate for history that Marchand kept these pages of memoirs, written in good and flowing language, filling in many details, correcting the mistakes of others. It is the true story of greatness, an eyewitness record to history and its aftermath. Indeed, Marchand's memoirs are one of the most important historical documents covering the life of this great leader.

Preface

Jean Tulard
Member of the Institute of France
Professor at the Sorbonne

*T*here is no doubt of the authenticity of these *Memoirs*, nor the truth of the facts which Marchand reports. He had nothing to hide, nothing to apologize for. He spoke with sincerity and simplicity of the everyday life of Napoleon. This body of work is the last of the important Napoleonic Memoirs to be translated into English. Marchand has provided precious memories that lead us into an intimacy with this Great Man.

However, one's curiosity is piqued by the previously published *Memoirs* of Constant Wairy, by Lavocat in 1830. That publication was quite successful until scholars began to have reservations about the composition of the work. To what extent had the editors embellished Constant's memories of his experiences? In the end, Constant abandoned Napoleon along with the Mameluke, Roustam, in 1814. For this, Constant was not forgiven.

It was Marchand who was chosen by Grand Marshal of the Palace Bertrand to replace Constant. The young man came from a good family from Eure-et-Loir and accompanied Napoleon to the Isle of Elba. Educated, discreet and devoted, Napoleon lets himself be won over. Marchand is at the Tuileries during the 'Hundred Days'; he accompanies the Emperor at Waterloo, and he embarks on the *Bellerophon* and then the *Northumberland* with him. They find themselves on St. Helena where Marchand exercises meticulous care to assure the comfort of the Emperor. Making every effort to provide a life better than reality, he was with him until the moment of his death.

Of course, he was not with Napoleon during the greatness of the Empire, nor was he the confidant in great Imperial decisions. He became attached to Napoleon at the moment of the Emperor's decline.

But his testimony of events during the Imperial twilight is nothing less than moving.

This is the first translation into English of Marchand's very important text on the epoch of Napoleon. It completes the ensemble of materials brought together by Dr. Proctor Jones to assist in the understanding of the real Napoleon, the intimate Napoleon. In this work, the Emperor speaks freely.

Listen.

ACKNOWLEDGEMENTS

Book Designer, James Stockton and Associates

Production Assistants

Kyle O. Eidahl
Frania Feldstein
Suzanne Goraj
Proctor Jones, Jr.
Edna G. O'Leary
Diana Nichols
Dhyan Raufa
Frederic de Sibert
Toni Thompson
Karen Tucker

Marchand I

Jean Bourguignon

*A*s modest as Marchand's position first was in Napoleon's service and during the painful exile, his devotion to the Emperor remains without par. As the great exile himself said, Marchand's services were "those of a friend."

Louis-Joseph-Narcisse Marchand was born in Paris on March 28, 1791.[1] His mother, born Marie-Marguerite Broquet, had become the first of the King of Rome's three nurses. She had the full trust of the "governess to the children of France," Madame de Montesquiou. She was designated to swaddle the imperial child, feed him, and watch over him at night, sitting by his bed. She was dressed as one of the Empress' chambermaids, those Napoleon himself called the black ladies, because they always wore black silk aprons, whereas he called the "wardrobe girls" white ladies, because they wore white aprons. Among the three wardrobe girls was Henriette Marchand, daughter of the first nurse, and sister of the faithful Marchand of the years of exile.

Thanks to the help of his mother, and especially that of Madame de Montesquiou, Louis Marchand entered the imperial household in 1811 as a domestic servant. We even know that, at the governess' request, he received from the Emperor in 1812 the sum of 4,300 francs, in order to purchase a replacement for military service.

---

[1]Louis Marchand's birth certificate:

"Saint Sulpice parish, Paris.—On March 28, 1791, was baptized Louis-Joseph Narcisse, born today, son of Charles-Joseph Marchand and Marie-Marguerite Broquet, his wife, residing at rue Saint-Placide; the godfather: Nicolas-Louis Marchand, paternal uncle of the child; the godmother: Marguerite-Elisabeth-Narcisse Broquet, wife of Claude Dessayeux, wine merchant; and the father have signed.

"Signed: Marchand, Broquet, Marchand and Aragonnés. Certified copy: Paris, December 23, 1867."

(Archives de la Seine, provided by M. F. de Vaux de Folletier, chief archivist of the Seine.)

The Marchand family comes from good solid French stock. Its homeland, like that of the various branches of its family, is the Beauce, the former Gallic land of the Carnutes, amid the rare and cool valleys crossing the open plateau where in summer the proverbial harvest opulence reigns. A county in Eure-et-Loire, the county of Maintenon, regroups the rural communities where can be found the ancestry of the Emperor's companion in exile: first Hanches, in a bright valley of the Drouette; and, further east, near Gallardon, Ymeray and Montlouet, in the charming Voise valley.

Interesting details: Euphrasie, a granddaughter of Anne-Brigitte Marchand, who was the aunt of the future Count Marchand, had wed Jean-Baptiste Painlevé, grandfather of Paul Painlevé, the great scientist and statesman whose remains rest in the Panthéon. In addition, Mme Paul Painlevé, born Petit de Villeneuve, had an aunt who was, through the Broquets, the grandniece of Louis Marchand's mother.

As soon as he entered Napoleon's service, Louis Marchand took part in the trip to Holland made by the Emperor and Empress. He was then barely twenty. He immediately distinguished himself by his intelligence and devotion. But his true character emerged mainly at Fontainebleau in 1814, at the time of the abdication. Constant, the first valet, and the mameluke Roustam, ran away like cowards before their master's misfortune. Marchand was then chosen by the grand marshal to replace Constant. While his mother accompanied the King of Rome and his governess to Vienna, he followed the Emperor to Elba. Full of zeal, clever, sensitive, and discreet, he soon gained the trust of the Emperor, who never had cause to regret it.

Having returned to France during the Hundred Days, his head was not turned by the sudden reversal of fate. In Paris as in Porto Ferrajo, he remained true to himself. After Waterloo, on the *Bellerophon* as on the *Northumberland*, and during all the painful and difficult times of exile, he showed himself to be as respectful, zealous, active, and attentive as he was at the Tuileries and the Elysée. At a time when misfortune and defections disband so many courtiers, Marchand tried to spare Napoleon as many annoyances and sorrows as he could. He was, in the full meaning of the word, a man of heart.

A continuous witness to the miseries and sufferings of the great man, his first concern was—if not to heal an incurable wound—at least to ease, through distractions and occupations, the prestigious and superhuman intelligence suddenly reduced to idleness, condemned to slowly devour itself. Conversations, reading, and dictation, in Napoleon's own words, were like flowers cast upon the path leading him to the grave. To provoke them, inspire them, even solicit them, were so many ways to draw him out of his melancholy and solitary thoughts, and to shorten the long and deadly hours of his captivity.

Marchand took part in these historical or literary distractions: the *Summary of Julius Caesar's Wars* was entirely written in his hand under Napoleon's dictation, as well as various other fragments published in 1836.

On his deathbed, the Emperor had bestowed on Marchand the title of count, and had named him a trustee of his will and the annexed codicils: he thus gave proof, through this supreme act of will, of the high esteem in which he held the faithful companion of his years of misfortune.

He had advised him and even ordered him to marry, on his return to France, the daughter of a general who had distinguished himself during the imperial wars. This was General Brayer, the very man who had led the Emperor's march on Paris in March 1815, and then brilliantly commanded a guard division.

Marchand complied with the imperial wish. On November 15, 1823, he married Mlle Mathilde Brayer in the church of Notre-Dame de Lorette.

I have before me a few of the letters of congratulation sent to him on this occasion by members of the imperial family, all of which are unpublished.

Here, dated Munich, December 11, 1823, is a letter from Prince Eugène: "I am greatly in favor of this alliance," he wrote, "and wish that it may contribute to your happiness. The princess also asks me to assure you she sincerely shares my feelings in this regard."

King Joseph's wife, Queen Julie, then Countess de Survilliers, wrote from Brussels on November 29, 1823, in this fashion: "I have heard with great pleasure of your marriage, the more so because you have fulfilled the Emperor's wish in marrying the daughter of one of his brave generals. I congratulate you on this, and fondly hope that you shall find happiness in such a union which does honor to your feelings. Please believe I shall always take an interest in one who has shown such touching devotion to him whom we shall always mourn, and never doubt my special esteem." King Joseph himself, a few months later, added his wishes to his wife's; he wrote from the United States on May 31, 1824: "I know Lieutenant General Brayer rather well, and I am charmed that his daughter has become your bride; I have no doubt she will find happiness with you, whose faithfulness and noble sentiments shall henceforth serve as an example to generous souls. Have no doubt that I shall always feel true satisfaction in hearing from you, and in expressing to you my attachment and my esteem."

Princess Pauline Borghèse expressed the same feelings in a letter dated Rome, December 22, 1823. "I shall always learn with pleasure," she says, "all that can be favorable and bring you happiness. I greatly hope that circumstances will allow you to come to Italy, so that I may tell you in person of all the esteem I have for you, and meet your wife." Here is another handwritten letter from the prince of Canino, Lucien Bonaparte, addressed to Count Marchand on December 23, 1823: "Dear Count Marchand, I have received your letter dated November 18, and learned of your marriage with all the interest I shall never cease having for you. Please convey to Countess Marchand all my wishes for her happiness. If anyone should be happy on this earth, you deserve it. Please believe in the sentiments you have earned for life, from myself, my wife, and my children."

Finally, a little later, comes a letter from Cardinal Fesch, dated Rome, January 10, 1824: "I have received," he wrote, "news of your marriage to the daughter of Lieutenant General Brayer, by which you have fulfilled the Emperor's last wish. This double interest has brought me great satisfaction. Please believe that I shall never cease to pray God, who alone can bring happiness, and who in blessing your union can make it perfectly happy.

"The greater part of our family, now in Rome, was delighted to hear the good news, and we are all convinced you shall make a happy couple. We further hope that happier times will allow you to come and see us, so that we may express to you the sentiment of attachment we feel for you, and with which I remain affectionately yours."

Felix Bacciochi, Princess Elisa's husband, expressed himself in similar terms in his letter dated December 28, 1823: "Count Marchand, I can only applaud this choice, which both fulfills the Emperor's wish and also promises you the happiness you deserve for so many reasons." We find the same feelings in letters from King Jérôme, and from Louis, who signs as Duke of Saint-Leu.

I wanted to reproduce the preceding quotations as they are taken from autograph and unpublished letters, faithfully kept by Marchand, which—through their dates and points of origin—remind us of the dispersion of the Bonapartes following the fall of the Empire. The feelings expressed in them are unanimous, without planned agreement. And one can only notice everywhere in that correspondence the outpouring of sympathy and consideration Marchand enjoyed from the imperial family. He was without hesitation given the title of count that Napoleon had bestowed on him in a theoretical and moral fashion, and that Napoleon III would later confirm through official documents. No doubt can remain in this regard, and we can only cite this passage from an unpublished letter from Louis Bonaparte, former king of Holland, then Duke of Saint-Leu, who wrote Marchand from Rome on August 2, 1823: "I seize this occasion to express my feelings of esteem and the gratitude of each member of my family for the faithful services you have rendered, with as much courage as perseverance, to its head and sovereign. You are no longer a stranger to any of us; we only can, and must, consider you a worthy and old friend. The noble reward bestowed upon you by the Emperor is worthy of him and of your feelings, and can only be approved and considered gratifying by all those with a sensitive and French heart."

From the marriage of Louis Marchand and Mathilde Brayer was born a daughter, Malvina, who married M. Desmazières, an auditor in the council of State. Their son, M. Desmazières, was Marchand's last heir; he died without issue.

Prior to leaving Saint Helena, on May 27, 1821—eighteen days after the funeral—Marchand had come, alone, to accomplish a last pilgrimage to the primitive valley, scattered with myrtle and wild roses, since named Valley of the Geraniums, and which sheltered under a nameless slab the grave of the great exile. Filled with sorrow, he knelt. He kissed for the last time the stone covering the man he had loved and served so well. He picked a small flower which he placed in his notebook. Then, casting a last look—an emotional and deep look he wished to penetrate all the way to the Emperor—he got back on his horse and returned to town. That same evening, with the other exiles, he sailed on the *Camel* that was to return them to Europe.

It was natural that such a man, so devoted to the Emperor, motivated by such high feelings, should accompany Napoleon's casket, returned to France at last in 1840, to its final burial place, the Invalides. Marchand was placed along with Bertrand in the foremost rank of the expedition which, under the command of the prince of Joinville, returned the imperial ashes to France. But Marchand did not make the journey on the *Belle-Poule*; he was placed aboard the *Favorite* which was part of the same naval squadron division.

After the return of the ashes, as during the long years preceding it, Marchand led a discreet and quiet life in Paris, welcomed with open arms by all who kept the imperial cult.

Among those close to the Marchand couple we must mention Valérie Masuyer, whose unusual *Memoirs* I have published.[2]

Goddaughter of Empress Joséphine, she had been Queen Hortense's last lady-in-waiting, shared her years of exile, and had

---

[2]*Mémoires, de Valérie Masuyer, dame d'honneur de la reine Hortense.* Introduction and notes by Jean Bourguignon (Paris: Plon, 1937).

shown her the most faithful and kind attachment. She was a charming lady, in heart and spirit. A single incident suffices to depict her. As she was about to leave the castle of Arenenberg after the queen's death, Prince Louis, the future Napoleon III, asked what her plans were. With some emotion in her voice, she replied: "To remember!" She had retired to Paris and lived with her friend Joséphine de Forget,[3] grand-niece of Empress Joséphine, best known as the "Consuelo" painted by Eugène Delacroix. On December 15, 1840, Valérie watched the passage of Napoleon's funeral cortege from a window on avenue des Champs-Elysées. The next day, December 16, she wrote to her aunt, Countess d'Esdouhard, a letter I published in my book *The Return of the Ashes*; the original text is in my possession, and gives a vivid impression of the unforgettable ceremony. She ends by adding: "That fine day was for me followed by a fine evening: M. Marchand came for dinner, along with Father Coquereau, who pleases me for he is prouder to have brought back the Emperor's ashes than if he had received a cardinal's hat! We remained all four together, rue du Colisée, as if in a sanctuary." And she then renders Marchand a memorable homage: "We remembered," she said, "my uncle's last words: 'My children, continue to faithfully and quietly serve the Bonapartes, for the sole satisfaction of having done so.'

"Is not M. Marchand himself a living example of this? This excellent man wanted to give me new and precious mementos of the Emperor, among them some of his hair, cut by Marchand after his death. I shall ask Joséphine de Forget, on her next visit to Ham,[4] to tell the prince on my behalf all the good deserved by this admirable man, whose intentional modesty is such that it exasperates me."

---

[3] Joséphine de Forget, daughter of Count de Lavalette (1769-1830), director of the postal system and councillor of State under the Empire, who was sent to prison for being faithful to Napoleon, and whose famous escape was aided by his wife, "a heroine of conjugal love," as she was called. She was born Emilie de Beauharnais, niece of Empress Joséphine's first husband. It was Bonaparte who decided she should marry Lavalette, his ADC, in 1799.

[4] Ham, where the future Napoleon III was imprisoned after the Boulogne affair.

It appears, according to this letter, that Marchand was then not fully understood by Louis-Napoleon and his entourage. We indeed can see Valérie Masuyer herself revert to the topic, in another letter she sends to the prince on January 8, 1841,[5] from which we extract this passage:

" 'To devote myself to the cause of those the Emperor left us is the only reward I seek,' M. Marchand said to me a few days ago, on his return from Saint Helena. And my heart repeats this to you, along with his. Allow me to say a few words to you regarding this admirable man. Is it true that people have attempted to belittle him in your eyes? I don't know this, nor do I wish to, but I feel it is my duty toward you—as toward this friend who is so rightly dear to us, my family and myself—to remind you of these words of your beloved mother: 'The Marchands and the Broquets must be listed in the golden book of the Emperor's memory.' I myself shall add the name of the Brayers,[6] having witnessed, as did my father, their feelings of disinterested faithfulness. I can hear you from here, my dear prince, cry out that Valérie is always the one to sound a trumpet. This does not displease me. I wish I could have had the honor of having this said to me by your uncle as by yourself! With this great evocation of memory I shall leave you, my dear prince; after assuring you once more of the perennial faithfulness of the Masuyers and the Esdouhards, I ask your permission to kiss you, as always in memory of my queen."

Valérie Masuyer's intervention was not a fruitless one. Prejudice against Marchand disappeared. Napoleon I's executor was regularly received at the Tuileries under the second Empire. Napoleon III insisted on confirming Marchand's title of count. He also made him an officer of the Legion of Honor. I made a point of exhibiting at Malmaison, in a small room on the second floor dedicated to Marchand, the documents making these nominations official.

---

[5]This is a letter from Valérie Masuyer that I have already made public in my book on the *Retour des cendres, 1840*, (Paris: Plon, 1941).

[6]Countess Marchand's parents.

Additionally, it is appropriate to recall it was Marchand who submitted to Napoleon III Article 32 of the instructions dictated to him by Napoleon I. This article stated: "Should a reversal of fortune restore my son to the throne, it is the duty of my executors to draw his attention to all that I owe my old officers and soldiers, and my faithful servants." In fact, the beneficiaries of the will had not received the full amount of their bequests. The beneficiaries of the codicils had received nothing. Napoleon III received this request favorably, and on May 5, 1855, an imperial decree called for the execution of Napoleon I's last wishes.

At the fall of the second Empire, Marchand remained faithful to Napoleon III, as he had been to his uncle. I find proof of this in Napoleon III's unpublished letter to Marchand, dated Campden Place, Chislehurst, September 10, 1872:

"My dear Count Marchand, I am deeply touched by the affectionate and devoted words you wrote to me on the occasion of August 15. Whenever I receive a testimony of your unalterable affection, I feel closer to the glorious period you witnessed, and of which you are the living reminder. Please believe, my dear Count Marchand, in my feelings of friendship."

Marchand, who had witnessed the two great imperial catastrophes, Waterloo and Sedan, died in Trouville on June 19, 1876, surrounded by those dear to him, in the house he owned, rue de la Cavée, where he spent the summer. He was 85 years old. His funeral took place in Paris, where he had his regular domicile, 5 place du Palais-Bourbon. The ceremony was a very simple one, but held amidst a great number of faithful friends. Valérie Masuyer, who had retired after Napoleon III's death to her Jura estate, at the Etoile, insisted on attending the religious ceremony in spite of her age. With emotion, she placed violets on the newly dug grave.

Marchand's life, apart from what is revealed through his Memoirs, does not lend itself to lengthy discussion. But his appealing figure shall survive as a magnificent example of greatness in the realm of faithfulness, righteousness, and devotion.

Memoirs of Marchand II

*I*n his *Recollections of Half a Century*, in the days of Louis-Philippe and Napoleon III, from 1830 to 1870, Maxime du Camp alludes to Marchand's *Memoirs*. "The valet Marchand, who remained with the Emperor until his death, and who, according to custom, slept across his door, has written a commemorative journal wherein the facts are accurately related. I believe, without being able to prove it, that this journal was purchased and destroyed by Napoleon III. This is regrettable from the standpoint of historical truth, which must take precedence over any consideration of propriety or self-interest.

"These memoirs," adds Maxime du Camp, "would have been a revelation."

Such a revelation is fortunately no longer impossible today, and the present work is proof of this.

Marchand's memoirs were neither purchased by Napoleon III nor destroyed on his orders. They were entrusted to me by his grandson, M. Desmazières-Marchand, and I am proud to ensure their publication.

Marchand's memoirs—written in his own hand, in a fine and compact handwriting—are composed of four files, each enclosed in a large envelope, loose but carefully numbered sheets.

The first envelope bears the title: The Island of Elba—Return to France. But the story in fact starts with the trip to Holland, when Marchand entered the service of the Emperor, in 1811. It continues with the trip to Dresden, the Russian campaign, the Malet conspiracy, and the 1813 Saxony campaign. This constitutes a first chapter. The second chapter deals with the 1814 Campaign of France, the abdication and the Fontainebleau treaty, the Emperor's departure for the island of Elba, and Marchand's own trip to Paris and Rambouillet, before joining Napoleon in Porto Ferrajo. Napoleon's arrival on the island of Elba and his settling there form a third chapter, entitled:

Organization of the Emperor's household. Details of his public and private life. His service. His health. We now come to Chapter Four, with the following title: The Emperor's construction projects in Porto Ferrajo. The Marciana hermitage. Purchase of San Martino. Death of Empress Joséphine. Arrival of Madame Mère, of Madame Walewska, her sister, brother, and son, of Princess Pauline. The Elba court. Tuna fishing.

Chapter Five shows the general dissatisfaction in France and the defense measures. Then he notes the incident of the little goatherd, the beaching of the *Inconstant*, the threats of confinement on Saint Helena or Saint Lucia, the news from Vienna provided by Cipriani, New Year's Day 1815, and the harassment inflicted on the entourage of the young King of Rome. It ends with retrospective details on Napoleon's divorce from Empress Joséphine.

Chapter Six brings news from France, the Emperor's resolve to leave the island of Elba, preparations for the expedition, M. Colonna's mission to the king of Naples, then the embarkation and departure. Chapter Seven takes us from the crossing and the landing at Golfe Juan to the march on Grenoble and the occupation of that city, after the first encounter with the royal troops.

Finally, a last chapter—Chapter Eight—relates the triumphal march on Lyon, Mâcon, Chalon, Autun, Auxerre, and Fontainebleau, up to Napoleon's entrance into Paris amid an enthusiastic crowd. It ends with Marchand's comments and a conclusion to the first part. This first part, thus made up of eight chapters, comprises 137 pages.

The second envelope, entitled The Hundred Days, contains 82 pages. Marchand had thought of dividing it into chapters. But he only executed the first one, with the following subtitles: My position at the Tuileries. The Emperor's conversation with the prince arch-chancellor and the Duke of Bassano. Creation of the ministry. The March 22 parade. The Elban battalion.

Starting with March 25, Marchand abandons the division into chapters, and in one single stretch relates the events he witnessed up to Napoleon's surrender to the British in July 1815.

Two large parchment envelopes hold the Saint Helena memoirs: one contains 158 pages, the other 278. Altogether there are four large envelopes.

The present volume utilizes only the contents of the first two envelopes. We shall speak again of the other two, relating to Saint Helena, in the introduction to the second volume.

Such a publication was awaited for a long time. Marchand himself did not seem opposed to it. As early as 1835, he published in Strasbourg the manuscript of *Caesar's Wars*, which he had written entirely in Saint Helena under the Emperor's dictation, and followed it with various unpublished fragments, also dictated by Napoleon: *Notes on Virgil's second book of the Aeneid. Comments on Voltaire's Mohammed tragedy. Note on suicide. Second codicil.* It is a small book, now very rare. I have in front of me the copy given by Marchand himself to Valérie Masuyer. In the preface, he underscores the recounting of Napoleon's last moments, such as they remained engraved in his memory, and as he found them in his notes.

He first had thought of appending to this book his recollections of the island of Elba, the Hundred Days, and Saint Helena. Then he changed his mind, judging that the dictation covering the *Commentaries on Caesar* should be published free of any context. In any event, he did not hesitate to add: "My recollections will come from the memory of the heart, which shall never fail. May the publicity I intend to give them someday reveal the Emperor such as I knew him: great through his genius, his talent and his glory upon the throne; great through his courage and resignation in adversity."

The acknowledgment is definite. At that moment, Marchand is clearly considering the publication of his memoirs. But he seems to later have restricted his ambition, since he himself relates, in the preamble we shall read later on, that he collected his memories for his daughter, his dear Malvina, and for those who loved the Emperor.

That is the interpretation which, since Marchand's death, his family seems to have adopted, especially his grandson, who had befriended me following the exhibition I organized at Malmaison in 1921 to commemorate the centennial of Napoleon's death. M.

Desmazières-Marchand, when he handed me his grandfather's manuscripts, asked me to extract from them a book entitled: "Napoleon, Based on Marchand's Memoirs". I showed him several times the inconvenience of such a method: there was a risk of plagiarizing the original work, and of ending by distorting the very thinking of the author of the memoirs.

Finally, during one of his last visits to Malmaison, he left me free to seek the publication mode best suited to the task. Bringing Marchand's manuscript to light without changing a single word thus became mandatory. That is the solution I have adopted, while accompanying the original text with notes and comments.

I have inserted these comments in places where Marchand's story seemed to me to need some clarification. I also had to resign myself to limiting my notes to satisfy the publisher's wishes, as he did not wish to overload the present book.

The great historian of the Napoleonic family, M. Frédéric Masson, had obtained from M. Desmazières permission to borrow Marchand's manuscript for a few days, promising he would only take a few notes. When M. Desmazières learned the promise had not been respected, and that a copy—though incomplete—had been made, he took back his manuscript, and his relations with M. Frédéric Masson were affected by this. I have these details from M. Desmazières himself.

The copy in question remains in the papers Frédéric Masson bequeathed to the Thiers Library. But the *Memoirs* remained unpublished.

They constitute a solid contribution to Napoleonic documentation. No doubt they bring no sensational revelations, and reiterate facts already known through other memoirs. But they contain the truth: they confirm accurate facts, and sometimes rectify many errors. Not only do they record Marchand's personal observations, but they reflect his deep feelings, and the very emotion that so many circumstances—sometimes tragic—made him experience. In any event, the author always expresses himself with moderation, in a clear style, devoid of any literary embellishments. His constant aim remains to refute all lies, or to rectify the slightest inaccuracies, through the simple telling of events.

The interest of these *Memoirs* is undeniable. They abound in details that might be unsuccessfully sought elsewhere. It is the Emperor's daily life that is spread in front of us, helping us to understand all the grandeur of soul of the man of genius who had fallen from so high into an existence as unjust as it was miserable. M. Ernest d'Hauterive, the author of the magnificent article in the *Revue de Paris*[7] on "Marchand and his Memoirs," has often expressed to me, through letters he wrote or through friends we had in common, his wish to see published the memoirs of Napoleon's most faithful companion in exile. "It would be," he said, "a fine page written to the glory of the Emperor."

Circumstances beyond my control prevented me from realizing such a wish sooner. I have great satisfaction in doing so today, and I am sure this publication shall soon be welcomed with thanks, not only by the erudite and historians, but by the public at large, always fascinated by the prestigious imperial legend.

Finally, as underscored by M. Ernest d'Hauterive, is it not to honor Marchand himself to disseminate the writings he made "not to glorify myself, but to leave a testimony to what I saw, and through this to serve my master beyond the grave"?

Jean Bourguignon.

---

[7]*Revue de Paris*, (December 15, 1939).

Introduction

*I*n the early evening of March 19,[8] 1821, seventeen[9] days before his death, the Emperor informed me very kindly of the choice he deigned to make of me as one of the executors of his will, along with some of his last wishes, and the arrangements he was making on my behalf; he then said to me: "You shall marry, and have children; they shall inquire about me, pursue you with questions, and you will be able to tell them you saw me die of misery on the rock of Saint Helena, STRUCK DOWN, BUT STILL STANDING."

It is for you, my dear Malvina, and for those who loved the Emperor, that I have collected my memoirs: they contain the truth. They shall show Napoleon in Saint Helena, just as great in adversity as on his throne, when he commanded over Europe, still equal to himself; STRUCK DOWN, BUT STILL STANDING.

My memoirs reproduce my observations, my feelings, and the emotions that events spurred within me. Much has been written about the Emperor on the island of Elba, during the Hundred Days, and his captivity in Saint Helena. All that has been printed is not always accurate. I am indebted to the Emperor's memory, not to his dignity, certainly little compromised by maneuvers due to cupidity or partisan spirit; I am indebted for his kindness toward me and for the honor he has done me in naming me one of the executors of his will, so that I may restore the truth in the facts I am aware of. I shall do so with moderation, often even without referring to the alterations it has suffered, and through the simple telling of events.

Although I have shared the enthusiasm that Napoleon inspired, I have not ceased to be truthful. During the ten years I spent in his personal service, six were spent in a more special way, during his captivity in Saint Helena and his stay in Elba. I was able to admire

---

[8] April 19—Ed.
[9] Sixteen—Ed.

such genius, talent, and glory on the throne; such courage, resignation and grandeur in adversity; and always and everywhere such sensitivity and kindness for his people! I have but one fear, and shall have but one regret: that my pen might fail my heart.[10]

---

[10]A facsimile of this introduction, which Marchand had placed at the beginning of his *Memoirs*, is reproduced here.

His signature, also reproduced here, which appears on the last page of his manuscript, is preceded by a date: October 18, 1842, the date the final draft was completed. He specifies himself that "his memoirs had been written for a long time." It is that draft, written in his own hand and signed by him, that we have used in its entirety for the present publication.

J.B.

PART ONE

Marchand's Beginnings in the Service of the Emperor

CHAPTER ONE

Entry into the Emperor's service — Trips to Dresden and Holland —
Campaign of Russia and Malet conspiracy —
1813 campaign in Saxony

In 1811, twelve young men were chosen among the families in the Emperor's personal service to serve as ushers in his apartments. My mother, attached to the household of the King of Rome as first nurse to the prince, requested this favor for me from the grand chamberlain, the Count de Montesquiou,[11] and it was granted.

The Emperor was then happy, at the peak of his glory. He had just had a son[12] whose birth fulfilled all his ambitions; he saw before him the establishment of his lineage while he was still young. He had the vision and the hope of placing his son's throne out of reach of the dangers which threatened his power daily.

The court was brilliant, with festivities, balls, shows, small trips, and hunts rapidly following each other. The former nobility sought the honor of attending the court, of being admitted to the Emperor's household, and serving the state in administration or the army. It was welcomed and obtained what was within the Emperor's power to grant it: honors and positions. The new nobility did not see this without some jealousy, but it knew the Emperor in the army, and there, only merit was rewarded. It was to be under the battle flags that duty and honor, valor and glory, led to a fusion of the old and the new

---

[11]Count Pierre de Montesquiou-Fezensac (1764-1834) was elected a deputy to the imperial legislative body, and succeeded Fontanes to the presidency of that assembly. In 1810, he replaced Talleyrand as the Emperor's grand chamberlain. That same year, his wife, granddaughter of the Marquis Le Tellier de Courtanvaux, himself a descendant of Louvois, was named governess to the Children of France. Maman Quiou accompanied the King of Rome to Vienna in 1814.

[12]The King of Rome was born in Paris on March 20, 1811.

nobility, the fusion of all parties, the Emperor's primary goal in his plans of glory and prosperity for France. A genius as active as he was powerful, the Emperor for his time had arrived, and was even ahead of it: he promptly replaced anarchy with order, by undoing the disasters of the Revolution.

King Louis, against the Emperor's wishes, but in the interest of his people whose suffering he knew, had just abdicated as King of Holland.[13] The Emperor decided to make the trip. Some time after that, the court went to Compiègne, and Their Majesties left that residence for the kingdom the Emperor had just annexed to France.

Since the Emperor was visiting the country, he arranged to meet the Empress in Antwerp. The princess went, along with her reti-

---

[13]Since his accession to the throne of Holland, King Louis' relations with Napoleon were more and more sour. The Emperor's correspondence is filled with criticisms of the King of Holland, regarding politics and his relationship with France. The sovereign of Holland was caught between his royal duty and his standing as a French prince. The growing tension between the two brothers had led to a decree, dated Rambouillet, July 9, 1810, whose first article stated: "Holland is annexed to the Empire." A few days before, in order to avoid such a solution, Louis had tried to abdicate in favor of his son "in the interest of his people, whose sufferings he knew." But Napoleon had opposed this. As a result, in opposition to the Emperor, in Holland, in Germany, and even elsewhere, his brother acquired the image of an unfortunate monarch, full of loyalty, justice and kindness. He became "the good King Louis."

In any event, following the annexation of the kingdom of Holland to France, one understands the need Napoleon felt to undertake the trip, lasting from September 19 to November 11, 1811. It is the first trip in which the young Marchand, aged only 20 at the time, took part. The previous year, similar concerns had already led Napoleon into the same regions. In April to June 1810, he had traveled throughout northern France, the Brabant province, and even extended his trip out to the Zeeland islands. Marie-Louise, whom he had just wed (April 1), had accompanied him.

nue, to the Laeken castle,[14] leaving the King of Rome in the care of Countess de Montesquiou. When she arrived in Laeken, she made several excursions in the vicinity, visiting manufacturing facilities and the Brussels theater, and purchasing a considerable amount of lace, which the Emperor had suggested, in order to bring new business to those factories that were encountering bad times. Everywhere she went, she was greatly welcome.[15]

In the meantime, the Emperor was visiting the entire northern coast from Boulogne to Flessingue, where he had ordered some construction work. While on board the *Charlemagne*, he was detained there for three days, without being able to go ashore because of violent

---

[14]The Laeken castle, in the Brussels suburbs, is the current summer residence of the Belgian royal family. Built in 1784, it was bought in the Year XII by the First Consul, who paid 518,853 francs for it. Bonaparte immediately undertook major repairs there, enlarged the grounds, put in gardens, and the following year purchased a million francs' worth of furniture, porcelain, and books. Under the Empire, Laeken became an imperial residence, with a governor, General Suchet. Empress Marie-Louise made two short stays there, in 1810 and 1811.

The following year, it was this castle of Laeken that Napoleon, through a decree, offered the former Empress Joséphine, in exchange for the palace of the Elysée he had given her at the time of the divorce (October 16, 1809). Joséphine accepted the exchange, but never came to Laeken, even to take possession.

The castle was destroyed by fire in 1890, and the greater portion of the artistic treasures, furniture, tapestries, and the library established by Napoleon were destroyed. The castle has since been rebuilt.

[15]The Emperor had left Compiègne alone, on September 19, at 3 a.m. Early on the 22nd, Marie-Louise left in turn for Brussels, where she arrived on the 23rd during the night. At the theater, she won over the public. When petals from her bouquet of tulips fell to the floor, people fought over them. She took pleasure in visiting the shops. She thus complied with the Emperor's recommendations. During this week-long separation, the Emperor wrote to Marie-Louise every day. On September 25, while he was on board the *Charlemagne*, he advised the Empress that he was writing to Estève, the crown treasurer, to send her 30,000 francs for her private purse. He added: "You may order or purchase 100,000 francs' worth of lace in Brussels." Marie-Louise complied. She did indeed purchase 144,035 francs' worth of lace, of which she distributed a great portion to the ladies of her court. Mme de Montebello received a needlepoint dress worth 5,000 francs, and other works worth nearly 4,000 francs.

winds; some persons in his retinue, who had gone on board small ships, met with great danger.[16]

The Empress left Laeken to join the Emperor in Antwerp; Their Majesties remained in that city a few days, visiting public establishments and attending festivities given in their honor, and left Antwerp after witnessing in a shipyard the launching of a vessel into the Escaut.[17]

The Emperor left town, letting the Empress proceed to Gorcum, where he rejoined her.[18] The various armed forces under the command of Marshal Oudinot were under arms, in spite of heavy rain;

---

[16]During those weeks, the Emperor's schedule, though quite busy, varied little: he inspected fortifications, naval shipyards, and coastal defenses, and passed troops in review, received officials, etc. After visiting Montreuil-sur-Mer, he slept in Boulogne. Via Calais, Dunkirk and Furnes, he reached Ostend on September 23.

That day, along with Caulaincourt and General Mouton, he went by small boat from Zwyn across the former North Sea body along the northern Flanders coastline. He slept in Breskens, the small port at the Escaut estuary. He then visited forts on the island of Cadzand (today part of the continent), stopped in Hulst, and at 1 p.m. passed in review the fleet anchored off Vlissingen. Napoleon went on board the *Charlemagne*, and was forced by the high seas to stay on board until the 27th, when he landed in Vlissingen. On the 28th, he visited Walcheren island, occupied, then evacuated by the British in 1809. He stopped in Middelburg, the present capital of the Zeeland province, and at city hall, the "stadhuis." He visited Veere, an important port in 1811, and on the 29th, departed Vlissingen. He sailed up the Escaut on board a yacht, stopped in Tarneuse, then Bath. On the 30th, early in the morning, he landed in Antwerp, and spent the morning granting audiences and conducting inspections. At 4 p.m. Marie-Louise arrived from Brussels.

[17]They stayed in Antwerp from September 30 to October 4. The sovereigns stayed at the residence of the mayor, M. Cornelissen. For a full three days, the couple did not part; they visited shipyards and vessels under construction, and traveled the Escaut on a boat. They heard a Te Deum in the church of Notre-Dame in Antwerp.

[18]On October 4, a new separation: At 2 a.m., the Emperor left on an inspection trip along the coast. He visited in turn Rosendaal and Willemstad, where he lingered over the fortifications with Berthier, Caulaincourt, and Decrès, the navy minister. He went by boat to the island of Goree, spent the night on board his yacht, went up to Dordrecht, on the Meuse, and arrived in Gorcum on the 5th.

Meanwhile, Marie-Louise left Antwerp to spend the night in Breda, and joined Napoleon for dinner in Gorcum. Now called Gorinchem, on the Meuse, it is connected by canals to the Lek and to Amsterdam. In Napoleon's days, it was still an important fortified town called "the key to Holland."

the Emperor reviewed them. When he returned, although wet, he granted audience to the town officials. The governor of the kingdom, arch-treasurer Lebrun,[19] Duke of Plaisance, had come to town to greet Their Majesties.

From Gorcum, the Emperor and Empress proceeded to Amsterdam, via Workum.[20]

Lebrun. Third Consul of the French Republic.

---

[19]Charles François Lebrun (1739-1824), member of the council of Elders, was named Third Consul after the 18 Brumaire, in charge of organizing finances. Under the Empire, he became arch-treasurer, prince, Duke of Plaisance. After Louis' abdication in 1810, Lebrun was sent by Napoleon to Holland with the title "the Emperor's lieutenant general." Thanks to his activity and hard work, he managed in 15 months to organize all branches of public service. Napoleon kept him in the Netherlands as governor general. In this function, he was present when the Emperor came in October 1811. His mission was quite successful, and he showed such deep interest in the Dutch people that they were quite thankful to him and called him the good Stathouder.

His son, General Anne-Charles Lebrun, ADC to the Emperor, was put in charge in 1809 of organizing the defense of the stronghold and forts of Antwerp, and supplying the strongholds of Breda, Berg-op-Zoom, and the islands of Cadzand and Walcheren. Two years later he was named governor of Antwerp.

They made a solemn entry into Amsterdam.[21] The Empress rode in a multipaned carriage, with an honor guard around her. The Emperor was on horseback, surrounded by a brilliant general staff, and was deliriously cheered by the entire population which had turned out to see him. The notables of the city, tradesmen and others, were surprised to see the Emperor speaking to everyone in his own terms, appearing to be perfectly aware of their interests, concerned with their needs, and not at all foreign to any of the details he knew would please them.[22]

---

[20]There seems to be some confusion in Marchand's mind regarding this town. Workum is much farther north and was not part of the itinerary followed by Napoleon while going from Gorcum to Amsterdam.

We know his exact itinerary. Having arrived in Gorcum on October 5, Napoleon and Marie-Louise left on Sunday the 6, after mass. Before 6 a.m. the Emperor had already inspected two detachments from Oudinot's army corps. But it was in Utrecht, which Marchand does not mention, that the Emperor was to meet and inspect Oudinot's army corps. The carriage proceeded via Leerdam and reached Vreeswyk, where Their Imperial Majesties went by boat, reaching Utrecht at 3 p.m. on October 6. They spent the rest of the day visiting the Zeist camp, then Amersfoort. Back in Utrecht, they remained there until October 9.

Utrecht is an important city, and because of its strategic and geographic situation, it was the seat of General Oudinot's command.

Nicolas-Charles Oudinot (1767-1847), Duke of Reggio, marshal of France since 1809, whom Napoleon called the Bayard of the Army, had since 1810 first commanded the army of the North, then the army of Brabant, and finally the observation corps in Holland. He remained at the head of the Utrecht camp from July to October 1811. Having succeeded in reconciling the rigorous orders he had received with the consideration owed the Dutch, he earned the gratitude of the latter, who offered him a sword of honor.

Napoleon spent October 8 and 9 with Oudinot's army corps. Along with the Empress he attended important maneuvers involving the entire infantry, artillery, and the four cuirassier regiments making up the Utrecht camp. After these maneuvers, the two sovereigns visited the Moravian Brothers facility in Zeist.

[21]Napoleon and Marie-Louise left Utrecht on October 9, arriving in Amsterdam at 3 p.m. The cortege Marchand mentions followed the Kalverstraat, the major business street in the city. The sovereigns stayed in the royal palace that served as city hall until 1808, when Louis Bonaparte converted it into a royal residence.

[22]See *Voyage to Holland in the Summer of 1806*, by Sir John Carr, a British poet and traveler (1772-1832). A splendid copy of that book was part of Napoleon's private library.

During the entire time the Emperor and Empress remained in Amsterdam, there were nothing but parties and excursions. In the absence of the Emperor, who had gone to Texel,[23] the Empress went to visit the village of Broek,[24] whose streets form a kind of mosaic upon which carriages could not ride. An exception was made for her Majesty, who was taken to the mayor's house; she was shown the door, which was only opened for christenings, weddings, or deaths. The Emperor also went to Saardam,[25] to visit the cabin where Peter the Great lived while he was studying shipbuilding.

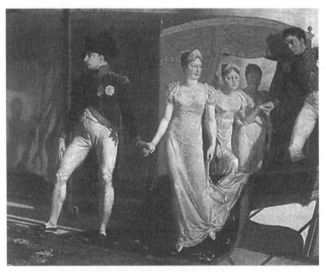

The Emperor and Empress arrive in Holland.

---

[23]Texel (Tessel), a Dutch island at the Zuydersee entrance, two miles from the continental tip of the Helder.

[24]While the Emperor left for Tessel, Marie-Louise visited Broek, six miles from Amsterdam. The streets are paved with colored bricks laid on edge, and arranged to form all kinds of designs. This is what leads Marchand to say the streets are covered with mosaic.

[25]Saardam (Zaandam), a small town in the northwest suburbs of Amsterdam, active in shipbuilding.
    Peter the Great did indeed live there, under the name of Mikhailov, as a carpenter, in 1696, while studying shipbuilding. His cabin can still be seen today.

During this trip, the Emperor and Empress were one day on a yacht; he went up to the helmsman, questioned him, and asked if the boat belonged to him. "Not at all," he replied; "if it were mine, I would consider myself very fortunate."

"Well, I am giving it to you," the Emperor said to him. The man responded with an incredulous smile, not understanding that the Emperor could give him something not belonging to him, and thus expressed no thanks to him for this. But when grand marshal Duroc summoned him that evening, and handed him the title to the boat and the receipt from its owner, "the man's joy," Duroc said to me, "was delirious, and that much more so because he had believed I was making fun of him." The Emperor said he thought the boat had easily cost him 6,000 francs. It was making a man's fortune and happiness quite inexpensively.

The Emperor did many similar things, which, he used to say, a sovereign could never do enough of. The people among whom they are done remain more attached to you; they trust that when misfortune strikes, they shall also be rescued in a providential manner.

The voyage was a brilliant one, and French actors came there to put on performances.[26] The people in that city missed King Louis, but this did not prevent them from showing their enthusiasm wherever the Emperor appeared. From Amsterdam, Their Majesties proceeded to The Hague, via Haarlem, and visited the port and the settlements. During a new excursion of the Emperor's,[27] the Empress went to the Loo castle,[28] where the Emperor joined her. Their Majesties then went

---

[26]Indeed, on October 12, returning from the trip to Saardam, the Emperor and Empress attended that evening a performance of Racine's *Iphigénie en Aulide*. Another play was performed on October 23.

[27]Napoleon had left the Empress to go to the stronghold of Zwolle, in Over-Yssel province, to inspect the troops at the Gröningen camp. He rejoined the Empress at the Loo castle.

[28]Summer residence of the Dutch royal family, in the Gueldre province, 15 miles from Arnhem.

to Nimègue and Dusseldorf, and crossed the Rhine in Cologne, where feasts were given in their honor. All the city guilds, carrying banners with the insignia of their professions, paraded below the Empress' windows, to cries of Long live the Emperor, long live Empress Marie-Louise! All the streets were festooned, decorated with tapestries, greenery, and strings of flowers. After leaving Cologne,[29] they proceeded to Dinant. During the night so violent a wind had risen that the pontoon bridge had been carried away. The Emperor wanted to cross, but the local boatmen thought the river too swollen for anyone to attempt a crossing for two or three days. The Emperor knew there were some British sailors garrisoned in the city, and he ordered that the cleverest and strongest of them be brought out. The water was rising constantly, and the current was swift and dangerous. The Emperor asked the sailors if they could join together enough boats to allow his entire convoy to cross the Meuse. They replied it was possible, but risky. His Majesty told them to begin at once. The weather was cold: on the Emperor's orders, hot wine was made plentiful. In a few hours they built a raft, upon which the Emperor, the Empress, and the retinue first went across. Before the sun was up, the entire convoy had gone across. The Emperor had each man given a full set of clothes, a bonus, and his freedom, with arrangements for them to go to England. There were forty of them. On November 11, Their Majesties arrived in Saint-Cloud, where they rejoined the King of Rome.

---

[29]Napoleon and Marie-Louise left Cologne on November 8. They stopped in Liège, and had headed for Givet, via Namur. They were halted on November 9 by the overflowing of the river Meuse. Marchand seems to place this halt in Dinant, but it occurred in Givet. The details given by Marchand appear so accurate that they are quoted in Givet by local tradition.

From Givet, via Mézières and Reims, the Emperor and Empress returned to Compiègne, where they arrived on November 11. They left the same day for Saint-Cloud.

France and Russia were at odds, the cause being the military occupation of the Duchy of Oldenburg[30] by the Prince of Eckmühl (Davout), on orders from the Emperor. No matter how justified such an occupation was because of the enormous amount of British products being channeled through that country, no matter how much damage the continental blockade established by the Emperor and recognized by Russia suffered because of this, the Emperor considered the invasion by his troops to represent a lack of consideration for a princess of Russian imperial blood. He was about to blame the action taken by his lieutenant and pull out his troops, when a threatening note arrived from the Saint Petersburg cabinet: it demanded the immediate

---

[30]The Duchy of Oldenburg was in the northern plains of Germany, stretching from the Weser estuary, in the Bremen territory, along the North Sea, and around the Gulf of Jade. It included the island of Vangervog.

The original county had been made into a duchy in 1777 by the Emperor of Russia. During the 1806-1807 war with Russia, the French had occupied the duchy, and vacated it after the Treaty of Tilsit.

The Continental Blockade policy forced Napoleon to growing encroachments in authority and occupation inside countries likely to favor British contraband, particularly Holland and the northern German shores. As a result of various senatus-consulti, Napoleon annexed a number of territories to France. In July 1810, it was Holland; in December 1810, the German shoreline that included the Duchy of Oldenburg. Napoleon had offered the Duke of Holstein-Euten, tutor to the reigning Grand Duke of Oldenburg and the tsar's uncle, an exchange of his territory for that of Erfurt, but he had refused. Later on, through a January 1811 decree, Napoleon ordered the taking of Oldenburg.

Marshal Davout, Prince of Eckmühl, in January 1810 was named commander in chief of the army of Germany; in December 1810, commander of the Hanseatic islands; and in April 1811, commander in chief of the Elban observation corps. He was thus assigned to occupy the duchy. Contrary to what Marchand implies, he had not exceeded the imperial instructions, and could only be blamed for the appearance, out of political cleverness. In any event, Russia too felt affected by this decision. First, Napoleon was becoming the dominating factor in the Baltic, over which Peter the Great had wanted to assure control for Russia. Second, the dispossessed prince of the Duchy of Oldenburg was, through his marriage to Catherine Pavlovna, the tsar's brother-in-law. And the Emperor was thus sending back to his ally Alexander his sister, stripped of her future crown! The tsar did try to negotiate, but Napoleon dragged the negotiations out, and offered only vague compensations. Alexander then sent to the courts of independent Europe a copy of his formal protest. Napoleon pretended to view this act as a new provocation. This is what Marchand refers to as a "threatening note."

evacuation of the duchy, and the turn-over of Danzig as a free city, in reparation for the occupation of the Oldenburg shoreline. This challenged the honor of France, disrupted the fine harmony existing between the two powers, and led the Emperor to back the Prince of Eckmühl (Davout) in the position he had just adopted.

The Emperor, concerned with the darkening political horizon, wished to have parties and balls to entertain the Empress and the young ladies at court. The most brilliant party was that given in the theater of the Tuileries palace: quadrilles were organized, and rehearsals took place several days ahead at the small theater in the Empress' apartments erected for that purpose. The Emperor's two sisters, both remarkably attractive, took part in this. Princess Pauline came dressed as France, creating an ideal of beauty enhanced by a ravishing costume; over a white tunic, her bosom was covered by a light breastplate covered with golden scales; she wore a light helmet of burnished gold, upon which fluttered a few white feathers; with laced boots on her feet, and a half spear in her hand, she made a most ravishing picture.

The Queen of Naples represented Italy: she wore a red coat embroidered with gold. As she was not as tall as her sister Princess Pauline, this admirably rich costume appeared heavy, and gave the other a fantastic appearance. The most charming ladies in court were noticed in the quadrilles. Countess Le Grand, Baroness de Mesgrigny, and other ladies just as attractive appeared as the Hours, following the Sun, represented by General Charles de Lagrange.[31]

---

[31]This is cavalry General Armand-Charles-Louis Le Lièvre, Count de La Grange (1783-1864). ADC to Berthier, he had accompanied him to Vienna when the Prince of Neufchâtel went to represent the Emperor at Marie-Louise's wedding. He became a brigadier general in 1812. He was to command the imperial quarters during the retreat from Russia, and distinguish himself during the Campaign of France. His name is inscribed on the Arch of Triumph.

The Emperor had always considered widespread peace to be necessary to the regeneration of Europe. His first objective as consul had been to achieve it, and he often said that he could not be blamed for the breach of the Peace of Amiens. When he became emperor, it was known to be his constant goal, and after the battles of Austerlitz, Friedland, Wagram, and even before crossing the Neiman, he always offered peace to England. He had no ambition to wrest the scepter of the seas away from that nation, but he wanted French vessels to be respected at sea, and protected by their flag. The Emperor therefore did no more than take part in wars that were waged against him.

Before leaving Paris on such a great enterprise, the Emperor held several food councils, whose objective was the provisioning of Paris. For the past two years, the harvests had been poor. The coming year was shaping up poorly.[32] Before leaving, he gave precise and strict orders that surplus storage facilities be filled, and that bread in Paris should be maintained at a moderate price for the workers, whom he was much concerned about. He knew that the rich would always manage to buy some, whatever price it might reach. The Emperor had known the effect of shortages in Paris; he knew that the people,

---

[32]It is strange to note that Marchand here seems to echo the Emperor's preoccupation, and to have been struck by the major economic crisis that had been worsening since 1810.

This crisis started in commerce and industry. France's exports had greatly decreased. Official reports mention "the terrifying condition of France's commerce." The 1810 harvest had been mediocre, the one of 1811 poor. That of 1812 was to be, as Marie-Louise feared in one of her letters, "a sterile year." It was indeed called "the year of costly bread."

Napoleon had tried to adopt measures to abort the crisis. He had granted major loans to industrialists and bankers, and organized a food council to supply Paris. To remedy the menacing increase in the cost of wheat, decrees had been passed to limit distillation of grain, regulate the marketing and sale of wheat, and limited the price of wheat to a maximum of 35 francs per hectoliter: in 1809, the price was 15 francs per hectoliter. Thus the price had more than doubled from 1809 to 1812. The result was that the price of bread in 1812 went from 10 cents a pound to 60 cents a pound in many areas. By resorting to the maximum, Napoleon had imitated the Convention. The consequences were naturally the same as in 1793: deserted markets, clandestine trade: the "black market," as we would call it today, was organized.

dominated by hunger, could be led to all kinds of disturbances, which he wanted to avoid during his absence.

Having thus established the mechanism by which his administration should operate, the Emperor and Empress, in the spring of 1812, left Saint-Cloud to go to Dresden, again leaving their son in the care of Countess de Montesquiou whom they greatly trusted, and deservedly so. Everyone knows that the Emperor, when handing his son, said to her: "Madam, I entrust you with the destinies of France; see to it that he becomes a good citizen and a good Christian." These words were spoken to a woman whose faith and piety were well known.

Every morning, Countess de Montesquiou was in the habit of bringing the King of Rome to breakfast with the Emperor, who would take him in his arms and place him in his lap. The Emperor took pleasure in holding him so, and playing with him, and even teasing him. One morning he was playing with him, and holding his small hand in his; looking at Madame de Montesquiou, he said: "Madam, when will you make this hand able to hold a solid saber?"

"Sire, before teaching him to do harm, we must teach him to do good."

"That is the reply of a woman of wit," said the Emperor.

Two days after leaving Saint-Cloud,[33] the Emperor and Empress arrived in Mainz, where they stayed, hosting the Grand Duke of Hesse and the Duchess of Darmstadt.[34]

---

[33]Napoleon left Saint-Cloud at 6 a.m. on May 9, 1812. He stopped in Mainz at 9 p.m. on the 11, leaving the next morning to arrive four days later in Dresden, on May 16.

[34]Louis V, landgrave of Hesse-Darmstadt since 1790, reigned 1790-1830. When he joined the Rhine Confederation in 1806, he had taken the title of grand duke and called himself Louis I. Marchand gives him his rightful title of grand duke. One should recall that Louis I was showered with rewards by Napoleon, but was among the first to join the Allies in overthrowing him after the Russian retreat. His son Louis II, who was to succeed him in 1830, had married the princess of Baden. He remained faithfully attached to Napoleon, who made him a grand duke. He was succeeded by his grandson, Charles-Louis-Frédéric, who had married Princess Stéphanie de Beauharnais on April 7, 1806, at the Tuileries.

From there, they went on to Frankfurt to see the Prince Primate,[35] and then to Dresden, being honored by the princes whose states they traversed.

Several sovereigns stayed in Dresden for a month: the Emperor of Austria came, along with the empress. She was said to be distant from Empress Marie-Louise, her step-daughter, and not to like the Emperor, who on this occasion was constantly gallant toward her. The archdukes of Austria came; the King of Prussia came with the royal prince, his son, asking the Emperor if he would allow him to accompany him as ADC. Empress Marie-Louise displayed great luxury of dress at all the parties given during that trip: through the elegance of her figure and the diamonds covering her, she eclipsed her stepmother, who was quite attractive, but mortified by her stepdaughter's success.

The Queen of Westphalia, along with many princes of the Rhine Confederation, went to the Dresden court, visiting the good and honest King of Saxony. The Emperor was like Agamemnon among all these potentates who never ceased to demonstrate their friendship toward him. It was the peak of his imperial glory. The time was not far removed when unheard-of reversals would occur. All the sovereigns parted, appearing to be in the best of harmony. If the Emperor counted little on Prussia that he was leaving behind him, he did not doubt the good faith of the emperor of Austria, his father-in-law, and went into Russia full of trust in the promises given that would not allow him to believe they would be forgotten at the first battle lost.

---

[35]He is referring to Carl Theodore von Dalberg, member of a noble family of the German Rhine region. He was one of the major figures in Germany during the Revolution and the Empire. He had entered orders after studying law and theology, and proved to be one of the more enlightened men of his time. In 1802 he became archbishop of Mainz, and was the last elector from that city. When the Holy Empire was abolished, he joined the Rhine Confederation, with the title of prince primate, and Frankfurt am Main as his capital. Napoleon had named him grand duke of Frankfurt in 1810.

In addition to these two men, among the princes "bent in adoration" (Vandal) before Napoleon, one should mention the King of Wurtemberg, the Grand Duke of Baden, the Duke of Anhalt, and the Duke, later King, of Bavaria.

Having taken his leave of the King of Saxony[36] and the princes of his family, the Emperor left Dresden on May 29; the Empress also left a few days later. The princess went to Prague to rejoin her family, with whom she spent a month enjoying parties. The Count von Neipperg[37] was posted as knight of honor in the service of the Empress. In the duty quarters, he spoke to me several times of his admiration for the Empress, and of his Italian campaigns, where he lost an eye. I was far then from imagining, in his respectful relations with the Empress—having reached a mature age, as he had, with a black patch over the eye that marred his face—the harmful influence he would have a few years later over the destiny of the young princess, steeped as she was in the most unquestionable virtue. Prince von Neipperg was a man of great wit, with a fine figure, as gracious as could be, and had kept a chivalrous soul and ideas.

Before arriving in Prague, the Empress had been complimented by both the civil and military authorities; all along her route, arches of triumph had been erected, and the population expressed great joy in seeing again the young archduchess who, in their minds, had been sacrificed to politics. Many cavalry squadrons accompanied her entrance into Prague, which took place to the sound of cannon and

---

[36]Frederick Augustus (1750-1827), King of Saxony by the grace of Napoleon since 1806. Grand duke of Warsaw in 1807. He paid a heavy price at the Vienna treaties for his faithfulness to Napoleon.

[37]Count Albrecht Adam von Neipperg belonged to an old Swabian family. Born in Salzburg in 1775, died in Parma in 1829, he served continuously in the Austrian army against France. Posted to the service of Marie-Louise in 1812, he became her lover and then her husband after the fall of the Empire. Marchand's testimony is very interesting: he points out not only the conditions by which Neipperg came close to the Empress, but the exact identity of the man. Some historians thought it might have been his brother Charles Vincent Jérôme. Marchand's testimony is as positive as it is accurate. Only a small error appears in the story: it was not during the Italian campaigns, but along the Rhine in Doelen in 1794, that Marie-Louise's future second husband lost an eye.

pealing bells; along her path were several religious orders and guilds, making the air ring with cries of Long live Empress Marie-Louise![38]

Throughout all the festivities, Her Majesty was given the place of honor. During the great galas her chamberlain, M. de Montesquiou, served her table, assisted by two pages, who in turn were assisted by two valets, from whom they received what was to be offered the Empress. The same was true for the emperor of Austria.

On July 1, the princess left her family for Carlsbad, where the emperor of Austria accompanied her. After a few days spent in that small town, she left her father to return to France, stopping near Metz at the home of Count de Pange,[39] her chamberlain, where she spent the night. A most brilliant and well organized reception had been prepared. Among the mementos left by the princess with her hosts, there is in the library a book in which she wrote gracious and kind words on their behalf. After spending the night in Châlons, she arrived on July 18 in Saint-Cloud, where she rejoined her son.

Having arrived in Poland, the Emperor still hoped the peace would not be disturbed. He awaited the successful outcome of Count

---

[38]Napoleon left Dresden on Friday, May 29, before 5 a.m., having received one last time the respects of the King of Saxony, and kissed Marie-Louise. She remained in Dresden another five days. On June 4 at 5 a.m. she left the Saxon capital and proceeded to Prague, where she was detained by continuous parties until July 1. Marchand did not follow the Emperor, who proceeded via Glogau and Posen toward Poland and the Russian campaign. He remained with the Empress, and this is how we find him in the duty quarters, talking to Count von Neipperg.

[39]Marie-Jacques-Thomas Songis de Pange, appointed the Emperor's chamberlain in 1809, and later detached to Empress Marie-Louise's service. He was made a count of the Empire in 1810, and owned an estate in Lorraine. It was there, a few km. from Metz, that he received Empress Marie-Louise.

de Narbonne's[40] mission to Wilna, but in vain. The French army crossed the Neiman on June 24.

While the Emperor was entering Moscow at the head of his army, General Malet[41] was rekindling old plots, with more audacity than means or assurance of success. Held in detention in a medical facility, he had succeeded in winning over a few officers of the reserve

---

[40]Count Louis de Narbonne-Lara (1755-1813) was said—rightfully so, it appears—to be a bastard son of Louis XV. A former student at Juilly, then at the artillery school in Strasbourg, he turned to diplomacy, and was a student of Vergennes'. On his return from exile, he joined the Empire and attracted Napoleon's attention. As ADC to the Emperor in 1811, he took active part in the Russian campaign.

On May 18, 1812, Napoleon sent him to Wilna to give Emperor Alexander a personal letter: a last and fruitless attempt in favor of peace. The Count de Narbonne did not leave the Emperor during the entire Russian campaign. He returned to Paris in January 1813, was sent by Napoleon as ambassador to Vienna, then, after the Prague congress, to Torgau, in Saxony, where he died in 1813.

[41]The extraordinary Malet affair, led by an obscure officer without contacts or means—and which almost succeeded—had considerable repercussions. The Empire had been shaken by the storm of the plot; Napoleon, along with his adversaries, gauged the frailty of the imperial edifice. It was as a result of this strange affair that after the Berezina, the Emperor decided to return to Paris and personally take up again the reins of power.

Claude-François de Malet, born in Dôle in 1754, served as a king's musketeer, then in the revolutionary armies, where he became a general during the Directory. During the Consulate and Empire, he held a number of other posts. Placed on inactive duty in 1805, he joined the army of Naples, and served as governor of Rome before General Miollis. Relieved of his duties in 1807 by the viceroy of Italy and sent back to France because of his republican propaganda, he was then imprisoned at La Force (July 1807), released without trial in May 1808, and retired. Connected with the Philadelphian Society, he was again imprisoned in 1809. For reasons of illness he obtained the favor of residing in Dr. Dubuisson's clinic, 333 rue du Faubourg-Saint-Antoine. He escaped from there over the garden wall in October 1812. He joined his accomplice, Fr. Caamagno, proceeded to the Popincourt garrison, rue Saint-Ambroise, and managed to take over the 10th national guard cohort, along with its commanding officer, Major Soulier, by announcing the Emperor's death and the constitution of a provisional government. After freeing Generals Guidal, recently involved in the Midi plot, and Lahorie, former chief of staff of General Moreau, from La Force prison, he broke into the home of General Hulin, governor of Paris, and wounded him in the head with a pistol shot. He was then arrested by Baron Pierre Doucet, the governor's chief of staff, and the garrison adjutant Laborde, his aide. Tried by a military commission, he was sentenced to death along with 14 accomplices on October 28, and executed by firing squad the next day on the Grenelle plain.

cohorts and of the Parisian guard. At 3 a.m. on October 19,[42] these officers took their troops and had them occupy the outposts. With great audacity, General Malet freed from prison a few obscure plotters, without any resources, and imprisoned the minister and the prefect of police,[43] announcing at the same time the Emperor's death and the formation of a new government. This conspiracy, halted through the presence of mind of General Laborde, only lasted a few hours, and changed nothing in the appearance of Paris. Had it followed its course and lasted twelve hours, it would have compromised many more people.

The prefect of the Seine, Count Frochot,[44] was a victim of his own gullibility in this amateurish affair. On his return the Emperor dismissed him, reproaching him for not having remembered that in France, the king never dies. The king is dead, long live the king! A few friends of the administrator tried unsuccessfully to appease the Emperor's anger against him. "How can you," said the prince, "speak to me on behalf of a man who at the first rumor of my death, instead of going to see my wife and son, on the orders of an unknown person clears the city hall conference room to install a new government? Is that proper conduct for a prefect of Paris? Don't mention him again!"

A court martial judged the leaders of the young soldiers, General Malet defended them and showed great courage, both during the

---

[42]Marchand commits a minor error here: the conspiracy started on October 23.

[43]The plotters had imprisoned, without resistance, Savary, Duke of Rovigo, minister of police; the police prefect, Baron Pasquier; and the prefect of the Seine, Count Frochot.

[44]When Napoleon returned, Count Frochot was solemnly dismissed from his functions as councillor of State and prefect of the Seine, by a decree dated December 23, 1812, "for having ignored the heredity and sanctity of the crown." Marchand recalls the rallying cry that Napoleon himself evoked before the senators who had come to greet him on his return: "Our fathers," he said, "had for a rallying cry: 'The king is dead, long live the king!' These few words contain the advantages of the monarchy." Frochot, born in Dijon, former attorney for the Burgundy parliament, member of the constitutional assembly, executor for Mirabeau who had been imprisoned during the Terror, councillor of State after 18 Brumaire, had been named prefect of the Seine in 1800, and had reorganized the entire administration of the city of Paris.

trial and at his death. The Empress was at Saint-Cloud when Prince Cambacérès came to inform her of the criminal plot that had just taken place; she immediately sent one of her pages to inquire about General Hulin,[45] who was severely wounded. The guard garrisons and those of the various regiments, the schools of Saint-Cyr and Saint-Germain rallied to the defense of the Empress, who demonstrated great levelheadedness, learning almost simultaneously of the conspiracy and the arrest of the conspirators. At eleven, the Duke of Rovigo (Savary) and the prefect of police were back in their homes.

In Russia, after a series of brilliant successes, unheard-of reversals of fortune were brought about by the climate. The Grand Army's 29th bulletin[46] had announced enormous losses. France was stricken with dismay. The Emperor had the courage to return only a few days after the publication of such disastrous events; his unexpected arrival was necessary, and bolstered public opinion. All the mechanisms of a vigorous administration were brought into play. Astonishing activity, comparable to that of the Hundred Days, succeeded in raising in three months armies that were both numerous and well supplied.[47]

---

[45]General Hulin suffered a broken jaw from the pistol fired by Malet.

General Pierre-Auguste Hulin was born in Paris in 1758. On July 14, 1789, he headed the citizens and French guards who marched on the Bastille. It was he who set up two cannons in front of the castle doors, bringing about the surrender of the fortress. One of the heads of the Parisian national guard, then adjutant general in Bonaparte's army in Italy, he took part in the 18 Brumaire coup, was named head of the foot grenadiers of the consular guard, and presided in 1804 over the court martial that sentenced the Duke of Enghien. He became major general, great officer of the Legion of Honor, and count of the Empire, and in 1812 headed the 1st military division and was governor of Paris.

In April 1814, he was to join Louis XVIII, but lost his command, resuming it in 1815 on Napoleon's return. In July 1815, he was banished by royal ordinance and went abroad. He was allowed to return to France in December 1819 and retire from the army. He died in 1841.

[46]The Russian disaster was announced to the Empire by the Grand Army's 29th bulletin, sent from imperial headquarters in Molodetchna on December 3, 1812. Anatole de Montesquiou was assigned to bring it to Paris, and arrived only a short time before the Emperor himself. The repercussions of this terrible news were all the greater as nothing of the French losses had been known previously.

The French retreat had been deplorable since Napoleon left the army. It can be seen through the notes made by the Emperor in the book written on the Russian 4th corps by M. Labaume, Prince Eugène's ADC, that urgent circumstances called Napoleon to Paris;[48] only from there could he impress Prussia and Austria, and should he delay going, his passage might be prevented. He left the army in the hands of the King of Naples and the Prince of Neufchâtel (Berthier).[49] It was a misfortune that the Emperor, during many important crises, needed to be with the army and in Paris at the same time. During his conversations in Saint Helena, the Emperor pointed out the government's mistakes at times when his presence was necessary with the army. At the time of the battle of Austerlitz, the financial and banking crisis; at the time of the battle of Essling, Fouché's intrigues; during the Russian expedition, the Malet affair which offered new proof of the negligence of all segments of the administration when he was not there to direct their moves. Everything therefore relied on him, on his own person; he had to be everywhere.

When the Emperor had ensured the means of setting off on another campaign, without telling anyone of his plans he asked the Prince of Neufchâtel (Berthier) to organize a hunt at Grosbois.[50] He had lunch there, and in the middle of the hunt left for Fontainebleau to

---

[47]Having arrived in Paris on December 18, 1812, the Emperor immediately reorganized an army. The entire artillery train that had crossed the Neiman had vanished. Napoleon wanted a new, larger one. On December 27, he was brought the inventories of materiel and artillery personnel throughout the Empire, and on the following day he dictated to General Gassendi, then head of artillery, and to Colonel Evain, his aide, a plan that was immediately put into action. Details of this had to be modified in January and February 1813. But Wesel and Mainz remained the rallying points for all that was located on the left bank of the Rhine, while Magdeburg was a forward arsenal.

[48]Labaume, Prince Eugène's ADC, indeed wrote, *Relation circonstanciée de la campagne de Russie, en 1812* (Paris: Panckoucke, 1815). Marchand knew in Saint Helena of Napoleon's annotations on this book.

[49]Murat became commander in chief of the army of Russia after Napoleon departed on December 5. Forced to evacuate in turn Wilna and Kowno, he handed over command to Prince Eugène on January 18, 1813. Berthier remained with them as major general.

spend a few days there. All were taken by surprise, and he and the others arrived in Fontainebleau with the clothes on their backs. The night was spent getting from Paris what everyone might need for the following day.[51] Immediately after his arrival, His Majesty went to visit the Holy Father, who was staying in the palace, and came back a little while later to his own apartments. The Pope almost immediately came to return the visit he had just received. The Emperor was informed of this, and showed his respect to the point of coming out to meet him in the Diane Gallery, then leading him into his study, where they remained closeted for almost an hour. When His Holiness came out, the Emperor accompanied him to the place where he had met him, chatting merrily with him, and they parted, calling one another *San Padre* and *figlio mio*. Some have nevertheless dared to suggest—and the rumor gained credit—that the Emperor had dragged the Holy

---

[50]This hunt took place on January 19. The Grosbois castle, a dozen miles east of Paris, includes a fine wooded park. This was part of the estate Napoleon had created for Berthier. The castle belonged in turn to the Count of Provence, Barras, General Moreau, and Berthier, Prince of Wagram.

[51]The hunt at Grosbois was only a pretext: nothing was prepared; however the premeditation of the Fontainebleau trip is certain. But Napoleon did not want to alert anyone. His goal was to see the Pope, whom he had had abducted in Rome, and who had been his prisoner at Fontainebleau since June 20, 1812.

The Emperor arrived with his retinue on January 19 at 6:30 p.m., unconcerned by the cold or the lack of dinner. He immediately sent an usher to ask His Holiness if he could see him. Having received an affirmative reply, he immediately proceeded to Pope Pius VII's apartment, walked right up to the pontiff, and embraced him, showing him nothing but signs of affection. Pius VII at once returned his visit. Marchand was there, and relates events he witnessed. That is why he energetically protests against certain pamphleteers or libel writers who accused Napoleon of having thrown violent fits of temper and even of having used physical violence against the Pope: if there was indeed violence, it was only verbal. Pius VII himself assured Count Paul van der Vrecken, on September 27, 1814, that Napoleon had never resorted to physical violence against him at Fontainebleau. "It is untrue," he declared, "and I invite you to say in my name to all those who speak to you about it, that he never committed any excessive acts against me. But one day, in the heat of the argument regarding renunciation to the Roman states he grabbed me by a button of my cassock, as he was known to do, and shook me so hard that my whole body was shaking. That is probably what people are talking about…"

Father to his apartment by the hair. No doubt such rumors are not worthy of a denial; but since I was a witness to this scene, I am pleased to point out to what extremes biased minds can go when they wish to slander a great man. How indeed can one imply that the Emperor—whose first concern when he took power was to restore the altars destroyed by the 1793 Revolution, and who, in addition to his religious faith, considered religion necessary as a means of governing—could have committed an act so little in keeping with his character and upbringing? Fortuitous circumstances[52] had brought the Holy Father to Fontainebleau. It was General Miollis' doing. The Emperor had not wished it, he said, but once done, it had to be accepted. Had reversals not occurred, it was his intention to surround the Pope with great spiritual power in the midst of the capital that would hereafter have become the Holy Father's residence. Paris thus would become the center of the religious as well as the political world, and the Emperor would work to achieve Italian unity.[53]

---

[52]After the peace of Tilsit, the Emperor's aims regarding Rome knew no limits. The idea of annexing the papal capital haunted his imagination more and more. As soon as his first successes during the 1808 campaign appeared to confirm his luck, he decided in Schönbrunn to attach the papal states to the French Empire. Pius VII then posted a bull of excommunication against those guilty of violence toward the Holy See. Napoleon, who was its direct target, responded by abducting the Pope, who was first taken to Savona, near Genoa. But he wanted him at hand. From Dresden in 1812, as he was launching the Russian campaign, he ordered him brought to Fontainebleau. After a difficult trip led by Major Lagorse, the pontiff arrived in the imperial palace on June 19, 1812, near death. Marchand blames General Miollis.

Miollis had started his career during the American expedition, distinguishing himself at Yorktown in 1771. He then served in the revolutionary armies, and was promoted to brigadier general in 1795. After a brilliant career, he was named in 1808 commander of the 30th division in Rome, and in that capacity had arrested the Pope in July 1809, taking him to Savona. During this episode, in accordance with the Emperor's orders, he fulfilled his mission with a moderation for which Pius VII was grateful to him.

Prior to leaving Paris to rejoin the army, the Emperor wished to put an end to the disagreements he had with the Pope. The bishop of Nantes[54] had informed him that the bitterness of the cardinals was no longer the same, and that personal intervention would bring about a complete reconciliation between him and the Holy Father, which was advisable because of his political interests and religious feelings. The Emperor, in the interest of religion, obtained that the Holy See would commit to deliver within a specified time the expedition of the bulls, and even that, by the 1801 Concordat, the sovereign would for a limited time nominate bishops to seat vacancies. Once these grounds were established, the Emperor dictated a new Concordat, and the Pope, who was present, verbally agreed to all the stipulations. On January 25, 1813, this Concordat was signed in the presence of the entire court along with that of the Holy Father, and with Marie-Louise present.[55]

---

[53]Marchand here expresses ideas conceived in the Emperor's imagination. Refer to Napoleon's conversation with Count de Narbonne, when he said to him: "If I keep Rome for my son, I shall give Notre-Dame to the Pope. Paris will then be elevated so high in mankind's admiration that its cathedral will become that of the Catholic world..." Furthermore, in the Memoirs he would later dictate in Saint Helena, Napoleon tried to explain his 1812 plans. He clearly stated he wanted to recreate the Italian homeland, and reunite its various peoples into one independent nation. This is what Marchand summarizes when he states that "the Emperor would work to achieve Italian unity."

[54]The French prelate who was bishop of Nantes was Baron Jean-Baptiste Duvoisin (1744-1813). He had become grand vicar and a canon of Laon at the time of the Revolution. Exiled as a refractory priest, he returned to France only in 1801. Named bishop of Nantes, he gained so much favor with Napoleon that the latter named him to reside with Pope Pius VII during his stay in Savona and Fontainebleau. The Emperor appreciated his cleverness and experience, and on his return from Russia put him in charge of negotiating with the Pope and his representative, Cardinal Doria. It is based on these negotiations that Napoleon decided to go to Fontainebleau to settle in person those points about which they had disagreed for so long. Note that the bishop of Nantes, who was to die a few months later, had dictated a kind of will: "I beg the Emperor to restore his freedom to the Holy Father; his captivity disturbs even the last moments of my life. I have had the honor of telling him several times how this captivity distresses all Christendom, and how disadvantageous it is to prolong it. I believe it is necessary to His Majesty's happiness that His Holiness return to Rome."

We know that the Pope left Fontainebleau only on January 21, 1814, and entered Rome on May 24.

To complete the reconciliation, the cardinals who were still prisoners were released, and those who were exiled were allowed to return. Once this Concordat was signed, the Emperor returned to Paris with all his court.

The King of Naples had left the army on the Emperor's orders. Prince Eugène, who had taken command, reorganized it along the Saale. After such a great disaster, the Emperor found himself facing all the European powers allied against him. His genius, along with new phalanxes of young soldiers, proved at Lutzen, Bautzen, and Wurchen[56] what the French nation was capable of in Napoleon's hands.

---

[55]Marchand is the only writer to mention Marie-Louise's presence at the signing of the Concordat at Fontainebleau on January 25, 1813. The Emperor had her write to Vienna an informal letter wherein the Empress congratulated herself on her husband "having arranged everything with the Pope." The Concordat contained ten articles filled with a great spirit of conciliation on Napoleon's part.

Napoleon had Marie-Louise write to her father Francis II, on the evening of January 25 (the very evening of the signing): "The Emperor has today settled the affairs of Christendom with the Pope. The latter appears very pleased. He is very gay and in a good mood since early this morning, and signed the treaty 15 minutes ago. I have just come from him, and found him in very good health... I am sure that you shall learn of this reconciliation with as much pleasure as I have."

Two days later, on January 27, Napoleon was back at the Tuileries.

The Pleswitz [Pleischwitz] armistice[57] put an end to our successes, and changed the fortunes of our armies; Austria, who advised it, was not ready, although it had fully decided to join the coalition. Negotiations therefore took place in Prague[58] in bad faith, and war resumed. The loss of the Vandamme corps negated all the results of the Dresden victory[59] and the entry into Bohemia.

---

[56]Lutzen, a small Saxon town southeast of Leipzig, was the scene of two great historical battles. The first was in 1632, the last victory over Wallenstein by the King of Sweden, Gustav, who was killed there.

It was also the scene on May 2, 1813, of the battle the Germans call Gross-Gertchen, a small nearby village. It started the 1813 campaign with a victory for Napoleon. The Russians and Prussians had to retreat to Dresden, where the Emperor pursued them on May 8, crossing the Elbe. The effect of this bloody victory on morale was considerable.

Bautzen, a Saxon town on the Spree, is mainly famous for the battle Napoleon won there on May 20 and 21, 1813, over the Russians and Prussians; they had fortified themselves along the Spree after their defeat at Lutzen. The Emperor attacked them with forces inferior in number and captured Bautzen on May 20. The next day the Allied troops had to withdraw so as not to be surrounded. A lack of cavalry prevented Napoleon from consummating their defeat.

Wurchen, a Saxon town 10 km. east of Bautzen, was the scene of the second day of the battle of Bautzen, on May 21, 1813, leading to the Wurchen victory.

[57]Metternich did not want to declare war on Napoleon at once: he wished to pick his own time. "Going from neutrality to war," he wrote, "will only be possible through armed mediation." After Lutzen and Bautzen, he felt the time had come to propose such mediation. He offered the Emperor an armistice intended to prepare the opening of a great European congress and the signing of a universal peace. Napoleon signed the Pleischwitz (a village in Lower Silesia in Germany) armistice on June 4, 1813, and it lasted until July 28. This armistice, extended until August 10, was beneficial to the Allies.

[58]It was during the Prague congress, at the expiration of the Pleischwitz armistice, that Austria was to mediate. But the congress was in fact aborted before it really began. On August 10 at midnight, the exact expiration time of the armistice, Metternich had pronounced the dissolution of the congress, and announced Austria's declaration of war against France.

The disastrous retreat at Leipzig brought our armies back to the Rhine, and the Hanau victory only served to guarantee their final moves. During this campaign, the turncoat Moreau was mortally wounded.[60]

Moreau.

---

[59]The military campaign interrupted by the armistice started anew. Schwarzenberg, with the Austrian army, headed for Dresden. But on August 26, 1813, Latour-Maubourg's cuirassiers and the old guard commanded by Mortier overwhelmed the Austrians and drove them out of town. Napoleon finished routing them and Schwarzenberg had to go back to Bohemia.

Napoleon was unable to capitalize on this victory. Kept in bed by illness for almost six weeks in Dresden, he had ordered his lieutenants to pursue the defeated army, but he could not prevent their rivalries and their mistakes. Vandamme, who had entered Bohemia and was about to cut off Schwarzenberg's retreat, failed in his maneuver for lack of proper liaison with Mortier and Gouvion-Saint-Cyr. Instead of cutting off the Austrians, he was surrounded himself and had to surrender at Kulm (August 29-30, 1813). Marchand alludes to this capitulation that indeed erased the result of the Dresden victory. Vandamme, Count of Unseburg (1770-1830), had come from the revolutionary armies. He was promoted to major general on February 5, 1799. He had taken the Pratzen plateau at the battle of Austerlitz (December 2, 1805), and for this had received a pension of 20,000 francs. On July 1, 1813, he had become commander of the 1st corps of the Grand Army of Saxony.

[60]The Allied armies had managed to close in their circle of iron and fire, and Napoleon was pursued into the Leipzig plains, where the destinies of the Empire and France came into play. This formidable engagement lasted four days, and was rightfully called the Battle of Nations. In spite of the guard's miracles, and because of the Saxon treason, Napoleon was thrown back to the walls of Leipzig and had to retreat at all costs. After Leipzig, Napoleon had no allies left. Germany was in full uprising, French troops were retreating via Weimar and Erfurt. There it was learned that the Austrians and Bavarians commanded by Wrede had taken up position on the Main to cut off Napoleon's retreat. He had to cut his way through the Bavarians. The last engagement was in Hanau, a town in Hesse-Cassel 15 km. from Frankfurt am Main. Drouot, with some 50 cannons that fired on the enemy only when he was 40 paces away, opened up a passage through the Bavarian armies. Napoleon said disdainfully of Bavarian General Wrede: "I was able to make him a count, but I couldn't make him into a general." It is this victory on October 30, 1813, that Marchand mentions in his brief, but very accurate, summary.

Marchand insists on mentioning the death of the "turncoat Moreau." General Moreau (1763-1813) had distinguished himself in the revolutionary armies. He succeeded Pichegru as head of the northern armies. At the end of the Consulate he was hostile to Bonaparte, and accepted the idea of overthrowing him, while refusing to serve the Bourbons. Sentenced to two years in prison and dismissed from the army rosters in 1804, he obtained permission to retire to the United States. He was called up by Tsar Alexander II in 1813, arrived in Prague on August 17, and took part in the Allied offensive on Dresden. But during that battle, on August 27, 1813, he was hit by a cannonball that broke his right knee and took off his left calf.

Transported to Lahn, he had to have both legs amputated. However, he died a few days later, on September 1. A Saxon priest, witness to his last moments, related that he cursed himself: "To think that I, Moreau, am dying in the midst of France's enemies, hit by a French cannonball!"

The Battle of Champaubert.

Napoleon enters Rheims for the last time.

The Battle of Montereau.

Napoleon in the field aims a cannon during the Battle of Montereau.

Top: In the bivouac,
the Emperor shares
a potato with one of
his guards.

Bottom: In a very
small room in the
Fontainebleau
Palace, Napoleon
signs his first
abdication, April 8,
1814.

Napoleon descends the great staircase in Fontainebleau to face an emotional farewell ceremony.

After the farewell, in the great court at Fontainebleau, the Emperor returns to the carriage which will take him into exile.

CHAPTER TWO

Campaign of France in 1814 — Abdication and Fontainebleau treaty — The Emperor's departure for the Island of Elba — My trip to Paris, Rambouillet, Porto Ferrajo

*T*hese were times of misfortune. A committee of active royalists was organized, and carried hopes to Louis XVIII.[61] At the end of 1813 our borders had been forced by the passage the Swiss opened for the armies of the coalition. Our allies were abandoning us. Before leaving Paris, the Emperor returned Ferdinand VII to Spain, and the Pope to Rome.[62] He entrusted the Empress and the King of Rome to the fidelity of the Parisian national guard. The enthusiasm generated by the Emperor when he took the young king in his arms to present him to the national guard officers, gathered together in the Hall of Marshals, can never be forgotten by its witnesses. Frenetic and prolonged cries of Vive l'Empereur! moved from the Hall of Marshals to the assembled national guard in the Carrousel. When the Emperor

---

[61]Although not many, the royalists were very active. As early as the end of 1813, there were posters in all the French cities favoring the return of the Bourbons, and even proclamations signed by Louis XVIII or the Prince of Condé. This increased in early 1814. On January 1, Louis XVIII issued from Hartwell, his residence 60 km. from London, a new proclamation promising to "guarantee their positions to those who held them" and to uphold "the code sullied by Napoleon's name." This edict was posted and circulated everywhere, and was followed by others in the same vein, signed by the Count of Artois and the Duke of Angoulême. It must not be forgotten either that Châteaubriand was starting to write his famous pamphlet *De Buonaparte et des Bourbons*.

[62]The Emperor had started negotiations as early as November 19, 1813, with King Ferdinand VII of Spain, interned in the château of Valençay. This had led to the treaty of December 11, in which the Emperor promised to free Ferdinand VII and recognize the integrity of Spanish territory, on condition that Spain return to neutrality and force the British army to evacuate. Due to regrettable delays, Ferdinand VII was sent back to Spain only on March 19, 1814.

passed in front of them to receive their oath of loyalty, the air was filled with a roll of cries of Vive l'Empereur! Long live the Empress, Long live the King of Rome. These demonstrations of so true a love for his son moved the Emperor: he kissed the young prince with a warmth that escaped none in the audience and moistened more than one eye.[63]

Each day, the Emperor followed the progress of France's enemies on his map. There was much concern among the wealthy classes; but for the common people, the Emperor was there, faith in his genius was great,[64] and a clever scheme could revive his star, obscured by two campaigns that were unfortunate but not devoid of glory for our

The Empress and the King of Rome put under the protection of the national guard.

---

[63]See the drawing by Baron Gros, showing the January 23, 1814, scene, when Napoleon placed the Empress and the King of Rome under the protection of the national guard: "I am placing my wife and son in their care..." (Musée Napoléonien de Bois-Préau, Edward Tuck Foundation).

[64]Marchand is right to differentiate between the state of mind of the well-off classes, i.e. the former nobility and bourgeois, and that of the common people in early 1814. The aristocracy and middle class agreed in condemning the folly of Napoleon's ambitions and the despotism of his government. But the opinions that reigned in the cities, from the salons to the shops, had not reached the factories or the countryside. Among the people they cried: "Down with combined taxes!" and "Vive l'Empereur!" Reliable witnesses back up Marchand's statement. Everywhere among the simple people, contemporaries note the same frame of mind. "The trust in the Emperor's genius is boundless," some say. "The people are for the Emperor," others say. And all this testimony confirms Mollien's statement: "The popular masses knew only the Emperor and the Empire." Marchand is correct in recording that Napoleon had in no way lost the people's affection, and that he maintained his prestige as a great captain.

armies. In vain were they negotiating in Châtillon-sur-Seine;[65] the
Emperor recognized in Saint Helena that it was not possible for the
negotiators to make peace there. So they fought, and the 1814 campaign was one of the more glorious for our troops and the Emperor,
but not the most successful. The Emperor made war with 40,000 men
against 240,000,[66] and defeated them; he said he would have driven

---

[65]In early 1814, from the Oder to the Aube, from the Mincio to the Pyrenees, everywhere the enemy armies were, if not in retreat, at least held back. In spite of inferiority
in numbers Napoleon had won several victories, however, he remained in a very critical position. The Allied sovereigns had entered France, although their armies appeared
partially demoralized. On both sides an agreement could have been considered, but it
was not possible. Brilliant days like those of Montmirail and Vauchamps prevented
the Emperor from submitting to humiliating conditions. In spite of their problems, the
Allies were determined to reject Napoleon's offers.

This explains the congress that took place in Châtillon-sur-Seine, during the
Campaign of France in February and March 1814. Such a diplomatic meeting obviously aimed at an arrangement between Napoleon and the great coalition formed
against him in 1813. It really ended as nothing but a dilatory conversation between the
two parties.

The congress opened on February 4, 1814, as Napoleon was waging battle after
battle in Champagne. None brought there any truly peaceful inclinations. Caulaincourt, Duke of Vicenza, represented Napoleon. He tried to drag out the negotiations,
as if to allow the Emperor to wait for the fortunes of the battlefield to turn again in his
favor. The low-ranking diplomats who represented the Allies at Châtillon were in no
greater hurry to succeed, and their deliberate slowness was easily felt. This was so true
that, having decided to grant no concessions, the Allied plenipotentiaries signed the
Chaumont treaty, backdating it to March 1: this was the death sentence of the French
Empire and the forerunner of the Holy Alliance. Indeed, by this treaty, Austria, Great
Britain, and Russia committed themselves through this solemn pact not to lay down
their arms until France accepted their conditions. The Châtillon negotiations were broken off and the Allies no longer hesitated to flaunt their intransigence.

[66]The figures given by Marchand are close to those reported by Henry Houssaye for
the beginning of the campaign; when they had crossed the Rhine in late December
1813, the Allied armies pushed back the French corps spread out along the border.
Marmont, Macdonald, Victor, and the Prince of the Moscowa had about 46,000 fighting men. The Bohemian army, led by Schwarzenberg, and the Silesian army, led by
Blücher, had about 250,000 soldiers.

As of February 26, the main army positions were as follows: Napoleon was master of Troyes, having concentrated between the Seine and the Aube 74,000 men and
350 cannons. Facing him, the main Allied army had about 120,000 men stretching
back to Chaumont and Langres. But one must add Blücher's 48,000 men who were
attempting a very hazardous march around Napoleon's left.

them from Paris, but for the treason of Marmont, Augereau, and Tall-eyrand.[67] He therefore made war, until the moment when the new Judas surrendered his master, and treason took away Paris and a part of the army from France.

The Emperor was quartered in Troyes at the home of Baron de Mesgrigny,[68] one of his equerries, when he learned during the night by

---

[67]The Campaign of France in 1814 shall remain one of the more glorious in French military history. From January 25 to February 8, the Allies made menacing progress. Napoleon won at Brienne, and held for 12 hours at La Rothière, 20 km. from Bar-sur-Aube, against superior forces: this was in vain, and he had to pull back to Troyes. On February 9, a brilliant period opened. Blücher and Schwarzenberg made the mistake of splitting up in order to better march on Paris. And suddenly Napoleon, in a remarkable move, again showed his marvelous genius. He fell on Blücher's columns, and in four victorious attacks, overwhelmed each in turn: at Champaubert, on February 10, where the "Marie-Louise" recruits shone like veterans; at Montmirail on the 11th; at Châ-teau-Thierry on the 12th; at Vauchamps on the 14th. He then rushed toward Schwarzenberg, whose vanguard was reaching Fontainebleau. He captured the Montereau bridge (February 18), and forced the main enemy body to retreat to Troyes and Chaumont. Then, continuing the maneuver, he turned back against Blücher, who followed the Ourcq to seek help from the approaching Bernadotte. But the Soissons stronghold, instead of preventing the two enemy armies from joining forces, surren-dered on March 4. The third period of the campaign had begun. Napoleon had restored equilibrium until late February; he had gone on the offensive, and was entitled to expect victory.

He would now attempt admirable maneuvers. His soldiers would accomplish miracles. But everything was to betray him.

He was forced to pull back before Laon on March 10, because of superior forces; the same at Arcis-sur-Aube (March 20). From the Oise to the Seine, the Allied armies now formed an insurmountable mass. They pushed back Marmont and Mortier at La Fère-Champenoise (March 25). Napoleon had moved toward Saint-Dizier, in the enemy's rear, to try to turn the invaders away from Paris. But on March 30 Paris sur-rendered, and Marchand tells us under what conditions Napoleon sought refuge in Fontainebleau.

[68]On March 28, 1814, Napoleon left Saint-Dizier in the morning. The campaign had started in that town, and was ending there. Now the only question was that of returning to Paris. Napoleon arrived at Doulevant-le-Château that same day around 5:30 p.m. He left the next day, March 29, very early. Having crossed the Aube over the Dolen-court bridge, he marched with the guard on Vendeuvre-sur-Barse. He arrived in Troyes during the night with the main cavalry body. The infantry had bivouacked at Lusigny. The Emperor stayed at the home of Baron de Mesgrigny, one of his equer-ries.

Adrien de Mesgrigny had accompanied him during the entire German campaign of 1813. They parted only at the Fontainebleau farewell.

a coded note[69] that the enemy army was approaching Paris. He went the following day, escorted by the service squadrons, as far as Villeneuve-l'Archevêque,[70] and arrived in great haste at midnight on the 30th at Cour de France,[71] to learn of the enemy's entry into Paris through a surrender, and the retreat of the government and the Empress to Blois.

---

[69]Mention of this "coded note" is found in no other contemporary source. It no doubt announced that Meaux had been evacuated on March 27. Bulletins followed at regular intervals, and in Doulevant, Napoleon found a note from M. de Lavalette, warning of new plots, the approaching enemy, and all sorts of dangers. Fain (*Manuscrit de 1814*) gives the following extract from this encrypted note: "The foreign partisans are on the rise; secret transactions are helping them. Napoleon's presence is required if he wishes to avoid the capital being handed over to the enemy. There is not a moment to lose."

Finally, at the Dolencourt bridge, on the road to Troyes, Caulaincourt notes that an agent of the minister of police and one of the postal service had caught up with Napoleon and told him that Marshals de Trévise and de Raguse had been forced to fall back on Paris, under pressure from Blücher.

[70]Napoleon left Troyes at dawn on March 30, on horseback. When his horse was exhausted, he arrived at Villeneuve-l'Archevêque, on the Vanne, 23 km. from Sens. With the Prince of Neufchâtel, he then climbed into a wicker cabriolet lent by a butcher; Bertrand, Flahaut, and Caulaincourt climbed into a second one. Schuermans and Louis Garros are mistaken when they indicate that Caulaincourt rode in the Emperor's carriage.

In Sens the small group lunched at the Hôtel de l'Ecu de France, then left immediately in a coach lent by M. de Fontaine. The Emperor wanted to make up for lost time at all costs and skipped relay stops, going on to Paris, Villeneuve-la-Guyard, Moret, and Fontainebleau, hoping to arrive in enough time to take charge of the troops of Marshals Marmont and Mortier.

[71]The hamlet known as Cour de France or Fromenteau, along the Paris-Fontainebleau main road, is part of the community of Juvisy, near the fountains known to all tourists. That is where Camille Flammarion set up the famous Observatory of Juvisy. It occupies the small château of Cour-de-France, rebuilt in 1728, where kings stopped in the old days on their way to Fontainebleau. Sold as national property in 1793, it became the post house of Fromenteau, managed in 1814 by M. Petit. Today's sitting room is the one where, on learning from General Belliard of the capitulation of Paris, Napoleon collapsed and remained a long time with his elbows on a table and his head in his hands. A small bronze statue of Napoleon can be seen there today.

The Emperor arrived there in the late evening of March 30. According to Fain it was 10 p.m. Gourgaud says 11 p.m., Marchand midnight. The next day, Thursday, March 31, Napoleon continued on to Fontainebleau. He got there around 6 a.m. and moved into the apartments bordering the gallery of François I.

Napoleon returned to Fontainebleau, where his guard soon joined him; they asked to march upon Paris,[72] and punish the traitors whose names were known to them. The Emperor was going to head them toward Pithiviers and Orléans; once reunited with the government and the Empress, he would be able to parley when someone came to announce there was a hope of negotiation. The Emperor thus remained at Fontainebleau and in this fashion lost his wife, his son, his treasure, the muscle of his power, and a very strong barrier.

On April 2, the act of forfeiture[73] was pronounced by the Senate. The Emperor learned about it in Fontainebleau, where he was surrounded by his guard, his marshals, and the senior officers of his household. His great heart must have breathed vengeance against this cowardly decision by the first body of state. Sinister rumors even circulated about His Majesty's life being threatened by men who, it was said, owed him their high positions. The Emperor must have then felt great contempt for the human race, and in particular for those who—forgetting the respect owed him—could be annihilated by a single call to his guard, who were totally devoted to him. The crisis had reached its peak, and could not last any longer. The marshals invited the Emperor to abdicate in favor of his son. He therefore sent a

---

[72]The old guard division led by Friant, and the young guard division led by Henrion, had arrived in Fontainebleau on April 2. Next morning, April 3, Napoleon reviewed them in the Cheval Blanc courtyard. He said to them: "In a few days, I shall attack the enemy in Paris. I am counting on you…"

The enthusiasm of the troops gave him every hope, but Marmont's defection was to dash these to naught.

[73]On April 2, 1814, the Senate had voted the decree declaring that Napoleon Bonaparte and his family were removed from the throne.

The president of the Senate, Lacépède, and the secretaries, who were the only ones who could convene the Senate and render the meeting legal, had left with the Empress. The act of forfeiture had been proposed by Charles-Joseph Mathieu, Count Lambrecht, from Saint-Trond in Belgium. A minority of senators who had remained in Paris supported this motion, although they had been showered with favors by Napoleon.

few of them, along with the Duke of Vicenza (Caulaincourt),[74] to
negotiate advantageous conditions for the King of Rome with the
Emperor of Russia, in the name of the army, telling them to take with
them Marmont, in whom he placed great faith. These gentlemen
departed; once in Essonne, they informed the Duke of Raguse
(Marmont) of the Emperor's desire to have him join them. The
marshal appeared embarrassed and unsure of what he should do, then
finally decided to get in the carriage with them. Once in Paris, they
went to Emperor Alexander's residence, and were strangely surprised
not to see Marmont accompany them. They were not aware that an
agreement had been made between him and Prince Schwarzenberg[75]
which no longer allowed him to defend the Emperor's interests. They
nevertheless obtained the Regency; the Emperor of Russia had
appeared favorably disposed toward Napoleon II, when an officer
handed him a dispatch[76] telling him that the Duke of Raguse's
(Marmont's) corps had withdrawn to Versailles, leaving Napoleon's
headquarters at Fontainebleau unprotected. Given that the
plenipotentiaries had come to negotiate with him in the name of the
army, he was amazed to learn through this dispatch that the officers of

---

[74]The plenipotentiaries designated by Napoleon at Fontainebleau on April 4, 1814,
along with the Duke of Vicenza (Caulaincourt), were Marshals Ney, Prince of the
Moskowa, and Macdonald, Duke of Tarento. The three plenipotentiaries arrived in
Essonnes around 4 p.m. They asked Marmont to come with them and left around 6
p.m. After stopping in Petit-Bourg, where General Schwarzenberg was, they reached
Paris and were received at dawn by Emperor Alexander. But a second meeting took
place in the afternoon of April 5. Marmont was present at the first, but had avoided
going to the second, as noted by Marchand. Caulaincourt stated: "His conscience was
so heavy that he was no doubt anxious to escape our stares."

[75]Charles-Philip, Prince of Schwarzenberg, Austrian field marshal and diplomat, born
and died in Vienna (1771-1820). He first distinguished himself in the Austrian army
during the wars of the Revolution. Lieutenant general in 1800, he cleverly escaped the
capitulation of Ulm in 1805. Austrian ambassador in Saint Petersburg in 1808, he was
posted to Paris after the 1809 campaign, for the negotiations of the marriage of Napoleon and Marie-Louise. It was on this occasion that he gave the famous party that
ended in a fire.
   Beginning in 1812, he resumed service in the army, and commanded the Allied
armies in Leipzig and during the battle of France in 1814.

that corps supported the act of forfeiture proclaimed by the Senate. The negotiators—themselves taken aback by such inconceivable news—tried to mitigate the bad impression this dispatch had just made on the emperor (Alexander), but nothing more could change his mind, and the meeting had to break up.

The marshals returned to Fontainebleau[77]and told the Emperor how Emperor Alexander's good intentions had suddenly altered when he learned of the defection of Marmont's corps, and of their useless efforts to convince the prince that the treason of a commander and a few generals did not represent the devoted feelings of that corps toward the Emperor, but the monarch had no longer wanted to hear anything.

The thought of being abandoned by a man whose fortune he had made, with whom he had shared his bread, upon whom he thought he could rely, was very painful to him, and must remain a tragic remorse in the heart of the man guilty of it, since that defection prevented the army from imposing its conditions, and the house of Bourbons was recalled to the throne.

---

[76]The afternoon conversation with Alexander started favorably; the tsar seemed "shaken" when one of his ADCs advised of a message brought by an officer of Schwarzenberg's. The emperor asked what he wanted; the ADC replied in Russian: "To inform you that the Duke of Raguse's corps joined our side this morning, and is before our outposts." Caulaincourt, who spoke Russian, had understood. The news brought a complete change of heart in Alexander. Caulaincourt attempted a last and emotional move: it was met with refusal. Napoleon had to "abdicate unconditionally."

[77]The three plenipotentiaries had returned to Fontainebleau during the night of April 5-6. They woke Napoleon at 1 a.m. to inform him of the failure of their mission.

Sending this marshal to Paris was unfortunate; General Souham,[78] who had remained alone to command that army corps, feared that knowledge of his treason might reach the Emperor, and that his head—as well as those of the others who, like himself, were part of the conspiracy—would pay the price. Those traitors precipitated the movement that was to take place only on orders from the Duke of Raguse (Marmont); they made the soldiers believe they were marching against the enemy. They left amid cries of Vive l'Empereur! and only discovered in Versailles the treason of their commanders, whom they sought in order to punish them, but these had withdrawn from the furor of the moment. This decision, the result of which was so fatal, might not have been made had the marshal remained with his corps. The Emperor abdicated with these fine words:

The Allied Powers having proclaimed that the Emperor Napoleon is the only obstacle to peace in Europe, the Emperor, true to his promise, declares that he renounces for himself and his heirs the throne of France and

---

[78]Joseph Souham (1760-1837) was a product of the armies of the Revolution; he was a major general in 1793, and seemed to have a great taste for politics. His close relations with Pichegru and Moreau brought him problems and various suspensions, followed by reinstatement. Napoleon gave him command of a division in Spain, where he was wounded. He served with distinction in Germany, and was wounded in Lutzen, then Leipzig. He was in 1814 Marmont's principal lieutenant in front of Paris, and his role in the Duke of Raguse's defection appears to have been a major one. Having joined the Bourbons, he was stricken from the rosters at the return from Elba; the royal government made him governor of Strasbourg. He retired in 1832.

[It is believed by some authorities that while he was First Consul, Napoleon had an affair with Souham's wife which resulted in the birth of a child, a daughter. The mother admitted to this. Though time had passed, Souham may not have been unhappy to participate in an act that would obviously injure Napoleon. See: André Gavoty, "Le Secret de Rosalie Souham," *La Revue des Deux Mondes*.—Ed.]

Italy, and that there is no sacrifice, even that of life itself, that he is not ready to make for the welfare of France.[79]

Executed at the Fontainebleau palace, April 11, 1814

During the night of April 11-12, the Emperor tried to kill himself with poison.[80] Since the retreat from Moscow, he had kept in his travel kit an envelope containing a substance meant to bring instant death. He used this, but—either because it had lost some of its potency, or because his stomach contracted too soon—he vomited everything, and the expected result failed to occur. At 11 p.m. he called for the Dukes of Bassano (Maret) and Vicenza (Caulaincourt), and for Counts de Turenne and Bertrand, and told them about the attempt he had made, saying: "God does not want this!"

---

[79]Without any transition Marchand cites the text of the Fontainebleau abdication, which he dates April 11, 1814. In fact it was written and signed by Napoleon on April 6. He gave it that same day to Caulaincourt, who was on his way to Paris to see the Russian emperor: "I am entrusting this abdication to your honor and faithfulness. Give me your word not to hand it over until the treaty has been signed, and you have received guarantees that the French government will abide by all its clauses."

Emperor Alexander received Caulaincourt during the night of April 6-7. He already knew Napoleon intended to abdicate, because of an indiscretion by Marshal Ney. Alexander demanded the abdication, and Caulaincourt had to show it. But he handed it over officially only when the treaty determining Napoleon's situation was signed by the negotiators on April 11. It is on that date of April 11, 1814, that the abdication appears in the *Bulletin des Lois*, and that date is given by Marchand.

No one knows where the original document is: the facsimile was traced by Baron Fain, and is kept at the Fontainebleau palace. The original appears nowhere, neither in the Archives nationales nor in the Bibliothèque Nationale.

The date and location of the signature ceremony is erroneously described to Fontainebleau visitors as being "April 5 in the king's study"; it was in fact April 6 in Napoleon's study.

[80]This poisoning attempt has been contested by certain historians. It is however confirmed by Marchand. Revealed for the first time by Norvins, it was mentioned by Thiers, Constant, Bourrienne, and Fain. But the best recounting of the episode is given us by Caulaincourt in his *Mémoires* (vol. III, chap. ix). The date is subject to dispute. Thiers, Constant, and Bourrienne say it was during the night of April 11-12. So does Marchand. But Fain and Caulaincourt say April 12-13, and they seem to be right.

The time for defections had arrived: Prince Berthier had left the Emperor, assuring him of his return. This old friend never appeared again. During the day, the Emperor called for his first valet Constant:[81] he had left, never to return either. His mameluke Roustam[82] had left for Paris, and was not seen again. His surgeon M. Yvan[83] had also abandoned him. Those he had the most right to count on, having heaped kindness on them at the peak of his power, were deserting him in adversity. His first valet Constant, whom he honored with his affection, and the slave Roustam, given to him in Egypt, both smothered with kindness, yielded to ingratitude and abandoned their master in his adversity; both were marked in a list Napoleon

---

[81]More exactly, Constant Wairy, a Belgian, born December 2, 1778, in Peruwelz, a community that later became part of the department of Jemmapes. He first worked for Joséphine, then, when Bonaparte was leaving for Marengo, became his valet. Although somewhat uneducated, he left his *Mémoires*. But these were written by several authors: Roquefort, Méliot, A. Luchet, Nisard, and mainly Villemarest. They must be consulted with reservation.

This ungrateful man dared complain about Napoleon's lack of generosity toward him. But here are some of the benefits he received: in addition to his salary of 6,000 francs and 2,000 francs in clothing allowance, he had a seven-room apartment, a dining accommodation for four, a carriage with horses and a coachman at his service, and access to all four major theaters; besides allowances in the field or during travels, he received from the Emperor between 1808 and 1814, 1,800 livres in income, an annual pension of 6,000 francs, and sums totaling some 260,000 francs. This did not prevent him from deserting at Fontainebleau, taking with him much money and jewelry, Napoleon said himself. I was able to collect a few mementos of Constant at the Malmaison Museum, among these his pastel portrait by Schmidt (1813) and the porcelain cup in which the Emperor's valet served him hot chocolate.

[82]The famous mameluke Roustam received by Napoleon in Egypt from Sheik El Becri. Having brought him back to France, he had the armorer Boutet teach him how to load weapons. He took him everywhere; Roustam was in all the parades, wearing surprising costumes covered with embroidery, and headgear made of blue or red velvet embroidered in gold and topped with a plume, galloping on a horse with an oriental harness, and clanging his saber. Roustam, paid 2,400 francs as a mameluke, also drew 2,400 francs as assistant weapon-bearer, without counting all the gratuities that at least doubled his wages. In the year XIII he had received a pension of 500 livres. At Fontainebleau in 1814, Napoleon gave him a lottery office with a sum of 50,000 francs. Such generosity did not prevent Roustam, in April 1814, from deserting along with his friend Constant.

established before leaving for 50,000 francs out of the 2 million assigned to him by the Fontainebleau treaty.

Next to these cowardly abandonments, it is a pleasure to record acts of devotion:

Countess Bertrand,[84] six months pregnant, left Empress Marie-Louise, whom she had accompanied to Blois and Orléans, to come to Fontainebleau, preparing to accompany the Emperor to Elba with her children when His Majesty was settled there. The war minister held back until the last minute the order that was to hand over Elba to the Emperor, and the devoted Duke of Vicenza (Caulaincourt) had to intercede with the Russian emperor to get the order expedited.

On his abdication, the Emperor kept an income for himself and his family, and retained his personal property for the latter. The principality of Elba was guaranteed to him. The Emperor had not demanded Corsica,[85] as close to the coasts of France as those of Italy. Corsica had to be either French or Italian, but only as part of France did it properly fit into the naval and commercial Mediterranean network.

---

[83]Yvan was Napoleon's regular surgeon. Attached to Bonaparte as early as the Italian campaign, he followed the Emperor throughout all his European travels. He treated the Emperor after he was wounded in 1809 at Ratisbonne. He appears in the Gautherot painting in the Versailles museum depicting that war episode.

In addition to his annual salary of 12,000 francs, Yvan was named head surgeon at the Invalides hospital. Napoleon made him an officer of the Legion of Honor and named him baron with an annual endowment of 9,000 francs, not counting the many bonuses that varied each year between 25,000 and 30,000 francs.

At Fontainebleau on the evening of April 14, when Napoleon had just given him 200,000 francs and the cross of commander of the Legion of Honor, Yvan—who seemed to have gone crazy—went to the stables, grabbed a horse, and galloped away toward Paris. Napoleon never forgave him.

[84]While only a major general, Grand Marshal Bertrand had married in 1808 Fanny Dillon, daughter of General Arthur Dillon, deputy from Martinique to the Etats Généraux and guillotined in 1794, and of Laure Girardin de Montgerald, widow of M. de la Touche, a cousin of Empress Joséphine. The family had roots in Ireland.

While the grand marshal made the perilous journey through southern France with Napoleon on their way to Elba, Mme Bertrand went to Châteauroux and waited at her father-in-law's for the appropriate moment to join her husband. In early July she started on her way with her children, a maid, and a servant.

Under Napoleon's sovereignty, it was only Corsica, and became dependent on British power that the Corsicans had repudiated. The Emperor's most cherished title was that of being French, and it remained intact at the moment when fate deserted him. Should he sacrifice this also? Should he extend it to the Corsicans? How would they look upon him? Would their government not before long become riddled with British, French, or Sardinian intrigues? It was wiser and showed more foresight to give up on Corsica, whose people he loved and held in high esteem. In his sacrifice for France, the Emperor wanted nothing; the Fontainebleau treaty was made not for himself but for his people. His abnegation was complete, the treaty of Fontainebleau could never degrade its grandeur, its glory remains entirely his. His friends' foresight, though frustrated, shall always do them honor. The violation of the stipulations they had negotiated only proves the immorality and lack of political sense of those guilty of it. It was also stipulated that a sum of two million francs would be taken from the personal holdings that he was surrendering to France, and be paid to the generals of his guard, his officers, and the members of his household. Napoleon assigned the sums, but nothing was paid out. The other financial terms of his abdication were also violated. MM. de La Bouillerie[86] and Dudon[87] delivered to Orléans the Emperor's private treasure[88] and his portfolio. The 38 million in gold was divided between two enemy commanding generals and four plenipotentiaries of

---

[85]We know through Caulaincourt's *Mémoires* (vol. III, p. 250) that Napoleon approved the action of his faithful ambassador to the Allied powers in not asking for Corsica instead of Elba, since Corsica was a French department that should not be stripped from France. The Emperor had said to Caulaincourt: "I agree with you entirely; poor France shall be stripped enough when they come to the peace treaty."

[86]François Roullet de la Bouillerie was born in La Flèche on April 27, 1764, and died there on April 7, 1833. He was the First Consul's private cashier, treasurer general of the expeditionary force to England, and treasurer general of the special domain. He nevertheless abandoned the Emperor in 1814. When the Bourbons returned, he became superintendent of the king's civil list and secretary general of the ministry for the king's household. La Bouillerie became deputy for the Sarthe in 1816 and 1820, and was made a peer of France in 1827, with the title of state minister. It can be under-stood that the Emperor refused to see him during the Hundred Days.

the Allied courts. M. Peyrusse,[89] the army treasurer, was sent to Orléans to retrieve the Emperor's portfolio, containing 40 million in various securities. He brought back only 2.5 million francs.[90]

---

[87]Jean-François Dudon (1778-1857), auditor in the council of State in 1813, general superintendent of the northern army in Spain in 1809; attorney general of the Seal council in 1810, councillor of State in 1815, he became deputy for the Ain and the Loire-Inférieure. Napoleon had made him a baron of the Empire on November 22, 1808.

[88]For details on the Emperor's treasure mentioned here, see Pasquier's *Mémoires* (11, 366), Peyrusse's *Mémorial et Archives, Mémorial de Sainte-Hélène* (IV, 135), Frédéric Masson's *L'Affaire Maubreuil* (March-April 1814).

[89]Baron Guillaume Peyrusse was born in Carcassonne on June 16, 1776. He was first paymaster for the crown treasury. On March 24, 1809, he was made paymaster for the crown treasury in the imperial army headquarters; in that capacity he participated in the campaigns of Germany, Moscow, Saxony, and France. He was made deputy inspector for the imperial guard and a knight of the Legion of Honor in 1814. After the Fontainebleau abdication, he became head treasurer in Elba. He returned to Paris with Napoleon, became a baron of the Empire, treasurer general for the crown, an officer of the Legion of Honor. Under Louis-Philippe, he became mayor of Carcassonne, and councillor general of the Aude. In 1853, Napoleon III made him a commander of the Legion of Honor. He died in 1860.

[90]Peyrusse's *1809-1815. Mémorial et archives de M. le baron Peyrusse* (published in 1869) gives good information on Napoleon's financial situation at the time of the abdication. On April 10, 488,913 francs remained in Peyrusse's money chest. The next day, April 11, the Emperor sent his treasurer to Orléans. In spite of difficult communications, already hindered by enemy partisans between Fontainebleau and Orléans, Peyrusse arrived there on April 12. He learned that six million had been saved, out of some 40 million. About 34 million had been handed over to the enemy, through Dudon's fault. Out of the remaining six million, he managed to take with him 2,933,600 francs, slightly more than Marchand indicates. After having the remaining chests holding the money covered with manure, Peyrusse left his servant to keep an eye on them. Then he undertook to return to Fontainebleau. Cossacks were patrolling the area around Orléans. He managed to send his servant to Grand Marshal Bertrand, to inform him of the situation and ask for troops to protect his return. A battalion under the command of General Cambronne was sent to meet Peyrusse who, informed of this, got under way. The funds he had taken were soon placed in safety in a wagon brought by Cambronne's soldiers. He arrived at Fontainebleau on the night of April 16, and on April 17 reported to the Emperor on his mission and the result.

When Napoleon left for Elba, he carried with him about 3.5 million francs.

The Emperor came down from his apartment by the great staircase, surrounded by the friends who had remained faithful to him, generals, and senior officers of the guard. After touching farewells to his guard in the person of General Petit whom he embraced, and having kissed the eagle, he departed for Elba at 11 a.m.[91] on April 20, accompanied by Generals Bertrand and Drouot, and by the Allied commissioners.[92]

Since I, along with curator of the wardrobe Gervais,[93] had been assigned the task of going back to Paris to pick up the Emperor's personal effects, we got under way, saddened by all that we had seen; and arrived there at 6 p.m.

Informed that the Empress was still at Rambouillet,[94] I left the following morning to go there; I wished to see my mother, who was accompanying the young prince to Vienna. Emperor Alexander was just leaving the Empress. The princess was informed that I was going with the Emperor, and she expressed her satisfaction to my mother. Countess Montesquiou, when handing me her letter, told me to assure the Emperor that she would always take care of his son. I was leaving my mother, when would I see her again? After such great misfortunes,

---

[91]The famous "Farewell" ceremony appears to have taken place a little later than stated by Marchand, probably between noon and 1 p.m. Cf. Jean Bourguignon, *Malmaison, Compiègne, Fontainebleau* (Paris, 1946), 234-38.

[92]Count Antoine Drouot (1774-1847), famous artillery officer of the Grand Army. After a splendid career, he insisted on going to Elba with the Emperor, who called him "the wise man of the Grand Army" and said of him "Drouot is the epitome of virtue." W. Serieyx, *Drouot et Napoléon* (Paris, 1931).

[93]The position of "curator of the wardrobe" had been created at the beginning of the Empire and given to Charvet, according to Frédéric Masson.

[94]When the Allies threatened Paris, Empress Marie-Louise left the capital on March 29 for Blois. She stopped at Rambouillet on the 30th, and only arrived in Blois the evening of April 2. She left there on the 8th to stay in Orléans until April 12. She was back in Rambouillet by the 13th, remaining there until April 23, before returning to Vienna. After the Emperor's departure from Fontainebleau, when Marchand went to Paris on April 20 and learned that the Empress was still at Rambouillet, he went there on the 21st and was thus able to see his mother, the King of Rome's nurse.

what was to be ours? The moment was heartbreaking. I wrenched myself away from her embrace, after holding her tight against me, and left.

I returned to Paris during the night, and on the 22nd Gervais and I were on the road to Lyon, hurrying our horses to catch up with the Emperor in Fréjus. We traveled by boat on the Rhône down to Avignon, thinking we would hasten our journey, but we only arrived in Fréjus on the 29th. The Emperor, accompanied by the commissioners, had sailed the day before from Saint-Raphaël on the frigate *Undaunted*.[95] While going through Orgon,[96] we heard that an uprising had been organized to assassinate the Emperor. Decent people were upset and indignant at this. In Avignon and Aix, the people were still excited; nothing had been spared in Provence to rouse the population against Napoleon and intimidate the upright citizens who would have rushed to his defense.

Some considered it strange that he decided to take the British ship, rather than the French one awaiting his orders. His Majesty wished to spare the officers of the French frigate *Driade* and the brig *Inconstant*, and M. de Montcabrié who commanded them, the embarrassment of taking him there and sharing the pain and humiliation of his deportation. Outside of France, was he still under the yoke of military surrender of the April 11 treaty? If so, was it up to the French navy to carry out that portion? If not, couldn't Napoleon

---

[95]This frigate, which the British commissioner Sir Neil Campbell had had come from Marseille at Napoleon's request, was commanded by Captain Usher; the Emperor went on board the evening of the 28th. The next morning at 11 a.m., the *Undaunted* sailed for Elba. On May 3 at 8 p.m., it was anchored at the entrance to the Porto Ferrajo harbor.

[96]Orgon, Bouches-du-Rhône, in the Arles district, is 6 km. from Cavaillon. Violent demonstrations occurred there on Monday, April 15, when Napoleon came through, which upset him. They were led by a peasant named Durel, head of a royalist group.

Cf. Paul Bartel, *Napoléon à l'île d'Elbe* (Paris, 1947).

pay a courtesy to the British navy and Captain Usher, and save the French frigate from entering Porto Ferrajo only with a flag of truce and under British escort? Peace had not yet been signed, and even the *Undaunted* carried only a truce flag.[97]

In Fréjus, all was quiet. We were busy finding a ship for Elba when Princess Pauline, who was in Muy,[98] advised us that a Neapolitan or British frigate she was expecting at any moment was to take her to Naples, and that it would stop in Porto Ferrajo and drop us off. We waited for a few days which seemed very long to us, in spite of a wonderful reception from the Colle family; its head had just been removed as mayor because of his Bonapartist ideas, which earned him banishment after the Hundred Days and 18 months in jail for his oldest son, ruining his health. M. Savournin, son of the owner of the castle where the princess was staying, came to Fréjus; like us he was going to Elba, to become the Emperor's secretary (not seeing him arrive, the Emperor took M. Rathery, the grand marshal's secretary, and M. Savournin remained with Count Bertrand). He told us the princess would board the Neapolitan frigate *Letizia* in Villefranche, and that we had no other course but to go to Nice, wait for the princess, and board the *Letizia* or the British frigate[99] that was to escort her to Elba.

All three of us left for Antibes and Villefranche; our passports had visas for Elba. We had hardly arrived in Villefranche when 12 or

---

[97]On the evening of April 27 the French frigate *Driade* and the brig *Inconstant* arrived in Toulon, instead of the corvette promised by the treaty. Peytes de Montcabrié who commanded them reported to Napoleon, telling him he had been ordered to escort him to Elba. But the Emperor, doubting the Bourbons' good faith, would have none of it. Since he was being refused the corvette he was entitled to, he would rather sail "equal to equal" under a foreign flag than "defeated and banished" under the Bourbon flag. He added: "I have given my word to the British, I shall not take it back."

[98]Princess Pauline had left Nice in mid-March to take the sulfur waters in Gréoux. Concerned about the turn of events, she had stopped in Luc (Var), where M. Charles, a deputy, had loaned her his house in Bouillidou, a mile from the village. Bonaparte had stopped there on his return from Egypt. There too Napoleon, before reaching Fréjus 37 km. away, met his sister. To make room for him she had moved to Rayol, near Muy, 15 km. from Fréjus, to the house of M. Savournin, a faithful servant of the Empire.

15 women, real harpies, came into the adjoining room and started to dance a jig, wanting us to join in. After they left, the harbor captain, a Corsican who never went out without two pistols in his belt, came to warn us not to spend the night in this town and to go to Nice, where we could quietly await the princess' arrival. We followed his advice. The British frigate and the *Letizia* arrived, we went on board the former, and the two frigates sailed in formation. The princess went on board the British frigate, where a party awaited her. On June 1 we arrived in Porto Ferrajo after a few days' crossing. I proceeded immediately to the palace, where the Emperor was lunching. Informed of my arrival, he had me come in. I handed him the letter the Empress had given to me, and that given me by Countess Montesquiou. After reading them, the Emperor asked me what had delayed me, and I explained. When he asked about Rambouillet, I told him that I knew through my mother that, as soon as the Bourbons' recall was known in Blois, all the high civil servants who had followed the Empress there promptly left her to go to Paris; this desertion was painful to see. General Schouwaloff had brought the Empress and the King of Rome back to Orléans, where she was subjected to the most shameful pilferage, so that she arrived at Rambouillet without a thing.

Returning to his private quarters, a few minutes later he asked me a number of questions about the Empress and his son, to which I replied by repeating what I had been told by Her Majesty's people: that the Empress had wanted to join him in Fontainebleau, but that as soon as her resolve was taken, a message had been sent to Count Schwarzenberg, who was in the area, and he had immediately sent troops to counter this meeting. I had been assured that her doctor, M. Corvisart,[100] had told her the air in Elba would not be good for her health; others had said that since the Emperor held many things against her father, he would not feel the same way about her; and finally, in the best interests of the King of Rome, it would be better for her to join

---

[99]This was the British frigate *Curaçao*, commanded by Captain Tower, who when referring to Napoleon used only the term the great man. It was on board this frigate that Marchand and his companions, Gervais and Savournin, sailed on May 30, arriving in Porto Ferrajo on June 1.

Napoleon enters Porto Ferrajo greeted by the townspeople and the Mayor.

Porto Ferrajo as it looked to Napoleon. Salt beds are in the foreground.

Under the walls of Stella Fort, the Mulini Palace is chosen by Napoleon for his household. His rooms are on the ground floor of the two-story building on the left facing the garden.

The Mulini Palace as seen from Fort Stella.

Salon at the Mulini Palace.

Napoleon's summer house, San Martin. He is quartered on the ground floor with reception rooms above.

Porto Longone in 1814. Napoleon maintains a residence in the fortress.

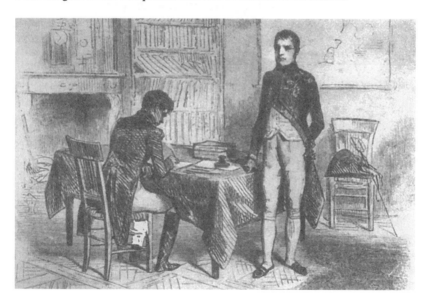

Orders of the day are dictated.

her father. The Empress, tired or ill because of all these contradictions, had talked it over with Countess Montesquiou, a woman of sage counsel. The latter had told her the dutiful path was that leading to the Emperor, and that, since she was being allowed to speak her mind, the Empress should heed her advice. The Empress responded: "That is indeed my intention." But once back within her entourage, Her Majesty had again listened to her advisers. It was decided she would go to Rambouillet, where she arrived ill and unhappy to see around her the people whose friendship she was entitled to count on urging her toward a conclusion of the drama that would then allow them to return to their own habits. I told His Majesty that when the Austrian emperor arrived at Rambouillet, the Empress had rushed in tears into her father's arms, presented her son to him, and asked him to look after him. The Austrian emperor had appeared very embarrassed and had taken the King of Rome in his arms to kiss him, but the prince, on returning home, had told his governess Maman Quiou: "Grandpa is not handsome." The Emperor got a good laugh from his son's observant remark.

I reported to him the observations I had made on the way; I told him that in Orgon, Avignon, and Aix, people were still very excited.

In the days that followed, I learned through Noverraz[101] of the obstacles set up along the route the Emperor was to follow, in order to assassinate him.

---

[100]Marie-Louise alleged poor health for not going to Elba. Was this real or a pretext? The Emperor wanted to know: to this end, he asked for a decisive opinion from Corvisart, the doctor he still trusted and whose attachment and gratitude he did not doubt, about the trip, the climate in Elba, and how the Empress would tolerate it [Cf. J. Bourguignon, *Corvisart, premier médicin de l'Empereur* (Lyons, 1937)]. The requested consultation was immediately written out in front of Mme de Montebello. It was highly pessimistic, and it forbid the Emperor to either order or even express a wish that Marie-Louise accompany him to Elba at this time. The doctor added that he doubted the Empress and the King of Rome could ever live there. In any event, it would be out of the question for her to stay there, no matter how short a time, before a long rest cure in Aix. Corvisart concluded: "Aix is salvation, Elba is death, for both mother and child."

The Emperor had left Fontainebleau on Wednesday, April 20, at 11 a.m., followed by 14 carriages and escorted by the imperial guard stretched out along part of the road. In his carriage were Generals Bertrand and Drouot, sometimes together, sometimes taking turns. He was accompanied by four commissioners of the Allied courts: the Russian Count Schouwaloff, the Austrian General Koller, the British Colonel Campbell, and the Prussian Count Waldburg-Truchsess, to whom we owe a description of this journey, during which any respect for adversity was totally absent.[102]

The Emperor slept in the following places: Briare, April 20; Nevers, April 21; Roanne, April 22, escort arrangements keeping him there for 12 hours. He went through Lyon on the evening of the 23rd and went on to sleep in Péage du Roussillon,[103] between Saint Vallier and Valence. On the 24th he encountered Marshal Augereau. They got out of their carriages and approached one another; the Emperor touched his hat, the marshal his cap, which he kept on. This general seemed very embarrassed; they walked away from the carriages to talk, then parted to proceed each on his way. The Emperor did not yet know of the indecent proclamation this marshal had made to his army.[104] In Valence, there were 150 Austrian chasseurs to serve as escort.

---

[101]Noverraz was Swiss, from the Vaud. He was admitted to the Emperor's household in 1809 and promoted in 1813 to footman in his personal service. He rode on the seat of the imperial vehicles during the campaigns of 1813 and 1814. He then took up the position of runner, and wore as a result a two-pointed hat with rooster feathers. This was a servant capable of risking his life for his master. He proved this, as later related by Marchand, when going through Orgon where, at great danger to himself, he had prevented a hostile population from approaching the vehicle he had under his care.

[102]Napoleon himself said in Saint Helena that the two books that had hurt him most were: de Pradt, *L'Histoire de l'Ambassade de Varsovie* (Paris, 1815), and Waldburg-Truchsess, *Relation de Waldburg-Truchsess* (Paris, 1815).

[103]In fact, during the night of the 23rd, Napoleon continued his journey in his sleeping-car. On Sunday the 24th, he breakfasted early, 20 km. past Vienne, at Péage du Roussillon (Isère).

The Emperor's first service had arrived in Valence, and were ready to eat, when two gendarmes came on behalf of the marshal to ask the people to leave town. In spite of arguments that they had just stopped to eat and would be leaving immediately thereafter, one of the marshals' ADCs came to force them back into their carriages, although the meal was on the table. They were obliged to leave, threats having turned to the use of force.

The Emperor heard about these details only in Valence, when he received a copy of the marshal's proclamation; after reading it, he said: "Still the same man, what a wretch!" The Austrian commissioner couldn't help telling the Emperor: "Your Majesty has treated with

---

[104]Charles Augereau, Duke of Castiglione, marshal of France; son of a manservant and a fruit merchant of the faubourg Saint-Marceau; born rue Mouffetard in Paris on October 21, 1757, died in 1816 of a "chest edema" on his lands at La Houssaye (Seine-et-Marne).

After serving in the royal army, he fought in the Revolution campaigns, became a major general in 1793, and distinguished himself under Bonaparte during the Italian campaigns in 1796. He won the battle of Castiglione. He then replaced Hoche at the head of the armies of the Sambre-et-Meuse and Rhin-et-Moselle (1797), and that same year assumed command of the Rhine army. He left that command in 1798, and in 1799 was elected deputy of the Haute-Garonne at the council of the Five Hundred. He opposed the 18 Brumaire, but supported the Consulate.

He commanded the Batavian armies in Germany (1800-1801), then the Bayonne camp (1803), and finally the Brest camp (1804). Marshal of the Empire, commander of the 13th cohort of the Legion of Honor, he commanded the 7th corps of the Grand Army (1805-1807). Wounded at Eylau, where his corps was decimated, he returned to France, and was named Duke of Castiglione in 1808. In 1809 he commanded the 8th corps of the army of Germany, then the 7th corps of the army of Spain, replacing Gouvion Saint-Cyr. In 1810, he took over as commander in chief of the army of Catalonia, but was soon replaced by Macdonald. In 1812 he commanded the Grand Army 11th corps in Germany, commanded in Berlin the following year, and soon became governor of Frankfurt. He took part in the battle of Leipzig. In 1814, he commanded the army of the East (from the Rhone to Lyon). Finally, beaten by the Allies in Saint-Georges (March 18, 1814), he pulled out of Lyon and retreated to Valence (March 23), abandoning Napoleon and insulting him in his April 1814 proclamations. He met Napoleon near Valence on April 26. He rejoined the king's cause, became a knight of Saint-Louis (June 1, 1814) and governor of Lyon (June 21). He was stricken from the list of marshals on the Emperor's return, though he took part in the Champ-de-Mai ceremony (June 1, 1815). He nevertheless came out in favor of the Emperor, offering his services to Napoleon, who turned him down. After the Hundred Days, Augereau came back to Louis XVIII, but the king also turned him down.

great kindness a man who scarcely deserves it." During the Hundred Days, Augereau wrote a long letter to the Emperor, assuring him of his devotion and denying he was ever a traitor. At the same time, he published in Caen a proclamation about Louis XVIII, just as indecent as the one in Valence about the Emperor.

Well-informed people have assured me that Augereau, once in Lyon, found himself in the theater surrounded by Austrian officers, and that a voice in the top balcony yelled: "Isn't there another town remaining to be betrayed?" The pit applauded, the Austrian officers stared at one another, and the marshal left.

While in Elba the Emperor occasionally spoke of this marshal: he wrote of him that when actually victorious he always thought himself on the verge of being beaten, and would call for more troops, claiming that otherwise he couldn't hold on. "I would arrive with a few of my staff officers, spread out a map, and show him that his position was excellent; his morale would then be restored, and he would become cocky. He was a good general who had captured many divisions in the Italian campaigns, but a mean man who had been badly brought up, having faults and vices that neither time nor his high position could correct."

The Emperor slept on the 25th in Montélimar;[105] all along the road the Emperor had received nothing but signs of affection from the population. In Avignon, they had been aroused; in Orgon, the same events occurred, the same assassination plots. A man rushed like a madman to open the carriage door. The Emperor's messenger Nover-

---

[105]In fact, the Emperor did not sleep in Montélimar on the 25th, but arrived there on Sunday the 24th around 6:30 p.m. He stopped there only a few hours, at the *Hôtel de la Poste*. The town officials, draped in their sashes of office, welcomed him. Napoleon pleasantly listened to the local news. Around 7:30 he sat down to eat with Bertrand and Drouot. His supper consisted of soup, fish, chops, stew, and asparagus; he drank a glass of chambertin and a cup of coffee. At the hotel he greeted M. Gaud de Rousillac and chatted with the hotel proprietor, M. Chabeaud. He got under way again around 8:30 p.m. and spent the night in his sleeping carriage. Via Donzère, he went through Orange at 3 a.m. and reached the Avignon relay station at dawn on the 25th. That morning he was insulted by the Orgon population. He spent the night of the 25th at the Auberge de la Calade, 8 km. before Aix.

raz, sitting on the seat, pulled out his saber with one hand and a pistol with the other, and paying no attention to the crowd, threatened the first man who dared come near the carriage. The grand marshal lowered the window and yelled at him to keep quiet. This brisk action by Noverraz and the grand marshal's wise recommendation quieted the first rabble movement, and allowed time for decent people to get them away from the carriage.

The Austrian commissioner got angry and said to the mayor: "If you don't put an end immediately to these disgusting scenes, I'll have 20,000 men here within two hours who will tear the place apart." The uproar was quieted. Orgon was too far from the center for the assassination attempt to be well organized. There too, however, some disgusting scenes occurred: a mannequin representing the Emperor was executed not far from the horse relay. The commissioners moved the crowd aside and put an end to the cries. He arrived, not without danger, at Princess Pauline's at Luc, and boarded the British frigate at Saint-Raphaël.

Until reaching the South, Napoleon's route had been peaceful.

Until reaching the South, Napoleon's route had been peaceful. On May 3, the *Undaunted* arrived in the Porto Ferrajo roadstead. The

Emperor dispatched General Drouot[106] to inform General Dalesme[107] and the local officials and population of his arrival. General Drouot informed the public officials of the new sovereign's intentions. No change was to be made in the administration, all employees were to keep their positions.

The Emperor invited the island sub-prefect, Balbiani,[108] on board. He named him superintendent, and asked him to research the

---

[106]In the manuscript margin next to Drouot's name, Marchand added the following note based on the general's own testimony, relating a familiar anecdote:

General Drouot said that from an early age he had liked to study. "When my parents, who were bakers, saw my aptitude, they agreed to provide me with teachers, and I thus reached the moment when I could apply for an artillery 2nd lieutenant's posting. My dress, my small size, and my discomfort contrasted with the elegant young men who were also applying; my coming seemed to surprise both the audience and my colleagues. I modestly sat down, awaiting my turn to be called. M. La Place was one of the examiners, and I was among the last to be called; I answered with assurance the questions asked of me. The examiner, quite surprised, took pleasure in extending the exam beyond what had been asked of the others, and proclaimed me head of the class. It certainly was the finest day of my life because of the happiness I was bringing my parents."

On Elba, when the Emperor spoke to him of his return to France, the change in color for the brig, and the provisions to be loaded aboard, he listened like a man surprised by such an endeavor. But once that moment had passed, he undertook by all courses and means to ensure its success, acting just as the entire battalion did: obeying the sovereign's orders.

[107]General Baron Jean-Baptiste Dalesme. Born in Limoges on June 20, 1763, died in Paris at the Invalides hospital on April 13, 1832. After being wounded on the Danube (June 22, 1809) he received a 4,000 franc pension. He became commander of the Ombrone department (May 22, 1810), baron of the Empire (June 23, 1810), and commanding general in Elba (October 24, 1810), succeeding General Dazémar who remained there only six months. Napoleon found him there in May 1814. When the Emperor returned for the Hundred Days, he named him major general and governor of Elba. But under the second Restoration, he was retired by royal ordinance (September 15, 1825). In 1830, after the fall of the Bourbons, he would become commander of the Invalides hospital and grand officer of the Legion of Honor.

[108]Balbiani, as Elba's sub-prefect, had greeted Napoleon's arrival with a proclamation couched in hyperbolic terms. Continuing in his post, he was then named superintendent, having authority over the island's entire judicial system. Under the sub-prefect came all the small kingdom's judicial organizations (court of appeals, supreme court of appeals, and the civil court). Paul Bartel, *Napoléon à l'île d'Elbe* (Paris, 1947).

color of Elba's first flag. It was found that the first house governing
the island as sovereigns had been that of the Appiani in Pisa; its banner
was white with bees, since appi means bees in Italian.[109] Having left
the Emperor, the sub-prefect informed all the island officials that His
Majesty would land the next day, and would receive them with pleasure.

The island of Elba,[110] located in the Mediterranean along the
coast of Greater Tuscany, opposite Piombino, is six leagues in length
and two leagues in width. Its population was then 13,700 inhabitants.
After having attracted the Romans because of its rich iron mines, it
became the property of the kingdom of Two Sicilies, then of the
Piombino principality, and finally of France, to which it belonged
when, through the Paris treaty of April 11, 1814, it was given in all
sovereignty to the Emperor Napoleon, who along with all members of
the imperial family retained his titles and authority.

At 5 p.m. Generals Bertrand and Drouot landed, along with
the Allied commissioners, and proceeded to the Etoile fort and the
offices of General Dalesme, commander of the island. On the spot, an
official report was made of the takeover—carried out by General
Drouot in the name of His Majesty the Emperor Napoleon—of the
island of Elba, its forts, batteries, buildings, military stores, and all
property falling under the crown's domain. Santini[111] was secretly sent

---

[109]The new flag was patterned after that of ancient Tuscany, dating back to Cosmo de
Medici. Napoleon's flag had two crimson horizontal bands separated by a white band.
In the upper left corner was a white field with a diagonal crimson band decorated with
three golden bees.

[110]The island of Elba in the Tyrrhenian sea, now belonging to Italy, province of
Livorno (Tuscany), is separated from the continent by the 15 km.-wide Piombino
canal. It covers 225 square km. and now has a population twice that indicated by
Marchand. This mountainous island has several harbors: Porto Ferrajo, Rio Marina,
Porto Longone, Marciana. Iron has been mined there since antiquity.

In the Middle Ages, Pisans were found there around the 10th century, then
Genoans. Later the Spaniards gave it to the Duke of Savoy, Prince of Piombino, of the
Appiani family. In 1736, it was annexed to the kingdom of Naples. In 1801, Bonaparte
made it part of the kingdom of Etruria, then three years later of the French Empire. It
constituted a special department, then was attached to that of the Méditerranée, until
Napoleon became its sovereign (May 4, 1814 to February 26, 1815).

ashore by the Emperor to sound out the feelings of the population; after returning on board, he reported they were full of enthusiasm that such a great man was becoming their sovereign.

Early in April, an uprising had occurred in Marciana and British troops had landed. On April 21, the Porto Longone Italian garrison had mutinied and killed or wounded some of its officers; the mutineers had been driven out of the fort. They were roaming the countryside, enticing peasants to join the British. On April 27, General Dalesme received from a British frigate the strange demand to hand over the island and its fort. Finally, on the 28th, the same frigate turned up with a truce flag and an ADC to the war minister debarked, carrying dispatches from His Excellency to General Dalesme. They announced the Emperor's abdication, his imminent arrival, and the fact that the island, forts, and artillery were to be handed over to him.

The frigate's captain was invited ashore, and General Dalesme showed him the dispatches he had just received. The captain said he had known of their content for two days, but had to obey the orders of Commodore Montrésor, who at the Livorno station did not yet know their contents. He then requested for himself and for the other ships of the Tuscany coast squadron permission to enter the harbor and salute the white [royal] standard that had just been raised. General Dalesme thanked him for this unaccustomed courtesy, but refused entry on the pretext that the appearance of British naval forces might cause trouble on the island. The minister's ADC went back on board, and by noon the truce ship was out of sight.

On May 4, the Elban garrison and the national guard turned out in full dress; the officials, the commanding general, and the sub-prefect, followed by an enthusiastic population, proceeded to the har-

---

[111] Jean-Noël Santini, born in Corsica in 1790, in the poor village of Lama, near Bastia. He was a Corsican infantryman until 1812, then a messenger at general headquarters. In 1814, he voluntarily followed Napoleon to Elba. He was made keeper of the portfolio and usher. He was a devoted servant of the Emperor, present again in Saint Helena. A very rare document was published under his name: *De Sainte-Hélène aux Invalides, d'après les documents manuscrits de Santini, par Joseph Chautard, son of the commander of the brig Inconstant that brought the Emperor back from Elba... etc.* (Paris, 1854).

bor. The Elbans sensed all the advantages for themselves and for the island of the Emperor's choice of Elba as his residence. The town cannons and those of the fort announced the Emperor's landing; as soon as he was spotted in the gig, he was recognized by his hat and green chasseur of the guard uniform. All arms were extended toward him. Cries of Vive l'Empereur! repeated a thousand times filled the air. It would be difficult to imagine more exuberant happiness. Such a reception must have compensated him for the disgusting scenes of Avignon and Orgon.

The Emperor stepped on shore and greeted the people and the officials. He received the keys to the city, presented by the mayor, with accompanying speeches. [112] The more prominent citizens, including M. Vincent Foresi,[113] hurried to make available to the Emperor all that he would need to get settled. M. Foresi, with enthusiastic zeal, saw to everything and gained everyone's esteem and thanks.

The white standard had been flying since April 28, and the Emperor ordered it taken down and replaced by his own, white with a red band bearing three golden bees. That flag was respected by the Barbary powers who, they said, would not make war on God.

An official report concerning the handing over of the island was immediately written in these words:

On this 4th day of May 1814, His Majesty the Emperor Napoleon having taken possession of the island of Elba, General Drouot, governor, had the island standard raised over the forts in the name of the Emperor: it has a white

---

[112]The mayor, M. Traditi, presented the keys on a silver platter. Napoleon took them, held them for an instant, then returned them, saying: "Take these back, Monsieur le Maire, I am entrusting them to you. I could not make a wiser choice." M. Traditi was subsequently chosen by the Emperor as one of the four chamberlains.

[113]Vincent Foresi, supplier to the naval forces, became a sort of supplier to the imperial court. He often served as a guide for Napoleon on his excursions throughout the island, and in particular accompanied him when the Emperor chose the site of his residence in San Martino. His nephew Emmanuel Foresi published in 1884 in Florence an interesting pamphlet entitled *Napoléon I, all'isola dell'Elba*. The Emperor is depicted therein in familiar and even bucolic terms.

*background with a diagonal red band adorned with three golden bees. This stan-
dard was saluted by the batteries of the coastal forts, the British frigate
Undaunted, and the French warships present in the harbor. In witness thereof,
we the Allied commissioners have signed this document, along with General
Drouot, governor of the island, and General Dalesme, high commander of the
island.*

Executed in Porto Ferrajo on May 4, 1814

    Signed: Koller, Campbell, Drouot, Dalesme

At the same time, General Dalesme had the following proclamation posted:[114]

Inhabitants of Elba:

    *Human vicissitudes have brought the Emperor Napoleon among you,
and he has chosen to become your sovereign. Before arriving here, your new
monarch spoke the following words to me, which I pass on to you as proof of
your future happiness:*

    *"General, I have sacrificed my rights to the interests of the nation, and
kept for myself sovereignty and ownership of the island of Elba. All the powers
have agreed to this. Tell this to the inhabitants, and the choice I have made of
their island, because of their customs and climate. Tell them I shall take the
greatest interest in them."*

    *People of Elba, these words require no comments: they are your des-
tiny. The Emperor has judged you well, I owe you that.*

    *People of Elba, I shall soon be leaving you, and this with great sorrow,
as I sincerely love you, but thinking of your happiness will soften the bitterness
of my departure; and wherever I may be, I shall always remember this island and
the virtues of its inhabitants, and wish them well.*

Porto Ferrajo, May 4, 1814

    Signed: Brigadier General Dalesme

---

[114]Among the authors who have covered Napoleon's stay in Elba, most do not mention
this proclamation, or allude only vaguely to it. The only one to publish it was Marcel-
lin Pellet in his book: *Napoléon à l'île d'Elbe* (Paris, 1888). But the wording, without
modifying the spirit of the proclamation, differs in many terms and phrases from the
text given by Marchand.

From the harbor, the Emperor proceeded under a canopy to the parish church to hear a Te Deum. The service was conducted by Father Arrighi, vicar general of the bishop of Ajaccio and Bastia. When the ceremony was over, His Majesty proceeded to the town hall amid a crowd eager to see him; windows were decked with flags and handkerchiefs waved in joy. The Italian imagination, in contrast to the simplicity and honesty of the Elbans, had an enchanting effect; all reached the highest level of exaltation. Once arrived at the town hall, the Emperor courteously received all who came. It was already a family celebration day. He invited the lay and religious officials to maintain union and concord. This was not necessary: as of April 28 order had been restored. General Drouot was named governor of the island, and the Emperor placed on his hat a cockade with the colors he had just adopted; the public officials and the national guard did the same.

The following pastoral letter[115] was published and posted in all the communities:

> *Joseph-Philippe Arrighi, honorary canon of the Pisa cathedral and the metropolitan church of Florence, etc., under the bishop of Ajaccio, vicar general of the island of Elba and the principality of Piombino.*
>
> *To our beloved in the Lord, our brethren of the clergy, and to all the faithful on the island, salutations and blessings.*
>
> *Divine providence, who through its good will disposes inexorably of all things, and assigns the nations their destinies, has decided in the midst of political changes in Europe that we hereafter be the subjects of Napoleon the Great.*
>
> *The island of Elba, already famous for its natural products, is now*

---

[115]Same comment as previous note. Besides Gruyer's *Napoléon roi de l'île d'Elbe* (Paris, 1906), and M. Pellet (op. cit.), who briefly mention this pastoral letter, no other author bothers with Marchand's text. It only appears as an appendix to Waldburg-Truchsess' *l'Itinéraire de Napoléon à l'île d'Elbe*. It should be noted Waldburg-Truchsess had nothing to relate about the stay in Elba, having stopped in Fréjus along with Schouwaloff. We know the Prussian commissioner used, for the final part of his story, the notes of Austrian General Koller, who had followed Napoleon to Elba.

It is about Arrighi's pastoral letter that Countess d'Albany, whose hatred for Napoleon is well known, wrote on May 20, 1814, to Ugo Foscolo: "Our neighbor had himself recognized as sovereign of his island, and some tramp of a priest thanked providence for it."

about to become illustrious in the history of nations through the homage it pays its new prince, whose glory is immortal. The island of Elba indeed takes its rank among nations, and its small territory is ennobled by the name of its sovereign. Elevated to such a sublime honor, she receives in her midst the man anointed by the Lord, and the other distinguished people accompanying him.

When His Imperial and Royal Majesty chose this island for his retirement, he announced to the universe what his choice was. What wealth is about to inundate our country! What multitudes will rush in from all points to behold a hero!

The first day he set foot on our shores, he proclaimed our destiny and our honor: "I shall be a good father," he said, "be you my beloved children."

Dear Catholics, what words of tenderness! What expressions of good will! What token of our future happiness! May these words charm your thoughts, and, deeply imprinted on your hearts, may they be an unending source of consolation.

Let fathers repeat this to their children! Let the memory of these words that assure the glory and prosperity of the island of Elba, be perpetuated from generation to generation.

Fortunate inhabitants of Porto Ferrajo, it is within your walls that the sacred person of His Imperial and Royal Majesty shall live. You have been known throughout the ages for your kindness of spirit and affection for your princes. Napoleon the Great now resides among you; never forget the favorable impression he has formed of his faithful subjects.

And all of you, faithful in Jesus Christ, heed your destiny:

Non sint schismata inter vos, pacem habete, et Deus pacis et dilectionis erit vobiscum (Let there be no discord among you, live in peace, and may the peace and love of the Lord be with you)!

May faithfulness, gratitude, and submissiveness reside within your hearts. Unite all in respectful feelings of love for your prince, who is more like your good father than your sovereign. Celebrate with holy joy the kindness of the Lord, who throughout eternity has reserved for you this happy event.

Consequently, we order that next Sunday be sung in all churches a solemn Te Deum of thanksgiving to the Almighty, for the favor he has bestowed on us in his abundant mercy.

Given in the Episcopal palace of the island of Elba, on May 6, 1814.

Vicar General Arrighi,

Francesco-Angioletti, Secretary

The Emperor spent his first days inspecting public buildings and making several journeys to various points on the island. He went to visit the Rio mines, stopping at the house of M. Pons,[116] the director, to have lunch with him.

The Emperor's belongings were unloaded; 20,000 francs were found missing from the treasury. Peyrusse had the funds he brought from Fontainebleau taken up to the lodgings prepared for him; they were in bags of 1,000 gold napoleons[117] packed in straw; the unpack-

---

[116]André Pons, called Pons de l'Hérault, left an invaluable memorial of the events that took place on Elba.

Born in Cette on June 12, 1772, son of a Spanish innkeeper and a French mother, he became in turn merchant marine captain, naval officer, and artillery captain. He had known Bonaparte at the Toulon siege, housed him for two days, and introduced him to bouillabaisse from Provence. An ardent republican, a supporter of Robespierre, and a Jacobin, in order to show the intransigence of his opinions he had abandoned his first name of André and chosen as sponsors two heroes of the cause of liberty, calling himself Marat-Lepeletier Pons. After Thermidor, he remained a passionate Jacobin. He had been jailed. He had fought the Directory. He scorned and rejected with disdain the offers of Barras, who was trying to win him over. At the time of 18 Brumaire, he was offended by his former Toulon comrade's "putting force ahead of the law." Disgusted by politics, he refused to serve under the Consulate and the Empire. He married and swore to his wife he would never accept service in the military. In 1809, he accepted the position of manager of the iron mines on Elba, whose income went to the Legion of Honor. This post gave him complete freedom. He set to work with conscience and understanding. The mines were almost abandoned; he restored production, wrote regulations, promised the workers financial and physical security; he had healthy lodgings built for them, giving the example of hard work, sharing their food, and taking an interest in their families. Within a year, this solid republican had acquired such notoriety that he was known throughout the island by the nickname of *il nostro babbo* (our papa). He had a townhouse in Porto Ferrajo, a country house in Rio Marina, near the mines, and was living a happy and quiet life when he learned that Napoleon, deposed from the imperial throne, had been named King of Elba.

As he was one of the more important civil servants of the island, on the arrival of the sovereign, he was designated to accompany the delegation that went on board the *Undaunted* to welcome Napoleon. On the evening of his solemn entry in Porto Ferrajo at around midnight, the Emperor—temporarily housed in the city hall—called for him and asked if he could put him up in his Rio Marina house, without disturbing Mme Pons. Pons accepted. See Pons' two books published by Léon-G. Péllissier.

ing was done hastily, with a sentinel at the door. He belonged to the island commando battalion, was a cobbler by trade, father of a large family, and poor, and thought how useful a small part of this gold could be to himself and his family. The gold was at last in the treasurer's quarters, the crates upended and abandoned, the straw still there; he was alone, and wished he could find a few coins in the straw he spread about with his feet. His surprise was great when his foot encountered some resistance, and he discovered it was a bag similar to those he had seen being brought up. His body shook all over; he did not know what to do, and hesitated for a long time. Finally, certain he had not been seen, he placed the bag in his tall hat, which he put back upon his head, and continued his guard duty. As soon as he was relieved, he took his treasure home. That same day he went to see the parish priest, asking him to display the Holy Sacrament for three days to thank God for the help he had brought him and his family.

The man, known to be poor, suddenly began spending above his means; it was felt this could only be at someone else's expense. Noticing the disappearance, M. Peyrusse informed the court of the amount and urged them to keep the affair secret, so that the Emperor would not hear about it.

The police conducted an inquiry, and the man whose sudden spending had already attracted suspicion was arrested. At first he denied all, then said the money he spent had been found in a ditch. Fear of a sentence kept him replying in the negative; but when he was assured there would be no punishment, and that M. Peyrusse had even promised to give him 2,000 francs if he told the truth, he admitted everything. The entire sum was not recovered: 4,000 francs remained in his hands or was lost. I received all these details from M. Poggi de Talavo, who was an examining magistrate at the time.[118]

After remaining a few days at the city hall, the Emperor moved into a house[119] where some engineering officers were quartered. It was there I found His Majesty; I took advantage of a moment when the Emperor was absent from this modest palace to familiarize

---

[117]1 napoleon = 20 francs—Ed.

myself with it. The house consisted of a low-ceilinged ground floor
with ten rooms. Four faced the town, with a commanding view: a front
hall, a small drawing room, a dining room, and a small gallery; the six
others faced the garden and the sea: a study, a library, a bedroom, a
bathroom, and two utility rooms for interior service. This house,
located at the top of one of the steepest streets in town, stood halfway
up the hill dominated by the Etoile fort, where General Cambronne
was quartered, and the Falcon fort, further away. These two forts, connected by a covered path, made up the city defenses facing the sea.

Positioned like an amphitheater, this residence dominated the
town, the harbor, and some pretty country houses in a fertile valley on
the other side of the harbor. It was the most agreeable, most practical,
and safest house for His Majesty.

The grand marshal continued occupying the common house;
General Drouot lodged near the Emperor in a building complex used
until then by the garrison officers. Those buildings served to house the
officers, the kitchens, and the domestics of the palace at the same time.

In town as at the palace, cisterns replaced fountains; they were
large and sufficient for all needs.

Until the imperial guard arrived, the Elban national guard was
on duty to serve the needs of His Majesty, who had nothing but praise

---

[118]When Napoleon arrived on the island, Poggi de Talavo held the post of judge
through the intervention of Lucien Bonaparte. This had at first aroused the suspicion
of the Emperor, who treated him coolly. But his refinement, intelligence, and cleverness soon earned him Napoleon's trust, and he was put in charge of the police.

It was from Poggi that Marchand learned of the incident just related. The same
event is recorded in Peyrusse's *Mémorial* with fewer details, but it does provide the
name of the thief, a certain Allery.

[119]Mayor Traditi had first put up Napoleon at city hall. But that residence suffered
from abominable hygienic conditions, and it was too easy for anyone to enter it. So the
Emperor immediately sought a residence where he would not be disturbed by street
noises or bothered by the fetid smell of the gutters that served more or less as sewers.
His choice fell on a small house built in 1724 by the Grand Duke of Tuscany, Gian-
Gastone, the last of the Medicis; enlarged, it had last been occupied by the commanders of the artillery and the engineers. It was the *casa dei mulini*, so called because of its
proximity to windmills. Napoleon rapidly had it transformed, overhauling it completely into the imperial palace of the Mulini.

for its precision and devotion. A few armed sailors from the frigate *Undaunted*, commanded by a noncommissioned officer, were made available to the Emperor by Captain Usher. They were on duty at the palace, alongside the national guard. The garrison barely sufficed to guard the fortifications and the city's outer gates; the national guard was already sharing that duty with it.

Captain Usher, informed at the time of the landing that the Emperor's table lacked many things not yet available on the island, most graciously and promptly sent part of the personal provisions he had on board, without allowing any reimbursement.

During the crossing and after the landing of the guard, the British were astonished by the Emperor's familiarity with the soldiers. This formed an amusing contrast with the aristocratic haughtiness they were accustomed to. When His Majesty left the frigate, he had a napoleon given to each sailor, and gave Captain Usher a small box decorated with his portrait surrounded by diamonds.

On May 23 the frigate *Driade*, commanded by M. de Montcabrié, sailed into the roadstead, bringing with it the brig *Inconstant*; and at daybreak the following day, five or six British transport were reported, carrying the imperial guard. M. de Montcabrié went ashore, saw the Emperor, the governor, and General Dalesme, and made all plans for the loading of the garrison.

The guard had been traveling for 25 days; this delay had worried the Emperor, who feared they might have been prevented from boarding. He went down to the harbor with the grand marshal, and was greeted there with cries of Vive l'Empereur! The next day these soldiers relieved the garrison, and thereafter began as a rule to take their off-duty walks so as to reconnoiter the road traveled by His Majesty. Finding them everywhere, the Emperor wanted to know the reason; he was told the agreement they had made among themselves. He could not control the emotion brought on by such attachment: "Tell them I have found children, they have nothing to fear on my behalf." These old soldiers were good, and were loved by the islanders; children were always about them, and drilled with sticks and paper hats. Lithography has captured such a scene and faithfully rendered it.

On June 4, the *Driade* and the transports left Porto Ferrajo. Napoleon had gone aboard that frigate a few days after her arrival.

The Neapolitan frigate *Letizia*, which had brought Princess Pauline to Porto Ferrajo on June 1, departed on the 2nd, promising the Emperor to return in a few months. His Majesty accompanied it to the harbor; the frigate sailed away, and soon was out of sight.

Napoleon greets his Polish Cavalry unit.

In dictating his view of recent history, Napoleon pores over maps of his former battles.

PART TWO

*Marchand's Beginnings
in the Service of
the Emperor*

FROM THE STAY IN ELBA TO THE HUNDRED DAYS
(JUNE 1814 TO JUNE 1815)

CHAPTER THREE

Organization of the Emperor's household — Details of his public life— Of his private life — His service — His health

$\mathcal{A}$s soon as the guard arrived, the Emperor's arrangements took on a certain amount of stability. This is a good time to describe living arrangements of the island's new sovereign, his court, his household, and details concerning him personally.

The officials of the church and the courts, the civic and community governments, and the civil servants saw no change in personnel.

General Drouot was governor of Porto Ferrajo and the whole island; General Cambronne commanded the guard. General Drouot ate each day with the Emperor. General Cambronne had regular contact with His Majesty, as did the port captain Filidor,[120] the gendarmerie captain Paoli,[121] his lieutenant Bernotti, and Taillade, captain of the brig *Inconstant*.

The grand marshal continued to head the Emperor's household. It consisted of four chamberlains: MM. Vantini, Lapi, Traditi, and Gualandi;[122] six ADCs: MM. Vantini Jr., Binetti, Bernotti, Pons,

---

[120]On June 4 the Emperor named M. Filidor port captain in Porto Ferrajo, and assigned him the position of naval inspector for the ship tonnage that was subject to sanitary inspection.

[121]Paoli, a Corsican, was a gendarmerie lieutenant in Elba when Napoleon arrived. On May 29, the Emperor made him a captain and attached him to his personal service. He appears to have distinguished himself by his dullness and blind obedience. His assistant was Lieutenant Bernotti.

and Perès, the sixth not having been named[123] (the Emperor remembered them in his last moments, as well as Vicar General Arrighi; he had always spoken of them and their services with gratitude); finally, two palace quartermasters: MM. Deschamps and Baillon;[124] the treasurer M. Peyrusse; the secretary M. Rathery; a doctor, Dr. Foureau,[125] a student of Corvisart; and a pharmacist, M. Gatte.[126]

---

[122]In the budget prepared by Peyrusse and adopted by Napoleon on June 24, 1814, these four chamberlains are listed by name with an annual salary of 1,200 francs.

Vantini was the most discreet: aristocrat, gambler, womanizer, and of poor reputation, he was said to live by expedients. But he was witty and elegant, although his biting tongue was something to contend with. His greatest merit was to have constantly favored French influence. Dr. Christian Lapi, who commanded the Elban national guard, belonged to one of the first island families; he was wise and prudent, with a certain reputation. His niece had married a French officer, Major Camille Gauthier. Along with his post of chamberlain, Lapi held that of director of all the island's domains and forests. For details on Traditi, see note 112. As for the fourth chamberlain, Gualandi, he was the most discreet of men, blind in one eye, and mayor of Rio.

[123]Marchand mentions only five ADCs, indicating the sixth had not yet been named. Peyrusse's *Archives* list six: Perès, Pons, Binet, Vantini, Senno, and Bernotti, all lieutenants. The list, signed by Bertrand, is dated May 15, 1814. It would therefore seem that the sixth name is Fortunato Senno. What is the origin of Marchand's statement? Is it an omission? Or perhaps Senno never took up his duties? Note that Frédéric Masson states five officers. The decree preceding the list specifies the ADCs will be paid 1,000 francs and their uniform will consist of a green coat with hussar-style cuffs, red trim, and bees on the lapel; green vest and trousers; riding boots; black collar; silver epaulets and shoulder braid on the right shoulder. When they are wearing shoes, the vest and trousers are to be white.

[124]Deschamps and Baillon, serving as palace prefects in Porto Ferrajo, were two of the four quartermasters at the Tuileries palace, where, starting in July 1808, they served under senior adjutant Augustin Auger, commander of the Tuileries.

They had been officers in the elite gendarmerie corps, and had won the Emperor's favor for their fine service and shown through their sustained devotion that they deserved it. The Emperor made them knights, captains, and awarded them the Legion of Honor. Both were experts in their trade and their honesty was scrupulous. In Peyrusse's 1814 budget, each is listed as drawing a salary of 6,000 francs.

The staffs for the bedroom, dining room, and stables were also organized. While passing through Fontainebleau, Gervais and I had learned that Constant, the Emperor's first valet, had not followed him, and that Roustam had not returned from Paris. Gervais, who was Constant's uncle, felt the shame of his nephew's misconduct: he ran to the latter's nearby country house, and found him prostrated by his own ingratitude. He tried to convince him to come with us, relying on the Emperor's great kindness toward him. But Constant knew the Emperor better than his uncle; he felt his failing was due to a lack of courage, and that it would not be forgiven by his master. He remained home, torn by shame and sorrow. If these two servants failed in their duty and gratitude, such was not the case with MM. Hubert and Pélard,[127] who accompanied the Emperor to Elba and only returned to France after my arrival. The former was going back to the bedside of his dying wife. Such men do honor to faithfulness.

---

[125]Dr. Foureau de Beauregard, a student of Corvisart who had followed the Emperor, was a doctor in the imperial infirmary. He had taken part in the 1814 campaign, and in the Fontainebleau awards list he figured for 30,000 francs. His name appears in Peyrusse's accounts for the Campaign of France. On March 24, the treasurer paid Foureau, "ambulance doctor," 3,000 francs for the needs of his work. In Elba, in the Emperor's household budget prepared by Peyrusse and adopted on June 24, 1814, Foureau's salary is shown as 15,000 francs.

[126]The pharmacist Gatte, shown in Peyrusse's budget with a salary of 7,800 francs, was Dr. Foureau's indispensable aide. He appears to have been a modest man, preparing his prescriptions with great care. He had married a reportedly very attractive woman, Bianchina Nici. In spite of his amiability, he sometimes had arguments with Dr. Foureau, and Napoleon had to intervene to subdue their quarrels.

[127]Under the Empire, Hubert and Pélard were the Emperor's two regular valets. They had followed him from Fontainebleau to Elba, but only to substitute for Marchand until his arrival in Porto Ferrajo.

These two valets figure in the Emperor's household budget, approved by him on July 3, 1814 (Chap. V, travel expenses): a sum of 600 francs each is allotted them for their return to France.

On his return there, Pélard became a château concierge.

As for Hubert, he was anxious to get back to his wife, who was dying in Paris. According to Count de Ségur, Hubert's education, wit, talents, and character made him the most distinguished of the valets. He drew "intelligently." We owe to him a portrait of the Emperor, an interesting document.

Remaining with me were the valets Gillis[128] and Noverraz,
and the wardrobe boy Denis. Saint-Denis,[129] delayed in Mainz, arrived
only after the surrender of that city; he brought several of the
Emperor's snuffboxes he had bought back at a sale of His Majesty's
personal effects.

At Fontainebleau the Emperor, knowing that Constant and
Roustam were not coming, inquired as to Ali's whereabouts: that was
the name that had been given to Saint-Denis when he donned the
mameluke costume. When told that Ali was detained in Mainz, he
said: "I'm sorry, that one would have followed me."

In the outer chamber were: MM. Dorville, usher; Gervais, in
charge of the linen room and furniture storage; Santini, keeper of the
portfolio; two Elban ushers, Mathias and Archambault,[130] heading the
footmen (the latter became head groom in Saint Helena); and Gaudron
and Léon, polishers. The food department included: MM. Colin, food
comptroller, who soon returned to France; his aide Quéval, who
replaced him; Totin and Cipriani, butlers (the latter followed the
Emperor to Saint Helena); Pierron,[131] pantry head (he became a butler
in Saint Helena after the death of Cipriani); Ferdinand, the chef, and

---

[128]Nicolas Gillis (sometimes Gellis), who had been the Emperor's valet for some time.

[129]Louis Saint-Denis, son of a groom in Louis XVI's stables. After his studies and a
short internship as a notary's clerk, he joined the imperial household in 1806 as
apprentice groom. In 1811, Napoleon wanted a second mameluke in addition to Roustam. He had tried to keep a certain Ali, brought back from Egypt, but he turned out to
be such a nuisance that he was relegated to the post of upstairs boy at Fontainebleau.
Saint-Denis was chosen to replace him, given an oriental costume, and renamed Ali.
He then performed the same duties as Roustam. During the campaigns of Russia and
Saxony, it was he who carried the spyglass and the silver flask containing spirits.

In Elba, Saint-Denis was a faithful and devoted servant of the Emperor, as he was
later in Saint Helena. He left his *Souvenirs*, published in 1926.

[130]Achille Archambault had been part of the stable personnel since 1805. He was an
exceptionally skillful coachman who knew how to drive the horses briskly, as the
Emperor liked. In 1814 he had insisted on going to Elba, where he served as chief of
the footmen. He too must be considered a first-class servant, who could be counted on
by his master.

In Saint Helena, at the end, he would care for the Emperor's linen and clothes.

two helpers: Chandelier and Lafosse. The stables had some 50 horses. Chauvin was in charge; Amodru was chief groom. There were also 18 or 20 stable boys, French or Elban;[132] Vincent was head of the tack room.

I was called on to perform an interior duty I was not familiar with, having up to that time been chamber usher. After M. Hubert's departure, His Majesty had called me in and asked me several questions I tried to answer as best I could. His kindness in talking to me prompted me to tell him that in 1812 he had exempted me from the draft; he said: "You are mistaken, I had no right to do so." I told him that had been his reply to Countess Montesquiou, who was asking this favor for me, but that he had paid for a military replacement out of his personal purse. "I believe I remember that, and am pleased that it was you."

I told him that at Rambouillet my mother had told me of the Empress' resistance to her entourage's advice that she leave Paris, and her desire to show herself to the people with her son. She said she did not doubt that as the daughter of one of the confederate sovereigns, she would be respected by the Allied troops, not believing that the Austrian emperor, her father, could remove her husband from the throne and deprive his son of a crown that was to be his. The King of Rome, I told him, grabbed onto each piece of furniture so as not to go to Rambouillet, which he deemed too ugly. Made impatient by the force used on him—and force had to be used to get him into his carriage—he said

---

[131]Pierron started as pantry aide in 1807 and became butler. He had taken part in the campaigns of 1813 and 1814. At Fontainebleau, he insisted on leaving for Elba to replace one of his superiors who had deserted. Taken along as pantry head, he never left Napoleon after that time.

[132]From the list of names given by Marchand, it can be seen that Napoleon's household had a large staff, and he only lists the main servants. He does not mention an Elban, Signora Squarci, who worked in the linenroom, and a Frenchwoman, Mme Pétronille, a laundress. Nor does he mention the head gardener, Claude Hollard, who had been Elisa's gardener at Piombino, or the head musician, M. Gaudiano, assisted by a pianist, M. Sepier, and two singers, Mme Béguinot and Mlle Gaudiano.

in anger: "I don't want to leave Paris, Papa is not here, I am the master here."

The Emperor asked me for what amount I had been listed out of the two million he had distributed at Fontainebleau. I told him I was the only one on Elba who was not included. "You won't be short-changed. I'll take care of you. I will marry you off. I am naming you my first valet. I entrust you with my private purse; it contains 800,000 francs in gold. Peyrusse will give you 3,000 francs a month for my clothing and pocket money. You shall submit to me an account of this each month, and I will settle it."

There was in the Elba palace a ceremonial like that at the Tuileries, but on a reduced scale. One was admitted to this small court upon presentation by the grand marshal or one of the chamberlains. Certain people were admitted. Each Sunday, mass was heard in one of the rooms in the Emperor's apartment, that before the drawing room; it was celebrated by Vicar General Arrighi. The Emperor was always present, and the civilian and military officials were invited; the Emperor would see them after mass. The town bells were often heard; he used to say that their sound reminded him of his youth, when Madame Mère took him to mass, and also of the time he had spent in Brienne. One habit I had occasion to notice was that whenever he wished to deny some accusation leveled against him on a serious matter, he would cross his forehead with his thumb and say: "I'm aware of no such thing."

As Madame and princess each had a chaplain, they heard mass at home. Every Sunday there was a family dinner, where some towns-people were invited. Every evening there was a salon gathering, held by Madame or the princess. All persons who had admittance to the palace could attend. At the stroke of ten, the Emperor would retire to his quarters. The salon generally ended at midnight. After the princess arrived, there was a theater in Porto Ferrajo.

These details may appear of little interest; however it was in his private life that the Emperor had to be seen. It is there that I learned of his kindness and the easy-going nature of his service; for me, his grandeur and glory are everywhere.

I have said that the Emperor had me handle his private purse, and that he would go over the accounts each month. In Paris, the Emperor rarely had any money on him; in Elba, he always had a purse containing 300 or 400 francs in gold. His alms were numerous, and all his outings were marked by acts of kindness. One day when he was riding his horse, he was accosted by an old woman from Marciana. She greeted the Emperor and told him, with the familiar and respectful honesty of the Elbans, that she was poor and had lost her son; she had less regret since he had died in his service, but she was in need and was appealing to him. His Majesty said: "I'll take care of you; have hope."

"At my age, Sire, we have no more."

"Well, have faith in me."

"Oh, I won't be lacking in that: faith came to me when I saw you." The Emperor pulled out his purse and gave her five napoleons. The poor woman, seeing so much gold, was still busy thanking him when he was far away before she noticed. She feared he had made a mistake, and that evening went to the grand marshal and asked if the Emperor realized it was five napoleons he had given her. When he heard of this considerate thought, the Emperor was touched, and told me that evening to put her name on the list of pensioners. The grand marshal had assured her that the Emperor had not made a mistake, and had indeed meant to give her that sum.

Among the pensioners was Grand Vicar Arrighi, a kind and excellent cleric, known for his virtues, insight, and advanced age; he was not rich, and the income derived from his job was not sufficient to relieve the misery he saw around him in so many forms. The Emperor told me to put him down for 3,000 francs from his own purse. Every month I would carry 150 francs to this worthy prelate; he would smile when he saw me, and show me all kinds of courtesies, which touched me. He would invite me to sit down, and would relate some historical stories of the Emperor's youth. He said the latter came from a great family of Florence which revolutions forced into exile, and which came to settle in Corsica; he added that a Bonaventure Bonaparte had been beatified, and had been a saintly man.[133] He told me that after the death of the Emperor's father, as Madame was a very young widow, Archdeacon Lucien[134] had assumed management of the household property. He was a highly respected man, and had foreseen the young Napoleon's rise, just as Paoli did. I had heard the Emperor say that the former hid his gold in his bed, and that before dying he had said to Joseph, "You're the eldest, but there is the head of the family," pointing to Napoleon. Paoli said of him that he was patterned after Plutarch's men and would make a great mark on his country. His Majesty said he used to have a great affection for Paoli, which waned when the latter sided with the British, necessitating his family's departure from Corsica.

---

[133]The Bonapartes very probably descended from a patrician family in Florence. In any event, one branch of the family settled in San Miniato, and another in Sarzane.

The last heir of the San Miniato branch, Canon Philippe, was in contact with the Corsican Bonapartes. Archdeacon Lucien, mentioned in the next note, was his host. Napoleon's father Charles also visited him when he came to take his law exams at Pisa University. During the Italian campaign, on June 29, 1796, General Bonaparte slept there on his way from Livorno to San Miniato. Canon Philippe gave a magnificent dinner for his guest and his staff. Then he took him aside, telling him that a Bonaventure Bonaparte, a Bolognan monk in the 17th century, had long ago been beatified, but could not be canonized because of the enormous expense. He asked Bonaparte to request that the Pope canonize him.

Napoleon, amused by this unexpected request, didn't even try asking. Later on, at the time of the coronation, the Pope spoke of this canonization project, but the Emperor turned a deaf ear. The remains of the blessed Bonaventure Bonaparte are kept in Bologna in the Santa Maria della Vita church. This amusing anecdote, told by Napoleon to Antommarchi, appears in that author's book *Les derniers Moments de Napoléon* (Paris, 1825).

[134]Lucien Bonaparte, archdeacon of the Ajaccio cathedral, born in Corsica around 1711, died in 1791, was the uncle of Napoleon's father, hence the Emperor's great-uncle.

Napoleon's father, Charles-Marie Bonaparte, orphaned at 13, had grown up under the tutelage of his uncle the archdeacon, who was an important man in Ajaccio, firm and enlightened. But he kept a close rein on his nephew, who was soon found to be a spendthrift. The archdeacon had sent his ward to the Corte high school founded by Paoli. Charles spent three years there, became a lawyer, and married Letizia Ramolino, niece of one of the cathedral's canons, a friend of the archdeacon.

Napoleon often spoke of his great-uncle with gratitude, even saying he had been a second father to him.

The Emperor said that when young he had been very boister-ous, quick, dominating all that surrounded him; when he acquired a taste for studies, which came early, reading became for him a passion he never relinquished. He had fond memories of Father Patrault,[135] his mathematics professor, and would say: "That man understood me."

I have many similar anecdotes that do as much honor to the generosity and sensitivity of the Emperor as to the character of the good Elbans. From time to time, His Majesty would tell me on his return about his distribution of his gifts; but more often I had the details from Saint-Denis or Noverraz, who accompanied the Emperor during his rides on horseback or by carriage, and were witnesses to them.

I must here deny all the absurd tales that have been told about Napoleon's temper, his harshness, the epileptic seizures he allegedly had that made him unmanageable, and declare the falsity of the rather widespread rumor that he wore armor under his uniform. I can attest to never having seen anything other than a flannel shirt.

Serving the Emperor was an agreeable task; he was good, easygoing, and gentle with all who surrounded him. If it happened that he had become cross while outside, and this ire was felt indoors, it was never violent; it was thus easy to approach without increasing its level. There was always good reason for his anger, which he expressed with great diplomacy. Whenever his bad temper was mentioned, those who had reason to feel guilty about causing it—and whom, out of caution, he had only mildly scolded—would recognize his moderation and

---

[135]Father Patrault was indeed mathematics professor at Brienne. When he left Brienne, he became a layman, going into the service of M. de Loménie, the bishop of Sens, who had him manage his financial affairs.

At the beginning of the Italian campaign, Patrault came to join his former pupil, now General Bonaparte. He was taken on as a sort of secretary and named director of national domains. In that post, Patrault soon amassed a fortune. He lived in grand style, had a hotel in Paris and a country house in Suresnes, and managed to lose all he had earned. Informed of this, the First Consul refused to see him. He merely bought a quantity of orange trees that adorned the Suresnes house, and had these taken to Mal-maison. Later, he provided him with a subsistence allowance.

their mistake, and would not do it again; the Emperor was just and always ready to forgive.

The first day of my service with the Emperor, he asked me for some tea. I sent the wardrobe boy to get some in the pantry, and he brought me a tray carrying all that is needed for tea; I took this from him and out to the Emperor who was walking on a garden terrace close to the sea. He poured himself a cup, put sugar in it, and was about to drink it when he said to me: "Where does this cup come from?"

"From the pantry, Sire," I replied. He threw the container and its contents against the wall, breaking the cup. "Henceforth use only those things in my kit, and no others." I apologized for my ignorance of the kit, as nothing had been told me about it. That first lesson was harsh; I was taken aback. I was not immune to the fear inspired by the Emperor, but I was sure of the devotion that had led me to offer him my services, and I remained calm after this moment of temper. I went to get from his kit the gilt tray and all that was related to tea, and came back to offer these to him; his face had changed, and he said: "That's fine." That was the only outburst I experienced with the Emperor. These lasted but a moment; that instant gone, he only seemed to remember them in order to give some indication of his satisfaction with your service or person. This was calculated, and was for him a means of testing a man and assessing his character. When he returned that evening, he greeted me with a kindness that dismissed any fear I had of displeasing him, which had worried me for that part of the day I did not see him. He questioned me about my studies, my family, my social habits. Only a short time was needed to convince me of the falsity of the palace rumors about his difficult temper. I have never understood the purpose it served those close to him to believe such rumors. Never did the Emperor commit acts of violence against any of his servants; he was far removed from such actions, and criticized them in others. He was not in the habit of saying he was satisfied, he even seemed to pay little attention to efforts made to please him, or greeted them with indifference; but this was only pretense. It often happened by the same system that if he had recompensed you, he would show during the day some sign of impatience, as if to say not to attach too much importance to the favor he had done you. If, after scolding someone and noticing that he seemed hurt, he would approach the person he had chagrined, and either pinch his ear hard or tug at it: this implied all was forgotten. These ups and downs of humor were rare, as we always found the Emperor in a bright and cheerful mood at home. When he had gotten attached to a man and was sure of him, of his affection and devotion, that man became invulnerable; he was under his protection. Only serious faults could threaten the friendship with which he protected him. His character leaned toward indulgence; it was easygoing, and he made large allowances for human foibles. Speaking one day of the abandonment he encountered at Fontaine-bleau, he said that among men there were good and bad ones, that one shouldn't generalize and put them in the same basket, and that he had seen some people worth much more than the act they had just committed. Our task was therefore not so much to anticipate his desires, but to search out what might please him. There was no shortage of these attentions and that care in Saint Helena, where he was so miserable. Each of us has a clear conscience about having softened the bitterness of the few days he had left during this harsh captivity, and can look to this memory of devotion to ease the pain caused by his loss upon that awful rock.

The Emperor was consistent in the dress he had adopted: a three-cornered hat, the uniform of the guard's mounted chasseurs (that of the grenadiers was for Sundays in Paris), riding boots, or silk stockings with buckled shoes. During the first months of his stay on Elba, he wanted to wear white breeches buttoned at the bottom, with cuffed boots; finding this accouterment uncomfortable, he reverted to white cloth trousers and buckled shoes. When his boots were removed on his return, he wanted to don his shoes right away without changing socks, which could be done without inconvenience as his boots were clean inside and he had a fresh change of clothes each day. The Emperor had acquired that habit in Paris where often, returning from a ride or from hunting, he would attend a council of State or one of ministers, and did not take time to change clothes. He was always clean all over, his hands were elegant, he tended to his nails carefully. He had fine teeth and they remained so until his death.

The Emperor slept little; I had my first opportunity to observe this. He rose several times during the night. He was so well organized he could sleep when he wanted. Six hours' sleep was enough, taken all together or in several naps. He was always happy when he awoke. "Open the windows, that I may breathe God's good air" were often his first words. He sometimes went out at night into the garden in his robe. The nights were clear, and he enjoyed their pure smell. The calm was interrupted only by the sound of waves breaking 200 feet below the terrace where he walked, and by the sentinel's "Who goes there?" or by the Emperor, should he start to sing, which he sometimes did while thinking of something else; he was rarely in tune and would repeat the same words for 15 minutes. It would be: Had the king given me Paris, his large city. He would change its ending and substitute for I prefer my beloved...Give me back Paris. And also: Yes, it's done, I'm getting married. Or even: Here's daylight, Colette is not coming. Or finally: Marat, the people's avenger. As I stated, his thoughts were on something entirely other than what he was singing. His voice was loud, and his laughter carried a long distance. When he sang in this way, he didn't care who heard him. He seemed to be urging the night to end and waiting impatiently for daylight. As soon as it dawned, he dressed, got on his horse, followed by Noverraz or Saint-Denis, headed for the harbor, picking up General Drouot on the way, and rode to the grand marshal's or to Pontial, or watched his guard exercise.

When it began getting warm, he would come home and lunch, sometimes alone or with Generals Drouot and Bertrand. He preferred the simplest dishes: lentils, white beans, green beans which he loved but was afraid to eat for fear of finding threads which he said felt like hair, the very thought of which would turn his stomach. He was fond of potatoes prepared any way at all, even boiled or grilled over embers. He commonly used chambertin, which he cut with a lot of water; he never, or rarely, drank fine wines or liqueurs; a cup of black coffee after lunch assured his sobriety. Back in his quarters, he would slip on a robe, go into his study, and wait for his bath, which generally lasted one to two hours. In Elba it was a saltwater bath, which suited him well; there he read, or dictated at times, but seldom. In that residence I saw the *Sovereigns' Correspondence with the Emperor*, bound in a red leather volume.

One day when I remained alone with the Emperor while he was in his bath, he asked me if I knew how to tell how much water his body would displace; I had to admit my ignorance. "Give me some paper and a pencil, I'll tell you." He calculated it, and I have forgotten the number. "The students of the polytechnic school were always happy to solve the questions I asked of them when I went to see them." The Emperor said he had always taken an interest in the polytechnic school. It had been founded by Monge, whom he liked; Laplace, Lagrange, and Prony, who were his friends, were its heads. Mathematical sciences, which he loved, were taught there. "The origin of the rumor that I didn't like that school is that the young students, mostly 15 or 16, were sowing their wild oats amid the corruption of the capital, so I placed them in barracks, which displeased them."

The Emperor had a habit of remaining in his bath an hour and a half or sometimes two hours. He would always get out with hot sheets, go to bed for an hour, shave, dress, and around 4 or 5 p.m. climb in his carriage and go pay a visit to Countess Bertrand, whom he sometimes took along with him. He would head for some point on the coast and return in the boat that was waiting for him there, manned by the guard sailors, with Gentilini, an island sailor, as pilot. That boat generally had provisions of oranges and candles for use at night.

When the Emperor, once dressed, emerged from his apartment, the first valet would hand him his hat; he would take it in one hand, and in the other a handkerchief sprinkled with cologne, which he would touch to his lips, forehead, and temples. He was then handed a snuffbox, a spyglass, and a candy box containing licorice. The Emperor never left his room without placing these objects in the various pockets of his uniform. If during the day he attended the council of State, the chamberlain on duty would not fail to carry these same items, so as to give them to him if he had forgotten one, either in his study or in the drawing room.

The Emperor loved luxury and magnificence, but at the same time wanted to see economy practiced within his household. He would say about someone who had violated his trust: "I am prepared to give away 100,000 francs, but I will not tolerate having one cent stolen from me."

One day he asked me the cost of the silk stockings he wore. I replied: "For His Majesty, they cost 18 francs."

"And why more for me than for others? I won't have that. Must I be robbed?"

"No, Sire, I like to think that the quality, coupled with the fact that it is for Your Majesty, is what raises the price."

"That's what I don't want, unless you make up the difference out of your own pocket," he said to me, pinching my ear hard.

This reminds me that once at a hunting party in Bagatelle, when the Emperor was lunching with all the guests, he asked his sister, the Queen of Naples—who was wearing on her lovely head a charming pink hat shaped like a helmet with white feathers—how much that finery cost her. She replied: "Three hundred francs."

"You're being robbed, madam; with such a sum, I would equip ten of the Empress' dragoons, more solidly than you are."

In Elba, the Emperor was 44 years old. In his youth he had been quite slender, his complexion sallow, his face long, his eyes deep-set: such was the fine head we knew when he was Consul, supported by a superb frame. The plumpness he had since acquired produced his fine imperial head, the face that had filled out, the whiter skin, and that countenance full of expression and genius that appeared taken from antiquity.

I recall that Princess Pauline's hairdresser, who had come one day to cut his hair, having finished his job, took three steps back from the Emperor like an artist in front of his masterpiece, and kneeling, said in Italian: "His Majesty has an admirable Roman head." It was true, but the Emperor had a good laugh from the exclamation and attitude of Rodamonte—that was the hairdresser's name.

Nothing indeed in the portraits I have seen of the Emperor matched the fine head I had before my eyes, except for David's portrait; and the etching has something heavy about it that the Emperor did not have. Chaudet's bust, in my opinion, must serve as model. The Emperor was of average height, broad-chested, and had a fine figure; his hands were fine and his feet well formed. The skin of his body was pink, contrasting with his face which had a Mediterranean tint to it. His head was large, covered with very fine chestnut hair, thin over the forehead but sufficient to form a characteristic curl; he shaved so as to have no whiskers.

A few people still believe the Emperor used a lot of tobacco, and that, like Frederick the Great, he would stuff it into his vest pocket instead of his snuffbox. Suffice to say, to counter such an assertion, that his vest pockets were fakes. The tobacco he used was coarse, and his handkerchiefs were rarely stained by it; it did happen that his snuffbox would open in his pocket occasionally, and a rare accident was presented as a habit.

Every morning at 7 a.m. M. Foureau de Beauregard, His Majesty's doctor, came when he got up. The Emperor would talk about his health, which was generally very good, chat with him about medicine, and question him about his previous evening's activities. His Majesty held him in high esteem, and liked him.

During his stay in Elba, the Emperor vomited twice in a manner similar to the way he did shortly after our arrival in Saint Helena, which worried us later. Were these the first symptoms of the illness that took him from us? I do not know. Dr. Foureau was immediately summoned, and His Majesty talked at length about the causes of such vomiting and the means to prevent it. He said to him: "Doctor, my father died of a problem with his pylorus. You must do all you can to save my son from this." This vomiting did not tire him; he would rinse out his mouth and return to the drawing room without any apparent alteration on his face. It is unfortunate that Dr. Foureau could not take care of the Emperor and follow him to our awful rock; perhaps he might have saved His Majesty for us. As he was a member of the chamber of deputies during the Hundred Days, the Emperor made him consider his duty to pursue the mandate received from his supporters, as well as the thought of serving the best interests of the King of Rome there.

The Emperor had streaky scars on his thighs. He was in the habit of scratching them, and was not distraught when they bled a little; he considered this good for the health, and a useful light form of bloodletting. One day the Emperor scratched them enough for blood to flow out; he pointed out to Dr. Foureau who was present the abundance of the blood, and told him the source of this itching, as well as the scar from a bayonet wound above the knee. He told him: "It was in Toulon, when I commanded the famous battery of fearless men. A gunner fell by my side; I grabbed his swab so that my gunfire would not slow down, and caught this man's scabies. I was poorly treated, the virus penetrated inside, and I lost a lot of weight during my Italian campaigns. Even my chest was affected. I was urged to see a doctor. I saw Corvisart, and his manner suited me; he said to me 'It's nothing, it's an ingrown humor that must be drawn back out.' He applied two vesicatories to my chest, which felt less oppressed. My cough disappeared. That's what made Corvisart, your teacher, rich. It is from that moment on that I put on weight. These little scars open up from time to time and it serves as a bloodletting; I always sense ahead of time when these attacks will occur." Though he did not have a high opinion of medicine, the Emperor liked to discuss it with his doctor. One day Dr. Foureau came with several anatomical charts he was explaining to His Majesty. The Emperor listened to him carefully and told him he had also wanted to study that branch of science, but had to give it up because of the repulsion and odor of cadavers, which he could not stand. Turning to talking about himself, he said to him: "For me to commit some excess that is contrary to my normal habits restores a proper balance in me; after a long rest, a day's hunting or several hours' ride does me good. What leads to my rarely needing your ministrations is that I know my limit, and if I exceed it, my stomach will immediately surrender the excess."

The Emperor had the same attacks in Saint Helena, but they disappeared during the last years of his life; the itching had no effect, he scratched but nothing would flow. His sweating, formerly quite abundant, disappeared.

CHAPTER FOUR

The Emperor's construction projects in Porto Ferrajo —
The Marciana hermitage — Purchase of San Martino —
Death of Empress Joséphine — Arrival of Madame Mère —
Of Madame Walewska, of her sister, brother, and son —
Of Princess Pauline — The Elba court — Tuna fishing

$\mathcal{E}$verything on Elba had to be created. The Emperor first attended to his lodgings in town and in the country, and to providing apartments for Madame Mère and Princess Pauline who came to join him, never to leave again: her affection for His Majesty attested to this. Foreigners were many on the island;[136] it was up to the inhabitants to provide practical lodgings for them. A number of distinguished Englishmen who came there and had the honor of being presented to the Emperor were struck by the clarity of his conversation.

As soon as the guard had arrived, the grenadiers and chasseurs not on duty were used to demolish furnaces near the house that had once served to heat cannon shot, as well as a large quantity of shacks that cluttered the periphery. They had to resort to explosives: these were bombproof buildings. A fixed-price arrangement was made with the soldiers; they had a very hard time, and asked the Emperor for a

---

[136]This fact is abundantly confirmed by all contemporary accounts, such as those of Campbell and Pons de l'Hérault. A crowd of visitors indeed landed each day in Elba. They came from all over Europe: Italy, Germany, Norway. French mothers brought their children to show them the "hero of heroes." Excitable old ladies, no longer able to bear the exile of "the Glory of France," left home to come and greet the Emperor. But the most frequent visitors were British: some came as simple tourists; others, important politicians or aristocrats, sought the honor of admission to the Mulini palace. Naval officers from the British warships in the Mediterranean would take leave from their ships to come to Elba, to such a point that the squadron commander had to forbid these trips back and forth which were contrary to regulations.

bonus, saying they would drink only water. The bonus was granted. In a very short time, a fine terrace and a garden replaced those shacks. Thus isolated, the palace dominated on all sides.[137] All kinds of workmen, distinguished foreigners, a great number of Englishmen, and French tradesmen traveling in Italy arrived on the island, and rentals became very expensive. A great deal of activity was noted everywhere. The palace could only be reached by a steep flight of stairs. His Majesty had a fine street laid out winding through the town, allowing people to reach the palace by carriage. Roads were laid out: one from Porto Ferrajo to Marciana was already progressing well; that leading to Porto Longone was completed. Another, heading for San Martino, was being finished.[138]

The Emperor had purchased there, from a man named Manganaro and a few others, a very spacious piece of land covered by a good

---

[137] The Mulini palace. Indeed the Emperor ordered pulled down a group of shacks and windmills cluttering the upper plateau of the Porto Ferrajo hillside, and cleared the surroundings of the two buildings occupied by the artillery and the engineers, before connecting these with a central building. He was the real architect of his domain, drawing all the plans. Rising from the rubble, the palace, where he moved in at the end of May, was only completed in September. The garden, which he had laid out in Italian style, overlooked the sea.

[138] All the island's roads radiated from Porto Ferrajo. The one to the west went to Marina and Monte Giove; the one to the south and east went to Porto Longone, Rio Marina, and the iron mines. Besides those two roads crossing the island from one end to the other, the only remaining important road usable by carriages was that going to Campo, the last large village in the south of the island, famous for its granite quarries that produced the columns for Pisa's churches and palaces. Besides these roads, which Napoleon found in poor condition, there were only mule trails, often poorly defined. It was this shortcoming that Napoleon worked to correct. He tried to give the island its first road network, and to carry out this plan, he named Leopold Lombardi inspector of roads and bridges.

vineyard. He had a charming country house built there.[139] During the time it was being built, San Martino became the destination of his outings, either on horseback with an ADC, or by carriage, escorted by a picket of Polish lancers. Thirty of these fine men, commanded by Major Balinski,[140] came from Parma with their horses to join their comrades of the guard.

These activities were interrupted by the sad news of Empress Joséphine's death on May 29, 1814.[141] The Emperor appeared deeply saddened; he locked himself up in his study and saw only the grand marshal a few moments during the day. Speaking about that princess, the Emperor said she had the elegance of a Creole, combining with infinite grace and charm a conviviality and evenness of temper that never failed. Everything she wore was elegant and set the fashion, and her night apparel was as elegant as her day's. While recognizing that princess' taste for spending, adding that he had several times had to settle her debts, he paid her justice by saying that among the debts she contracted there were some that helped make friends for her through little things given at the right moment with her habitual grace. Either in Elba or in Saint Helena, the Emperor always spoke of her with the

---

[139]The Mulini palace was not yet completed when Napoleon wished for another house in a more restful country setting. He had a house built in San Martino.

It is reached by the Marina road. Four km. from Porto Ferrajo, a road branches off into a valley dominated by a steep mountain with vineyards at its base, and oak groves above. The road then rises, and halfway up offers a fine panorama. Napoleon bought this from an officer in the 35th line regiment named Manganaro, and put Foresi in charge of the negotiations. The San Martino property was in fact bought by and for the account of Princess Pauline, with the proceeds of some diamonds she sold.

It was a modest house: four whitewashed walls, with five windows in the front; a ground floor with a narrow door, and a second floor whose rear—due to the slope of the terrain—was on a level with the garden, filled with a variety of trees, oaks, mulberry trees, acacias, and a Mediterranean elm planted by Napoleon himself.

[140]In 1807, Napoleon had formed a unit of Polish light cavalry in the grand duchy of Warsaw. In 1809 they became the Polish lancers, and by late 1811 they numbered three regiments. It was a group of these who followed the Emperor to Elba. They were commanded by Baron Jermanowski, a major, assisted by two captains, Schultz and Balinski. The names of these three officers appear at the bottom of the guard's proclamation to the army at the time of Napoleon's landing at Golfe Juan.

same outpouring of feelings. He would say: "Joséphine exceeded all others by the grace of her manners when she gave. She loved the arts and protected them, and would do battle with Denon to have a few paintings to decorate her gallery. My instructions to Denon would put all in proper order." The first time the Emperor saw her, he was

---

[141]Empress Joséphine died at Malmaison at noon on May 29 of an infectious flu, her last word being Napoleon's name. She died in her room, draped in red with gold embroidery, still visible today on the second floor of the château, which has been converted to a museum. The bed where the Empress drew her last breath is still there.

On the manuscript of his *Mémoires*, Marchand added in the margin the following note:

The Emperor learned with annoyance of the favor requested by Emperor Alexander of Louis XVIII for this princess and Queen Hortense; he thought it would have been better to take part in her sorrow.

Marchand appears to have shyly, almost regretfully, added this footnote imposed on him by his desire for accuracy, as he worshipped the first Empress as well as Queen Hortense. One can indeed understand Napoleon's "annoyance," had the rumors repeated to him been in line with the truth. But Napoleon, who was better informed later on, knew nothing of the circumstances that had put Joséphine in contact with Tsar Alexander. It was the latter who had spontaneously written to Joséphine asking to be received at Malmaison. "I was consumed," he wrote to her, "by a desire to see you, Madame: since I have been in France, I have heard your name blessed by all. In the simplest huts as in castles, I have gathered details regarding your angelic kindness, and I will take pleasure in bringing Your Majesty the blessings I have collected on her behalf."

Is this document not the most decisive response to all the slanders that have been heaped on Joséphine's memory? Some historians have forgotten the beautiful letter written by the rejected Empress to Napoleon, condemned to exile on the island of Elba: "Should I learn that, against all appearances, I am the only one willing to fulfill her duty, nothing shall hold me back, and I shall go to the only place where happiness can exist for me, as I will be able to console you when you are isolated and unhappy there. Say but one word, and I shall leave." How can we not underline the difference between this attitude and that of Marie-Louise, who so soon forgets Napoleon in the arms of a Neipperg or a Bombelles?

It has therefore been an error to hold against Joséphine her relationships with those who had contributed to destroying the Empire. She solicited nothing: it was the tsar who extended his hand to her at a time when she was encountering difficulties of all kinds, and when the future of her children and grandchildren caused her legitimate anxiety.

Caulaincourt's invaluable testimony in his memoirs sets matters straight. It was he who never ceased to attend to the business affairs of Joséphine and Queen Hortense. "The Emperor of Russia," he says, "was in all these circumstances a most useful defender and supporter. His intervention helped me triumph over all difficulties."

charmed more by her wit and graciousness than by her beauty; she was appealing. Marriage followed soon after that first impression, which, far from waning, gained more strength every day, and after the divorce turned to affection full of esteem. A visit paid her by Emperor Alexander and the Prussian king was the cause of her death; she had been ill for some days, and rose and dressed up a bit to receive the two sovereigns. A blocked fever, followed by a sore throat, led her to her grave.

With her kind disposition, excellent heart, and true sensitivity, she would pity other people's misfortunes, and cry with those who came to tell her their troubles, which, the Emperor said, often made her the prey of manipulators good at exploiting such sensitivity. The Emperor wanted to stop this tendency toward spending. He had threatened to put in jail a certain person he suspected of encouraging the Empress on that path: this was Mlle Despeaux,[142] a dress or hat maker. Spotting her one day, he ordered that she be expelled from the palace, and taken by four gendarmes to Vincennes. The order given to the Duke of Rovigo (Savary) was carried out in force, and this woman was already walking at the end of the avenue de Saint-Cloud, very worried about what could have earned her such treatment, when Marshal Duroc, hearing that the Emperor's joke had been taken seriously, ordered that Mlle Despeaux be allowed to get into his carriage. She arrived in Paris sickened by the Emperor's prank. At the palace, where

---

[142]Joséphine readily bought everything without inquiring the price, and some merchants took advantage of this. We know through Mme de Rémusat that "the Emperor would have liked no merchant to be able to reach the Empress, but he had to yield on this point."

Mlle Despeaux was already famous under the Directory. A newspaper of the day, the *Semaines critiques*, called her the "Michelangelo of fashion." She had kept her maiden name for her business, as she was married to an employee at the war ministry.

If one were to believe the highly suspect *Mémoires et souvenirs d'une femme de qualité*, she was an ardent royalist, working for free for all the great families ruined by the Revolution, and allegedly acted as go-between to obtain a private meeting between Joséphine and a friend of the Bourbons, who came to plead the cause of the Duke of Enghien. The *Mémoires* of Mlle Avrillon, first chambermaid to the Empress, are more trustworthy. In the latter, a detailed account of the anecdote reported here by Marchand can be found.

the story was much repeated, the Empress' women called this action a bit too barbaric.

Memories of the Empress were connected with the finest moments of the Emperor's political career, the Italian campaigns, the Montebello negotiations, Campo Formio, the Consulate, the first years of the Empire. With Joséphine, his star rose; she had during her second marriage an extraordinary brilliance. She was then the evening star.

Marie-Louise's purse amounted to 50,000 francs a month; 20,000 francs were for the poor, her reserve fund was 20,000 francs. With less money than Joséphine, she accomplished more, being better organized; her alms were plentiful, but she did not know how to give as Joséphine did.[143]

The island of Elba, where the Emperor was settling, was a place for calm and philosophical thought; how stable would it be? Was there not already something vague in his hopes, something uncertain in his future? He dared not admit it, and sought to distract himself; the work he had undertaken brought him back to something solid he wished to hold on to, and which each day escaped him.

After a few days of sorrow, the laborers, masons, and carpenters once more occupied his time. He could be found among them very early, sometimes wearing silk stockings and buckled shoes, listening to and laughing at their comments.

In order to receive Princess Pauline,[144] the Emperor had a very fine apartment constructed above the ground floor he occupied, and a

---

[143]Regarding this difference in allowances given to the two Empresses, Mme de Rémusat gives the following explanation in her *Mémoires*: "The reason was that Mme Bonaparte had to hand out much help to poor members of her family who asked for it frequently, and that, having relatives in France as the archduchess did not, she had to spend more. Mme Bonaparte gave much; but since she never took presents from her own belongings, but always bought them, this vastly increased her debt."

[144]Princess Pauline arrived on Elba November 1 to share her brother's exile.

very large building[145] close to the palace fixed up as a ballroom and small theater; the best painters in Italy came to decorate them, as well as the theater in town. The Emperor had to leave the palace for a short while; he went to live in the hermitage of the Madonna de Marciana.[146] He took only a few people with him: Paoli, captain of the gendarmerie, and the ADC Bernotti accompanied him there. A few grenadiers and three mamelukes camped nearby.

Marciana Marina sits at the foot of the tallest mountain on the island, Mount Campana. That village is inhabited by fishermen; a long and steep hill leads to Marciana. The town is small; a climb just as long leads to the hermitage of the Madonna. There, under a chestnut

---

[145]This was the Mulini palace, where transformations were carried out with energy. The central building first consisted only of a ground floor with seven rooms, including the Emperor's bedroom, library, study and the ADCs' drawing room. Above this ground floor Napoleon had built a large salon with tall windows, which could be used as both a ballroom and reception room. To the right of the central building stood the former engineers' building, with pantry and kitchens on the ground floor; on the second floor, eight rooms or apartments. To the left stood the former artillery building, featuring on the ground floor a movable partition, separating the room in two to serve as a dining room and theater; in addition, there were five rooms. On the second floor of this building were the apartments intended for Marie-Louise and the King of Rome, where Pauline moved in with her party. Finally, the large building mentioned by Marchand is that connected at right angles with the former artillery building through a gallery, where a greenhouse, offices, and the Emperor's bathroom would be set up. It connected with the former theater, which Napoleon would furnish as a theater for Pauline, while waiting for the construction of a municipal theater. Today the casa dei Mulini is white with green shutters. The exterior has changed little.

[146]The western road heads toward a high mountain blocking the horizon, with the two neighboring peaks of Monte Capanne and Monte Giove. This is what Marchand calls Mount Campana. The road first goes to Marciana, which, like many Mediterranean towns, consists of two villages: Marciana Marina (Marciana-by-the-Sea) and Marciana Alta (Upper Marciana). It is above Marciana Alta, that at the end of a rather steep climb, the Madonna chapel can be found in the middle of a chestnut grove. In front of the porch, four fountains flow into a small stone basin. The chapel facade is decorated with frescoes. A few yards from it stands the small house that once sheltered the hermit, and which attracted Napoleon's attention when he first visited this isolated spot at the beginning of August. It was inhabited by the sanctuary keeper, Romiti. The Emperor immediately decided to purchase it and convert it into a summer residence.

He returned to Marciana Alta on August 20 and lived in the small house by the chapel for the balance of the month. It was there he hosted Mme Walewska.

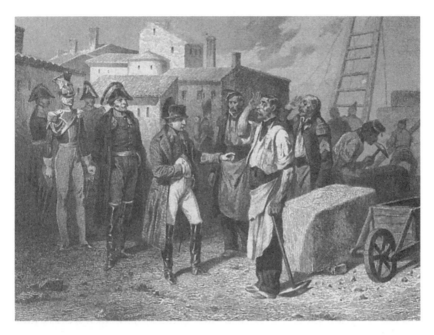

On Elba, the old guard has volunteered to work on the roads. Here they are greeted by the Emperor.

The house at Madonna de Marciana as it looks today.

grove, stood a well-built chapel, suitably decorated inside; next to it was a one-story structure consisting of four interconnected rooms which were made suitable for housing the Emperor by painting the walls and washing the tile floor. Two hermits had retired there, far removed from the world and its faults, living off the alms they went to collect each day in the town and surrounding villages. They moved into the house cellar which was dug into the rock, as the house nestled on a gentle slope. They were helpful and devoted, helped their neighbors and set a good example by their virtues. They served this chapel, which at one point during the year attracted from the neighboring communities a pilgrimage of the inhabitants, who never failed to drop an offering into the alms box.

The man whose name had spread across the universe, and whose kindness and virtues were of a different nature, had come to occupy their modest abode. The fickleness of fortune and political friendships, the passions of men, and public opinion were for him subjects of meditation just as rich and fulfilling as those adopted by the two good hermits. Near the chapel, facing the main door, a building had been erected, semicircular in shape, of Doric design, its entablature held up at regular intervals by pilasters. Out of this flowed an abundant spring of clear and pure water born of the mountainside, that went gurgling along to vanish into the chestnut grove, maintaining its coolness. Lilies of the valley, heliotrope, and violets filled the shade and dampness of the forest with their aroma. It was a delightful site. The calmness of the nights and the soft moonlight led to melancholy dreams, of which the Emperor appreciated all the charm. Not far from the fountain, climbing further up toward the peak of Mount Campana, one encountered a totally bare rock,[147] and the view from there

---

[147]This rock was called the Affacciatoio. Napoleon sat there for hours on end, his eyes riveted on the island where he was born.

dominated the Tuscany archipelago, the Corsican sea, Pianosa,[148] and
Monte Cristo.[149] These two islands appear to be at the foot of Elba.
From that point, the Emperor could imagine the paternal roof in
Ajaccio, and far beyond, that beautiful France whose destiny he had
abdicated. The Emperor liked that solitary rock; he went there, and one
day felt like taking a nap there. Captain Mellini[150] who was with him

---

[148]The island of Pianosa in the Tyrrhenian sea, now belonging to Italy, province of
Livorno (Tuscany), is 15 km. from Elba, and is inhabited today by a few hundred fishermen. It is the famous Roman Pianasia where Agrippa was exiled, then murdered by
order of Tiberius.

When Napoleon reigned in Elba, the island was uninhabited. It was visited by
residents of Rio, Porto Longone, and Campo, who went there to collect hay. In 1803,
France under the Consulate had made it into a fortress. In 1805, the Emperor's sister
Elisa, Princess of Piombino, had a small fort built there with four guns and a 150-man
garrison, whose mission was to repel pirates. But in 1809 the British had demolished
the fort and captured the garrison. The few colonists had fled, and only some wild
goats remained.

In May 1814, the Emperor decided on the military occupation and colonization of
the island. He went there several times, chose the location of the fort, and decided on
the most advantageous crop, namely wheat.

But if he failed to organize agriculture there, he made of the island such a strategic stronghold that Colonel Campbell became worried and realized that no mention
had been made of Pianosa in the Fontainebleau treaty. The Emperor took no notice of
his objections. When he returned to France, the war material he had transported onto
the island served to round out his flotilla's armament.

[149]Monte Cristo is a tiny island in the Tuscan archipelago in the Tyrrhenian sea, with a
surface of ten square km. There are ruins of a Benedictine monastery destroyed in the
16th century by the Barbaresques.

[150]Mellini was Elban, born in Porto Ferrajo in 1766. After serving with the troops of
the King of Sardinia, he went to Bastia, Corsica, in 1788. He became a gunnery officer
in the national guard, and in 1793 a lieutenant in the 16th light infantry, then in the
engineers. He was a good artist, and readily gave his drawings to his benefactors.

He became an engineering captain in Year II, served again in Corsica, and then in
the army of Italy. In Year V, he returned to Porto Ferrajo, where Admiral Brueys had
him undertake some important map work: the Tuscany coast, harbors, anchorages,
depth soundings and shoals, the islands of Gorgone, Elba and Giglio; of Porto Ferrajo,
the harbors of Elba, the forts, and Longone. While doing this work, he was taken prisoner by the British who interned him on Elba, having stripped him of his belongings
and instruments. He resigned in Year IX, was put on disability pension, and four years
later became keeper of the pyramid erected at Marengo in Year XIII. In 1814 he joined
the Emperor on the island, and became commander of the engineers there.

did a charming sketch of the scene; he soon abandoned his pencil and grabbed a hammer and chisel, carving into the rock the hour, date, and year when the prince had slept there. We owe to this engineering officer a few sketches of Elba made by him, among them the departure of the small Porto Ferrajo fleet for the coast of France.

The Emperor spent his time in trips to the surrounding villages; everywhere he relieved unhappiness. I was often the minister of his charities to the poor, the pastors of Marciana and Poggio making the distributions. The Emperor had been at the hermitage for a few weeks, when on August 2 he was told of Madame's arrival in Porto Ferrajo. He immediately left the table, and to rejoin his dear ones more quickly, went down to the Marciana marina and got into his boat. I went with him, while the servants proceeded on land. The sea was rough, but he arrived in Porto Ferrajo just as Madame was landing; he kissed her several times, thus drying the tears flowing from his mother's eyes. So many things had happened since their separation!

The Emperor took Madame to her lodgings. A spacious house near the palace had been prepared for her.[151] Madame was in good health, and still showed great beauty. She was then sixty; she had kept her figure, and appeared ten years less than her age. A woman of great character, she had endured with courage and resignation the loss of a husband she adored, whose portrait went with her everywhere. From that point on, she devoted herself entirely to her children. The Emperor would say: "Madame is full of nobility and pride, she is worthy of all veneration. The care she took of us and our education sets a rare example of a family where so many clever and capable children are found."

Madame was sharing her husband's perils while she was pregnant with the Emperor. She bore thirteen children; widowed at 30, she was left with five boys and three girls: Joseph, the oldest, who was king of Naples and Spain; Louis, King of Holland; Jérôme, King of Westphalia; Pauline, Princess Borghèse; Caroline, Queen of Naples;

---

[151]The house chosen for Madame Mère was located on a street rising from the Grand-Place to the Etoile fort and the Mulini palace. It was the house of chamberlain Vantini; with its spacious rooms, it was considered one of the finest residences in Porto Ferrajo. The rent was set at 200 francs a month.

Elisa, Grand Duchess of Tuscany; and Prince Lucien, whose op
kept him apart from the Emperor, and who during the Hundred
came back to him. The Emperor often told how his mother, preg..ant
with him, had wanted to go to mass on August 15, Assumption Day.
She had to come home in haste and, unable to reach her room, gave
birth to him on a rug showing great men of legend. I had occasion to
see at Madame's house in Porto Ferrajo a full portrait of the Emperor's
father, Charles Bonaparte. He was a very handsome man. The
Emperor spoke of him as a superior man. He died of stomach cancer in
Montpellier.

Madame brought with her a chamberlain, M. Colonna, two
lady's companions,[152] and her household staff. Among her servants
was quite an old woman who walked bent over, and who had brought
up all of Madame's children. Her name was Saveria. Madame trusted
her, and she lorded it over the household. She was prone to much
miserliness, which was then attributed to Madame. The latter was
quite well-ordered, but not parsimonious as people liked to say.

Mme Saveria came one day and asked to see the Emperor,
who was then in his bedroom. I informed him of this, and he said at
once: "Have Saveria come in." The Emperor said to her in Italian,
laughing: "Well, Saveria, are you still as miserly as I've always known
you to be?" She replied in the same language: "Sire, it is not miserliness, it is prudence." She was very pleased with the kind reception
given her by the Emperor, and the promise of a job for one of her
grandchildren who had just arrived in Elba. The honorable Father
Bonavita became Madame Mère's chaplain.

The Emperor returned home happy after the few hours spent
with his mother; he went to bed, but was sick during the night. In Marciana he had asked one of the mamelukes of his guard to prepare a
Turkish-style pilaf;[153] the garlic present in part of the food he was

---

[152]The two ladies were Mme Blachier and Countess de Blou de Chadenac.

[153]The Emperor had ordered the pilaf—of Turkish origin and made of highly spiced
boiled rice—from one of the three mamelukes he had brought to the Marciana hermitage.

offered whetted his appetite, but during the night he had trouble digesting; a few cups of tea helped. Laughing the next day about the dinner prepared by the mameluke, he confessed having never eaten as much or with such good appetite.

On August 15, the Emperor's birthday was celebrated on the island; the civilian, military, and church officials came to pay their respects to His Majesty. A large dinner was given on this occasion, attended by: Madame; Countess Bertrand, her husband, and General Drouot; General Cambronne; Colonel Malet,[154] Grand Vicar Arrighi, and M. Senno, mayor of the city; the president of the court; and M. Pons de l'Hérault. After dinner the Emperor asked me for a little box containing some jewels he had had sent from Genoa. Each guest shared in his generosity; General Drouot received a pin shaped like an eagle. The guard was not to be outdone by the town, and wanted to give a party also. When evening came, the artillerymen set off some very fine fireworks they had prepared themselves. That night there was a public ball. Having watched its beginning, His Majesty went home, changed from his uniform into civilian garb, donned a round hat, and went off with Count Bertrand to mingle with the crowd. He had ample proof of the love the good Elbans felt for him: exuberant and open gaiety lasted well into the night. That same day the Emperor had attended a meal with his guard, who were never happier than when he was in their midst. As soon as he appeared, cries could be heard of Vive l'Empereur!, coming from the heart, and a deputation of non-commissioned officers came to offer him a glass of wine, with which he toasted their health; it was for all these old warriors a moment of enthusiasm approaching delirium. The Emperor went home only at midnight, pleased with his day.

---

[154]Anselme Malet. Soldier, drum major in the consular guard, lieutenant, then captain in the light infantry, major in the "old guard" chasseurs, chief of staff of the guard in Elba, he was killed at Waterloo. He had fought in all the campaigns from 1793 to 1815. He was wounded at Saint Jean d'Acre, at Lodi, and at Essling. He was an officer of the Legion of Honor, and a typical grognard. He was a major, not a colonel, and his assistant on the staff was Captain Laborde. He is remembered for his run-in with some Austrian officers in Lyon who had insulted the tricolor cockade, and whom he wanted to challenge.

Since Napoleon's arrival, Porto Ferrajo was no longer recognizable, and its peaceful residents were very thankful for the work being done everywhere. Streets heretofore impassable were opened up for carriage traffic, now able to reach the palace and also go to Ponticel. A theater, christened the Fortunati, was finished; its decoration was completed. All that was needed was the arrival of the Italian artists who, for a slight stipend, were to move in. Rumors even circulated that Mme Grassini[155] and Crescentini,[156] along with the famous com-

---

[155]Giuseppina Grassini (1773-1850) became famous through a great success at La Scala in Milan in *Roméo et Juliette*, when the French army entered Milan in May 1796.

In Saint Helena, Napoleon would say: "In spite of their deploying all their charms, I was not moved by the beautiful Italian women." And on May 23, 1796, he was able to write to Joséphine: "Five or six hundred pretty and elegant women sought to please me, but none resembled you... I saw and thought of no one but you..." It would seem that, at least then, the pretty Grassini could not win Bonaparte's heart away from the absent Creole, and she pursued her brilliant singing career without succeeding in seducing the victorious general. But four years later in 1800, Bonaparte was returning from Egypt, went over the Saint Bernard pass, and on June 2 entered Milan again. Concerts were given in honor of the First Consul. Grassini deployed her marvelous talents, and on the morning of June 5, Berthier, entering the First Consul's bedroom, found the pretty singer there. She managed, before and after Marengo, to capture the attention of the hero: not only did he succumb to her charms, but he brought her back to Paris.

It can be seen that it was not in Milan in 1805, at the time of the coronation, as Marchand states, but as early as the second Italian campaign that Grassini had captured Napoleon's attention. Marchand errs in good faith.

But the episode with Grassini was only short-lived. She consoled herself with the violinist Rode. Napoleon had cared so little about her that he held no grudge against her for her infidelity, and had her hired in 1808 at the Empress' theater, at a salary of 35,000 francs. She attended all social events at the end of the Empire. In 1811, she sang in the private apartments of the Tuileries. The marshals' salons all vied for her. However, when Napoleon fell from power, in spite of all the favors accorded her, she found herself close to need.

In 1814 she was singing in London, and before as after the Hundred Days, was much seen with Wellington, becoming his singer and lover. Having divided her existence between Paris and Milan, she lived until 1850. Under the dome of the Invalides, at the time of the Return of the Ashes, she may have heard her niece Judith Grisi head the musical program of that great ceremony. Cf. André Gavoty, *La Grassini* (Paris, 1950).

poser Paër,[157] were due to arrive for its inauguration. The Emperor had always been very kind to the artists he protected. Those just mentioned had been the object of his munificence. The first artist could not forget that at the time of his coronation in Milan, she had attracted his attention. At that time, His Majesty had summoned her, and after the first moments of their meeting, she reminded him that she had made her debut at the time of his first exploits in Italy: "I was then," she said, "at the peak of my beauty and talent; I appealed to all eyes; I set all hearts on fire. You alone remained aloof, and yet you alone attracted my interest. When I was worth something, when all Italy was at my feet, I scorned all that for one glance from you, in vain; and it is now that I am no longer worthy of you that you finally look at me." The Emperor liked to recall that episode in his life, and the woman whose speech had charmed him as much as her person.

---

[156]Girolamo Crescentini, famous Italian (castrato) singer (1769-1846). He achieved great success in Italian cities and also in Vienna, in Zingarelli's *Roméo et Juliette*. Napoleon was struck by his talent, and while at Schönbrunn signed an order bringing him to Paris, where he made him first singer of his court and his private chapel, with a salary of 30,000 francs. In 1809, after hearing him sing, the Emperor sent him a lavish gift, the decoration of the Order of the Iron Cross which he had just created in Italy to be the equivalent of the French Legion of Honor.

[157]Ferdinando Paër, famous Italian composer (1771-1839). He wrote an opera, *Circé*, in 1791 in Venice. Between 1789 and 1799, he wrote no less than 25 operas for all the Italian theaters. Then famous, he was called to Dresden in 1801 as chapel master for the elector of Saxony. When during the 1806 campaign Dresden was invaded by French troops, Paër had just produced his *Achille*. Napoleon saw this, and liked it so much that he wanted to have this musician, whose reputation was one of the most brilliant of his time, join his service. On his orders, a contract dated Warsaw, January 1807, and signed by Talleyrand was awarded to Paër. The contract named him lifetime composer of the Emperor's household, in charge of directing the music of the court's concerts and theaters. Napoleon therefore brought him to Paris with his wife, a talented singer, and the tenor Brizzi; he formed, along with them and Crescentini, Mme Grassini, and other virtuosi, the Emperor's private singing group.

Preoccupied by shows and concerts, Paër wrote almost nothing for several years. In 1811, his genius seemed to reawaken, and he wrote the score for *Agnese*. Shortly thereafter, in 1812, Napoleon chose him to succeed Spontini as director of the Italian theater.

Under Louis-Philippe, Paër was in charge of the king's chapel music, a post he held until his death.

In addition to gifts, Crescentini had received the Iron Cross decoration. This decoration was foreign, and so was the man. People highly disapproved of such a deed, but all the clamor was drowned out by a remark that becomes successful when uttered by an attractive woman like Mme Grassini. People were talking indignantly in front of her, in a salon where she was, about the awarded decoration, when she rose majestically and said: "And his wound, sir, does it count for naught?" There was such a brouhaha that she was embarrassed by her success. That was the end of it.

M. Paër, music master to Empress Marie-Louise, had also been showered with kindness by the Emperor. These three people felt a debt of gratitude toward him, and during the Hundred Days they told me that had the Emperor remained in Elba, they would certainly have come there to entertain him.[158] Talma and Mlle Georges[159] also proposed to do so.

---

[158]It is difficult to share Marchand's sentiment and confidence on this point. Paër, Grassini, and Crescentini during the Hundred Days undoubtedly assured Marchand they would have come to Elba. Crescentini perhaps, but Paër was to be named by Louis XVIII his chamber composer, prior to becoming the Duchess of Berry's singing master. As for Grassini, she sang "and did more than just sing" for Wellington.

[159]There is no need to dwell on these two well-known names casually mentioned by Marchand. The great tragedian Talma (1763-1826) was covered with favors by Napoleon, who had him play in Erfurt before "an audience of kings." Mlle Georges (1787-1867) excelled in the roles of queens, was a great actress with the Comédie-Française, and also became the object of Napoleon's most tender interest. Talma remained faithful to the Emperor to his very deathbed. Talma himself recalled an event worthy of recounting: "When the Emperor returned from Elba, he had the goodness to speak to me about a letter I had written him at Fontainebleau at the time of his abdication, when all were abandoning him, both men and fate. 'It did not surprise me, my poor Talma,' the Emperor added: 'you were very unhappy when you wrote to me, but fate has its good sides: I am bringing my reply in person, and we will see one another again.' "

During his terminal illness, the doctors caring for him found on his chest a small gold medallion bearing the portrait of the Emperor. Below it the following three words were engraved: *Tibi semper fidelis*. No greater testimony can be given of his Napoleonic faithfulness.

As for Mlle Georges, although she was cast aside by Napoleon after 1813 and no longer came to the sun-filled apartment at the Tuileries, she was the only one of his mistresses who remained faithful to his memory in times of adversity as in times of power.

That autumn a few garrison officers, General Lebel[160]—who
had just arrived with his charming daughter who was honored by
Napoleon—and a few local ladies put on a performance of the *Calif of
Baghdad*.[161] This was well done and quite successful, given in a small
theater erected in a large hall the Emperor had built near the palace in
order to give balls there during the winter. The Emperor expressed his
satisfaction and his desire to hear them again.

The musicians hired in Genoa by Captain Loubers[162] were
mediocre; the Emperor had heard them in Longone when they arrived,
and was not pleased with them. An excellent artist from Milan,
Gavodiano, who had spontaneously come to offer his talents to the
Emperor, was named conductor, and as the basic elements were good,
he turned them into an excellent band that accompanied the Elban battalion to Paris. Gavodiano was then named head of the guard band, and
also worked in the chapel: it was a just reward for his disinterestedness
and his love for the Emperor.

Captain Loubers' mission in going to Genoa was also to show
off the brig and the Elban colors. It was manned by 50 grenadiers in

---

[160]Antoine Lebel, born in 1765, enlisted as a gendarme in 1784 and was a cavalryman
all his life. He was made adjutant major in 1813. He seems to have arrived in Elba of
his own free will with his wife and charming daughter, and there was talk of making
him commander at Longone. His daughter was placed by Napoleon with Princess
Pauline, as Countess Molo, but her father did not remain in favor with Napoleon. He
was a colonel during the Waterloo campaign, and joined the king's cause on July 18,
1815.

Details on Lebel are given in Pons de l'Hérault's *Souvenirs et anecdotes de l'île
d'Elbe*, op. cit. But we should note therein a double error, probably due to the fact that
Lebel readily adopted inaccurate titles. He was not adjutant general, as Pons states, but
adjutant major. Neither was he a general, as Marchand states. He only became a general after joining the king in July 1815.

[161]The *Calife de Bagdad*, a one-act comic opera (by Adrien Boieldieu), first shown at
the Favart Theater on September 16, 1800.

[162]Captain Jules Loubers (1785–d. after 1840) commanded the 4th Imperial Guard
company on Elba. Well-born but a snob pretending to be an aristocrat, he was not popular. He was assigned by the Emperor to be Princess Pauline's official dancing part-
ner, which was a good choice. He retired as a lieutenant colonel in 1830, and was still
living in Gascony in 1840.

fine uniform, who greatly impressed the population when they went ashore; all wanted to see them and host them. Glory was written on their tanned faces, and they were the object of everyone's admiration. They resisted the extended invitations, spoke of the Emperor with enthusiasm, and returned on board ship after behaving with admirable wisdom.

Cipriani, one of the Emperor's butlers, went along also. He had been secretly sent to thank several tradesmen of his acquaintance who had offered the Emperor their services and any money he might need. Some furniture was purchased to better cover up the purpose of this mission.

When the brig returned, the Emperor went on board and chatted with his old soldiers who were all happy to see him again, and delighted by the Genoa furlough. He inquired whether they had been well treated during the crossing. One of them, a wine-lover nicknamed La Comète, replied: "Sire, that was quite a party!"

"Any complaints? You didn't lack for wine, judging by your color."

"That's only a sunburn, Sire; but the finest thing on me is this (pointing at the eagle badge on his cap); it has never faced the rear." The Emperor left the ship, and when he got home that evening, was still laughing about the witty quips of his old grognard, who a few months later would die at Waterloo, repeating the words of his leader: "The guard may die, but it never surrenders!"

In July, Countess Bertrand arrived in Porto Ferrajo with her children, accompanied by the general's brother. The lady was pregnant and gave birth in August to a boy, who died in October because of a deplorable error by the pharmacist. Understanding such legitimate sorrow, the Emperor would often visit her with words of friendship and encouragement to ease her pain. It was he and Empress Joséphine who had brought about the marriage of that lady to General Bertrand, for whom the Emperor had much esteem and affection. He gave them each a dowry, with the generosity the Emperor brought to all he did: 200,000 francs to the countess, 50,000 francs in diamonds, 30,000 francs for her trousseau, 200,000 francs to Count Bertrand and the La

Jonchère villa. Such was the couple's dowry. These details were given me by the countess herself, who liked to relate the Emperor's kindness toward her.[163]

Countess Bertrand had brought with her the Fontainebleau treaty,[164] which was burned along with other papers when the Emperor left Elba.

This lady had charming conversation, an elegant figure and charming feet; although not beautiful, her appearance was pleasant. Her entire person was imbued with a distinction which her children inherited.

Madame Mère's arrival had brought the Emperor back to Porto Ferrajo. After spending a few weeks there, he returned on August 20 to La Madonna, and Madame came to stay in a small house

---

[163]The La Jonchère villa, given to the Bertrand couple, was next door to the Malmaison estate. It was on the road that starts at the end of the property and leads to the hamlet of La Jonchère and La Celle-Saint-Cloud. It was an unpretentious structure which, with its main building and a wing on each side surrounding a large central terrace, had the appearance of a small castle. The interior decoration by Percier and Fontaine remains in some of the rooms, particularly the dining room. The estate now belongs to M. Maurice Bérard. Bourguignon was fortunate to be able to save the castle and its interior decoration during the German occupation in World War II.

[164]On his departure from Fontainebleau, Grand Marshal Bertrand had written to Caulaincourt on April 19 to ask him to look after his wife: "As soon as I arrive in Elba, I shall write to my wife to join me; please provide her with a passport for herself, two maids, and her children. Please also provide a separate passport for my brother Louis, who will bring her and come back at once..."

Caulaincourt obtained the requested passports, and took that opportunity to send the Emperor a letter dated May 28, 1814, containing copies of the various Allied ratifications, and another letter dated June 2, containing England's act of adhesion to the treaty of April 11. These were the letters and the diplomatic documents they contained that Countess Bertrand brought with her to Elba.

in Marciana.[165] The Emperor dined every day at her house, and received a few people from the city there, returning in the evening to his hermitage. His Majesty had been there a few days when Mme Walewska,[166] who was going to Naples, asked his permission to stop and see him on the way. Having been granted permission to do so, she came with her son, sister, and brother.[167] She remained 24 hours at the hermitage, and did not go to Marciana where Madame Mère was staying. On the island, people thought it was the Empress and the King of Rome, and became excited. The Emperor had gone to meet her with Paoli, the gendarmerie captain, and Bernotti, one of his ADCs, followed by two mamelukes. Bernotti got off his horse when they met the two ladies, picked up the child, and carried him to the hermitage, allowing no one else the honor of carrying the presumed King of Rome. He was certainly two years older, but the beauty of his features and the curly blond hair flowing over his shoulders made him look very much like Isabey's portrait of the King of Rome.

The rumor had spread throughout Porto Ferrajo, and Dr. Foureau, whom the Emperor had not taken with him, went to see

---

[165]Madame Mère followed the Emperor when he returned on August 20 to the hermitage at La Madonna, and she settled in Marciana Alta with her chamberlain, superintendent, two lady's companions, two maids, her cook, and four servants. She occupied a house that still stands today and bears a commemorative plaque on its facade. From La Madonna, Napoleon wrote on August 23 to the grand marshal in Porto Ferrajo: "I brought my three iron beds. I want one sent to Marciana for Madame Mère. She will be comfortable in the assistant's house…she will have a room for herself, and three for her staff. The necessary basic furniture already exists in the house. I shall have a dresser added. I believe there are enough kitchen utensils, candles and lamps. Send three curtains for her room; the rods are there. Send us a fireplace set, as I think they are right to say it is necessary to light a fire at night." The Emperor had not planned on staying more than four or five days at La Madonna. He remained there almost two weeks, and left only on September 4 or 5, after Mme Walewska's visit.

[166]The reader will be familiar with Mme Walewska's name.

"The child of Wagram," as he was called, the son of the Emperor and Marie Walewska, became during the second Empire a most important person, as ambassador and minister of foreign affairs, under the name of Count Walewski (1810-1868).

[167]Mme Walewska's sister was Emilie Laczinska, and her brother Colonel Teodor Laczinski.

General Drouot to ask him if it might not be a good idea to come and offer his services to the Empress; the next day at dawn he was at the hermitage. The Emperor had turned over the three small rooms he occupied to the two ladies; beds had been set up, and he had taken refuge for the night in a tent erected a distance away under some chestnut trees. Saint-Denis and I slept in the walls of the tent. It was there that Dr. Foureau found me. Surprised to see him, I asked what brought him there; when he promptly congratulated me on the pleasure I must be feeling at seeing my mother, I understood his mistake, and without having time to correct it, went in to see the Emperor who was calling for me. I mentioned this to the Emperor, who had a good laugh. When the Emperor was dressed, he came out of his tent, where he had spent a rather poor night; a heavy rain with much wind had prevented him from sleeping, but sunshine announced a fine day and had already dried up the surrounding area. He found Mme Walewska's child playing, called to him, sat on a chair he had asked me to bring, and put him on his knees, then called for the doctor who was strolling in the vicinity. When he had arrived, he asked: "Well, Foureau, how do you find him?"

"But Sire, I think the king has grown a lot!" That child was two years older than the young Napoleon, but had the same kind of face. The Emperor laughed heartily over the doctor's mistake, teased him a few moments, and thanked him for his eagerness to come and offer his services.

The Emperor had no household staff with him to serve his guests; lunch was brought all prepared from Marciana, as was dinner. If there was a shortage of luxury at the table, there was plenty of mirth. The Emperor wanted the child, who had not lunched with him, to have dinner there. Mme Walewska said he was far too unruly, but His Majesty was not surprised by children's mischievousness. He claimed to have been very stubborn and unruly himself, saying: "I would hit Joseph and then force him to do my homework. If I was punished and put on plain bread, I went and swapped it for the shepherd's chestnut bread, or I would go find my nurse who would give me some little squids I was quite fond of!"

"Sire," said Mme Walewska, "I believe that if these were offered to Your Majesty, you would not like them as much."

"Not at all, I would eat some with pleasure."

The day was spent strolling through the area until dinnertime, as the ladies were to sail out that same evening. The Emperor placed Mme Walewska's son next to him; he was very good at first, but that didn't last, and as his mother was scolding him, the Emperor said: "Aren't you afraid of the whip? Well, I urge you to be: I felt it only once, but have remembered it always." He told how this had happened: "My grandmother was quite old and stooped, and seemed to me and to Pauline like an old fairy godmother. She walked with a cane, and her affection for us always led her to bring us candy; this didn't prevent us from walking behind her and mimicking her. Unfortunately she noticed this and complained to Madame, telling her she was raising us without any respect for grandparents. Although she loved us very much, Madame put up with no nonsense, and I saw that I was in for it. Pauline got hers first, because skirts are easier to pull up than pants are to unbutton and pull down. That evening she tried to get me, but in vain; I thought I would get off scot-free. The next morning she pushed me away when I tried to kiss her, but I had forgotten all about it when during the day Madame said to me: 'Napoleon, you are invited to lunch at the governor's house, go get dressed!' I went upstairs, quite happy at the idea of lunching with officers, and got undressed rapidly. But Madame was like a cat waiting for a mouse; she suddenly entered my room, closing the door behind her. I realized the trap into which I had fallen, but it was too late, I had to submit to the spanking." And as the child had listened with great care, the Emperor said to him: "Well, what do you think of that?"

"But I don't make fun of Mama," he replied with a contrite look on his face that pleased the Emperor, who kissed him, saying: "That's a good answer!"

During the day, the gendarmerie captain told him he had just received a report that two soldiers in the Corsican regiment had exchanged blows with their swords; the Emperor asked: "What was the cause? No doubt some whore?"

"Yes, Sire."

"Which man was wounded?"

"The one who appears to be guilty, having insulted the woman whom the other was holding by the arm, and wanted to appropriate her for himself."

"That's only just; even the meekest animal will bite anyone who tries to take its food away from it."

Mme Walewska (later Countess d'Ornano)[168] was a ravishing beauty at the time the Emperor knew her in Poland. She bore him a son, was always very devoted to him, and never failed the Emperor in difficult times, either at Fontainebleau in 1814[169] or at Malmaison in 1815. At the time I am writing of, when she arrived on Elba, she had put on a little weight, without her waist showing it too much. An open and calm expression on her face revealed the sweetness of her character. Her sister who was with her appeared to be 18; she was slender, with the head of an angel. Two days after their arrival, these ladies went back on board the ship that had brought them and sailed for Naples. The Emperor accompanied them to the Marciana marina, and was most courteous. He said that in his day men were far more amia-

---

[168] After Napoleon's departure for Saint Helena, Mme Walewska considered herself free, and on September 7, 1816, in Brussels, she married General Count d'Ornano (1784-1863), a distant cousin of the Bonaparte family, and former colonel in the guard dragoons, who was to become a marshal during the second Empire. Mme Walewska died on December 11, 1817.

[169] Reference to Mme Walewska's visit to Fontainebleau at the time when the Emperor tried to end his life. She waited the whole night in an anteroom for his call. But Napoleon remembered her only in the morning, when the unhappy woman, tired of waiting, had just gone away. He said: "Poor woman, she will think she was forgotten!" And in the depth of his disaster, he found time to reassure her in a note dated April 16: "Marie... the feelings that move you touch me greatly. They are worthy of your fine soul and the kindness of your heart. When you have settled your affairs, should you wish to go and take the waters at Lucca or Pisa, I shall see you with great pleasure, as well as your son, toward whom my feelings never change. Take care of yourself, think of me with pleasure, and never doubt me!"

In August 1814 she was in Florence, then Naples, and it was from there that she went to Elba.

ble than they were today. Camp life had not made him cynical; in all matters relating to the fair sex, he used poetic expressions or words.

The September rains drove the Emperor from that residence to Longone,[170] and Madame left Marciana to go to Porto Ferrajo. In Longone, the Emperor lived in the upper part of town, which is a fort built on a rocky peak; the view from the Emperor's apartments was admirable. Colonel Jermanowski[171] was governor of the town and of the castle. As such, he came to greet the Emperor and take him to his quarters, which were roomy and extensive, but totally devoid of furniture. The camp bed that accompanied the Emperor was erected; a few chairs and a table made up the bedroom furniture. Colonel Jermanowski, as gracious as he was gallant and brave, was much liked by the townspeople, for whom he gave small parties and dinners. During the few weeks the Emperor spent in that residence, he was always joined at table by the governor and a few town officials. The evening gatherings lasted until 10 p.m., at which time the Emperor went home. Two days before the departure from Longone, princess' secretary, M. Marie,[172] brought the Emperor a letter announcing her imminent arrival. The Emperor's questions came so fast that the messenger was dumbfounded, asking the Emperor to excuse him for his confusion of mind, caused by the emotion of being in his presence. After allowing him to calm down, the Emperor listened to him and told him to go wait for him in Porto Ferrajo where he would be in a few days.

---

[170]A small harbor on the east side of the island, in the iron ore region. Today it numbers nearly 3,000 people. Above the harbor on a rocky spur rises the citadel, built by the Spaniards in the early 17th century. The Italians have since made it into an "ergastule," i.e. a prison.

[171]Colonel Jermanowski, born in 1779, enlisted as a volunteer in 1800 in the Polish legion serving France. After 1806 he served in the Polish light cavalry. He went to Elba with Napoleon, was entirely devoted to him, and came back with him. He commanded the imperial guard lancers at Waterloo, where he was wounded. He was a commander in the Legion of Honor, and a baron of the Empire.

[172]This was probably a Frenchman who lived in Naples, and whom Princess Borghese often used to convey things belonging to her.

During the Emperor's stay in Marciana, a rumor circulated that General Bruslart,[173] governor in Corsica for Louis XVIII, had sent an emissary to Algiers to induce the pirates to kidnap the Emperor during one of the excursions when he left Porto Ferrajo and returned there by sea. Spotting one morning from his bedroom some small ships within sight of Porto Longone that he thought were Barbary ships, he asked me for his spyglass, rested it on my shoulder, and soon realized he was not mistaken. Their presence so close to his residence, at a time when such rumors were circulating, led him to order the brig *Inconstant* to set sail from Porto Ferrajo where it was and come drop anchor at Longone.

As soon as it arrived, Captain Taillade, the brig skipper, came to receive his orders. A note then addressed to Colonel Jermanowski said this: "Colonel, you shall take on board ship one officer, one sergeant, four corporals, and twenty-four men from the chasseurs battalion, being careful to select those who are not prone to seasickness. You shall also take one sergeant, one corporal, and ten men from the commando battalion, with the same stipulations, and personally supervise the embarkment."

Once the embarkment was completed, the brig sailed out immediately. The Emperor kept it in sight for a long time, but the vessels vanished when they saw it, and the brig returned to port that evening.

Mme Dargis[174] also arrived at that residence from

---

[173]General Louis-Guérin de Bruslart (1752-1829) was an officer of the old monarchy. Emigrated in 1791, he became ADC to the Duke of Bourbon, and in 1814 prepared the arrival of the Duke of Berry on the Normandy coast. During the first Restoration, Louis XVIII made him governor in Corsica. His official orders directed him "to get rid of Buonaparte at any cost."

[174]Pons de l'Hérault also mentions this lady in his *Souvenirs et anecdotes de l'île d'Elbe*. He spells the name Dargy. He describes her as being accompanied by a young child, saying she was his aunt. He mentions she looked barely more than 25, spoke well, had a pleasant face, and was a compatriot of General Drouot's.

Prangins,[175] a place four leagues from Geneva along the lake, where King Joseph and his family lived. She brought letters from the king. She asked permission to remain on the island, and the Emperor didn't know what to do, as she was without means. San Martino was being built, and the position of concierge was about to become available; she asked me to solicit that position for her, and the Emperor granted it. This woman came from Nancy and was rather quixotic. She felt obliged to write me a poem to thank me for the position I had obtained for her. I read this to the Emperor, who laughed over it, and after that whenever he referred to her, he would call her "My lunatic," although she was not that; but she had a mania for writing and expressing herself in rhyme.

The various journeys made by the Emperor had provided all the time required to complete the modifications to his residence: the princess' apartment, the ballroom, and the theater were finished. The Emperor returned to Porto Ferrajo. A pretty garden had been planted and covered with sod, and flowers were growing everywhere.

On his return, he had fine certificates handed out to a few grenadiers who were asking to go back to France. The Emperor had been able to tally up his revenues and expenses since he had been on the island, and felt the need to bring about some changes in his household. These were made in the food arrangements and a few salaries that were too high. Some messes were eliminated, and replaced by allowances; only his mess remained. I continued to have mine. This resulted in a substantial saving in the service. He was kind enough to tell me himself that he could now only give me 2,500 francs out of the 5,000 francs he used to give me. I told him it was much more than I needed, that 1,000 francs was more than sufficient for my needs. That

---

[175]Prangins, district of Vaud, on the road bordering the lake, halfway between Geneva and Lausanne. The castle was built around 1750 by M. Guiguer, a banker in Saint-Gall, who took its name. His grandson, General Guiguer de Prangins, sold it to King Joseph, exiled from France after the first Restoration. The former King of Spain enlarged the place, and built the elegant residence known as La Bergerie between the forest and the shore. The Prangins villa, once inhabited by Prince Napoleon (Jérôme), still belongs to the head of the Napoleonic family.

evening at bedtime he told me: "You will make up the 5,000 francs out of my private purse." I tried to protest this, but he said: "That is my will."

The last pieces of furniture were being placed in Princess Pauline's apartments when the frigate bringing her was announced. The Emperor went down to the harbor to wait for her. He had been strolling there for a moment when he thought he recognized a gendarmerie sergeant placed there to keep away the crowd that was anxious to see him. The Emperor went up to him and asked if he wasn't a Corsican.

"Yes, Sire."

"From where?"

"Bocognano, Sire."

"What's your name?"

"Marcaggi." The name was familiar to the Emperor. During the Corsican civil wars, he had been arrested in that vicinity by brigands and locked up in a room. A young man named Marcaggi,[176] from Bocognano, offered to rescue him and accompany him until he was out of danger. The Emperor remembered that favor and even recalled

---

[176]The name Marcaggi was associated with an episode of the revolutionary days' internal fighting between the anti-French Paoli partisans, aided by England, and the commissioners of the convention, whom the Bonaparte family supported; Bastia was the seat of the department, as Ajaccio was entirely in the hands of the Paolists. This episode dates from late April or early May 1793, during Napoleon's fifth stay in Corsica, where he had arrived in October 1792 and from where he departed in June 1793 with his entire family, "thrown out of the homeland he had so dearly loved."

Napoleon—whom Paoli called a "rascal"—feeling he no longer was safe there, decided to leave Ajaccio and rejoin the commissioners of the convention in Bastia. He set off on foot with one of his shepherds. Between Vivario and the Vecchio bridge, he became certain that, should he proceed any further, he would unavoidably be arrested. It was better for him to go back, discreetly return to Ajaccio, and proceed to Bastia by sea. He returned to Bocognano. But Paolist peasants seized him and locked him up in a ground-floor room. Fortunately a window opened onto the road. That evening, in the darkness, Napoleon jumped out unseen and ran away, guided by two of his partisans: one was Felix Tusoli, the other Marcaggi, whom he found again in Elba as a gendarmerie sergeant.

it in Saint Helena in one of his "conscience bequests."[177] He continued to chat with the sergeant, who showed him two of his very young children. The Emperor gave them each two napoleons to buy pastries. Once back in France, the Emperor made him a lieutenant. This soldier, forgotten on the island where he had been for so long, had a good service record: he awarded him the cross of the Legion of Honor and promised to take care of his children as soon as they reached high-school age.

When the frigate[178] had dropped anchor, the Emperor went out in his gig to meet the princess, brought her back to shore, and drove her in his carriage to Madame's. She then came to take possession of the apartment the Emperor had prepared for her. She was very thankful and happy about it. That same day, the Emperor, overseeing the installation of furniture in the princess' apartment, burned his fingers badly on a small dish where aloe was burning. Without paying attention, the Emperor had wanted to move it away from in front of a marble bust. As an inkwell was handy he dipped his fingers in it, without complaining of having felt the slightest pain; his fingers healed without his having said anything. I was the more saddened by this accident as it was I who had placed that burner there, and the Emperor was moving it only to reply to the grand marshal. He was contemplating the Canova bust of himself: what he reproached the artist for in that statue was the athletic figure he had been given, as if it had been his arm that had won battles, instead of the use of his head.

---

[177]In Napoleon's will, a codicil dated April 24, 1821, mentions the following item among some 20 distributions:

"I bequeath 100,000 francs to Marchand, of which he will deposit 50,000 francs with the treasurer, to be used for 'conscience bequests' in accordance with my instructions." It was one of these bequests that benefited Marcaggi.

[178]This was the brig *Inconstant* which Napoleon had sent to Pauline to bring her to Porto Ferrajo. She had boarded it in Portici on October 29, escorted by four senior officers the Emperor had assigned to accompany her. The *Inconstant* sailed into the Porto Ferrajo harbor on November 1, 1814. The princess was greeted with salvos from the forts' batteries.

Princess Pauline's arrival initiated a new way of life in Porto Ferrajo. Parties, balls, and concerts were given at her house; evening receptions were held at the Emperor's and at Madame's, replacing the activities of all kinds that had taken place until then. The small court of the sovereign of Elba took on a less military look. The princess, whose every charm was at its peak, lent an air of gallantry and mirth to all who surrounded her. The Emperor was quite right in naming his two sisters, the Queen of Naples and even more so Princess Pauline, whose beauty was more austere, as the two prettiest women of his court in France. Nothing was as perfectly beautiful as this princess. It could be said that, in creating her, Nature had borrowed from Praxiteles those points with which he determined the perfect shape of his Venus, for her beauty was that remarkable. She had brought her retinue, taking as lady's companions Mme Colombani and Mme Bellini,[179] wives of senior officers, and Mlle Lebel, daughter of the adjutant general by that name. All three had a remarkable appearance and distinction. The princess dined every day with the Emperor and General Drouot; she had herself transported from her apartments to the Emperor's. She went on her excursions in a sedan chair, in preference to a carriage; she was always accompanied by officers of the guard, who all vied for the honor. The Sunday invitations for dinner continued. It happened at one of these dinners that Countess Bertrand, who was not always on time, entered the dining room when the Emperor was already seated. She had forced people to wait for her and wanted to apologize, but the Emperor, knowing her weakness, said to her: "Madam, it is neither

---

[179]Mme Colombani was the handsome wife of an Italian army major whom Napoleon found in Elba and took in his service. The Emperor placed the young woman as a lady's companion with Pauline; she was not only gracious and pleasant, but her conduct was also exemplary. Her brother-in-law Colombani, a former war commissioner, seems to have been employed by the Emperor for different missions to the continent.

The second lady's companion mentioned by Marchand was the Spanish wife of a Polish major. She seems to have been very charming, and danced the fandango beautifully. The following year, on June 29, 1815, she would come to see the Emperor at Rambouillet to ask permission to follow him to Saint Helena. She later went to South America, and founded in Lima a large boarding school for girls where she made a fortune.

appropriate nor polite to make people wait for you." Saint-Denis, who was serving the Emperor, told me that those words were spoken in a rather curt manner; she had been quite taken aback, and the handkerchief she used attested to the tears in her eyes. Princess Pauline hastened to soften the impact on her feelings by asking news of her charming children. During that dinner, the Emperor announced that twice he owed his life to the fact that he measured only 5 feet 2 inches.[180]

Some forty Polish cavalrymen, sent by the Emperor to the Empress in Parma under the command of Major Balinski,[181] landed in Porto Ferrajo; the Austrian government had not wanted them to remain with this princess. The Emperor received them on the castle terrace, and they were quartered in the Etoile fort.

A few days after she had settled in, the princess was kind enough to send for me; she handed me a letter from my mother,[182] and the Emperor was present. That night when he went to bed, he asked me what she had written. I told him she gave news of the Empress and the King of Rome, who was very much liked by the Austrian emperor; and that a few days ago, when he got cross with her, he told her he would send her to take care of Louix XVIII. She also said that while the prince was very busy one day observing troops parading under his windows, the Empress went near him and asked him if he thought those soldiers were as fine as French soldiers; he replied: "No, if they were French, they would salute me." She told me that the Empress was going to Aix for the baths, to restore her health which was much affected by recent events, and told me her wish that the Empress would go to Parma so that I could come and see her there.

---

[180]French measure; English 5 feet 7 inches.

[181]Balinski is listed as a captain in the Polish cavalry lancer squadron. Joining it in 1807, he spent most of his career in this elite unit. He was wounded at Wagram. At the second Restoration, he went to serve in the Russian army.

[182]Marchand's mother held the position of nurse to the infant King of Rome.

During this trip, the King of Rome remained in the care of
Countess Montesquiou[183] and my mother, who wrote to me morning
and night; she made sure that the Emperor's name was mentioned in
the prince's prayers. Several of these details made the Emperor laugh,
and pleased him. That evening they were repeated in the salon. Princess Pauline said at this point that she had been told that in Vienna,
when the Prince de Ligne[184] had been introduced to the King of Rome,
he had asked his governess if this was one of the marshals who had
betrayed his father; when he received a negative answer, he had then
held out his hand.

The Emperor used the most flattering words when speaking of
Countess Montesquiou. As I was retiring, he said to me: "Doesn't she

---

[183]By a decree dated October 22, 1810, Countess Montesquiou had been named "governess to the children of France." Born Le Tellier de Louvois de Courtanvaux and a
direct descendant of Louis XIVth's grand minister, she was the wife of Count de Montesquiou, who on January 29, 1809, had replaced Talleyrand as the Emperor's grand
chamberlain. After the Fontainebleau abdication, she faithfully followed the King of
Rome to Vienna, continuing to honor her promise to the Emperor.

The King of Rome called her "Maman Quiou" and was very fond of her. She
never left his side, from the time he arose until bedtime. But as increasing measures
were taken at the Vienna congress against the sovereign of Elba, Mme de Montesquiou and her faithful followers felt the danger growing. On March 20, 1815, Baron de
Wessemberg informed her of "the elimination of her position and the need for her to
leave Marie-Louise's court." Marchand's mother, to whom we owe the touching
details related here, suffered of course the same fate.

The memoirs of Anatole de Montesquiou, daughter of the countess, make very
interesting reading.

[184]This is the famous prince of Ligne (1775-1814), one of the more brilliant men of his
time, in whom can be found the international mentality of the 18th century, and author
of the famous *Mélanges militaires, littéraires, sentimentaires* (*sic*). Field marshal in
the Austrian army, related to the imperial family, he nevertheless did not hide his
admiration for Napoleon. He died during the Vienna congress, in which he took part.
The anecdote related by Marchand must have taken place at the very end of his life.

mention Méneval?"[185] He expected to learn from this faithful aide the contents of the secret resolutions reached at the congress of Vienna. It wasn't long before he had news. Through this correspondence, the Emperor was able to follow the Empress' trip to Switzerland, as well as the side trips that took her to see King Joseph in Prangins.[186]

It was on her return from seeing this prince that she found in Aix Count Neipperg,[187] who was coming on orders of the Austrian emperor to join her household as chamberlain—but in fact to spy on that princess' moves and oppose any attempt that might suggest to her the thought of going to Elba. Had she come to this residence, she would have found portraits of herself and of the King of Rome hanging in the Emperor's bedroom.

---

[185]Claude, Baron de Méneval (1778-1850). First served as secretary to Joseph Bonaparte during the negotiations preceding the treaties of Lunéville and Amiens. Joseph offered him as secretary to the First Consul, replacing Bourrienne. Napoleon always appreciated his services and his devotion, and assigned him to Marie-Louise when she was named regent. Méneval followed the Empress to Vienna in 1814, and managed to keep Napoleon informed of what was going on at the congress. But, like Mme de Montesquiou, he in turn was sent back to France. He spent a day in Prangins, which had become a kind of communications center between Elba, Austria, the kingdom of Naples, and France. He related in his *Mémoires* his visit to King Joseph. "I had a great desire to see again this noble family who had welcomed my youth with so much kindness. I found King Joseph just as he had always been, kind, pleasant, and unpretentious, having like Cincinnatus returned to his plow, more interested in the details of country life and the Emperor's fate than in memories of the brilliant and stormy career he had led..."

[186]It was through Méneval that Napoleon heard about Marie-Louise's trip through Switzerland and her visit to Prangins. Marie-Louise's visit to her brother-in-law Joseph, in July 1814, led to comments and objections voiced by the French minister in Zurich to the two deputies from Vaud, MM. Muret and Monod. The latter relates: "The minister tells us that the former King Joseph does not behave in our midst with the circumspection France would expect. When Marie-Louise came, he should have worn his decorations, among them the Golden Fleece; he should have accompanied her, and this upset the people; there were cries of Vive l'Empereur! Vive Napoleon! These cries were heard in Lausanne too."

[187]Marchand mentions Neipperg when he comes to Aix-les-Bains in the service of Marie-Louise. He had said, when leaving for his new post: "Before ten months are up, I shall be her lover, and soon after, her husband." It didn't take six months.

Tuna fishing takes place twice a year in Elba; it is an island celebration that starts with a sort of ritual. The men who carry out this fishing, which produces much revenue for the sovereign's estate, are required by treaty to sell the islanders one quarter of their catch at very low cost. The autumn fishing was off to a good start; it began at daybreak. A large number of boats crisscrossed the roadsteads where the fishing was taking place; all eyes were on the enormous net. Fishermen were harpooning the fish that surfaced; the waters were soon reddened by their blood. When the tuna lose their strength, they are gathered and taken ashore. The Emperor went out to harpoon a few, and came back from this activity covered with salt water and a few drops of blood. The fishing that year was most abundant.

In spite of the resources brought about by the Emperor's constructions on the island, the residents of Capoliveri[188] refused to pay their taxes when the tax collector came to their homes. The Emperor criticized at great length the gendarmerie lieutenant in charge of the collection, who had just told him about this minor rebellion. He said to him: "Go tell them that if they haven't paid within 24 hours, I will send a battalion to lodge and eat in their homes." This refusal by a rich parish was setting a bad example, and this first mutiny had to be repressed vigorously. The taxes were paid.

---

[188]The first village encountered on the main road to Porto Longone and the iron mines. Its appearance was unappealing, and it had a bad reputation. The Romans in antiquity and the Pisans in the Middle Ages had made it an asylum for insolvent debtors, forgers, bankrupts, and those hiding from the law, but a place recognized under the law as such, hence its name "free place." A suspicious population had gathered there whose evil acts were for a long time a source of terror on the island.

Napoleon had always tried to ensure order throughout his small principality. Some trouble occurred in a few areas because of taxes. In Capoliveri, no one wanted to pay. Gendarmes were sent out, but were chased away. The Emperor then threatened to send, under the command of Colonel Jermanowski, a mobile unit consisting of 200 Corsican chasseurs, 20 Polish lancers, and 15 gendarmes. This unit was to lodge with the inhabitants until the taxes were fully paid. They were paid that same day.

CHAPTER FIVE

General discontent in France — Defense measures — The goatherd —
The Inconstant runs aground — Threats of confinement on
Saint Helena or Saint Lucia — News of Vienna from Cipriani —
New Year's Day 1815 — Troubles in Vienna —
Details on divorce from Empress Joséphine

*O*fficers and travelers or tradesmen arriving from France, Italy,
and Corsica gave His Majesty an exact idea of France's position and the general discontent caused by the new government. People
feared for the Emperor's person. News arriving from Vienna, via
Livorno and Naples, was not reassuring. Tradesmen from Genoa and
Lyon, knowing that the Emperor's and his family's pensions were not
being paid, offered him money. There was talk of Saint Helena.

The Emperor thus decided to send back to the continent, to
Genoa, Captain Loubers of the guard, who had gone there before with
Cipriani, one of his butlers. Cipriani, a trusted aide of Saliceti,[189] the
police minister in Naples, knew many people in Genoa and Vienna he
had previously seen in Naples, with whom he had established contact
during his first trip. Captain Loubers had a sensitive mission, and carried it off with tact and success. The brig arrived in the Genoa harbor
under the pretext—as in the past—of buying things necessary for the
battalion, and some furniture and crystal for the palace. Letters from
the Emperor to the Empress were sent and received, and the replies
arrived in Elba; intelligence contacts were established in that city, and
offers of money and devotion to the Emperor were made to Captain
Loubers.

Cipriani's mission was to find out, through persons whose
names had been given to him, what was going on in diplomatic circles
in the capital and in the congress itself; to watch for the departure of

any sovereigns gathered there, and to immediately so inform the
Emperor; and to establish in Genoa with his friends a news network
that would send the Emperor a bulletin each week on affairs in Vienna.
He soon reported that the congress was talking about the danger of
having Napoleon so close to the coasts of Italy and France, and of the
need to move him further away, the name of Saint Helena having been
mentioned. The Emperor couldn't believe it, but this was confirmed by
another source, and a copy of the secret resolution on this subject was
provided; newspapers were openly talking about this plan. True or
false, this information brought back by the brig forced the Emperor to
take certain precautions. Navy commander Chautard was ordered to

---

[189]Cipriani had been a trusted deputy of Saliceti. Christophe Saliceti was born in Bastia in 1757, of a Plaisance family, and had studied law at the University of Pisa. He returned to Corsica and became an attorney for the Corsican upper council. Elected as deputy of the third estate to the Etats Généraux in 1789, that same year he drafted the decree of the constitutional assembly declaring Corsica an integral part of France. After the assembly was dissolved, he represented Corsica at the convention. Having broken off with Paoli, he had to flee his birthplace for a time. He sought refuge in Provence, joined Carteaux' army, and allied himself with Barras, Robespierre, and Fréron to crush the enemies of the Republic in the south. In 1796, he was named by the Directory as government commissioner to the army of Italy. There he showed himself to be very devoted to Bonaparte, and served him well at the time when the armistice with the Pope was signed. In 1797, he was back in Corsica where he collaborated with Lucien Bonaparte. Elected a member of the council of Five Hundred, he did not join the partisans of 18 Brumaire, but the First Consul did not hold this against him: he knew Saliceti's talents as an administrator, which he had appreciated in Italy, and wanted to put them to use. He sent him on a mission to Tuscany, then Genoa, to create a party favorable to France there. He attracted the attention of Joseph Bonaparte, who had become king in 1806, and who named him minister of police. In this post, Saliceti showed great qualities and a firm character. During the Calabria uprising, a frightened Joseph thought of fleeing, but remained on the entreaties of his police minister: he then added to his title that of war minister. Murat's arrival in Naples changed the situation. The new king knew Saliceti was backed by his wife Caroline, whose influence he feared. He did not keep him in his position, and Saliceti returned to Paris. But the Emperor sent him back to Italy to be part of the Consultum that was to take possession of Rome (1809). Just as he had settled there, an Anglo-Sicilian army landed in Calabria, so he proceeded to Naples, which was threatened by the enemy. He resumed his former duties and saved the situation. But in spite of all these services, Murat did not keep him, naming Maghella police minister. Saliceti died suddenly (1809) as he left a dinner party offered by his successor. Such was the man of valor, much appreciated by Napoleon, whom Cipriani had loyally served: Cipriani could offer Napoleon no better reference.

keep a vigilant watch on the navigation of ships cruising near Elba. British newspapers coming from Livorno[190] gave a confirmation of sorts of the news brought back by the brig. The Emperor, on receiving

---

[190]In Napoleon's time, Livorno was, after Genoa, the second port of western Italy. It remained a free and neutral city until the creation of the Italian kingdom. When Napoleon was sent to Elba, his sister Elisa abandoned Tuscany, whose grand duchess she had been since 1807, and the former sovereign Ferdinand III resumed possession of his states. At the beginning of his stay in Porto Ferrajo, Napoleon had sent Pons de l'Hérault as emissary to Ferdinand, who greeted him very kindly, expressing a real interest in the Emperor, whom he always called his "dear nephew." He said he had had great difficulty dissuading the reactionaries who wanted to completely dismantle the Napoleonic code.

The grand duke's minister, Fossombroni, was also very friendly and respectful toward Napoleon. He asked Pons to beg the Emperor "to be very careful," adding "it is up to you to look after him, as they want to kill him." While Napoleon remained in Elba, Livorno served as a center for both espionage and counter-espionage.

Because of recent events, Elba had become the focus of attention of all Europe. Louis XVIII's government in particular wanted to keep a close eye on the deposed Emperor. As early as July 1814, he decided to reestablish near the island the Livorno consulate, eliminated in 1808 at the incorporation of Tuscany into the French Empire. He named to the post a trustworthy man, adjutant general Mariotti, who received confidential instructions and considerable secret funding.

Mariotti was a Corsican from Bastia who had served as brigade commander in the French army in 1799, and whom Napoleon had made a knight, then an officer in the Legion of Honor. The Emperor had then lost interest in him. It is probably because of the spite he felt about this, and his solid knowledge of the Italian language and habits, that Talleyrand chose him. Mariotti had moved to Livorno in early August 1814. On September 13, Talleyrand informed him of his departure for the congress of Vienna, urging him to keep an eye on Elba and "its owner."

Mariotti wasted no time, and set up agents in all the small ports between Livorno and San Stefano who kept him informed of the slightest incidents, and all the moves of those coming to or going from Porto Ferrajo. Bruslart, the military commander in Corsica, was in constant correspondence with the Livorno consul; the latter had not neglected the surveillance of Porto Ferrajo itself. The many visitors whom curiosity attracted to Elba have been reported in a previous note (136). Mariotti understood the need for reliable observers amid this cosmopolitan crowd. Among these, one deserves special attention: coming from Livorno, he landed in Porto Ferrajo under the guise of an oil dealer. His name remains a mystery, but he was always designated as "the oil merchant." Under the pretext of doing business, he made useful contacts. He was in contact with all foreigners coming through, all the island civil servants, and all the Corsican, French, and Italian officers. He wrote down in his notebook everything he heard, and reported on this to Mariotti in the form of a diary. His reports, written in Italian, are of rather uneven interest.

[See the detail reports of the "oil merchant" in the forthcoming *Napoleon: 1814-1821, "Prelude to Conclusion"*–Proctor Jones Edition.—Ed.]

this first news, said: "I do not believe that Europe wishes to take up arms against me; I would however not suggest they attack me here, they could pay dearly for their endeavor. I have six months' provisions, good artillery, and brave soldiers to defend me. I was guaranteed the sovereignty of Elba; I am at home here, and I do not advise anyone to come and disturb me." Some defense measures were decided on for the outer gates. The Emperor ordered the British fort armed, as it was separated from the stronghold's fortification system. One day when he was having a well dug at the foot of the fort, a child of some dozen years came up to him, and was looking at him carefully, a happy look on his face; the Emperor asked him in Italian why he was there.

"I came to see you, they say you are the Emperor Napoleon, is it true?"

"But what are you doing?"

"I am tending my goats."

"Are they yours?"

"No, they are my master's."

"Are you pleased with him?"

"Not too pleased, he is rich and gives me little."

"Would you be happy to have another job?"

"Yes, if it was with a good master."

"Well! come to town tomorrow and ask for the grand marshal, he will find you a job. Bertrand, send him to Chauvin, he will put him in the stables." That same evening the little goatherd turned the goats over to his master, did not complain about him, and asked for his blessing, which he gave more readily than the small amount of money he owed him.

When the Emperor left Elba, this young child followed his retinue. The Hundred Days took place, a small sum was given him to learn a trade, and the little Elban goatherd got married and is well settled in Paris.

The Emperor also went to Pianosa, a small island attached to Elba where he was having a fort constructed under the supervision of Captain Larabit,[191] an engineering officer (later a deputy). He camped there several days in his tents, then returned to Porto Ferrajo after quieting a rather violent altercation[192] between the young captain and Major Ruhl,[193] ADC to the Emperor.

It was at about this time that notices from London informed Napoleon that the plan to take him away from Elba did not originate

---

[191]Marie-Denis Larabit, born in 1792, was a 21-year-old lieutenant of engineering when he volunteered to go to Elba in 1814, there being no other engineering officer available to go. He had previously served with distinction in Saxony and France, and in 1814 was attached to the imperial guard general staff.

He landed in Elba in June 1814, and Napoleon greeted him with marked cordiality and placed him under the orders of Captain Raoul, commanding the military engineers.

Once back in France and promoted to captain, Larabit entered politics, where he remained very active, eventually becoming a deputy. He always remained faithful to the Napoleonic family, and became a senator in 1853 by imperial decree. He returned to private life after the September 1870 revolution.

[192]We know through other witnesses, namely Pons de l'Hérault, of the incident mentioned here by Marchand. When Napoleon decided to organize Pianosa militarily, he ordered Lieutenant Larabit to proceed to the island and construct there a fort for 100 men and 8 cannon, giving him four eight-inch pieces and four four-inch, a detachment of grenadiers, one of artillery, and 100 men from the commandos. Napoleon had shown Larabit the exact location for the barracks and the fort. He even showed him on a map the high rock dominating the harbor: "That's where you must set up your artillery," he said; "place all your guns in position within 24 hours, and fire on anything that tries to land in spite of you."

But Napoleon had previously named as island commander Major Gottmann, who opposed the construction of the barracks and wanted a house built instead. This led to endless and violent arguments. When Napoleon visited again to see how things were progressing, he complimented Larabit and faulted Gottmann. The Emperor's chief aide, Major Ruhl, came to Gottman's defense. There then was a violent argument between Ruhl and Larabit. The Emperor prevented the duel that was about to settle the argument, saying to Larabit: "I forbid you to fight." But to show that he approved of his conduct, he removed Major Gottmann from his command.

[193]Ruhl was a rowdy officer who arrived in Elba after Napoleon. He claimed to be an artillery major, showed great enthusiasm for Napoleon, was welcomed warmly by the guard soldiers, and was made chief ADC to Napoleon. It was soon learned that he was in fact only a captain, hence his many altercations with guard officers.

with the British minister; Lord Liverpool had in fact written to Wellington in this regard. The Princess of Wales had just asked His Majesty if she could come to Elba.[194] The Emperor, deeply involved with construction and workmen, could not receive her graciously, and asked her to put off this little trip. The princess had seen Empress Marie-Louise in Bern, during her trip to Switzerland: he learned she was being noticed there for the strangeness of her dress and behavior.

In early December, the Emperor sent the brig to Naples carrying M. Ramolino[195] as official representative to the king. It was through the queen and her ambassador, the Duke of Campo Chiaro,[196] that he had contact with Vienna. They were trying to bypass the Neapolitan ministers. They had their own court's interests to defend at the congress. The confinement of the King of Saxony and the occupation of Dresden and Leipzig by Prince Repnine[197] as governor general served to separate the interests of the courts of Austria and France

---

[194]Caroline Amélie Elisabeth, born May 17, 1768, second daughter of the Duke of Brunswick (died in 1805 from wounds received at Auerstaedt) and Princess Augusta of England, sister of George III. In 1805 she married the Prince of Wales, who in 1820 became George IV; the marriage was not happy, though they had a daughter, Charlotte-Augusta. The princess traveled extensively on the continent; Commander M. H. Weil's book *Les Dessous du congrès de Vienne* (Paris, 1917) shows she was in Milan in November 1814, then a few days later in Naples, staying in the palace occupied by Saliceti. She must then have planned on visiting Elba, Marchand being the only one to mention this.

[195]Ramolino, a relative of the Emperor, held the position of tax director in Ajaccio. He had come to Elba to offer his services to the Emperor.

[196]The Duke of Campo Chiaro was a Neapolitan statesman of Spanish origin whose family settled in Naples in the 18th century. In 1806 he was called to the council of State by King Joseph, then became minister for the royal household and was given several diplomatic missions. At the congress of Vienna he represented King Murat.

[197]The Repnine princes belonged to a very old Russian family: among them was Prince Nicolas Vassilievitch, well known during the reigns of Catherine II and Paul I. He became a field marshal under the latter.

The prince mentioned here by Marchand, Nicolas Volkonski, was the grandson of the field marshal. He fought as a colonel at Austerlitz. Later, after Napoleon's first defeats, he was governor of Saxony in 1813-14, and is mentioned by Marchand as such.

from those of Russia and Prussia. It was obvious that the cards were being reshuffled; it was then in Vienna a time of anxiety and alarm. In Elba it was not the moment to complain of the non-execution of the Fontainebleau treaty.

Later the Emperor learned that the congress had been about to dissolve; an alliance was being formed between France, Austria, and England against Russia and Prussia, and the house of Bourbon was asking Austria for full reinstatement to the Naples and Parma branches of their holdings. Emperor Francis was already agreeing to violate the Fontainebleau treaty articles that ensured Marie-Louise and her son the duchies of Parma and Plaisance.

Returning from Naples, the brig almost sank on arrival. It was too late to enter the harbor. Captain Taillade waited until the next day. During the night a terrible storm came up; very early the next morning, a muffled sound was heard: it was cannon shots of distress. The weather was so bad that it was impossible to see or launch anything. The Emperor was in bed; I entered his room and informed him of the condition of the sea and the help being called for. He immediately donned his robe and wanted to go out to his garden terrace. He was almost knocked over by the wind when he stepped out, and we reached the terrace wall with difficulty, holding on to it so as not to be blown away. His Majesty could only hear the muffled sound of the cannon, which he judged to be coming from the Etoile fort, but could see nothing: the waves were furiously breaking on the rocks below the terrace, covering it with water and creating a spray that prevented seeing anything. The violence of the wind had knocked down the sentry boxes located near the palace. He had barely returned inside when General Drouot came to tell him it was his brig the *Inconstant* calling for help, and that it was barely holding on with only one anchor. It was feared the anchor would slip and the ship would break up, and it would have done so, save for the presence of mind of Lieutenant Jarry. At an instant when the storm-tossed vessel had its bow pointed toward a small nearby cove and the waves were pushing the ship toward it, this intrepid sailor cut the cable with a single ax blow and allowed the ship to beach itself. The Emperor, alarmed over his sailors' peril, called for horses while he was dressing and galloped off, arriving near the cove where the brig had just beached itself with only little damage. The sailors were exhausted. M. Ramolino was put ashore, where he fell to the ground, thanking providence for saving him from such great peril. His Majesty ordered a large fire lit, and all the provisions that could be found locally brought out. He returned to the palace happy that the brig's crew and the brig itself had been saved.

On New Year's Day, the Emperor accepted the good wishes of the island officials and the assembled officers' corps. He received a letter from the Empress giving news of his son. She wrote that he was charming, and would soon be able to write by himself. His Majesty also received letters from Prince Eugène, Queen Hortense, and other members of his family. The King of Naples assured him of his gratitude and complete devotion. Countess Bertrand, long kept at home by ill health, came for the occasion, and there was no end to the graciousness extended to her by the Emperor. All these people, after being received by the Emperor, then went to see Madame and Princess Pauline. That evening there was a family dinner party, to which were invited Grand Marshal and Countess Bertrand, General Drouot, General Cambronne, Colonel Malet commanding the national guard, the mayor of the city, Colonel Jermanowski, the president of the court, Grand Vicar Arrighi, chamberlains Vantini and Senno, Mme Vantini and her daughter, and M. and Mme Pons de l'Hérault. In the evening there was a social gathering lasting until midnight, attended by many city residents and officers from the various corps. At 10 p.m. the Emperor retired to his own quarters.

In the morning on his awakening, I presented my respects to the Emperor, who asked me what I was giving him as a New Year's gift. I replied that I knew of nothing worthy of him and could only wish to see him reunited with the Empress and the King of Rome. "Poor child," he said as he got up. He then proceeded to wash and dress. The princess and Madame came to see the Emperor; at a moment when they were alone, they called for me, gracefully accepted my respects, and each gave me an opal of equal value.

Through his secret correspondence, the Emperor knew about the small rivalries existing in the Empress' household between Mme de Montesquiou—who was said to be too great a lady to be worried by the harassment of the new lady-in-waiting—and Mme de Brignole.[198] According to such news, doubts were being cast in the Empress' mind about the legitimacy of her marriage to the Emperor, to push her into a divorce which she was vigorously resisting. The new lady-in-waiting was no foreigner to these intrigues. Rumors of removal from Elba and confinement on Saint Helena continued to be given credence. As to the divorce, the Emperor merely laughed, knowing only too well Marie-Louise's attachment to himself and their son; he never doubted her having courageously declared she wished to keep her title as his wife. The emperor of Austria was too religious not to firmly oppose the idea. "All the circumstances of my divorce were known in Vienna before Marie-Louise got married, it was legal, valid, unchallengeable. All these rumors are therefore without foundation, all this harassment and plotting will fail; they do not worry me in the least. I was thankful to Countess de Brignole for accompanying the Empress to Vienna, and she would drop in my esteem were I certain that such advice came from her."

In 1809, when the Emperor was to marry Archduchess Marie-Louise, the Vienna court had wanted to know all the circumstances of the divorce, the dissolution of his marriage with Joséphine. The civil bond was a public act, pronounced with all the solemnity required by our laws and the senatus consultum of the imperial family records.

---

[198]Countess de Brignole held the title of "palace lady" to Marie-Louise. Born in Genoa, she had been used there by Napoleon in several negotiations. She was close to Talleyrand, and through him had married off her daughter to Baron Dalberg, nephew of the archbishop-elector of Mainz. Baron Dalberg had been showered with favors by Napoleon, which did not prevent him from helping restore the Bourbons to power. His mother-in-law, who followed Marie-Louise to Austria, remained primarily the faithful friend of the Prince of Bénévent. He relied on her and her daughter to harm the Emperor. It was she who had the evil idea of having Constant and Roustam come to Rambouillet to undermine Marie-Louise's marital faithfulness with stories of Napoleon's mistresses. As stated by Octave Aubry, she was a born procuress, ready to push the Empress into Neipperg's arms.

Vienna was provided with the official court decision stating there had been no marriage between His Majesty and Joséphine. The official court had based its decision on the fact that the council of Trent, our own traditions, and especially our royal ordinances, to compensate for this council not having been recognized in France, demanded the presence of the contracting parties' own parish priest, under penalty of annulment. This had not happened. The Emperor was far from wanting to use a means that could only injure his dignity.

In 1804 the court was at Fontainebleau. The Pope was coming for the imperial anointing; the marriage with Empress Joséphine had not been blessed by the church. The Empress was pressing the Emperor to have this done; for it to be made public would have caused a scandal. Cardinal Fesch offered to perform the ceremony privately in the castle chapel, claiming to substitute for the actual parish priest, as did several cardinals: in his capacity as grand chaplain, he considered himself the court parish priest. He did indeed bless the marriage in the chapel in the presence of Grand Marshal Duroc and two or three other witnesses. All he had done was totally null and void. The official court, after hearing the witnesses, declared it so, and fined the Emperor 20,000 francs because of his imperial position. The fine was passed on to Cardinal Fesch for payment, so that he would learn about the council of Trent and the Blois and Moulins ordinances. He certainly would not have been foolish enough to pay it, he said.

CHAPTER SIX

News from France — The Emperor's decision —
Preparations for the expedition —
M. Colonna's mission to the king of Naples —
Embarkation and departure

The news from France was becoming worse from day to day, and dissatisfaction was general. In Vienna, plans were made to abduct the Emperor and restrict his freedom. The first day of a faction's triumph is a day of happiness; all is clemency, amnesty is on every tongue, even in every heart. On the second day justice is invoked, there is a pretense of reasonable conduct; the third day is already that of vengeance and reactionary deeds. Who was asking for this? As always, those who had contributed neither a drop of blood nor a penny to victory. It was now the third day. Those who had acquired national property were being harassed, the army was ignored and insulted, and a marshal of that same army proposed a Quiberon commemorative column. The exile mentality present in all government acts was spoiling all the good the Revolution had accomplished. The Emperor groaned over this fine France he had labeled a great nation twenty years before. The thought of returning to France was taking root in his mind. For the past eight months, the Emperor's days had been spent in the midst of construction and of his family. As San Martino was completed and furnished, the Emperor was able to spend a few days there. Madame and Princess Pauline came for dinner. The princess, whose apartment was ready, settled there, accompanied by Mme Bellini, her lady companion. A few days later, the Emperor returned to Porto Ferrajo for the approaching winter that came early that year. Soirées were held at the princess'. A few balls were given in town, the officers had their own, and all were most successful and well attended. The princess gave one that outshone all others, in the large ballroom built close to the palace: she and the many guests enjoyed it greatly, and the Emperor came. At midnight he went home, the ball continuing until daybreak. These festivities were at great expense to the town inhabitants who had been invited.

On January 8 it snowed so much in Porto Ferrajo that no one could recall a similar thing happening before. Just as General Bonaparte had been credited with the abundant rain that fell during his stay in Cairo, some wanted to see something mysterious about the snow that fell in Porto Ferrajo, and attribute it to the Emperor's presence on the island.

In the midst of all these pleasures, the Emperor became certain that Louis XVIII did not want to comply with the Fontainebleau treaty, and regarded the Republic and the imperial dynasty as usurpers. With secret joy he observed that the mighty of the day—themselves insulted by the many libelous pamphlets then flooding Europe that showed the Emperor as a coward, or some French Nero or Caligula—considered him a man in need of protection rather than a source of concern. These false notions led to the powers maintaining no agent in Porto Ferrajo. Only England ordered Colonel Campbell to divide his time among Florence, Livorno, and Piombino.

The Emperor knew and stated that outside of a few thousand schemers, the entire nation remained attached to him in spirit, opinion, and heart, just as it was attached to the principles of national sovereignty and French honor; that it had only submitted to the necessity imposed by its enemy and the new Judas; but that out of 30 million inhabitants, 29.5 million kept alive in their hearts the hope of overthrowing the princes, who were but enemies of the nation and foreign proxies. He knew that if ladies with embroidered lace handkerchiefs had called out "Long live the king!" when the guard entered Paris, the people were moved on seeing them and cried out "Long live the old guard!" The thought he had of returning to France, and the bad weather, caused him to suspend all construction except for roads, where it continued to provide work for idle hands that would have had to be helped in some other fashion. His activities became more internal. He waited in silence for the moment when public spirit in France reached the pitch where it would hail his return with acclamations.

Such was the Emperor's frame of mind when M. Fleury de Chaboulon,[199] a former auditor in the council of State, arrived in Elba. He was sent by a few of the Emperor's friends to bring him an accurate report on French public opinion, beyond what he could gather from newspapers. He had two long meetings with the Emperor, after which he departed for Naples. Napoleon's friends in France wanted him to know that the people were dissatisfied, and that a movement aimed at overthrowing the government was taking shape. In favor of whom? The Duke of Orléans was being named. Fouché pointed to the core of this plot that offered Europe, said the Emperor, the sad example of a king being overthrown by his own cousin. All these reports strengthened in the Emperor's mind a resolve nurtured by his imagination: that of crossing over to France with the small number of troops he had available, and striking the soil of France with his foot as Caesar had done, producing armed legions.

Everything said in front of me caused me to believe that the Emperor in leaving Elba, with the congress disbanded, was almost certain to win the emperor of Austria to his cause. Nevertheless, in leaving Elba much would be left to chance. The moment to attempt such an expedition seemed to have been reached; for eight months all expenditures had been drawn on the funds brought from Fontainebleau by M. Peyrusse. Madame and the princess had paid into that fund the moneys they had with them, and I preserved intact the 800,000 francs in gold of his private purse. France was refusing to carry out the treaty of April 11; this was not the time to complain, but to profit from it.

The Emperor had in his guard a Captain Haureau de Sorbet whose wife was a reader to the Empress, and was with her. This officer left Elba with verbal instructions which were successful, and he returned during the Hundred Days to bring news of the Empress and the King of Rome. He took part in the battle of Waterloo as a battalion commander.

For some days, the Emperor was silent and thoughtful at home. Generals Bertrand and Drouot were summoned much more frequently than usual, as was General Cambronne, and the map of France remained spread out in the study; pins were stuck in it. Taking

---

[199]Pierre A. E. Fleury de Chaboulon, born in Paris on April 1, 1779. In various historical documents, many variations of his name appear (de Fleury, Fleury Chaboulon, Chaboulon de Fleury, Fleury de Chaboulon). He published his memoirs under the last name, which is used here.

He entered public service early, became an auditor in the council of State and sub-prefect of Château-Salins in 1811, and distinguished himself in late 1813 and early 1814 by his administrative skills and his courageous behavior during the foreign invasion, causing Marshal Ney to term him "the intrepid sub-prefect." During the Campaign of France, he joined the Emperor in Montereau, who sent him to Reims as sub-prefect to organize the resistance. During the first Restoration, he returned to private life and traveled to Italy, which led him to attempt the visit to Elba mentioned by Marchand. He had two meetings with Napoleon, and was back in Lyon on March 3, 1815, to greet the Emperor on his return.

On March 20, 1815, he became Napoleon's fourth secretary, and was sent on a mission to Basel on May 1. He sought refuge in England after Waterloo, and published in 1819 the curious *Mémoires pour servir à l'histoire de la vie privée du retour et du règne de Napoléon en 1815.*

This shows him as a careerist, putting himself forward, courting, flattering, and slandering as needed. The immoderate love of the word "I" characterizes his work. His assertions and stories were refuted by Napoleon himself, when he received a copy of the *Mémoires* in Saint Helena. As soon as it was in his hands, he covered it feverishly with notes and observations indicating his irritation. The copy of the *Mémoires* containing Napoleon's annotations now belongs to the city of Sens, and was published by M. Lucien Cornet, former mayor of Sens (Paris 1901).

To give an idea of Napoleon's opinion, here are the unpleasant and humiliating corrections the Saint Helena exile wrote after the author's name, and of the label he had taken when he called himself "Ex-secretary to the Emperor Napoleon and his cabinet":

"This auditor was unknown to Napoleon in 1815. He joined the cabinet as second secretary in Lyon on March 13, and became fourth secretary, which is to say the last, in Paris on March 20. He was sent to Basel on May 1; he remained 40 days with my cabinet. Only the first secretary worked inside the cabinet. This young man, full of fire and merit, was not mature and steady enough for that job. He often went out to chat with the aides and young men in the duty quarters, thus contrasting with Méneval and Fain, who led such retiring lives that some chamberlains, after serving four years in the palace, had never seen them. All the speeches and statements attributed to Napoleon must be regarded as inventions. The author makes him speak and think in accordance with his own opinions."

The inaccurate information often given regarding Fleury de Chaboulon made it necessary to develop this extensive note.

advantage of the return of good weather, he decided to resume or initiate several construction projects. Leaving his worrisome thoughts behind in his study, outside he put on a show of much mirth: he laughed with the princess, visited Madame, had dinner with her, went to inspect his guard, instructing it to put in a garden around the barracks, decided with the engineers on new improvement projects around town; in other words, he did everything to throw people off the track regarding the plan he was contemplating.

A few days later M. Colonna d'Istria, Madame Mère's chamberlain, was sent to Naples to warn King Murat of the Emperor's resolve to return to France, where the Bourbons were governing contrary to the nation's interests. He told him that the motherland was calling him and he owed it to his love for her to respond to her call. He urged him to remain quietly in his kingdom, have his army take up good positions, and await developments. He told him he was assured that the Austrians would not make a move, Italy must remain neutral, and he would be leaving within a few days. Unfortunately this prince did not heed the sage advice he was being given. He knew he had wronged the Emperor by his conduct in 1814. He did not hide from M. Colonna his idea of assisting the Emperor's return through a strong diversionary action in Italy. M. Colonna begged him not to do it, saying it was the Emperor's wish; he promised—but not strongly enough to prevent M. Colonna from revealing his fears on his return to Porto Ferrajo. He brought with him a letter from the king of Naples filled with devotion, giving the news he had just received from his minister in Vienna of the closing of the congress and the departure of the Russian emperor for his territories. This news, impatiently awaited by the Emperor, made his departure almost immediate. He was however worried about the king of Naples' idea of entering Italy: he saw in this action, if it were to take place, how his affairs could be ruined by him in 1815, just as he had ruined them in 1814. Before leaving the island, he therefore reiterated his wish that no action be undertaken without his order. King Murat, after having participated in the Russian campaign with that quality of chivalry that made him shine so on the battlefield, had left the army in Wilna, unhappy over a bulletin that left to the viceroy of Italy the reorganization of the army. Taking advantage of his discontent, the Allies made overtures to him. He listened to them, but nevertheless served in the 1813 campaign and only returned to his kingdom after the battle of Leipzig. England renewed its pressure on him and the queen, stressing to both their own interest and that of their people, if they did not want to be dragged down by the Emperor's fall. Their hearts had been cruelly torn apart before abandoning the cause of France and the Emperor, but they finally did so on January 11, 1814. The prince joined the coalition and numbered among our enemies, a sad page we would like to tear from this fine story of life on the battlefields.

The Emperor did not feel he had to wait for confirmation from Vienna itself of the news conveyed by King Murat. He decided on his departure and prepared for it. During one of the evenings preceding his departure, he summoned M. Poggi de Talavo, whose character he admired, brought him into his study, and told him about his plan to return to France and his wish that he come with him. He urged secrecy about what he was confiding to him, especially toward Madame and Princess Pauline, saying: "If Galeazzini[200] is still here, engage him under any pretext, I will give him a prefecture. Pons has been notified: he is a man as energetic as he is devoted, and he is coming with me." When M. Poggi returned to the drawing room, Madame and the princess tried to find out from him what the Emperor could have said, but he eluded their questions and remained impenetrable.

The brig, which had been repaired, was painted a different color and loaded with supplies for a voyage of several months. Two nights before, the Emperor had dined in his room with General Drouot, talking to him about the war ammunition to be loaded on board the brig, the personnel that could be embarked on it and those to be placed on the other vessels, and Madame Mère's carriage to be loaded on board one of the xebecs to fool people into thinking that princess was going to Naples. Ending the conversation on that subject, he then talked about the Egyptian campaign, "country of memories, where we traveled Bible in hand." He analyzed the Moslem religion and our own: "The first is all sensual, promising blue-eyed houris, verdant copses, streams full of milk. It's nothing but sensuality. Ours on the contrary is all spiritual, the mind and charity rule. One is the religion of love, the other is all earthly and sensual. I was perfectly suited to settle in that country, given the little religion of my army." He said that in Italy monks had shown him a manuscript by the historian Joseph where the entire life of Jesus Christ had been inserted on a page with two or three lines, and said it had been a mistake for them not to delete that page.

That evening the Emperor was very talkative; he told of several youthful pranks, both at Brienne and at the military academy. He said: "Rarely was I caught in the traps that were set. Among us there were some sons of great families; parents invariably urged their children to make friends with them, in order to use their support later during their careers. We were merciless toward those who did, calling them all sorts of names, which led to fights where blows were given and received." He recalled his days as an artillery officer, expressing surprise at the quality of their mess and how little it cost them. He told

---

[200]Baron Galeazzini was a Corsican, born around 1760, who adopted the revolutionary principles. In 1790 he was in the Corsican department, and it was on his initiative, backed by Mirabeau, that the island was declared an integral part of French territory. He was mayor of Bastia in 1794, and participated in the heroic defense of that city against the British. Forced to capitulate for lack of food, he sailed for France with his family. After the victorious Italian campaign, Bonaparte named him superintendent of the conquered provinces of Reggio and Modena, then sent him to Rome. After taking part in the expedition that took back Corsica from the British, Galeazzini returned as mayor of Bastia. He then became prefect of Liamone, one of the two Corsican departments. In 1803 the First Consul named him commissioner general for Elba and its dependencies, with extensive powers. His brilliant service there earned him praise and the title of baron. But he was surrounded by envious people and enemies. He was blamed for having a road constructed that endangered the island's security. Napoleon summoned him to Paris for explanations. Disgraced, he remained unemployed until April 1814, when Napoleon was exiled to Elba. Galeazzini then wrote to Napoleon, begging him to go and observe on site the injustice of the disgrace he had suffered. The new sovereign of Elba made inquiries in Porto Ferrajo, and had Count Bertrand write to Galeazzini exonerating him.

His enemies did not give up, and a Corsican named Sandreschi then accused him of plotting to assassinate the Emperor; but Magistrate Poggi had no trouble demonstrating the accusation was without foundation. On his return to France, Napoleon received Galeazzini and named him prefect of Maine-et-Loire. After Waterloo, Galeazzini retired to Corsica, where he died.

of the care he had taken regarding his expenditures, and the privations he forced on himself through careful economy, in order to do what his richer friends did. He stated his success in Toulon did not surprise him; it was only during the first Italian campaign that he acquired great ambition. The recounting of all these details was of great interest to me and prompted my admiration for the man who, from a humble artillery officer, had through his genius made himself into the ranking man in the world.

During these last days, the great map of France was spread out over the drawing-room rug, and the Emperor on his knees would trace the route he proposed to follow: the grand marshal and General Drouot were the only ones allowed to know about it. Saint-Denis, Noverraz, and Santini had been sent to different points on the island to learn from the harbor captains the number of ships that were there; several were chartered and were to proceed on a given day from the various points along the coast to the Porto Ferrajo harbor. M. Pons de l'Hérault, director of the Rio mine, was specifically charged with this mission and with placing an embargo on all the island ports, as soon as the departure date was definitively set. Thus the Emperor had an inventory of all the ships in each port and what they could carry, so that he could pick the best ones, as there were more than he needed to transport the guard, the Corsican battalion, and the required equipment.

During the night of the 25th to the 26th, all the chartered ships proceeded to Porto Ferrajo, and an embargo was placed on all others in the ports where they were located. It was a Sunday; mass was celebrated as usual, with many people attending. According to his practice, after mass the Emperor received people in the drawing room, and told those who were there of the decision he had reached to return to France, where he was being called. Already, without any explanation, a great deal of activity was taking place in town. When at 1 p.m. the guard was ordered to go on board, there was a real explosion, and all were running to pick up their scattered gear. Although I suspected some great plan, the Emperor only mentioned it the day before at bedtime, saying he was going to France and to prepare everything for this trip while taking very little. He said to me: "One chasseur's and one grenadier's uniform, some shirts, and nothing else." Without really complying with what he told me, I spent part of the night preparing things, taking an inventory of what remained to give to Madame, and I was careful to keep with me as he had directed a tricolor cockade to hand him when he requested it.

Since the Emperor had urged me not to mention anything until noon, and since all these arrangements could not be made in his quarters without being noticed by the staff, I answered all inquiries by saying the Emperor was going to spend a few days in San Martino. Even the members of his household were so far from believing in this expedition that no one doubted the reason I gave was the truth. Opening his bedroom door and coming into my room, the Emperor saw me busy at my inventory. Finding at hand a Lépine watch similar to the one he carried, he said to me: "Take this watch with you, it is a present from me. It dates back to my Consulate." Attached to the watch was a gold chain and a key. I thanked the Emperor for his present, and for connecting it with such a brilliant period in his life. It is today among the relics I kept of this great man, and which I gave to the Museum of Sovereigns.

On the day of departure, the Emperor arose like any other day. Dr. Foureau came in as usual as His Majesty was about to shave. "Well, Foureau, is your bag packed? We're going to France." The doctor smiled and replied: "I would like nothing better, but I see nothing that would lead me to believe it!"

"What! Since I am telling you, it is so! Be ready by this evening." Saint-Denis, who was holding the mirror the Emperor was using to shave, smiled at me, thinking it was some form of joke the Emperor was playing on his doctor. When the Emperor had dressed and gone into the garden, they were much surprised when I told them nothing could be more true, and that they should make arrangements so as not to be taken unaware; I assured them of this departure only because the Emperor had spoken of it, but not until noon would it be known throughout town. Until then, the secret of the expedition was known to only a few. After mass, the Emperor told those people who had attended, and the guard received the order to depart. All preparations were finished when suddenly the British corvette was spotted. First it was feared it might have some knowledge of the plan. The grand marshal, who was with His Majesty, went down to his quarters. A large number of grenadiers were ordered to continue working. As the Emperor had just dictated to his secretary, who was absent for a moment, the door to his study was open. He called me and told me to sit down, pointing to a small table in a corner of the study near the window: it was that used by M. Rathery. This was the first time I wrote under the Emperor's dictation, which he gave with such volubility that I couldn't keep pace with him. Then he went into the drawing room, where he had just been informed that General Drouot was waiting for him; I had barely written down the first few words when he disappeared, telling me to send that off immediately to the grand marshal. It was an order for him, I had retained its meaning in spite of the disarray of my mind. I went to tell Count Bertrand what had happened to me, and informed him verbally of what I had been unable to write. It directed him to order the brig's captain to set sail and leave the harbor; and if the British captain should ask him where he was going, to answer that he had just caulked the brig's hull and wanted to know if it was leaking. The idea of capturing the corvette, in the event it was aware of the plan, had also been expressed. The British captain, while passing the brig, did ask where it was going, and was given that reply.

The captain went to see Count Bertrand, who pretended to be in a great hurry to go up and see the Emperor who was calling him. The grand marshal as usual invited the captain to dinner; he refused, stating he had to be in Livorno that same evening. Half an hour later he was at sea, having crossed the harbor without anything striking him as odd: all was just as usual.

Madame, Princess Pauline, Countess Bertrand, and a few wives of employees were to stay on the island and await developments. The princesses dined with the Emperor who was perfectly calm, nothing on his face revealing he was about to embark on such a perilous venture. After dinner he went into the drawing room and told his butler who was pouring his coffee that he was to be on board without too much fuss in one hour. The people who were to accompany him were gathered there. A town delegation came to see him; one of them, the chamberlain M. Vantini, spoke and expressed the pleasure and sorrow the Elbans felt on seeing His Majesty depart: the sorrow of having him no longer among them, and the pleasure of knowing that greater destinies were calling him to the continent. They wished for the success of his endeavors, and hoped that His Majesty would not forget the good people of Elba.

The Emperor told them that Elbans could count on his gratitude, and that their memory would always be dear to him. Grand Vicar Arrighi, along with his clergy, told him on leaving that he would pray to heaven for the success of such a vast undertaking. The Emperor remained alone with Madame and the princess.

That day all papers had been burned, even those dealing with his memoirs, which he was already dictating. On the previous days, the Emperor had worked on providing for the defense and safety of the island. He had named M. Lapi, a colonel in the national guard, its governor, with the title of brigadier general. He organized with M. Poggi a junta for Corsica, and designated eight people on an executive committee. He handed these gentlemen the decree naming the twelve members of this junta. The former were in charge of announcing the Emperor's departure from Elba and having the tricolor raised over Corsica, with the recommendation they avoid any disorder and accomplish this quietly. They were not to leave until three days after His Majesty.

Having settled all this, the Emperor had to part with his family. The princess and Madame were in the throes of pain; full of fear and hope, they couldn't let the Emperor out of their arms. All those who were going with His Majesty were allowed to kiss these ladies' hands. I was in the Emperor's room, awaiting his final orders, when Princess Pauline entered, her beautiful face covered with tears; she came up to me, holding a diamond necklace worth 500,000 francs. She wanted to speak, but sobs choked her voice. I myself was moved by the state she was in. She said: "Here, the Emperor sent me to hand you this necklace, as the Emperor may need it if he is in trouble. Oh! were this to happen, Marchand, never abandon him, take good care of him. Adieu," she said, offering her hand for me to kiss.

"Your Highness, I am hopeful this is but au revoir."

"That is not what I think." Some secret premonition seemed to tell her she would never see the Emperor again. His Majesty walked in at this point, speaking words of consolation, and took her out into the garden. In the drawing room I found Madame alone and in tears. Marchand, I am putting my son in your hands. Here," she said, handing me a candy box bearing a very good likeness of her, "may this replace the one he now uses; should fate turn against him, do not abandon him!" She raised both hands to her eyes, and I heard nothing more but sobs.

From the palace to the harbor, the street was full of people wishing to say a last goodbye to the Emperor. The Italian imaginations were excited. The Emperor's glory appeared to them in new forms and with richer and brighter colors.

The entire guard was on board; a few Poles who were late remained on the island. One mameluke had been confined to Pianosa, having fought a duel with a gunner whose hand he had cut off; he was forgotten there. I arrived on the brig; it was crowded, one could barely move around. The guard was divided between the brig, the sloops *Etoile* and *Caroline*, and four transport ships: about 1,000 men, 600 of the guard, 300 from the Corsican battalion, 60 or 80 passengers, and a few Poles. The flotilla was commanded by Commander Chautard, with Lieutenant Jarry under him.

Cries of Vive l'Empereur!, first from a distance in the upper part of town, announced that the Emperor was leaving the palace. At 7:30, they accompanied him down to the harbor, swelling with the whole population, and stopped only when the brig was reached. Those on the brig saluted the island one last time while leaving it. The moon was full, its bright face lighting up the scene, lending majesty to the progress of our little fleet; the sea was calm, and an offshore breeze pushed us rapidly toward the coast of France.

Madame Mère, Princess Pauline, and Countess Bertrand were to proceed to Rome, and from that capital come to Paris if the enterprise succeeded. Countess Bertrand, impatient to get back to France and not doubting the expedition's success for a moment, sailed a few days after our departure in spite of Madame's advice and landed on the coast of Antibes. There she was arrested with her children, her servants, and a few wives of the household personnel, taken to Marseille under guard, and kept under arrest, with the consideration due her rank. She only recovered her freedom when the Emperor had reached Paris and orders to that effect were sent to Marshal Masséna. Madame, more cautious, went to Rome with the princess, and arrived at the same time that Countess Bertrand was landing at Antibes. Princess Pauline, too ill to undertake such a long voyage, returned to Italy.

CHAPTER SEVEN

Crossing — Landing in Golfe Juan — March on Grenoble —
Encounter with royal troops — Occupation of Grenoble

The die was cast. A great decision, based on the most honorable and powerful motives—the welfare of France—had just been made. Napoleon was crossing the Rubicon; his was not to conquer or die, but to conquer for the motherland or see her torn by anarchy; such was the alternative offered by his position, and his goal to free her. The errors of the king's government were hastening its execution. As soon as the Emperor had boarded the brig, the flotilla set sail, with the moon shining and emphasizing the outline of the island and the Porto Ferrajo forts. We soon lost sight of it.

The Emperor remained on deck until 11 p.m., when they started clearing the brig's deck. His Majesty went down to his cabin and went to bed in one of the small camp beds that had been prepared for him. Count Bertrand slept on a mattress on the floor in the Emperor's cabin. I spent the night fully dressed on a mattress placed across that door.

Early the next day, the 27th, the Emperor went up on deck, had all the people accompanying him line up in two rows, and had their names taken down. Some clutter still existed, a few useless items that couldn't be stowed were thrown overboard, and order was established on the ship.

Around 10 a.m., a British corvette was spotted sailing in our direction. His Majesty ordered the guard to man the guns along with the sailors; he positioned the men needed for each piece, and had them go through the exercise. The grenadiers were eager to fight and board the other ship, but the corvette entered Porto Ferrajo. His Majesty said:

"Campbell will be disconcerted when the commander of that corvette tells him I have left the island of Elba."

The news of Napoleon's departure for France was therefore known after dinner on the 27th, in Livorno, and that night in Florence, at the residence of Lord Burghersh.[201] The news must have reached Vienna on Saturday, March 4. It is therefore not surprising that Talleyrand succeeding in obtaining on March 13 that Napoleon be outlawed by all nations. It has since been learned that the proclamation by the powers was ready on March 9. A few plenipotentiaries and Emperor Alexander himself thought they were being overly hasty. But letters arrived from Turin on the 8th, telling of the landing in Cannes; and others from France announced that in order to stop the disturbance caused by Napoleon, they had an army headed for Naples which Talleyrand put at 80,000 men, divided between Grenoble and Dôle, and other troops that were gathering in Lyon. There was no doubt that Napoleon would be tracked down, cut off, or captured; hence they obtained Russia's consent to the declaration of March 13.[202]

---

[201]Lord John Fane Burghersh, eleventh Earl of Westmoreland. Sent in 1813 to Allied headquarters, then assigned in 1814 to Schwarzenberg, Burghersh was then a plenipotentiary minister in Florence.

[202]The dates assumed by Marchand are inaccurate. It was on March 1 that an express courier from Campbell confirmed in Florence the departure of Napoleon, whose destination was unknown. The first news of the escape, sent by the Austrian consul general in Genoa, reached Vienna during the night of March 6-7. It caused general consternation, and rumor said Napoleon had landed in Naples. It was only on March 9 that Vienna learned of the landing in Golfe Juan.

A declaration was indeed signed on March 13 by the plenipotentiaries of the eight nations represented in Vienna. This manifesto, or banning order, "unique in its content and form among all diplomatic acts," read: "Although intimately certain that the whole of France, rallying behind its legitimate sovereign, shall resign to oblivion this last attempt by a criminal and impotent delirium, the European sovereigns declare that if against all expectations any danger should arise from this event, they are prepared to offer the king of France and the French people the help necessary to restore tranquility... The powers declare that in breaking the agreement that had established him on the island of Elba, Napoleon Bonaparte has destroyed the only legal title attached to his existence, and that by appearing again in France, he has placed himself outside civil and social relations, and that, as an enemy and disrupter of the peace of the world, he has exposed himself to prosecution and conviction."

After the British corvette had appeared, the Emperor ordered the flotilla to head for the island of Capraya,[203] which was within sight.

Around 11 a.m. on the 27th, we spotted a brig sailing out of Saint Florent and below Cape Corse, heading for Livorno and toward us. The Emperor ordered a close eye kept on it; soon afterwards he was informed it was a merchant brig. But as it grew nearer, we realized we had been mistaken and it was indeed a combat brig. As it continued toward us, the Emperor had everyone not needed on duty go below deck. He remained on the duty bridge and gave orders that all be positioned in case of attack, but the brig changed heading and disappeared.

In the afternoon we spotted the two frigates of the Corsican station, and continued on our course without their bothering us.

Shortly before sundown the flotilla encountered Captain Andrieux; the flag of Elba was raised, and the corvette passed within hailing distance. When it was close enough, the Emperor told Captain Taillade, the former brig commander who knew Captain Andrieux, to offer to talk with him. The latter responded to the inquiry made of him through a megaphone that he was on a mission to Livorno where he had to be that same evening. All he asked was: "How is he?"

"Fine," came the answer.

"Have a safe journey," he said as he moved away. When that ship came close, the Emperor had ordered the grenadiers and chasseurs to remove their bearskins.

The Emperor dined on deck, surrounded by the civilian and military officers who shared his rations. After dinner, sitting on the bridge bench with Count Bertrand (General Drouot was bedded down, seasick), the Emperor told the officers of all ranks surrounding him about some of the difficult times in his life: he talked of French army campaigns, their victories, the spirit moving the soldiers, the love of

---

[203]Volcanic island in the Gulf of Genoa, 40 km. from Corsica. Part of Corsica until 1507, and since, part of the Genoa republic. Colonel Campbell, who only learned in Porto Ferrajo on the 27th of Napoleon's departure, wanted on March 1 to sail around Capraya in his frigate the Partridge. He thought Napoleon might have halted his flotilla in some cove of the island, ready to descend on Livorno. But the Emperor was that very day dropping anchor in Golfe Juan.

glory and of the motherland. He said to them: "There is nothing you cannot get the French to do through their taste for danger: it is their Gallic heritage. The love of glory and courage are in the French an instinct, a sort of sixth sense. Many times in the heat of battle I have seen our young conscripts jump into the fray: honor and courage came out their very pores." He then listed the qualities necessary to make a good officer, and observed how difficult it was to train him. Nature had to have roughed him out first, and given him coolness under fire, giving him mastery of himself and his decisions, a quick eye, and determination. He told them what had been said of his fatalism: "Few men have had greater influence on the masses than I have, but it would be stupidity to have me say that all is written on high and that were a precipice placed in my path, I wouldn't have to alter my course not to fall in. My belief is that of any reasonable being, that in war, where danger is equal almost everywhere, we must not leave a place known to be dangerous to go and stand where death can also reach us, and we must resign ourselves to our fate. Once you have that thought well in mind, you become master of your courage and composure, which is communicated to the men under you; the most cowardly among them will then pride himself on courage."

He stated that conscription was a national institution, and already had become part of our customs. "The time will come when a girl will want no part of a man who has not paid his debt to the motherland. That institution will be at its peak when it is no longer considered a duty, but a point of honor envied by all; then will the nation be great, glorious, and strong." As grenadiers three or four ranks back listened with admiration to the words flowing out of the Emperor's mouth, he said this, capable of setting afire their bubbling courage at the time of such a perilous venture: that his army of Italy might be duplicated, but certainly never surpassed, and that with his guard built into a corps of 40,000 men, he would be sure of crossing all Europe.

He then went on to portraits of some of his marshals. Next he told how, after he had been brought to the throne by the unanimous wish of the nation, treason had caused his downfall, and how Marmont, whom he had every right to count on and had sent to Paris to

At one point in the crossing, the *Inconstant* is hailed by a passing English ship, the *Zephyr*. The expected boarding attack does not take place.

When the odd-looking little navy of Napoleon puts in at Fréjus only a few surprised people witness the occasion.

Debarkation of Napoleon in France, 1 March 1815.

In the middle of the night, Napoleon studies the route to Paris.

negotiate on his behalf, had gone there only to ruin his affairs. He said that the majority of people and parties were more faithful than was believed to the sentiments of national honor, glory, and independence, and that the nation could never have enough guarantees against the Bourbons and the feudal lords. "The constitution of 1793, which left executive power in the hands of the Bourbons, did not provide the people with enough of a guarantee. Suppose the men of the League had recognized Henry IV as a Protestant: think of the charters, the constitutions, the guarantees they would have demanded in order to reassure their consciences and ensure their faith! They would never have felt they had enough. This is the same. No matter what they say or do, wolves can never gain the trust and faith of sheep." He then talked of the duties of a good general, who must never neglect any kind of foresight, and must always be sure that his forces are so situated that they can face anything. "There is not one of my generals whose depth I don't know; some have it up to the belt (pointing to his own), some up to the shoulders, but those who have even more are few." There was in that scene, flooded by moonlight, something reminiscent of Plutarch's great men. What a school to learn about war, the officers were saying. They would have spent the night listening. At 11 p.m. the Emperor retired to his cabin.

On February 25, the guard's proclamation to the army and that to the French people had been dictated. Perhaps because the Emperor deemed it appropriate to make certain changes, on the morning of the 27th, in sight of Golfe Juan, he dictated in his cabin the two proclamations as they appear below. He dictated in fiery fashion; his entire soul was painted on his face. When speaking of the motherland, of the misfortunes of France, he was electrified; genius was at work. *Deus ecce Deus*. I have seen the Emperor on many occasions; I never saw him look as superb.

PROCLAMATION OF HIS MAJESTY THE EMPEROR TO THE FRENCH PEOPLE

Golfe Juan, March 1, 1815

Napoleon, Emperor of the French, by the grace of God and the State Constitution.

Frenchmen,

The defection of the Duke of Castiglione (Augereau) delivered a defenseless Lyon to our enemies. The army I had entrusted to his command was, by the number of its battalions and the bravery and patriotism of its troops, in a position to defeat the Austrian corps facing it, and to descend on the rear of the enemy army that threatened Paris.

The victories at Champaubert, Montmirail, Château-Thierry, Vauchamp, Mormans, Montereau, Craonne, Reims, Arcis-sur-Aube and Saint-Dizier; the insurrection of the courageous peasants in Lorraine, Champagne, Alsace, Franche-Comté, and Burgundy, and the position I had assumed in the rear of the enemy army—cutting it off from its stores, its reserves, its convoys and all its transport—had placed it in a desperate situation. Never were the French nearer to being more powerful, and the elite of the enemy army was lost without its resources; it would have found its grave in these vast lands it had ravaged without pity, when the treason of the Duke of Raguse (Marmont) surrendered the capital and disorganized the army. The unexpected behavior of these two generals, who betrayed at once their motherland, their prince, and their benefactor, changed the destiny of the war. The disastrous position of the enemy was such that at the end of the engagement that took place before Paris, it was left without ammunition because of its separation from its stores.

In the midst of these new and grave circumstances, my heart was torn, but my soul remained unshakable. I considered only the interest of the nation; I went into exile on a rock in the middle of the sea. My life was and should again be of use to you. I did not allow the great number of citizens who wished to accompany me to share my fate; I believed their presence would be of use to France, and I took with me only a handful of brave men necessary for my own protection.

Elevated to the throne by your choice, all that was done without you is illegitimate. For 25 years France has had new interests, new institutions, a new glory, all of which can only be guaranteed by a national government and a dynasty born of these new circumstances. A prince who would reign over you, seated on my throne thanks to the same armies who ravaged our land, would vainly seek to bolster his position with the principles of feudal rights; he could ensure the honor and the rights of only a small number of individuals, enemies of the people who have over the past 25 years condemned them in all our national assemblies. Your domestic tranquillity and your consideration abroad would be lost forever.

Frenchmen! In my exile I have heard your complaints and your wishes; you call for this government of your choice, which is the only legitimate one. You reproached me my long slumber, you accused me of sacrificing the greater interest of the motherland to my own rest.

I have crossed the seas amid all kinds of perils; I have arrived among you to reclaim my rights which are yours. All that individuals have done, written, or said since the fall of Paris, I shall take no notice of; it shall in no way influence the memory I retain of the important services they have rendered, for there are events of such a nature as to stand above human arrangements.

Frenchmen! There is no nation, no matter how small, that has not had the right to escape the dishonor of obeying a prince imposed by a temporarily victorious enemy. When Charles VII returned to Paris and overthrew the ephemeral throne of Henri VI, he admitted owing his throne to the valiance of his soldiers and not to a prince regent of England.

It is likewise to you alone, and to the brave men of the army, that I pay the homage of my duty, and shall always do so.

Signed: Napoleon

The following proclamation to the army also develops with dignity and strength the purpose of the venture Napoleon came to undertake; in writing it, he was assured of the success of this great endeavor, and he did not put forward the many violations of the Fontainebleau treaty; such motives were personal to him. It would be up to the council of State later on to submit its application to the powers of Europe.

The proclamation to the army was dictated with the same speed.

PROCLAMATION OF HIS MAJESTY THE EMPEROR TO THE ARMY
Golfe Juan, March 1, 1815
Soldiers!

We have not been vanquished. Two men from our ranks betrayed our laurels, their country, their prince, and their benefactor.

Would those we witnessed for 25 years traveling all over Europe to provoke enemies against us, who spent their lives fighting against us in the ranks of foreign armies while cursing our beautiful France, now claim to command and place our eagles in chains, they who could never withstand their stare? Shall we suffer that they inherit the fruits of our glorious labors? That they snatch our honors and our lands, that they slander our glory? Should their reign last, then all will be lost, even the memory of those immortal days! See with what tenacity they belittle them! And if there remain some champions of our glory, it is among those same enemies against whom we fought on the battlefield!

Soldiers! In my exile I heard your voice! I have arrived, despite all obstacles and perils! Your general, called to the throne by the people's choice, and raised upon your shields, has been returned to you: come and join him!...

Seize these colors that the nation has proscribed, and which for 25 years served as rallying point for all the enemies of France! Wear the tricolor cockade! You wore it during our days of glory.

We must forget that we have been the masters of nations; but we must not suffer that any meddle in our affairs!

Who can claim to be master on our own soil? Who could hold such power? Take again those eagles you carried at Ulm, Austerlitz, Jena, Eylau, Friedland, Tudella, Eckmühl, Essling, Wagram, Smolensk, the Moscowa, Lutzen, Bautzen, Montmirail. Do you think that handful of Frenchmen, so arrogant today, could withstand their stare? They will go back from whence they came, and if they care to, reign as they claim to have reigned for the past 19 years.

Your lands, your rank, your glory, and those of your children have no greater enemies than these princes imposed on us by foreigners; they are the enemies of our glory, because the recital of so many heroic actions which made famous the people of France, fighting against them to free themselves of their oppression, is their very condemnation.

Veterans of the Sambre-et-Meuse, the Rhine, Italy, Egypt, the West, the Grand Army, are being humiliated. Their honorable scars are scorned; their successes would be crimes and these brave men would be rebels, if—as the enemies of the people claim—legitimate sovereigns were amid foreign armies.

The honors, rewards, and adulation go to those who served them against the motherland and against us.

Soldiers! Come and rejoin the flag of your leader. He exists only because of you; his rights are but those of the people and your own; his interest, honor, and glory are no other than your interest, honor, and glory. Victory shall arrive on the run; the eagle along with the national colors shall fly from steeple to steeple up to the towers of Notre-Dame: then shall you be able to show your scars with honor; then shall you be able to boast of your exploits; you shall be the liberators of the motherland.

In your old age, surrounded and admired by your fellow citizens, you will be listened to with respect as you recount your great deeds; you shall be able to say with pride: "I too was part of this Grand Army which twice entered Vienna, entered Rome, Berlin, Madrid, Moscow, cleansed Paris of the blot which treason and the presence of the enemy left upon it."

Honor to these brave soldiers, the glory of the motherland! And eternal shame to the criminal Frenchmen, whatever the rank of their birth, who fought for 25 years alongside the enemy to tear apart the soul of the motherland!

Napoleon

There is as much inspiration in this proclamation as in the previous one; the speech of the generals, officers, and soldiers of the Elban battalion, given further on, does not lack in it either; it was dictated with the same speed. Open any Greek or Latin author, you cannot find a speech superior to these three. To think that Napoleon was accused of not knowing how to write, as he was of lacking in courage!

When these proclamations were read on the upper deck, they were greeted with enthusiasm. All hurried to make copies and multiply them, to have a larger quantity to hand out on landing. The Emperor regretted not having taken with him a portable printing press, as he felt that printing lent a more authentic character that would impress the people more.

As we were about to raise the tricolor, the Emperor handed me his hat through the hatchway to replace the Elban cockade with the national cockade, which took only a moment. The Emperor donned his hat: at the sight of that cockade, of the little hat where the colors of

Austerlitz shone, the excitement was so great that the Emperor, who wanted to speak, couldn't get in a word.

It would in fact be difficult to describe the joy, the enthusiasm, the emotion that were expressed on the brig: the cheers, the clapping, the foot stomping were so loud that it seemed all the brig batteries were firing at once. It was delirium. Knowing that the guard rations were used up, the Emperor ordered his butler to bring out the provisions made for his own retinue and share them with the grenadiers. A signal was sent to the flotilla to close in and hoist the tricolor, which was greeted with the same enthusiasm as on the brig.

Promotions were announced in the guard, and medals were distributed to those who had earned them. The entire battalion became legionnaires. A few Poles received no medals, Colonel Jermanowski objecting that they had too little service, and asking His Majesty to wait for them to distinguish themselves before awarding them this mark of courage and honor. General Drouot did not appear on deck during the crossing, as he was seasick and had to remain in bed.

Less than a mile from Golfe Juan, the Emperor ordered Captain Lamourette to set out to sea with some 30 men and secure the battery at the point along the coast where the landing was to take place. This battery lay between Golfe Juan and Antibes, and was not manned.

They carried a few copies of the guard's message to their brothers-in-arms, worded as follows:

The generals, officers, and soldiers of the imperial guard, to the generals, officers, and soldiers of the army.
Golfe Juan, March 1, 1815

Soldiers and comrades,

We have saved your Emperor for you, in spite of the many pitfalls placed in his path; we bring him back to you across the seas, amid a thousand dangers. We have landed on the sacred motherland with the tricolor cockade and the imperial eagle. Trample the white cockade under your feet, it is a symbol of shame and of the yoke imposed by foreigners and by treason. We would have spilled our blood in vain if we were to tolerate the vanquished (sic) imposing laws on us!

In the few months the Bourbons have reigned, they have convinced you that they have forgotten nothing and learned nothing. They are still governed by prejudices hostile to our rights and those of the people.

Those who bore arms against their country, against us, are heroes! You are rebels whom they are willing to forgive until they are sufficiently strengthened by the creation of an army corps of former exiles, the introduction of a Swiss guard in Paris, and the progressive replacement of new officers among your ranks! Then it will be required to have borne arms against the motherland to have any claim for honors and awards; it will be necessary to have been born in conformity with their prejudices to become an officer. The soldier will have to always remain a soldier: the people will bear the taxes, and they will reap the honors.

Until such time as they dare destroy the Legion of Honor, they have handed it out to traitors and granted it in prolific quantities in order to degrade it. They stripped it of all the political prerogatives we had earned at the cost of our own blood.

The 400 million in special assets from which our endowment was drawn, and which were the heritage of the army and the reward for our success, have been appropriated by them.

Soldiers of this great nation! Soldiers of the great Napoleon! Will you continue to be the soldiers of a prince who was for 20 years the enemy of France, and who boasts of owing his throne to a prince regent of England? All that has been done without the people's consent and our own, and without consulting us, is illegitimate.

Soldiers! Retired officers! Veterans of our armies! Come with us to conquer this throne, safeguard of our rights. May posterity someday say: "Foreigners, assisted by traitors, had imposed a shameful yoke on France; brave men rose up, and the enemy of the people and the army vanished and disappeared into nothingness."

Soldiers! The drums are beating! We are on the march! Run to your weapons, come and join us, join your Emperor and our tricolored eagles.

(The 1815 *Moniteur* gave the list of signatures.)

At four we dropped anchor in Golfe Juan. The flotilla was reunited, the tricolor raised. The crossing had been most fortunate; it could have turned disastrous had the British corvette, the two frigates on station in Corsica, and the *Zephyr* done their duty, or had they received orders. They wanted to remove Napoleon from Elba, and did not imagine he would be so informed and would escape before this last violation of the Fontainebleau treaty. At that time, letters from the prefect of the Var mentioning unusual activity in Elba, the stories told by the grenadiers returning to France, and the influence they had on public opinion in his department had remained unopened for several days. It was considered fortunate at the time that Napoleon would have to face an army of 30,000 men: no weight was given to the discontent of the people and the troops. Finally, no one could believe that the entire army would go over to his side as soon as he appeared before them.

The landing took place as soon as the flotilla had dropped anchor. At this point, the Emperor summoned General Cambronne and ordered him to take some forty men to form the advance party along the road to Fréjus, before Cannes. Already the previous day, he had stated he wished to return to the throne without spilling a drop of blood. When he gave his orders to the general, his last words were heard: "General, I am putting you in charge of my finest campaign: you won't have to fire a single shot, you will find nothing but friends."

At five, the flotilla artillery announced the Emperor's landing. All troops were ashore. The Emperor saluted this cherished soil. "Soil of France! Fifteen years ago, I christened you Homeland of the Great Nation. I salute you again, under the same circumstances: one of your children, the most worthy of this fine title has come again to deliver you from anarchy. Nothing for myself! All for France!"

Camp was established between the sea and the highway, under some olive trees. The Emperor urged that care be taken to pay for all that was used, and to respect the property which we passed through. Twenty-five men under the command of Captain Lamourette were sent to take possession of Antibes. They found the garrison drilling outside; instead of seizing it and announcing the Emperor's arrival, they entered the town while neglecting to secure the door. The commander of Antibes, surprised at first, got hold of himself, had the doors shut, and held them prisoner. The Emperor soon heard about this state of affairs; he was annoyed, but did not try to free them. The goal of the enterprise would not allow him to waste time in taking Antibes, or even in communicating with the garrison and its governor. The latter, after placing the captain and his grenadiers in a safe place, had the garrison which had been left outside come in immediately, for fear that, on hearing of the Emperor's landing so nearby, they would join him. It was only after the doors had been closed behind them that the soldiers learned of the attempt at taking Antibes, and of the Emperor's landing.

A few officers voiced the opinion that they should immediately proceed to Antibes and try to take it, to avoid the bad impression that might result from this city's resistance. The Emperor replied that Antibes played no role in the conquest he was planning, and that the way to remedy the effect of this development was to move faster than news of it. He sent M. Vauthier, war commissioner, to evaluate the situation. As he was on horseback, he soon returned, and reported that the town doors were shut.

MM. Pons, Poggi, and Galeazzini were sent to Cannes to procure horses: M. Pons returned that night and described the astonishment of the residents on seeing the grenadiers. He had found General Cambronne with the mayor of Cannes, but he had left and must be near Grasse.

A few surprised people witnessed our landing. When they learned it was the Emperor who was planning to march on Paris, they expressed their amazement that he had so few troops with him. That evening a great fire was lit, and the Emperor sat in front of it and fell asleep wrapped in the coat he wore at Marengo, his feet up on a second chair. The guard gave way to joy; they did not sleep; they awaited the time of departure. The baggage had been unloaded; a few mules were bought nearby to carry the treasure. One of these was made available to me to carry the 800,000 francs in gold of the Emperor's purse, his camp bed, and some baggage which I entrusted to Saint-Denis. Few saddle horses had been put on board. Generals Bertrand and Drouot were the only ones riding at first, all others went on foot. The Poles were forced to carry their saddles, bridles, and lances. Among the ADCs who had followed the Emperor, Perès,[204] from Longone, could not be found. No doubt fearing the consequences of the venture, he had gone into hiding so as to go home at the first opportunity. When he got there, I was told he had to flee the wrath of the local people and retire to the continent.

Orders had been given to Commander Chautard to go to Naples and provide news of the Emperor.

On March 1 at midnight we broke camp; Saint-Denis kept an eye on His Majesty's baggage, and I tried to walk not too far from the Emperor. The guard had intercepted a courier from the prince of Monaco, and he assured the Emperor that once through Provence he would find everyone ready to follow him. These words from a common man reflected exactly the thinking of the Emperor, who ran into the prince of Monaco[205] near Cannes. First embarrassed, he relaxed when he faced the Emperor who greeted him as an acquaintance; he had been first equerry to Empress Joséphine. A large fire was lit, and he and the Emperor approached it. During their entire conversation, he held his hat in his hand. The Emperor dismissed him and wished him a safe journey. The prince had not hidden from the Emperor all the perils involved in such a venture. The rather large circle that had formed around him and the Emperor prevented my hearing what they were saying; however the Emperor's mirth implied he was satisfied with the

---

[204]It is worth mentioning the testimony of Pons de l'Hérault in connection with this man who came to serve Napoleon on Elba as ADC:

"Perès, from Longone, Neapolitan by birth, was a very stupid boor, almost an imbecile; the Emperor had stooped to that choice because he wished to have on call someone to whom he could give orders whose execution required an almost total lack of intelligence."

[205]By a decree dated June 7, 1809, in Schönbrunn, Napoleon had named "M. Honoré Monaco" equerry to the Empress. He was the oldest son of the former Prince Charles of Monaco, Duke of Valentinois, who reigned until February 14, 1793, as Honoré IV, and had married Louise d'Aumont.

Born in 1778, he had entered the Emperor's military staff as an aide, then joined Murat's staff as ADC. After the second Restoration, as heir to his father, he reigned over Monaco as Honoré V until his death in 1841.

details he was given about Paris and the mood in France. The prince had given the opinions of the salons, while the courier offered those of the people, who would all rise up as soon as he appeared.

The Emperor passed through Cannes[206] during the night, and few people were seen along his path, although some windows opened and lit up; a few cries of Vive l'Empereur! were heard. His Majesty picked a guide from among the local people and was much amused by the man's conversation, which he encouraged through playful questions. Once near Grasse, a halt was called until the entire battalion had caught up; we then went through town: all was silent, the people were gone. The Emperor wanted to have lunch in Grasse: his lunch was prepared there. The town officials had all been replaced with royalists. This deep silence prompted him to prefer lunching on the hill overlooking the town. The entire population soon followed him there; the mayor did not appear. Horses and mules were purchased; a few Poles and some people in his retinue were given horses. During the day, at the various halts, kegs of wine were tapped to refresh the guard and help it endure such great fatigue.

After lunch the Emperor talked to the women, and made a few jokes that amused them. The generals addressed the men, talking to them about the motherland and the evils threatening it if such a state of affairs continued much longer; little by little the crowd warmed up, and cries of Vive l'Empereur! were heard. One of the townspeople then spoke up, saying to the grand marshal: "General, His Majesty has indeed punished us by not doing us the honor of lunching in our town. If he knew the bad treatment we have received from the returned exiles, our silence would not have been interpreted so harshly, and His Majesty would see we are worthy to be part of his faithful subjects."

---

[206]Napoleon's first concern on landing had been to send General Cambronne to Cannes, with 40 chasseurs and grenadiers, to stop all couriers, and requisition for cash the horses and mules he could find. He said to him: "Cambronne, I am giving you the vanguard of my finest campaign. You won't have to fire a single shot. Remember that I want to regain my crown without spilling a drop of blood." (From Cambronne's testimony during his trial.)

The grand marshal replied: "Remain quiet, that is the only way to serve him well."

Proclamations were printed in this town; several residents of Grasse offered to accompany the Emperor and serve as guide through the difficult and snowbound passes he would have to negotiate. He chose two of them designated as good patriots. The Emperor had brought with him a coach and two small artillery pieces. The roads were about to become impassable for these, and he abandoned them in town, until such time as the road through Antibes would be open.

Sometimes on foot, sometimes on horseback, the Emperor reached the village of Séranon[207] on March 22 at 2 a.m., having covered 20 leagues on his first day. He had walked for more than an hour in the snow and on the ice, helped by Colonel Ruhl. I had continued following the Emperor along with his young military aide, Vantini. Our baggage was far behind us. The Emperor was quartered in the mayor's house; all had been prepared to receive him, but the mayor was not there. We had had a horrible journey; the cold was intense. The Emperor was very tired, his boots were soaked, and he had much difficulty taking them off; he stretched out on two chairs in front of a big fire. The battalion arrived a few hours later. There had been some places that were difficult for men to get through, and even more so for horses and beasts of burden; one of the mules loaded with battalion baggage rolled over into a bottomless precipice. I was worried about the mule carrying His Majesty's purse and bed, but it arrived safely in the care of Saint-Denis and Noverraz. We immediately set up the Emperor's bed, and he slept for three hours. At daybreak His Majesty got dressed, and was kind enough to say to me: "You must be tired, take one of my horses until we find some to buy." I then heard him say to the generals: "The battalion must be exhausted! Well, courage! The main thing is to get past Sisteron. Masséna can't be aware of the speed of my progress, and his orders will reflect his uncertainty." The

---

[207] A small village perched at more than 1,000 meters, 40 km. from Grasse. Known for its rock formations in the shape of organ pipes.

Emperor had sent M. Pons to see him, and the marshal promptly jailed him in the Château d'If.

The Emperor spent the night of the 3rd in Barrême;[208] along the way we bought some mules, which served to mount the people in his retinue. On the road His Majesty met a peasant riding a horse, and asked how much he would sell it for. This man, not knowing who was making the offer, said: "1,000 francs." The Emperor replied: "My friend, the price is too high for me."

On the 4th, between Castellane and Digne, the peasants who heard about the Emperor's march were running down the mountain in droves; from the way they were talking, it was evident they feared the return of tithes and feudal rights. The Emperor, knowing of the inflammatory proclamation of the prefect, sent out some emissaries to assess the mood of the people in Digne. He was soon informed that the prefect and the few troops he had in town had left, and that the residents had torn up the posters and proclamation and were impatiently waiting for him: His Majesty was indeed received with delirium. He had dinner there. Baroness Desmichels (the general was away)[209] came to see the Emperor and assured him that the further he proceeded, the more he would find the population ready to rise up in his favor. A young cavalry officer, M. Desmichels, a nephew of the general, wanted to follow the Emperor; his offer was accepted, and he remained as a mil-

---

[208]A city in the Basses-Alpes [now Alpes Maritimes], 18 km. from Digne.

[209]General Baron Louis Desmichels (1779-1845), born in Digne, retired there during the first Restoration. His army career began with Bonaparte in Italy, then Egypt. He served with the consular guard grenadiers, then with the imperial guard chasseurs, where his colonel, Prince Eugène, befriended him. In 1805 he served brilliantly near Nuremberg, earning an accolade from Murat and congratulations from the Emperor, who promoted him to captain and made him an officer in the Legion of Honor. He served in all the imperial campaigns, and as colonel commanded the 31st chasseurs regiment. In 1813 he went back to Italy on the orders of Prince Eugène, who promoted him to acting brigadier general. But Napoleon's abdication did not allow his confirmation, and he was put on inactive duty. He took up active duty again when Napoleon returned, and he joined him in Lyon. Heading the 4th regiment of chasseurs, he served with great distinction at Waterloo, and the second Restoration sentenced him to seven years of retirement at half-pay.

itary aide to the Emperor throughout the Hundred Days. Proclamations were printed in that city.

On the morning of the 5th, the advance party of 100 men and General Cambronne captured the bridge and fortress of Sisteron; the small garrison of that city was forced to evacuate it. The Emperor dined there and went on to sleep in Gap, preceded by the advance party, and accompanied by the Poles and mamelukes on horseback. Additional proclamations were again printed and sent out in all directions. The battalion head surgeon, M. Emery, preceded the Emperor to Grenoble and arrived there to prepare the people. The soldiers and officers of the Gap national guard fraternized with those of the imperial guard. All who had followed the Emperor were now on horseback.

The Emperor left Gap only after dinner on March 6, with all the troops now together, rested and refreshed. At his departure, the entire population lined the Emperor's path, and expressed its joy by shouting: Down with combined taxes! Vive l'Empereur!

When he arrived in Saint-Bonnet,[210] the local population offered to gather together the surrounding villages and accompany him. The Emperor said: "No, your sentiments show me I was not mistaken, and they are for me a positive guarantee of my soldiers' feelings. Those I meet will side with me, and the more we are, the better my success will be assured."

One of the battalion grenadiers had asked permission to go on ahead and see his father. When His Majesty passed by on the road, he presented this blind old man of 90, and his young brother who wanted to join the battalion. That family was poor, the scene was touching. After saying some flattering words to the old man, the Emperor pulled out his purse containing 25 napoleons and gave it to him. All day long, the local population had lined up along the Emperor's way.

---

[210]A town in the Basses-Alpes [now Alpes-Maritimes], 16 km. from Gap, along the Drac.

His Majesty arrived in Corps[211] and slept there; the advance
party went on to La Mure. As the Emperor progressed, the entire population came out loudly in his favor and lined the road he was to take.
The Emperor was moving as fast as lightning, saying to the grand marshal and General Drouot: "Success lies in the speed of my progress
and in my arrival in Grenoble." There were a hundred leagues between
the place we had landed and that city; they were covered in six days.
The advance party encountered a mounted line battalion on the main
road to Grenoble. It had came to halt the Emperor's progress. General
Cambronne asked to talk with them, but the commander refused. General Cambronne sent word to His Majesty that he was being stopped
by a battalion of the 5th line regiment, a company of engineers and one
of sappers, 700 to 800 men in all. This battalion had turned up in La
Mure with a few barrels of powder, to blow up the bridge; the population had opposed that move, and it had pulled back to Laffrey.[212] As
during the entire journey, I was lying asleep fully dressed in the
Emperor's bedroom when Saint-Denis, sleeping in the anteroom,
knocked at the door and told me the grand marshal wished to speak to
the Emperor. I opened and announced him to His Majesty, and he read
him General Cambronne's report. The Emperor asked if the grenadiers
had arrived, and the reply was affirmative. "Let them rest, and tell
Cambronne to wait for my arrival before undertaking anything."

At daybreak the Emperor dressed and set off with the guard
following; he met the advance party, and went on ahead. At a distance
away, he had his battalion halt and line up in columns by platoon. On
the left side of the road was a hill that the Corsican battalion was getting ready to occupy; already a few companies were climbing it. To

---

[211]Corps, in the Grenoble arrondissement, a day's march from that city. Napoleon
spent the night of Monday, March 6, there, at the Dumas inn.

[212]Small community in the Grenoble arrondissement, 24 km. from Vizille on the plateau of La Matheysine, near Lake Laffrey. The episode related here is well-known,
marking March 7, before the arrival that evening in Grenoble.

For details on a commemorative statue of Napoleon erected under the second
Empire, its destruction in 1870, and its restoration, cf. G. Faure and M. Deléon,
Napoléon à Laffrey (Grenoble, 1929).

The route Napoleon.

Napoleon encounters French troops sent to stop him. He stands before them. "Here Iam," he says, "You recognize me. If there is a soldier who wishes to kill his Emperor, shoot. This is the moment." With one great shout, the troops yell, "Vive l'Empereur."

the right there was a small plain into which he sent the Poles, a few mamelukes, and all his retinue on horseback. The Emperor sent his ADC Colonel Ruhl to inform the 5th line regiment of his arrival; its commander told him he was forbidden to communicate with them, his hands were tied. But a faraway cry reached us, that of Vive l'Empereur! Colonel Ruhl came back, informed His Majesty of the general feeling, leaving no doubt: all that was needed to take over the troops and remove their commander was for him to show himself and speak to the soldiers. War commissioner Vauthier was sent to advise the battalion commander that he was holding him responsible toward France and posterity for the orders he gave; meanwhile he ordered the guard to place their weapons under their arms. He had the tricolor unfurled, and the band marching ahead played *Allons enfants de la Patrie*.[213] All were electrified, both our battalion and the Grenoble

[213]*La Marseillaise*, "the war song of the army of the Rhine," was until 1815 almost banished from the official repertory. Napoleon was generally greeted by *Veillons au salut de l'Empire*, and the slow rhythm of *La Victoire est à nous* accompanied any march by troops on foot.

troops. The Emperor, wearing the little grey overcoat that so many times had had a magical effect on soldiers, accompanied by Generals Drouot, Cambronne, and the grand marshal, walked up to the 5th line regiment. His Majesty was soon recognized, and he said to them: "Kill your emperor, you may do so." Vive l'Empereur! was the only reply. An old soldier, with tears in his eyes, walked up to him and clicked the ramrod into his rifle: "You can see how much we wanted to kill you!" In an instant, the tricolor cockades they had in their packs replaced the white cockades, which after the battalion departed marked the place where it had stood, and they fraternized with the guard.

When order was restored, the Emperor said: "I come with a handful of brave men, for I am counting on the people and on you. The Bourbon throne is illegitimate because it was not erected by the nation; it is contrary to the national will, because it is contrary to the country's interests, and exists only in the interest of a few families. Ask your fathers, ask all these people coming from nearby, you shall learn from their lips what the Bourbons have in store for France." Then, turning to the crowd of people who had come to see him, he said: "Is it not true that in your communities you are threatened with a return of the tithe, of privileges, of feudal rights, and of all the abuses from which your successes had delivered you?"

"Yes, Sire, we were threatened with these, our parish priests were already having storage sheds built."

An ADC to General Marchand[214] was with the troops coming from Grenoble; when he saw the enthusiasm and attachment of the people and troops for the Emperor, he left to go inform his general. A few officers took after him to catch him, but he had a better horse and escaped.

The 5th line regiment and the engineers and sappers asked to make up the advance element; the crowd of residents pressed along the route and provided accompaniment by singing songs honoring the Emperor. He had been on horseback all day, he was very tired and had a cold, but His Majesty insisted on taking advantage of the ever-growing enthusiasm to enter Grenoble. When his ADC arrived, General Marchand, commanding the division, ordered the city gates closed.

Should he not be afraid of any communication between the king's troops and those of the Emperor? What had occurred before La Mure assured him of what would happen as soon as his division recognized the Emperor and saw the tricolor. A young officer in the Grenoble national guard, M. Dumoulin,[215] came forward and offered the Emperor his sword and his wealth. He had left Grenoble a few hours previously, and informed the Emperor that he could count on Colonel La Bédoyère, the goodwill of the garrison and that of the population. He provided news of Dr. Emery, who had actively prepared the town patriots. M. Dumoulin stayed with the Emperor as military aide and received the cross.

Between Vizille and Grenoble, the adjutant major of the 7th line regiment came to tell the Emperor that his colonel, M. de La

---

[214]General Count Jean Marchand (1765-1851). An attorney in Grenoble, he joined the army at the time of the Revolution and became a captain in the Isère volunteers. He took part in the Italian campaigns under Bonaparte, who had the Directory promote him to brigadier general in 1799. He commanded a division of Marshal Ney's corps, and distinguished himself in numerous battles from 1805-1807. After Friedland, he was named a grand eagle of the Legion of Honor and count of the Empire. He then served in Spain, and in 1812 in the Russian campaign, where he shone during the capture of the great redoubt at the Moskowa. In 1813 he served at Lutzen, Bautzen, and Leipzig. In 1814 he was put in charge of raising an army in Isère, and headed the 7th military division in Grenoble. He remained there during the first Restoration, where Napoleon found him on his return from Elba. But Marchand preferred to flee rather than fight under the imperial flag.

In spite of the name, he was no relation to Marchand, author of these *Mémoires*.

[215]Jean Dumoulin was a rich Grenoble glove maker, a friend of his compatriot Emery, surgeon of the guard and part of the Elban battalion.

Dumoulin is reported by Berriat Saint-Prix (*Napoléon à Grenoble*, written 1815, published 1861) as having corresponded with Emery by hiding his letters in packages of gloves sent to Porto Ferrajo. Montholon claims Dumoulin came to see Napoleon in Elba in October and in November 1814.

In any event, while going through Castellane on March 3, Napoleon had demanded that the mayor give him three blank passports. One was filled in with the name of surgeon of the guard Emery, allegedly on leave. And he had told him: "Go ahead of me. Go to Grenoble and tell them I'm coming."

Bédoyère,[216] was bringing his regiment to him. Half an hour later he appeared, carrying the former eagle of his regiment stuck on the tip of a tree branch. The Emperor took the eagle, kissed it, and after congratulating this young colonel on his patriotic courage, embraced him. The 7th was lined up along the road, and he inspected it and went on his way. This regiment of 1,800 men doubled the Emperor's forces, the crowd of people quadrupled them, and cries of Vive l'Empereur! Down with the priests! Down with combined taxes! accompanied this triumphal march up to Grenoble.

Having arrived before Grenoble at 9:30 p.m., the Emperor found the city doors locked and the troops restricted to their barracks. The cries of Vive l'Empereur! shouted on the ramparts by the soldiers and inhabitants left no doubt regarding their sentiments.

The ramparts were crowded with soldiers from the 3rd engineering regiment of 2,000 men, the 4th artillery regiment where Napoleon had become a captain twenty years earlier, the two other battalions of the 5th, the 11th line regiment, and the 4th hussars. The soldiers yelled from the top of the ramparts, that the powder was wet. Torches were lit everywhere, but they were ordered put out.

The Emperor summoned General Marchand to open the city

---

[216]Charles Huchet de La Bédoyère, born in 1788, joined the armed forces in 1806 in the ordinance gendarmes. He served during the campaigns of Prussia and Poland (1806-1807), and was made Lannes' ADC in 1808, captain in 1809, and ADC to Prince Eugène that same year. As a colonel, he commanded the 112th infantry regiment in 1813, and was wounded in the left thigh at Golberg in Silesia. In 1813 he married Georgine de Chastellux. He was offered command of the 1st division, 2nd brigade in Paris in February 1814, but preferred keeping the command of his regiment; in March 1814 he went to Fontainebleau and offered his services to Napoleon. As colonel commanding the Chambéry 7th line regiment in October 1814, he was in Grenoble when Napoleon approached the city. He and his troops sided with the Emperor, and joined him between Tavernolles and Brié, 8 km. from Grenoble. During the Hundred Days he was promoted to brigadier general and ADC to the Emperor in March 1815, and made a peer of France and count of the Empire in June of that year.

After Waterloo, La Bédoyère was excluded from the amnesty by name, sentenced to death, and shot by a firing squad in the plain of Grenelle. This execution had long and heated repercussions.

Bourguignon was able to obtain from the La Bédoyère family and preserve at Malmaison a few precious souvenirs of the general, notably a portrait by Lefèvre (1802) and a miniature by Guérin.

After the first confrontation near Grenoble, and the enthusiastic welcome given him
by his old troops, Napoleon walks among them smiling and giving personal greetings
not only to the soldiers but to their families as well.

doors. Half an hour later, the general asked that he be given until the next day. The sappers then undertook to break down the door with their axes. The first blows had barely landed when the door was opened. His Majesty made his entrance amid an army and population full of enthusiasm. In Grenoble, the Emperor became a power to contend with. He could sustain a war if necessary, he could count on the troops and population who were greeting him with such a show of happiness. The Emperor lodged at an inn. After his supper, the citizens of Grenoble brought him the doors to the city, as they couldn't offer him the keys. The next day His Majesty received the town officials and the corps heads. All the speeches were unanimous; all stated they had no obligation toward princes imposed by foreigners.

The Emperor's former mathematics teacher arrived and asked if he could see his former pupil. The Emperor, who was in his room, came to the door to greet him, embraced him, and remained a few moments chatting with him: this kind old man was enchanted with the flattering reception he had just received. Colonel Ruhl, born in the vicinity of Grenoble, came to present his father whom the Emperor took great pleasure in meeting, saying that he would see to the future fortune of his son, who had been one of his guides in Egypt. During his stay in Elba this officer, along with Dr. Emery, the battalion surgeon-major, maintained a very active correspondence with the city's patriots. Countess Marchand, wife of the general, had not left with him; she came to see the Emperor and told him that her husband could not join his cause without being a traitor to his oaths, but would do so as soon as the king had left the kingdom. The Emperor showed this lady all the graciousness he was capable of when he wished to please, assuring her that he would have taken great pleasure in seeing her husband. The general did not see fit to present himself. As the prefect M. Fourier,[217] a member of the Egyp-

---

[217]Jean-Baptiste Fourier (1768-1830). A distinguished mathematician, he was engaged at the Ecole Polytechnique by Lagrange and Monge. Because of his varied and great knowledge, he was included among the scientists who accompanied Bonaparte to Egypt. As perpetual secretary of the Egyptian institute, his brilliant administrative qualities led to his heading the justice department in Egypt, and to reward him, Napoleon named him prefect of Grenoble, member of the Legion of Honor, and baron. In 1815, as Napoleon was approaching Grenoble, Fourier had a proclamation published on March 5 calling for respect for the king's government. When the Emperor arrived, he left town. In a shrewd political move, the Emperor named him prefect of the Rhône on March 12, but Fourier arranged to be dismissed on May 12. Under the second Restoration, he became perpetual secretary of the science academy.

tian commission, had left town, the Emperor found a replacement in the person of a prefecture councillor, and he named as commander of the national guard a former major in the imperial guard. At two, the Emperor passed the troops in review, to cries of Vive l'Empereur! Down with the Bourbons! The 6,000 soldiers had the previous day donned the old tricolor cockades which they had kept in their packs as mementos of their past glory. The Emperor said to the officers who reported this that it proved the troops' opinion in a striking manner, that they had held on to them as a treasure when they were forced to accept the anti-national flag of the Bourbons, and that the latter had committed a grave mistake when they proscribed these colors that had been forever French. Immediately after the parade, these troops set out for Lyon, preceded by a population singing patriotic tunes. The first point of the venture had been scored; the Emperor was master of Grenoble where he had arrived with lightning speed, and which was the center of an important province, with all kinds of resources gathered in the arsenal. He was leaving behind him a patriotic and devoted population, and could proceed to Lyon without fear. What had just occurred in the Grenoble division he could expect from that of Lyon, and he was not mistaken.

As the key to the gates of Grenoble is not available, citizens tear the gate down and present it to the Emperor.

CHAPTER EIGHT

March on Lyon — On Mâcon — Châlon, Autun, and Auxerre —
Fontainebleau — Arrival in Paris —
Comments and Conclusion of Part II

*O*n March 9 the Emperor went on to sleep in Bourgoin, preceded by the 4th hussars and followed by the entire garrison. The crowd and the enthusiasm were ever growing, in spite of the rain and bad weather that day. Ever since the landing, cries of Down with the priests! Down with combined taxes! had accompanied the Emperor, who never answered anything to such calls. The Emperor was in his coach, tired and with a cold, and went to bed as soon as he arrived. That night he received news of Lyon through a staff officer, M. Moline de Saint-Yon,[218] sent by General Brayer.[219] The sentiment in this great city was not at all uncertain; but the presence of Monsieur the Count of Artois, who had just arrived there, restrained its outburst, and prevented the citizenry from going out to meet Napoleon. He learned from the same person that the population had objected to the bridges of La Guillotière and Morand being blocked, and that Monsieur and Marshal Macdonald wanted to defend Lyon, against the

---

[218]Alexandre Moline de Saint-Yon, born in Lyon in 1786. He graduated in 1805 from the Fontainebleau school as a second lieutenant, and took part in all the campaigns of Austria, Prussia, Poland, and Spain, earning his promotions on the battlefield. Wounded in 1813 at Saint-Jean-de-Luz, he became a major and returned to France with Marshal Soult.

When Napoleon returned from Elba, he was named his military aide and accompanied him at Waterloo. Retired at half-pay under the second Restoration, he became a historical writer. Recalled to active duty after the July revolution, he was promoted to colonel, and eventually to lieutenant general. He became a peer of France, a grand officer of the Legion of Honor, and war minister (1845-1847), and retired in 1848.

As a writer he published opera librettos, fragments of military history, an article on Prince Eugène, and a history of the counts of Toulouse.

advice of the war council. They had no artillery; he said to the young officer: "Go back and assure Brayer of my friendship." The Emperor immediately gave orders to Count Bertrand to gather some boats at Mirbel and close the Paris road to the prince and the marshal who wanted to prevent him from entering Lyon.

On the 10th the Emperor set off for Lyon, the army ahead of him, and it was not long before he was in the midst of the column, his saddle horses following his coach; he climbed on horseback and appeared at the head of his troops. Residents of Lyon were continually arriving to join His Majesty, describing the agitation in town. The people were waiting for but one word to demolish the bridge barricades that even the troops did not wish to defend. The Emperor was informed that Monsieur, while inspecting the cavalry, had stopped in front of an old soldier from the 13th dragoons wearing several chevrons, and said to him: "Come, my good man, cry out Long live the king."

"No, my lord, I cannot do it, we shall not fight against our father." That response said everything; turning toward General Brayer who was near him, he said: "There is nothing more to hope for," and he departed with some of his courtiers and a single national guardsman who accompanied him on horseback. General Brayer, informed of his departure, sent a detachment of the 13th dragoons to serve as escort. The Duke of Orleans, who had come with him, had already left Lyon.

Marshal Macdonald insisted on defending the city. Two battalions posted at the Guillotière bridge were to prevent its being crossed; a reconnaissance party from the 4th hussars and a few Poles

---

[219]General M. S. Brayer (1769-1840) enlisted in 1800 and served brilliantly throughout all the campaigns of the Empire, at Austerlitz, Friedland, in Spain, and in Germany. He was the general commanding the 19th military division in Lyon for the king in 1815. He along with his troops joined the Emperor on his return from Elba and took command of the small imperial army's advance party. He was given command of a division of the young guard, named a count and peer of France, and governor of Versailles and the Trianon. Sentenced to death in absentia after Waterloo, he went to America and served in the military in the U.S., Brazil, and Chile. Pardoned, he returned to France in 1821 and returned to service. His daughter married the author of this book, Marchand.

led by Colonel Jermanowski showed up, crying Vive l'Empereur! The two battalions were ordered to open fire, but they put down their weapons and also cried Vive l'Empereur! The marshal, who was present at this defection, headed for Paris, riding a horse lent by General Brayer. At the outskirts of Vaize, he was stopped by two hussars from the 4th, the marshal being alone, wearing a blue coat and only a colonel's epaulets. General Baron Dijeon, arriving, identified him and had him released.

As early as March 6, Napoleon and those following him were outlawed by the following proclamation which Chancellor Dambray had borrowed from ancient legislation, perhaps that used against Mandrin.

King's ordinances relating to general security measures.
(Moniteur, March 7, 1815)

Louis, by the grace of God, king of France and Navarre, salutations to all who read this.

Article 12 of the constitutional charter has charged us with making rules and ordinances regarding the security of the state. It would be severely compromised should we not take prompt measures to repress the venture just undertaken against our kingdom, and put an end to the plots and the attempts at inciting civil war and destroying the government.

Because of this, and on the report made to us by our beloved and faithful knight chancellor of France, Sir Dambray, commander of our orders, and on the advice of our council, we have ordered and order as follows:

Art. 1.—Napoleon Bonaparte is declared a traitor and rebel, for having entered the department of the Var under arms. All governors, military commanders, national guard, civilian authorities, and even simple citizens are enjoined to seek him out, arrest him, and promptly bring him before a court martial, which after identifying him shall pronounce against him the penalties provided under the law.

Art. 2.—Shall be likewise punished as guilty of the same crimes, all military and employees of all ranks who have accompanied or followed Bonaparte in his invasion of French territory, unless—within eight days following the publi-

cation of this ordinance—they surrender to our governors, commanders of military divisions, generals, or civil administrators.

Art. 3.—Shall also be sought out and punished as agitators and accomplices of rebellion and attempts to change the form of government and provoke a civil war, all civil and military administrators, heads and employees in said administrations, payers and collectors of public funds, and even ordinary citizens who would either directly or indirectly provide aid and assistance to Bonaparte.

Art. 4.—Shall be likewise punished, in accordance with article 102 of the penal code, those who—through speeches given in public places or meetings, posters, or printed writings—have taken part or encouraged citizens to take part in the revolt, or abstained from stopping it.

Our chancellor, our ministers, secretaries of state, and our director of the police, each as far as he is concerned, are charged with the execution of this ordinance that shall be inserted in the evening bulletin, and sent to all governors of military divisions, generals, commanders, prefects, subprefects and mayors of our kingdom, with orders to have it printed and posted in Paris as well as elsewhere and wherever needed.

Given in the Tuileries château on March 6, 1815, the twentieth year of our reign.

Signed: Louis

For the king: the chancellor of France
Signed: Dambray

In the eyes of those who had published such a proclamation, the Emperor's landing and his march on Lyon and Paris were to be considered hostile acts against the people's rights; troops joining him were in a state of rebellion. In the face of this same rebellion and Napoleon's immense influence, they were forced to commit the heir apparent to the throne, as the king could not come himself.

As the Emperor said in Saint Helena, nothing was wiser and better conceived than sending out the princes to meet Napoleon, as the king could not come himself; it was a way for a city of 100,000 not to fall to 800 men, as Paris remained in the hands of the king. But the fall of the second city in the kingdom must have foretold that of the capital.

Around 7 p.m. the Emperor entered Lyon, surrounded by officers and generals of all ranks who had come out to meet him; at his side could be seen Lieutenant General Brayer, commanding the Lyon division, who had come to meet him with a large staff. The enthusiasm of this great city was at its highest, and happiness and its exhilaration were painted on all faces.

It is impossible to imagine the crowd of men, children and old people who ran out onto the bridges and embankments, at the risk of being crushed. Everyone wanted to see him, hear him, be certain that it was indeed him and not some imaginary person, the object of their hopes and not one of disastrous illusions. Cries of Vive l'Empereur! Down with the priests! Down with the exiles! Down with feudalism! rang through the air like a drum roll. The Emperor was touched and shared in this public elation, but did not fail to note these accusations against the royal government, which offered him a sure guarantee of the success of his plans, as well as proof of the call sent out to him by the French people—humiliated by foreigners, belittled by their government, and concerned about their future. His Majesty stayed at the archbishop's residence, where all had been prepared to receive him, and put his own safety into the hands of the dismounted national guard.

No doubt he privately approved of the mounted national guardsman who had accompanied the prince; but in Saint Helena he declared it untrue that he asked to see the man and gave him the cross, as had been claimed. It is also false that he refused the help of the mounted national guard because it had failed to do its duty and accompany Monsieur as it should have done. It was rather because the institution did not recognize a mounted national guard.

On March 11 the Emperor, accompanied by a few generals and a picket of hussars, went to Place Bellecour and reviewed General Brayer's division. His Majesty saw with pleasure this square that 15 years before he had restored from its ruins, and whose first stone he had laid. The crowd was augmented by the surrounding population who had come to see him. The cries of Vive l'Empereur! and the enthusiasm were the same as the day before. When the Emperor returned to the archbishop's residence, he found the gallery full of generals, colonels, and magistrates; he spoke to each in his own language, and went into the drawing room where he received the imperial court, the municipal authorities, the corps leaders, and the heads of the national guard.

His Majesty ordered all the commanders of corps stationed in the surrounding countryside to proceed to this or that point along his route or the adjoining departments. He wrote to Marshal Ney, who was at Lons-le-Saulnier with his army, to get under way and come join him. From Lyon the Emperor was already issuing decrees and administering the country. That day General Brayer's division formed the advance party leading the way to Paris.

After issuing a proclamation to the people of Lyon, the Emperor departed on the 13th, deeply moved by the sentiments shown him. The simple words: "People of Lyon, I love you!" perfectly expressed the emotion he felt.

The Emperor had a carriage purchased to continue his journey, and gave me the coach. M. Fleury de Chaboulon joined the Emperor in Lyon. He was employed in the cabinet to work in Paris under Baron Fain. His Majesty named him senior counsel, and thus rewarded through this first favor a staunch devotion during his missions in Elba and Basel.

His Majesty stopped in the afternoon in Villefranche and went to the city hall, where a large number of wounded soldiers was presented to him.

During the night the Emperor arrived in Mâcon, and was lodged at the Hôtel du Sauvage; he complained about not having been put up at the prefecture. The next day he received the congratulations of the municipal authorities and the national guard. He spoke often to one of the aides, whose candor amused him; this aide had just told him that "from the moment he learned of his landing, he had considered him mad." He was not the only one, and the Emperor's alleged madness was one of the reasons for the success of his venture. The

Emperor said to them: "During the last war, you did not uphold the honor of Burgundy!"

"Sire, it was not our fault, you had given us a poor mayor!" The prefect, M. Germain, one of the chamberlains presented to him by Paris in 1804 whom he had made a count, had left. The Emperor said: "Germain thought he had to run away from me; his person is not so important that we can't do without him." From one town to the next, the population lined the road.

The Emperor learned in Mâcon that the Parisian national guard wanted to defend the king, and that this prince refused to leave the Tuileries. He replied to the man bringing the news: "The national guard will maintain order in Paris, and the king will not be there waiting for me.—What do you think, Brayer?" he asked the general who was present, and who replied: "Sire, let them talk; they won't find a single soldier who will fight against you, and the enthusiasm of the population is such that you will arrive with 500,000 men if you wish." The Emperor did not know General Brayer very well, and the mission of one of his staff officers, M. Saint-Yon, to Bourgoin, had surprised him. He said in Saint Helena: "His career had been spent far from me, I was hesitant, but the openness with which he greeted me when he came to join me at the head of a large staff of officers dispelled all my doubts. It was especially during our trip from Lyon to Paris that I was able to appreciate all the force of his character."

The Emperor arrived in Châlon on the 14th. Rain was pouring down, but the population still came out all along the way. As he was about to enter the city, he was shown some artillery intended for use against him that had been captured by the people; he congratulated them, and seized this occasion to tell them he would always remember their fine conduct in 1814. He sent the Legion of Honor to the mayor of Saint-Jean-de-Losne, saying: "It was for good people like him that I created the Legion of Honor, and not for exiles pensioned by our enemies."

In Châlon His Majesty received a deputation from the city of Dijon; the inhabitants had driven out the prefect, and the Emperor removed the mayor and named another one.

On the 15th, the Emperor slept in Autun; he received the municipal authorities and severely chided the mayor who was being dominated by a handful of nobles. "Who are you, sir, to let yourself thus be governed by a privileged few? Aren't you yourself a plebeian, must you abandon the care of the people you administer to the hatred of the nobility?" The Emperor removed him from office.

On the 16th we slept in Avallon. The Emperor was welcomed there like everywhere else, and the national guard officers provided his personal service. He reinstated several civil servants who had been removed for having participated in the defense of the country against foreigners; he issued orders to have the subprefect of Semur arrested and sent to jail in Avallon for persecuting the patriots.

The Emperor arrived the next day, the 17th, in Auxerre, having lunched in Vermenton. The prefect M. Gamot, Marshal Ney's brother-in-law, had remained at his post. His Majesty stayed at the prefecture, and found in the drawing room a life-size portrait of himself wearing the imperial garb, as well as busts of the Empress and his son. The Emperor received congratulations from the authorities, and talked about the nation's interests. A few retired officers came to offer their services; during the day, he received an officer from Marshal Ney announcing his imminent arrival.

His Majesty summoned M. Viard, vicar of the cathedral, who from his pulpit was preaching fidelity to the established government and organizing the resistance against the Emperor's army. It was indeed late, dangerous, and atypical of the character and prudence of a priest. The Emperor chided him for inciting civil war in the name of a God of peace and mercy, told him he should only concern himself with spiritual matters, and quoted several passages of the Holy Scriptures, to which the vicar did not and could not respond.

It was again confirmed to the Emperor that the king wanted to defend Paris. "The only army on which he could depend is now mine. Ney is coming. I crossed Provence and the upper Dauphiné with 900 men, I now have 30,000. Three million peasants ran out along the way and showered me with blessings. Why? Because I have honored France and governed in the spirit of the nation. The Bourbons have brought the foreign yoke and the spirit of exile. France is rejecting these. I am confident about Paris, Louis XVIII is too astute to wait for me at the Tuileries."

During the night the grand marshal came to knock at the Emperor's bedroom door, and I opened. He had come to tell the Emperor of the marshal's arrival in town. The Emperor put off receiving him until the next day, the 18th. The marshal's first moment was uncomfortable: was he remembering his promise to the king? It didn't last long; the grand marshal had written him that he would be greeted as on the day after the Moskowa. The Emperor's arms opened, he threw himself into them, and they embraced. Left alone they talked at length, the marshal admitting he had been carried along by his army, he could not have kept it in the service of the king, and he had left Paris with the full intent of fighting against the Emperor.

His Majesty ordered that boats be gathered to transport a part of the army that was exhausted as far as Fossard. The Yonne was swollen, one of the boats sank, and a few of those in it were drowned. This loss that greatly affected General Brayer, who commanded them, was deeply felt by the Emperor, who prided himself on his return not costing a single human life.

That morning the Emperor had reviewed the 14th line regiment. He then mingled with the crowd anxious to see him, and returned to the prefecture accompanied by the same cries of Vive l'Empereur! Down with the priests! Down with combined taxes! he had heard since his landing. A few royal emissaries sought and even gained entrance to the prefecture building. They were recognized, and one of them would have been thrown out the window had not Count Bertrand intervened. The Emperor, informed of a few uprisings in the south and of the first movements of the Duke of Angoulême, before leaving took measures to suppress these. Generals Suchet, Gérard, and others sent emissaries to inform the Emperor of their devotion. The Emperor sent a letter to Lecourbe, who was eager to place his patriotism at the Emperor's service. The Emperor left Auxerre, and the people accompanied him far beyond the city. The Emperor was anxious to arrive in Fontainebleau and enter Paris on March 20.

Everywhere the greatest happiness prevailed along his way. In Fossard, he found a regiment of dragoons who, without officers, were coming to join him: he inspected them and gave out compliments and promotions. He was astonished that young Moncey who commanded the 3rd hussars had felt obliged to run away from him, while sending a message that he would never fight against him, but that he had taken an oath from which he had not been released. Several officers and hussars from that regiment followed the general trend and came to join the Emperor. His Majesty had me go ahead of him and ordered me to wait for him in Fontainebleau. A palace quartermaster, M. Deschamps, had arrived there and all was prepared to receive the Emperor; the former concierge was still there, but was on the verge of being dismissed. I arrived at 11 p.m. The rumor had been circulated that in the forest there were 1100 or 1200 men ready to abduct the Emperor. His Majesty stopped four hours in Moret, and left only when he received a report that the forest had been searched, and that guards were at every outlet in the direction of Paris, Orléans, and Melun. We were then close to the king's army, and I had seen nothing along my way. His Majesty arrived at 4 a.m. escorted by a few hundred cavalrymen: Colonels Jermanowski and Ruhl, and a palace quartermaster, M. Buisson, galloped by his carriage door. The Emperor appeared pleased to find himself again in this palace which treason had forced him to leave eleven months before. A good fire was lit in his bedroom; he summoned the concierge, one of his former servants, who told him that as soon as the Bourbons came back, they had busied themselves removing all the symbols reminiscent of the imperial regime, but the crowned N's sculpted on the bed had escaped their attention and were still there. Having assured him of his continued benevolence toward him and his family, and dismissed him, His Majesty went to bed. At 7 a.m. he dressed, and soon learned of the king's departure, which the grand marshal who had just heard the news came to tell him.

Before leaving for Paris, the Emperor ordered that the Elban battalion be given a day's rest, and told me to go straight to Paris. Between Fontainebleau and Essonnes, His Majesty was inspecting a regiment. The coachman who was taking me stopped; the Emperor asked what coach that was, and on learning it was mine, ordered me to proceed.

At the Cour of France I found the Emperor's carriages, equerries, and household staff. I arrived at the Tuileries at 6 p.m. There was no sign that another sovereign had inhabited this palace: the reception and household staff were at their posts; it merely looked as if His Majesty were returning from a trip. The Emperor arrived only at 8 p.m. on March 20, having been detained by the crowd gathered along his way and by the congratulations of the generals who came out to greet him. The army that had been assembled in Villejuif to fight him served as his escort.

When the Emperor got out of his carriage, a thousand arms carried him up to his apartments; the giddiness of joy was everywhere. Queen Hortense, dressed in black, was waiting for him in her drawing room. The Emperor embraced her affectionately, providing the consolation she was entitled to expect from the friendship of His Majesty toward her and Empress Joséphine. After these first moments of most legitimate sorrow and regrets, he proceeded into his own drawing room, and talked with dignitaries of the Empire. All were delighted, even elated, and he shared these sentiments without restraint. His Majesty retired to his own quarters only at midnight, exhausted.

Many people have claimed that the Emperor's return was blemished, that he should have been surrounded by the brave Elban battalion that had forced its march to arrive with him. This is what I heard His Majesty say in Saint Helena: "I entered Paris as I did Grenoble and Lyon, at the end of a long day's march and at the head of the armies sent to oppose me; I arrived in Paris just as when I returned from Marengo, Austerlitz, Tilsit. I had too many other things to do to waste two days preparing a ceremonial entrance; I would not have sacrificed fifteen minutes for that."

The Emperor's return to the Tuileries, the retaking of power with 900 men, without firing a shot or spilling a drop of blood, and without any internal conspiracy by the country's inhabitants, shall always remain among the marvelous events of which the history of nations offers no or very few examples. Be it audacity or the result of genius, it matters little; we saw it with our own eyes, and it remains unbelievable nevertheless. The Emperor had just covered in 20 days a route requiring 40 days' march. The Emperor had been quietly settling down in Elba in his new situation, but the conditions stipulated by the Fontainebleau treaty were not fulfilled, they were even violated. An attempt was to be made on his life, the plan originating in Corsica, and the Emperor was informed of this by his friends. There was a plan to restrict his freedom and confine him on Saint Helena. He was no longer obligated to abide by stipulations he alone honored; force was all that mattered to his enemies, while justice, respect of treaties, blood relations, and the memory of honorable friendships meant nothing anymore. The goal he had set, the welfare of France, the motives which had led him to abdicate had become meaningless. He recognized that the government succeeding his own was ruling opposite to the nation's interests, that the exile spirit dominated it, and was leading it each day from serious errors to even more serious errors, ruining France. He recognized that, if he had committed mistakes, he owed his fall less to these than to intrigue, treason offered or solicited, but always backed by foreigners and the misfortunes of the 1814 invasion; France missed him and would welcome him with open arms... As long as only his personal interest was compromised, he hesitated. But when it was the salvation, honor, and glory of the motherland, there was no hesitation: belonging entirely to France, he would do everything for her. The Emperor landed at Golfe Juan on March 1 and marched on Paris; every three days, his military forces doubled; at every point along his path, the people showered him with their blessings and hopes, and showed their willingness to defend him if he were attacked. Peasants and soldiers, civil servants and magistrates, all told him that they were finished, had he not come. In 20 days he was before the walls of Paris, at the head of 60,000 men; and the king, who could not prevent the evil that his courtiers, his ministers, and the privileged classes had brought to France, had the painful wisdom to leave his palace in the middle of the night. Thus were verified the Emperor's words to M. Poggi when speaking of the Bourbons: their government of 19 years was so weak that even with miracle on top of miracle, it could not stand.

The only thing lacking in this great enterprise, for it to have been fully successful, would have been for the Emperor to have left Elba two weeks later: his landing would no longer have found the sovereigns gathered in Vienna, and the declarations of March 23 to 25 would not have been made. Many events then supporting his determination to return to France would have been affected. Unfortunately M. Colonna d'Istria arrived from Naples, bringing him the king's message announcing the closing of the congress and the departure of Emperor Alexander for Saint Petersburg. Had the Emperor left Elba only on receipt of the message he was expecting from Vienna, which Cipriani was bringing in person and which arrived in Porto Ferrajo on the 27th, the Emperor would have delayed his departure for a few days. Unfortunately, the Emperor had left the island on the 26th. Cipriani, saddened not to find the Emperor and delayed in reaching France, only caught up with us in Paris.

On his arrival at the Tuileries, the Emperor is carried on the shoulders of the crowd to the great staircase of the palace.

Top Left: Louis-Joseph Marchand
Top Right: Caroline Murat
Bottom Right: Pope Pius VII

Top Left: Empress Joséphine
Top Right: Marshal MacDonald
Bot. Left: Field Marshal von Blücher
Bottom Right: Marshal Grouchy

Top Left: Count de Montholon
Top Right: Countess de Montholon
Bottom Left: General Bertrand
Bottom Right: Countess Bertrand

Top Left: Captain Ussher
Top Right: Pozzo di Borgo
Bottom Left: Pauline Bonaparte
Bottom Right: Pons de l'Hérault

Top Left: Lazare Carnot
Top Right: Lucien Bonaparte
Bottom Right: Jérôme Bonaparte

Top Left: Banker Laffitte
Top Right: Countess Walewska
Bottom Left: Madame Mère

Top Left: Madame Grassini
Top Right: Madame Pellapra
Bottom Left: Prince Schwarzenberg
Bottom Right: Joseph Fouché

Top Left: Prince Murat
Top Right: General Duroc
Bottom Left: General Marmont

Top Left: Baron de Cambronne
Top Right: General Becker
Bottom Left: Charles de La Bédoyère

Top Left: Hortense de Beauharnais
Top Right: Baron Peyrusse
Bottom Right: Count von Neipperg

Top Right: Pauline Bonaparte
Bottom Left: Sir Neil Campell
Bottom Right: General Drouot

Top Left: Captain Maitland
Top Right: Count de Las Cases
Bottom Right: General Gourgaud

Top: Mrs. Abell
Bottom: Betsy Balcombe

Top Left: Mr. William Balcombe
Top Right: Mrs. Balcombe
Bottom Left: Lord Holland

Top Left: Admiral Sir George Cockburn
Top Right: Sir Hudson Lowe
Bottom Right: Rear Admiral Plampin

Top: Sir Pulteney Malcolm
Bottom: Sir George Bingham

PART THREE

The Hundred Days

CHAPTER NINE

My position at the Tuileries — The Emperor's conversation with the
prince arch-chancellor and the Duke of Bassano—
Creation of the ministry — Parade of March 22 — The Elban battalion

*T*he kindness and trust shown me by the Emperor turned my service into my fortune and glory. However, after His Majesty returned to the Tuileries, I was less frequently near him than in Elba. I was generally present only when he awoke and when he went to bed, but I continued for a few days to sleep across his doorway, as I had during the trip; then I took possession of my apartment. If the Emperor had orders to give me, it was when he got up; I would report back to him when he retired to his quarters, usually at 10 p.m.

I benefited from all the prerogatives of my position: a table for four, a carriage with a coachman at my disposal who came in the morning for instructions, and access to the four great theatrical shows sent to me by the grand chamberlain, Count de Montesquiou. He was kind enough to inform me that on the remuneration list he put me down for 6,000 francs' salary and 2,000 francs for clothes, which is what my predecessor received, and that His Majesty had increased the first figure to 8,000 francs, while leaving the second one standing.

I spent my time visiting friends, observing the mood of the public. In the evening the Emperor generally asked me what I had done during the day; it was more out of curiosity than because of any special importance he attached to it. Be that as it may, during the first few days I spoke only of happiness and enthusiasm, which seemed to move him a great deal. If some important revelations reached me through my friends, just as devoted as I was to the Emperor and his glory, I would submit these to His Majesty.

As I have already stated, the evening of March 20 was given over to joy and to Queen Hortense in mourning for Empress Joséphine. That princess had come to the Tuileries to greet the Emperor. His Majesty had learned on Elba of the steps taken with Louis XVIII so that she could keep her property and receive the title of Duchess of Saint-Leu. When they were alone in his study, he could not help saying a few words that chagrined this princess, who nevertheless remained attached to the Emperor. He deemed that people had forgotten rather quickly what was owed his memory. After this first moment, he assured her of all his affection, and went into the drawing room to receive his friends' congratulations. It can be understood that such moments had to be brief, as the Emperor was impatient to devote himself to the salvation of the nation and the care of government. He remained alone in the drawing room with the arch-chancellor[220] and the Duke of Bassano (Maret),[221] two of his former ministers, from whom he confidently expected to receive accurate information on the state of things in France. His Majesty had indeed culled a large quantity of individual observations on Elba, but they could lack in accuracy and particularly in uniformity. He said he would never have signed the treaty of Paris, but as it had been signed, he would respect it, and would inform Vienna of this. He was uncertain if the powers would be satisfied with that, no matter how sincere the commitment he was making; doubtless their best interest would advise them to uphold that treaty, and he advised the Austrian emperor that nothing would be changed in the current state of Italy. This conversation was reported to me by one of the two people present, on my return from Saint Helena. He said to me: "The Emperor talked to us about the nature and shape of the government he wished to restore." He asked for their opinion. The two men outlined for him the course of the king's government,

---

[220]The position of arch-chancellor was foremost among the great officers of the crown. Cambacérès (1753-1824) held it without interruption until the last days of the Empire. Although he was Duke of Parma, his title was "prince arch-chancellor."

[221]Hugues Maret, Duke of Bassano (1763-1839). Secretary of state, he was one of the closest collaborators of the Emperor, who in 1811 put him in charge of foreign affairs.

and the errors into which it had been led by M. de Blacas and the exile spirit on one hand, and on the other hand that the carelessness and lack of experience of the ministry had neither the ability nor the power to prevent.

After hearing the opinions of the Duke of Bassano (Maret) and the prince arch-chancellor, whom he called a man of sound judgment, the Emperor said to them: "One does not recommence a political career such as mine twice; it is in my best interest to live quietly and use the remainder of my days repairing the evils brought on France by 20 years of war ending in invasion. The misfortunes of our motherland have robbed me of my retirement; the certainty that I would be disturbed in my possession of the island of Elba made me hasten matters. I came to France without any agreement with the powers, but strengthened by the divisions existing between them. What position will Vienna take? We will soon hear of it. When the powers learn of the unanimous fashion in which I was welcomed back to France, that the Bourbons could offer no resistance, and that no one or nearly no one took up arms to ensure their retreat to the limits of the kingdom, they will think it over before responding, and if they act in haste, they may regret it. Let us not forget that the sovereigns in congress are not my only enemies: the European oligarchies fear me, and they have enough representatives in Vienna. Castlereagh and Wellington will stir them up against me and they will come to a decision to make war, so we must prepare for this."

His Majesty took both these ministers in with him, and after leaving the table, addressed the matter of organizing a ministry. The prince arch-chancellor accepted the justice portfolio, which he had held during the Directory. The Duke of Gaëte (Gaudin),[222] Count Mollien,[223] and Duke Decrès[224] resumed respectively those of finance, the treasury, and the navy. The war portfolio was given to the Prince of

---

[222] M. M. C. Gaudin, Duke of Gaëte (1756-1841).

[223] François-Nicholas, Count Mollien (1758-1850).

[224] Admiral Duke Decrès (1761-1820).

Eckmühl (Davout),[225] whose patriotism and attachment to the Emperor, untiring zeal, and strict honesty were well known in the army. The Duke of Bassano (Maret) again became minister, secretary of state. The position of foreign relations minister remained vacant; a few days later it was given to the Duke of Vicenza (Caulaincourt),[226] who only accepted it to give the Emperor further proof of his devotion.

Count Carnot[227] received the interior portfolio, being proposed as the most able to reconcile the old patriotic party within the government. The Emperor knew his talents and his strength of character, and remembered his noble request to serve against the enemy in 1813, and the brilliant fashion in which he had defended Antwerp; he only regretted that he had been circumvented by a few schemers.

The Emperor was also being asked to appoint the Duke of Otranto (Fouché) minister of police; he knew this minister's taste for intrigue and his desire to get mixed up in everything, ready to jump at every chance, always sticking his foot into everyone else's shoes, said the Emperor. The Emperor showed a real aversion to using this minister, but the Duke of Bassano (Maret), the arch-chancellor, Counts de Lavalette[228] and Réal,[229] and even the Duke of Rovigo (Savary) agreed for various reasons to praise his behavior in 1814. For some it was an

---

[225]Marshal Davout, Duke of Auerstaedt, Prince of Eckmühl (1770-1823).

[226]Caulaincourt, Duke of Vicenza (1773-1827). Grand equerry. His duties brought him in constant contact with the Emperor, who trusted him entirely in spite of some friction. Napoleon gave him important diplomatic missions. He was ambassador to Saint Petersburg, then in 1814 was put in charge of Napoleon's interests at the Châtillon camp in connection with the Allies, after the capture of Paris. His *Mémoires* were prepared by Jean Hanoteau and published by Plon.

[227]Lazare Carnot (1753-1823), engineering officer, member of the Committee of Public Safety, in charge of military affairs. He earned the name "organizer of victory." Napoleon did not share his liberal ideas, and kept him in the background until 1814, when he put him in charge of defending Antwerp. Paying homage to his talents and great integrity, he made him minister of the interior during the Hundred Days.

[228]Count Antoine de Lavalette (1769-1830). Director of the imperial postal system. Sentenced to death during the second Restoration, he escaped from the Conciergerie prison thanks to the ingenuity of his wife, a niece of Empress Joséphine.

additional guarantee for Carnot's party; for others, it was because he had consistently opposed Louis XVIII's government. He had done this, it was said, without hesitation and without ulterior motives for the Emperor's return. In the opinion of these gentlemen, the Duke of Otranto had jeopardized his own safety. They won out over the Emperor's visible reluctance: he was put in charge of the police. It was only later the Emperor learned that this minister, hearing of his landing in France and arrival in Lyon, had hurried to orchestrate the uprising of the troops under the command of Count d'Erlon,[230] Lefebvre-Des-nouettes,[231] and the brothers Lallemand,[232] so as to be worthy of him and return to favor.

That same evening the Emperor deliberated whether he should start hostilities by marching on Brussels, surprising the coalition as he had surprised France, and taking advantage of the animosity of that country's inhabitants toward the British to drive them out of Belgium and conquer the banks of the Rhine before the Allies were in a position to oppose this. Some considerations stopped him, and His Majesty put off until two months later what he wanted to do immediately.

The Emperor returned to his quarters only between midnight and 1 a.m., and called for me. MM. Sénéchal, Pelard, and Hubert, his former valets (the last two had accompanied him to Elba), came in

---

[229]Count P. F. Réal (1757-1834). Prefect of police in the days of the Empire.

[230]J. B. Drouet d'Erlon (1765-1844). Supported the Empire, of which he was a distinguished soldier, and covered himself with glory at Waterloo. He became a marshal of France and governor general of Algeria.

[231]General Lefebvre-Desnouettes (1773-1822). Supported the Empire, and in spite of his brilliant conduct at Waterloo was sentenced to death in absentia, but managed to reach America. He died in a shipwreck.

[232]General C. F. A. Lallemand (1774-1839) was a brigadier general commanding the department of Aisne in March 1815. He along with his brother joined the Emperor's cause, was made a major general, and tried in vain to accompany the Emperor to Saint Helena. Condemned in absentia, he managed to flee to America, where he headed the chimerical Champ d'Asile. The July monarchy reinstated him in his rank and made him a peer of France.

with me. His Majesty greeted them with kindness; wishing to know about public opinion in Paris, he asked them various questions while undressing and then dismissed them, inviting them to let him know their needs. He kept M. Hubert to complete his personal staff, while the other two received posts as concierges to châteaux which they had asked for and which were vacant at the time. I waited for them to leave before submitting to His Majesty a petition by Roustam, his mameluke, that had been given me by his father-in-law Douvil, formerly a chamber usher for the King of Rome. No matter what I said to him regarding the inappropriateness of a request that was going to remind the Emperor of his son-in-law's behavior at Fontainebleau, he would not concede, and insisted so much that it be presented—saying that Roustam was counting on my not refusing him that favor—that I agreed to do it.

When I presented the petition to the Emperor, telling him from whom it came and the request that had been made of me to present it, he answered: "He's a coward! Throw it in the fire, and never mention him again." Constant had a better understanding of the enormity of his error, and too much good sense to attempt such a thing.

I told the Emperor how surprised I had been on my arrival to find all the personnel at their posts, even the gala staff in the drawing room, and that for my part, arriving from Elba, I had wondered if His Majesty wasn't just returning from a trip in France, as so little appeared to be changed. Each had returned in uniform and resumed his duties as if they were a personal right. A few had remained in the service of the king, a small number: they merely changed uniforms. One of these had remained as an office usher, and the Emperor said to him: "Well, Denis, you remained in the service of the king?"

"Yes, Sire, but in order to better serve Your Majesty!" That reply displeased the Emperor, and after the Hundred Days caused trouble for its author. It would be difficult to express the sensations felt by the various persons I encountered; it seemed to everyone that the Emperor's reign had not been interrupted at all, and satisfaction appeared on all faces. In talking to all with affectionate kindness, the Emperor was recapturing the influence he knew how to exert on all

who approached him. During the night of the 20th, the Elban grenadiers and the Corsican battalion arrived.

On the morning of the 21st, those who were in the habit of
being received by the Emperor were present when he arose. The first
to enter was the grand marshal. The Emperor, catching sight of him,
said: "Well, Bertrand, did you find your bed as comfortable at the
Tuileries as in Elba?"

"It is at least the best I have found since we left there." After a
few moments, the grand marshal told him that M. Fontaine was there.
He had him come in and, as he shaved, asked him various questions to
which the skillful architect replied. Taking advantage of a lull in the
conversation, he told him all that he found prestigious in his march
from Cannes to Paris, and that in his opinion that last feat surpassed all
others. The Emperor said: "You think so? Well, I have no other merit
than having accurately judged the state of affairs in France. As for my
secret of marching with the masses, had I wanted to drag two million
men along with me, I could have brought them right up to the Paris
walls; public opinion was the sole conspirator in my venture. Two men
helped me immensely along the way: La Bédoyère's great enthusiasm
in Grenoble, and Brayer's in Lyon. But at times such is the fate of man
that—had my decision to leave Elba not been crowned with success—
my venture would have been considered that of a madman."

M. Fontaine[233] spoke to the Emperor of the statue of Henri IV
on the Pont-Neuf terrace, saying that all of Paris had contributed by
subscription to the erection of that monument; the Emperor replied
that it was in a fine location, and nothing more. He talked about the
work ordered by the king's household, and said in speaking of
members of that family that besides Louis XVIII, the only man of
means was the Duke of Orléans. When M. Fontaine had left, I advised
the Emperor that his doctor, M. Foureau, and M. Yvan, his former
surgeon, were there. He told me to show the first in, but would not see

---

[233]Fontaine (1762-1853). Famous architect whose name is associated with that of Percier. Successive regimes put him in charge of various improvements in Paris and the
upkeep of the sovereigns' residences.

the second, as this man had left him unexpectedly at Fontainebleau. He never returned. M. Foureau continued to come each day while the Emperor was washing and dressing, as he used to do in Elba. When leaving his room, the Emperor asked him if Corvisart was in Paris: the famous doctor was not there.

That same day the Emperor reviewed the Paris garrison, as well as the Elban troops, all gathered in the Tuileries courtyard. He delivered a strong speech full of energy, beginning with these words:

Soldiers! I came to France with 600 men because I was counting on the love of the people and the memories of old soldiers! I was not disappointed in my expectation; soldiers, I thank you! The glory of what we have just done goes entirely to the people and to you, all I did was to know and appreciate you!

He ended the speech in this fashion:

Soldiers! Only the imperial throne can guarantee the people's rights, and above all the foremost of our interests—that of our glory. Soldiers! We shall march to drive from our territory the princes subservient to foreigners; the nation shall not only support us with its wishes, it shall follow our lead. The French people and I count on you. We don't wish to meddle in foreign nations' affairs, but woe to those who meddle in ours!

He then introduced to them General Cambronne and the guard officers who had accompanied him in Elba, and the former guard eagles appeared in the middle of the square. He then said:

Soldiers! They bring you their eagles. Let them be your rallying point: in giving them to the guard, I give them to the entire army! Treason and unfortunate circumstances had covered them with a funeral veil, but thanks to the French people and to you, they shall reappear shining in all their glory. Swear that they shall always be wherever the motherland's interests call them! May traitors and those who would invade our territory never be able to withstand their gaze!

"We so swear!" the soldiers replied with enthusiasm. They then paraded to cries of Vive l'Empereur! The Elban battalion, having arrived after covering 240 leagues in 20 days, was quartered in the Elbeuf barracks, on the Carrousel square; the following day these words were written over the door in large letters: "Lodging of the Brave." By chance I caught sight of this inscription and mentioned it to the Emperor as he was going to bed, not as something that could bring about dissension in the guard, but only as a flattering homage to that battalion. The next morning, I was surprised to hear the Emperor speak of it to Count Bertrand and tell him to have the inscription removed: since all the guard could not be quartered there, it was not just to say that. He added that the Elban battalion was only a deputation of the guard; all had offered to be part of it. There were therefore nothing but drawbacks and no advantages to leaving an inscription that might bring about discord. Nighttime was chosen for its disappearance.

The battalion grenadiers who manned the guard posts at the Tuileries during the night of the 20th to the 21st had been designated for such duty at Pont-sur-Yonne on the 19th at 8 p.m.; they covered 25 leagues in 24 hours and arrived at their post without having left anyone behind. All this battalion received the Legion of Honor; the Emperor gave each soldier an additional pension of 300 francs, and the officers who were already legionnaires advanced one rank in the order.

At the audience on Sunday, March 26, the Emperor received congratulations from the ministers of the council of State, the supreme court of appeals, the finance court, the imperial court, and other tribunals, and the ranking public servants. The speeches reflected the character of their writers and speakers; all spoke of liberty, and the independence and honor of the motherland. Count de Fermont's speech in the name of the council of State was a declaration of principles. The Emperor's replies were all contained in the one he had made to the prince arch-chancellor.

The sentiments you have expressed are my own. All for the nation, all for France, such is my motto. I and my family, whom this great people have ele-

vated to the throne of France and maintained there in spite of political upheavals, do not want, must not, and can never claim any other titles.

M. Poggi, present that same evening when the Emperor was retiring, told him that in all the speeches there was an almost deliberate intent to speak of liberty and constitution, as if asking for promises to be made in this regard. The Emperor replied:

The country is more eager for equality than for liberty; their concept of liberty is poorly digested, they forget that I love it as much as and more than they do. But one must not be facing 800,000 enemies who want none of it; I am above all, and more than they are, devoted to the salvation and welfare of France. I want equality for all in the means of succeeding; that is the ruling passion of the century, we must not crush it. As to liberty, if it comes about, it will be due to circumstances, and I won't be involved.

Every day since the Emperor had come to the Tuileries, the population, eager to see him, gathered in droves in the garden under his windows and never failed, whenever he showed himself, to welcome him with a cheer, the only one heard at that time, of Vive l'Empereur!

A few days hence, the Emperor went to the faubourg Saint-Antoine, where he was soon recognized and surrounded by a crowd that accompanied him to the Tuileries. Those in his party were separated from him, and were worried by this mass of people, from which a man with bad intentions could emerge. Only cries of love were heard.

During this period of the Hundred Days, the Emperor was overwhelmed with work, and yet nothing was put aside. He had Baron Fain and his former secretaries back in his cabinet, kept M. Rathery with him, and took in M. Fleury de Chaboulon. His Majesty did not sleep more than three hours at a time. He then went into his study, worked for a few hours, and got into a bath that was ready as soon as requested; the water was kept constantly hot. At 6 a.m., he had his shutters opened and called for his mail, opening it sitting in front of his fireplace wrapped in his robe, and remaining that way until he was ready to wash and dress. The interesting letters were set aside to be taken up later, the others were tossed on the carpet; these he called his "answered." He was also given newspapers which he perused, noting at times those where he found good articles, inquiring who had written them. After this first round of work, he would dress: this was the time when the grand marshal, his doctor, the architect, and his librarian M. Barbier would come in and receive their orders; he would then dismiss them and go into his study.

At one of these morning sessions, Dr. Foureau advised a little less work and more exercise. The Emperor replied: "There you are, doctor: you think I stand around as you do with both hands in my pockets; where do you expect me to find time to exercise?"

"But Sire, the Elysée-Bourbon would offer Your Majesty the opportunity for both work and a stroll in the gardens!"

"You're right, but I have no time to think about a trip. I was born and built for work, not to handle a pickax," he said, showing one of his hands: it was quite handsome, and he was at that moment tending to his nails with great care. "My body does not know any limit to work, my presence of mind after midnight is such that I can awaken instantly; I get up without anyone guessing from the condition of my eyes that I have just been sleeping, and my dictation has as much freshness of mind as at any given moment during the day. I have inside my head a drawer for each matter: when I am through with one, I open another, and they never get mixed up."

On April 8 when he awoke, the Emperor received from the Duke of Bassano (Maret) the important news of the Duke of Angoulême's capitulation, transmitted by telegraph. His Majesty decided it would be carried out, and sent the following letter to Marshal Grouchy:

Count Grouchy, the king's ordinance of March 6 and the declarations signed in Vienna on March 13 by his ministers would authorize me to treat the Duke of Angoulême just as this ordinance and declaration wanted me and my family to be treated. But consistent with the decision that led me to order that the Bourbon family be allowed to freely leave France, I intend that you give orders

for the Duke of Angoulême to be taken to Cette where he be put on board a ship.
You shall see to his safety and prevent any ill treatment of him. You shall only
see that the funds taken from public deposits are returned, and ask him to give
back the crown jewels which are the property of the nation. You shall also make
him aware of the laws of our national assemblies which have been re-confirmed,
and which apply to members of the Bourbon family who would enter French ter-
ritory.

You shall thank the national guard in my name for the patriotism and
zeal they have shown, and for the attachment to me that they have demonstrated
during these important events.

Having said this, I pray God, etc...

General Exelmans, whose mission it was to follow the king
and princes, had advised that the king and his family had left Lille to
go on to Ghent. Marshal Masséna had proclaimed the Empire in Toulon; all over France, the tricolor was flying.

In the midst of his many occupations, the Emperor did not forget the zeal and devotion of a few of his public servants in Elba. M.
Poggi de Talavo was foremost in his trust, which was all the more honorable for the magistrate as it was deserved. It was especially in the
evening when going to bed that the Emperor would receive him and
chat with him. It was through this magistrate that the Elbans and Corsicans had their requests for jobs and help submitted to the Emperor;
all received jobs, bonuses, or allowances. Paoli, Brignoli, and
Marcoggi shared in his generosity: For Brignoli's son I asked for
admission to boarding school, with a full scholarship and clothing
allowance, which the Emperor granted.

When M. Pons de l'Hérault, detained in the Château d'If by
Marshal Masséna, returned to Paris, to reward his zeal and devotion
the Emperor named him prefect of Lyon, with an allowance of 20,000
francs out of his purse; Baron Galeazzini received the prefecture of
Angers, with 10,000 francs from the purse. In addition, these gentlemen received their travel and relocation expenses. M. Poggi received a
temporary salary of 12,000 francs.

Two men whose distinguished services were recognized by the Emperor, General Baron Brayer and Colonel de La Bédoyère, were made counts and peers of France. The former received command of a young guard division, was made a chamberlain, governor of the Château of Versailles and the Trianon, and commander of the Lyon national guard; his pay amounted to 100,000 francs, to which the Emperor added an income of 6,000 francs drawn on the Orléans canal. The second was made a general, ADC to the Emperor. Both are mentioned in the Saint Helena will for 100,000 francs each.

Informed that a purge had just taken place in the palace of a few former servants who did not inspire enough trust for the job of porter of the inside stairs—because, it was said, they had remained in the service of Louis XVIII—I mentioned this to the Emperor. I told him that among them was the father of a man who had accompanied him to Elba; I had been told of this by him, and couldn't help being touched by the sorrow he felt over it. The Emperor was much upset that he should thus be ridiculed, and ordered that those employees be retained in their positions. Although all services had resumed just as if the Emperor had never left France, His Majesty wanted the chief servants on Elba to remain as such in Paris: thus Totin remained as first butler, Pierron head of the pantry, Chauvin head of the stables, and Archambault and Mathias in charge of the footmen.

A caricature insulting to Louis XVIII was brought to the Emperor's quarters without anyone knowing how it had gotten there; the person who had left it obviously had access there, but didn't boast of it. It was only that evening I learned it had been found by the Emperor on his mantelpiece, and he had tossed it into the fire after a scant look. The Emperor had been too much exploited for the past eleven months by the press and similar pictures not to know how little importance one should assign to such trash.

The haste with which the king had departed forced his staff to neglect some of his furniture and belongings. The furniture was sent back into storage; the prince's portfolio was still on his table, open letters in the drawers. The Emperor had a look at them, learning from them that many people who showed him a great deal of zeal had

shown no less for the Bourbons. It was of little interest for his purposes, but what will give a perfect understanding of the Emperor's
kindness is the fact that he revealed nothing of this, and continued to
consider as sincere the sentiments expressed to him. It was part of the
Emperor's wisdom and experience of men not to judge them too
severely, and to take into consideration the inconstancy of their
impressions and feelings. His Majesty had all these letters locked up in
the king's portfolio, and kept all the status reports or memoranda that
had been published in the past nine months. When he had a free
moment, the Emperor would glance through them: there were, he said
in Saint Helena, not mystical books as had been said, but more than
500 secret reports and major petitions.

Five boxes were also found inside the drawers of this table.
One of these, in malachite lined with gold, contained the portrait of
Madame de Savoie, wife of the prince; another, made of turtle shell,
showed a picture of a hunt at Fontainebleau, and on the other side a
map of that residence; the third, a landscape drawn in ivory on an
enameled gold box, was the work of Dieppe. The fourth, made of
black turtle shell, had on its lid a picture in ivory showing the queen,
Louis XVI, the dauphin and dauphine surrounded by angels; the fifth
was an enameled gold box containing a medal of the king, newly
minted, and a silver medal of Pius VII. The Emperor handed me these
snuffboxes, telling me to take good care of them; they went to Saint
Helena, and were returned to the imperial family after the King of
Rome's death.

M. de Blacas' correspondence and that found in the trunks in
the bodyguards' quarters were inspected by four commissioners from
the senior justice department, the police, and the ministry of the interior. The Emperor did not want the police alone to be in charge of this,
not wanting the signers of the letters to be exploited, and sensing they
might be.

In the same papers was a letter from a chambermaid of Princess Pauline's that seemed to have been written in a fit of temper: the
princess' habits were described, her dress, her wardrobe, all that could
concern a woman seeking to please. A guard artillery officer who had

obtained her favors was named. It also mentioned the Emperor, whose hands were handsome and well-kept. The incident was related of the time when, while supervising the furnishing of the princess' quarters, he had badly burned his fingers on a brazier without showing the slightest emotion, but finding an inkwell at hand, had dipped his fingers in it, then wrapped them in his handkerchief. That was true. Many other things were said also, but what was an atrocious libel and had been added in another handwriting was that the Emperor was sleeping with the princess, and in the same hand the words: to be printed.

M. de Talleyrand's assets had been sequestered. At his residence letters addressed to the Duchess of Angoulême were found, still sealed.

Prince Joseph, who lived in Switzerland, arrived in Paris as soon as he learned of the Emperor's arrival. Of all his brothers, this was the one the Emperor liked best. He had not left a good impression with the Parisians of his conduct in 1814. One day in Elba, the Emperor said of him to Count Bertrand that he had one of the more enlightened minds, honest hearts, and noble characters to grace a throne, but that nature had destined him to private life, as his virtues, education, and talents were much too refined for business matters. The prince was a living image of the Emperor, with finer features and a fresher face, perhaps too a narrower forehead. The interview was most touching in their hurry to fall into one another's arms when they first caught sight of each other. In Saint Helena the Emperor always spoke of this prince with a deeply felt affection.

Recognition of the Empire throughout all of southern France had put an end to the captivity of Countess Bertrand and a few wives of civil servants who had boarded the same vessel she had, and soon they arrived in Paris one after the other. Cipriani and Mme Bellini also arrived: the latter, wife of a Polish colonel attached to the army staff, had been on Princess Pauline's personal staff in Elba. Her husband had been ordered to return to his station, and she was alone in Paris. As she knew no one there, she wrote to me about her problems and told me of her needs. The Emperor had noticed her at the princess', and I mentioned her to His Majesty that same evening; he told me to remit to her

4,000 francs out of his purse, and to have her let me know if she was again in difficulty. She asked me to convey all her thanks to the Emperor. A few days later she received a dinner invitation, and was able to offer her thanks to His Majesty in person.

From all sides, speeches and proclamations by the troops and the generals were reaching the Emperor. Baron de La Bouillerie, former treasurer to the Emperor, asked to be allowed to justify his actions to His Majesty, who would not forgive him for having handed over his treasure to Orléans. The Emperor felt that if he received him, M. de La Bouillerie would easily convince him that his conduct had not been a matter of courage but all a matter of circumstances; and as it was his intention to keep M. Peyrusse, his treasurer in Elba in this post, he refused to see him. Marshal Augereau wrote him a private letter assuring him of his sincere devotion, denying he had ever betrayed him. Having read it, the Emperor threw it in the fireplace, no doubt recalling the marshal's lack of politeness during their meeting in the south on his way to Elba, and the infamous proclamation by which he insulted him in his misfortune, and which the Emperor only learned of later. This same marshal sent a letter to the 14th military division, which he commanded for the king, that was just as indecent toward the Bourbons. It was the time for regrets over errors committed.

The Emperor offered his regrets on the death of the prince of Neufchâtel (Berthier), who had fallen out a window at his Bamberg palace where he was staying. The prince had left him rather unexpectedly at Fontainebleau, promising to return, and had never reappeared. Was this death intentional or an accident? The first conclusion was that which prevailed among the public. The Emperor was assured of the contrary by the prince's butler, who was in Paris and whom the Emperor summoned in order to know the truth. Before this catastrophe, the Emperor had said jokingly: "What I wish to see is Berthier in his bodyguard uniform." The Emperor did not approve of the major general of the Grand Army donning the uniform of a captain in Louis XVIII's bodyguard; but had Berthier come to him, he would have welcomed him and opened his arms to him, offering his trust and restoring his rank of major general, for which he was so well suited, said the Emperor.

Since returning to Paris the Emperor had gone out on foot only twice, in the evening with the grand marshal, both in overcoats. His Majesty wore a green one with a round hat, and the grand marshal a blue one, also with a round hat. The two of them would stroll along the Paris boulevards and streets without being recognized. It would have been difficult to recognize the Emperor dressed this way. This exercise for his legs pleased him. It was during one of these walks that he stopped and told the grand marshal to have the Elysée-Bourbon prepared, for there he could at once take the exercise he needed without business matters suffering, as he could attend to them while walking in the gardens of that large and airy residence. The Emperor mentioned this to me that evening as he was retiring, saying that it would only take place after the review of the federated troops. I had received that day an invitation from Mlle Georges[234] of the Théâtre-Français, to go and see her. I told the Emperor I had gone, and she had told me of important papers she had in her possession, compromising the Duke of Otranto (Fouché) to the highest degree. I told the Emperor she assured me that all who were attached to His Majesty disliked seeing the trust he placed in this minister. The Emperor laughed and replied: "I have my eye on him! Did she not tell you she was having difficulties?"

"No, Sire, she only mentioned her desire to hand these papers over to Your Majesty in person."

"I know what it is, Caulaincourt mentioned it to me, and said she was experiencing some difficulties: give her 20,000 francs from my purse." A few days later he received from her the information she wished to hand over herself, and she was able to thank the Emperor for his generosity to her. The Emperor often came to the rescue of major artists in the capital, or even awarded them indemnities without their requesting it. Talma and some other artists were honored several times by his munificence. The Emperor liked the arts and sciences, but was

---

[234]Marguerite Joséphine Wemmer, known as Mlle Georges (1787-1867), an actress with the Théâtre-Français, with whom Napoleon had a famous affair.

too busy during the day to give any time to them. He had chosen lunchtime to receive distinguished artists and scientists, and he then talked with them of science or literature, which were of great interest to him. During the Hundred Days, at one of these luncheons he told Talma to whom he had shown some kindness: "Well, Talma, it was reported to me in Elba that you had taught me how to behave on the throne!" Talma replied, laughing: "Sire, it does the master too much honor, for assuredly Your Majesty behaves very well in that position, and people forget that I am the one coming here to profit from Your Majesty's comments." Isabey[235] was among the artists the Emperor rewarded; he and others had been received at Malmaison during the days of the Consulate. It is untrue that these artists allowed themselves the liberties in bad taste attributed to them, which later forced the Emperor to keep them at a distance. All of them recognized in the chief of state too high a position and mind to allow themselves liberties in speech or action. The times for their visits were changed, but the Emperor remained no less their protector; far from being kept away, Isabey became the drawing master of Empress Marie-Louise, and during the Hundred Days several received bonuses which I was charged with distributing.

During the first weeks after the Emperor's arrival in Paris, the apartments of the Empress and the King of Rome were opened, workmen were assigned there, and work continued. It was believed at first that the princess was about to arrive with her son, but soon the opposite became obvious, and it became known that we would have to face a formidable coalition being assembled against France, in which Austria was taking part. Even while dealing with the foreign powers, the Emperor was fully convinced he needed an outstanding victory in order to dissolve that coalition, so he neglected nothing at home or abroad to ensure its success. Special commissioners were sent out to the 23 military divisions. Military aides and generals were sent to all

---

[235] Jean-Baptiste Isabey (1767-1855). Painter of miniatures. Tradition has it that at the beginning of the Empire, he and Bonaparte studied at Malmaison the costumes for the coronation, using small models.

points of the kingdom, to inspect and strengthen the forts and the threatened locations, and to take advantage of the national spirit. The arms manufacturers and the Paris armorers were busy day and night manufacturing weapons.

In the face of such great danger, our most renowned citizens seemed to doubt success. Marshal Masséna said one day to Cipriani, who told me of it in Saint Helena: "Everything must be begun again, I can see but one way to escape this: as the sovereigns want no part of the Emperor, let him surrender his crown at the Champ de Mai; the war will become a national war. He is young enough to succeed in such a great venture, and to make the kings regret not having recognized that he alone can be mediator between the old and new ideas…" I replied: "But this would be a republic; it would no doubt make kings tremble, but could not this revolutionary hydra—cut down once by the Emperor—surface again? The Emperor's powerful hand could fail, bringing back the Jacobinism of '93 that all still remember. It is better to accept the sacrifice the Emperor has made of his person, and for us to share his Calvary."

Prior to leaving the Tuileries for the Elysée, the Emperor reviewed the federated troops. An awkward precaution had been taken: the Emperor was passing along the front row on horseback when he noticed some grenadiers running to follow him. He stopped immediately and angrily told them to go away, while he proceeded alone slowly among the federated troops. I was standing at one of the Tuileries windows. Hurt by a precaution offensive to the men being reviewed, I cannot say how happy I was to see the Emperor put an end to a proceeding that gave the impression he was suspicious. Cries of Vive l'Empereur! emanating from all ranks greeted his passage. He recognized among these a gunner who had served with him in Toulon, asked him about his assignment, and promised to look into it. The Emperor's enemies were circulating the most offensive rumors about this review; he said: "Let them talk, they are not decent people, but the sort we must endure." Others criticized the Emperor for stopping this popular movement, to which he replied: "The popular movement was not halted, it was normalized. It was just as large as between 1789 and

1792, but then we had three years to arm ourselves, and here we had but forty days; then we were attacked by an army of only 80,000 men, this time by 600,000 men. If in 1792 we had been attacked by as few as 300,000 men, Paris would have been captured, in spite of the nation's energy and the three years it had to get organized."

On May 21 the Emperor moved into the Elysée. It was there that Prince Lucien, whom the Emperor had not seen for many years, came and threw himself in his arms. His opinions had often been contrary to the Emperor's, but he admitted in truth that no heart ever beat more patriotically for France than that of his brother Napoleon. Power had been offered him by the Emperor during his stay in Italy. The prince always refused it, not only because he considered it a pitiful present, but because the offers were made under conditions that offended his domestic feelings. Faced with the Emperor's prestigious return, and the imminence of the danger which threatened France, he did not hesitate to come and offer his help to the Emperor. The arrival of the prince was a great joy for the Emperor's friends and the patriots. Time away from the motherland had modified his principles, he had come to appreciate the great character and leadership of the man he had left as head of the French Republic; and he became convinced that in ascending to the imperial throne, his brother had never for a moment ceased to be a patriot. In these difficult times, he brought the assistance of his popularity and his talent, so to speak. The meeting was most touching; all the past was forgotten in the embrace of the two brothers, joined by Prince Joseph, witness to this fraternal scene. The three spent an hour together; the Emperor summoned me and told me to bring his great sash of the Legion of Honor, which I brought on a silver platter. The Emperor took it and put it over the neck of the prince, who embraced him and thanked him, and a few moments later they parted. Prince Lucien, who had entered the room without any decoration, left it with the great sash. This insignia bore witness to all he met of the reconciliation that had just taken place, and the prince's modification of his principles. A staff was awaiting him at the Palais Royal where he then went; Count de Las Cases was part of it, and an entire household organization had been made available to him. This residence soon became a meeting place for literary figures, artists, and patriots: he spoke to each in his own language, reminding the most ardent of these friends what Jacobin democracy had been, and the setback it had caused the people's emancipation; in this moment of danger to France it was necessary to work together toward the constitutional order the Emperor wished to establish. The Emperor was pleased by this unexpected return of his brother.

The prince was taller than the Emperor whom he resembled very much, with less regular features. His smile seemed pleasant to me, and he appeared happy to be among his family.

The Emperor had placed in his drawing room the Fox bust sent to him by Lady Damer.[236] This lady received in exchange a snuffbox decorated with a portrait of the Emperor surrounded by diamonds.

One evening as he was retiring, the Emperor spoke to me of paintings he wished to commission—and that were ordered—of a few scenes that had occurred along his way: he mentioned the moment when he came up to the 5th line regiment; that when the Elban grenadier introduced his blind 90-year-old father and his young brother who wished to follow him; and that when Colonel de La Bédoyère presented him with his regiment's eagle that he had kept, which the Emperor grasped and kissed.

Since the Emperor's arrival in Paris, he had tried to win over men who, because of their social position and intellect, justly claimed to have influence on the opinions of the Paris salons. M. Benjamin Constant[237] was among and at the head of these, and the Emperor had long talks with him at the time of the Additional Act of the Empire, of which they were both proud. The Emperor said: "He was no longer the 20-year-old lover; his friend Mme de Staël no longer had the influence

---

[236]Lady Damer (1748-1828). Famous British sculptress. After the peace of Amiens, she had promised the First Consul a bust of Fox.

[237]Benjamin Constant de Rebecque (1767-1830). He is known to have been intimately connected with Mme de Staël, and as a result was suspect to the Emperor. But Napoleon appreciated the suppleness and elegant subtlety of his mind. It is said that it was he who in 1815 was charged with writing the *Additional Act to the imperial constitution*.

over him that forced me to banish both of them because of their prejudice in constantly opposing me."

On April 22, the Additional Act to the imperial constitution
was published; this declaration paralyzed the momentum that I had
noticed since my arrival. That day I saw men sincerely attached to the
Emperor speak to me of it with bitterness. Had the Emperor asked me
about the effect produced by this act as he sometimes did, I would
have told him; but that same evening he went to bed appearing preoccupied, and did not mention it to me.

During his stay at the Elysée, the Emperor would come and
attend mass at the Tuileries, receiving people afterwards and then
going back to his residence. It was during one of these trips back that I
told him Mme Pellapra[238] had notified me of her arrival in Paris.
Countess Walewska[239] was also there; the Emperor had learned this
through the Duke of Vicenza (Caulaincourt). She arrived from Naples;
the Emperor had not seen her since her visit to Elba. He sent me to
inquire how she was and tell her to come during the day with her son.
Mme Pellapra was then a ravishing beauty, and had been noticed by
the Emperor during a trip he made to Normandy in 1812. She was
staying with her family in Lyon when the Emperor arrived there on his
return from Elba; she shared in her heart and soul the excitement of the
Lyon population, and the Emperor sent me to her house. The lady had
been in Lyon for only a few days, and he had much to learn by talking
to her: the difficulty was to find an hour in the midst of all the bustle
around him and the orders he was sending out in all directions. He was

---

[238]Mme Pellapra, a handsome woman from Lyon. She had a daughter who became
Countess de Chimay. Princess Bibesco published the countess' correspondence and
memoirs, with a long introduction, in April 1950. Cf. Princess Bibesco, *A daughter of
Napoleon; memoirs of Emilie de Pellapra, comtesse de Brigode, princess de Chimay*
(New York, 1922)—*Lettres d'une fille de Napoléon (Fontainebleau et Windsor) 1853-
1859* (Paris, 1933). Cf. also the article by André Gavoty, in the *Bulletin de l'Institut
Napoléon*.

[239]Countess Walewska. Regarding the Emperor's last days spent in France and free at
Malmaison, from June 25 to 29, 1815, see Jean Bourguignon, *Les Adieux de Malmaison*, illustrated brochure (1947).

only able to grant her an audience at a late hour in the evening, business having prevented an earlier time. The Emperor's relations with Countess Walewska had preceded his marriage to Empress Marie-Louise, those with Mme Pellapra came after. If these affairs were rare in Empress Joséphine's time, they became more frequent during the second marriage. He concealed these affairs, saying that more than once he had avoided falling into traps set for him, knowing well that a precipice could be hidden under flowers.

It must be said that the Emperor was very much in love with - Empress Marie-Louise; the only reproach he made to that princess was not making enough effort to please the ladies of the court, who, accustomed to Joséphine's graciousness, noticed this difference. Perhaps they forgot that, born to the throne, used to homage and respect, she didn't feel obligated to please them, and the natural shyness she showed in public was taken for aloofness. She had a great deal of affection for her lady-in-waiting the Duchess of Montebello, but showed only kindness toward the others. The Emperor attributed to her all the qualities that would make her loved: he said she was kind, gentle, affable, and even playful in her normal relations. Here is the opinion of Queen Caroline, sister of the Emperor. This princess' judgment will not come under suspicion: she did not much like either of her sisters-in-law Empresses Joséphine or Marie-Louise. When she was in Paris in 1838, she had her lady companion write to me: "Today, May 5, the anniversary of the Emperor's death, the queen wishes to spend the evening and have dinner at home; she is inviting you, Mme Marchand, and your daughter to come dine with her. M. Méneval will be there also." The conversation was entirely devoted to memories of the Empire. She told us the advantage Joséphine had over Marie-Louise was in understanding the French mind, and having been able to make good use of this in the Emperor's interest. She was infinitely kind, and Marie-Louise not less so, but people talked less about it. The aim of one of them was to achieve the maximum impact, whereas the other, who was opposed to any form of affectation, did not strive for this. Being nineteen years old, she had a charming figure, her bearing was full of dignity, freshness—perhaps too much; she had charming blond hair, and hands and feet leaving nothing to be desired. She was cultured, and from Braunau to Compiègne she responded to all speeches addressed to her with a facility and ease that attested to this. The word "ninny"[240] she was said to have used as a compliment when addressing the prince arch-chancellor is entirely a lie: she was too familiar with the French language not to know the meaning of the expressions she used. The queen (Caroline), who had been named superintendent of the Empress' household and sent by the Emperor to greet her, said that the princess had been most gracious toward everyone; she did not part from the people who had accompanied her from Vienna without some emotion, which did honor to her kind heart, but she did so with courage. During the journey she covered only small distances each day and was greeted with receptions wherever she went. Every morning when she arose there was a letter from the Emperor, brought from Paris by a page who would return with the reply.

She told us that the Emperor was very anxious to meet her, and several times cursed the ceremonies and feasts that delayed this meeting which occurred only in Soissons, where a camp had been set up to receive the princess. But the Emperor was growing impatient, and proceeded there one day before the Empress. When he learned she was only ten leagues away, he left along with the king of Naples to go meet her. The Emperor often said that when the two carriages met, he jumped out of his and into hers, and the princess' first words after a moment of silence had been that the portrait brought her by the Prince of Neufchâtel was not very flattering. The Emperor had been enthusiastic about this flattery, and asked her what advice she had received when coming to meet him; she replied: "To obey you in all matters." After stopping a few moments in Soissons, Their Majesties, accompanied by the king and queen of Naples, arrived in Compiègne. The Emperor, whose appearance was always very neat, had taken even greater care than usual to appear to his best advantage.

---

[240]"Ganache" in French.—Ed.

At one of his morning receptions at the Elysée, I informed the Emperor that M. Corvisart, back in Paris, was in the next room with Dr. Foureau. The Emperor had him come in; not seeing him dressed as head doctor, he said to him: "Ah, Corvisart, you're wearing the garb of the Institute?"

"Sire, I have retired, but remain always available to Your Majesty." The Emperor complimented him on his student Dr. Foureau, whom he said he believed to be as enlightened as he was modest. Then a moment later he said to him purposefully that he had seemed in a great hurry to leave the Empress in Vienna in spite of her health requiring his care, since he had prescribed her taking the waters in Aix rather than facing the climate in Elba that could have harmed her. M. Corvisart, slightly embarrassed, replied that indeed he had recommended taking those waters so that if she went to Elba, the Empress would arrive there in better health. The Emperor talked about one thing and another with him, and as he was ready to go into his study, M. Corvisart asked permission to present his nephew, his former page, now a captain in the cuirassiers. The Emperor had him come in, and M. Corvisart said in introducing him: "Sire, this is the stuff majors are made of."

"I shall give him the opportunity to become one," replied the Emperor, after speaking kindly and encouragingly to the young officer.

The Emperor was impatiently awaiting the arrival of M. Ballouhey, former superintendent to Empress Joséphine, whom the Emperor had assigned to Empress Marie-Louise because of his strict honesty. He knew he had had to leave Vienna, stop in Munich to see Prince Eugène, and return to France via Belfort; orders had been given so that the telegraph in that city would inform Paris of his arrival there. Having been so advised, the Emperor calculated how much time it would take to travel from Belfort to Paris, and had a sentry posted at his house so that he would come immediately to the Elysée as soon as he arrived, no matter what the time or his travel clothing. On April 28 M. Ballouhey arrived in Paris; he came immediately to see the Emperor, who kept him almost two hours. The Emperor had a great deal to learn from him about what was happening in Vienna, and all that Prince Eugène had passed on to him on the subject was of the utmost interest to him. He learned about M. de Talleyrand's activities with regard to the March 13 declaration, and the commitments he had made with the coalition; he again was told that had his departure from Elba been delayed by a few days, the sovereigns would have already departed for their realms, M. de Talleyrand would not have obtained the March 13 declaration, and His Majesty's landing would have had maximum impact. Prince Eugène informed him that the Allied forces could not enter France before July; the Emperor then said to M. Ballouhey, with a look of great satisfaction: "Then I don't give a damn about them, my affairs will have been settled by then." The prince also advised him to arrange to make the war a national issue as much as possible, at a time when he would have all Europe stirred up against him, and to beware of the Duke of Otranto (Fouché) who was already plotting in Vienna. He informed him of the names of a few generals and colonels whom he should not trust, and gave him details on invading enemy forces and the points that appeared most likely to be attacked. M. Ballouhey brought all these details committed to memory, and many things might have escaped him, so the Emperor said to him: "Go get some rest, and tomorrow bring back to me our conversation of today in writing." As he left, M. Ballouhey reiterated his fears about the Duke of Otranto Fouché); the Emperor said he had him under surveillance, and would already have had him arrested and his papers seized, but was delaying until the return of an agent he had in Basel, as that minister's disgrace could undermine his mission.

The Emperor learned many particulars about the people who were close to Empress Marie-Louise and her entourage. Twelve days later, in early May, his former secretary Baron de Méneval, now on the Empress' staff, confirmed to him what M. Ballouhey had said; the Emperor had a meeting with him also lasting several hours, and told him to come and see him every day at his levée. He handed me a letter from my mother expressing her fears that the Emperor might not succeed in withstanding the formidable coalition that was forming with Emperor Alexander as its head. Nothing in all this news gave any indication that Marie-Louise, in this gathering of kings, was putting forth her rights as wife and mother to turn aside the storm that was gathering against France and the Emperor. Was this princess already unworthy of the great name of Napoleon, as she was later?

The Emperor's fears regarding the king of Naples were unfortunately justified, in spite of His Majesty's wish expressed prior to leaving Elba that he should not quit his kingdom; no sooner had he learned of the Emperor's entrance into Paris than he decided on his own to advance into Italy. Did he fear the Emperor's resentment, did he wish to undo the immense harm he had done to France in 1814 by separating his interests from those of the Emperor? Be that as it may, he marched into Italy calling for independence, at the head of 80,000 men; he had no doubt he could instill into his soldiers' souls the fiery courage that filled his own. He was mistaken. At first he had success against troops taken by surprise, but soon afterward, this fine and brilliant army was beaten on May 2 and 3, near Ancona, and was never able to rally again. The Emperor was extremely upset by his brother-in-law's invasion; he sensed all the advantages the coalition against him could derive from it. Had this army, that a single month was enough to destroy, remained on the defensive as the Emperor had recommended to its leader, while commanded by a man as brave as Murat, it could have brought pressure to bear on Austria, saved its power for the Emperor's interests, or at least weighed heavily in the ensuing negotiations. Instead, Austria refused to believe the sincerity of the Emperor's promises regarding Italy, thought he was deceiving it, and from that premise decided to crush him with all the power of its monarchy.

After his failure, King Murat had sailed to seek refuge in France, and the Emperor learned of his landing in Golfe Juan with Madame Mère, Cardinal Fesch, and Prince Jérôme. The unfortunate prince remained hidden along the coast of Provence. War was imminent; he let the Emperor know of his desire to serve in the French army as a general, but France could still remember the treaty of Naples and the declaration of war by this king or viceroy of Italy, at a time when all the powers were against her. The Emperor did not accept. Had he arrived in person on the eve of battle, the Emperor could have opened his arms to him and afforded him the opportunity to right his wrongs. France, being generous, would have forgotten the king of Naples' error, remembering only the glory of one of her children on twenty battlefields, ready again to shed his blood for her. It was, I believe, about such conditions that the Emperor added in Saint Helena: "I would have entrusted him with the command of my cavalry; it would have achieved marvels under his command." All know the tragic end of this brave and unfortunate prince. The Emperor in Saint Helena felt that the Calabrians had been less cruel towards Murat than the British government was being toward him.

The Emperor, satisfied with the actions and conduct of General Grouchy in Lyon and the confidence he had inspired, made him a marshal.

It was said before and during the Hundred Days that the Emperor continued to mistrust the great lords of old, who were said to have betrayed him. The Emperor responded to that criticism in Saint Helena, saying that the great lords of old under Napoleon were Frenchmen like anyone else, and those who were devoted to him had behaved well. He cited Choiseul-Praslin, Montesquiou, Beauvau, Ségur, and others. He said: "I brought former noblemen into my army, and even exiles, without it ever being the worse for it, and why? Because it was known that in the army everything is granted on the basis of merit; it is not enough to be a great lord, one has to be brave— and in this respect, the old nobility was no less so than the new. What had I to fear from them, had I not stricken them all from the list of exiles?"

As soon as the Emperor heard of Madame's arrival in Paris, he got into his carriage and went to her house, where his brothers had gathered. It had been a long time since Madame's heart had throbbed with happiness as great as during this family reunion. Princess Pauline, too ill to undertake this voyage, had remained in Italy.

On June 1 the Emperor opened the Champ de Mai, his three brothers with him, in imperial dress just as he was. It was both a patriotic and a religious celebration. The Emperor was in a good mood; he had gone from the Elysée to the Tuileries for this solemn affair, to don there the garb in which he was to appear in public. Count de Montesquiou in full costume presided over the dressing, and the Emperor had the goodness to praise me to him in the most flattering terms. Once the Emperor was dressed, Count de Montesquiou put around his neck the collar of the order of the Legion of Honor, and fastened on his sword.

The weather, undecided in the morning, turned fair, and the Emperor left the Tuileries to the sound of artillery, to proceed to the École Militaire. I was already there when he arrived; a throne had been erected in front of the building. A semicircular wall had been built in front of this throne, forming an immense hall with the sky as its ceiling. There were rows above which the names of the department were written, showing the deputies where each was to go, and many tiers of seats had been reserved for the public, where a large number of women in brilliant apparel could be seen. After a speech to the deputies, greeted with cries of Vive l'Empereur!, he climbed down from the throne with his brothers, surrounded by his senior officers, and proceeded to the center of the Champ de Mai. An altar had been prepared there at the top of many steps, where it could be easily seen. After offering thanks, the Emperor, his hand on the Gospel, took an oath of fidelity to the imperial constitution. He distributed eagles to the national guard and the imperial guard, who swore to defend. There were deputations from all the army regiments gathered together on the Champ de Mars. When they returned with their eagles to their brothers-in-arms, all were able to confirm the magical influence the Emperor exercised over the masses: all spirits were electrified and cries of Vive l'Empereur! were heard coming from the troop deputies and the huge crowd. The same spirit was present as that of 1790 that led the nation to such great results.

After the parade of troops, the Emperor went to the Tuileries to the sound of artillery. That evening he returned to the Elysée, tired but happy in the enthusiasm he had inspired. There were huge banquets where the army and the national guard fraternized.

The Emperor's life during the period of the Hundred Days was most active, and not, as some claimed, given over to slumber by reason of his corpulence. But a change had occurred in society: it was easy for him to see that men were less docile than before.

The words of some people I met surprised me, and I noticed with sorrow that they were no longer as confident as in the past; I was chagrined by this. However, we were approaching the time to launch our campaign, and I said to myself that if the Emperor emerged victorious from this struggle that was about to begin, those people would change their tune.

After a period of incredible activity, backed by the nation, the Emperor had put it in a state of defense; he was leaving behind him a few seeds of dissent, but counted on a victory to dispel them.

The chambers convened on June 8; on the 11th, the Emperor received a deputation from the chamber of deputies at the Elysée. These deputies thanked the Emperor for relinquishing the extraordinary powers he held, in order to proclaim the beginning of a constitutional monarchy; they assured him of the chamber's cooperation in the defense of national independence, and promised him to actively support the constitution. The royal charter, not having been approved by the people, could not be considered an obligation by the nation.

Regaining that day full exercise of its rights, rallying around the hero to whom its faith again entrusted the state government, France was surprised and saddened to see armed sovereigns asking it for justification of an internal change which was the result of national will and threatened neither existing relations with other governments nor their safety. France could not accept the conditions with which the Allied nations were trying to veil their aggression. To attack the monarch of its choice was to attack the independence of the nation. It was fully armed to defend this independence and to repel, without exception, any family or any prince they would dare impose on it. The Emperor replied:

Monsieur Le Président and deputies of the chamber, I find with satisfaction my own sentiments in those you have just expressed. In these grave circumstances, my thoughts are absorbed by the imminent war, to whose success are tied the independence and honor of France.

I shall leave tonight to place myself at the head of my armies: the movements of the various foreign enemy corps make my presence there indispensable. During my absence, I would be pleased to see a commission named by each chamber to reflect on our constitution. It is our rallying point, and must be our North Star in these stormy times. Any political discussion that would tend to directly or indirectly diminish the necessary trust in its measures would be unfortunate for the state; we would find ourselves navigating among shoals without compass or rudder. Our present crisis is a major one; let us not follow the example of the Lower Empire which, pressed on all sides by barbarians, made itself the laughingstock of posterity by concerning itself with abstract concepts at the very moment when battering rams were breaking down the city gates.

Independent from the legislative measures that internal circumstances necessitate, you may find it useful to concern yourselves with laws instrumental to the upholding of the constitution. These can be the subject of public work, without any inconvenience.

Monsieur Le Président and deputies of the chamber, the sentiments expressed in your speech show me sufficiently the attachment of the chamber to my person, and all the patriotism that moves it. In all my undertakings, my step shall always be straight and firm. Help me to save the motherland. As the last representative of the people, I have contracted the obligation that I now renew, to use in quieter times all the crown's prerogatives and the little experience I have acquired to help you improve our institutions.

That same night at 10 p.m. the Emperor went home accompanied by Prince Joseph, who handed him a large quantity of diamonds—I learned later they amounted to 800,000 francs. They were each wrapped separately. Giving these to me, the Emperor told me to lock them in the secret compartment of his traveling kit along with Princess Pauline's necklace, estimated at 300,000 francs. This kit had its place in the Emperor's carriage. He also handed me two thick packages sealed with his crest, telling me to take one to Countess Walewska and the other to Mme Pellapra. I returned to the Elysée only at 1 a.m. During the day, the Emperor had been kind enough to grant my father a position as state messenger, vacant through the death of one of these, and told me to have the decree to that effect prepared by the Duke of Bassano (Maret). The unfortunate events of Waterloo prevented the execution of that decree.

On the 12th at 4 a.m., the Emperor left to rejoin the army (taking with him his ADCs, military aides, and two pages, MM. Gaudin and de Cambacérès). He left a regency council composed of Prince Joseph as president, Prince Lucien, the eight ministers with portfolios, and four ministers of state, all of whom were to decide by majority vote; in the event of a tie, the president's vote would decide.

On leaving Paris, the Emperor visited the fortifications in Soissons and slept in Laon. On the 13th he arrived in Avesnes, where all the troops were concentrated, and on the 14th reminded them in a proclamation that the anniversary of Marengo and Friedland had twice decided the destiny of Europe. The Emperor, who had given a command to General Bourmont only at the request of General Gérard, soon learned that this general, followed by Colonel Clouet Villoutreys Dubareuil and two general staff officers, had gone over to the enemy; he knew his battle plan and was able to apprise the enemy of it. He immediately made changes in his plan of attack. On the 15th, the French army crossed the Sambre at Charleroi, encountered some light troops on the other side, and crushed them, taking prisoners. At 10 a.m., the Emperor entered Charleroi and the army took up position before that city on the road to Fleurus. An enemy division of some eight to ten thousand men straddling this road was pushed back, the infantry overwhelmed by the cavalry, but France lost General Letort. That evening when the Emperor returned to his headquarters, he was thoughtful and troubled by the death of his ADC, saying not a word while undressing. He gave orders for the army divisions to enter the plain of Fleurus that had been distinguished 20 years earlier by the finest military feats of the French army. On the 16th the enemy army, arranged in the shape of an amphitheater on a hillside behind the villages of Saint-Amand and Ligny, was ready for battle. At noon it began with the greatest enthusiasm. The leaders' fervor and the soldiers' valor triumphed over the energetic resistance offered, and they remained masters of the battlefield. Such a fine beginning to a campaign led to the greatest hopes. The next day when I crossed the battlefield, I saw what the horrors of war had brought about: it was covered with the dead and wounded, the latter being tended by medical officers left there for that purpose.

The enemy army, split in two, took off in two directions. On the 17th, the Emperor pursued the British heading for Brussels, and slept in Plancenoit at a small farm where he established his headquarters, while Marshal Grouchy, at the head of an army corps of 40,000 men, followed the Prussians toward the Meuse. The Emperor said he could have hoped for more from the brilliant success he had just achieved, and the outcome of the battle could have been decided had Marshal Ney carried out his orders by bearing on the rear of the enemy army. Saint-Denis told me that during the most intense moment of the Ligny battle, hearing laughter behind him, the Emperor turned around sharply and said to the young military aide who had attracted his attention: "Be a little more serious, sir, when faced with all these brave men killing each other."

I arrived at headquarters much later than the Emperor; my carriage had overturned in a stream, and it had taken several hours to get it out. Night had fallen, it was very dark, and heavy rain made the roads difficult to manage. We went past headquarters and the coachman drove me to the main guard post, where I was stopped. I turned back and finally arrived at the Caillou farmhouse; the Emperor had gone to bed an hour before, telling Saint-Denis of his astonishment at my not having arrived. I had been there barely two hours when he called me and asked what the weather was like: I told him of the accident that had delayed me, the poor condition of the roads, and the rain that continued to fall. At 3 a.m. he summoned his senior military aide, Colonel Gourgaud, telling him to go reconnoiter the terrain and see if the artillery could maneuver; his impatience to attack was visible. The enemy had remained in position before the Soignes forest. It had been believed the previous night that it had taken up that position only to give its convoys time to cross the forest. Supplies had not arrived, the weather had been awful all night, and several days' march, a great battle, and other combats had tired the troops; they needed to see the sun at daybreak to dry out and recover from the night's fatigue. Colonel

Drouot reported the roads were so damaged and the ground so wet that he didn't believe the artillery could maneuver until things dried out a little. After this report, the Emperor remained in bed but arose early, pleased to see the weather clearing. He was quartered in a small square room, the furniture that had been there having been tossed into the courtyard, and it served as bedroom, study, and dining room. He paced back and forth in that room a long time, hands behind his back; then he took a pair of scissors and ran them around his nails, appearing much more concerned with the battle that was about to begin than with this detail of his appearance. He often went to the window and looked at the skies; once he had shaved, he dressed and summoned General Gourgaud, who wrote under his dictation.

At 9 a.m. the Emperor asked for his breakfast, which he shared with Prince Jérôme, General Reille who commanded the 2nd corps under the prince, and a few other generals who were invited. The Emperor said to them cheerfully as he got up from the table: "Gentlemen, if my orders are carried out well, we shall sleep in Brussels tonight." He told Saint-Denis to bring his horses and mounted, followed by his general staff. The Emperor's arrival was greeted all along the line by a thousand cries of Vive l'Empereur!, cries of love if ever they were. When the Emperor felt the ground had sufficiently dried to permit maneuvering, he ordered the 2nd corps to attack the Hougoumont woods located before the enemy's right. At noon, Prince Jérôme's division moved forward to take it, was driven back, and regrouped for a second attack: the prince was able to take it only after a very stubborn battle, in which he was wounded. At the same time this attack was going on, the 1st corps moved into the houses of Mont-Saint-Jean while approaching the enemy's position. The British, left to themselves, seemed to me unable to hold out against the combined efforts of the French army; the Emperor was waiting for an opportune moment. I returned to headquarters sure that a great battle was about to be won, when around 5 p.m. Noverraz came to tell me that a Prussian corps had joined the British, General Lobau's division was facing it, and the battle raged on. I was worried in spite of myself by the enemy's persistence, and became more so when Saint-Denis came gal-

loping in to fetch something for the Emperor, saying to me in great
haste: "Things are going badly. We just saw masses of troops in the
distance: we first thought it was Marshal Grouchy, and a joyful cry
went up; but it is Marshal Blücher's corps, and we have no news of
Marshal Grouchy. The Emperor cannot understand why he did not
arrive at the same time." And he left at a gallop. It was then 7 p.m. I
was reflecting sadly: General Bülow had already added his numerical
force to the British army. The Emperor had shown no anxiety over it,
since he had dispatched a courier to Paris to announce that the battle
had been won. But the arrival of Marshal Blücher's army increased
this numerical strength excessively against a tired army; it could
change a day that was to raise the French army's glory to new heights
into a day of sorrow, if Marshal Grouchy did not arrive.

I mentioned my fears to General Fouler, the Emperor's
equerry, who told me that we should take great care to show nothing,
adding that it was against his advice that the equipment train was
located so close to the battlefield, but since it was there, nothing short
of an order from the Emperor would make it withdraw. About an hour
went by, and the noise of the artillery and rifle fire seemed to be coming appreciably closer to us. Night had not yet fallen when we saw the
road filled with artillery trains and wounded soldiers being held up by
men who were not; this retreat was taking on an alarming character. I
had the Emperor's bed placed temporarily in its case, shut the travel
kit, and readied myself for any eventuality. The Emperor's carriage
was on the battlefield; this did not worry me in spite of its containing a
large sum of gold, Princess Pauline's necklace, and the diamonds
added by Prince Joseph the night of the departure from Paris. Believing that the carriage could always make it through, I even congratulated myself on not having all these valuables with me: I was already
quite encumbered by those I had in gold, amounting to 100,000 francs,
and 300,000 in banknotes which I kept locked up in the large travel kit
that fitted in my carriage. Soon we no longer heard the gunfire
approaching; but someone came to ask the officer and the men
assigned to guarding the carriages to move into the nearby woods and

prevent the enemy from entering it, to give time for them to be moved away.

Fate had just turned the outcome of the battle against us. The best plan devised to vanquish and destroy the enemy's hopes, to bring him to peace, was overturned by the nonexecution of the Emperor's orders to one of his lieutenants, Marshal Grouchy. Had he forced the enemy at swordpoint as he had been told to do, he would have arrived on the battlefield at the same time, to take part in victory rather than bringing about the army's defeat. Fate had it that the guard was engaged in battle at the moment Marshal Blücher's corps arrived, as were the service squadrons that were never deployed except by order of the Emperor. Thus at the most critical moment the Emperor no longer had under hand the reserve that he so brilliantly utilized at a given moment to recapture a victory that might elude him. General Fouler, hearing the gunfire in the woods getting closer to the carriages, had taken it upon himself to order them pulled back; it was already a little late in view of the congestion along the road. I had the Emperor's bed placed on a mule and the travel kit put in my carriage; it was hitched to a powerful team and was soon pulled out from where it had been parked, but once on the road had to travel like everything else. I nonetheless thought it was saved until arriving at the Quatre-Bras intersection where the congestion became such that it couldn't get through. I wanted to see what was causing this problem: an accursed mortar blocked the way and was stopping all that arrived, which meant that in an instant a mass of carriages were across the highway and prevented passage. The enemy, also stopped, was looting the last cars, and mine was about to fall prey. At once I opened the travel kit, grabbed the 300,000 francs in banknotes, placed these on my chest, buttoned up my uniform over them, and abandoned the rest. With much difficulty I managed to go from one carriage to another and emerge from the bottleneck in which I was caught. The Duke of Bassano (Maret) and Baron Fain took off on foot, their carriages remaining in the middle of this mess; like me, they were without news of the Emperor, whom some said had been killed and others, that he wished to sleep on the battlefield. How could we believe any of them, considering the disorder in which they were retreating? I was unsure, and waited until I saw the guard that was following the movement, but in somewhat better order. I asked several officers if they knew the route taken by the Emperor: none of them could tell me. I therefore set off with them; the cannon had long ago become silent. This guard so brilliant the day before, so enthusiastic that very morning, was now hurrying along the road, bleak and silent. Full of worry, I followed it and marched all night and all the next day. Passing through Beaumont and Charleroi, I arrived at nightfall in Avesnes: its gates were closed. I learned that Prince Jérôme, wounded, was inside, as were the Emperor's horses. I spent the night at a dragoon bivouac, moving up close to one of the fires; luck would have it that I recognized an old comrade among the officers, who offered to share with me a piece of bread he was eating. I thanked him, and we chatted about our misfortunes and our fear that our unfortunate motherland would once more be exposed to the ravages of foreigners.

I thus waited for the Avesnes gates to open, and before long saw the service horses coming out, led by Amodru, the Elban groom. I ran up to him and asked: "What happened to the Emperor?" "I don't know," he replied with tears in his eyes. I got on one of the horses and rode to Laon, sad and worried at not knowing what route the Emperor had taken. Once there, I dropped down on some straw to get a little rest. I hardly had stretched out when I was told the Emperor was at the post house in town. My fatigue vanished instantly. The Emperor was alive! France could still be saved, the army might perhaps rally near this city. I ran to the post house; the first person I saw was Saint-Denis, who told me the Emperor's carriage had been captured along with all that was in it. The loss of the battle had been too much on my mind for that of the diamonds and money to make much of an impression; I was sorry only about the loss of Princess Pauline's necklace, which had been moistened by her tears, and her words "The Emperor may need this" came back to me and made me sad. I went in to the Emperor. Count Bertrand was with him, both were very calm, but appeared absolutely exhausted. I told him how my carriage had been seized at the Quatre-Bras intersection, and how I had only been able to save the banknotes that were in it, having come from there on foot all the way to Avesnes; and that I was deeply saddened to learn that His Majesty's carriage and the valuables it contained had been seized. "It's a misfortune," he replied and went on enumerating the resources left to France if he was backed by the chambers: the equipment lost as well as the supplies would easily be replaced, and by rallying the army in Laon the enemy could be contained, giving the nation time to pull itself together. Having heard only bits and pieces of the Emperor's conversation, I recall this spoken to General Bertrand as I came out: "If I return to Paris and dip my hand in blood, I will have to plunge it in all the way to the elbow." The name of Fouché was then brought up, and seemed to be a target for his vengeance. When he left the Waterloo battlefield, the Emperor had proceeded to Philippeville, where he arrived with a handful of cavalrymen from all units, and there he found the Duke of Bassano (Maret) and a few officers of his staff. After spending the night sending out staff orders, he wrote to Prince Joseph and headed for Laon, along with Grand Marshal Bertrand, the Duke of Bassano, his ADCs Generals Flahaut and La Bédoyère, and M. Gaudin, his page. Another page, M. de Cambacérès, had been taken prisoner the day before.

As the Emperor wished the chambers and the country to know the whole truth about the situation, he prepared the battle report and sent it to Paris by courier. If in rallying his army near Laon the Emperor had intended to stay there, it was doubtless only for a moment: for he ordered me to take a stagecoach and go to the Elysée, where he intended to be the next day. I preceded him by only a few hours. His friends, fearing for his safety, saw danger in a decision that would place him in the midst of factions where passions were brewing, and thought he was in a much stronger position at the head of the army than he could possibly be in Paris. The Emperor, solely concerned with saving the country and not his person, felt that a rapid and truthful account of events would awaken the patriotic sentiments of the representatives, and that with him there the chambers would not despair of the salvation of the motherland. Backed by them, the nation would rise as a man and the Emperor would restore good fortune to our flag.

Imbued by this feeling of love for the country, he feared losing neither his throne nor his life. The nation and the army did not fail him, but the chambers failed the country.

On June 21, the Emperor arrived at the Elysée at 5:30 a.m. He was greeted on the steps by the Duke of Vicenza (Caulaincourt) to whom he could pour out the sorrow in his heart and the intensity of his spirit. He summoned Count de Lavalette, who arrived promptly. The Emperor had not removed his boots since the battle, and the officers accompanying him, as well as he, were exhausted. I asked if His Majesty wished to have a bath prepared, and he said he needed one to refresh himself. Paris, which had fallen asleep in the enthusiasm of the victory at Ligny, could not understand this unexpected return of the Emperor. The word treason was beginning to be repeated from mouth to mouth when the Waterloo bulletin arrived, telling of our misfortunes and our alternatives. The bulletin, once known in Paris, caused agitation, and the passions which the Emperor was sure to extinguish with a victory released their full fury against him on his return.

Once the bath was ready, the Emperor entered it. The Duke of Vicenza (Caulaincourt) and Count de Lavalette accompanied him to the bathroom. As he was getting in, the Emperor told the Duke of Vicenza to assemble the council of ministers, and sent reprimands to Marshals Ney and Grouchy for not carrying out the orders they must have received. He said: "What a strange destiny, where three times I saw France's assured triumph slip through my hands: but for a traitor's desertion, I would have annihilated the enemy at the outset of the campaign, crushed it at Ligny if the left flank had done its duty, and crushed it at Waterloo if the right flank had not failed in its duty. Well, all is not lost. After great feats of valor, panic seized the army. I am going to present to the chambers an accurate account of what happened, and I hope that the presence of the enemy on French soil will restore the deputies' sense of duty, and that my honesty will rally them around me." At the first rumor of the Emperor's arrival, Baron de Méneval had rushed to the Elysée; he was shown in to the Emperor as he was about to return to his bedroom. I thought the Emperor was going to go to bed for a moment, as he habitually did, but he said he was going to dress and shave. At the same instant Princes Joseph and Lucien were shown in, and he talked to them about the preceding events. Prince Lucien told him that as soon as our misfortunes were known, people became agitated, and that the worst could be expected from the deputies' deliberation, because of the ill will of a few members. The Emperor replied: "You must count La Fayette among those: he will not fail to stir up people against me. They imagine that the Allies are only after me personally, and do not see that in parting with me they will lose France."

The Emperor was informed that the council of ministers had assembled. The Emperor went in, followed by Princes Joseph and Lucien. I have been told it was easy to see on the faces of a few ministers the consternation, fear, and discouragement of this council where such important matters were being debated. There was mention of an abdication in favor of the King of Rome. Wanting above all to save France, and learning of the state of insurrection in the chamber, the Emperor allowed the possibility that he would agree to this; but still confident in the patriotism of many of its members, he sent out as representatives Prince Lucien and ministers Carnot, Fouché, Caulaincourt, and Davout, who left the Elysée at 3 p.m. The Emperor said to them: "Go, speak to them of France's interests, which must be dear to all its representatives; when you return, I shall make the choice my duty dictates."

Prince Lucien, tasked with giving an account of the events and results of the battle, asked the chamber for its help in taking the measures necessary in this time of danger. The chamber appeared to rally to the eloquence of this orator, when La Fayette restored discord to the point where the chamber could no longer be counted on. Filled with noble indignation against the representatives who misjudged to such a point all that was great, generous, and devoted in the conduct of the Emperor—who had the power under law to dissolve a chamber hostile toward him—Prince Lucien urged him to overturn it. The Emperor did not, but was indignant over the violence being done to him.

An anxious crowd had gathered in the Marigny avenue. I was returning in a carriage along the Champs-Elysées, when at that intersection the crowd prevented me from going any further; I got out and told the coachman to return to the stables. I allowed the crowd to carry me to below the terrace where the Emperor was strolling with Prince Lucien. The crowd was huge, and each time the Emperor appeared at the end of the long path where he was strolling, cries of Vive l'Empereur! issued from all these indignant people who were demanding weapons and a single word, to crush the domestic enemy and march against the one approaching Paris. Only a word; certainly the victims were chosen and would fall to the vengeance of the people. It certainly required a superhuman courage on the part of the Emperor not to let himself be carried away by the popular enthusiasm. His great spirit remained calm, and France shall forever remain thankful to him for this: for it would have meant civil war on top of foreign war. I remember perfectly a moment when Prince Lucien and the Emperor reached the end of the path; Prince Lucien seemed to be saying: "Will you allow so many powerless cries without taking advantage of them to serve France." This prince, in a pamphlet published in 1835 called *La Verité sur les cent-jours*, tells us what was going on in his heart and that of his brother. "Facing 20,000 cries of Vive l'Empereur! and the sublime expression that spread over the features of Napoleon captivated by the event, I interrupted a silence of several minutes by saying to him: 'Well, do you hear the people? It is the same all over France! Will you abandon it to the factions?' Halting, and responding with a wave of the hand to the crowd's cries of enthusiasm, he said to me: 'Am I superhuman to be able to return one-thousand wayward deputies to a union that alone can save us? Or am I a miserable party leader who will needlessly start a civil war? No, never. In Brumaire, we had to draw the sword for the good of France, today for the good of France we must cast that sword away from us. Go and try to win over the chambers: I can achieve anything with their support. I could do much in my own interest without them, but I could not save the motherland. Go, I forbid you when leaving to address these people who demand weapons; I will attempt everything for France, I will attempt nothing for myself.' "

The prince (Lucien) adds: "Those are the words spoken by Napoleon. My eyes filled with tears, and for the first time in my life I fell to my knees before him, admiring from the bottom of my heart this father of the nation, betrayed and misunderstood by misguided representatives."

Let us add that such a supreme sacrifice earned this great man the rock of Saint Helena for a prison.

As I have quoted the Emperor's words preserved for us by the prince, let it also be mentioned that in the same pamphlet he indignantly refutes an accusation rather widespread at the time that he urged the Emperor to abdicate in favor of the King of Rome, in order to become regent.

The prince (Lucien) states: "Have I ever committed a cowardly act to acquire a throne? Had Napoleon II succeeded his father, what claim could I have had to the regency? Did not our family have at its head my older brother, Prince Joseph, one of the most enlightened minds, this brother who was like a father to me in my childhood? We are not of a blood to respond to affection with ingratitude, to undermine the head of our family in a cowardly fashion by secret maneuvers, and to sacrifice memories and conscience to the sad rage for power.

"Everyone knows that during my retirement in Italy, I received several offers to return to power, either in France or on a foreign throne, and letters from my family, from Talleyrand and Fouché, who were in turn trying to get me to accept Napoleon's offers. I do not believe it is very common to refuse such offers, and it is at least a likely presumption that one is not devoured with ambition." Having mentioned the article that refutes the rumor circulating at the time in which he absolves himself of this libel, I return to the chamber of deputies where he had been sent by the Emperor. What did he find there? A continuous session, in violation of the charter: fear of dissolution had led it to this decision at the instigation of General La Fayette, whose misplaced patriotism made him serve the cause of the enemy rather than that of his country. The chamber of peers, where Marshal Ney had stirred up trouble by an exaggerated description of our losses at Waterloo, did not prove any wiser. Strengthened by our dissensions and by assurances given to it, the enemy marched on Paris at full speed.

At 11 p.m. a council was held with Prince Lucien presiding; the resolution arrived at there was taken to the chamber and opposed by M. de La Fayette, who said it did not meet the general expectation, and that only an abdication could put an end to the crisis that existed in France. Thus, while Carnot saw in the Emperor's abdication the ruin of France, others were pressing for it with all their might.

Not exercising his right to dissolve the chambers, the Emperor drew back only before civil war. As the supreme judge of the French people, with his goal of order and well-being for France, he could only proceed with help the chambers refused him. He abdicated: nothing was more constitutional, or proves better that the aim of his politics was a monarchy based on those principles. Had he acted otherwise, and civil war ensued, his name would have been cursed, and he would have been held responsible for all the blood shed as a result.

When the Emperor learned of the resolution reached by the chamber, and that his offer of devotion to the country was being ignored, he said to Prince Joseph: "They are insane, and La Fayette and his friends are naive politicians: they want my abdication and fear that I will not give it to them. I shall do so, and hold them responsible for the evils that descend on France. They want me to abdicate in favor of my son, but that is a farce when the enemy is at the Paris gates, and the Bourbons right behind them. United, we could save ourselves; divided, we are helpless."

It was nearly 1 a.m. when the following "Declaration to the French people" was taken to the two chambers, the chamber of peers by Count Carnot, and the chamber of deputies by the Duke of Otranto (Fouché):

People of France! In undertaking war to defend national independence, I was counting on the unity of all efforts, all wills, and the help of all national authorities. I had reason to hope for success, and I had challenged the declarations of all the powers united against me. Circumstances appear to have changed. I offer myself in sacrifice to the hatred of France's enemies. May their declarations be sincere, and may they want only my person. My political life is at an end, and I proclaim my son Emperor of the French, under the name of Napoleon II. The ministers shall form a provisional government council, and on behalf of my son I urge them to organize without delay a regency by means of law. Unite for public salvation, and to remain an independent nation.

> *Signed: Napoleon*
>
> *June 22*

While the act of abdication was being finalized, the Emperor was strolling in the Elysée garden with his brothers; like the day before, the Marigny avenue was filled with people shouting Vive l'Empereur! a thousand times. His Majesty was greeting this multitude eager to see him, when he was informed there only remained for him to sign; he quickly went in and came back to the garden to join his brothers and continue his stroll. A few cries of Down with the priests! could also be heard. The chambers thus received this abdication so badly desired, they deliberated about it, and in the afternoon a deputation from each came to express the thanks with which they accepted his noble sacrifice.

The Emperor replied to both these deputations:

I thank you for the sentiments you have expressed. I wish my abdication could bring France happiness, but I have little hope of this, as it leaves the state without a leader, without any political existence. The time wasted on overthrowing the monarchy could have been used to place France in a position to crush the enemy: I recommend that France promptly reinforce its armies. Whoever wishes peace must be prepared for war. Do not place this great nation at the mercy of foreigners, and beware of seeing your hopes deceived. Therein lies the danger. Whatever position I find myself in, I shall always be at ease if France is happy; I entrust my son to France, and hope it will not forget that I abdicated only for him. I have also made this great sacrifice for the good of the nation. It is only through my dynasty that it can hope to be free, happy, and independent.

That evening when he went to bed, the Emperor asked me what effect his abdication caused in Paris. I said to him, with deep sadness and great emotion: "Sire, the people don't understand it, they are astonished that Your Majesty does not overturn the chamber and assume dictatorship at so serious a time. Paris fears the enemy's approach, it has no faith in the men in charge of its affairs, and all whom I saw today state that it is like handing them over bound hand and foot. The ministry is accused of treason, they are so angry that they seem to want victims. Only a word is needed from Your Majesty, and they will find some in the ministry and the chamber. Sire, all are convinced they will not get the King of Rome, and will have to endure the Bourbons' revenge." The Emperor explained: "Only the abdication can save France, faced with the abandonment of the chambers; to act in any other way than I am doing would bring about a civil war, and I would have its blood on my conscience: this I do not want."

After the abdication, the Emperor remained a few more days at the Elysée. The next day and the following there were many carriages in the courtyard. The third day they decreased, but the public turmoil around the residence increased. The Emperor thought that such demonstrations could hinder negotiations, and that his abdication could be slandered by his enemies who feared the people's manifestations in favor of their elected choice, and thus withdrew almost stealthily from so much proof of love and affection by retiring to Malmaison. Before leaving, he sent to his former comrades in arms the following proclamation. It never reached the army, as the sentiments it expressed frightened the new governing bodies too much:

Soldiers!

When I yielded to the necessity that forces me to leave the courageous French army, I take with me the happy certainty that through the eminent service the motherland expects from it, it shall justify the praise even our enemies cannot deny it. Soldiers! Although absent, I shall follow your actions: I know each corps, and none can win some reported advantage without my doing justice to the courage it displays. You and I have been slandered, and men unworthy of appreciating your work saw in the signs of attachment you showed me a zeal of which I was the sole object. Let your future services teach them that it was the motherland above all you were serving in obeying me, and that if I share in any way in your affection, I owe this to my deep love for France, our common mother. Soldiers! Only a few more efforts and the coalition shall dissolve. Napoleon will recognize you through the blows you strike. Save the honor and the independence of France, remain to the very end as I have known you for the past twenty years, and you shall be invincible.

Two days before leaving Paris for Malmaison, I spoke to the Emperor when he was retiring about a letter I had received that morning, in which I was invited to go to Saint-Philippe-du-Roule. The place where I was to meet the person was given and, the fanciful nature of the letter having awakened my curiosity, I had gone there, as my ego led me to believe this regarded me. I had approached the meeting place, letter in hand; a woman was there praying. At the noise I made in moving a chair to approach her, she turned around sharply; in addition to the elegant and slim figure I had noticed at first, she revealed a face that was veiled, but not enough to disguise that she was young and pretty. I told the Emperor: "I bowed respectfully as I came near her, and asked in what way I could be of service to her. She remained silent for a moment, then, much embarrassed, confessed that the Emperor's misfortunes were of great concern to her, and increased in her a feeling of attachment she had had toward him for a long time. She would be very happy if in this moment of adversity she could express this to him. She was highly moved. I said to her: 'Madam, I can promise you to tell His Majesty this evening when he retires of your admiration for him, but I cannot assure you that the audience you request will be granted.' 'See to it that it is,' she said, quickly taking my hand, pressing it firmly between hers, and lifting it to her bosom, 'you would make me so happy; you will do it, won't you? Promise me!' 'Madam, I can only repeat what I said to you, and add that the timing is not propitious; however I promise you to faithfully convey to the Emperor the enthusiasm with which you are filled.' " I said to the Emperor: "We parted, with a promise to meet tomorrow at the same time and place to convey the answer. I await Your Majesty's reply."

The Emperor smiled over the whole thing and said to me: "Is she French? Her speech is more that of an Englishwoman."

"What can she want of me? It is an admiration which is bound to lead to an affair, and we must not allow it." I wrote to the unknown woman my regret that circumstances did not allow me to bring her my answer in person; but the Emperor was leaving for Malmaison and I was obliged to go there ahead of him. I gave my letter to a discreet man to take to her, and never heard from her again.

The provisional government had been named: names like Caulaincourt and Carnot reassured decent people, but that of the Duke of Otranto (Fouché) as president gave cause for concern. That minister was habitually surrounded by intrigue and treachery. No sooner did he hold the Emperor's abdication in his hands than he approached royalist agents, with whom he negotiated the Bourbons' return to France; and while La Fayette headed a deputation sent to the enemy camp to try to halt the march on Paris, the Duke of Otranto was inviting the heads of the same armies to come there posthaste. He had been able to master the council, and had drawn within his spiderweb even Marshal Davout, who lost more than his popularity in handing over Paris without a fight. If in such sad circumstances there are names lacking in patriotism, there are others who did not lack it at all: men like Béranger, Manuel, Boulay de la Meurthe in the chamber of deputies carried the day against the royalists, the Orleanists, and the republicans, and had Napoleon II proclaimed; while in the chamber of peers men like Drouot, La Bédoyère and Count Regnault de Saint-Jean d'Angély also carried the day for their side. These two chambers seemed to forget that the elevation of the King of Rome to the imperial throne was the condition for the sacrifice the Emperor was imposing on himself.

On June 25 at 12:30 p.m., the Emperor left the Elysée without escort and climbed into the grand marshal's carriage that stood waiting for him at the garden gate on the Champs-Elysées; Count Bertrand was with him, and Noverraz on the seat. At the same time, the Emperor's carriages rode out on rue du Faubourg-Saint-Honoré, taking to Malmaison Generals Gourgaud and Montholon, the Emperor's ADCs, and his chamberlain, Count de Las Cases. Baron de Mesgrigny, the Emperor's equerry, was on horseback at the door of the first carriage which, followed by the escort, led people to believe that the Emperor was in it. It was only after passing the city gates that the Emperor, leaving the grand marshal's carriage, climbed into his own to proceed to Malmaison; there he was greeted by his adopted daughter, Queen Hortense, with an affection as respectful as it was touching. Twenty-five men from the imperial infantry guard, commanded by one officer, were there to watch over the Emperor's safety in this residence.

Prior to leaving Paris, the Emperor had requested from the provisional government two frigates and passports to go to America. He had his secretary M. Rathery burn letters, memoranda, and petitions that could place the signers in jeopardy. I remained at the Elysée-Bourbon a few hours later than the Emperor, to gather up all his belongings and wait for some purchases I had made which had not arrived. My family was with me, dismayed by a departure that was perhaps separating us forever, and also by the misfortune gripping the country. The moment of separation was a cruel one; I embraced in turn my father, sisters, brothers, and brother-in-law, and left asking them to control a sorrow that was causing me to lose mastery of my own. We parted, promising to see each other the next day and those that followed at Malmaison, if the Emperor stayed there a few days.

After they left, I wandered through the Emperor's apartments, so full of eager courtiers a few days before, and today so empty that I found myself alone there with my wardrobe boy. I took some small portable furnishings that could be useful to the Emperor where he would go, such as gilt incense-burners, small marble busts of the King of Rome, small framed pictures, the work of Isabey representing the prince at various ages, others of Empress Marie-Louise, and a small bronze statuette of the Emperor produced during the Hundred Days, made by the Galles workshops. There was in the Emperor's bedroom a superb silver washstand on a tripod in the shape of swans' necks, with a pitcher of the same material, the work of the silversmith Biennais; my desire to take it was battled by my fear of committing a reprehensible act. The Emperor had praised that piece while using it, I knew how much it would deprive him not to have it, as he liked to plunge his face into much water after shaving; this one was 15 inches in diameter, and could hold a large quantity of water. The thought of pleasing him dispelled any scruples I had about taking it. I had it transported to my carriage, and placed my coat over it in order not to arouse the curiosity of passersby in Paris or along the road. I arrived at Malmaison at 6 p.m., my carriage full to breaking. That evening as he was retiring, I told the Emperor of the state of ferment in which I had left the Paris population, and about my visits to Mme Pellapra and Mme de Walewska; the latter proposed to come to Malmaison the next day with her son. Mme Pellapra had asked me to convey all her regrets about not daring to come there without his instructions. At the time of this departure, there was a theft at the grand marshal's of a small case containing jewelry and snuffboxes valued at 60,000 francs, without anyone noticing this pilferage. Count de Montholon, in his *Memoirs of Saint Helena*, relates that there also was a theft of a considerable amount of negotiable securities in the Emperor's study, which no one was aware of. I knew of the first theft, but neither in Paris nor in Saint Helena did I ever hear of the second one.

Thus had just come to an end the period of the Hundred Days, so great in its beginning and so unfortunate in its end.

Had the Emperor known in Elba of the conspiracy that the army heads were plotting in his favor against the Bourbon throne— brought about by the weakness of the new government and the outmoded pretense that was as blighting to the French people as it was dangerous to the interests of the past 25 years—he would have left Elba only one month later: he would have avoided the March 13 declaration and the crusade against France headed by Emperor Alexander, and March 20 would have achieved all its goals.

The Emperor was ignorant of this movement, and knew about it only after arriving in Grenoble; he had neither the will nor the power to anticipate it. He knew that an army which was the glory of France, often the terror of its enemies, and always, even in its setbacks, the object of Europe's admiration, could not stand to be scorned, insulted, and decimated, and could only be waiting for the moment of revenge.

He therefore had in his favor his ability to assess conditions in France and the mood of the nation.

His arrival in arms on French territory was not the result of a conspiracy. There were no plotters there where everyone else was plotting: the king because of his loss of confidence, his ministers because of their incompetence, the exiles because of their conceit and the combination of ignorance and presumption that was to be their downfall, and with them that of the country. Those were the conspirators.

If, as he wanted, the Emperor had been able to wait for a lasting peace and ensure the promulgation of a constitution, he would have eliminated the most important source of division brought about by our first misfortunes, and taken away from the enemy powerful means of creating trouble and internal dissension. Deeply moved by love and gratitude toward his country, and by the heady welcome he had received, he wanted to please France: he tried to satisfy public opinion, to flatter the public spirit, and those around him who attempted to be its interpreters erred and misled the Emperor

It was believed during the Hundred Days that Napoleon did not show the force of willpower that had led him to such great success. As I have said, people did not sufficiently take into account his desire to please the people. The Emperor had dictatorship in hand: he should have kept it. His shrewdness was almost never at fault, he often pointed out what had to be done, and events proved him right. But in this case he had to yield to objections coming from his advisors, who were most attached not only to his person but to the welfare of France, its independence, honor, and the glory of the state.

The Emperor said in Saint Helena that the steel of several generals had lost its temper in the events of 1814: they had lost something of the confidence, audacity, and resolve that had earned them so much glory. What he said about the generals was true of everyone. The Allied declaration of March 13 had caused the loss of much assurance among members of the ministry and the council of State. That declaration became generally known in Paris a few days after the Emperor's arrival. It was to weaken its influence that the council of State, in its

March 29 speech, retracted commitments the Emperor had made in his proclamations to the nation and the army to produce a constitution, and inserted this paragraph: "To better establish the rights and obligations of the people and the monarch, the national institutions must be reviewed by a major assembly of representatives, already announced by the Emperor."

This promise warded off the dangers of the March 13 declaration and directed the mind of the public away from it; but it lent strength to the arguments of those who wanted any kind of constitution in spite of the times and events. .

At Malmaison, which reminded the Emperor of his early years of glory and happiness, he was surrounded with care and love by Queen Hortense, and the devotion of the generals and other officers who offered to accompany him in his misfortune. Count Bertrand, the Duke of Rovigo (Savary), Generals Lallemand, Montholon, and Gourgaud shared the duties of ADC; Majors de Résigny and Planat, joined by Captains Mercier and Schultz, those of military aide. This last had accompanied the Emperor to Elba; he and several others, on the eve of the departure for Malmaison, solicited the honor of following the Emperor there. Baron de Montaran served as equerry there, Count de Las Cases as chamberlain, and his son and M. de La Pagerie as pages. The food service was quite extensive, and the household service the same as in Paris.

During the few days spent at Malmaison, the Emperor received visits from his friends, who traveled out at all hours of the day to bring him news; he questioned them anxiously. Among those who came were Count de Lavalette, the Duke of Bassano (Maret); Generals Flahaut, La Bédoyère, and Caffarelli; M. Poggi; and the Emperor's brothers, Princes Joseph, Lucien, and Jérôme. The ladies who had remained deeply attached to him did not fail him either. Queen Hortense's drawing room was filled in the evening with Countesses Bertrand, Montholon, and Caffarelli. The Duchesses of Rovigo (Savary), Bassano (Maret), Countesses Regnault de Saint-Jean d'Angély, Walewska, and others whose names escape me, came to Malmaison and shared in the sorrow. Mme Pellapra came also to bring consolations of the heart that were much appreciated by the Emperor; on the rock of Saint Helena her memory served sometimes to chase away the boredom of captivity, when he remembered her soul and her beauty.

Before leaving Paris, I had packed a trunk of things now useless to the Emperor, made up of imperial clothes from the Champ de Mai, His Majesty's lace, weapons, an antique hilt, and a small medal collection; in accordance with the Emperor's orders, I had sent it all to Count de Turenne, grand master of the wardrobe, who remained its custodian. I had brought with me the large medal collection; the Emperor told me to give it to Count de Lavalette, who gave me in exchange 30,000 francs in gold which were deposited with M. Laffitte. Before leaving Paris the Emperor had opened an account with this banker with a credit of four or five million through M. Perregaux, one of his chamberlains; this having been accepted, such a sum was deposited that same day. It was the Emperor's entire fortune. On this occasion His Majesty saw M. Laffitte, and in Saint Helena said that he had found in him not only a financier, but a man with a very good grasp of important political questions.

The Emperor was waiting rather impatiently for the arrival of the passports he had requested, as well as the order making two frigates available to him to go to America. When on June 25 General Becker[241] came to Malmaison to take command of the imperial guard, and see to both his protection and the respect owed him, Queen Hortense thought they were going to arrest the Emperor. She was frightened, and was about to throw herself between His Majesty and the man charged with this mission, when she was told the enemy was approaching Paris. The general was only sent to see to the Emperor's personal safety.

As soon as he arrived, General Becker asked to be shown in to the Emperor, and handed him a letter from the minister of war, Prince of Eckmühl (Davout), worded in this fashion:

---

[241]General Becker, Count of Mons (1770-1840), sent to Napoleon to represent the provisional government, accompanied him to Rochefort.

Paris, June 25, 1815, 4 p.m.

General,

 Please be advised that the government commission has named you to command the guard of the Emperor Napoleon at Malmaison.

 The honor of France requires that his safety and the respect owed him be assured. The interest of the nation demands that malicious people be prevented from using his name to foment trouble.

 General, your acknowledged character is the government's and France's guarantee that you shall fulfill both tasks. You are invited to proceed immediately to Malmaison, take command of the guard, and take all dispositions required to accomplish these goals.

 Sincerely, etc.

 Minister of War Prince of Eckmühl (Davout)

This measure, dictated by the Duke of Otranto (Fouché) and agreed to by the minister of war, was nothing but a disguised way of monitoring the Emperor's actions; this had become the more necessary as both these statesmen had already been in contact with Baron de Vitrolles, the king's agent, regarding the return of Louis XVIII.

The Emperor did not fail to point this out to General Becker, who behaved most honorably in these circumstances. On my return from Saint Helena I had the honor of seeing the general frequently, and this is what he told me about the situation:

"When I accepted this mission, it was only in order to serve the Emperor and protect him; I did not then suspect what was revealed to me a few days later, that the Duke of Otranto (Fouché) and the Prince of Eckmühl (Davout) were negotiating with royalist agents. The Emperor was hurt by the manner in which I had been sent to him, he would have liked for the government to inform him officially of an act he considered a formality and not a measure of surveillance to which it was useless to subject him. The idea that the Emperor could believe that I could lend myself to any role other than that of a good soldier who had come to look after his safety appalled me, and I told him that if my presence at Malmaison could awaken such a suspicion, I would immediately resign the mission I had been entrusted with. The Emperor saw how hurt I was, and said to me: 'Set your mind at ease, General: had I been given the choice of an officer, I would have designated you by preference, as I have long been aware of your loyalty.' He took me out into the garden and we talked about Paris."

The general reminded me that on board The *Saale* I had given him one of the Emperor's shirts, which he cherished.

The Emperor was worried to see the enemy army moving closer to Paris without any resistance being offered or measures taken to defend the city. He spoke of this with his entourage; light troops could reach Malmaison; it was said that the enemy army was near Paris. What he had predicted was coming true. The French commissioners complained about the bad faith shown by the Allies during negotiations, the anxiety of the government was increasing, and the Emperor's delay in leaving Malmaison made them fear that a spontaneous decision might lead the Emperor to take command of the army and destroy the entire scaffolding of treason that was handing Paris over to the enemy. It was only on the 27th that the grand marshal, who was in Paris to secure two frigates from the government commission to take the Emperor to the United States, wrote to His Majesty that the minister of the navy was making available to him two frigates in the Rochefort harbor, and that all orders relative to relay posts along the way had been given; the frigates were not to leave the Rochefort roadstead before the safe-conducts had arrived. The Duke of Otranto (Fouché) gave verbal authorization to Count Bertrand to take from the Tuileries—where orders had been given not to let anything more be taken—a complete table service of twelve settings, the porcelain known as 'Headquarters,' six sets of table linen for twelve in damask cloth, six sets of kitchen linen, twelve pairs of high-quality sheets, twelve pairs of ordinary sheets, six dozen towels, two travel coaches, three saddles and bridles for general officers, three saddles and bridles for grooms, 400 books to be taken from the Rambouillet library, various maps, and 100,000 francs for travel expenses. This was what the government was granting to the man who had governed France with so much glory, and given considerable fortunes to those who surrounded him; the very man who was allowing these modest belongings to be taken had received from him an income of 200,000 pounds.

In spite of the provisional government's urging the Emperor both by letter and by oral communications to leave Malmaison, the Emperor was paying no heed. General Becker was ordered to appear in Paris in front of the commission, who ordered him to depart incognito that same evening with the Emperor for Rochefort. At the same time he received a passport authorizing the general to go to that city with his secretary and servant. The secretary was to be the Emperor!

This ridiculous order was no more heeded than the preceding ones; it led the Emperor to have General Becker tell the provisional government commission that he gave up the idea of going to Rochefort. As communications were not free, he did not think his personal safety had enough guarantees; furthermore, once at that destination, he had to consider himself a prisoner, since his departure from the island of Aix depended on passports to go to America that would no doubt be refused. Therefore, the Emperor was determined to await the decision regarding him at Malmaison; he would wait until the Duke of Wellington issued a ruling on his fate, and the government was free to announce this. He was therefore remaining at Malmaison, certain that nothing unworthy of the nation and its government would be attempted against him.

Since June 25, frequent messages had passed between the government and General Becker at Malmaison. The Emperor's friends came in great numbers, but on the 28th, the closing of the barriers and the erection of a barricade at the Neuilly bridge presented some difficulties in reaching him. However on that same day I again saw my brother-in-law and sister, who told me of the agitation in Paris; people did not understand the Emperor's calm at the approach of the enemy. That afternoon Mme Pellapra sent a message to me through her servant that she was waiting for me on a street in Rueil, and I went there at once. She assured me that she knew, without a doubt, that the Duke of Otranto (Fouché) was currently negotiating with M. de Vitrolles, Louis XVIII's agent, and that the Prince of Eckmühl (Davout), while concentrating his forces around Paris, was paralyzing their action. She told me to warn the Emperor of this; the first of those two ministers was a man who would hand over the Emperor if there was a profit in it for him. While I was with that lady, part of the guard that was in Rueil fell out with their weapons. Worried about what this could mean, I left her to return to Malmaison, where I learned that at the approach of the enemy General Becker had received orders to destroy the bridges at Chatou and Bezons, and to maintain a military guard on those roads. He was firmly resolved to defend the Emperor with the few hundred men he had under him, joined by the generals and military aides who were with him.

Saint-Denis had been sent to Versailles by the Emperor to fetch some shotguns, saddle pistols, and a box containing two pairs of fine pistols; he had found the road free, but there was concern that the Emperor was remaining so quietly at Malmaison where patrols could find him without warning. MM. de Bassano (Maret) and Lavalette, the Duke of Rovigo (Savary), and General Bertrand were with him. That evening when the Emperor retired to his quarters, I told him what I had learned of the mood in Paris, and the will to defend itself should His Majesty appear, but that in his absence there would be total inertia and the Bourbons would be accepted. Mme Pellapra whom I had seen in Rueil had asked me to tell him that the Duke of Otranto (Fouché) was negotiating with M. de Vitrolles, and the commissioners sent to the enemy camp were not listened to. The Emperor replied: "All that I have told them is coming true, La Fayette is a simpleton, and those people who do not know the French spirit are ruining the country."

During the night of the 28th to 29th, Duke Decrès and Count Boulay de la Meurthe came to Malmaison. The Emperor had been in bed for several hours when I quietly entered his room to tell him these gentlemen had arrived. When they were shown in, they told the Emperor that the enemy army around Paris gave rise to fears for his personal safety. The government had decided to consider as null and void the paragraph in the ordinance that, in putting the frigates at his disposal, forbade them to set sail without a safe-conduct. The interests of the state as well as his own demanded imperatively that he leave at once; passports had been brought for all those who proposed to share the Emperor's exile. His Majesty talked to them for a moment of the evils he saw descending on the motherland, then dismissed them both. On receiving his farewells, they left in a state that bore witness to the deep sorrow in their hearts.

That day M. Corvisart had come to Malmaison with one of his pupils, a young practitioner he brought to present to the Emperor. M. Foureau de Beauregard, his doctor in Elba, intended to rejoin the Emperor later, but having been elected deputy in his department and having to pursue his legal obligation could not for the moment relinquish the mandate he had received from his fellow citizens. This young man, M. Maingault, had been called on to replace him. After he was introduced, the Emperor told him to take his orders from the grand marshal, and remained walking in the garden with M. Corvisart for a full half-hour. On leaving him, the Emperor went back to his rooms and summoned me, as he usually did. He handed me a small vial about fifteen lines long by four or five wide[242] containing a red liquid, and urged me to let no one see it, adding: "See to it that I have it on me, either by attaching it to my jacket or some other part of my clothing, so that I can always reach it easily." At that same moment word came that the Duke of Bassano (Maret) or Count de Lavalette was in the drawing room. I remained alone with the vial, which doubtless contained instant death; my thoughts were very sad until that evening, when I again saw the Emperor when he retired. After telling him what Mme Pellapra had said, I was about to leave when he asked me what I had done with the vial he had given me. I showed him the end of his left suspender strap, which he could easily reach with his right hand, and under that strap I showed him a small leather pouch containing the vial, which could easily slide in or out, kept in place by an eyelet with a small cord through it. He examined it all, took the vial out and put it back in, then looked at me and said: "That's fine." And as he noted how distressed I was, he pressed his hand on my cheek and told me to

---

[242] About 1 1/4 inches by 1/3 of an inch—Ed.

get everything ready for his departure, which would probably take place the next day.

Allowing for a sudden departure, I made an agreement with M. Colin, comptroller of the Emperor's household, a man both honest and devoted to the Emperor: he would see that the two carriages that were to transport the silver and the so-called 'Headquarters' porcelain were always ready to be hitched to the post horses and got under way; he handed me an inventory of their contents. He had not stopped at the 12-piece silver set, as the Duke of Otranto (Fouché) had generously done with his master; he added all the silver of the Emperor's set at the Elysée to that brought from the Tuileries. This explains how, after selling a great deal of it in Saint Helena, much still remained after His Majesty's death.

On the morning of his departure, the Emperor talked to me and told me to assure those servants who were coming with him that their existence was taken care of. I took the liberty of answering him that they all considered themselves fortunate to be able to offer their devotion. An allowance was given each of them by the grand marshal for travel expenses. I learned that Ferdinand, the cook in Elba, was not going with the Emperor, and that King Joseph had promptly placed his own at his disposal. He placed around his body the diamond necklace which Queen Hortense had begged him to accept, as it might be of use to him in this moment of great misfortune. Having determined which roads the carriages would follow to go to Rochefort, the Emperor had 1,800 francs issued to General Montholon and 1,500 to General Gourgaud for relay post expenses between Paris and that city. A few sums of 10,000 francs were distributed to people he could not take with him, and who were in serious financial straits, M. Poggi and others. Generals Chartran and Piré came to ask for the means to escape the persecution they were threatened with. There was exasperation in their voices. The Emperor was warned of this, he noticed it, and said it was only fair that people who had sacrificed themselves for him should come to him; he had 10,000 francs given to each of them to attend to their immediate needs, and regretted that he could not do as much for all who were going to suffer because of him.

Since the return from Waterloo, the people surrounding the Emperor had been advising him to go to England. The Emperor, who said his political existence was at an end, preferred the United States, and it was for that destination he was about to set off. In the morning, cries of Vive l'Empereur! Down with the Bourbons! Down with traitors! were heard along the road. It was a division returning from the Vendée who, knowing the Emperor was still at Malmaison, had stopped in front of the park and refused to take another step without seeing the Emperor or taking him with them. This cry that reached us of Vive l'Empereur!, so often the certain sign of victory, rekindled in the souls of the warriors surrounding the Emperor their love of combat. The Emperor too allowed his great heart to be seized with enthusiasm, because after talking to the general commanding that division, he summoned General Becker and told him he was delaying his departure by a few hours, enough time to submit to the government his proposal to take command of the army in the name of Napoleon II and outline for them a plan of operation that gave every chance of success in driving the enemy beyond the border within a few days. General Becker gave proof of his devotion by agreeing to undertake a mission which could bring him criticism from the government, but he saw a chance of salvation for the country in the plans proposed by the Emperor, and he departed. He had great difficulty reaching the commission because of obstacles on the way. The Duke of Bassano (Maret), who had come to work with the Emperor, left him shortly after the general's departure to work for the Emperor's return, should his offer be accepted.

Such was not the case. The proposal was received with dread; they had thought the Emperor far from Paris, and the offer he was making would completely undo the negotiations so painfully worked out with the royalist agents to make them acceptable to the president of the council, and also to the members of the commission who now would only be guided by him. First a reply was made by the Duke of Otranto (Fouché) that his offer was unacceptable; then they criticized the general in bitter terms for having taken on this mission when he ought to be on the road to Rochefort; it was urgent for him to leave at once, as the Emperor was no longer safe in the vicinity of Paris. As the general requested that he carry a government decision on the result of his mission, the Duke of Otranto immediately wrote the following note to the Duke of Bassano (Maret), whom he supposed to be still at Malmaison:

> *As the provisional government cannot accept the proposal that General Becker has just made on behalf of His Majesty, for reasons that you yourself will appreciate, I pray you to use the influence you have always had on him to advise him to leave without delay, as the Prussians are marching on Versailles, etc.*
>
> *Signed: Duke of Otranto*

While General Becker was in Paris, Count de Lavalette, the Emperor's faithful friend, had arrived at Malmaison and was giving His Majesty a report on the frame of mind in the capital. All were anxiously waiting for the moment when the Emperor would call for his horses to place himself at the head of the army, when General Becker returned and put an end to our illusions of happiness: the provisional government had refused the Emperor's offer. His Majesty read the note addressed to the Duke of Bassano (Maret), then, without revealing any emotion, gave orders for his departure. Once back in his quarters, accompanied by the grand marshal, he said: "Those people are destroying France." He removed his guard chasseur's uniform, donned a brown coat with blue pants and riding boots, and placed a round broad-brimmed hat on his head. The Emperor was chatting while dressing, with the calm of a serene soul that had wished until the very end to defend the interests of the country. He went into the drawing room where he found Queen Hortense, whose tears moved him, and who proved full of devotion and kindness. He went out with her into the garden, but did not want her to go any further. He embraced the princess for the last time, said a final goodbye to the few friends who were there, as well as to Mmes de Vicenza (Caulaincourt), Caffarelli, and Walewska, handed his horse to his equerry Baron de Montaran, and walked away from friends who were all bursting into tears as he approached the small park gate. A coach hitched to four post horses that was to be preceded by Amodru, a groom acting as outrider, had been waiting there for nearly an hour. The Emperor climbed in, followed by General Becker, the grand marshal, and the Duke of Rovigo (Savary), who were accompanying him, all three dressed in civilian clothes. Saint-Denis, who was to ride on the top seat, had put in ample provisions and as many pairs of pistols as there were passengers, keeping two pairs for himself. I had placed 20,000 francs in gold in a small coffer, to be used as needed on the way. Leaving Malmaison by this transverse road, the Emperor came to Rambouillet. In spite of all the precautions taken, His Majesty could not escape the eyes of the good people stopped near his coach who cried Vive l'Empereur! It was now 5:30 p.m. on June 29, 1815. Horses were hitched to the coaches and the supply vans loaded with silver and linen belonging to the Emperor. Knowing that the baggage was to leave as soon as His Majesty's coach had departed, I had in great haste picked up all that belonged to the Emperor, to place it in my carriage and climb in only after seeing the vans under way. I shook the hands of a few people present who embraced me with tears in their eyes and despair in their hearts. There were two convoys: the one with three carriages, the Emperor's coupé in which General Gourgaud rode, mine, and a supply van, headed for Rambouillet; the other convoy, with carriages bearing the imperial coat of arms under the guidance of Count de Montholon, carrying Mme de Montholon and her son, Count de Las Cases and his son, and all the rest of the entourage, headed for Angoulême and then to Rochefort. Countess Bertrand and her children came alone by another road. All were to rendezvous in Rochefort.

General Gourgaud headed the convoy, and we followed. In spite of the crowded conditions in my carriage, I made room for M. Maingault, the Emperor's doctor, and Totin, the head butler. So as not to have too large a sum of gold with me, I gave part of it to General Gourgaud, who kept it with him and gave it back to me later. On each of the outside seats of our two carriages were a footman and a wardrobe boy. These different routes had been ordered so that we would not run short of horses.

On the hill before arriving in Gressey, the Emperor spotted Amodru, his groom, next to his coach; he was to order the horses along the road followed by the Emperor. Over his civilian dress he wore a hunting knife and the belt of the household grooms. The Emperor had him told by Saint-Denis to remove that knife, which would only serve to have him recognized; civilian dress did not include it. Amodru obeyed, but angrily; he went on ahead to prepare the horses in Coignères where the Emperor was to change teams, but in actuality took the road for Versailles and disappeared. When he arrived at that post house, the Emperor was strangely surprised not to find horses ready. He asked Saint-Denis where Amodru could be, as the master of the post had seen no one; it was thought he had taken the wrong road and would be found at Rambouillet, but he never showed up. This man whose conduct had always been perfect, who had followed the Emperor to Elba and throughout all his campaigns, had abandoned his master for no reason. Santini, who was in this convoy, got on a horse and served as outrider from Rambouillet to Rochefort.

The postilions who brought the Emperor to Coignères had a good idea that the Emperor was in that coach, but said nothing to the others. They were paid only the regular price along the way to avoid drawing attention. On the road some distance from Rambouillet, His Majesty encountered a Polish cavalry unit wearing the uniform of the Vistula legion heading for Versailles. Although the orders of the provisional government were that the Emperor was not to stop in any town, when His Majesty arrived at the main gate of the Rambouillet park, he expressed the desire to stop there. Saint-Denis had the park gate opened, and the Emperor went down the drive to the château; there he was greeted by M. Hébert, one of his former valets in Egypt, who had asked him for that post as concierge. He hastened to make everything available to the Emperor. Saint-Denis, to whom I owe the details of this journey, told me that once supper was served, the Emperor sat down but no one spoke. After 15 minutes the Emperor got up from the table and went back to his room, followed by the grand marshal who emerged half an hour later, saying that the Emperor was not feeling well, had gone to bed, and would wait until the next day to continue his journey. The Emperor had arrived at that residence at 8 p.m.

The convoy led by General Gourgaud arrived much later. The Emperor was in bed; during the night he asked for some tea, which restored a little perspiration. His agitation ceased, sleep came to him, and the next day this slight illness had vanished. The grand marshal, the Duke of Rovigo (Savary), and Generals Becker and Gourgaud took the room next to his and spent the night there. In circumstances such as these, the stomach calls for little food; the sorrow shown by M. Hébert, the Emperor's worthy servant, was so great and deep that Saint-Denis and I sought to restore calm to his spirit and did not think of eating. I ate little, and spent part of the night reflecting on the destiny that brought us to a hunting lodge where I had known the Emperor so powerful, on a throne he was now leaving, not knowing what land of exile he would reach—for at this time Saint Helena, which had been mentioned in Elba, was far from my mind.

The next day, June 30, I told the Emperor my fear of having been separated from him when I found no horses prepared along the road, and my surprise at Amodru's disappearance. I told him that as I was about to get into the carriage, his secretary M. Rathery had told me his wife's health was too deplorable to allow him to leave her all alone; he asked me to assure His Majesty that the 3,000 francs' pension the Emperor proposed to give him when he planned on accompanying him would not be drawn by either him or his wife. The Emperor nevertheless told the grand marshal to cancel that pension that was to be paid by M. Laffitte; he also told me to help Count Bertrand choose some good books from the library of this residence, as well as a selection of maps, and to send it all to Rochefort. He sent a letter to the furnishings administrator to have a van sent to Rochefort, and another to his librarian M. Barbier[243] to have him send 2,000 volumes from the Trianon library, as well as the great opus on Egypt.

---

[243] Antoine-Alexandre Barbier (1765-1825), an erudite librarian. He was in turn librarian to the Directory, the council of State, and primarily to Napoleon himself. The Emperor, who valued him highly, put him in charge of creating the portable library and the historical library in 3,000 volumes, pet projects of his.

That same night Colonel Bellini and his wife arrived at Rambouillet: both had been in Elba; they proposed to follow him to the United States. Mme Bellini was dressed as a man. Though very grateful for this proof of attachment, the Emperor appeared disturbed by it, and told the grand marshal that his retinue was already very large and they should be encouraged to return to Paris. I told the Emperor they were penniless and unable to return there without help from His Majesty. The Emperor had me give them 3,000 francs to attend to their more pressing needs. I saw Mme Bellini, who was in deep despair. She reminded me of the Emperor's kindness to her in Elba, and could not understand his refusing to let her accompany him in his second exile when she had come to find him in the first; she calmed down however and said she would make preparations to go to the United States.

Before getting into his coach, the Emperor had M. Hébert come in, said a few consoling words to him, and promised not to forget him. This was not an idle promise: on his deathbed, the Emperor listed him in his will for 50,000 francs, and had 10,000 francs in gold given to him, foreseeing he would not be left for long in the position of concierge he had given him. In the morning the Emperor had me tell Santini to have horses readied along the road he was to take from Rambouillet to Rochefort.

At 11 a.m. the Emperor left this residence. The population had been rushing to the château gates since morning, waiting to see him; when the carriage pulled away, they cried Vive l'Empereur! His Majesty went through the park to rejoin the road to Chartres. The next day, July 1, he was in Tours, where he stopped only a moment. One of his former chamberlains, M. de Miremont, whom the Duke of Rovigo (Savary) had sent for, came immediately to invite the Emperor to come rest at the prefecture; he assured him he had nothing to fear from the population, who were full of gratitude for all he had done in the region. The Emperor thanked him and continued his journey as far as Poitiers, where he stopped to dine at the Hôtel de la Poste, just outside of town. Until then, nothing had come to disturb the safety of the travelers, except for a point between Saint-Amand and Tours where several horses were heard galloping. It was night, very dark, and they

could see nothing; it was only when the riders drew close that Saint-
Denis recognized two gendarmes, and so advised the Duke of Rovigo.
They asked Saint-Denis, who was on the top seat, who was in that
coach; he replied that they were general officers going to Niort. Both
gendarmes moved closer to the coach, removed their hats, and
informed the Duke of Rovigo, who asked them what they wanted, that
a few brigands were in the vicinity and they had been ordered to warn
travelers of this. They offered their services, which were not accepted,
and moved off, wishing them a safe journey. After resting for a few
hours from the oppressive heat, and freshening up to get rid of the
troublesome dust, the Emperor left the Hôtel de la Poste around 4
p.m.; he had arrived there at 11 a.m. When he arrived in Saint-
Maixent, the local population was stirred at seeing a coach drawn by
four horses stopped in front of the post house. They were eager for
news, hoping to have some from travelers coming from Paris, and the
crowd was getting larger as happens in these cases. The passports had
been demanded, and had not come back; General Becker signaled a
gendarmerie officer who was trying to get through the crowd to come
over to him. The officer soon recognized General Becker, under whom
he had served; complying with the wish that had been expressed, he
went to the city hall and soon returned with not only the passports, but
a safe-conduct issued by the municipality. This crowd wished no
harm, Saint-Denis said to me, but their curiosity to see the travelers
bordered on indiscretion; it could very well happen, in spite of the
Emperor's disguise, that someone in the crowd might recognize him
and he would thus become the object of an ovation he did not wish. As
soon as the passports were returned, the horses left at a gallop for
Niort, through the crowd that moved aside to let them pass. Along the
way there was a rather long hill to climb; the Emperor stepped down as
well as his companions and they walked some distance behind the
coach. Saint-Denis was walking alongside it when he was joined by a
neighboring farmer who, traveling on the same road, had looked at the
Emperor closely. He approached Saint-Denis, asking who the travelers
were. Saint-Denis answered: "They are generals going to Niort." As
they walked he asked him for news of Paris, with anxious curiosity

about the Emperor's fate. This man had served under the Consulate and the Empire; wounded in the early campaigns, he had returned home and tended his fields. He told Saint-Denis his joy at seeing the tricolor flying again from the church steeple in his village, and his disappointment at perhaps seeing again the white flag, considering that party's hatred of the "blues." While conversing they reached the crest of the hill; the coach stopped and so did the farmer, hat in hand. He greeted the travelers who were getting back into the coach and they returned his greeting, speeding off as fast as their horses would take them. At 8 p.m. the Emperor arrived in Niort very tired and expressed his desire to rest there: the coach was taken to the Boule d'Or inn. Up to that point, the Emperor had not been recognized along the road. On July 2 he arrived in Niort where his brother Joseph joined him.

The most comfortable room in that modest hotel was located above the kitchen: a simple wooden floor separated the two rooms, allowing all that was said there to be heard. The supper was mediocre, and the bed prepared for the Emperor quite uncomfortable, in spite of all Saint-Denis did to make it bearable. No one in the hotel suspected the importance of the travelers. After supper, the Emperor went to bed and told Saint-Denis to put a night-light in the fireplace, which was contrary to his habits. As usual, Saint-Denis slept across the door, so as to be awakened at His Majesty's first call. The noise from the room below the Emperor's bedroom did not allow him to sleep. At 3 a.m. someone knocked at the door of the room where Saint-Denis slept: he went to open it and ask what they wanted. They were two gendarmerie officers who wanted to talk to the Duke of Rovigo (Savary) and General Becker: he pointed to the rooms of those gentlemen. The Emperor, who couldn't sleep, asked Saint-Denis what it was, and he told him. Soon afterwards our carriages, held up at the Niort gates for passport verification, arrived at the Boule d'Or and roused the whole hotel. The Emperor summoned General Gourgaud immediately and asked how we could be so much later than he. The general told him that our carriages, stopped in Saint-Maixent, had been impounded at an inn until our passports were examined; only then did he realize that nothing had been filled in on any of them. He had hastened to fill them all in before someone came to ask for them, and this official examination had wasted two hours, spent having a rather poor lunch. The Emperor learned how Colonel Bourgeois of the gendarmerie, on recognizing General Gourgaud, had rushed over along with General Saulnier to offer his services to the Emperor.

The prefect M. Busche, informed of the Emperor's presence in town, came immediately to place the prefecture building at his disposal, as well as his carriage, hitched up in the inn courtyard, to take him there. Soon the news of his presence spread all over town; the 2nd hussars mounted their horses; everywhere excitement prevailed, changing the Emperor's resolve to leave that same morning as he had planned, and leading him to accept the prefect's hospitality and rest at his house, as he had not been able to do at the Boule d'Or. As soon as he arrived at the prefecture the Emperor went to bed, but while he slept the population awoke and joined in the happiness of the two regiments garrisoned in that town. They talked of nothing short of begging the Emperor to join the army of the Loire commanded by Generals Lamarque, Clauzel, and Brayer, along with a division of the young guard. Since my carriage contained considerable sums, I did not want to leave it in the courtyard of the inn: I had requested horses to have it taken to the prefecture. I was strolling as I waited, when General Lallemand arrived to join the Emperor. Surprised to see him alone, I asked how it happened that General de La Bédoyère was not with him; he replied that, yielding to family pressure, he had remained in Paris, confident about the terms of the surrender, and all he had said to him could not make him change his mind. He went to join the Emperor at the prefecture. A 48-hour halt in this town allowed King Joseph to join His Majesty there, as did Countess Bertrand. The arrival of so many eminent people in the city of Niort had stirred the whole population, and the acclamations of the people every time the Emperor appeared gave him a well-deserved feeling of pride, and spoke highly of his administration in that department.

All the staff carriages had remained in the courtyard of the inn, and the Emperor's and mine were brought to the prefecture. I was waiting for the Emperor to wake up before I went in when he called for me. It was 11 a.m.: General Lallemand, who had just arrived from Paris, gave him news of that city that spurred the imagination, and King Joseph, arriving later that day, added to it. General Clauzel[244] joined without hesitation in any plan that meant a march on Paris. General Brayer had given proof of his devotion from Lyon all the way to Paris during the return from Elba, so his cooperation could be counted on; only General Lamarque[245] showed little enthusiasm, which could well have changed had the Emperor's mind been firmly made up. He was at present yielding to the influences around him, and let others approach these generals.

That evening there was a dinner at the prefecture to which the town civil and military authorities were invited; bands from the various regiments were heard, and a large crowd sang patriotic tunes in honor of the Emperor; in the evening the town was illuminated. That evening General Gourgaud was sent to Rochefort to inquire if it was possible, when leaving the Gironde, to avoid the British cruisers by going through the Maumasson pass on a light ship, and joining at sea an American vessel whose captain's assistance had been assured by King Joseph.

In returning home that evening, the Emperor told me he had thought of sending me to wait for him in Rochefort, but that I would leave with him only on the following day. The evening at the prefecture had lasted until 11 p.m.; as he retired, the Emperor told me to come in at 3 a.m., to be in the coaches at 4.

---

[244]Bertrand, Count Clauzel (1772-1842) served brilliantly under the Empire, but in July 1815 was stripped of his rank. Sentenced to death in absentia, he managed to sail for America. The conquest of Algeria after 1830 gave him again the opportunity to distinguish himself. Marshal of France and governor general in Algeria, the disastrous 1836 campaign against Constantine left him in a state of disgrace.

[245]General Maximilien Lamarque (1770-1832) is less known for his brilliant military exploits than for his political role. During the Hundred Days, he succeeded in the difficult task of pacifying the western departments, where a new royalist movement was starting. Deputy of the Landes, he enjoyed a great reputation for liberal eloquence. General Lamarque's funeral in 1832 served as a pretext for the violent uprising of the Saint-Merry cloister.

Taking advantage of the Emperor's stop in Niort, General Becker wrote the following report to the government:

In order to hasten my report to the provisional government, I am informing it by special courier that the Emperor has arrived in Niort, tired and very concerned about the fate of France.

Without having been recognized, the Emperor was greatly touched by the concern with which people were inquiring of him along the way, and the expressions of interest made him say several times: "The government doesn't know the mood in France, it was too anxious to have me leave Paris, and had it accepted my proposal, things would have turned around: I could still exercise in the name of the nation a great influence on political matters, by backing up the government's negotiations with an army for which my name would serve as rallying point."

Arriving in Niort, His Majesty was informed by the Rochefort maritime prefect that, by doubling its cruisers and its vigilance since June 29, the British squadron had rendered impossible any exit by vessels. The Emperor had General Becker write the following letter to the prefect:

In these conditions, the Emperor wishes the minister of the navy to authorize the captain of the frigate he will be boarding to communicate with the commander of the British squadron should extraordinary circumstances render this move indispensable, as much for the Emperor's personal safety as to spare France the pain and shame of seeing him removed from his last refuge and delivered into the hands of his enemies.

Under these difficult circumstances, we are anxiously awaiting news from Paris. We hope the capital will defend itself and that the enemy will give you time to see the outcome of the negotiations undertaken by your ambassadors, and to reinforce the army to cover Paris (this sentence and the last were dictated by the Emperor). If in this situation the British cruisers prevent the frigates from departing, you may call upon the Emperor to serve as a general, as his only consideration is being of use to the motherland.

Signed: Lieutenant General Count Becker

On the 3rd at 4 a.m. the Emperor thanked the Niort prefect for his cordial and frank hospitality and climbed into his coach, escorted by a platoon of the 2nd hussars commanded by an officer galloping next to the door. His Majesty—unable to escape the eagerness of the population that had spread beyond the city and was hailing him with cries of Vive l'Empereur!—once a few leagues out of town, did not wish the escort to go with him any further; he thanked the officer and the platoon, and had each man given a gold napoleon. Early in the afternoon of the same day, the Emperor arrived at the subprefecture building in Rochefort; the carriages under the command of Count de Montholon arrived that night, and on the next day, July 4, all the retinue was together. On the 5th King Joseph arrived too.

While in this town, the Emperor remained in civilian dress, but the population was soon informed of his arrival, and the most enthusiastic demonstrations gave testimony to the affection the people had for him. The population that had gathered under his windows waited to see him in order to express to him with the national cry of the day, Vive l'Empereur!, their feelings of love and sorrow. He showed himself several times at the balcony of his apartment, and each time he was welcomed by the crowd with the same enthusiasm. He remained removed from the personnel of his retinue, who saw him no more than had he been at the Tuileries. Those near him were the grand marshal, the Duke of Rovigo (Savary), and General Gourgaud. The Emperor was calm and appeared indifferent to what was going on.

In this city, the Duke of Rovigo arranged to negotiate 100,000 francs' worth of drafts he had for the account of the Emperor, and exchanged them for gold. I had twelve deer-hide belts made, in order to divide among them the 100,000 écus[246] in gold that constituted the treasure, which thus became easier to transport by a dozen members of the retinue.

His Majesty learned in Rochefort that the provisional government had refused the furniture he had requested, and that his librarian M. Barbier had not been able to obtain that his Trianon library be sent to him. Deputations from towns and the army came to plead with the

---

[246]The 'écu' was a silver coin worth 5 francs; hence 100,000 écus = 500,000 francs. —Ed.

Emperor not to abandon them. The Emperor replied that it was too late; his advice, opinion, and services had been scorned and rejected, the enemy was in Paris, and it would mean adding the horrors of civil war to a foreign invasion. He could certainly, with the Aix garrison augmented by the Rochefort troops, respond to the invitations of Generals Lamarque and Clauzel. But it would be of no use for the motherland; this decision could only serve to stipulate conditions advantageous to himself, and his patriotism was too great to be concerned with his own person when so many evils were about to befall France. The Emperor asked the grand marshal to collect the names of the army officers who made up this deputation, and those of the town deputies who likewise came to express to him their regrets and devotion.

The telegraph between Rochefort and Paris was in constant contact during the five days the Emperor was in that city. He was being pressed to embark. The navy had not lagged behind the army in offering its services to help His Majesty elude the surveillance of the British cruisers. Captain Bodin offered his help, and Captain Besson, commanding a Danish ship, placed himself at the disposal of the Emperor, promising to take him to the United States and to hide him so as to escape all searches of the cruisers: but hiding in the hold of a vessel if it were taken was not a method he found worthy of him.

On July 8 the Emperor left Rochefort and proceeded to Fouras to board the frigate *Saale*, commanded by Captain Philibert; the entire town lined his way, having but one cry for him: Vive l'Empereur! At 10 p.m. he was on board.

On the 9th, he left the ship to go visit the fortifications of the island of Aix, where he was greeted with great enthusiasm by the population and the garrison. He then returned on board for lunch. On the 10th and the 11th, the Emperor did not leave the frigate; he sent the Duke of Rovigo (Savary) and Count de Las Cases to find out if the safe-conducts promised by the provisional government had arrived so that he could proceed to the United States. These gentlemen ascertained that they had not arrived and that the frigates would be attacked if they tried to sail out. They told the Emperor that if he wished to go to England, the captain of the *Bellerophon* had assured them he would be welcomed there. After this meeting, the British vessel came close to us and dropped anchor in the Basques roadstead. The safe-conducts had not arrived, and it was obvious that they wished His Majesty to give himself up of his own accord.

The household horses had just arrived in Rochefort, led by Chauvin, head of the service staff, along with a large number of male personnel. He came on board to take orders from the grand marshal, and to request the money needed to pay the grooms and settle the expenses incurred during the trip. The means to transport such a large amount of material were lacking, the Emperor was short of money, and he was told to sell them, and take from the proceeds the money needed to pay the men.

On the 12th, the Emperor left the *Saale* and went to stay on the island of Aix, where various ploys were suggested to escape the British cruisers. The Emperor had been greeted with enthusiasm by the population lining the shore. The dispatches from Paris invited him to depart without delay, for fear of dire consequences; on the contrary, the population begged him not to leave, saying they would defend him against his enemies. King Joseph, whose attachment never failed the Emperor, came on the 13th to offer to give himself up to the British while pretending to be His Majesty, thus giving the Emperor an opportunity to escape. The Emperor embraced him and rejected this proposal while saying goodbye and urging him to look after his own safety. Young naval officers came to propose to the grand marshal that the Emperor go on board a coastal sloop: they were MM. Gentil, Duret, Pottier, Salis, and Châteauneuf, and all warranted they could slip through the British cruisers without being seen by them. The Emperor was touched by so much devotion, and for a moment decided to trust their courage and share their dangers, and a few personal effects were carried on board. The drawback of such a vessel was that for want of water and food it would be forced to stop somewhere along the coast. They did not follow through with the plan, and the personal effects were unloaded. The Danish ship, with Captain Besson, offered a much better chance: Count Bertrand and the Duke of Rovigo

(Savary) went to visit it, and food was brought on board along with weapons and some of the Emperor's personal effects; the departure time had been settled, when other decisions were reached.

On the 14th, Count de Las Cases and General Lallemand were sent on board the *Bellerophon*. Captain Maitland told them he had orders to take on board Napoleon and his retinue, and to treat him with the greatest courtesy. These gentlemen came back and reported to His Majesty on their mission: Captain Maitland did not guarantee that passports for America would be granted. Before that, General Lallemand had been sent to the Bordeaux River to secure passage.

Much time had been wasted in Rochefort, and the delay can only be blamed on the uncertainty of the orders issued by the provisional government, the passports that were expected, the unfavorable winds, and the blockage of the exit by British vessels.

Had he been alone, the Emperor would not have hesitated on the choice to be made; as early as Niort he had said: "As soon as Marchand arrives, I will go to Rochefort and board the first ship I find there sailing for America, where people can come and join me." Steered away from this solution, he came to have with him women and children, hence his hesitation.

Before reaching a final decision, the Emperor wished to have the advice of the people around him: he gathered them together, and submitted to their deliberation whether he should surrender to the British; several opinions were given. One of the witnesses told me that Count de Las Cases, the Duke of Rovigo (Savary), and Count Bertrand, with their loyal and generous feelings, put themselves in the place of the British ministry, and thought His Majesty would be greeted in England with all the respect due adversity. The others, Generals Lallemand, Montholon, and Gourgaud, did not share that opinion: less confident of British hospitality, they advised against it and begged His Majesty not to come to such a decision. General Lallemand, who had been sent to La Rochelle, said that there were in the Bordeaux River several vessels without sails that had offered their services, and stated they would escape the British cruisers: all vied for the honor of saving the Emperor and taking him to America. He had seen the captains of these vessels, men of resolve, and the Emperor could easily reach them by land: it only required tricking the surveillance around us by pretending to be ill. To make it more believable, His Majesty only needed to leave Marchand behind to answer the questions that would be asked regarding the Emperor's illness for 24 hours. He was certain he could take the Emperor by land to Saintes and get him on board ship before anyone became aware of his escape. This plan was disputed, the opposition won out, and the Emperor returned to his room, saying to the grand marshal who accompanied him: "Bertrand, it is not without danger to place oneself in the hands of one's enemies, but it is better to risk trusting their honor than to fall into their hands as a rightful prisoner."

The tug-of-war he had been subjected to for several days had ceased, and the fatal decision to turn himself over to the British had been reached. No one then foresaw Saint Helena, and Count Bertrand told me that during this council meeting, General Lallemand was the only man who had opposed this decision with all his strength.

The Emperor's decision to give himself up to the British has mainly been attributed to Count and Countess Bertrand. Certainly Countess Bertrand did not hide her desire to see the Emperor go to England, and never doubted he would be received there with pomp and circumstance. It was because of her generous spirit, inspired by the greater glory of the Emperor. She did me the honor of talking to me about it, but such sentiments had no influence on the decision His Majesty had just reached. In Saint Helena, while browsing through a small book entitled *Recollections of Madame Durand*, a lady on the staff of Empress Marie-Louise, the Emperor read that accusation in it: he took a pencil, marked the passage and wrote: Untrue. I have already stated that men he could consider to be his good friends, the Duke of Vicenza (Caulaincourt) and Count de Lavalette, had given him the same advice at the Elysée before leaving Paris; this advice was renewed by the older people among those he had just consulted. A large entourage which he would have had to part with, had he made a different choice, perhaps contributed to the decision he reached.

The Emperor then wrote to the prince regent the following letter that shall be admired throughout the centuries and be the shame of the British government of that time:

Your Royal Highness, faced with the factions that divide my country and the enmity of the greatest powers in Europe, I have ended my political career; I come like Themistocles to sit by the hearth of the British people. I place myself under the protection of their laws, which I request from Your Royal Highness, as the most powerful, the steadiest, and the most generous of my enemies.

General Gourgaud, charged with taking this letter to the prince regent, went on board the British cruiser; he was accompanied by Count de Las Cases, who informed the captain of the *Bellerophon* that on the next day, the 15th, the Emperor would come on board.

Indeed, the next morning at 6 a.m., the brig *L'Epervier*, flying a truce flag, took the Emperor on board and conveyed him to the *Bellerophon*. The deepest sadness showed on every face, and when the British gig approached to take the Emperor on board, the most heartrending cries were heard: officers and sailors saw with despair His Majesty trust his fate to the generosity of a nation whose perfidy they well knew. Having said goodbye to the crew and cast a final look on this beautiful France whose destiny he was abdicating, the Emperor climbed into the gig. Cries of Vive l'Empereur! mixed with sobs accompanied him until he arrived on board the *Bellerophon*. Despair was so great among some that they pulled their hair out, while others trampled their hats with their feet, out of rage.

It is regrettable that the Emperor did not board the *Méduse* rather than the *Saale*; the two captains did not have the same amount of vigor. The latter was a cold man who perhaps had orders to attempt nothing to save the Emperor; he had kept the fleurs-de-lys on the panes that separated the dining room from the salon, which could attest to his small measure of Bonapartism. The captain of the *Méduse* on the other hand was bursting with it. To save the Emperor or to die was his motto, and he envisioned that possibility by attacking the *Bellerophon* with both frigates while *L'Epervier* got through. That act of devotion was still possible on the day he went on board, but the next day the presence of Admiral Hotham made it impossible. Learning of the Emperor's decision to surrender to the British, good Captain Ponée cried: "Ah Ah! why did he not come on board my ship, rather than the *Saale*! I would have gotten him through in spite of the cruisers. In what hands is he placing himself! Who could have given him such vicious advice? That nation is nothing but perfidy! Poor Napoleon, you are lost, a terrible premonition tells me so!"

When the Emperor left *L'Epervier*, General Becker went up to the Emperor and asked if he should accompany him to the *Bellerophon*. The Emperor said to him: "Do nothing of the kind, they would certainly say that you gave me up to the British." The general seized the hand the Emperor offered him, covered it with kisses, and rising with his eyes full of tears, said: "Sire, may you be happier than we!"

Note. General Becker has said—and M. de Vaulabelle has repeated—that while sleeping on board near the Emperor, separated from him only by a thin partition, during the night he had heard cries brought about by an attack of hemorrhoids that had tormented him at Waterloo. The general was mistaken, for neither in Elba, nor during the Hundred Days, nor in Saint Helena did the Emperor ever complain of such a problem.

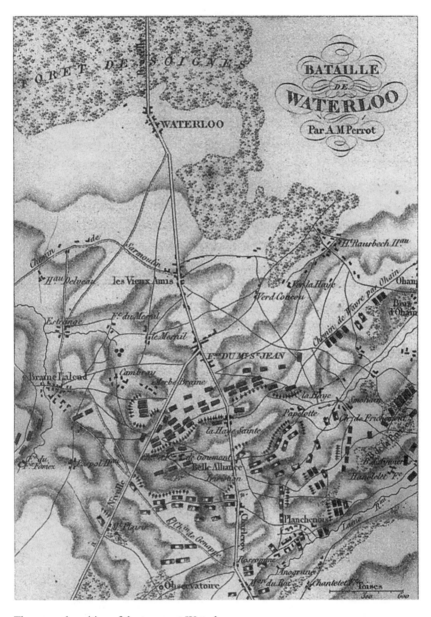

The general position of the troops at Waterloo.

The Battle of Ligny. By careful marshaling of his troops and a good understanding of the lay of the land, the first day's fight is won.

Departure of Napoleon from Waterloo after the battle of the Belle Alliance.

The assembly is received with disdain as their acts have brought down the government.

As things fall apart around Napoleon, his staff begins to leave him. The loyal ones stay. Napoleon is grateful and does what he can to relieve their concerns.

The Elysée Palace in 1815. After Waterloo Napoleon sets up his residence here.

Because Paris is unsafe, Napoleon returns to Malmaison to wait for promised passports. They do not come. His friends including the Countess Walewska, mother of Napoleon's son, and Madame Pellapra, mother of Napoleon's daughter the future Princess of Chimay, come to say farewell.

In the guise of being in charge of Napoleon's security, General Becker is sent by Talleyrand to keep an eye on him.

The view at the port at Rochefort.

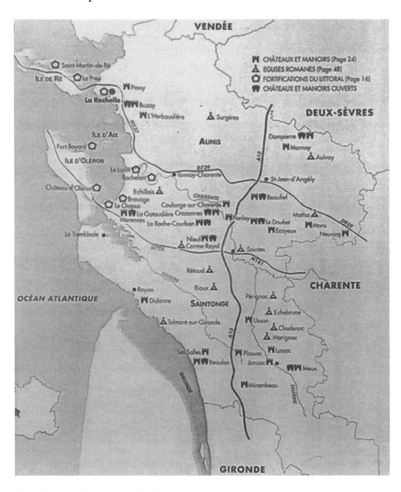

Map showing the route to Rochefort.

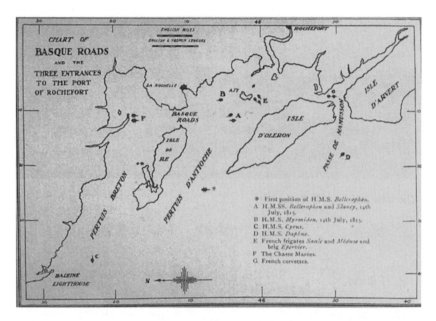

The Basque Roads and the three entrances to the port of Rochefort showing positions of British and French ships which will prevent Napoleon from going to America.

While waiting to make his decisions, Napoleon goes to the Island of Aix which had been a navy post. He makes the commanding officer's house his headquarters.

BOOK TWO

SAINT HELENA

PREFACE TO BOOK TWO

*J*ean Bourguignon died before having finished his work. Men of his caliber are strangers to rest, working without respite and dying while still at their labors without having completed the task whose boundaries have yet to be defined.

Interested in everything, fascinated by history, enamored of the Napoleonic epic, and an artist and writer, Jean Bourguignon devoted his life to Malmaison and its inhabitants, from the lowliest to the most famous. France owes to him the most delightful of its palaces, the most vibrant and exciting of its historical museums.

I had the great privilege of working alongside him, and I was able to benefit firsthand from his vast knowledge, his legendary kindness equalled only by his unselfishness, his generosity, and his ability to forgive, if not to forget, the evils and ingratitude of this world.

The political life he had sampled among the great, or so-called great, had taught him to know men. He judged them without severity, with the good nature and benign philosophy that lent such charm to his conversation. But perhaps ministerial work had brought out in him a natural facility to sidestep the obstacles which prevented him from reaching his goals—to lay siege to collectors, for the sake of his beloved museum. Some of them, having made a gift to Malmaison, considered themselves in the debt of the kindly curator who had approached them, and expressed their gratitude to him for having allowed them to be of service.

As Chief Curator of the Napoleonic Museums, a guiding force behind the great national palaces, a member of the Institute, and one concerned with the future of the Army Museum, Jean Bourguignon carried out his work in accordance with the larger picture his vast intelligence and extensive knowledge afforded him. Yet for all this, he never neglected the telling details brought to his attention by a sure taste for the colorful and a desire to portray people and events as accurately as possible.

That is why Marchand's character, his intelligence, his uprightness, his integrity, and above all his loyalty to the fallen Emperor appealed to Jean Bourguignon.

In memory of Napoleon's brief stay at Malmaison before his departure for Rochefort and his tragic fate, he brought together for the museum touching mementos of the Emperor, his captivity, and the return of his body, before offering to the public his two moving and definitive works: *Les Adieux de Malmaison* and *Le Retour des Cendres*. He also wanted that the noble figure of Marchand, considered a friend by the dying Emperor, be evoked in the last palace Napoleon had inhabited in France.

Count Desmazières-Marchand, grandson of the executor of the Emperor's will, responded to the wishes of Malmaison's curator by offering the museum not only invaluable souvenirs of the Emperor, but of his grandfather as well. To Jean Bourguignon personally he entrusted the memoirs that the faithful Marchand had written for his daughter, "to better teach you," Marchand wrote, "and later your children, what the Emperor meant to me, to better show you this man who was the arbiter of kings, equally as great in adversity as on the throne when he ruled Europe, and to tell you of his resignation in dying on the rock of Saint Helena."

The publication of these memoirs was in a way the crowning achievement of Jean Bourguignon's career; they were the last memoirs yet unpublished of those people who had been with the Emperor up to his final moments. Jean Bourguignon published the first volume which relates the events of the island of Elba and during the Hundred Days. In the fine and substantial introduction with which he prefaced Book One, Jean Bourguignon draws a vivid portrait of Marchand and prepares the reader to find in the faithful valet's story, if not "sensational revelations," at least information on facts that had remained obscure or distorted, depending on the leanings or the opportunism of the witnesses and memoir writers—details which "correct many errors, and contain the truth."

Jean Bourguignon intended to give the public the major part of Marchand's memoirs, that which deals with the Emperor's captivity, when death overtook him, so to speak, pen in hand before a blank page. He left his daughter, Mme Roland Hélène Rooke-Bourguignon, Marchand's manuscript and the task of publishing it. The courageous young woman saw to this sacred duty despite mourning, sorrow, and all the difficulties overwhelming her due to the almost simultaneous loss of a dearly loved father and mother.

Because I was her revered father's colleague, Mme Hélène Rooke-Bourguignon asked me to finish his work. With legitimate pride I accepted this token of confidence and the honor accompanying it, without daring to claim that I could replace the illustrious man deceased.

The memoirs that Marchand devotes to Saint Helena are the most important and the most captivating. They are in five parts.

The first three take the reader from the embarkation on board the *Bellerophon* to the end of Napoleon's sustained battle against Hudson Lowe, his jailer, until illness and voluntary seclusion had diminished the physical resistance of the indomitable captive.

The last two parts are given to the final moments of the Emperor's life and to his death. His last hours are documented in a manner particularly detailed, accurate, and touching.

Marchand actually took daily notes which, incorporated into a narrative always minutely exact and captivating, leave the reader breathless and supply him with details hitherto unknown. The decent valet tells the truth; he describes what he did, what he said, what he heard, without claiming to judge anyone. Count de Las Cases, the grand marshal, Generals Gourgaud and Montholon, and Countesses Bertrand and Montholon come to life naturally under his pen; Marchand refrains from commenting on their behavior to each other, even to the Emperor. He rarely associates himself with the opinion the "French of Longwood" held for the "English of Plantation House and London." If he complains of their decisions, it is because the Emperor's physical and mental life are affected and suffer from them. Badly mistreated himself by Hudson Lowe, Marchand fears being sent to the Cape of Good Hope, because he would have to leave the Emperor and deprive him of his care. But he never complains of the fatigue or the lack of sleep imposed on him those final months by his almost constant attendance on the distinguished invalid.

His affection, his devotion, his reason for living all revolve around the Emperor, whose words he notes carefully. He copies them directly, and we can hear the short, precise sentences expressing teeming thoughts and implacable good sense by turns.

However, Marchand's memoirs do bring to light some problems for the historians of the future to examine. The story of the Hundred Days and Saint Helena will not be complete until the British archives have been studied by French specialists. The captivating, fascinating, perhaps revealing "clandestine history" of this period, whose veil Marchand lifts slightly, remains in shadow: the Allies' intentions and behavior regarding Napoleon as sovereign of Elba; the role Cipriani and his agents play in Vienna; the secret trips between the island and the continent; the spy network in Livorno; the events and information leading to the Emperor's departure; the Flight of the Eagle and the royal army, etc., without forgetting the Duke of Feltre's (Clarke's) schemes at Ghent, the actions of Fouché's police, and the behavior of Countess Bertrand and her family in May and June 1815.

On the other hand, we become lost in conjecture trying to justify Napoleon's decision to give himself up to the English. "As soon as
Marchand arrives," the Emperor says in Niort, "I will go to Rochefort
and get on board the first ship I can find sailing to America, where you
can come to join me." It is a decision, almost an order. But after the
discussion on the island of Aix, he says to Bertrand: "It is not without
risk to put yourself in the hands of your enemies, but it is better to trust
their honor than to fall into their hands as a rightful prisoner." What
happened in between times? Apparently there exist in England some
secret documents, originating from Admiral Decrès in particular.

Even on Saint Helena, the Emperor seems better informed
than is generally believed regarding what happens on the island, and
even in Europe. There exist, in Jamestown or elsewhere, one or more
"mailboxes." Cipriani, of whom Gourgaud is jealous, reprises his role
as spy; he has contacts with the people of Saint Helena, with sailors...
Marchand piques our interest in the life and character of this man, who
is much more than a butler; he leaves us with the desire to learn more
about him.

Santini awaits a historian to bring him out of the mists of legend. His stay in London is quite extraordinary...Has all been told
about the commissioners and their circle? About O'Meara? About the
officers at Deadwood? About the visits paid to Countess Bertrand,
whom the Emperor avoided for a time? About the relations among the
"French of Longwood" with certain leading citizens of the island, for
example Mr. Doveton, a knight of the Order of the Bath, landowner
and magistrate of the island of Saint Helena, whom, in a letter dated
January 13, 1826, General Bertrand calls his "respectable friend"?
Cardinal Fesch's behavior is equally inexplicable, as is that of the
Emperor's family living in Europe, with the exception of Pauline.

But there is no archives concerning the captivity; who will
take charge of establishing them? Like the documents, the souvenirs of
Saint Helena are far-flung; who will create a Museum of Saint Helena?

In an article in *Le Temps* on August 17, 1929, Georges Mon-
torgueil, seconded by Ernest d'Hauterive, the late René Vivie de
Régie, and my friend Pierre Chanlaine, called for the publication of

Marchand's complete memoirs. In support of Jean Bourguignon's efforts, he wrote: "The few stylistic errors or awkward phrases found in them are negligible, and in no way tarnish the author's memory."

Decidedly, Louis Marchand, loyal executor of the Emperor's will, and the essential interest of his memoirs are far above a few liberties taken with syntax, with the result that the solution adopted by Jean Bourguignon in Book One has been respected here. Just as he did, I have attempted to clarify, with the help of necessary punctuation and some minor corrections, certain sentences whose length made them difficult to understand.

Notes expanding various passages have been kept to a minimum, as the biographies of the principal protagonists are well known; I have preferred unusual information to often-repeated details. It is, after all, Marchand's text that is far more important than commentaries of his editor.

The reader can refer to the works of Mme Marie-Antoinette Pardée, in particular to her *Sainte-Hélène*, for which she specifically studied the Lowe Papers at the British Museum; to the recent and definitive version of the *Mémorial du comte de Las Cases* edited by Marcel Dunan of the Institute (Flammarion); to his many notes and commentaries drawn from the best sources; and to Dr. Arnold Chaplin's *A Saint Helena Who's Who* (London: Arthur L. Humphreys, 1919).

Marchand's memoirs completes the list of documents written by Napoleon's companions in Saint Helena. They follow the *Mémorial* of Count de Las Cases, the *Journal* of General Gourgaud, the memoirs of Antommarchi, the writings of General and Countess de Montholon, the *Souvenirs* of the mameluke Ali (published by Professor G. Michaut), and section of General Bertrand's journal, *Cahiers de Sainte-Hélène* (vol. I: January-May 1821; vol. II: 1816-1817), deciphered and annotated by Paul Fleuriot de Langle.

Covering the entire span of the captivity, written by a man of courage, good sense, and fine mind—he who was the most sincere, modest, unselfish, devoted, and loyal of all the members of the captive

Emperor's entourage, Marchand's memoirs, in which all his fine qualities are reflected, constitute an authoritative work.

In closing, I wish to express my affectionate and respectful gratitude to Mme Roland Hélène Rooke-Bourguignon, for the trust she has shown in me and the friendship with which she honors me.

I thank my friend René Varin, the distinguished cultural attaché at the French embassy in London, whose goal is to make known on the other side of the Channel everything associated with France's greatness; no historian and researcher ever appeals to him in vain. I thank my lifetime friend Georges Mauguin, erudite historian of the Napoleonic epic and author of many colorful, well-documented, and lively works; Alain Decaux, the well-known historian, whose demanding work unfortunately kept him at a distance from me during the publication of these memoirs; Mlle Madeleine Tartary, librarian at the Bibliothèque nationale, whose kindness and competence in all concerning the Epic are legendary, and who offered to take on the task of indexing proper names in these memoirs; M. van der Kemp, chief curator of the Versailles Museum, and his colleague Mlle Langlois; thanks to them, Marchand's memoirs are illustrated with unpublished documents; Lieutenant-Colonel Santini, medical corps, a mine of information on Corsican celebrities and curiosities, the historian of Corsican regiments and battalions; Mme Sevestre, Dr. Jean Delmare, and the great-grandnephews and nieces of the loyal Coursot, the Emperor's butler in Saint Helena; Dr. Rouyer de Vitteaux (Côte d'Or), Coursot's birthplace; Colonel Marc Troude, medical corps, the historian of General Bacler d'Albe; M. Charles Maillard, well informed regarding Marchand's descendants; my friend Jacques Arnna, autograph expert and impartial critic; Marc-André Fabvre, eminent documentalist, director of the war ministry library; Major Chalmin, of the historical archives; Jean-Claude Devos, archivist and librarian of the army's historical services; André Cambier, curator of the war ministry administrative archives; Colonel Barrère, kind and knowledgeable administrator of the "Napoleon at Saint Helena" exhibit organized at the Hôtel des Invalides; M. Dominique Paoli; and all those who have helped me with the arduous task entrusted to my care.

Henry Lachouque.

Because Napoleon expected the British government to provide him sanctuary, he surrenders himself to the commanding officer of H.M. Frigate *Bellerophon*, Captain Maitland. He is taken out to the ship by English sailors.

After much soul-searching, and in an effort to be correct, Napoleon and his party board the *Bellerophon* hoping to be taken to England.

Gourgaud.

Montholon.

Bertrand.

Las Cases.

Some drawings by Denzel Ibbetson
made on the *Northumberland*.

PART FOUR

*Toward Saint Helena,
the Briars, Longwood*

CHAPTER TEN

The Emperor on board the Bellerophon — Torbay — Plymouth —
Napoleon prisoner — Vexations — The Northumberland —
Toward Saint Helena

*W*hen the Emperor arrived on board the *Bellerophon*,[247] he
was received at the top of the stairs by Count de Las
Cases,[248] who introduced him to Captain Maitland.[249] The troops were
under arms and the ship's company was out on the yards. "I come,"
said the Emperor to Captain Maitland, "to place myself under the protection of British laws." The captain answered with a deep bow and
took him down to the main stateroom, where a few moments later the
ship's officers were introduced to him. Countesses Bertrand and
Montholon, as well as their children, were left on deck; they then took
possession of their quarters. The Emperor, having entered the room
which was intended for him, re-emerged. Captain Maitland urged him
to examine all parts of his ship, where an admirable state of order and
cleanliness prevailed. The brig *L'Epervier*, which had brought us, was
about to leave. Before its departure the grand marshal gave the captain
of that ship a letter for General Becker which read as follows:

---

[247]This was an old vessel with 74 cannons. It had fought in the battle of Aboukir in
1798. At Trafalgar it fought against the Eagle and both captains were killed. Having
lost its masts, the *Bellerophon* had been forced to leave the line. This old ship was
incapable of making a long cruise. Did the French sailors in Rochefort know this?

[248]See Count de Las Cases' *Mémorial de Sainte-Hélène*.

[249]Captain Frederick Lewis Maitland, born in 1777, had served on the staff of Lord
Saint Vincent. His conduct toward Napoleon was hotly debated in England. The British admiralty deprived him of his command until 1818. He died a rear admiral in 1838
in the Bay of Bombay and was buried in the cathedral of that city.

15 July 1815—My dear general, we have arrived on board the British [ship]. We can only praise the welcome we have received here, and thank you for the good care you have taken of us. Please inform Madame and Princess Hortense, who must be near Paris, that the Emperor is well. Please also inform Prince Joseph, who must be near Rochefort.

I have given you a copy of the letter which the Emperor has written to the prince regent; I need not remind you to show this to no one for at least two weeks. You will sense how improper it would be for it to be known before the British papers have published it.

Please believe, etc.

/s/ Bertrand

That afternoon while sailing for England we saw the *Superb* arrive, commanded by Admiral Hotham[250] who gave the order to drop anchor and came alongside the *Bellerophon*. This general officer immediately came on board to pay a visit to the Emperor, and begged him to do him the honor of visiting his vessel and accepting a small collation there. The Emperor, after talking to him for some time, said as he left that he would accept his invitation.

The following day, as the Emperor was coming out of his bedroom to go on board the *Superb*, he found the marines under arms. Stopping in front of them, he requested them to go through some weapons drills, including that of crossing bayonets, which they did with precision. The Emperor, approaching one of the men, pushed down rather hard on the barrel of his rifle, in order to judge the man's strength. Not finding adequate resistance in this position, he seized the rifle and demonstrated the movement, to the great surprise of all who were there.

When the Emperor arrived on the admiralty vessel, the entire ship's crew was in parade uniform and standing on the yards, and the

---

[250] Admiral Hotham (1777-1833) had served in the Navy since 1790 and had fought at Trafalgar. From 1810 to 1812, commanding the *Northumberland*, he had participated in the blockade of the French coast. He was then named to the North American fleet. He became a rear admiral June 4, 1814, and in 1815 raised his colors on the *Superb*, a vessel with 72 cannons built in 1798.

soldiers were under arms. On his vessel Admiral Hotham rendered the Emperor the honors due a crowned head. Saint-Denis, who accompanied the Emperor, told me on his return that the reception had been most sovereign in tone; the Emperor had been very gracious toward the admiral during the visit he made to his ship, and on leaving thanked him for his frank and cordial reception.

That evening we were sailing again toward England. Such great care taken by the British to please us led us to hope that the reception in England would be no worse. But alas! It was to be entirely otherwise.

The officers in the Emperor's retinue were placed in cabins in the first gun battery. The Emperor was settled in the large room on the poop deck; the room just before it was both a dining room and a drawing room, in which every night one of the Emperor's ADCs slept, just as in Paris. To be closer to the Emperor I slept in his bedroom, and Saint-Denis just outside across the doorway.

Count de Las Cases had been a naval officer and was often called by the Emperor, who would query him regarding the course of the vessel. It was evident to him, although the wind was not favorable and navigation difficult, that the ship was not sailing as fast as it was supposed to; we were about to learn the reason. It was during this crossing that the Emperor noticed that Count de Las Cases had only the decoration of the Order of the Reunion and gave him the cross of the Legion of Honor; telling him to wear it if he still recognized his right to repair this omission in not presenting it to him earlier. During these first days of navigation the Emperor did not become seasick, but it was not the same for his officers and the personnel in his retinue, who were almost all sick at the beginning of the crossing. On July 24, arriving in Torbay[251] at 8 o'clock in the morning, the Emperor learned that General Gourgaud had not received permission from the admiralty to disembark, and that any communication with shore had been forbidden him. This general soon came and informed the Emperor, who deduced nothing good from the refusal to allow his ADC to personally deliver to the prince regent the letter he was carrying, which he had had to relinquish. The captain of the *Slany*,[252] upon which he was

Invited to make an inspection, no part of the ship is missed by the experienced eye of
Napoleon.

When it becomes known at Torbay that the *Bellerophon*, carrying Napoleon, is in the harbor, hundreds of English people come out in small boats to see him.

Important government officers have informed Napoleon that he is to go to St. Helena. He boards the *Northumberland*, commanded by Admiral Cockburn. He is received politely and the members of his party who are to accompany him are chosen.

At Plymouth, when Napoleon sees the curious crowd surrounding the *Bellerophon* in small boats, he presents himself at the rail.

embarked, having dropped anchor in the Torbay, informed General Gourgaud that his orders were not to allow him to communicate with shore, and that he himself would deliver the letter Gourgaud was carrying to London. No matter how much the general protested, he was unsuccessful; the *Slany*, on which he was under surveillance, could be considered quarantined until the *Bellerophon* came to drop anchor in this bay. As soon as he arrived Captain Maitland sent a courier to Lord Keith,[253] who was in Plymouth. While dressing, the Emperor looked out of his bedroom's porthole at the shoreline covered with charming houses, in which he said he would be pleased to live in solitude under the name of Muiron, one of his ADCs killed while covering his body

---

[251]On July 21 Lord Liverpool wrote to Lord Castlereagh: "We are all of the same opinion: we must not let Napoleon reside in this country. The very delicate legal questions that would be raised on this subject would be highly embarrassing."

In fact, it was necessary to prevent the Emperor from having any means of invoking British law and obtaining from a judge a writ of habeas corpus.

This was Lord Liverpool's main concern. As it turned out, this writ was obtained on July 31. A lawyer was on his way to inform the proper authorities, and Liverpool wrote to Castlereagh:

"Bonaparte is giving us a great deal of trouble in Plymouth."

A strange race began between the lawyer and Lord Keith; and became quite eventful. On August 4 the admiral precipitously left his domicile, jumped in a rowboat, went on board the *Tonnant*, then abandoned this to regain the *Prometheus*, and disappeared.

[252]This was Lieutenant Commander Sartorius, commanding the *Slany*, a corvette mounting four guns and eight cannons.

[253]George Elphinstone, Lord Keith (1746-1823), was an old sea wolf who had participated in every naval campaign from the end of the 18th century until 1815; he had convoyed the corps of General Abercromby to Egypt in 1801. If he did not achieve renown as a great admiral, important captures made during lucky cruises had made him a considerably richer man.

Ever unable to sleep quietly at the mere thought that a French rowboat could still be floating on the ocean other than keel up, Lord Keith, inelegant guardian of Napoleon, whom he called the 'reptile,' had spent fifty years of his life chasing the French. But at the age of seventy, he was forced to accept one of them at his table and be nice to him: Charles de Flahaut, ADC to the Emperor, the most seductive and representative of the gentlemen of the race he detested, had just become his son-in-law!

with his own, or that of Duroc,[254] of whom he had been very fond. Fruit was sent to him by the owner of one of the houses he was admiring. On leaving his room, he went on the bridge in the company of Count de Las Cases. A large number of boats carrying a population anxious to see him were gathered around the ship. The Emperor, approaching the side, saluted them, and was answered with cheers. No matter how benevolent these demonstrations were, they did not succeed in dissipating the ominous feeling that had seized our souls.

During the night of the 25th to the 26th, we sailed for Plymouth where we arrived on the 26th, ten days after our departure from Rochefort, and twenty-seven after our departure from Paris. A much larger throng of people and small boats gathered around the ship. The sea was obstructed by them out to a great distance; it was easy to see, through the welcome the Emperor received when he showed himself, that interest was mixed with curiosity on the part of this multitude. No doubt it was feared that it might become even greater, for orders were given to push these boats some distance away from the vessel. The people in charge of this task did so with revolting brutality, showing no concern whatever for the accidents that might result from the impact of their own boats against those they were ordered to push back, full of men, women, and children all crying out in terror. These precautions had their reason: the faces around us had changed, the name of Saint Helena was being heard. Two honor guards had been stationed on either side of the dining room door since the Emperor came on board; one of these, an Irishman by birth, at a moment when he believed he was not being watched, crossed himself to let me understand he was a Catholic and said to me in a low voice: "No good for Emperor Saint Helena." Captain Maitland's first steward, who had gone on shore and come back on board, said the same thing to me. I

---

[254]One of Bonaparte's oldest companions-in-arms, Muiron had been an artillery officer during the siege of Toulon. He was ADC to General Bonaparte and was killed in Arcole while covering him with his own body. The frigate which had brought Bonaparte back from Egypt was called *La Muiron*.

Duroc, Duke of Friuli, grand marshal of the palace, ADC to the Emperor, had been killed at his side by a stray cannonball in Silesia on May 23, 1813.

kept this sad news to myself, but I believed in the possibility of deportation, a rumor that had circulated on the island of Elba as being the idea of the congress of Vienna. At this point, they were going even further; they were deliberating in council whether they might not hand over the Emperor to the vengeance of Louis XVIII. The Duke of Sussex,[255] it is said, saved his country from such an infamous action. We tried to read the fate that was awaiting us in the faces of those who had gone ashore. Captain Maitland, when he came back on board, was appalled and extremely upset by the sad news he had to convey. His silence on every subject was too significant to be mistaken, and if there had been any illusions left, a letter from Lady Clavering[256] to the Count de Las Cases and a report that secretly reached the Duke of Rovigo (Savary) did not allow any doubts regarding the destiny the Allied sovereigns had reserved for the Emperor.

On the morning of the 27th, the frigate *Eurotas*[257] dropped anchor next to us; rumors spread at once that it was to carry off the Emperor during the night. The Emperor was aware of the rumors that were circulating, but he showed nothing that could lead people to believe he put any faith in such treacherous gossip, and appeared confident in his trust of British fairness. On this same day, Captain Maitland advised the grand marshal that he had just received the order to have transported on board the *Eurotas* all the officers who were not

---

[255]The Duke of Sussex, sixth son of the king of England, George III—whom madness had kept from the throne since 1810—was the regent's brother. A liberal, he put his talent as an orator at the service of the opposition, and conducted a spirited campaign in the high chamber in favor of Napoleon.

[256]Lady Clavering was an old and faithful friend of Mme de Las Cases, writes Montholon. Of French origin, good and helpful, she had in London aided a large number of exiled families. "It is thanks to her that I was able to come back to France," said Las Cases to the Emperor in 1816.

[257]The frigate *Eurotas* left Torbay on August 8, having on board Generals Lallemand and Savary, as well as six officers. All expected to be put ashore in France and shot; but *Eurotas* took them to Malta, where they were detained until 1816. Lallemand went to the United States; Savary wandered through the Orient until 1819 and then returned to France, where he had been condemned to death in absentia. Acquitted by court martial, he was reinstated in his rank in 1830 and died in 1833, at the age of fifty-nine.

part of the personal service of the Emperor. This decision of the ministry was to be announced by Lord Keith during the day; anxiety
mounted among us. Lord Keith did indeed come on the 28th to pay a
half-hour visit to the Emperor, but it was a courtesy visit and he
revealed none of his government's intentions. It was only three days
later, on the 31st, that this admiral and undersecretary of state Bunbury[258] came on board the *Bellerophon* and petitioned the honor of
being received by the Emperor. They were introduced, remained alone
with him for about half an hour, and departed, leaving on the table the
following declaration, after giving him an oral translation of its contents:

> *As it is appropriate for General Bonaparte to learn, without any further
> delay, the intentions of the British government toward him, Your Lordship
> (Admiral Keith) conveys the following information to him:*
>
> *It would be little in keeping with our duty toward our country and the
> allies of His Majesty that General Bonaparte retain the means or opportunity to
> again disturb the peace of Europe. This is why it is absolutely necessary that he
> be restrained in his personal freedom, insofar as this primary and important
> goal requires.*
>
> *The island of Saint Helena has been chosen as his future residence; its
> climate is healthy and its location will allow him to be treated with more indul-
> gence than would be possible elsewhere, in view of the mandatory precautions
> that would have to be employed to secure his person.*
>
> *General Bonaparte is authorized to choose among the people who
> accompanied him to England—with the exception of Generals Savary and Lalle-
> mand—three officers, who along with his surgeon and twelve servants will be
> permitted to follow him to Saint Helena, and will never be allowed to leave the
> island without the approval of the British government.*

---

[258]Sir Henry Bunbury (1778-1860), general and distinguished historian, was secretary
of state for war in the cabinet of Lord Liverpool.

Rear Admiral Sir George Cockburn,[259] who is named commander in chief of the station at the Cape of Good Hope and the adjacent oceans, will take General Bonaparte and his retinue to Saint Helena, and will receive detailed instructions governing the execution of this duty.

Sir George Cockburn will probably be ready to leave in a few days, therefore it is desirable that General Bonaparte[260] immediately choose the people who are to accompany him.

The Emperor listened to the government's message with great calm, without showing any emotion. When Lord Keith and Sir Henry Bunbury had ceased to speak, he said to them: "I am the guest of England and not its prisoner; I came freely to place myself under the protection of British law. The government has violated the laws of its country, the rights of the people, and the sacred rights of hospitality in regard to me. I protest and appeal to British honor."

The admiral and the undersecretary of state assured the Emperor as they left that they would immediately convey the words they had just heard to the ministers.

That same evening, Captain Maitland sent the following letter to Admiral Keith:

---

[259]Sir George Cockburn, then aged forty-three, had distinguished himself during the war in America. During his march on Washington, he had been able to rout the Bladensburg militia before capturing the federal capital. On August 24, 1814, he had given the order to burn the Capitol, the White House, the navy yard, and several other public monuments. His reputation for "energy" had earned him a decoration and the mission of "transporting" the Emperor.

The admiral's division included the *Northumberland*, which was his flagship, the frigate Havana, the Bucephalus, the Ceylon, and the Furet. The 2nd battalion of the 53rd infantry regiment was on board these ships. Only one company was aboard the *Northumberland*.

[260]The original text reads "Buonaparte." Marchand did not respect this spelling, probably because the pamphlet writers under the Restoration wrote the name of the Emperor this way to remind people of his Italian origins. In fact, the Emperor's baptismal certificate says "Bonaparte," but his father considered this spelling erroneous, as the Emperor declared in 1790 to the genealogist d'Hozier. The last Italianate signature of Napoleon is probably that shown on his marriage certificate on March 9, 1796. In any case, the document signed on March 14 of the same year reads "Bonaparte."

Milord, I have carefully read the extract of the letter you have sent me.
I have informed you of my protest: I am not a prisoner of war; I am the guest of
England. I came to this country on the British vessel Bellerophon, after having
informed its captain of the letter I was writing to the prince regent, and having
received from him the assurance that his orders were to receive me on board and
transport me to England with my retinue, if I so requested. Admiral Hotham has
since reiterated the same assurances; from the moment I was freely received on
the Bellerophon, I have found myself under the protection of your country's laws.
I wish to live freely in England, under the protection and supervision of the law,
taking all engagements and measures which might be deemed appropriate. I do
not wish to have any correspondence with France, or to partake in any political
affairs. Since my abdication, my intention has always been to reside in the
United States or in England. I flatter myself that you, Milord, and the undersec-
retary of your government shall make a faithful report of these facts. It is in the
honor of the prince regent and the protection of your country's laws that I have
placed, and place my trust."

    31 July 1815
    Napoleon

    Immediately after the departure of Lord Keith and Sir Henry
Bunbury, the Emperor summoned the grand marshal. No sign of this
indecent declaration could be perceived on his face; his soul rose high
above this monstrous decision that made a calvary of Saint Helena,
and a martyr of the Emperor. Accompanied by the grand marshal, he
went up on deck and showed himself to the eager crowd, with the
same expression as on the preceding days. But a painful scene awaited
us; a few ships carrying our wounded prisoners taken at Waterloo was
sailing by, some distance from the *Bellerophon.*

    Back in his quarters, the Emperor remained alone with the
grand marshal a long time, talking vehemently and pacing rapidly.
When the grand marshal left, he told me to bring down to his stateroom a few cases containing silver and jewelry, as well as some securities which he designated to me, and which I knew to be in the travel
kit. The Emperor came in and repeated what the grand marshal had

said; after having satisfied his orders, I came back with him as he had asked. As I entered, I found the curtains over the windows drawn very tight; they were of red silk, which lent a mysterious hue to the room. The Emperor had already removed his uniform, saying that he wished to rest a little. Continuing to undress, he told me to go on reading where the bookmark remained in *Lives of Illustrious Men*, which was on his table. I had been struck by the arrangements the Emperor had just made in sending these things to the grand marshal's quarters. I knew he had on him that which would allow him to escape his enemies, if he unfortunately fell into their hands, or if someone tried to commit a dishonorable act against his person. The thought of destruction came to me as suddenly as lightning; I felt a moment of indescribable anguish. I was troubled by the drama that could occur in front of me. Feeling all my blood flow back toward my heart, when the Emperor without opening the bed-curtains said to me: "Read," I took the book and read with enough firmness to not let him guess the suspicion that had arisen in my soul. After a half hour of reading, ending with the death of Cato, the Emperor came out from behind the curtains with a calmness that alleviated all my fears and slipped on his bathrobe. Regarding the circumstances of Cato's death, the Emperor alluded to it one day: "He was wrong; after the death of Caesar, united with the sons of Pompeii, he thus became the first man of the Republic." This memory of the death of Cato could not be applied to the position of the Emperor who, a new Prometheus, was sailing to Saint Helena.

Within him a great determination had been reached, that of living and showing civilized Europe what a great soul can do in the grip of adversity. The Emperor had summoned the grand marshal. I left when he entered, and discovered in the drawing room the Duke of Rovigo (Savary) and General Lallemand, who were speaking together of this exclusion that deprived them of sharing the Emperor's fate. Neither doubted they were about to be handed over to the French government; both appeared disdainful of the death awaiting them. They regretted however not having found death on twenty battlefields, rather than at the hands of Frenchmen on the plain of Grenelle. "You

know, Savary," said General Lallemand, "we have escaped death so
often that it had to catch up with us sooner or later." The tranquillity of
these two generals speaking of their impending end was reminiscent of
something old-fashioned in their character.

On leaving the Emperor's quarters, the grand marshal held in
his hand the list of the people who, more fortunate than others, were to
accompany the finest, most complete genius of modern days to Saint
Helena. This choice fell upon the grand marshal, who expressed his
desire to follow the Emperor everywhere he went, along with his wife
and children.

The Emperor had written the name of General de
Montholon[261] and his family; Count de Las Cases, whose wit and
knowledge he had greatly admired in the past, along with his son;
General Gourgaud, attached to the personal service of the Emperor as
first ADC, and who could with reason count on the Emperor's
affection, ended the list of selected people. The government only
granted three officers; the Emperor designated four. Admiral Keith
agreed to this wish of the Emperor's by adding the Count de Las Cases
as cabinet secretary. To this list was attached that of the household

---

[261]Charles-Tristan de Montholon, son of Mathieu and Angelique-Aimée de Rostaing.
Born 1783 in Paris. Married on July 23, 1848 to Mlle O'Hara. (The first marriage of
the count to Albine Roger does not appear on his service record.) He joined the army
on October 7, 1799, served in many wars, and became a marshal on August 23, 1814.
He went to Saint Helena with the Emperor Napoleon on July 17, 1815, was stricken
from army rosters on that date, returned to France on October 18, 1821, and finally
died in Paris on August 20, 1853.

His campaigns included 1799 Italy, 1800-1801 Batavia, Vendémiaire An XIV,
1805-1807 Grand Army, 1808 Spain, 1809 Germany, 1814 France.

He became a member of the Legion of Honor on March 14, 1806, and knight of
Saint Louis on July 8, 1814.

His title was count of the Empire; he received on August 15, 1809 a pension of
4,000 francs. Chamberlain to the Emperor in 1809.

On July 12, 1812, he married Albine Vassal, a handsome young woman who had
been married to Daniel Roger, a financier from Geneva, but divorced from him in
1809.

On December 19, 1812, the minister of foreign relations wrote to him that "His
Majesty has judged the marriage that you have contracted incompatible with the honorable functions entrusted you." Montholon therefore ceased to be chamberlain and
ambassador to Wurzburg, and returned to the service of the War Ministry.

staff: MM. Marchand, Saint-Denis, Noverraz, Cipriani, Pierron, Lepage, the two Archambault brothers, Rousseau, and Gentilini; all except Lepage had been with the Emperor on the island of Elba.[262]

The grand marshal was granted two servants, Bernard, his

---

[262]For details on Noverraz, see Book One, footnote (101); Saint-Denis, (129); Pierron, (131); Cipriani, (189).

Lepage, King Joseph's household cook, was to have followed his master to America. But at the last moment Ferdinand Rousseau, the Emperor's chief cook on Elba and during the Hundred Days, had an unpleasant conversation with the grand marshal over his salary. He left, placing everyone in an awkward situation. Lepage agreed to go without much enthusiasm. He was an indifferent cook with a bad temper and doubtful loyalty.

Rousseau was an entirely different matter. In the Emperor's household he held the colorful title of tinsmith and candle maker, which defined his duties. In Saint Helena he was in charge of the upkeep of the silver, no simple task! Later deported by Sir Hudson Lowe, he entered Joseph's household.

Gentilini was a Corsican sailor of 33. Pilot of the Emperor's dinghy on Elba, he had come to Paris as a footman, a position he kept in Saint Helena. He was married to Juliette Collinet, a laundress. Here is the certificate given Gentilini by the grand marshal at the time he left Longwood: "He has served with precision, loyalty, and devotion. Having contracted a respiratory infection, he left Saint Helena only for reasons of illness. He deserves the protection of all persons attached to the Emperor, who grants him a lifetime pension of 600 francs dating from this day, to be paid by Madame Mère or any other member of his family.

"Longwood, Sept. 30, 1820
"Count Bertrand."

The brothers Archambault were faithful servants, skilled horsemen, and masters of daring driving. The elder, Achille-Thomas, having entered the stables in 1805, sacrificed the career he loved to follow the Emperor to Elba. Bertrand named him brigadier of the footmen, and in this capacity he served at the Tuileries, the Elysée, and Waterloo. The morning of the battle, Saint-Denis entrusted the Emperor's carriage to him. Archambault was unable to save it, but he carried away two portfolios he considered particularly important. His younger brother Joseph-Olivier, loyal and devoted as well, was a footman under his brother's orders.

Both returned to the stables on Saint Helena and as drivers or guides led the Emperor's carriage at a gallop, narrowly skirting the terrible precipices on the island to the joy of Napoleon and the terror of the ladies accompanying him. Like all good drivers, the Archambault brothers never refused a glass of wine. Deported from Saint Helena by Hudson Lowe, Archambault the younger left his brother with the Emperor. Achille cared for his ailing master, dressed him for the final time, kept watch over his body, and attended the exhumation, before becoming an impassioned partisan of Prince Louis-Napoleon.

wife, and their child. For Mme de Montholon, Mlle Joséphine,[263] and for General Gourgaud, a servant whose name did not appear on the roster when they left, and thus was not authorized to get off the ship when they arrived in Saint Helena, and had to return to France by the first ship leaving.

The fate of each had thus been decided, and everyone began preparing for the long crossing. Calm succeeded the anxiety which the decision taken regarding the Emperor had caused everyone.

The judgment to surrender to the British, counseled by some and disapproved of by others, had nevertheless not led anyone to believe such an outrage would occur; but for those who deceived themselves that a brilliant reception was waiting for the Emperor on his landing, the disappointment was cruel. Countess Bertrand was overcome by these dark sentiments; Saint Helena awakened in her the loss of a child who had died the preceding year on Elba, and about which she could not console herself. She saw in this new exile the graves of her surviving children, whom she loved passionately. She became so distraught that she came to see the Emperor and entered without being announced. She begged him, were he to go to Saint Helena, not to take her husband with him, because she would lose her children there. The Emperor, who was with Count de Las Cases, was taken aback by this unexpected presence, yet seeing that she was in such great distress, he tried to restore calm to her mind. However, the nervous exasperation of this lady was such that, leaving with the same impulsiveness with which she had entered, she ran to the porthole of her room and would have thrown herself into the sea had she not been stopped in time. This act of despair gives a measure of the more or less strong internal agitation felt by each of us. Countess Bertrand overcame her repugnance for Saint Helena, mastered the fear she had of losing her children there, followed the Emperor to his land of exile, and was by his side when he died.

---

[263]The Heyman couple were in the service of the grand marshal. The husband Bernard was Count Bertrand's valet, and his wife Colette was the countess' maid.

Joséphine Brulé, twenty-five, was chambermaid to Countess de Montholon.

Three or four days were spent waiting for the *Northumberland* to finish its preparations, and nothing indicated that the British government intended to change anything in its previous resolutions. The Emperor dictated to Count de Las Cases the following protest, and asked Captain Maitland to send it to Admiral Keith:

At sea on board the Bellerophon, August 4, 1815

I hereby solemnly protest, before heaven and mankind, against the violence which is being done to me, and against the violation of my most sacred rights, in disposing by force of my person and my freedom. I came freely on board the Bellerophon, I am not a prisoner, I am the guest of England. I came here myself at the instigation of the captain who had orders from the government to receive me and take me to England with my retinue, if that were my desire; I presented myself in good faith, to come place myself under the protection of its laws. As soon as I set foot on board the Bellerophon, I was among the British people. If the government in giving orders to the captain of the Bellerophon to receive me and my retinue had only wanted to set a trap for me, an ambush, it has forfeited its honor and blemished its flag.

If such an act were consummated, it would be in vain for the British in the future for their loyalty, their laws, and their freedom; British faith would be lost with the hospitality of the Bellerophon.

I appeal to history; it shall say that an enemy who made war for twenty years against the British people came freely, in his misfortune, to seek shelter under their laws—and what greater proof could he give of his esteem and trust? But how did England reply to such magnanimity? She pretended to extend a hospitable hand to this enemy and, when he gave himself up in good faith, she slaughtered him.

Napoleon

During the night on the 4th, we left our anchorage in Plymouth and proceeded to Start Bay to await the *Northumberland*, that was being fitted out in Portsmouth. The sea was rough and I was suffering horribly. We were escorted by the ship *Tonnant* and the frigate *Eurotas*. Although the anchorage in Start Bay was awful and the sea continued to be rough, the Emperor did not suffer.

On the 6th, they signaled the arrival of the *Northumberland*, which was to take us to Saint Helena. The preparation of this vessel was not yet completed and it could not, they said, head to sea for another six or eight days. Until then we were to hold by tacking back and forth. On this same day, Admiral Keith came to introduce Admiral Cockburn, and advised us that before leaving the *Bellerophon*, instructions from the minister required a general search of belongings.

Here are the instructions given by Admiral Keith to Captain Maitland:

At anchor on Start-Bay, August 6, 1815

All weapons of any kind shall be taken from the Frenchmen of all ranks who are on board the vessel that you command. They shall be carefully collected and will be in your care as long as there are Frenchmen remaining on board the Bellerophon; they shall then be placed in the care of the captain aboard whose ship which they are transported.

Captain Maitland took it upon himself to leave the swords and seize only the firearms.

The instructions from the ministry given to Admiral Cockburn went into much greater detail and are shown in the following extract:

When General Bonaparte is transferred from the Bellerophon on board the Northumberland, it will be an appropriate time for Admiral Cockburn to conduct the search of any belongings the general may have.

Admiral Sir George Cockburn shall allow furnishings, books, and wines. In the furnishings is included silverware, providing it is not in such great quantity that it could be considered less for personal use than as property convertible into cash.

He will have to abandon his money, his diamonds, and all his negotiable notes, whatever their nature.

The admiral shall explain to him that the British government has no intention of confiscating his property, but only taking over the administration of it, so as to prevent him from using it as an instrument of escape.

The search must be made in the presence of several people designated by General Bonaparte, and an inventory of these effects shall be made and signed by these people, as well as by the admiral or any other individual designated by him to assist in this inventory. The interest or the capital, depending on the sum, shall be applicable to his needs and its disposition will remain largely up to him. On this subject he shall communicate his wishes from time to time, first to the admiral and then to the governor, when he has arrived, and unless there is reason to oppose it, they will give the necessary orders and pay the expenses by drafts drawn on His British Majesty's Treasury.

In the event of death, the disposition of General Bonaparte's belongings shall be determined by his will; he can be assured his dispositions shall be strictly observed. As it could be that part of his property came to be that of persons in his retinue, these shall be subject to the same rules.

The admiral shall take on board for Saint Helena no person belonging to the general's retinue without the consent of such person, and after explaining to him that he will be subject to whatever regulations are deemed suitable to secure the person of the general. The general shall be informed that should he attempt to escape he would expose himself to being put in jail, along with anyone in his retinue who is discovered attempting to further his escape.

All the letters that shall be addressed to him, as well as to his retinue, shall first be given to the admiral or the governor, who shall read them before handing them over; the same will apply to letters written by the General and those in his retinue.

The General must know that the governor and the admiral have received a definite order to address to His Majesty's government any request or complaint he deems suitable to communicate. Nothing in this regard is left to their discretion, but the paper on which these representations are made must remain unsealed, so that they may add any observations they feel are appropriate.

Certified copy, in the harbor of Start Bay, aboard the Bellerophon,

> *August 6, 1815*
>
> *Admiral S. George Cockburn*

The grand marshal informed me of this search of the Emperor's personal effects; he told me the time chosen would be that of the transfer of these same belongings from the *Bellerophon* to the

Northumberland, and that I should leave only 80,000 francs in one of the silver chests: the balance would be distributed to each of us, and given back to me later. On the appointed day, the admiral came as he had announced with Mr. Glover,[264] his secretary, and a customs officer. I had gathered in the same room all the trunks containing silverware, giltware, Sèvres porcelain, table linen, and bathroom linen; they were opened for them, and I declared 4,000 gold napoleons, which they took. Seeing that I was alone during this search, the admiral departed before the operation began, and left me with the customs officer and his secretary to proceed with the inventory of everything belonging to the Emperor. They appeared astonished at the small amount of baggage offered for their search; no doubt gauging the Emperor's fortune by the height of his glory, they expected to find themselves faced with mountains of riches, where only a few remnants hardly worth showing were displayed. They did not know that, concerned exclusively with France, the Emperor had attended only to the greatness of the motherland and the fortunes of the country. His disinterestedness would have left him without a cent after Waterloo, had not such friends as the Dukes of Vicenza (Caulaincourt) and Bassano (Maret) and Count de Lavalette, with M. Laffitte, busied themselves securing for him a few million, which six years later would serve to establish the bequests in his will.

Once the inventory was made, I signed it jointly with these gentlemen who handed me a receipt for 4,000 napoleons to serve the needs of General Bonaparte on his arrival in Saint Helena. My ear, even more than my soul, was severely shocked by this title, and my national pride deeply wounded. Until then it had not entered my mind that the British government, who had recognized France's right to make Napoleon a general, a consul, and an emperor—since this power had its own representative at the Congress of Châtillon in 1814 to negotiate with him—could today contest this title and give him that of

---

[264]J. R. Glover, secretary to Sir Hudson Lowe, left a diary entitled *Napoleon—Last Voyages*, published in 1893 and 1895.

General Bonaparte, leaving him in their eyes not the Emperor Napoleon, but merely the head of the French government.

After reading his receipt, I told Mr. Glover I could not accept it without referring it to the grand marshal; that the title of general given the Emperor was eminently glorious, but this qualification appeared to me so inconceivable and in such contradiction with history that I could do nothing but go to seek out orders. "These are," said Mr. Glover, "the terms of the declaration." I left him and went to see Count Bertrand who said to me, resting his hand affectionately on my shoulder, "Let them call him what they want, they shall not prevent him from being what he is. Take what they are giving you." I therefore accepted the receipt and a copy of the inventory that were given to me. I understood then that with such behavior anything could be expected on the part of that government.

During this visit Lord Keith, accompanied by Admiral Cockburn, had come and entered the Emperor's quarters to present him with the last instructions of his government; that of turning over his weapons. Bowing in front of the Emperor, in a voice deep with emotion he said to him: "England requests your sword." Saint-Denis, present at this scene, told me the look on the Emperor's face had been dreadful and that proudly placing his hand on the hilt of his sword, he appeared to defy anyone who would try to take it from him. The two admirals, who were clearly executing an order going against their characters, saluted respectfully as they left; the Austerlitz sword remained suspended at the Emperor's side. Only the firearms were taken: these gentlemen[265] kept their swords, although they had also been demanded of them.

The Emperor had learned from the grand marshal that the surgeon assigned to him by Baron Corvisart prior to leaving Malmaison would not be following him. He said to me while preparing for bed:

---

[265]Throughout the entire book, Marchand frequently uses the expression "these gentlemen"; by this he refers to the four senior members of Napoleon's personal staff, Generals Bertrand, Gourgaud, de Montholon, and Count de Las Cases. Marchand also frequently uses the expression "these ladies"; by this he refers to the two wives who accompanied their husbands, Countesses Bertrand and de Montholon.—Ed.

"Maingault must be very frightened by the instructions of the British government; is that why he is not accompanying me?"

"Sire," I said to him, "he did not allude to that reason; he said to me that apart from the honor of being attached to Your Majesty's service, a personal interest had interfered; that of completing some affairs in America where his family was to go, and that he could not go to Saint Helena without compromising these same interests."

"He is afraid of the life of seclusion in Saint Helena," replied the Emperor; "besides, he was only with me temporarily. Foureau shall come and join us, but he has declared very clearly to Bertrand that nothing in the world could persuade him to leave; he is evidently frightened by the stern nature of these instructions."

The Emperor had me count out to each of the people who could not accompany him a sum of money in gold to take care of their immediate needs, and a year's wages to those servants who would remain behind. He dictated to me a note for 3,000 francs payable at M. Laffitte's for one of his valets, Gilles Pélissier, whom he could not take with him. The 250,000 francs which had been hidden from the British investigation were spread out in eight belts that we placed around our bodies and were returned to me when we arrived in Saint Helena. The Emperor called this sum of money "his reserve" or "a pear to quench thirst." Each month I would add a few savings to it. At the Emperor's death this special fund amounted to 300,000 francs and was used for the first codicil's stipulations in Saint Helena.

Since the Emperor had been on board the *Bellerophon* he had talked several times to Dr. O'Meara,[266] surgeon on this vessel, who spoke Italian very well and whose demeanor was frank and open. This surgeon had been to Egypt, and conversed with the Emperor about his recollections of the glory and the administration he had left in that country. This circumstance in conjunction with his ability to express himself in a language known to the Emperor rendered him more inter-esting to the Emperor who, when he spotted him on deck, would call him over and question him on the health of the crew or on other aspects of his art. During the crossing we had just made, Dr. O'Meara had attended to several people in the Emperor's retinue who had become seasick (M. Maingault was very ill himself). All praised his kind, affectionate manner. All attempts, even those of the admiral, having failed to convince M. Maingault to follow the Emperor, he considered having Dr. O'Meara join him: and instructed the Duke of Rovigo (Savary) to ask if he would follow him to Saint Helena as surgeon attached to his person. The doctor replied that he would accept that honor very gladly if his government did not oppose it, and if he could continue to benefit from his rights as an Englishman. Admiral Keith, advised by the grand marshal of the Emperor's desire, promptly granted Dr. O'Meara an unlimited leave of absence with full pay and permission to accompany General Bonaparte to Saint Helena in the exercise of his medical functions.

On August 7, after having forgiven Captain Maitland the hatefulness which his government was expressing, the Emperor prepared to leave the *Bellerophon*. He received those of his officers who could not accompany him. The separation was very sad: on one hand, tears and despair; on the other, calm and consolations given to those who were not to follow him; then finally resignation. As he left the stateroom, the Emperor affectionately saluted the officers of the British vessel who were lined up along his path; all were sad at the fatal outcome that henceforth would be associated to the name of the

---

[266]Barry Edward O'Meara, aged 33, had been assistant surgeon in the 62nd infantry regiment, but had to resign because of a duel, and had then joined the navy. He was the surgeon on the *Bellerophon* when the Emperor arrived on board. As doctor at Longwood, he was under suspicion, mistreated by Hudson Lowe, and after his departure from the island on August 2, 1818, stricken from the rosters of naval surgeons.

In 1822 O'Meara published two volumes: *Napoleon in Exile and A Voice from Saint Helena*. These works, translated into several languages, revealed the treatment the Emperor was subjected to by the British minister and his subordinate.

O'Meara retired in London and died there on June 10, 1836. In his will, registered at Somerset House, can be read: "I take advantage of this opportunity to declare that with the exception of few insignificant and involuntary errors in the *Voice from Saint Helena* the book is a true and faithful narration of the treatment imposed on a great man by Sir Hudson Lowe and his subordinates, and that I even eliminated a few facts which, although true would have been considered exaggerations, to the point where people would not have believed them."

On his grave in St. Mary's Church, in Paddington Green in London, can be read: "Barry Edward O'Meara, surgeon to Napoleon."

Bellerophon: that of a lack of hospitality. He got into the small boat that had been prepared for him and his following and reached the *Northumberland*, saluting with one last look those he was leaving, and whom he knew to be devoted to him heart and soul. Once on the *Northumberland*, the Emperor remained on the bridge to chat with Lord Lowther and Littleton,[267] who were on board, and the conversation was very lively. Only a few moments remained: I used them to write some departing words to my father and mother in Vienna, my family whom I perhaps would never see again.

At the moment of sailing, those Frenchmen who had accompanied the Emperor on the *Northumberland* and had to leave him embraced him with an outpouring of affection, which attested to the separation being forever. The Duke of Rovigo (Savary) and General Lallemand, spotting me, came to me with tears in their eyes, and shaking my hand affectionately, entrusted the Emperor to my care.

A cutter that was circling the vessel to keep away boats loaded with curious spectators sank one, and several people perished. Two women owed their lives to silk dresses that held them afloat in the water. These two unfortunate women were brought unconscious aboard our ship to be given first aid, but they were then sent back to the cutter that had sunk them. A few men were saved by hanging onto ropes, suspended above the water; there was time to come to their rescue, but the rest of them drowned.

The reception given the Emperor on board the *Northumberland* was neither the one he received on the *Bellerophon* when he arrived, nor the one he received on board the *Superb*. Here the orders from the government were strictly adhered to in every respect: much politeness, even graciousness on the part of the admiral; but for him it was General Bonaparte who was on board and not the Emperor Napoleon. The title of Excellency replaced that of Majesty.

---

[267]Littleton, a relative and friend of Cockburn, had obtained permission to travel on board the *Northumberland* from Portsmouth to Plymouth. The *Mémorial* describes the essence of the Parliamentarians' conversations with the Emperor: fox hunting, the Emperor's treatment, his politics regarding Spain and England, the condition of France, the slave trade, etc.

On the 8th, two frigates and several brigs having joined us with troops on board, the admiral gave the signal to get under way; after thirteen days in Plymouth and forty days since our departure from Paris, we were sailing for Saint Helena.

On the 9th, the shores of France became visible through the clouds, and we saw it one last time. The Emperor, who was on deck, removed his hat and remained motionless, saying with intense emotion in his voice: "Adieu, land of the brave! Adieu, France! Adieu!"

CHAPTER ELEVEN

Life on board ship — Arrival in Saint Helena — Jamestown —
The road to Longwood

𝒯he vessel, which had been only hastily prepared, required order to be established. It was necessary to accommodate all the troops that were on board, and also a few wives of military personnel; the taking on of provisions had not been completed and had to be done on the way. One thousand eighty people were on board this magnificent ship commanded by Captain Ross,[268] a man of much merit and courtesy. The poop deck had been set up for the Emperor, who occupied the room to the right while entering the main stateroom, and for the admiral, who had the room to the left. The stateroom, which was to be common to both, remained out of courtesy for the use of the Emperor, who only occupied it part of the day. The admiral only appeared at mealtime. The Emperor's iron bed was erected in place of the one that had been prepared for him; a washstand, small table, and an armchair made up the furniture of this small room lit by a porthole. During the entire crossing I slept in that room on a mattress provided

---

[268]Captain Charles Bayne Hodgson Ross (1778-1849) was the brother-in-law of Admiral Cockburn and served under him during the war in America.

In Saint Helena he lived in Ross Cottage located next to Longwood. He left the island on June 19, 1816.

In a letter addressed to W. J. Hall in Kingston, Jamaica, on July 26, 1816, he gives information regarding the surveillance organized by the navy in Saint Helena: "No ship is allowed to drop anchor unless it needs water or provisions. Then a guard is placed on board. All the ships that are anchored are placed in safety at sundown under the surveillance of the guard. No one in town can be outside after 9 p.m. without a password, and all the bridges and doors are closed at sunset except one. The coast guard are always outside; one ship cruises constantly in one direction, another in the other. Consequently, as long as this present system lasts, it will be impossible for him to escape; the security in the place is very tight."

on board ship. I was often awakened by the Emperor, who would ask for his shaded lamp in order to read and take a few notes; the first he took were in Lacretelle. Saint-Denis, as on the *Bellerophon*, slept in the adjoining room across the doorway.

The Emperor, wanting to give himself more freedom, said he would have lunch at 10 o'clock in his room, and only emerge around 3 or 4 p.m. He would call these gentlemen in turn to chat with him, maintaining a preference for Count de Las Cases, who better than the others, could tell him what was happening on board, and whose conversation was most enjoyable for him. I had taken with me six small mahogany cases containing what was called a field library, provided by M. Barbier,[269] the Emperor's librarian. These crates consisted of good works, and were of great assistance in fighting the boredom of such a lengthy crossing.

The Emperor, entering the stateroom after he was dressed, generally remained there until being told dinner was served. Then all those invited gathered. The place of honor at the table was reserved for him; to his right was Countess Bertrand and to his left the admiral. He was served by Saint-Denis on his right and Noverraz on his left; other people were arranged in the order of their ranks. He only remained at

---

[269]Barbier, a former priest, was named librarian to the Emperor in 1807.

We do not know the makeup of the Saint Helena library. The Emperor wanted to take from Paris 10,000 volumes as well as works on America, everything that appeared concerning him, the campaigns, etc., atlases, dictionaries, his campaign library completed with modern works...

He was only able to take with him 588 volumes from his libraries in Le Trianon, Malmaison, and a few books taken in passing from that of Rambouillet. Following a number of private shipments, and those made every year by Lady Holland, the library in 1821 contained 1,814 volumes, 1,226 of which had been shipped from England. Saint-Denis took care of them.

In compliance with the Emperor's desires, 400 volumes, "chosen among the ones that have served me most," were given to Saint-Denis to be handed over to the King of Rome. Then the exiles helped themselves. The balance was sold to the London bookseller Bossange who, after making a few careful selections, organized a public sale on July 23, 1823, the catalog containing 123 items. A few volumes were given to members of the imperial family.

At Bertrand's death, the volumes belonging to his estate were partially sold for scrap, except a dozen or so that were saved from disaster.

the table a half hour or forty-five minutes at most: if he remained there longer, it was a concession on his part to the admiral, who ordered that the service be accelerated so that the Emperor would not be inconvenienced in his habits. On the first day only, the Emperor suffered through the duration of an English dinner; Saint-Denis told me that the following day and as long as the crossing lasted, he habitually got up before dessert was served. He would go out on deck, followed in turn by one of these gentlemen, most frequently Count de Las Cases. Apart from the regulars at this table, one land officer and one naval officer were invited and, weather permitting, one from the squadron sailing with us. The Emperor would ask them a few questions about their careers and always showed them great courtesy. One day, having left the table to walk on deck, he called the master, who though responsible for directing the ship did not hold the rank of officer. He took pleasure in chatting with him, and ended by saying: "Come tomorrow and have dinner with me." The master had this invitation repeated to him twice, as it was completely outside of normal discipline and etiquette, and he believed his captain and the admiral would not agree to it. This was not the case: when the admiral learned from the Emperor what he wanted, he was most gracious in assuring him that whoever he had invited to the honor of sitting down at his table would be welcomed to dinner. It is probable that the Emperor would not have had any complaints about Admiral Cockburn, had he not felt obliged as soon as he arrived in Saint Helena to carry out the instructions from the British minister, dictated by hate for any human spirit and the rights of man. During the entire crossing, he always showed himself to be very courteous toward the Emperor. If he should leave the table to come out on deck where the Emperor already was, he would rush up if the weather was bad and offer him his arm, which was always accepted. The Emperor had adopted a cannon against which he would lean when he was not walking about; the young midshipmen who kept guard around him so he would not be hurt during maneuvers named it the Emperor's cannon. When night came, the Emperor would return to the wardroom, where he would engage in gambling at which he always lost. Between 9 and 10 p.m. he would retire to his room. Those were the Emperor's habits on board the *Northumberland* and during the entire crossing; feelings of respect and admiration filled the crew whenever they saw him appear on deck. They admired his noble resignation with respect to the hateful instructions from Lord Bathurst, and were thankful to him for having honored a man's worth in the person of one of the crew.

On August 15, these gentlemen came individually to wish the Emperor a happy birthday; the Emperor had forgotten about it, and was quite touched by this attention which, without demoralizing him, took him back to happier days. He spoke touching words of kindness to one of them. I am told by Saint-Denis that the admiral, informed of the circumstances, that evening at dinner proposed a toast to the health of the Emperor, in which all the Englishmen joined. That same evening, it was remarked that he constantly won at gambling, and had he wanted to follow up on his luck, the sum could have been considerable. "My luck was such," he said to me on returning, "that my winnings reached 80 napoleons." The Emperor had played twenty-one. This luck seemed to me all the more extraordinary, as every day I was obliged to replace in his purse the few napoleons he had lost while gambling the previous night.

During this long crossing, the Emperor's health did not suffer; he was of a perfectly even temper, appeared to be entirely indifferent to what went on around him, and never complained.

On the 23rd we arrived in Madeira, a charming town built on the side of a mountain; houses surrounded by wonderful gardens rose one above the other, creating a most agreeable, picturesque sight. It was on this island that our provisions were completed. The sirocco was blowing strongly, soon becoming quite furious; a real tempest. The admiral ordered that we put to sea, for fear of being thrown against shore; our topmasts broke, but the damage was quickly repaired. I had the admiral's butler, who was going ashore, buy me a box of watercolors to help pass the time in Saint Helena. During the two days we remained at Madeira, I was made quite ill by the pitching and rolling of the ship. Mr. Glover, who had gone ashore along with the ship's purser, reported that the island had suffered horribly from the storm. The inhabitants, who were Portuguese, superstitiously attributed the arrival of this sirocco on their island to Napoleon.

On the night of the 24th to the 25th, when all damage had been repaired and provisions completed, we set sail for the Canaries, leaving behind us Tenerife Peak, which we were able to view through our spyglasses for a long time. When we arrived at the tropics we saw a great number of flying fish. Below this latitude, a mulatto from Guadeloupe jumped into the sea during the night, and the sharp cries of "Negro, Negro!" which he was shouting turned the entire ship upside down. The wind was severe, and the sea was quite rough. As quickly as they dropped the sails and lowered a gig to go to his rescue, they could no longer hear the screams which would allow anyone to locate him. Flares were lit to illuminate the gig searching for this poor man, but in vain: he had disappeared beneath the waters. This man had been led to such an act of despair by the lashes he had received that very morning; unable to resist the urge to drink, he had again gotten drunk, and in order to avoid the punishment his lack of temperance would bring on him, he had jumped into the sea. As a great deal of commotion had occurred on board ship, the Emperor was concerned, and I recounted the circumstances to him.

I had been present as one of these punishments was being executed on board ship; the number of lashes, administered to the shoulders of the sailors, was proportionate to the magnitude of the crime. I had no idea this flagellation could be so barbaric; I could not understand how men would not revolt from such punishment. It seemed to me that the ensuing degradation for the man who received it was such that I could not believe his soul was still capable of any feeling of honor. I am led to believe this turns men into brutes, because I saw a tailor who, having been cut loose after just receiving twenty lashes, still danced a jig. I concluded there was a kind of man who could tolerate such lashings, but that this population could not, like the French nation, give birth to great citizens it could justifiably be proud of, those who had come out of the ranks of the army.

British newspapers that had arrived gave the Emperor the idea of learning this language; he mentioned it to Count de Las Cases, who promised him that in a very few lessons he would be in a position to read these public documents himself. An hour each day was assigned to this lesson, which also served to fight boredom during this long journey.

On September 23, we arrived at the equator; at this latitude, the sea's calmness allowed the sailors to hold a celebration for crossing the line.

We call this the celebration of Old Man Equator; to the British it is "the Great Beard." The oldest of the sailors becomes Neptune, and those who make up his retinue, in the most ridiculous of dress, carry him on a seat made of a gun carriage decorated with draperies. On the carriage he is taken around the ship, then, stopping before the captain's quarters (because the normal order of things is reversed on this day), he asks him the names of the passengers who have not yet been initiated into his empire. Addressing himself next to the admiral who was on the poop deck, he asked about General Bonaparte: the admiral laughingly replied, "He has already passed the equator." Five hundred napoleons given to Neptune by the Emperor caused the whole crew delirious joy, under whose auspices the festival began. Neptune advanced to the throne which had been erected for him at the foot of the main mast; one approached him by climbing ten steps and there each one was judged, not according to his deeds, but by the greater or lesser goodwill he showed in presenting himself. All the passengers had to submit to this ceremony, Captain Ross and the ship's chaplain along with the others. Near Neptune were two men, remarkable for their Herculean power, bodies tattooed like savages and, like them, wearing only trunks. One of them was armed with an enormous razor and the other with a pot containing tar destined to be put on the chins of those who appeared the most disobedient. It was they who prompted the greatest delight; buckets of water were thrown on them from high on the topmasts after they had undergone the bearding process, then they were chased around the ship everywhere they sought refuge, without being able to escape the buckets of water that were constantly being thrown on them. This festival—where the order of things is completely turned around, where all on board is confusion, where it seems that order will never be restored—after having lasted all day, magically ceased at a signal given by Captain Ross. At once discipline and order returned to the ship, and the arrival of a breeze which had just manifested after twenty days' calm was greeted with joy.

We continued to sail with a forceful wind, in formation with the squadron, with nothing remarkable occurring along our route except for the fishing of a few dolphins and the sight of some whales in the distance. At the latitude of the Congo, the admiral—who took great care to see that the Emperor's table was always well provided for—sent one of the brigs out to go find fruit and poultry, which it brought back in large quantities. The crossing was becoming quite extended; the admiral had decided to take a route which was not that ordinarily used by trade ships. It followed the coast of Africa instead of that of Brazil, where strong winds invariably led to either Saint Helena or to the Cape, toward India. Admiral Cockburn's attempt to follow an unusual route caused us to remain at sea seventeen days longer than we should have; the brig and the frigate, which the storm in Madeira had separated from us, arrived in Saint Helena seventeen days before the *Northumberland*. This crossing was becoming tedious for the Emperor who, accustomed to much exercise, could not find an opportunity to take any; a few dictations to General Gourgaud or to Count de Las Cases were the only distraction during the day, and even then he was not set up well for this type of affair. He was anxious to arrive in the place of his exile, no matter how sad the scene might be.

For several days dolphins had been appearing in abundant quantities, and the sailors caught a few of them, which they ate. The Emperor wanted to eat some and found the flesh quite good, but that was not the case with shark meat, which he found disgusting. Everything was cause for distraction on board. One day there was a remarkable noise on deck caused by the capture of a shark some six feet long, and the Emperor asked me what was occurring. When I told him that the fish just caught weighed one hundred eighty pounds, he wished to see it and took pleasure in the struggle that it was waging against the sailors. They began to skin it, and the tail thrashing against the deck was so frightening that the Emperor, who had moved in a little too close, was almost wounded. Inside this young shark were found remnants of human clothing.

Every day I was present at the taking of the ship's position, and although quite slowly, we were closing in on Saint Helena. On October 14, we were to see this island; in the afternoon someone cried: "Land!" and immediately all eyes turned in the direction given, looking for Diana's Peak, which we were told was the highest point on Saint Helena. We spotted it under a clear sky, fifteen leagues away, but it could only be seen through a spyglass on the horizon. At 9 p.m. the *Northumberland* dropped its sails for the night; a corvette sent out from the convoy on orders of the admiral approached the shore to announce our arrival.

On the 15th, seventy days after our departure from the coast of England, and one hundred and ten days after our departure from Paris, we were dropping anchor in Saint Helena, which appeared repulsive to us. Contrary to his normal practice, the Emperor got dressed early to go up on deck and get an overall view of the island, which he could only see imperfectly from the porthole in his cabin. He had before him a sketch of that part of the island where we were; he had told me to bring it along, and I had given it to him, heavy with sorrow. Once dressed, he went up on deck with his small spyglass in hand. One could not see the town, hidden by a terrace that followed the contours of the bay; one could only see the square church tower through the foliage, sitting between two enormous bare rocks that rose perpendicularly above the sea to a considerable height and seemed to be equipped with gunnery units on several levels. The governor's palace, surrounded by trees, appeared a pleasant residence; everything else was a large rock devoid of any vegetation.

No matter how great my desire to see land, I could only greet this like a grave. After watching for a few moments, the Emperor went back into his cabin without comment, allowing no one to guess what was transpiring in his soul.

As for myself, I was so weary of this floating house, so tired of the titles of General and Excellency given to the Emperor, that no matter what the place where we would have to live, providing that we would be there alone, I would prefer it to the *Northumberland*. For two days the inhabitants remained on the piers, waiting to see the Emperor at the moment he disembarked. Each evening at sundown they would go back home, disappointed in their expectations.

A harbor gig came alongside soon after our arrival; the admiral and Sir George Bingham,[270] the colonel commanding the 55th line infantry regiment, went ashore to look for a dwelling that would be suitable for the Emperor and his retinue while waiting for a proper residence to be found. A few hours later the admiral came back on board with Colonel Wilks,[271] governor of Saint Helena for the East India Company, and introduced him to the Emperor. Colonel Wilks answered promptly and respectfully the many questions the Emperor asked of him, and did so like a man of heart and intelligence. The India Company was turning this island over to the British government for the duration of the Emperor's captivity.

The brig *Furet* and the frigate *Havana*, separated from us by the storm in Madeira, had been at anchor in Saint Helena for the past seventeen days; the Brazilian route taken by these two ships was far preferable to that taken by the admiral.

After such a long crossing it would have been agreeable to disembark as soon as we arrived, but we understood that it was necessary to find a house large enough to suitably accommodate so many people. Everyone was awaiting the return of the admiral, who would decide on the time of debarkation. It was not to be, and the whole days of the

---

[270]Brigadier general Sir George Ridout Bingham (1776-1833). He distinguished himself during the war in the peninsula, and was sent to Saint Helena to command the entire garrison. He remained there until May 24, 1820. There are letters from Bingham addressed to Hudson Lowe showing that the relationship between the two was not always cordial.

[271]Colonel Mark Wilks (1760-1831) was governor of Saint Helena for the East India Company. He had arrived in 1813 and lived there with his daughter, Miss Laura. When the Emperor arrived, Wilks had just been remarried to an attractive girl from the island, Miss Dorothy Taubman. Intelligent and well-educated, Colonel Wilks seems to have been appreciated by the Emperor, who took pleasure in chatting with him.

15th and 16th were spent before setting foot on this damned island, as Countess Bertrand called it. The admiral and Colonel Bingham again went ashore, and in the evening on their return, they announced to the Emperor that they had found a small house in town for him and his retinue to live in, while awaiting the completion of Longwood. Although the instructions from the ministry stated the Emperor was to remain on board until such time as he could be housed in a manner assuring his detention, the admiral, more humane than the ministers, took it on himself to have him come ashore.

On the evening of the 17th, prior to leaving the *Northumberland*, the Emperor summoned Captain Ross to take his leave of him, and asked him to express his gratefulness to the officers and the crew. His goodbyes were received with great interest by those who heard them, and deeply touched those to whom they were repeated. The Emperor got into the gig, accompanied by the admiral and Count Bertrand, and was quartered in a small house belonging to M. Porteous: it was extremely clean. It was however not practical, because of its smallness and its position, and did not allow the Emperor to move about inside without being seen by passersby, nor to go out without finding himself suddenly in contact with the inhabitants of the few nearby houses making up what was called the town.

The admiral, accompanying the Emperor to the drawing room, told him that this installation was temporary, and that he was going to speed up work at the lodgings designated by his government. He again repeated that though it was up to him that he be as comfortable as possible, he was short of resources to finish the work as promptly as he wished. I had gone ashore before the Emperor and had already looked over the place. The drawing room was on the ground floor, the bedroom on the second floor; this house had neither garden nor courtyard. I saw sorrowfully that my dream during the entire voyage was not going to be realized: complete isolation and a practical house with shade and water for the Emperor. I would have liked for him the "Madonna of Marciana" from the island of Elba, with its cool, dense shade and its charming stream. Instead, we had a sun beating down on us burning our skulls in the city.

By 8 p.m. everyone had left the *Northumberland* and had gathered in this house, where no one found himself much more comfortable than on board ship.

I had arranged the Emperor's room according to his customary habits as much as possible. But the little room which was destined for my use had no exit except into that room, making it quite impractical for me. The Emperor slept poorly; he asked me for his covered lamp, slipped on his robe, and took a book. He spoke to me of the impracticability of this house, and his desire that Longwood, located near a forest on an elevated plateau, be ready soon so that he could move in there. "I shall go tomorrow with the admiral to look at this house, and it will have to be in very inadequate shape indeed for me not to find a way to lodge there." These words gave me immense pleasure, as my soul had filled with such great sadness when we entered the door to the city that I had bid an eternal farewell to my family. In the evening I learned that the admiral had opposed the landing of General Gourgaud's servant; he was not included on the official government list, and no matter how much the general insisted on keeping this servant to whom he was attached, the admiral was inflexible. He was put on board the brig sent to Europe to announce the arrival of the Emperor in Saint Helena.

The next morning at 8 o'clock the Emperor, the admiral, and the grand marshal, followed by Saint-Denis, mounted horses to go examine the house the Emperor had talked to me about during the night. I learned in his absence, from the present house's owner, that the temperature on the plateau was quite inconsistent; there were constant changes from fair to bad weather, and the milder climate of the town would be far preferable, if they were willing to give the Emperor the government house. The apartments were spacious there, a fine terrace overlooked the water's edge; however, the Emperor could not enjoy the freedom which would be given to him in any other part of the island, for fear of his escape. I was little attracted by the advantages of the Emperor staying in the city; in my point of view, the condition which destroyed them all was the restriction of his freedom.

On his way to Longwood, the Emperor saw a small house located in a place that seemed to him rustic and charming. He was told it belonged to a Mr. Balcombe;[272] he continued on his way but intended to stop there on his return. If Longwood was not habitable, he indeed preferred its smallest shack to a house in town, where he was not able to move about without being seen by passersby.

The Emperor arrived at Longwood, and was not particularly enchanted with the house that enjoyed no shade or water, and was exposed to the southeast wind that prevailed there constantly, and was quite strong at the present time. He immediately realized all the work remaining to be done for him to take up residence there, and paid little attention to everything the admiral would say regarding construction projects and improvements. The only advantage he saw there for himself was that it was a plateau extending several miles that would allow him to ride and even go out in his carriage if they were willing to cut paths through the woods of gum trees that stood a short distance from

---

[272]William Balcombe (1779-1829) was a tradesman for the India Company. In addition he headed the main firm on Saint Helena and supplied all ships with everything they needed.

Balcombe and his wife, who somewhat resembled Empress Joséphine, received the Emperor graciously during his stay at The Briars, and Marchand confirms that he was pleased with it. Designated as supplier to Longwood, Balcombe came there frequently, and was received several times by Napoleon, either alone or with his family. He left the island in March 1818, and was suspected by Hudson Lowe of having taken with him letters from the French—which is quite probable. He never returned to Saint Helena, in spite of many requests addressed by him to Lord Bathurst.

See in the Lowe Papers a letter from Balcombe in which he hopes the governor has forgotten their differences.

The Balcombes' younger daughter Betsy, a mischievous tomboy who amused the Emperor, in later life as Mrs. Abell published several editions of her *Recollections of the Emperor Napoleon*.

the house. The lieutenant governor Colonel Skelton,[273] who had resided at Longwood, had been extremely pleasant when he greeted the Emperor, but he could not prevent the disagreeable impression it made. They had taken great care not to show the Emperor the other part of the island where the governor's residence, Plantation House, lay, and in which they could very well have placed him. Plantation House was then the same house that I saw twenty-five years later, when I had the honor of retrieving the Emperor's mortal remains, under the leadership of the Prince of Joinville. It was pleasantly situated, sheltered from the easterly winds, surrounded by water and cool shade, dominating a well-cultivated valley with magnificent trees and well-marked paths. On seeing the elegance of the interior arrangements of this residence, I could not prevent my memory from returning to the barbaric process that had presided over the choice of Longwood as the Emperor's residence, when there was such a charming one on the opposite side of the island. There his life could have lasted longer, yet they wanted the severity of the climate to extinguish it as quickly as possible. Eternal shame upon the British government!

Here is some information regarding our discovery of Saint Helena that will be of some interest to the reader, now that this island—henceforth famous—had become the state prison for the Emperor, as well as his grave.

Jamestown, located on the chapel bay, is surrounded by denuded rocks rising more than six hundred feet above sea level. The island is guarded against anything unexpected; not only because of the lookouts who can spot any approaching ships as far as fifteen leagues out to sea, but also because of the formidable defenses that could prevent any access. From the bay, the town is hidden by a wall that

---

[273]The Skelton couple was quite pleasant. John, 52, was a lieutenant colonel in the Indian army, and had been lieutenant governor of the island since 1813. His wife was about 40; she spoke French quite well, and the Emperor received her with pleasure. She was invited to dinner several times, and also to go for a carriage ride. She died in 1866, at age 91, in Cheltenham, and often referred to her conversations with the Emperor.

Hudson Lowe had accused Skelton, like many others, of having taken to England letters from the Emperor when he left Jamestown in May 1816.

follows the contour of the bay up to the government palace; between that barrier and the sea stretches a pier where six artillery corps are located at water level, providing cross fire and defending the entrance to the harbor; no vessel can enter without passing under their barrage. Gunnery units no less considerable are established at various levels along the almost sheer cliffs that dominate the town; on each of these platforms are forts covering Jamestown, the bay, and the harbor, transforming that area into a veritable fortress, impossible to approach.

From the pier, the town is entered by a covered road cut through the boundary and leading to a narrow door closed off by a drawbridge; beyond is a large, level square planted with trees on the right and left. The government house is luxurious within and is bordered on the left by the East India Company's gardens of abundant trees and exotic plants, while the church is on the right. Private houses and stores, painted and clean, surround this square and constitute the street that extends in the direction of the valley and the road to Longwood. The whole of this little town, made up of about one hundred houses, is clean and elegant. When following the valley that rises to Balcombe Cottage, one finds the East India Company stores, an airy garrison, and country cottages. On account of the stream, fed by a waterfall coming from the mountains enclosing the southern valley, the vegetation is lush, and whether ascending the Longwood road or that of Plantation House, the scene is quite picturesque. The stream provides ships with a watering spot, allowing them to take water on board at the shore without entering town.

When we arrived, there were no island roads suitable for carriages. All connections were by country lanes, and the island counted only about five hundred white residents, including the garrison, and about three hundred slaves. In 1821, there were about eight hundred whites, three hundred Negroes, and as many Chinese or Indians, some of whom were employed at Longwood as servants in the kitchen, pantry, and wardrobe. At the beginning of our stay, water was brought by barrels, so the Emperor could not take baths as he would have wished. It was only much later that Sir Hudson Lowe, having undertaken the construction of a very large cistern at the foot of Diana's Peak, made it possible to gather water there during the rainy season; Longwood and the camp were then sufficiently supplied. The island resources were so small when we arrived there that the garrison, for close to one year, had drawn rations as they did on board ship. The inhabitants took from the company stores the articles they might need and were allowed to kill neither cattle nor sheep without the governor's permission.

The period when the inhabitants obtain luxuries in exchange for the fresh items they offer travelers, is that when the vessels from the East India Company, on their way from India to Europe, arrive in Saint Helena. This period lasts a few weeks and lends Jamestown a holiday spirit; after a long crossing, the foreigners are pleasantly surprised to find a retreat which offers them water, fresh meat, green vegetables, and fruit, and allows them to take long rides on horseback throughout the island, where there are pleasant residences such as Plantation House, Rosemary Hall, and Sandy Bay. The cottages of The Briars, Dewton, and Mason[274] present them with fine hospitality and cool shade to rest from the hot sun. These advantages were nonexistent at Longwood. This land possessed no more than a plateau on which a few unsuccessful attempts had been made to establish grain plantations. That part of the island was constantly beaten by southeasterly winds. As good as it might appear to travelers who have just com-

---

[274]Plantation House, the governor's residence, dates from 1601. The house is huge, with numerous lodgings and two wings. Facing the north, it is sheltered from southern winds by a series of hills running east-west, planted with pines and oaks. When coming out of the great vestibule, one passes under a portico and down steps leading to a vast meadow surrounded by woods. Well-kept and irrigated, it is pleasant and lush. A gate placed in a semicircular retaining wall opens on the path leading to the road linking Sandy Bay to Jamestown.

Sir Walter Runciman wrote, "The tragic farce of sending the Emperor on the poisonous plateau of Longwood, and giving Lowe Plantation House as a residence is a phenomenon that few people who did not know the facts and the circumstances are able to comprehend."

Rosemary Hall, about nine km. from Jamestown, was occupied by the Austrian and Russian commissioners.

Mason Cottage was owned by Miss Mason. She was asked to rent it to Hudson Lowe to shelter the Emperor, and refused, having been offered 100 francs per month.

pleted a long crossing, the climate of Saint Helena is generally unhealthy, particularly in the area occupied by the Emperor.

Therefore nothing that the admiral was projecting in the way of improvements on the Longwood plateau could appear attractive to the Emperor: it was simply a matter of making additions to a dilapidated, single-story house of stone that had served as residence for the lieutenant governor.

CHAPTER TWELVE

Installation at The Briars — The Balcombe family —
Admiral Cockburn — Dr. O'Meara — Departure for Longwood

*W*hile approaching town on his return from Longwood, the Emperor expressed to the admiral his wish to see The Briars; he promptly took him there. On their way, the Emperor told him that if the owner of the house did not object to it, he would like to occupy the pavilion that was about twenty-five paces from the main building: he preferred living there to his accommodations in town. When they arrived at the cottage, the request was made of the owner, who granted it wholeheartedly; although taken to his bed with gout, he expressed his desire to relinquish his entire house. The Emperor conveyed his appreciation but did not wish to accept; he told him that he would occupy the pavilion separated from the main house with pleasure, on condition that the family's habits would not be disrupted. After pointing out to the Emperor the cramped nature of this lodging in which he would be waiting for the work at Longwood to be completed, the admiral promptly acquiesced to his desire, and the grand marshal returned to town alone. He advised me of the Emperor's decision to settle temporarily at The Briars, and ordered me to have his things brought there, and to have Noverraz accompany me. At the same time he gave instructions to Cipriani, the butler, to have dinner brought from town every day during his stay. The Emperor also invited Count de Las Cases, who thought he should come without his son. But the Emperor, noticing this, said to him: "I do not wish to separate those who are so close: go send for young Emmanuel."

I had a moment of joy when I learned of this decision. After arranging everything and putting Noverraz in charge of bringing the baggage, I went to join the Emperor. No matter how gratifying the sensation was that I experienced upon entering Jamestown; the sight of these pretty, little houses so attractively painted which pleasantly decorated the only street and public square; no matter how beautiful, well landscaped and shady the botanical garden were, I abandoned it all without regret for isolation, because I imagined in town nothing more than a somber residence, annoying and impractical in view of the Emperor's habits. Finally, the family life for which I yearned, in which there would no longer be any Englishmen, had much to be said for it. The road I followed to go to The Briars was that which led to Longwood; cut into the side of the mountain, it oversees the town and the little valley, which from there continues to the foot of the sheer cliff where it ends. There, a silver stream falls from the top of this black rock and arrives at the base in a light mist, giving birth to a stream covered with watercress that meanders down to the town. The Emperor's pavilion looked out over this small valley, where here and there were strewn a few small houses, surrounded by seemingly well kept gardens. The town and the ships in harbor, with the whole ocean as a horizon, presented a picturesque view not devoid of charm. The aridity of the rocks that dominated the town and extended out to The Briars gave even more value to the vegetation covering this small, narrow piece of ground.

I found the Emperor sitting at the door to his pavilion chatting with the admiral, who had remained with him. He called me over and asked if the baggage was being attended to; I replied that it would be there within an hour. Nothing could be more cramped than this small pavilion, which I immediately explored: a small anteroom, a large room with four windows, and above two small rooms under the roof that were reached by a small staircase from the antechamber. Such was the entire lodging that would be occupied by the Emperor, Count de Las Cases, his son, Saint-Denis, Noverraz, and myself. The outbuildings of the main house were meager, but a fresh lawn spread in front, the garden was well kept, water and shade were not lacking, and the Emperor's solitude was never disturbed there. The lady of the house and her two charming daughters offered everything that could be of assistance in furnishing the room reserved for the Emperor. I accepted a few chairs, an armchair, and a table; what arrived from the city with Noverraz would allow the Emperor to settle into his usual habits. At The Briars, one had to consider oneself camping; the Emperor found around him the furnishings of a field tent.

As soon as the things had arrived, we took care of assembling his bed; the table was placed in the middle of the room with a rug. It was to serve as desk and dining room table, just as the room itself was to be bedroom, study and dining room. It was impossible to be more confined than the Emperor was, but he was free to move about and the rest could be forgotten. A dresser was offered to me with so much insistence on Mr. Balcombe's part that I had to accept. I spread out on it the Emperor's travel kit which, once opened, decorated the room a little. I sent for a crate from town containing the silver washstand taken from the Elysée-Bourbon, work of the silversmith Biennais. This piece of silver was very elegant, had cost 10,000 francs, and was the source of the Balcombe family's admiration. Portraits of the King of Rome and Empress Marie-Louise were hung on the wall, and a few pieces of cloth stretched on ropes across the windows completed the furnishings of the room. Count de Las Cases settled in with his son upstairs; Saint-Denis, Noverraz, and I slept in the hallway, wrapped in our coats on field mattresses that were sent from town.

It was there that the master of the world, abandoned to his fate, was to reside for two months. He would have to wait for his intended house, located in the most sterile portion of the island, to be finished. Faced with such great misfortune, we understood that the time for self-denial had arrived. We did not fail in this, we took care of everything, and the Emperor was served in Saint Helena with the same zeal, the same care, and the same attentiveness as at the Tuileries in his time of splendor. Nothing was too much for us to achieve this end, the single and only goal of our desires, happy to prove to him such a well-deserved devotion at any price. Artillery Captain Greatly[275] moved into The Briars with two orderlies to keep an eye on the Emperor. But

---

[275]Captain Thomas Greatly, royal artillery, commanded the detachment of gunners aboard the *Northumberland* who were to serve the guns used to defend the island.

St. Helena and Jamestown as viewed from the anchorage.

Jamestown from the air.

The main street, Jamestown. Napoleon spent one night at the nearest house on the left.

no matter how much care he took to avoid being in the Emperor's way, he always was, and this had unfortunate results; it characterized the beginning of the faltering of relations between the admiral and the Emperor.

The dinner came from town brought by Cipriani, the next day's luncheon being made up of a part of the previous night's dinner. It was evident that the Emperor would live very poorly in this arrangement. Count de Las Cases and his son had to do without napkins the first day, as the table linen had not yet arrived. Everything that was brought from town to The Briars by slaves arrived cold; the Emperor did not complain the first days, blaming the poor dinners on awkward organization. However, he talked to me about it one evening as he was going to bed. I told him he had a butler and a pantry head in town: one of the two could be with him and do his cooking at The Briars; and without disturbing Mrs. Balcombe, it would be possible to use to good advantage a small room where the slaves cooked their food. This way he could have a hot dinner. Two days later Pierron, the pantry head, and Lepage, the cook, came on orders of Count de Montholon, whom the Emperor put in charge of the service of the grand marshal, and they moved into The Briars. The silver and linen also arrived in sufficient quantity; the service for the Emperor's table took on a regularity it had heretofore lacked. In town, Cipriani was put in charge of provisions for The Briars, where they arrived every morning, and of providing for the officers lodged with their families in town. He kept with him the two Archambault brothers, Gentilini, and Rousseau, and Santini for serving at the table.

Admiral Cockburn, attempting to maintain the rapport that had been established between himself and the Emperor on the *Northumberland*, came from time to time to The Briars to offer his good services. But the surveillance measures taken by his officer, considered by the Emperor vexatious and totally useless, were weakening this rapport rather than strengthening it. Since the establishment of the kitchen at Longwood,[276] the Emperor, when one of his officers came up from town, could keep him for dinner and have him nearby longer; he thus managed not to have a day go by without seeing them. In this solitude, the Emperor kept the habits he had acquired on board ship; he would remain in his room until 4 o'clock, dress, and, followed by Count de Las Cases, go into the garden to wait for the moment when he was informed that dinner was served. General Bingham, coming one morning to pay a visit to the Emperor, exclaimed over the cramped condition of his lodgings and offered to send him a tent that could be erected in front of the pavilion on a piece of land leveled for this purpose. This tent became the dining room and the study, and was of great use during our stay at The Briars. Finally, after such a long crossing and such great misfortune, the Emperor seemed to appreciate the calmness of the deep solitude that surrounded him. He did not seem to notice the privations from which he suffered, and passed the long hours of boredom in conversations with Count de Las Cases on the Italian campaigns, which he was dictating to him.

The Balcombe cottage sheltered the head of the family who had gout, Mrs. Balcombe, kind, sweet, and affectionate, and two young ladies of whom the younger, Miss Betsy, promised to become pretty. Both of them were pleasant and gracious; they spoke a little

---

[276]The Briars.—Ed.

French; as Count de Las Cases spoke perfect English, relations were established with this family. The Emperor sometimes went to their house to be amused by the naiveté of these young people, and to partake in a game of whist that they offered him. He was moved by the great care this family took in offering their services and would have gone there more often, had he not noticed that curiosity brought to this house a few people desiring to see him. I have said that an artillery captain, M. Greatly, a sergeant, and a few soldiers had moved into The Briars and were carrying on a wearisome surveillance. After remarks were made to the admiral, the sergeant and the soldiers were taken away, but the captain continued to stay, in civilian clothes. The surveillance did not remain any less active, although it was disguised. In town it continued to take place with the same rigor. These gentlemen could not take one step without being followed by an officer or a sergeant; it was the same when they came to The Briars to see the Emperor, and even the ladies noticed it. Although all of them were better lodged than the Emperor, who had left them his butler, they felt isolated. The ladies came to dinner on Sunday expressing their sorrow, and the men talked to him about the harassment this meticulous surveillance was causing them. The Emperor sympathized with their complaints deeply, urged them to be patient, and promised that a good family life would offset the annoyances that they were suffering as soon as they were established at Longwood.

Count de Las Cases' position was envied by all and with reason; an intimacy based on witty conversation and a very courteous nature was forming between the Emperor and himself, further strengthened by their similarity in ages. Those whose devotion had been demonstrated on the battlefield, and whose love for him was no less great, feared they would lose a part of this affection that was becoming their sole consolation on this miserable rock. Here they sought neither titles nor greatness, but a friendship whose worth everyone felt in this land of exile. Certainly I would not have exchanged my shipboard mattress—although I felt the floor through it—for the most comfortable bed in the Porteous household.

The Emperor knew the best way to fight boredom was work; to this end he arranged to have one of these gentlemen every day. I have said that the Italian campaigns were dictated to Count de Las Cases, those of Egypt to the grand marshal; General Gourgaud had the Consulate, the island of Elba, and the Hundred Days; Count de Montholon had the Empire and, as if it were necessary to have two people to copy and clean up all these dictations, once corrected, the Emperor found nothing better than to put Saint-Denis and myself in charge. Later, when the Emperor had me write under his dictation, Saint-Denis found himself alone in this work.

The Emperor had tried to write himself, but his hand could not follow his thoughts that were so quick, concise, and full of fire; his fingers did not respond to the speed of his imagination. Then he attempted abbreviating, but in such a fashion that it was illegible to everyone, and sometimes even to himself. Confused one day by a few words inserted between two lines, I went to show it to him so he could read them to me; he was unable to read them himself and told me to leave them blank, commenting that he would remember them later.

During our stay at The Briars, the admiral gave several balls and a great dinner party, and came to invite the Emperor to do him the honor of attending. He intended, on this occasion, to introduce to him unofficially the civil and military officers of the island. Such gatherings did not suit the Emperor, who thanked him graciously for his invitation. These gentlemen and these ladies, even M. de Las Cases, in response to the Emperor's wish, attended all these small parties. A similar invitation was extended to the Emperor a few days later by Colonel Bingham and Major Fehrzen,[277] in the name of the officers who were giving the ball. The Emperor thanked them, refused, and sent Count de Las Cases; the latter went out of obedience, saying he was led more by the desire to be able to give an account to the Emperor of how the work was coming along at Longwood, than by the

[277]Major Oliver George Fehrzen commanded the 2nd battalion of the 53rd infantry regiment. A young officer of 29, he had served with distinction in the peninsula wars. He made a very good impression on the Emperor. He left Saint Helena in July 1817 with his battalion and died of cholera in India in 1820.

attraction of a pleasure that was not meant for a man of his age. He took his son with him and came back exhausted during the night. The following day he spoke of the house and the work being done there in the words of a man who was not at all attracted by the house's location nor the barrenness surrounding it: "Sire!" he said, "here we are camped. There we shall be penned in."

The Emperor was beginning to tire of his prolonged stay at The Briars; going out in short britches and silk stockings for walks in the garden after sundown, he had caught cold and was coughing a great deal. Mrs. Balcombe, to whose home he sometimes went toward the end of the evening, offered to make him an infusion of four flowers with a little honey from her own hives. The Emperor thanked her and showed her a small candy box containing licorice, the only remedy he said that he wished to use. The Emperor stayed at home for a few days, and the cold disappeared.

One evening when the weather was too bad for him to go out, he was sitting near a table with Count de Las Cases and his son and asked me to bring the box containing his snuffboxes. I brought it to him open, revealing the first compartment. Count de Las Cases and his son were not familiar with them; they marveled at the opulence of the boxes, and the resemblance of the imperial family in the portraits, which they looked at each in turn: "It is an evening with the family that I am giving you, my dear Las Cases," the Emperor said to him, "I had a great many others that Constant stole from me at Fontainebleau in 1814." The boxes in the second compartment were no less beautiful; they were decorated with antique cameos, very rare gold and silver coins, paintings by Petitot, portraits by Turenne. After examining the contents of the box, and after M. Emmanuel Las Cases had read to the Emperor several Greek inscriptions around the medals decorating some of the snuffboxes, I was about to close the box when the Emperor told me to also put in those he had been using since he was at The Briars. One was decorated with the portrait of Empress Marie-Louise, the other with that of the King of Rome. He replaced them with two others with silver medals. On one was the head of Caesar and that of Timoleon, on the other that of Alexander. "Come," he said, "don't you have anything more to show me? Show me my riches." I brought him another case containing twelve gold boxes with the imperial coat of arms, intended to give as presents, and two others decorated with his portrait surrounded by large diamonds. In the same box there were two small spyglasses for wartime use. Having seen these objects, he asked me for one of his small field travel kits; he examined all of its pieces in front of Count de Las Cases, and after closing it, gave it to him with these words: "It served me on the morning of Austerlitz, and shall go to Emmanuel when he is thirty or forty years old."

Since the Emperor had been at The Briars, he had not attempted to extend his excursions beyond what he called his favorite path. One day he felt like riding on horseback and covering an area of the island; horses were immediately sent from town. M. de Las Cases and Saint-Denis were getting ready to accompany him; but as he was about to mount his horse, the Emperor learned that the duty officer, who the day before had allowed him to ride alone if he did not want to be accompanied by him, had just received orders to comply with his instructions. The Emperor was irritated by this, and told Saint-Denis to send the horses back: he would not be going out. After his dinner he went out in the garden, as was customary. In roaming about, he spotted a small path used only by slaves. He set out down the path to reach the little valley seen from the windows of his pavilion. Although the path was dangerous, the Emperor, M. de Las Cases, and his son followed it, and arrived not without difficulty at the house of Major Hodson,[278] the aim of their stroll. When the Emperor left the major, night had fallen;

---

[278]Major Charles Robert George Hodson was a giant nicknamed "Hercules" by the Emperor. He was an infantry regiment major, and judge advocate, and acted as town mayor in Jamestown. His property visited by the Emperor on November 20 was called Maldivia. Major Hodson was present at Napoleon's funeral and at the exhumation ceremonies in 1840.

Mrs. Hodson was the daughter of Sir W. Doveton, member of the island council, who owned Mount Pleasant in Sandy Bay, about three miles south of Longwood. The Emperor visited Sir Webber Doveton in January 1816 and made his last excursion outside the limits there on October 4, 1820; accompanied by Generals Bertrand and Montholon, Napoleon had lunch in the garden with his host.

they could not come back by the same path and accepted the horses that were offered them. They arrived at The Briars quite late, which had kept us wondering where the Emperor might have been, as he was neither in the garden nor at Mr. Balcombe's. The next day the Emperor was delighted by his previous night's excursion and spoke in very honorable terms of Major Hodson and the cordial welcome he had received. There was something behind this pleasure: it was to have deceived his guard, who could not imagine the Emperor and Count de Las Cases attempting to follow such a dangerous path.

Admiral Cockburn, in spite of the restrictions that he imposed, remained nevertheless full of consideration for the Emperor and his retinue, and of courtesy for the ladies. But in town the surveillance had become intolerable, due to the adoption of new measures that took these gentlemen by surprise and disturbed them in their daily routines. The following is an example: the Frenchmen who were not residing at The Briars were henceforth to be back in town before 9 p.m., lest they be arrested by sentries who had orders to prevent any traffic at that hour between Jamestown and The Briars.

Here are the orders of the port authorities as they were communicated to the Emperor:

PORT REGULATIONS

1. The commanders of the honorable East India Company's ships and the masters or commanders of all merchant ships who are permitted to anchor at this island may not go ashore or allow anyone belonging to their vessel or ship to go ashore until these regulations have been communicated on board said ships. They must first send a list of all people on board to the governor so that he may indicate who is permitted to come ashore.

2. Firstly, it is required of all commanders of ships or vessels to declare whether any illness, contagious or otherwise, has taken place on board ship, and whether there have been any deaths in the course of the voyage and if so, to state the causes.

3. All letters and packages addressed to residents of the island, except those arriving by regular mail, must be given to the officer bearing these regulations. He will leave them with the government secretary, where the persons to whom they are addressed may come to claim them.

4. If the commander, one of his passengers, or anyone on board carries any letter, packages, etc., addressed to one of the foreigners on the island, they are requested to inform the governor himself, giving him the note or letter in its envelope or awaiting his orders, if the package is sizable.

5. Only the commander of the ship, once these regulations have been read and published on board, may come ashore if he wishes and go directly to the governor's, should he be in town. If not, he will make his arrival known at the quarters of the deputy chief of staff.

6. The commanders, officers, and any passengers who are then permitted to debark will go at once to the office of the major in town, to read and sign the island regulations before going to their lodgings or visiting any house or individual whatsoever.

7. No passenger or other person debarking from a vessel at the coast may leave Jamestown Valley without permission. To obtain permission they must appear at the deputy chief of staff's office.

8. No individual whatsoever having permission to debark may visit The Briars or Longwood or their adjacent boundaries, nor have any verbal or written communication with the foreigners detained on the island, without having directly informed the governor of his intentions and receiving his authorization to do so. If any individual should receive a letter or package from said foreigners, he must immediately bring it to the governor before replying to it. The same rule applies to any packages that may be received or whose delivery is attempted.

9. The commanders of the East India Company's vessels and the masters of all types of merchant ships who are permitted to anchor on the coast of the island may not allow anyone to go ashore on leave without the authorization of the governor. No passenger may sleep on shore without his knowledge.

10. No vessel belonging to the East India Company or any merchant ship may debark between sunrise and sunset, nor at any moment of the day whatsoever, without the officer in charge being present. If a ship for any reason whatsoever receives an order not to land, it must take care to stay at some distance from the harbor in order to allow other ships to land without interference. The greatest haste must be taken by ships loading or unloading merchandise to not obstruct the path of other ships.

11. All boats belonging to the East India Company or any merchant vessels must leave the island at sunset and passengers must immediately return on board their respective vessels, except under circumstances designated by the admiral.

12. No boat belonging to the vessels of the East India Company or to any ship whatsoever may come alongside or send a boat to any other vessel arriving in the harbor. No boat may land anywhere except in the harbor.

13. No vessel of the East India Company or any merchant ship whatsoever may drop anchor at this island between sundown and sunrise, nor set sail after sundown or before 10 a.m. They must not set sail until the clearance flag has been raised for each vessel and ship.

14. If the clearance flag is raised for a vessel shortly before sunset and it does not weigh anchor quickly enough, it may not set sail until the signal has been repeated the following day at 10 a.m.

15. It is expressly forbidden to all commanders of vessels or merchant ships to allow any fishing boat of the island alongside his ship without a permit signed by the governor, or to allow any boat belonging to his vessel to approach the numbered craft of island fishermen or to communicate with them.

16. If a fishing boat seeks to communicate with a vessel heading for the island which is already at anchor, or if it communicates with a boat belonging to the vessel, its commander or its officers are required to immediately make this known to the governor and the deputy chief of staff, taking the boat's number and detaining it if circumstances so dictate.

17. The commanders of vessels carrying newspapers which may contain recent news worthy of interest are required to give them to the person reading these regulations, for the surveillance of the governor, who will then carefully return them.

18. It is forbidden to debark gunpowder without first having alerted the commissioner of supplies and the master attendant, so that all necessary precautions may be taken to prevent accidents.

19. No stallions, mares, or geldings may be debarked without permission from the government secretary.

20. No wine of any sort may be debarked without a permit from the government secretary.

21. As the honorable council of directors has prohibited the importation of spirits coming from India, it is ordered that anyone in violation of this ordinance will pay a fine of 100 pounds sterling. Brandy, mead, rum from the West Indies, cordials, etc., may only be debarked in very limited quantities, after having obtained permission and paid a tax of twelve shillings per gallon. The debarking of any spirit in any quantity without a permit will subject the offender to the above-mentioned penalty.

22. Whaling vessels may not cast their harpoons while they are in the vicinity of the island, under penalty of a fine of fifty pounds sterling. Half this sum will be given in reward to the person reporting the infraction.

23. All commanders of vessels or masters of merchant ships must announce their departure 48 hours in advance, and do the same if they wish to remain longer than the time agreed on. This announcement must be given in writing to the government secretary and to the master attendant between 10 a.m. and 2 p.m. The topsail must be lowered 48 hours prior to the vessel's departure. No commander or master of any vessel or ship whatsoever may leave any person on the island or take any person away under any pretext without having requested in writing permission from the governor.

24. No commander, passenger, or any person whatsoever on board one of the vessels of the honorable East India Company or any other vessel that has anchored at the island may take possession of letters or packages to transport them to Europe, the Cape of Good Hope, South America, or anywhere else, except those arriving by post or which have been consigned to them by the secretary or the deputy chief of staff.

The commander of the vessel or merchant ship is to sign the attached form and return it to the officer reading these regulations.

The acrimony that was already appearing between the admiral and the Emperor only increased on reading this document. Among the people in town who suffered most from being separated from the Emperor was General Gourgaud. He was alone, deprived even of his servant who had been refused permission to land. In order to receive him at The Briars it would be necessary to find him a room. The Emperor informed him of this, and the general immediately overcame this obstacle by replying that all he needed was a small tent set up close to his. A few days later the general moved to The Briars.

Dr. O'Meara came from town to offer his services to the Emperor. The first time he witnessed his getting dressed, the Emperor showed him the flannel undershirt he kept on while shaving: "Well, doctor, this is what your pamphleteers call the coat of mail I used to wear in the days of my power." And then he pointed out to him what lay on the chair: "Here is the hat they say was lined with steel; it is through such lies that your compatriots were deceived on my account.

But their relations with France will soon make the truth known, and they will be enlightened." The doctor replied that the truth had been demonstrated here, and that the ladies who had the honor of seeing him at the Balcombes' remained delighted with his graciousness toward them. The opinion they retained of him was completely different from the one they had formed before having met him. "They must have imagined I was some sort of dark beast," the Emperor said, laughing.

The doctor informed him that a British vessel had just arrived that morning. The Emperor told him he had already known this, because of the newspapers that had immediately been sent out by the admiral, whose intentions had touched him. It was therapeutic for him, as well as for Count de Las Cases, who read them to him. This attentiveness had somewhat soothed the Emperor's bad mood at receiving the admiral's reply to a letter written by the grand marshal, in which he complained about the Emperor's situation and urged changes within the sovereignty of his position. However, the letter had been submitted to the Emperor before being sent out, and he had approved its wording. The admiral, no doubt upset by the comments made to him, had replied that he knew of no Emperor in Saint Helena. This reply, as curt as it was offensive, had been brought to the attention of the Emperor, who hid the discontent it caused him.

It was during the stay at The Briars that the Emperor heard the story of Tobie, an old slave serving in the Balcombe household. He had him tell him how, caught in a trap, he had been captured and taken on a ship that brought him to Saint Helena. The Emperor wanted to restore him to his home and family by freeing him; he asked Mr. Balcombe to tend to this negotiation, but it did not receive approval from the authorities, and poor Tobie remained a slave. When we were at Longwood and Tobie brought food, he never failed to ask news of the Emperor, having known of his good intentions toward him.

The Emperor had found one more source for conversation in General Gourgaud, who had moved nearby. If with Count de Las Cases he could broach any subject in conversation, he now had the option of discussing wars and campaigns with an officer who had been an eyewitness, and whose aptitude and erudition he knew. In addition, this man was always available and ready to take dictation, which eased the workload on Count de Las Cases, whose eyesight was weakening as a result of this assiduous work. It was also an opportunity to look back on the past; some anecdotes of the imperial court, wittily recounted by the general, made the Emperor laugh, and he found himself saying: "Ah, women, women, there are many things that, without them, I would never have known."

On this small piece of land, the inhabitants often gave feasts and parties that always ended with a ball. Invitations were not only extended to the ladies and gentlemen of the Emperor's retinue, who had no heart for taking pleasure and attended only on the Emperor's orders, but also to the Emperor himself; he always refused with kind words. The Emperor gladly received any visits that were paid to him, but refused any invitation that would take him outside his self-imposed retreat. The last ball given during the Emperor's residence at The Briars was that of Colonel Wilks, governor of the island for the East India Company. The Emperor, fatigued by the climatic variations, had not felt well for some days. The gentlemen and ladies of his retinue sent their gratitude for the received invitations, but did not go.

No doubt affected by the prevailing weather and the inconvenience of his lodgings, the Emperor sent General Montholon and General Gourgaud to survey the progress of work at Longwood, and to determine when it would be possible for him to move in. They returned and told the Emperor that the work on the house was completed; however, there still remained a very strong paint odor throughout the residence, particularly in his bedroom. They urged him to postpone moving for a few days. As for the buildings that were to serve as lodgings for these gentlemen, they were still far from completion. At that time it was November 28. On this same day the Emperor abandoned the chasseur of the guard uniform that he had been wearing since boarding the *Bellerophon*. He donned a green tail coat, and the only decoration he affixed to it was the emblem of the Legion of Honor. He continued wearing the sash of the Legion of Honor between his waistcoat and suit coat, which he always kept closed so that no one could see it. A pair of white cloth uniform trousers, silk stockings, buckle shoes, and the little hat that has become famous was the apparel he adopted at Longwood.

On the following day, the 29th, Dr. O'Meara informed the Emperor while he was dressing in the morning that the *Havana* had arrived from the Cape, where it had gone to secure provisions and other objects necessary for the establishment at Longwood, and had dropped anchor in Jamestown harbor. Letters and newspapers announced the assassination of Marshal Brune in Avignon, the execution of poor General La Bédoyère, shot by order of court martial, and other massacres provoked by the fanaticism of men such as Trestaillons[279] and others. Such tragedies were strongly felt by the Emperor and all of us who, on our way to the island of Elba, had known and beheld all the bloody upheaval of the Orgon population; they would have assassinated the Emperor, without the courageous intervention of General Koller, the Austrian Commissioner, and the fearless devotion of Noverraz.

On December 8, the admiral, carrying newspapers and letters that a transport ship had brought from Europe, informed the Emperor that everything was finished at Longwood. He wished for the Emperor to notify him which day he could return to accompany him and to give him instructions regarding specific arrangements, so that he could move into his new residence. The Emperor was anxious to leave The Briars and designated the following day, the 9th. Escorted by the grand marshal and the admiral, he offered a few details regarding the arrangements, asked for some pieces of furniture he would need, and personally thanked the admiral for the prompt execution of all the work that he had had done. The Emperor found the odor of paint to still be noticeable; but not wanting to prolong his stay at The Briars any further, he said to the admiral: "If you wish to come tomorrow, I

---

[279]Trestaillons, whose real name was Jacques Dupont, in August 1815 headed royalist bands that spread terror in the region of Nîmes. It was said he swore to cut into three pieces every Bonapartist in the department, hence his nickname of Trestaillons ("carve into three pieces"). He was arrested in October 1815, but was released because there were no witnesses courageous enough to testify against him.

shall move to Longwood." The admiral could not have received a better invitation; he himself was impatient to see this new installation completed before the arrival of the governor expected from England, and he was anxious to establish, according to his instructions, surveillance measures that would reassure him against any possibility of escape.

On the following day, December 10, after six weeks of camping at The Briars, the Emperor parted after expressing his gratefulness to the hosts. He had the head of the family given a gold box with his coat of arms, invited him to lunch and urged him to come see him with his daughters and wife once we were settled at Longwood. As all the preparations for departure were attended to, I left Noverraz in charge of accompanying the baggage in an oxcart and proceeded to Longwood alone. I desired to arrive before the Emperor in order to receive him.

The first pleasure Napoleon has on St. Helena is the company of the two young Balcombe daughters.

Napoleon gives Betsy Balcombe her lesson.

CHAPTER THIRTEEN

Longwood and its surroundings — Precarious setting —
Montholon's family — Count de Las Cases —
Grand Marshal Bertrand — General Gourgaud — The retinue —
Everyday life — Piontkowski

J ascended toward a previously unknown part of the island in order to reach Alarm House,[280] and I found only volcanic terrain without a trace of vegetation. From that vista point, the scenery was forbidding, yet at the same time captivating. A graceful road wound around a valley that led to Longwood; the house, visible on a plateau from the distance, behind which one could distinguish the forest called Deadwood, formed a rather inspiring scene. The valley that lay between us was a deep, tortured chasm called Devil's Hole. It was made of lava which had cooled in different states of fusion, the layers having superimposed themselves on one another. Pockets of soil spread by time gave birth to a few, stunted trees and patches of greenery. Beyond the ravine lay the camp, situated on a sprawling lawn, its barracks dominated by Goats' Mountain. This completed the overall Longwood scenery quite pleasantly. Resuming my way toward Hutt's

---

[280] Alarm House, on the road from Jamestown to Longwood, was three km. from the Emperor's residence. Colonel Wynyard, military secretary to the governor, and his wife lived there.

A guard post was established nearby, as well as the cannon that sounded at sunrise, at sunset, and whenever a ship approached. A signaling system with flags allowed it to communicate with the governor through relays at Rupert's Hill and Ladder Hill. The blue flag announcing that General Bonaparte had disappeared was never raised.

Gate,[281] I passed Geranium Valley, unsuspecting that six years later it would become the Emperor's graveyard. A small house, a few willows near a little fountain, and some garden plots could be seen; this vegetation reached as far as Hutt's Gate, where a small house stood with outbuildings. This is where the grand marshal and his family were to live while waiting for the lodging being constructed for them at Longwood to be finished.

This house, which the road leading to Longwood passed, seemed to bestride the two valleys it overlooked. That on the right was dominated by Diana's Peak, whose green summit was the highest on the island and separated Longwood from Plantation House, and offered more vegetation. It was strewn with a few country homes, the most noteworthy being those of Miss Mason and the Balcombe cottage. This valley extended from Diana's Peak to the ocean, following the Longwood plateau and then disappearing in some folds of terrain at the seashore. It became inaccessible due to the sheer cliffs. The vegetation in this valley did not extend beyond the small house belonging to Miss Robinson, located below Longwood; after this there was only volcanic rock in the same state of fusion as that of Devil's Hole. That part of the island could truly be called desolate.

For one who had remained at The Briars for six weeks without going outside, this countryside was not without charm; but this favorable impression dissipated more and more the closer I approached the house. The trees forming a green roof were really very stunted, with such sparse foliage that they provided no shade. The lawn that appeared fresh was so only by comparison with the rocky ravines and volcanic land separating me from it. Scorched by the sun, it was, on the Longwood plateau and at the camp, more like a field of straw than

---

[281]Hutt's Gate was, in 1815, a modest house located on the Jamestown Road, one mile from Longwood. Five companies of the 53rd settled near the cottage before moving, along with the artillery facilities, to Deadwood Camp.

The space in which the Emperor was allowed to circulate without being accompanied by the duty officer was enclosed in a polygon with a tortured perimeter varying from 4 to 12 miles. Outposts and sentries marked the periphery set up for infantry riflemen. A system of trenches dug inside the domain turned it into a real garrison. Traces of this still exist today.

of grass. The house itself was not surrounded by trees, as it had appeared to me on the way from Alarm House.

After familiarizing myself with the rooms that made up the house, my first concern was to prepare a bath for the Emperor, who used to take them so frequently and had not enjoyed one since Malmaison. The baggage and Noverraz arrived long enough before the Emperor that we were able to prepare his quarters and arrange it according to his habits. That morning the Emperor had donned his uniform of chasseur of the imperial guard for the day. At 3 o'clock, I heard a drumbeat at the entrance gate. The outpost, commanded by an officer, was under arms. It was the Emperor, accompanied by the admiral and the grand marshal, entering Longwood. He was followed by his officers, and the admiral by a few officers from his staff. Arriving in front of the house at the verandah door preceding the parlor, the admiral dismounted his horse and surrendered the reins, to help the Emperor get down. He took great care to make himself civil; he accompanied the Emperor into the drawing room and continued to offer his services. The Emperor took his leave, expressed his gratitude again, and told him everything was in order. With the way things were going, it was easy to perceive the cooling taking place between them, and it was to be feared that surveillance at Longwood would become more stringent.

The Emperor changed nothing in my arrangement of the furniture. In place of a large bed that had been put in his room, he told me to substitute his field bed, as it was an old friend he preferred to all others. This change was made while he was in his bath into which he had jumped with childish joy. The bathtub was a tremendous oak chest lined with lead. It required an exceptional quantity of water, and one had to go a half mile away and transport it in a barrel. I informed the Emperor that it had taken an extremely long time to heat this bath, as the furnace was much too inadequate for the bathtub. A few days later, due to Dr. O'Meara's efforts, another bathtub was brought from town that held less water; it was used until the arrival of one sent from London for the new house.

The whole time the Emperor remained in his bath, he kept Count de Las Cases at his side; when he came out, he climbed into bed for a while. When he got dressed, he donned the civilian clothes he had taken off that morning and never wore a uniform again. No matter how barren the surroundings and modest the house that the Emperor was required to live in, it must be agreed he was more at ease here than in the places of a few feet square in which he had lived for ten months, at sea or on land. This house, consisting only of a ground floor, was a former farmhouse belonging to the East India Company, which the lieutenant governor Mr. Skelton had assumed as his residence. Some wooden constructions had just been added to expand the building; others, attached to a separate building housing the kitchen, and destined for Count de Montholon, General Gourgaud, Count de Las Cases, Dr. O'Meara, and the duty officer, were nearing completion. These lodgings were all on the ground floor and situated next to each other.

In this new residence, the Emperor was housed alone; he had two small rooms each ten feet square; one of them was to serve as his study. In each of them, a small field bed was set up; the walls of both were decorated with nankeen bordered with a paper rose edging, and they were lit by two small windows known in France as the "guillotine" type. The view from these two rooms looked out upon the camp about a mile away. The window curtains were of white calico; a carpet in both rooms concealed severely rough flooring. In the room fashioned into the bedroom, there was a small fireplace made entirely of wood painted grey; a small iron grate inside indicated that coal was to be burnt in it. The fireplace was decorated with a small wooden frame with gilt columns, and a small mirror about eighteen inches tall and fifteen inches wide was attached above it. The two rooms were nine feet high, and were furnished with a few chairs and armchairs with caned backs painted green, a dresser, a settee, and a table covered with green cloth, to be used as a desk. I decorated the mantelpiece with torches taken from the Emperor's travel kit, a gilt cup and its saucer, and an incense burner made of the same metal. On either side of the mirror I hung two small portraits of the King of Rome; above them hung Frederick the Great's alarm clock on one side and the Emperor's watch on the other. To the left of the fireplace, I placed the Emperor's travel kit on a small table, opened it in order to decorate the room a little more, and hung over it a third portrait of the King of Rome, by Isabey. On the right side of the fireplace, the Emperor had his settee placed so that it protruded into the room. He then had it surrounded with a folding screen, so that air would not strike him in the face when the door to his bathroom was opened, as all the service had to be done through that door. Above the settee I hung a portrait of Empress Marie-Louise holding the King of Rome in her arms. A mahogany table was placed at the foot of the settee; a table covered with green cloth to be used as a desk was placed between the two windows although it extended beyond them on either side, and the bed was erected in a corner of the room facing the windows. These two rooms and the bathroom were called the Emperor's private quarters. A small antechamber opening onto a corridor leading to the kitchens completed the design.

When the Emperor left his chambers to go to into the drawing room, he first entered a room a little larger than the ones he occupied; it was called the map room, as all the maps were spread out on a large table stood in the middle. The room, lit by a French window, was quite dark. The bed the admiral had sent for the Emperor had been relegated to this room, which later became the dining room; one door opened into the drawing room, another into the corridor to the kitchen, and a third into the Emperor's bedroom. Beyond that was a large room lit by two windows. It had a small study with an exit into the kitchen corridor, allowing it to be entered without disturbing the Emperor in his quarters, although it really was part of it. The Emperor had at once designated it as a lodging for the grand marshal, whom he wanted to have close by. But Count Bertrand pointed out that he, his wife, and his three children would be very overcrowded in this one room, and since the admiral had no objection to his living in the small cottage at Hutt's Gate until his own lodging was completed, he asked permission to settle there with his family. "Do whatever you wish," replied the Emperor, "Montholon will lodge with me."

The Briars and Pavilion.

The Briars, St. Helena.

The Briars.

Balcombe's House, The Briars.

House of the Bertrand family.

Longwood in 1815.

Longwood.

Longwood as painted by Marchand.

Longwood, showing the position of the New House built (the White Building).

After a good deal of criticism by British leaders of the treatment of Napoleon by his captors, the government built a new house for him. Napoleon looked at it once and never inhabited it.

Longwood as seen in 1840.

Longwood today from the air.

Bertrand's House at Hutt's Gate.

New Longwood house.

The Governor's mansion, known as Plantation House, which should have been turned over to Napoleon; it is located in a pleasant part of the island.

Longwood Plantation House.

The guard house at the entrance at Longwood.

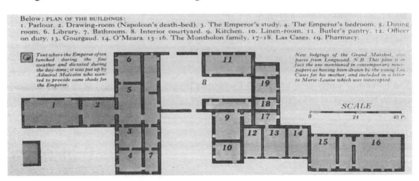

Below: PLAN OF THE BUILDINGS:
1. Parlour. 2. Drawing-room (Napoleon's death-bed). 3. The Emperor's study. 4. The Emperor's bedroom. 5. Dining room. 6. Library. 7. Bathroom. 8. Interior courtyard. 9. Kitchen. 10. Linen-room. 11. Butler's pantry. 12. Officer on duty. 13. Gourgaud. 14. O'Meara. 15-16. The Montholon family. 17-18. Las Cases. 19. Pharmacy.

Floor plan of the Longwood buildings.

Napoleon dictates to Gourgaud.

As the Emperor wanted to know how each of the people with him were getting settled in at Longwood, he left his room after dressing, and went straight to the lodgings of Mme de Montholon, separated from his own only by the room I mentioned. He knocked lightly and the countess opened, sliding aside a bolt that locked this door. She and the general expressed their embarrassment at being surprised in the disarray of moving in. "Sire," said the countess, "it is both my drawing room and my bedroom." The Emperor thanked them both for being satisfied with so little in order to lodge with him; he urged General Montholon to push the work being done on their apartment in order for them to move in there as soon as possible. The Emperor left, and told Count de Las Cases to take him to his temporary lodgings. It was a room close to the kitchen. The admiral had it arranged as best he could, but it was still in such a state that the Emperor said: "My dear friend, you shall sleep in the map room; there is already a bed, and you are not sufficiently comfortable here." Count de Las Cases thanked the Emperor, but out of discretion, never took advantage of this. He then went to General Gourgaud's tent erected in front of the house under his windows. Believing that in a climate where the temperature changes so suddenly after sunset, the roof on his tent was too light, he advised him to have a bed set up every evening in the parlor; the general could keep his tent to retire to during the day. The general thanked him for his offer, and said that in this manner he could very well wait for the work to be completed on his lodging. Dr. O'Meara and the British officer commanding at Longwood were also housed in tents: the Emperor was touched by the devotion of one and all, who preferred a poor lodging near him to a comfortable apartment in town. The Emperor returned to the drawing room, going through the parlor that was preceded by a small verandah: these two rooms stuck out from the main building, as can be seen on the map. The drawing room was lit by two windows, of the same type as those in the bedroom. The view looked out over the guard building located at the entrance to Longwood, and further out on Diana's Peak. The road between Hutt's Gate and Alarm House closed off the horizon on that side; with his spyglass, the Emperor was able to recognize those people who went to or from town. This drawing room, fourteen feet in length and twelve in width, was decorated with a marble fireplace with a large mirror above it, some chairs, armchairs, and a settee; a rug covered the floor, and white curtains with colored draperies hung at the windows. A piano was brought several days later to help distract Countess de Montholon, whose amateur talent was quite remarkable.

The wooden parlor that the admiral had had built was much larger. It was lit by five windows. Those on the left, when leaving the drawing room, had the same view as the latter. Those on the opposite side were located on either side of the fireplace, and opened on the gum tree grove located about a shotgun distance away, above which the ocean could be seen. This room, with a double door at one end facing the drawing room door, was the main entrance to the chambers and the waiting room for foreigners who solicited the honor of being received by the Emperor. The verandah, raised three steps above ground level, ran the entire width of the building; it was of trelliswork painted green, shaped like a portico, six feet wide and sixteen feet long. From there the view extended to a shallow valley where Count Bertrand's house was being constructed, not far from the farm and garden of the East India Company that made up the backdrop. It was dominated on one side by the camp, and on the other by Goats' Rock. The India Company garden consisted of very little; the gardener's lodging and the stable for the oxen were called a farm; at home this would have been the poor lodging of a peasant. The grass we walked on around the Longwood building was, like that of the camp, damaged by the wind and sun; although the dew was quite abundant at night, it was not enough to refresh it.

In sum, this place was sad, and the wind that prevailed constantly made it quite unbearable; but the plateau was completely dominated by the surrounding hillsides and could be easily watched: and this particular situation had determined its choice. The large parlor, twenty-four feet by sixteen feet, would have been the most practical room for the Emperor; when the weather was bad he could have strolled there. But the fireplace was poor, and it was impossible to make a fire in it. On the other hand, when the weather was good, the sun beat down on the roof with full, tropical force, and the heat in that room was unbearable. In the attic of the old building, they had made small cells for servants; these rooms were lit by skylights. My own, located just above the Emperor's room, was paneled on both sides; at the peak, they had cut a window decorated with shutters. The view extended over the most pleasant part of the plateau, encompassing the camp, the road from Alarm House to Longwood, Diana's Peak, and the prettiest part of the valley where Miss Mason's house and the Balcombe cottage were located. As I have already said, the grand marshal was lodged at Hutt's Gate, approximately two miles from Longwood.

That same evening at dinnertime began the family life that everyone so desired. The day after his arrival, the Emperor wished to look over the Longwood enclosure; he was accompanied by General Gourgaud and Count de Las Cases, who spoke English very well. He was of great help to him for engaging people he might meet in conversations, should he take a fancy to question them during their stroll. Poorly interpreted orders stopped the Emperor during his walk. The area to the left of him was not so large that he had to believe he would be free to move around without being stopped. He came home quite disgusted, and complained justifiably about the hindrances to his outings. When Colonel Bingham was informed of this misunderstanding, he came at once to apologize for the error committed by the sentry. The admiral also came during the afternoon and listened to the Emperor's comments on the uselessness of so many outposts that every instant confronted him with a bayonet. He assured him that nothing of the kind would happen again, and that he was taking great

Longwood: view of the Emperor's house.

care to make his stay in Saint Helena as bearable as possible.[282] Since our arrival on the island, nothing had yet been organized. Once at Longwood, the Emperor wanted his household staff to be organized; he assigned certain tasks to each one, to avoid friction that would have arisen otherwise, aptly saying that where everyone gives orders there is nothing but disorder. Although the grand marshal did not give up his title, it was Count de Montholon who fulfilled his duties. Cipriani, the butler under his orders, arranged with him for the distribution of food, both at Longwood and at Count Bertrand's at Hutt's Gate. Mr. Balcombe became the supplier, and the government allocations appeared reasonable. Sometimes there was reason to complain about the quality, but generally it was due more to a lack of resources than the admiral's fault, and when he was informed of this, he would immediately remedy it as much as he could, always expressing his regrets for a state of affairs that he tried to improve.

The stable consisted of ten horses: four draft horses and six saddle horses. A carriage purchased at the Cape of Good Hope by the admiral was there for the Emperor's use; it was the only one on the

---

[282]In the middle of the 18th century, Longwood consisted of a farm and a shed. In 1787 Colonel Robson, governor of the island, had an addition built outside the stable consisting of four rooms, and added a fifth room perpendicular to the building. Behind this a courtyard, a chicken coop, and some servants' quarters were also set up. The stable was a separate building.

The house was located at an altitude of 1700 feet, five miles from Jamestown, four miles from Plantation House, half a mile from Deadwood camp, and 200 yards from the Bertrand house and New House.

When landing in Jamestown, the admiral had convinced the French that Longwood would be a marvelous place to live.

Immediately on his arrival in Jamestown, Gourgaud wrote to Countess Caffarelli: "They are preparing for us a small country house five miles from here; as soon as it is repaired and furnished, we will take up residence there. It is said to be in a marvelous location. May it remind me of Malmaison."

Gourgaud begs the countess to reply to him, and specifies the way in which correspondence should be addressed. "Write to me as I do, without sealing your letters, and address them thusly: 'To General Baron Gourgaud on the island of Saint Helena.' Place this open letter in an sealed envelope addressed to Admiral George Cockburn, commanding the naval installation of His British Majesty in Saint Helena. Finally, make a last envelope on which you write 'The Secret.' Furthermore, I believe you must frank this letter as far as England."

island. Sailors taken from the crew of the *Northumberland* were dressed and assigned to the stable, under the orders of the Archambault brothers. The elder of the two brothers had been head footman on the Island of Elba but both of them came from the stables, and had already driven the Emperor in a carriage; it was therefore easy for them to organize that service. They drove the Emperor until the men under their orders were able to do so, and took care of training the saddle horses used by the Emperor. General Gourgaud was in charge of supervising the stable staff.

Besides the six sailors in the stables, six others were assigned to different services; the silver, under Rousseau's orders, had two of them, the kitchen had three, and the pantry, one. The Emperor did not want any in his private apartments, but on my suggestion, he agreed that I take a Chinese as wardrobe boy. My attendance on the Emperor was continuous, even at night. Saint-Denis and Noverraz each had one day on duty which consisted of staying in a small room preceding the bathroom used as an entrance to the Emperor's private apartments, and sleeping there at night in front of the Emperor's door, as I did myself. In addition, Saint-Denis continued to recopy the Emperor's dictations to prepare his manuscripts.

Santini was assigned to the map room as usher, opening the drawing room door when the Emperor came out of his bedroom, and acting as liaison with the outside staff. Gentilini became the footman, and was in charge of setting the table. Each of them wore the uniform matching his assignment; when this attire became too frayed, it was not replaced, and only the outer coat continued to be worn. Table service was handled with the silverware and the porcelain brought from Paris. In addition I had with me, in leather boxes, a magnificent dessert service from Sèvres representing the various battlefields of Egypt and Europe; beautiful vases and a collection of twenty-four cups from the same manufacturer completed this beautiful set, which the Emperor did not want to use for fear they would break. The Emperor's table was served by his butler, the pantry head who would offer him dessert himself; Saint-Denis and Noverraz were placed on the right and left of the Emperor, and served only him. Santini, Gentilini, and several footmen served those who had been honored with an invitation to dinner. If the Emperor dined in his private quarters, the butler would carry the dinner as far as the bathroom, the valet on duty would bring it in, and with his help I had the honor of serving it myself.

Count de Las Cases was assigned the job of taking inventory of the furniture, but it was of so little importance that he didn't even bother. The Emperor started working at Longwood, as he had at The Briars. Specific times were assigned to each of these gentlemen: the grand marshal had his, and every day a horse was taken to Hutt's Gate so that he could come to Longwood, where he and Countess Bertrand dined only on Sundays.

Lunch was first served at 11 a.m. and dinner at 7 p.m. Because he was obliged to dress to be present at lunch, the Emperor decided to lunch in his bedroom, and so extended the morning in his robe until 2 p.m. He then went into the drawing room, and if weather permitted he would call for the carriage to go on a tour of the Longwood plateau, or to Hutt's Gate to see the marshal's wife. During these trips he was accompanied by Countess de Montholon, Count de Las Cases, and by General Gourgaud, who went on horseback.

Dinner was at 7 p.m.; the Emperor had gotten into the habit of ending his evening in the dining room with some reading. All the staff would leave; he would then have Saint-Denis, who was in charge of the library, bring him either Corneille, Racine, or Molière and depending on the work selected he would say: "We will hear Talma or Fleury." At 10 p.m. he went back into his own apartment, taking with him Count de Las Cases. He would undress, chat with him, and dismiss him when sleep began to overtake him. If one adds to the preceding description a few horseback rides with General Gourgaud, the presentation of a few people from town, passengers coming from China or India and returning to Europe, a few dinner invitations extended to the admiral, Colonel Bingham, and some officers of his regiment, one will have a relatively accurate picture of the monotonous existence led by the Emperor in Saint Helena. Fortunately, intellectual resources were not lacking; thanks to his extraordinary mind and the diverse aptitudes of those surrounding him, he was entertained by conversations that rendered more bearable the awful rock where the hatred of kings kept him detained.

When all the construction was completed, everyone settled in his own corner as if he were to remain there until the end of his life, and embellished as best he could his modest lodgings. I had the carpenter from the *Northumberland* build two closets in my bedroom, in order to put the Emperor's clothing there. I placed them on either side of the window, and had paper bought in town. I was sent a Chinese paper with a blue background, decorated with roses and gilt highlights; there was no other, and I had it pasted on the walls. I had oilcloth representing a parquet put down to hide the poor condition of the floor, and a white bedspread made to cover my bed, although I did not sleep there. On a simple little settee that was there, I threw a percale sheet that gave it an enviable air of cleanliness; a small washstand and two chairs completed my furniture which my Chinese man took good care of, so that when I went there to wash, I spent the time there with pleasure. My shutters remained closed for coolness, but the sun bore down with such strength on the slates, only separated from me by lathing, that during the day this bedroom was uninhabitable.

The circumference allowed the Emperor his strolls around the house, without his being followed by the duty officer, could have been six or eight miles, but in truth, there was only the Longwood grove, the garden belonging to the East India Company, and Deadwood (the location of the camp, which he never visited), where he could stroll, and this area was certainly not much more than four miles. The rest consisted of ravines that he would cover on horseback with great care, so that his horse would not fall. One day when he was strolling on foot through one of these valleys, accompanied by Count de Las Cases and General Gourgaud, the Emperor almost disappeared in some sort of a bog; when he came home, he told these gentlemen who accompanied him to his bedroom: "It was the marsh of Arcole! What would they have said in Europe," he added laughing, "had I disappeared in it? That it was a just punishment for all my crimes!" As his boots were muddied all the way to the top, I asked Saint-Denis the reason for this. He told me that the Emperor, having climbed down from his horse to proceed on foot in a valley he did not know, had been mistaken about the nature of the terrain that appeared to be covered by fresh grass, but in reality had no consistency whatsoever. In that same area some time later, Saint-Denis, on horseback, found himself stuck in the mud and was only able to get out with great difficulty, assisted by General Gourgaud. The Emperor stopped his stroll, and only resumed it when General Gourgaud came to tell him that Saint-Denis had been able to get out.

In this valley stood the small house belonging to Miss Robinson. This lady has two daughters; the older was fifteen or sixteen, and both of them had gotten into the habit, when the Emperor passed their house, of approaching and offering him some flowers. Without being pretty, they were pleasant, but there was little financial ease under that roof. The Emperor would greet them with kindness, and was in the habit of calling the older one "the Las Cases nymph," and the valley "the Valley of Silence." The two young ladies thus acquired a certain amount of fame that soon reached town; this fame caused a naval captain from the East India Company to seek out the older daughter for his wife when he came through Saint Helena, and he married her. Before leaving the island the young couple came to see the Emperor, who congratulated the husband on his choice and wished for the young woman to become the mother of a fine, numerous family.

The Emperor had gotten into the habit of taking this stroll, because in that way he went up to Hutt's Gate, where the grand marshal lived. He would stop there, then come back to Longwood, having covered the entire area that was reserved for him, as he was not allowed to go any further without being accompanied by the duty officer. The Emperor could not accept that, sent 2,000 leagues away from Europe, on a rock 600 leagues from both the continents of Africa and America, he would not be allowed to roam this entire island, which was so narrow and unhealthy as a prison and impossible to be entered without authorization from the admiral or Sir George Bingham. The outpost beyond which he was not allowed to go was six hundred paces from the house and had orders to present arms to the Emperor. Apart from these precautions, all the peaks that dominated

Longwood were occupied by men who communicated between themselves by signals, and watched the Emperor during all his strolls. At 9 p.m. sentries fifteen paces apart took up position around the house, in such a way that it was impossible to get out. The patrols crisscrossed in various directions, and this state of affairs lasted until the day the duty officer was given a special assignment to do whatever was needed to catch sight of the Emperor twice every twenty-four hours. To these precautions must be added those taken at sea. From Diana's Peak and Alarm House, vessels could be seen twelve leagues out to sea; before they could approach, signals were sent to the two ships that constantly cruised around the island. If the ships spotted were not British, they were accompanied into the harbor by a cruiser, and the ship could not drop anchor until it had gotten permission and received on board a detachment commanded by an officer to keep an eye on its crew. Such were the precautions taken to assure the detention; they were soon to be augmented by those invented by the suspicious mind of the new governor, who was expected.

It can be imagined how unbearable these restrictions appeared to the Emperor, and how they generated complaints on his part. Instructions given on so many different points were often poorly understood; it was possible to arrest the Emperor during his strolls, and this would have happened, had General Gourgaud not restrained a drunken sergeant who wanted to prevent the Emperor from passing. Deeply resenting these injustices, the Emperor dictated to Count de Montholon a series of complaints addressed to Admiral Cockburn. The letter was quite strongly worded, that from the admiral was no less so, and the coolness that existed between them in their contacts increased all the more. The admiral claimed all the measures taken were based on his instructions: "But," the Emperor said, "there is an immense difference between the instructions and their execution. The person who gave these orders in London would oppose them, had he to execute them here; they are totally absurd."

An argument, after which one could have thought the admiral would temper his harshness regarding these limitations, took place between him and the Emperor, who soon relinquished his illusions.

Wanting to go on horseback to Sandy Bay, he gave up the idea when he was told that the duty officer proposed to accompany him. He did not find in this conduct the frankness which he attributed to the admiral's character, and refused to receive him during several visits he came to pay him, claiming he was ill when he was not. This desire to go to Sandy Bay had come about because General Gourgaud, accompanied by an officer, had visited that part of the island and gone as far as Plantation House. The contrast that existed between that site, covered with lovely vegetation, and the aridity of Longwood underscored even further the cruelty of having the Emperor lodged on this plateau: "It is an infamy!" said the Emperor. "It is barbaric savagery to have placed me under these tar paper roofs, when they could have lodged me a few thousand feet from here in a house where I would have found shade and water!"

Some petty rivalries which time only increased came about because a little more closeness was granted to Count de Las Cases, whose age was nearest to that of the Emperor. They were an obstacle to the good relations so necessary, that lead to trust and often bring charm in the midst of the greatest misfortunes: but among all these gentlemen the count was the only one who spoke English well and could translate the newspapers when they arrived. The Emperor was taking lessons in that language, and for Count de Las Cases it was an opportunity to spend one more hour with him. Then, too, let it be said that the Emperor was a man of habit, and although his fondness for the others was in no way diminished, the habits acquired at The Briars continued at Longwood. If he did not really suffer from this, the Emperor saw with regret that the voyage and the stay on the island had not generated the friendship so desirable in captivity among the gentlemen of his retinue.

When the Emperor organized the household staff, he decided there would be two tables for meals: my own and a pantry table for the servants of the Emperor's retinue. Some complaints followed, but nothing came of them because I had had a similar table on the island of Elba and in Paris during the Hundred Days, and there was no reason to complain about what the Emperor had decided. What had caused this small dissatisfaction was that with the exception of a few of these faithful servants, the Emperor had decided the butler would dine with me and the other servants would dine in the pantry, where a single table brought together the servants of the officers surrounding the Emperor; the food supply did not permit any other arrangement.

One day when Count de Las Cases was present while he was dressing, the Emperor showed him the bayonet scar he had received during the siege of Toulon, which had almost cost him his leg. I told him that an officer on board the *Northumberland* had told me with some pride that it was an Englishman who had been the first to wound Napoleon, and had hit him in the knee. I had answered him that this wound was still visible, and had been received at the very moment when, with his own hand, he was taking General O'Hara prisoner. "Although people thought I was not," replied the Emperor, "I was just as vulnerable as the next person."

The Emperor had heard that my bedroom was arranged with great taste. Knowing that he had gone out, I had gone upstairs to attend to a few things, when someone knocked at my door; my embarrassment was great to see the Emperor and Count de Las Cases, who accompanied him. "But," he said on entering, "it is not cleanliness, it is elegance, it is like the private apartment of some young mistress. Is this where all my riches are locked up? Come, open the dressers, they must not be very considerable." However, on seeing them, he was surprised to be so rich. He complimented me on the neatness of what he saw there, and seizing two pairs of spurs, asked me which were the oldest. I pointed to one set, and said he had worn them during the Dresden campaign. "Very well," he said, taking them and handing them to Las Cases, "these are for you."

"Sire," replied M. de Las Cases, bowing deeply, "I have only one regret, and that is not being able to do anything to earn these. I have only my love and my devotion left; both belong to Your Majesty." As he was descending my small staircase to leave, the Emperor said to him: "What is the grand marshal doing today, could he be ill? Why did he not bring me his work? I think, my dear, that it will be necessary for you to call your son, as your eyes no longer allow you to write under my dictation. It will train him for a task he will have to get used to." But Noverraz, who was at the foot of the stairs, told him that the grand marshal was in the drawing room; he went in and told Count de Las Cases to go out for a walk.

Around the end of December ships arrived from the Cape and from Europe: the *Doris* brought from the Cape two fine horses for the Emperor. One, called "Bonaparte" in that town, had won prizes in several races there; he was christened "Numide" at Longwood. Newspapers and letters were on board; although they were three months old, they were nevertheless anxiously awaited by those who hoped to receive them. Only those who have endured the suffering of captivity can understand how much the soul is moved by the memory of family, and what feeling of happiness is generated at the thought of the consolation to be brought by a letter from a mother or a sister. Those that the Emperor received from Madame Mère and Princess Pauline, whom he loved so much, must certainly have awakened painful memories in him, for he remained sad and thoughtful all afternoon. The admiral, who had presented himself several times without being received, took advantage of this circumstance to be received, when he announced he was carrying these two letters. When leaving the Emperor, he asked his permission to introduce to him the daughters of a British Admiral who had died in India, and who were returning to Europe. The Emperor granted this. These ladies, like all the other people who had been introduced to him under similar circumstances, took away with them the memory of great misfortune, and that of the great courtesy that had been extended them. There came a time, however, where he refused this kind of request: he said he did not wish that in Europe they could believe that at Longwood he was surrounded with great courtesy and care, when on the contrary he was suffering the harshest of captivities. It was in this vein that one day in a bad mood he told the grand marshal, to whom all foreigners who wished to be introduced had to submit their request: "Answer them that dead people do not receive visits."

On one of the ships arriving from Europe was Captain Piontkowski[283] whom I had known in the Polish squadron on Elba, commanded by Colonel Jermanowski. The Emperor hardly remembered
him, but the grand marshal told him who he was; the Emperor could
not understand how this officer had managed to obtain permission
from the British government to be sent to Saint Helena without his
having asked for him, whereas he had been refused the right to bring
with him men he would have liked to have. When this officer came to
Longwood, brought by the admiral, he was wearing the uniform of
ADC. The Emperor was hurt by this and said to the grand marshal:
"What does this uniform mean? He was never my ADC. Tell the admiral I shall not see him." Then, after a few seconds' reflection, he
decided he would receive him after all. That evening the Emperor
received him kindly, and told me as he was going to bed that he would
have preferred such a favor had been granted to an officer who could
offer him resources that he would not find in this one. He told me to
give him 500 francs to pay for his first necessities, and to pay him 250

---

[283]Piontkowski was a Polish officer, 29, who had been with Napoleon in Elba and was
a second lieutenant in the lancers of the guard at Waterloo. He was at Malmaison
when the Emperor bid goodbye to everyone, and accompanied Mme Bertrand and her
children during the trip to Rochefort. He had embarked on the *Myrmidon*, but was not
allowed to follow the Emperor, and waited in Plymouth with his young wife until
August 14, when he received permission to go to Saint Helena. He arrived there alone
on board the *Cormoran* on December 29, 1815.

He was assigned under Gourgaud to stable service. In Jamestown he was always
seeking out news, and on the Longwood plateau he insisted on hunting problematic
turtledoves. When Hudson Lowe demanded that all persons in the Emperor's retinue
sign a declaration expressing their specific desire to remain on the island and to submit
to restrictions, Piontkowski wrote a scathing letter describing the abominable conditions and the poor treatment the Emperor was subjected to there, although he agreed to
submit to the restrictions.

The letter, dated April 19, 1816, made Hudson Lowe absolutely furious, and he
wrote to Lord Bathurst: "When he came to England, Piontkowski solicited, as a special favor, authorization to come to the island; he had no sooner arrived than he started
developing a political character, and showing it in his declaration, full of reproaches
for the government who had acceded to his request."

The reply arrived from Lord Bathurst: "You shall remove from General Buonaparte at least four people, and I am including in those Captain Piontkowski."

He went back to London, where he rejoined his young wife, but ended up in jail.

francs every month. Captain Piontkowski ceased wearing the uniform of a ADC and resumed the uniform of the corps to which he belonged. He was quartered in a tent close to Dr. O'Meara and the captain of the guard, while waiting to be housed under a tar paper roof.

The feelings of devotion and respect that on August 15 had led these gentlemen to celebrate the Emperor's birthday on board the *Northumberland* led them to also celebrate January 1, 1816; the horizon had not gotten any better since that time. The Emperor tried to make this day less gloomy, by bringing an air of gaiety to the heartfelt wishes of each of them. Children had their turn, and he gave them some New Year's gifts and spent part of the morning being amused by their childish pleasure. After lunch he got into his carriage and invited Captain Piontkowski to accompany him.

No matter how much care the Emperor took to distract himself with work, and no matter how many horseback rides he took within the boundaries or around the island with the grand marshal or General Gourgaud, there were still many moments when painful thoughts haunted him. He would then say his enemies would have been less barbaric had they had him shot rather than bringing him to Saint Helena. His mental suffering must have been great. The restrictions imposed on him were also a source of aggravation; one would have thought that a conversation between the Emperor and the admiral, following a luncheon where the latter expressed the desire to please him and to improve the state of affairs, would have brought the admiral to get rid of the duty officer during the Emperor's excursions outside the boundaries, but this never happened. The only change he made was to order Captain Poppleton to follow the Emperor dressed in civilian clothes instead of in uniform. It was not the uniform that displeased the Emperor, but the constant surveillance made of his speech or his actions by the person wearing it. He had maintained the habit of questioning people he met. M. de Las Cases was his interpreter, but he could not do so without the duty officer knowing about it, since, without being close to him, he had orders never to let him out of his sight. Even his generosity towards a few unfortunates was halted for fear it might compromise them. If he had been free in his actions, he would have liked to enter cottages he encountered along his way, to talk about farming with some, to know the needs of others, and to offer financial help where it was needed without it being known. The memory of a good deed associated with one of his outings would have made him cheerful when he returned.

One day, when everything had been prepared for a small excursion to one of the farthest points on the island to have lunch, the Emperor was about to get on his horse early in the morning. A pack-horse with canteens had been prepared by General Gourgaud who, wishing to surprise the Emperor, cut up a large leather bag and succeeded in making a saddlebag similar to the ones that had contained the Emperor's meals in the army. Preparations had been kept secret; the Emperor hoped to mount his horse, gallop away, and escape the surveillance of his guardian. But the moment he was about to get on his horse, he was told that Captain Poppleton was already in the saddle, prepared not to let him out of his sight as he had done a few days before. When this was reported to the Emperor, he abandoned the excursion, and the horses were sent back to the stables.

The time he spent dressing was allotted to Dr. O'Meara to come and see the Emperor. One day, the doctor told the Emperor he had been told in town that the Emperor handled the plow no less well than the sword. They had learned how, seeing the East India Company farmer cutting furrows in a field to plant wheat, he had gotten off his horse to cut a furrow himself, and astonished the farmer by the regularity with which he had managed to do so. This field was a few acres of land located on the Longwood plateau. "The farmer," the Emperor said to him, "was making an attempt that will not succeed: the soil is too poor. Whether you plant oats, barley, or wheat there, the crop will fail; it shall be burned by the southeasterly winds that blow violently in this part of the island, to which it is exposed; any planting on this plateau is impossible, the wind will burn and kill all vegetation. If I had gone to America, I would have gone into agriculture, I would have taken care of my garden. I would have welcomed a few remnants of my army who would have come to join me, and we would have lived there together. This makes you laugh, doctor! My tastes are simple, and I need little; I have always envied the fate of a good bourgeois in Paris, drawing a pension of 12,000 pounds, able to pursue his interests in the arts and letters. I add to that the pleasure of a family atmosphere, without which no happiness is possible, whatever class one belongs to." The Emperor had learned through the newspapers that had arrived the day before of the death of the King of Naples and that of Marshal Ney. This news had saddened him, and I heard him talking to Dr. O'Meara, which renewed this pain as he spoke. He said nothing about the King of Naples' wrongs toward him, adding that to go down to Calabria with fifty men was the action of a madman, but those who had ordered his death were monsters. As for Ney, his death was a crime: Louis XVIII and his exiles had used him to seek revenge for the shame of their flight.

The time at which the Emperor got up on Saint Helena depended on how much rest he had gotten the previous night; generally he slept poorly, there were few nights when he did not go from one bed to another. If he asked me for his covered lamp, then he worked or read and went back to bed, waiting for daylight to arrive so he could get dressed and go riding. He had lunch when he came back, went back to bed if he was tired enough to do so, took his bath at two o'clock, using the hours he spent there to chat or to dictate to one or the other of these gentlemen, then got out, dressed, and got into his carriage with the ladies and Count de Las Cases, followed by General Gourgaud on horseback. These were the Emperor's habits during the first years of our stay at Longwood; they changed later due to his health. If he went to bed during the day, then the darkness had to be absolute; in the evening when he went back into his apartment, which occurred regularly at 10 p.m., either he went to bed or wanted to chat with the person who had accompanied him. He would have his covered lamp taken into the adjoining room, and chat with that person until he fell asleep or dismissed him, never exceeding a half hour or forty-five minutes.

The construction to house the Emperor's retinue had been completed. General Gourgaud abandoned his uncomfortable tent to move into the lodging intended for him, Count de Montholon settled in his, and the room he had been occupying under the same roof as the Emperor became the library. Count de Las Cases and his son changed their lodgings, but were not much better off than they had been. The Emperor offered them the one that General Montholon had just left, but the count refused, finding that what he had been given was adequate.

Since we had moved to Longwood, General Gourgaud was stricken with dysentery for the second time. This time the illness resisted treatment, and Dr. O'Meara informed the Emperor, who immediately asked him if there was any danger. The Emperor attributed the illness to General Gourgaud's having spent a prolonged amount of time under a tent since we had been at Longwood. Worried by alarming symptoms mentioned by the doctor, he expressed the desire that Dr. Werling from the artillery be called in consultation. The admiral offered to have both the naval doctor as well as the town doctor sent. The thought of death connected with the general's critical condition saddened everyone in the colony. For twenty days he made many people anxious. The garrison and the inhabitants of the island showed great concern for him; the Emperor's affection and that of his companions in exile did not fail him either. It was a joyous day that marked his convalescence, and also one of unity in all spirits.

PART FIVE

Hudson Lowe

CHAPTER FOURTEEN

Governor Sir Hudson Lowe — Harassment — Visitors —
The struggle begins

The grand marshal had left Hutt's Gate to come live at Longwood, being as his house had been completed. The Emperor would have liked him to come along with Countess Bertrand to join him every evening at the family dinner, now that he lived closer. But Count Bertrand pointed out that his wife was generally in poor health, and the Emperor knew she was never on time. He therefore asked permission to live in his new house as he had lived at Hutt's Gate.

The newspapers, brought by a storeship coming from England, gave the Emperor an opportunity for distraction through Count de Las Cases' translation. The same newspapers announced that the governor of Saint Helena, Sir Hudson Lowe, was about to leave England to go to his post. As a newspaper that had arrived in Saint Helena, the *Morning Chronicle*, openly faulted the British ministry's conduct toward the Emperor, it was deduced that the new governor would perhaps arrive with instructions to extend the prison to the entire island. He was expected quite impatiently, and with each ship that was announced, all wondered if it might perhaps be the *Phaeton*, the frigate on which it was known he had sailed. On April 14, the Emperor was about to go out in his carriage with the ladies, when he was told by Colonel Bingham that the *Phaeton* was in sight. Leaving Colonel Bingham, the Emperor changed the direction of his outing in order to see this frigate drop anchor in the Jamestown harbor.

That same day, which could be called one of detestable

remembrance, Lieutenant General Sir Hudson Lowe,[284] his wife, and her two daughters from a previous marriage landed in Saint Helena. During our stay in Saint Helena the older daughter married the Russian commissioner, Count Balmain. The governor's staff was composed of Sir Thomas Reade, chief of staff, Major Gorrequer, an aide, Lieutenant Colonel Lyster, inspector of the militia, Major Emmett and Lieutenants Wortham and Jackson of the engineers, these last three in charge of the construction of the new house, and Dr. Baxter, inspector general of the hospital.[285]

As soon as they had landed, the governor had Longwood informed that he would be there the next morning at nine o'clock to see General Bonaparte. It was a time at which the Emperor did not generally receive guests. Even if it had been otherwise, he was too hurt by this improper manner of announcing himself to receive him. The Emperor told Count de Montholon: "He can come whenever he wants,

---

[284]There is some disagreement regarding Hudson Lowe's physical appearance. There are several portraits that are quite different. The Emperor said, "I have seen Prussians, Tartars, Cossacks, and Kalmucks, but never have I seen a man as ugly and as repulsive. He has crime written all over his face."

A pencil sketch made by Wywill, a reproduction of which is in the castle at Jamestown, does not show Hudson Lowe in this horrible fashion.

In any event, Lady Lowe, sister of General Sir William Howe de Lancy, was a very handsome woman, aged 34, "attractive, amiable, a bit of an actress," said Napoleon. Sir Henry Russell writes "very elegant, looking like a model but wearing too much makeup and showing too much cleavage." These descriptions explain why the attractive Susan was not popular among the women on the island. Was it out of jealousy that she never paid a visit to her compatriot Countess Bertrand?

There are many biographies of Sir Hudson Lowe, who died poor, abandoned, and paralyzed in January 1844, aged 74, and is buried in London in Saint-Mark's Church on North Audlay Street.

His papers, known as the Lowe Papers, constitute 160 volumes that have been sold and divided among various places.

[285]Janisch, Reade, and Gorrequer made up the trio of jailers sharing a common hate for Bonaparte and the French; Austrian commissioner Stürmer said of Gorrequer, who spoke perfect French, that he was "a sly one." In July 1818 Lyster and Count Bertrand exchanged sharp words, and the Englishman wanted to fight a duel with the grand marshal. Lyster's stay at Longwood lasted two weeks. The governor wanted to impose Dr. Baxter as the general's doctor, and because of the use of that title, the Emperor refused to be attended by him.

but I will only receive him when he asks properly." The Emperor was convinced for a moment that the admiral, with whom he was not on good terms, had not informed the new governor that in order to be presented the request had to be addressed to the grand marshal, and that he had wanted to establish bad relations between Hudson Lowe and the Emperor from the outset, to make himself missed later on. "Certainly," he said to Dr. O'Meara who was present, "he knows very well that I never receive at nine o'clock, and if he wanted to talk to Lord Saint Vincent or Lord Keith, he certainly would not have failed to inquire the time at which these gentlemen were able to receive him. I hope," said the Emperor laughing, "that I am as worthy as they are: it is lacking in generosity to add insult to misfortune." The doctor assured him the governor had acted without wanting to hear the admiral's advice. "If you say so. I am willing to admit his strong and loyal character, but nevertheless he is a real shark. I have sought refuge among you, and I have found nothing here but poor treatment and insults. If the governor wishes to be presented to me, let him put in his request through Bertrand."

As he left the Emperor, Dr. O'Meara said to me: "I wish the 'shark' could remain with us; be certain that we will regret his departure." The doctor had gone into town, seen the governor's entourage, and learned that the instructions given him by his government were much more severe than those the admiral had put into effect until that time.

On April 15 at nine o'clock sharp, Sir Hudson Lowe, followed by his staff, galloped into Longwood and dismounted at the door to the Emperor's lodging, no doubt believing that at the sight of the jailer, the prison doors would open and reveal the prisoner to him. Orders had been given; Saint-Denis answered, to the request made of him to see the general, that the Emperor was ill and had not yet risen. Lowe retreated and walked with long strides under the windows of the Emperor, who saw him without being seen; he walked around the house and entered the duty officer's quarters to wait for the moment when he could be received. Obtaining no answer, he went in search of one; he was told the Emperor was sleeping, and no one could enter to see him. The governor then went to see Count Bertrand and asked him to announce his arrival to General Bonaparte, and ask when he would be willing to receive him. The weather was poor; there was a strong wind, and he was able to experience the Longwood climate. Sir Hudson Lowe's debut in his new government was not a fortunate one.

The Emperor chose the following day at 2 p.m. for the meeting. He had caught a glimpse of Sir Hudson Lowe through his shutters, but it was not enough to form an opinion about his person. He could not know the heart that beat beneath this outer shell; it was by talking to him that he proposed to judge him. The grand marshal told him he was a man 45 to 50, a little below average height, with graying hair and such bushy eyebrows overhanging his eyes that he had not been able to see the expression in his eyes, but he spoke with intelligence. He gave the Emperor the newspapers brought by the *Phaeton*, and told him he had received a letter from his father, and that General Gourgaud had gotten one from his sister. The Russian, Austrian, and French commissioners who had been believed to be on board this ship were to arrive with the new admiral some two weeks later.

The next day at 2 p.m. we saw Sir Hudson Lowe arrive, followed by his entire staff and accompanied by Admiral Sir George Cockburn, who intended to present his successor to the Emperor. They got off their horses and were let into the parlor; these gentlemen received them and waited for the moment when the grand marshal came to escort them in to be introduced.

The Emperor had been in the drawing room for ten minutes chatting with the grand marshal when he was told of the governor and the admiral's presence in the parlor. At this point there was an unfortunate misunderstanding: Noverraz was on duty at the door to the drawing room. When the Emperor was receiving people, the practice was to allow only the person requested into the room where he was. The grand marshal opened the door slightly and said to Noverraz: "Have the governor come in." The admiral was at the other end of the room, talking with his back turned; he did not see Sir Hudson Lowe enter, and when he presented himself, Noverraz did not dare open the door again, saying to him that only the governor had been requested. The admiral, offended, went out to the saddle horses the grooms were watching, took his horse, and went back to town. Before leaving, Sir Hudson Lowe asked permission to introduce the officers on his staff. Having granted this, the Emperor was surprised not to see the admiral, whom he knew had come with the governor, and asked that he be shown in. It was only then the Emperor learned of Noverraz' mistake; he expressed his regrets for this, and asked Dr. O'Meara to convey this to Sir George Cockburn. In addition, he sent one of his officers to clear up, if possible, the unpleasantness of such an involuntary lack of courtesy. Although he had cause to complain about the admiral, he used to say of him: "Under his uniform beats the heart of a soldier."

When he went back into his quarters accompanied by the grand marshal, the Emperor, speaking of Sir Hudson Lowe, said: "This man has a repulsive appearance and does not have an honest gaze. We must not rush to judge him, but I need to have his behavior reassure me about his physical appearance. His looks," said the Emperor laughing, "remind me of a Sicilian thug; what do you think, Bertrand?" The grand marshal replied he could not pass judgment, that perhaps he had only seen him through the prism of the qualities attributed to him, those of an honest man, a good administrator, a good father, and an undeniable intellect. The Emperor had remained worried, and Dr. O'Meara's words came back to my mind: "I wish the shark would remain with us. We shall regret his departure, be sure of that." It would not be long before we understood the meaning of the doctor's words. Sir Hudson Lowe's acts, from the time of his arrival on the island until the Emperor's death, would be a series of outrages and useless vexations, proving the Emperor had judged him perfectly when he said of him: "This man is not only my jailer, he shall be my executioner."

His first act on the island was the following communication, as inappropriate as it was insulting to the Emperor:

Napoleon receives Sir Hudson Lowe.

When Sir Hudson Lowe finally finally arrived to take over the military government of
St. Helena, his manner did not recommend itself to Napoleon who took an instant
dislike to him.

The billiard room at Longwood.

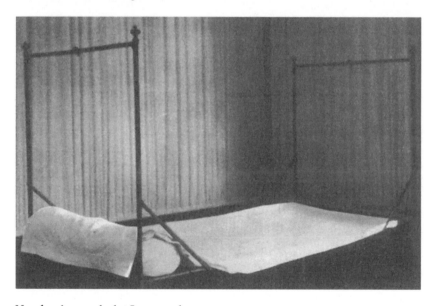

Napoleon's camp bed at Longwood.

Napoleon receives Sir
Hudson Lowe.

Count Emmanuel Las Cases and his son are not only companions of the Emperor, they
take his dictation. After great problems, Las Cases publishes a masterpiece.

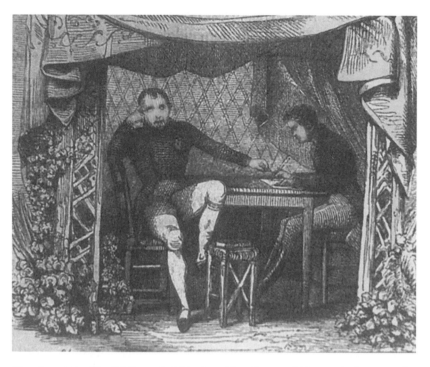

Napoleon generally dictates material to Count Las Cases and his son. A clean copy is made and read to Napoleon for correction.

"Respect the burden," Napoleon says to Mrs. Balcombe and Mrs. Stewart.

Longwood is overrun by rats. Arsenic is available to kill them. Will it be used on Napoleon as well? (See *Assassination at St. Helena Revisited,* Dr. Ben Weider)

The British officers and soldiers on duty in the nearby encampment are honored to be presented to Napoleon.

Downing Street, 10 January 1816

I must now inform you of the wishes of his Royal Highness the Prince Regent, which is that on your arrival in Saint Helena you will inform all the persons in Napoleon Bonaparte's following, including domestic servants, that they are free to leave the island immediately to return to Europe, adding that no one will be allowed to remain in Saint Helena except those who declare, in a written statement to be deposited in your hands, that it is their desire to remain on the island and submit to all the restrictions necessary to impose on Napoleon Bonaparte personally. Those among them who decide to return to Europe must be sent at the first favorable opportunity to the Cape of Good Hope. The governor of that colony shall be charged with providing them the means of returning to Europe.

Signed: Bathurst

The Emperor, rightfully irritated by an offense that he said was intended for him, forbade anyone to sign anything. The grand marshal was sent to Plantation House to reply verbally to this communication and to agree on the wording of a statement, but he returned without having obtained anything.

The Emperor dictated the following declaration to Count de Montholon:

We the undersigned, wishing to remain in the service of the Emperor Napoleon, agree to remain here, no matter how horrible the stay in Saint Helena, and to submit to the restrictions, no matter how unjust and arbitrary, that have been imposed on His Majesty and the personnel in his service.

"Montholon," said the Emperor, "let those of my servants who wish to sign, sign, but don't try to influence anyone." The statement was signed with joy by all of us who so deeply resented how insulting the British government's communication was to the Emperor.

Hudson Lowe declared he refused any imperial qualification in the declarations, he wanted no other designation than that of Napoleon Bonaparte, under penalty of being sent to the Cape of Good Hope; there was no way of refusing to sign it in the form indicated. The governor did not limit himself to this: he sent Sir Thomas Reade, his chief of staff, to assure himself the solidarity we had given was truly the expression of our free will; he took care to repeat to us we were making a commitment not to leave the island until after the death of General Bonaparte. "Colonel," I said to him, "we all came here to share in the Emperor's misfortune, to serve him, and to lighten his chains as much as possible. What could these restrictions possibly mean to us? We are all here to live and die with him."

"That is fine," he replied, "I will so inform His Excellency the governor." We left, leaving him with the captain of the guard in whose quarters he had called us.

Not satisfied with the report given him by his chief of staff, the governor, whose suspicion bordered on monomania, came himself to Longwood, had us appear before him, and returned fully convinced that our declaration to Sir Thomas Reade, and that sent to him by Count de Montholon were truly the spontaneous expression of our attachment to the Emperor, and our full determination to share his captivity. These gentlemen also signed: it had to be done, or else they would have to leave the Emperor. They did not hesitate a moment. The grand marshal tried to establish some conditions for his wife and children, but a few days later he signed as they had. During all this time the Emperor was deeply saddened; his great soul seemed to hesitate between the sacrifice he would have to make in letting these gentlemen leave, and the complete isolation he would find himself in after their departure. So religious a devotion on the part of all, when he learned of it, eased the pain that had filled him. Such was the first act of Sir Hudson Lowe on his arrival in Saint Helena: it was the prelude to the arsenal of restrictions to be established out of hatred for the Emperor, and which he intended to put into practice no matter how valueless they were.

Until he moved to Longwood, the Emperor had remained more or less indifferent to everything going on around him; he let matters run their course, and seemed to notice very little the deprivations surrounding him. At The Briars however he had strongly resented the harassment inflicted on his officers, and he had suffered from not being able to remedy the situation. But once he was at Longwood, faced with the restrictions imposed on him, he rejected the outrages and the persecutions, his soul full of indignation, and behind this moral barrier he had imposed on himself, he demonstrated what a great man is like in adversity. From that moment on, it can be said that Napoleon's martyrdom began, and that Saint Helena was to become his calvary. The hatred on the part of the ministry shall be a stain on British honor forever.

The Emperor had resumed his work with these gentlemen and his trips on horseback and by carriage with the ladies; the only distractions he had to fill those long, dreary days. If during one of these outings, he met people he knew from the town or the regiment, he would invite them for dinner and set a specific day. This state of affairs, for a man as suspicious as Sir Hudson Lowe, could not endure for long; for him, the security of the detention was compromised by each of these invitations and by each of the conversations between the Emperor and the people he encountered during his outings. If the Emperor had not been seen during the day by the duty officer, he would come at once to Longwood to the grand marshal's, declaring his instructions included witnessing the presence of General Bonaparte every day. Then, wanting to make all communications more difficult, he sent his aide, Mr. Gorrequer, to the tradesmen in town, informing them they were not to grant any credit to the French; they could not sell them anything unless they paid in cash, nor have any communication with them without the governor's permission. This proscription was official and posted throughout town.

The officers of the 53rd regiment had gotten into the habit of going to Hutt's Gate to see Countess Bertrand; they continued that practice when she lived inside the Longwood grounds. But they came to tell her that men of honor could not accept the conditions imposed on them to come and see her. Fear seized the inhabitants, and those who formerly, when they met us on the road, stopped to inquire about the Emperor, now did so only as they walked by, because if they struck up a conversation they were threatened with being forced to leave the island.

The governor, whom the Emperor had not seen since his first visit, came to Longwood and requested the honor of being shown in. The Emperor had someone reply that he was ill and could not receive him, but 15 minutes later he climbed into his carriage with the ladies, so that Lowe would clearly understand he had not wanted to see him. Another time, as he was about to get in his carriage, he spotted Hudson Lowe arriving at Longwood; he went back inside and did not come out again. He sent me to get a copy of *Paul et Virginie* and asked me to read it to him; the Emperor felt this novel contained the language of the soul, and had it read to him in whole or in part several times.

The arrival of the *Adamant* on May 7 provided another opportunity for the governor to come to Longwood and request to be received by the Emperor, in order to inform him, he said, of dispatches from his government. From any other man, one would have thought from his urgency in communicating the information, that he was bringing his prisoner some news likely to ease the hardship of his captivity. But coming from Sir Hudson Lowe, one could expect quite the contrary, and the Emperor hesitated to grant him an audience, but finally did so. The conversation that followed was long and animated. The Emperor listed all the complaints he had against him during the month he had been on the island. They parted more angry with each other than ever. Dr. O'Meara reported to the Emperor that as he went out, the governor had said to him, "General Bonaparte is not satisfied, it appears, to have created for himself an imaginary France and an imaginary Poland, as the Abbé de Pradt says, but he now wants to create an imaginary Saint Helena here."

I told the Emperor that when leaving this discussion, the governor had inspected the moat he had had dug around the property, and noticing in one corner a tree on the bank whose branches crossed the ditch, he had given orders that it be cut down, believing it could be used to jump across to the other side. "The reason," I said to him, "seems all the more ridiculous, as there isn't one of us who doesn't cross his ditch to go in or out of Longwood, and this means destroying a tree where there are so few of them."

"He came," said the Emperor to Dr. O'Meara, "to talk to me about a house sent by his government, about which the newspapers give many details. He asked me where I wished it to be located, and I replied: 'I want nothing from you, I ask only one thing, and that is that you leave me alone. You tell me your instructions are more severe than those given to the admiral; well, have the courage to put them in effect. I expect anything from your ministers. As for threatening to beat down my door to allow your aide to come in, I tell you he shall come in only over my body; the obligation of being accompanied by one of your officers is a vexatious measure. It is neither the man nor the uniform that bothers me. Poppleton is a good soldier whom I esteem, but I do not wish by any of my actions to give you the right to recognize that I am your prisoner. You know very well that the only surveillance needed to keep me here is that provided by your cruisers, and that to place an officer galloping behind me is absurd. But what you do not appear to know is that you are covering your name with shame and that your children will be ashamed to carry it.' "

The doctor told the Emperor that officers from the *Adamant* whom he had seen in town had told him that public opinion in England had been quite moved on learning that the driest part of the island had been given him as a residence, and that they had housed him in shacks when he could have lodged at Plantation House seemed inhuman. "You may be certain," the Emperor had replied, "that the announcement of a wooden palace—of which today's newspapers give details that are so many lies—is only placed there to fool people and let them believe my next home will have all the facilities and luxuries worthy of a lord." Having dismissed the doctor, the Emperor went into the drawing room. He intended to go out in his carriage, but the wind was blowing quite forcefully, and he remained on the verandah, amusing himself by watching maneuvers in camp. The *Adamant* contained not a wooden palace whose construction was going to proceed by enchantment, according to the British papers, but lumber, stones, and furnishings, some of which were sent to Longwood either to equip the rooms lacking them or to replace a few pieces no longer usable.

Thus the parlor received a table, a few chairs, and a mahogany billiard table. The Emperor did not play billiards, but when walking by he would amuse himself by rolling the balls around. The furniture in the drawing room was changed: a carpet to hide the floor, a chandelier for the ceiling, and a large mirror placed above the chimney. Two settees, six chairs, and six armchairs in black wood with gilt bronze ornaments on a dark green velvet background were sent; a table with a marble top was placed opposite the fireplace between the two windows, which received colored valances and curtains. A large mahogany table and chairs came to furnish the dining room; three mahogany library cases on stands were sent, the upper part of the doors containing gilt grillwork with green curtains to hide the shelves. These were put up in the room previously occupied by Count and Countess de Montholon. A large wooden table already there was topped with a green cover, and the large map of Italy made by Baron d'Albe was spread out over it;[286] a few mahogany chairs completed the furnishings. The supervision of the library was entrusted to Saint-Denis. The Emperor allowed us to replace a wobbly table he had in his room with a dresser that was sent which he felt he needed. A side table replaced the one he had; its legs were in bad shape, and everyone feared that sooner or later the lunch served to him would fall to the floor when he leaned on the table while getting up. I asked for a mahogany armoire that I placed in a room, to store all the Emperor's linen, and free some space in the ones I had built. The furniture that had been replaced was distributed among the various lodgings occupied by these gentlemen, who may not have had these things.

The passage of the East India Company fleet at Saint Helena is marked each year by festivities. A great number of passengers on board these ships, the officers, and the crew come ashore and spend much money purchasing vegetables and poultry that the inhabitants always sell at the highest possible prices. It was also a good time for shopping. Dr. O'Meara, at the Emperor's request, purchased a very fine ivory chess set for him. Among the people of distinction on board was Lady Moira, wife of the governor general of India. She was to stay on the island for two days at Plantation House, and undoubtedly expressed her desire to see or be introduced to the Emperor. The grand marshal came one morning to see the Emperor with a letter from Sir Hudson Lowe that an orderly had just brought him, in which he invited General Bonaparte to come and have dinner with Lady Moira the following day. The strangeness of this invitation first had the Emperor laughing, then he said to the grand marshal: "But in truth, this man has no common sense whatsoever: it is one more insult to be recorded, do not answer it! Were this lady sick, I might yield to her wish by going

---

[286]Baron Bacler d'Albe was a geographer and an engineer of great repute; Napoleon had met him during the siege of Toulon and in 1796 put him in charge of his topography office. From that time on Bacler d'Albe never left the Emperor. Soldier, officer, cartographer, artist, painter, engraver, lithographer, he died in 1824 at the age of 64. His map work is considerable. His famous map of Italy was the one used by the Emperor in Saint Helena. It was published in forty-two sheets, and there exists a complete collection of these in the Archives Nationales. Three paintings by Bacler d'Albe are exhibited in Versailles. A portrait of Bonaparte, which must look like him as Bacler d'Albe lived in such proximity to him, appears in the collections of Malmaison. Another bust of Bonaparte painted by the artist and engraved by Sallanches was used by Gros to execute his painting of the battle of Arcole.

to see her. He knows perfectly well that as I must be followed by an officer, I shall not accept the invitation. He thus prevents this lady from coming here and making herself a comparison between his luxurious residence and my miserable lodging. Lady Moira is free, why doesn't she come and visit your wife and Montholon's!"

In the hope of being introduced to the Emperor, a considerable number of passengers came to see the grand marshal. The Emperor was outside at that moment, and he chatted for a long time with one or the other. In dismissing them, he said to one of Lord Moira's ADCs: "Tell Lady Moira that had she been within the confines of Longwood, I would have paid my respects to her." The day before, among the visitors had been an officer who was a relative of Lord Saint Vincent; he asked him to assure him the admiral was one of the men for whom he had the highest esteem.

General Bingham had come to Longwood, and the Emperor was hesitant to receive him. Then he decided to do so as he had not seen him since he was promoted to the rank of general and wanted to congratulate him. When he was announced, it was at a moment when the soul is filled with disgust for men and things, as a result of reading a document Sir Hudson Lowe sent to Longwood, entitled: Agreement signed in Paris on August 2, 1815, by England, Austria, Prussia, and Russia. Better than the sovereigns of those powers, the Emperor foresaw the enormous mistake they had made by uniting against him to overthrow him. As a natural mediator between kings and peoples, he could avoid bloody upheavals, and arrange the social reorganization of Europe without difficulties. They did not understand this. Such a concept was too far above these sovereigns' geniuses; they believed they were strong enough to suppress the revolutionary ideas that would swallow them up someday, and decided on the monstrous deed of having Napoleon transported to the rock of Saint Helena. Here is the agreement:

Napoleon Bonaparte being in the power of the Allied sovereigns, their majesties the King of the United Kingdom, Great Britain, and Ireland, the Emperor of Austria, the Emperor of Russia and the King of Prussia have decided in accord with the stipulations of the treaty dated March 25, 1815, on the most appropriate measures to make it impossible for him to attempt any enterprise against peace in Europe.

Article 1. Napoleon Bonaparte is considered, by the powers having signed the treaty of March 26 last, to be their prisoner.

Article 2. His guard is specifically entrusted to the British government. The choice of the place and the measures that can best assure the purposes of the present stipulation are left to His British Majesty.

Article 3. The imperial courts of Austria and Russia and the royal court of Prussia shall name commissioners to proceed to and live in the place the British government assigns as Napoleon Bonaparte's residence, without being responsible for his security, and will ensure that he remains there.

Article 4. His Most Christian Majesty is invited, in the name of the four courts mentioned above, to send a French commissioner to Napoleon Bonaparte's place of detention.

Article 5. His Majesty the King of the United Kingdom, Great Britain, and Ireland hereby undertakes to fulfill the commitments assigned to him by the present agreement.

Article 6. The present agreement shall be ratified, and the ratification shall be exchanged within a few days or sooner if possible.

In witness thereof, the plenipotentiaries have signed the present agreement, and have affixed their seals.

Executed in Paris on August 2, 1815.

Signed: Prince Metternich, Count Nesselrode, Lord Aberdeen, and Prince Hardenberg.

Certified copy.

Signed: Lieutenant General Sir Hudson Lowe, Governor of the island of Saint Helena and commissioner for His British Majesty.

The lieutenant governor of the island for the East India Company and Mrs. Skelton, whose welcome the Emperor had appreciated when the day after landing he had come to Longwood with the admiral, came to Longwood to take their leave before sailing for England on one of the company ships. The Emperor had always received with pleasure Colonel and Mrs. Skelton, who had many times had the honor of dining with him. He could not entrust more honest people with the grievances he had against the governor, in order for them to reach high places in London. Wishing to add to the trust he showed them, he asked me for one of the lovely cups of his Sèvres porcelain, which he offered as a memento of his esteem to Mrs. Skelton. This lady thanked him warmly, while expressing her admiration for the paintings on it.

As can be seen, the Emperor continued to receive not only the island notables and the officers of the garrison, whom he invited either to dinner or to lunch under his tent if it was morning, he also received all the distinguished people landing on the island. The uneasy mind of the governor was rather alarmed by this. The slightest details coming out of Longwood took on great importance in his eyes, but he was worried to the highest degree about Dr. O'Meara's constant errands into town, over whom he could not and dared not exercise any control. Being free to communicate with the island inhabitants and the officers of ships in the harbor, he could convey to General Bonaparte news of Europe that the governor wished to have him know only after it had been filtered through him. Toward this goal, he did everything he could to convince the Emperor to take in his service Dr. Baxter, who he said spoke French, and was far more worthy than Dr. O'Meara. He failed however in his attempt, for the Emperor told him he was perfectly satisfied with his doctor and wished to keep him. As can be readily imagined, the Emperor was not fooled by the governor's expressed interest in his health being better cared for by Dr. Baxter than by Dr. O'Meara; he saw in this persistence the governor's desire to have near him a man of his own choosing.

It can be imagined that Dr. O'Meara, who was not subject to any of the Longwood restrictions, was too precious a resource for the Emperor to voluntarily part with him. Although a marked change had occurred since restrictions had been placed on the colonists and the garrison officers in communicating with us, the Emperor nevertheless knew what was going on both on the island and elsewhere. Hudson Lowe, in his desire to see only men of his choosing around the

Emperor, wrote to the grand marshal that he was going to replace the sailors working as servants either in the stables or the household with soldiers, believing no doubt that he could exercise more influence on them than on the sailors from the *Northumberland*. The Emperor refused this, and the sailors remained until the vessel departed. They each received a good bonus and were then replaced by soldiers from the 53rd regiment, who served very well and gave no occasion for complaint.

One matter that concerned the Emperor was the lack of compatibility between Generals Gourgaud and Montholon. Time had only increased this disagreement, to the point where they were going to fight a duel. A duel at Longwood between two men who, on arriving, were motivated by the same goal of easing the Emperor's captivity, was quite impossible. The Emperor intervened and summoned them: he preached conciliation, and disarmed them both with his paternal words. A few words uttered by General Gourgaud annoyed the Emperor, and he said to them: "Much as I like to have you near me if you live together in peace, you disturb me if you cannot share with me the few joys that are left to us; I would prefer to see you both go. It would be quieter if I were alone with Marchand." It is not very modest on my part to recall this last sentence that concerns me; if I do so it is because I must attribute it to a burst of temper on the part of the Emperor, occasioned by the general's reply. The Emperor, if left alone, would have quickly realized the deep solitude in which he would have found himself with only me near him when everything that surrounded him barely sufficed to occupy the prodigious activity of his mind.

One day when the Emperor had received distinguished foreigners who were passing through the island, Dr. O'Meara told him the next day as he was dressing how much these people had been charmed by his conversation, and how ashamed they were to have believed the libelous lies written about him. He added this impression was widespread among all the people who had the honor of being received by him. "Doctor," the Emperor said to him, "your compatriots imagine that I am some kind of ferocious horned beast? It is true the press had lashed out against me as it has done to no one else; it has described me as cowardly and bloodthirsty. All this slander will disappear of its own accord; these Englishmen coming from India will go to France and there they will learn to know me even better. Your governor asked me to receive him; I was in my robe, I did not want to, but I allowed him to come and disturb me. He made the most animated protests about his wish to make my position more bearable; he reverted to his adored theme of placing Baxter near me. He was going out of his way to please me, but he is a man in whom I could have no trust whatsoever. My disgust for him is such that when he left I told Marchand: 'Throw away this coffee, it is not fit to be drunk because it was near him.' In spite of myself, I mistreated him, but how could it be otherwise? He forbids us to write, and he worries our words might be heard elsewhere than on this rock, and might reach Europe! He has it in for Las Cases who he says writes lies to Europe, which I am quite certain is not true; he claims he attempts to send him down in my esteem. He has not spoken to me of his quarrel with Bertrand, who was forced to drive him out of his house because of the rudeness he displayed. It must have been very great indeed for Bertrand to have reached that point, for he is the most conciliatory person one could ever meet. Doctor, he would like to regain lost ground, but he shall not succeed; all that I ask of him is not to annoy me with his odious presence."

It had occurred to the government to build a more suitable house than the one in which the Emperor was living. When the grand marshal brought the plans, the Emperor said to him: "I would much prefer four or five hundred books. I would enjoy them. It will take five years to build this house, and by that time all I will need is a grave." The Emperor turned out to be a good prophet. Five years later he had reached the last days of his life, when they came to offer him the keys to this new house. "I have seen," he said, "all of the trouble taken by these poor sailors and soldiers to manage to achieve very little at Longwood; they were under the orders of the admiral, who is an active and intelligent man. I do not want them to be overwhelmed with work that I will not be in a position to benefit from, and have them curse me because of it." The grand marshal thought however that he should ask

him which location on the island would please him most; he answered
that The Briars appeared to be best, because there he would find shade
and water, or else Rosemary Hall or Colonel Smith's property. Finally
he said any other part of the island where he would be sheltered from
the southeasterly winds that consumed Longwood, covered with rain
and fog or overwhelmed by a sun that cooked his brains. "But can't
you see, Bertrand, this request is nothing but a joke! Any other part of
the island than this one, they will not give to me! It offers too many
advantages for them to take me away from it; I cannot take one step
without being noticed. It took a year to build your house, how long do
you think it will take to finish this one? If he speaks to you of it, tell
him that he can put it wherever he wants, and leave me alone."

The Emperor was perfectly right; some time after this the governor, free to choose the location, decided this house should be built
below and near that of Count Bertrand, sheltered from the southeast
wind by a fold in the terrain, close enough to the company gardens to
enjoy them, and within sight of the camp so that he could not take one
step without being spotted. There would be abundant water when the
construction of a huge cistern at Diana's Peak was completed; this reservoir was to collect during the rainy season all the water needed not
only to supply Longwood, but also to supply the island and the ships
coming from India that stopped there to take on water.

The Emperor's life on this rock was almost always the same,
divided between work, reading, and trips on horseback in the morning
in the company of General Gourgaud and Count de Las Cases. If he
took his carriage in the evening, it was in the company of one of the
ladies, or sometimes both of them. If it happened he should deviate
from this type of existence, it was because he was ill, and remained at
home. The sudden changes in the weather, against which he took no
precautions, were often the cause of bad colds that would set in and
keep him to his bed. Dr. O'Meara then offered his pharmacy, but the
Emperor always countered this with his candy box of licorice: "My
method, if I am ill," he said, "is to fast, take a little chicken broth and
in order to work up perspiration, I cover five or six leagues on horseback and then put myself to bed."

One day the Emperor was ailing and kept to his bed. He summoned the doctor: "Yesterday you had company for dinner. How many of the men were drunk?"

"Not one of them," the doctor replied laughing.

"You are not telling the truth. There must have been a few of them under the table. Was our friend Captain Ross not slightly inebriated?"

"Feeling good, yes, but inebriated, no; the only one exceeding mere happiness was Captain Piontkowski, whom I had invited to dinner."

"Piontkowski, who sometimes dines at the camp with officers of the 53rd, says that once the tablecloth has been removed, they pay so much an hour to drink, and this lasts late into the night."

"I can assure you," replied the doctor, "that is utterly untrue, and that there are officers in the camp who only drink wine twice a week."

"This is how," replied the Emperor, "when you do not understand a language well, a false interpretation is ascribed to the habits and actions of other people."

The Emperor had gotten into the habit of having lunch in his bathtub quite frequently, and I had made a small mahogany table which, held by hooks at each end, would fit into the bathtub at his desired height. On this table he was served his lunch, then afterwards, he was given his book or papers. He never remained in his bath less than an hour and a half, and kept the bath warm by letting a trickle of hot water run into it. One of the gentlemen was called to work or converse with him; often after having chatted with one of them, he called for another. His baths did him good, and he said that they decreased a dull pain in his side that he had begun to complain about.

CHAPTER FIFTEEN

Admiral Malcolm — The foreign commissioners —
Details of life at Longwood — The matter of money —
Vehement protests by the Emperor

On June 18, the Emperor was informed of the arrival of the frigates *Newcastle*[287] and *Oronte*, which were carrying on board the new admiral and the French, Russian, and Austrian commissioners. Count de Montholon also came to tell him that Mme de Montholon had just given birth to a daughter; the Emperor, knowing that she was pregnant, had sent me several times to ask how she was. He congratulated Count de Montholon, and told him he would give her the name Napoléone. During the afternoon the Emperor was able to visit Countess de Montholon, who presented her daughter to him.

The two frigates had barely dropped anchor in the harbor when they sent ashore the new admiral and his family, the Marquis de Montchenu, commissioner for France, Count Balmain for Russia, Baron Stürmer for Austria, and Captain Gors, ADC to Marquis de Montchenu. Dr. O'Meara had gone into town immediately and spoke with several passengers. When he returned to Longwood he told me that an Austrian botanist who had arrived on one of the frigates had seen my mother in Schoenbrunn before his departure and was carrying a letter for me. To fully understand all the happiness I felt on learning there was a man in town who had seen my mother, one would have to envision the fantasies of a prisoner's imagination. I immediately went

---

[287]The 60-gun HMS *Newcastle* arrived in Saint Helena on June 17, 1816. On board were Rear Admiral Sir Pulteney Malcolm and Lady Malcolm, John Irving, secretary to the admiral, the foreign commissioners and their aides: Count Balmain and Heinrich Peyle for Russia, and Marquis de Montchenu and Captain de Gors for France. Baron von Stürmer and his household arrived the next day on board the *Oronte*.

to see the Emperor to inform him of this; he thought he might also be the bearer of a letter from the Empress for him. I had to wait until the next morning and never had a night seemed so long to me.

Since I had left town to join the Emperor at The Briars, I had never returned to Jamestown. Without giving the reason I was going into town, I asked Captain Poppleton for a noncommissioned officer so I could go there, and General Gourgaud for two horses that were sent to me from the stables. I proceeded to town where no one knew me, gave the officer my horse to keep, and went directly to the house Dr. O'Meara had pointed out as that of the botanist. It was early, I found him in bed and apologized for this, but he understood my anxiety and handed me the letter from my mother, urging me to maintain absolute secrecy about this. He had left the Empress in good health, and gave me the most charming description of the King of Rome. I asked if he had a letter from this princess for the Emperor: he replied that he didn't, but hoped he would be fortunate enough to be presented to the Emperor and be able to speak to him of her. Fearing that too long a stay might compromise him, I left, happy in my good fortune. As I was getting on my horse, I spotted the commissioners strolling about town, staring at the enormous rocks dominating it. Without stopping to take a better look at them, I recognized in each of them the nation he represented. Followed by my officer, I returned in great haste to Longwood, and as I was going up the incline leading to it, Sir Hudson Lowe was coming down to town on the opposite side.

As soon as I arrived at Longwood I turned the horses over to one of the grooms on duty. I proceeded into the Emperor's quarters with my unread letter in hand. The Emperor allowed me to open it and told me to read it to him. I found in the envelope a carefully folded piece of paper, on which was written: King of Rome's hair; on another similar one was written: To my son. "This belongs to you," the Emperor said to me, "and this one is mine." After opening it and seeing the beautiful blond hair of his son, he told me to place it in his travel kit. I placed it next to a lock of hair of Empress Joséphine's sent to him on the island of Elba after this princess' death. These are the two locks of hair that are today in my reliquary. My letter contained many interesting details about the King of Rome, gave news of the Empress, but nothing gave any inkling that my mother had told the princess about the letter she was writing to me. I told the Emperor that the botanist had taken this letter on my mother's repeated insistence and that had anyone known about it, he would not have been allowed to leave Vienna.

The Emperor learned through the newspapers of the acquittal of General Drouot, whose noble character and selflessness he greatly admired; it was always with the highest praise that he would speak of him and his fine conduct at the battle of Hanau.

The doctor reported to the Emperor that when the governor arrived in town, he had asked where I had gone: no one knew at first what to tell him, but he soon learned I had spent fifteen minutes with the botanist (I very much regret I can no longer remember his name). He scolded everyone around him, and complained about the lack of surveillance exercised on the Frenchmen when they came into town. He threatened the botanist with sending him away from the island, and would have done so had Baron Stürmer not opposed it, but finally he calmed down, the harm—had there been any—being without remedy. The governor's ire made the Emperor laugh when he heard about it.

The arrival of the new Admiral Sir Pulteney Malcolm,[288] who came to take command of the naval forces, implied the departure of Sir George Cockburn, whom the Emperor had never seen again since the day when, coming to introduce Sir Hudson Lowe, he was quite

---

[288]A distinguished sailor, former commander of the squadron operating under Wellington in 1815, Malcolm was a gentleman full of talent and delicacy. He would try to smooth out the difficulties that were poisoning the atmosphere at Longwood and Plantation House, but the governor at once suspected him and had him watched. The admiral's visits to the Emperor were seen in a bad light, and Malcolm was harshly criticized by Lowe in a letter to Lord Bathurst on May 13, 1817.

Lady Malcolm was the sister of the East India Company governor who had sent Napoleon the famous chess set. *Lady Malcolm's Diary* published in 1899 was written at least partly under the admiral's dictation; the journal relates his talks with the Emperor far more than those of his wife, who actually understood very little French. Napoleon's vivacity, even his mirth, are frequently mentioned, as well as his striking opinions on a large number of subjects: Waterloo, the Bourbons, Egypt, Corsica, Ney, Soult, Whitworth, the Duke of Orléans, etc.

unintentionally treated impolitely. Before leaving the island, he came to take his leave of the grand marshal; he expressed regret that such a circumstance had closed the Emperor's door to him, and that he could not take on his duties. Nothing the grand marshal said to him on this subject could change his determination not to come and introduce his successor. As for myself, when I learned the admiral was leaving Saint Helena without seeing the Emperor, I regretted it. The Emperor would have had no reason to complain about him, had his instructions not been hatefully directed at him; and what was happening since Sir Hudson Lowe's arrival would cause us to miss the admiral. He was a man of heart and integrity, but his severe nature and demeanor made it difficult to approach him. The care he had taken on board ship each time we met to ask if the Emperor had everything he needed made me feel friendly toward him, and made me recognize that the eyes in this stern face were not without a certain kindness, inviting trust. The sailors on duty at Longwood were sent away and replaced by soldiers.

Admiral Malcolm therefore came without his predecessor, asking the grand marshal to be presented to the Emperor. His audience was put off until the following day, June 21, and the same protocol took place for him and his staff as that for Sir Hudson Lowe. Admiral Malcolm from the first was friendly to the Emperor who, when he had left, said he found he had "an open and honest face." "This man," he said, "must have a good heart. He expresses his thoughts frankly, and would inspire trust in the most suspicious man." Before leaving the Emperor, he asked permission to come and present Lady Malcolm, who had remained in town. The Emperor replied he would be most pleased to meet her.

Several crates of books arrived on the *Newcastle* and were sent to Longwood. It was a real joy for the Emperor who, as soon as they arrived, helped us open them to more rapidly satisfy his impatience to know these works. He then spent part of the night reading. The next morning when I went into his room, I found a large quantity of the books on the floor that he had thumbed through, he said, which probably held little interest. For several days he busied himself scanning them and then organizing them in his library.

Various toilet articles had arrived on the ship and were sent to Longwood: perfume, cologne, lavender water, Prince Regent tobacco, white cloth, and fabric for suits and shirts. The Emperor told me to keep the cologne for him, as it could not be secured in town at present, and distribute the rest among the household. He wanted to wear his clothes as long as possible, as he did not wish to receive anything from the British government. Two percussion shotguns[289] were sent to him in a box; he told me to give them to Saint-Denis who was already in charge of the Emperor's shotguns and pistols that Admiral Cockburn had given back to him since our arrival at Longwood. When speaking of the shotguns that were sent to him, the Emperor said that it was a joke in a country where there was no game.

There were a number of turtledoves on the island, but it was difficult to hunt them, as they would fly from one valley to another and it took an intrepid walker to follow them. Santini, whose chores were limited to serving the table or announcing visitors when the Emperor was in the drawing room, spent his morning at this exercise; he shot very well and managed to kill some. Two or three times a week they were served for the Emperor's luncheon, and he found them excellent. General Gourgaud tried to introduce rabbits into the Longwood woods by releasing a few of them; they were seen for a time, then they disappeared completely. A pheasant, very rare on the island, shot around Plantation House, was offered to the Emperor by the hunter. When the governor learned the Emperor had wanted none of the objects he had sent and knew of the distribution he had made of them, he got very angry; but the Emperor had seen the objects as an insult to both himself and his officers.

The men they were anxious to see and hear were the French, Russian, and Austrian commissioners. It was possible to learn the true state of affairs in France through them, if they were given to talking. During their horseback rides these gentlemen attempted to see them, and managed to engage them in conversation. The Marquis de

---

[289]The term percussion shotgun is incorrect. Perhaps the author meant shotguns with percussion caps, which British armorers had made very early on.

The great man is eyed by some of the soldiers.

The hat worn by Napoleon can be seen at the Malmaison Museum.

Montchenu[290] had letters for Countess Bertrand and Count de Las Cases. The commissioners did not hide their desire to be received at Longwood. The Emperor declared he would receive them as private individuals, but not in their official capacity of commissioners.

The first time they came to Longwood, they came up to the gate in the moat between the guardhouse and the house. The governor was not anxious for the commissioners to come to Longwood, but did not dare forbid this officially; they in fact did not attempt to come in any farther. The Emperor, informed by one of his staff that they were there, asked me for his spyglass, and through a slit in the shutter saw them perfectly. The grand marshal, General Gourgaud, Count de Las Cases, and General Montholon went out to talk with them. They felt that Longwood was the worst part of the island, and the last place in which to live because of the temperature variations. The Russian commissioner said they would be the laughingstock of Europe when people heard that, having come to Saint Helena, they had departed without seeing the Emperor. Boredom was already catching up with them, and they complained about the cost of supplies and the poor food. The Marquis de Montchenu spoke of asking for a new allowance from the king's government. The Emperor later told these men that he could offer them the books in his library, if reading would help them fight off boredom.

A pneumatic machine was sent to Longwood, and the Emperor put General Gourgaud in charge of its operation. He and Admiral Malcolm came to see it work. The general offered each one a cup of ice water, the surface of which had frozen within fifteen minutes. The Emperor took it, and as he chipped the ice, he spoke of the pleasure they would have felt putting such a piece of ice in their

---

[290]Montchenu was then 58. He was a marshal, and would stroll around the island in uniform, wearing his sword. "I know the man," said the Emperor, "he's an old dotard, a 'carriage general' who has never heard a shot in his entire life." Montchenu complained bitterly about the dearness of life and the meagerness of his salary. He was a big eater, and Dr. Henry relates the painful consequences of this for his liver and stomach. His secretary, Captain Gors, who had been assigned to him by the king's government, had a sharp wit and always added a postscript to each of his reports.

mouths, when they were crossing the desert on their way to Syria. This machine, the first seen on the island, was taken to General Gourgaud's quarters on the Emperor's orders, so he could conduct some tests. He made an unsuccessful experiment with lemonade and others with milk, that did not succeed any better.

The favorable first impression Admiral Malcolm had made on the Emperor when he was introduced continued as long as he was on the island. The Emperor regretted that he had not been placed in command, for he was sure his life would have been much easier than it could ever be with Hudson Lowe. As he was so friendly with the Emperor, Admiral Malcolm was received every time he came. Even when he was sick, he would grant him access to his bedroom. As he was going out with him one day, the admiral noticed the tent placed a few yards from the house was in very bad condition: he had it replaced immediately with another one taken from his ship. As the Emperor had no shade around his house, he often went under his tent to seek shelter from the sun; he also had lunch and worked there. The entrance faced the guardhouse, so that he could see the people coming to Longwood: if it happened to be the governor, the Emperor immediately returned inside the house. "That man," he said, "turns my stomach. He is devoid of any politeness or learning, I cannot bear to see him!"

On August 15, these gentlemen and the ladies came as they had the year before to pay their respects to the Emperor, who kept them all to lunch with him. The children were also invited, as well as Dr. O'Meara. According to his custom, the Emperor gave presents to the children, who were quite happy and contributed to making this family luncheon joyful.

Dr. Baxter, who had come to the island to care for the Emperor, had Dr. O'Meara request on his behalf the honor of being presented. The Emperor accepted and asked laughing whether the other doctor had killed as many patients as he had. The Emperor had very little faith in medicine, which he said had not advanced, because it worked in the shadows, whereas surgery was destined to make many brilliant discoveries. Having learned his cook was sick, the Emperor asked Dr. O'Meara for news of him; he replied that, although young, he was a worn-out man who did not have many years to live, and that it was necessary to replace him for a few days. The governor, informed of this circumstance, offered a Belgian woman he had in his service who spoke French and knew how to cook. No matter how repugnant it was for the Emperor to accept anyone from the hands of Hudson Lowe, he authorized Cipriani, his butler, to use her. Her cooking was not bad; she had a recipe for soup that the Emperor liked very much. It consisted of two egg yolks beaten with a little flour, making a light paste that she dropped in the bouillon when it came to a boil. For the duration of Lepage's illness she remained at Longwood, and when he began his convalescence, the Emperor decided to keep her. A few months later, she married the cook and a daughter was born. But afterwards the woman's health, formerly excellent, became poor; that of her husband was not any better, and both of them were obliged to leave the island to return to France, where Lepage died a year later. He was replaced by an Englishman, whose cooking was mediocre, but who remained in the position until the arrival of Chandelier, sent by Princess Pauline.

Under Admiral Cockburn, if supplies were not of good quality and complaints were brought to his attention, the admiral took care that they should be delivered in better condition, and would express his regret that the island did not offer more resources. Under the new administration it was not the same: not only was the quality often poor, but the quantity decreased. Cipriani complained of this to Sir Thomas Reade, who did not, like the admiral, use the vigilance required to correct the supplier's negligence, so that we resorted to buying in town with the Emperor's funds what was lacking for the household needs. The governor was informed of this, and told Count de Montholon that the supplies were quite sufficient, but they were not used economically. He came himself to tell the grand marshal that his government allotted only 8,000 pounds sterling for the expenses of Longwood: he had taken it upon himself to add another 4,000, but they had to decrease the expenditures. He added that 8,000 pounds had been granted for the Longwood expenses, in anticipation of a decrease in the household personnel; but as that had not taken place, any cost in excess of the 8,000 pounds sterling would have to be compensated by him. The Emperor replied to the grand marshal that he was ready to pay all the expenses, if he were given the opportunity to do so by contacting a banking house either in London or Paris, and if he could receive his letters unopened: "Don't answer anything definitively: we don't have to bother with such details, let him worry about it!" the Emperor concluded. Admiral Malcolm, whose mind was quite conciliatory, took advantage of the trust the Emperor showed him to ask him to try to come to an agreement with the governor, and if possible through mutual concessions to reach a state of affairs more desirable for both of them. "You do not know that man," the Emperor told him, "his mistrust is such that if I ask you to come riding with me—as you already have come riding in my carriage—you will no longer have his trust. Believe me, he is a devious man; full of deceit and completely heartless."

Whether this was pure coincidence or something agreed on by them, when the Emperor came out into the garden, he saw the admiral and the governor arriving together and did not go inside as he usually did. He greeted the admiral graciously and the governor with cool politeness. The meeting would probably have proceeded smoothly had they only chatted about general topics; but the governor took advantage of this occasion to talk to the Emperor about the necessary reduction in the Longwood expenses. The Emperor, who did not expect anything less than this overture, did not give him a chance to finish his sentence, and lost his temper in such a way that he came to regret it. The next morning he told the doctor while he was dressing: "But how could it be otherwise, when faced with the rudeness of such details. I told him: 'Settle this matter with my butler: don't send anything if you like, I'll go and sit at the table of the officers of the 53rd regiment: I'm sure there is not one of them who would refuse to share his dinner with an old soldier like myself. You have,' I added, 'full power over my body, but my soul shall always elude you. Know well that I am as proud on this rock as when I commanded all of Europe. Had you any honor, you would request your transfer.' I believe he answered that he had requested it. Would you believe, doctor," the Emperor added, "that in front of the admiral he dared claim he had changed nothing of what had been established by Admiral Cockburn! It was then no longer possible for me to hold back: I used very harsh words with him. I am not in the habit of insulting anyone, but the effrontery of this man was too much for me; I could not prevent myself from telling him exactly what I thought of him. The admiral had imagined I might change my mind about him! Never, I said to him, I judged him the very first day I saw him. His honest and loyal soul is taken advantage of by the other's deviousness. He thought he would justify himself by replying to my complaints that he was only obeying orders, and even then, not as harshly as he could. Sir, I said to him, there are certain professions that are given only to men who have qualified for them by dishonoring themselves. The executioner, just like you, says when he is torturing the man he is about to kill: 'I am only obeying orders: were I less adept, I would make you suffer a great deal more!' " It was with these scathing words that the governor left the Emperor, his heart filled with rage; he went to the grand marshal's house to talk to him about the fit of anger directed at him, but Count Bertrand refused to listen to him.Dr. O'Meara, who had spent the day in town, told the Emperor he was with Colonel Reade when the governor arrived there, and that addressing him personally he had told him in tones of violent anger: "Let General Bonaparte know that it depends on me to make his situation easier, but if he continues to show me no respect, I will make him experience my power. He is my prisoner, I have the right to treat him in accordance with his conduct, and if needed, I have the power to lock him up." The doctor added that Sir Hudson Lowe had told the officers of the 53rd with whom he had dinner that the Emperor no longer wanted to see them, because a red uniform made him sick. The Emperor, who had finished dressing, went into the drawing room taking the doctor with him, and called me to summon Captain Poppleton. "Sir," the Emperor said to him when he arrived, "you are, I believe, the oldest captain in the 53rd; please tell your comrades that they have been lied to, when it was insinuated that I no longer wanted to see them and that the sight of a red uniform made me sick. Tell them that I shall always see them with pleasure: I have great esteem for the 53rd, it is a regiment of brave men who have fought against me valiantly; I like brave soldiers who have received the baptism of fire, no matter what flag they fight under." Captain Poppleton thanked the Emperor for what he had just told him, and assured him that the 53rd, full of respect and admiration for his person, would never believe such statements if they were made in front of his officers and his soldiers. In order to cover for the governor, he added he had no knowledge that such words had been spoken.

The ice had been broken and the battle began. Sir Hudson Lowe had arrived in town, trembling with anger. He had previously given official communication of the bill dated April 16, 1816, by which the parliament sanctioned the treaty of August 2, 1815, and all the British government's acts towards the Emperor. He availed himself of the discretionary power given to the ministry that determined the punishment incurred by anyone violating the restrictions prescribed for the Emperor's safekeeping. He was not long in making use of these: not abandoning his project of reducing the supplies, he sent Major Gorrequer to Count de Montholon to ask him for a reply to his letter concerning the household expenses. The Emperor at that time was engaged in preparing a reply to the communication of that same bill; he also did so for the letter. After making the corrections and having had it read back to him, he charged first me, then Saint-Denis, whose handwriting was much smaller than mine, with making copies on silk in order to secretly transmit them to Europe. That letter was dictated to Count de Montholon, signed by him, and sent to Plantation House. It contained the following:

Longwood, August 23, 1816
General,

  I have received the treaty of August 2, 1815, concluded between His British Majesty, the emperor of Austria, the emperor of Russia, and the king of Prussia, which was attached to your letter of July 23. The Emperor Napoleon protests against the contents of this treaty. He is not the prisoner of England. Having abdicated in the hands of the nation's representatives, for the benefit of the constitution adopted by the French people and in favor of his son, he went voluntarily and freely to England, in order to live there as a private individual in retirement, under the protection of British laws. The violation of all laws cannot constitute a right. In fact, the person of the Emperor Napoleon is in the power of Austria, Russia, and Prussia. Even according to the laws and customs of England which has never brought into the balance of prisoners the Russians, Austrians, Prussians, Spaniards, and Portuguese, although allied with these powers through treaties and making war jointly with them, the agreement of August 2, made two weeks after the Emperor Napoleon had arrived in England, can have no power under the law. It only offers the spectacle of the coalition of the four largest powers in Europe for the oppression of a single man, a coalition that disavows the opinion of all peoples, and all the principles of sound morals.

The emperors of Austria and Russia and the king of Prussia had in fact no right to take any action against the person of the Emperor Napoleon, and therefore they could not make a ruling regarding him.

Had the Emperor Napoleon been in the power of the emperor of Austria, that prince would have remembered the relationship that religion and nature have placed between father and son, a relationship that is never violated with impunity. He would have remembered that four times Napoleon had restored his throne to him: in Leoben in 1797 and in Lunéville in 1801, when his armies were at the Vienna walls, in Pressburg in 1806 and in Vienna in 1809, when his armies were in control of the capital and three quarters of the monarchy. This prince would have remembered the protestations he made to him at the Moravia bivouac in 1805 and during the Dresden meeting in 1812.

Had the Emperor Napoleon's person been in the power of Emperor Alexander, he would have remembered the ties of friendship contracted at Tilsit, at Erfurt, and for five years as a result of daily contact. He would have remembered the Emperor Napoleon's conduct on the day after the battle of Austerlitz where, able to take him prisoner with the remnants of his army, he was satisfied with only his word, and allowed him to retreat. He would have remembered the dangers that the Emperor Napoleon personally incurred to put out the Moscow fire and save his capital. Certainly this prince would not have violated the duty of friendship and gratitude toward a friend in adversity.

Had the person of the Emperor even been in the power of the king of Prussia, that sovereign would not have forgotten that it was up to the Emperor, after Friedland, to place another prince on the Berlin throne; he would not have forgotten, before a disarmed enemy, the protestations of devotion and the feelings he expressed to him in 1812 at Dresden. It can be therefore seen in Articles

2 and 5 of said treaty of August 2 that, in no way able to influence the fate of the Emperor Napoleon's person who is not in their power, these same princes deferred on this matter to what His British Majesty would do, and he took it upon himself to carry out all these obligations. These princes have criticized the Emperor Napoleon for having preferred the protection of British laws to their own. The false ideas which the Emperor Napoleon had of the liberality of British laws and the influence of a great people, generous and free, on its government, led him to prefer the protection of these laws to that of his father-in-law or his former friend.

The Emperor Napoleon was always free to ensure what was his own property through a diplomatic treaty, either by placing himself at the head of the army of the Loire, or at the head of the army of the Gironde, commanded by General Clauzel; but seeking only retirement and the protection of the laws of a free nation, either British or American, any stipulations appeared to him needless. He believed that the British people would be more bound by a frank, noble and trusting step, than by the most solemn treaties. He was mistaken. But this error shall be a cause of shame for true Englishmen, and, in present as in future generations, it shall be proof of the disloyalty of the British administration. Austrian and Russian commissioners have arrived in Saint Helena; if their mission's goal is to fulfill a part of the duties the emperors of Austria and Russia have contracted through the treaty of August 2, and to make certain the British agents, in a small colony in the middle of the ocean, are not lacking in the respect due a prince connected to them through the ties of relationship and many other reasons, one can recognize in this move the mark of the character of these two sovereigns; but you, Sir, have stated that these commissioners had neither the right nor the power to have any opinion about what occurs on this rock.

The British ministry had the Emperor Napoleon transported to Saint Helena, 2,000 leagues from Europe. This rock, located below the tropics, 500 leagues from any continent, is subject to the extreme heat of this latitude, and is covered with clouds and fog three quarters of the year. It is at once the driest and the dampest country in the world. This climate is the worst possible for the Emperor's health.

It is hatred that has governed the selection of this place, as it has the instructions given by the British ministry to the officers commanding in this country. They have been ordered to call Emperor Napoleon 'General,' wanting to force him to recognize he had never reigned in France; this has decided him not to adopt an incognito name, as he had resolved to do when he left France.

First magistrate for life of the Republic, under the title of First Consul, he con-
cluded the London preliminaries and the treaty of Amiens with the king of Great
Britain; he received as ambassadors Lord Cornwallis, M. Mery, Lord Whitworth,
who have resided in this capacity at his court. He has accredited to the king of
England Count Otto and General Andreossi, who resided as ambassadors at the
court of Windsor. When, after an exchange of letters between the ministers of the
two monarchs, Lord Lauderdale came to Paris with the full powers of the king of
England he negotiated with the plenipotentiaries holding the full powers of the
Emperor Napoleon, and remained several months at the Tuileries court. Since, at
Châtillon, when Lord Castlereagh signed the ultimatum that the allied powers
presented to the plenipotentiaries of the Emperor Napoleon, he recognized by
this the fourth dynasty. This ultimatum was more advantageous than the treaty of
Paris, but demanded that France give up Belgium and the left bank of the Rhine:
this was contrary to the Frankfurt propositions and to the proclamations of the
Allied powers, and contrary to his coronation oath in which the Emperor had
sworn the integrity of the Empire.

The Emperor believed the natural limits were necessary to the security
of France as well as the equilibrium of Europe. He believed that the French
nation, in the circumstances in which it found itself, had better run the risk of
war than abandon this.

France would have obtained this integrity, and with it conserved its
honor, had treason not served the Allies. The treaty of August 2, the bill of the
British Parliament called the Emperor Napoleon 'Bonaparte,' and granted him
only the title of general.

The title of General Bonaparte is doubtlessly eminently glorious: the
Emperor wore it at Lodi, Castiglione, Rivoli, Arcole, Leoben, the Pyramids, and
Aboukir; but for the past seventeen years, he has carried the title of First Consul
and of Emperor. It would mean agreeing he never was first magistrate of the
Republic nor sovereign of the fourth dynasty. Those who believe nations are
herds that, by divine right, belong to a few families, are neither of this century,
nor even of the spirit of the English legislature, which several times changed the
order of its dynasty; this because major changes in opinion which the reigning
princes had not shared in had made them the enemies of happiness and of the
greater majority of that nation; for kings are nothing but heredity magistrates
who exist only for the welfare of nations, and not the nations for the satisfaction
of kings. This same spirit of hatred ordered that the Emperor Napoleon not be
allowed to write or receive any letter without its being opened and read by the

British ministers and the officers in Saint Helena. In this manner he was forbidden any possibility of receiving news from his mother, his wife, his son, his brothers; when he wished to avoid the inconvenience of seeing his letters read by low-ranking officers and send sealed letters to the prince regent, he was told they could only let open letters go through, for those were the instructions of the ministry.

This measure requires no comment. It will give a strange idea of the spirit of the administration that dictated it. It would be disavowed by the Bey of Algiers.

Letters have arrived for general officers in the retinue of the Emperor: they were open and were handed to you. You did not pass them on because they had not gone through the British ministry. It was necessary to have them travel another 4,000 leagues, and these officers learned with sorrow there was on this rock news from their wives, their mothers, and their children, and that they could receive it only in six months. This turns the stomach. It was not possible to subscribe to the Morning Chronicle, the Morning Post, or a few French newspapers. From time to time, a few censored issues of The Times have been sent to Longwood at the request made on board the Northumberland, a few books were sent, but those pertaining to the affairs of recent years were carefully excluded.

Since then, we have wanted to correspond with a bookstore in London, to order directly the books we might need, and those relative to current events. This was prevented. An English author having written A Voyage to France, and having had that book printed in London, took the trouble of sending it to you to offer it to the Emperor; but you did not believe you could give it to him, because it had not reached you through your government's channel. It is also said that several books sent by their authors were not handed over because they contained the inscription "To the Emperor Napoleon" and others "To Napoleon the Great." The British ministry is not authorized to order any of these violent acts. British Parliamentary law, though immoral, considers the Emperor Napoleon a prisoner of war, and never has it been forbidden for prisoners of war to subscribe to newspapers or to receive printed books. Such an interdiction applies only to the dungeons of the Inquisition. The island of Saint Helena is ten leagues around, it is inaccessible from any direction, brigs surround the coastline, outposts placed along the shoreline are in sight of one another and make it impractical to communicate with the sea. It is only through the little town of Jamestown that ships can drop anchor and depart. To prevent any individual from leaving the island, it is enough to watch the coast by land and by sea. In forbidding access to the interior of the island, the only goal can be to deprive the Emperor of an eight or ten-mile ride easily made on horseback, whose lack, according to the opinion of men of the art, will shorten his days.

The Emperor has been settled at Longwood, exposed to all winds, on a land that is sterile, uninhabited, without water, and incapable of sustaining crops. There is an enclosure of about 7,000 feet totally without vegetation; a thousand feet away on a hillock there is a camp, and another one has just been established at the same distance in the opposite direction, so that in the midst of the tropical heat, no matter where one looks, only camps can be seen. Admiral Malcolm, having understood the usefulness of a tent, in such a position, had one erected by sailors 20 paces in front of the house. It is the only place where shade can be found; however the Emperor can only be satisfied with the spirit moving the officers and soldiers of the 53rd regiment, as he was with the crew of the Northumberland.

The Longwood house was built to serve as a storage shed for the farm of the India Company; since then the lieutenant governor of the island had a few rooms built there. It served him as a country house, but it was in no way suitable as a permanent residence. Since we have been here, work has gone on without stopping, and the Emperor continuously bears the inconvenience and unhealthy atmosphere of a house under construction. The room in which he sleeps is too small to hold a bed of normal size, but any new construction at Longwood would only prolong the inconvenience of having workmen around. However, on this miserable island there exist some beautiful locations, offering fine trees, gardens and houses; and among them there is Plantation House, but the specific instructions of the ministry forbid you to give this house, which would have spared your treasury a great deal of expense used to build at Longwood some shacks covered with tar paper which are already uninhabitable. You have forbidden any contact between ourselves and the inhabitants of the island; you have in fact placed the Longwood house in total isolation; you have even prevented communication with the officers of the garrison. It appears that great care has been taken to deprive us of the few resources offered by this miserable land, and it is exactly as if we were on the wild and uninhabited rock of Ascension Island. For the four months that you have been in Saint Helena, you have, Sir, worsened the Emperor's position.

Count Bertrand has pointed out that you were violating even the laws of your legislature, trampling underfoot the rights of general officers, prisoners of war; you replied that you knew only the letter of your instructions, that they were

even worse than your conduct appears to us.
        Signed: General Count de Montholon.

        PS—I had signed this letter, Sir, when I received your own dated the
17th. You attached to it the detailed account of an annual sum of 20,000 pounds
sterling that you consider necessary to meet the expenses of the Longwood estab-
lishment, after having made the reductions you felt were possible. A discussion
of this itemized list can be in no way of any concern to us. The Emperor's table
offers the bare and strictest minimum. All the provisions are of poor quality and
four times as expensive as in Paris. You ask the Emperor to provide a fund of
12,000 pounds sterling for all these expenses. I had the honor of telling you the
Emperor had no funds, that for one year he had neither received nor written a
letter, and that he knew nothing of what was going on or could be going on in
Europe.
        Transported by force to this rock, 2,000 leagues away, without being
able to write any letter, he is today entirely at the discretion of British agents.
The Emperor had always wished and wishes to provide for all these expenses
himself, and he shall do so as soon as you make it possible for him, by removing
the interdiction whereby the island inhabitants may not be used for his corre-
spondence, and when it shall be submitted to no inquisition on your part or that
of any of your agents. As soon as people in Europe know the Emperor's needs,
those who take an interest in him will send the necessary funds.
        Lord Bathurst's letter which you have shown me gives rise to some
strange thoughts. Are your ministers not aware that the spectacle of a great man
faced with adversity is the most sublime of them all? Do they not know that
Napoleon in Saint Helena, in the midst of persecutions of all sorts to which he
opposes nothing but serenity, is greater, more sacred, more venerable than the
foremost throne in the world, where he was for so long the arbiter of kings?
Those who in this position do not show Napoleon respect, only debase their own
character and the nation they represent.
        Signed: General Count de Montholon

        In order to have an idea of the power bestowed upon Sir Hud-
son Lowe by the bill of April 16, 1816, that determined the penalties
for violating the restrictions prescribed for the Emperor's confinement,
it must be known that for us, it meant immediate transportation to the
Cape of Good Hope, where we would remain under surveillance at the

disposal of the government. For the island inhabitants, it meant banishment without indemnity and the loss of any fortune they might have; for slaves it meant the whip. Any officer guilty of the slightest infraction of the general restrictions and outside of his duty was to be sent back to England without employment; finally, it was a crime of high treason for anyone who did not immediately take to the governor any letter, written document or verbal message he received from us, or procured money or objects of value for us without having received previous authorization from the governor. The inhabitants were warned of these measures by several notices posted throughout the town and signed by Sir Hudson Lowe. As can well be imagined, this letter brought some recriminations from the governor that led to correspondence between him and Count de Montholon in which he complained bitterly about being accused of intercepting letters, and wished to be told which letters he had intercepted.

Since the Emperor had been at Longwood, it was enough to ask the grand marshal to have the honor of being presented to the Emperor, if His Majesty granted this. Sir Hudson Lowe, citing as he usually did the terms of his instructions, advised everyone that this right belonged to him alone, and had strict orders given at the camp that no officer could communicate with Longwood without a special permit from him. The correspondence became even more bitter, and the Emperor—justifiably hurt by measures that were unnecessarily vexatious and changed so brutally what had been established by Admiral Cockburn—declared that if the conditions before he moved to Longwood were not restored, he preferred to receive no one. Nothing could have served better the desires of Sir Hudson Lowe, whose principal goal was to place Longwood in complete isolation. He immediately made it known that as General Bonaparte declared he no longer wished to receive visits except through the intermediary of General Bertrand, he must conclude that any other method of arrival at Longwood would disturb him, and consequently he was adopting all measures necessary so this would not occur. Here Sir Hudson Lowe's soul was fully revealed: it was that of a tiger who, seeing his prey fall in the trap laid out for it, holds it in his bloody claws, and says before devouring it: "You are mine."

The Emperor now had only Dr. O'Meara to find out what was happening on the island, and which foreigners were coming through; he alone, like a nightmare, troubled the governor's sleep by his regular presence in town, and the news that he could bring. It was he who reported that senior officers had arrived on the *Cornwallis*, and having expressed a desire to be presented to the Emperor, had not been authorized to do so; and that Sir Hudson Lowe, in town or with strangers getting off ships, misrepresented the idea that had led the Emperor not to receive anyone anymore.

The bad weather as well as his health, which was suffering from the climate, prevented the Emperor from going out. He had complained for some time of a pain in his side; he would rub it briskly with a soft brush, then with his hand put cologne on it. Finding this massage helped him, he one day asked the doctor what he thought of the remedy he was applying to his side. Then, without giving him time to answer, he asked him the causes that led to liver disease. The doctor replied that drunkenness, coupled with heat and humidity of the nights, were responsible for much of it in camp. "If drunkenness is one of the causes of liver disease, it is not because of that I will ever have it," replied the Emperor. "This *galleriano*[291] of a governor must be very fearful that it will get back to me that a few of his compatriots have some esteem for me, since he has not sent me the story of my reign entitled To Napoleon the Great. What a pity! A printed book! It is with the same spirit that the newspapers are censored before I receive them; he fears I might find something in those he holds back to comfort my misfortune. I never want to lay eyes on that man again. He came to Longwood yesterday: when I saw him, I turned my back and returned inside. He was coming, Montholon said, to take away the British servants in the different services of the establishment, and to get from me the necessary funds to make up the deficient to the 8,000 pounds sterling allocated for Longwood expenses. He has written several letters

[291]Bandit or brigand.

regarding this subject without receiving an answer. I prefer making him write than having to talk to him; it suits my dignity better to suffer than to give myself up to a fit of anger, as I did the last time I saw him. He is a man of bad faith with an evil nature, and it is a waste of time to try to evoke better feelings from him. He has no heart."

When he left the doctor and entered the drawing room, the Emperor called for Count de Montholon with the intention of dictating to him a reply to the letters he had received from Plantation House. My freedom only began when the Emperor went into the drawing room; if the Emperor then asked for something from his private quarters, the valet on duty was there to satisfy him. I never went outside the Longwood enclosure during my walks, and I always had my notebook and pencil with me. I knew the plateau of Longwood so well that I could draw a view of the house from whatever point I wanted, without being obliged to go place myself there to draw it. The view that appeared most striking to me was that seen when crossing the first perimeter moat. The box of watercolors that I had had someone buy for me when we stopped in Madeira was about to be put to use. I wanted to fulfill a promise I had made to young Tristan, Countess de Montholon's son, who asked me for a drawing every time he saw me. This illustration that cost me nothing to create exceeded my hopes, and when it was completed, I gave it to the child, who was very happy and took it to his parents.

Mr. Balcombe, who had seen me put the finishing touches on it, found it so perfectly accurate and the color so true that he offered me 25 pounds sterling for it, if I were willing to give it to him. Tristan, who was next to me, dealt with the question when he cried out: "No, it is mine." I had grouped in the foreground, around the Emperor, the two ladies and these gentlemen, in the position they almost always assumed when going out for a walk; the Emperor stopped and put his spyglass to his left eye. It is the instant I had chosen: that picture was so familiar to me that each individual's small flaws and the Emperor's stance were perfectly accurate. General Gourgaud was arriving from town on horseback, and was heading toward the Emperor. Mr. Balcombe had offered me that price because he wanted to send it to England to make a profit.

I was far from expecting such a complete success with my painting, and even less that it would be shown to the Emperor. He had it brought when he returned from a ride in his carriage with Madame de Montholon, who had mentioned it to him; everyone made flattering comments about it. General Gourgaud alone remained cool, and confessed with understandable sorrow that he was not part of the group but set apart from it. That evening when he went back into his private quarters, the Emperor spoke to me of that drawing with great praise, which it certainly did not deserve. "You have caused poor Gourgaud grief," he added, "by not putting him near me, as all the others are." I replied to the Emperor that I had placed General Gourgaud on horseback heading toward him as if he was arriving from town to bring him news, in order to explain the pause in the walk, and to show him watching him through his glass as he approached. I said that I deeply regretted having caused the general sorrow, but I could change this easily. This small drawing, which Mme de Montholon prized, later came to an unfortunate end: it disappeared during a fire that occurred at her home in Brussels when she went back to Europe. The Emperor had found it remarkably accurate in its lines, and with perfect colors: "It is exactly the poor vegetation of Longwood and its wilted lawn. You have missed your calling," he said to me, placing his hand on my cheek.

"Sire," I said to him, "I have nothing to complain about in this position which fate has placed me, and more people envy me for this than would be the case with my painting." After that time, if it happened that I was not there when he called for me, he never failed to say: "If you chase away that which comes naturally, it gallops right back: he has probably returned to his paintbrushes." This often turned out to be true.

CHAPTER SIXTEEN

Sale of the silverware — The governor sends away Piontkowski
and several servants — Draconian rules; stricter regime —
The Emperor is ill — Removal of Las Cases

$\mathcal{D}$r. O'Meara had become the intermediary through whom all matters were handled between Longwood and the governor. "I am," he said to me one day, "caught between the anvil and the hammer: I will have great difficulty getting anything settled properly, there is too much bitterness on both sides." He reported to the Emperor that the governor had him summoned to Plantation House through an orderly. He had gone there and found the governor reading a letter he had just received from Count de Montholon. The governor had told him his intentions were misunderstood at Longwood, his acts were misrepresented, and it was not his fault if his instructions forbade him to allow the title of Emperor in his official correspondence with Longwood; if he was forced to ask the Longwood establishment for funds for the expenses, it was because his government refused to send him any more.

The Emperor replied: "There is an easier way to settle any argument regarding the title of Emperor. I have already proposed it, and I again propose taking the name of Duroc or Muiron, both of whom were killed at my side." The doctor asked him why he had kept the title of Emperor after having abdicated: "Why? Because I abdicated the throne of France, but not the title of Emperor that the nation had given me. I am not called Napoleon, Emperor of the French, but the Emperor Napoleon. They want people to believe the French nation has no right to make me a sovereign. If she had no right to make me an Emperor, she had no right to make me a general." All these negotiations were in vain; they suspended the measures Sir

Hudson Lowe proposed to put into practice for some time, and forced obstinacy so far that the Emperor ordered his silverware to be broken up. The letter dated September 9, dictated by the Emperor to Count de Montholon, which the governor had in his hands when Dr. O'Meara arrived at his home, contained the following:

Longwood, September 9, 1816
Governor:

> *I have received your two letters of August 30. One of these I was not able to pass on. Count Bertrand and I have had the honor of telling you several times we could not be responsible for anything that would go against the Emperor's noble character. You know better than anyone, Sir, how many letters had been sent by the post office to Plantation House. You have forgotten that, regarding the complaints we have submitted to you several times, you replied that your instructions forced you to allow nothing into Longwood, either letters, books, or printed matter, if these objects had not gone through your government channels. A lieutenant from the Newcastle had been the bearer of a letter for Count de Las Cases; you kept it, but since this officer had believed his discretion to have been compromised, you then provided the letter 30 days after it arrived on the island, etc. We are sure that our families and friends write to us often; until now, we have received very few of their letters. But based on the same principles you disavow today, you kept back the books and the printed matter addressed to you, and nevertheless you keep them.*

> *Your second letter of August 30 does not reply, Sir, to the one I had the honor of writing to you, complaining about the changes you had brought about during the month of August, which upset all the bases of our establishment in this country.*

> *1. There is no part of my written instructions more definitive, or to which my attention is more pointedly called than that no person whatever should hold any communication with him (the Emperor) except through my agency.*

> *You give your instructions a Judaic interpretation; there is nothing in them authorizing or justifying your conduct. Your predecessor had these instructions, and you had them during the three months before the changes you brought about a month ago. It was not difficult for you to reconcile your various duties.*

> *2. I have already acquainted him (the Emperor) personally of this.*

> *3. In addressing all strangers and other persons except those whose duty might lead them to Longwood, in the first instance to Count Bertrand (or*

asking myself) to ascertain whether the Emperor would receive their visit, and in not giving passes except to such persons who had ascertained this point or were directed to do so.

4. It is not, Sir, in my power to extend such privilege as you require to Count Bertrand, etc.

I am forced to declare to you, Sir:

1. That you have passed on nothing to the Emperor.

2. That for more than two months you have had no communication with Count Bertrand.

3. We are requesting no privilege for Count Bertrand, as I only request that matters continue as they have been for the past nine months.

4. I regret to learn that he (the Emperor) has been incommoded with the visit, etc...

What irony, this is bitter indeed!

Instead of attempting to reconcile your various duties, you appear, Sir, determined to persist in a system of continuous vexations. Will this do honor to your career? Will it earn the approval of your government and your nation? Allow me to doubt this.

Several general officers who arrived on the Cornwallis had expressed a desire to be introduced at Longwood; had you sent them to Count Bertrand, as you had done until now with all foreigners arriving on this island, they would have been received. You no doubt had your reasons for preventing people of some consideration from coming to Longwood. Claim if you wish—as you usually do—the terms of your instructions, but do not distort the Emperor's intentions.

Young Las Cases and Captain Piontkowski went into town yesterday. A British lieutenant accompanied them into town, where, in conformity with orders existing until now, he left them free to go see the people they wished. While young Las Cases was chatting with some young ladies, the officer came and—extremely upset about being tasked with such a disagreeable errand—informed him you had ordered him not to lose sight of him. This is contrary to what has taken place until now. I believe it would be appropriate for you to inform us of any changes you are introducing; this forbids us any trip into town, and through this you openly violate your instructions. However, you know that scarcely one person from Longwood goes into town once a month, and there is no circumstance authorizing you to change the established order. It is pushing persecution a bit far. I cannot imagine what prompted your letter of September 8. I am refer-

ring, Sir, to the postscript of my letter of August 23. The Emperor is ill as a result of the poor climate and privations of all kinds, and I have not brought to his attention all the fastidious details coming from you; this has been going on for two months, and should have ended long ago. Since the postscript to my letter of August 23 is quite specific, it is high time this came to an end, but it appears to be a text written to insult us.

I have the honor, Governor, of being your very humble and obedient servant.

Signed: General Count de Montholon

As I have already stated, any attempt on the part of the admiral to bring about a reconciliation between the Emperor and Sir Hudson Lowe was impossible. The negotiations undertaken between himself and Longwood through the intermediary of Dr. O'Meara ended in repeated words and letters, but achieved no result. The governor again put forward the necessity of being provided with adequate funds for the needs of Longwood, otherwise he would have to put the reforms he had indicated into effect. The Emperor, impatient and wanting to end such tiring insistences, told Count de Montholon: "Have all my silverware broken up with an ax by Noverraz, and send it to him so that he leaves me in peace." It was said in the flush of anger, and we were careful not to execute these instructions. But the following day Count de Montholon, having asked me for the list silverware, agreed with Cipriani on the pieces that could be broken up without affecting the Emperor's personal service. Had we acted contrary to this prudent measure, it would have meant depriving him of long-standing habits. Therefore the next day, on orders of Count de Montholon who had it confirmed by the Emperor, Cipriani had 65 pounds, 6 ounces of silverware broken up. As this operation took place in a small courtyard in sight of everyone, the captain of the guard was immediately told of this, and the telegraph informed Sir Hudson Lowe.

The destruction of so many fine pieces of silver was painful to see. The eagles and coats of arms that decorated it were given to me, in compliance with orders from the Emperor, and the following day Cipriani carried all this debris into town to sell it and turn over the proceeds to Mr. Ibbetson,[292] commissary for wars, who had been designated by the governor to receive it. When Cipriani came back from town, he told the Emperor the impression made on the inhabitants and the garrison officers at seeing this silver broken in order to ensure the needs of Longwood, as the British government was not able to do so. Indignation and shame, said Cipriani, was written on every face: they said they were humiliated to be the subjects of such a government. The Emperor said: "Every time you are asked for money, you will have to sell an equal value, until we have sold everything." The governor had not anticipated the reaction this broken silver produced in town; had it been possible, he would like to have hidden the extremes to which the baseness of his government had pushed the Emperor. If he was dismayed at the reaction, his surprise soon turned to rage. He said that this event had been a clever comedy; General Bonaparte had money, but rather than part with it he preferred to put on this pretense of poverty and inspire pity by having his silverware broken up. It can be seen with what shrewdness and bad faith he found ways to color his persecution; in this circumstance, he reaped only the scorn of the population and the garrison.

Three successive lots, weighing together more than 400 pounds, were sent to town to Mr. Ibbetson; the governor gave orders so that the shipments would not be visible to the population, as the first one had been. The proceeds of the sale served to bring into balance the governor's account, which showed a deficit compared to what he was allocated for the expenses of the establishment. Sir Thomas Reade deeply regretted that the pieces of silver were broken up and said he would have bought some of it by weight. However, the Emperor had foreseen this intention on the part of some of the more prominent people on the island, and for that very reason had ordered it broken up, removing the eagles and coats of arms so they would not be kept as trophies.

---

[292]Denzil Ibbetson arrived on the *Northumberland*, and remained until 1823. He made an excellent sketch of the Emperor.

Count de Montholon had Cipriani retain a sufficient quantity of silverware for the daily service of the Emperor and his household. According to the list Cipriani gave me to be submitted to the Emperor, it consisted of the following:

His Majesty's silverware.

96 flat plates with palmettos

18 soup plates

96 flat field plates

24 soup plates

6 oval platters

6 serving platters

24 dessert platters

2 serving platters

3 oval balls

6 round balls

2 soup tureens with lids

2 gravy bowls with platters

12 cream dishes with lids and bottoms

His Majesty's giltware.

28 forks

27 spoons

28 knives

32 coffee spoons

6 dessert spoons

2 sugar spoons

1 tray with feet

1 punch ladle

1 tray

18 bottle servers

8 salt cellars

2 mustard holders

2 oil cruets

1 small soup tureen for morning soup

2 dessert dishes

34 knives

96 spoons

96 forks

3 serving spoons

2 soup ladles

48 coffee spoons

8 salt spoons

1 mustard spoon

2 coffee pots

1 chocolate pot

His Majesty's porcelain.

60 Sèvres plates with views of cities or battlefields

12 soup plates

8 compote dishes

4 table settings

2 ice cream dishes

12 dessert plates

24 coffee cups with saucers

This service was the product of the Sèvres factory and was quite beautiful. There was not a single piece that did not represent a city or an event connected with the glory of the Empire.

As can easily be seen, the governor since his arrival had made a point of imposing one restriction after another. He had succeeded, if not in locking up the Emperor as he claimed to have the power to do, at least in depriving him from receiving anyone without his orders. He was not the kind of man to stop there: the frigate *Eurotas*, that had just dropped anchor in the bay, gave the Emperor hope of some distraction thanks to the newspapers he would receive that Count de Las Cases would read to him. The news we wanted to hear was not always the news read, but it led to discussions and helped pass the time.

The governor, whom the Emperor had already refused to receive, came to Longwood on October 1, the day following the arrival of the *Eurotas*. No matter how much he insisted on being admitted in order to communicate the new instructions he had just received, the Emperor persisted in his refusal, saying he was ill. He believed that if the governor came in person, he was only bearing bad news. It was only too true; giving up any attempt to communicate these instructions himself, Sir Hudson Lowe assigned Sir Thomas Reade to take them to Longwood, and the Emperor received him in the garden. The British officer approached him with the deference and seductive manners that disguise an evil soul. He informed him of Lord Bathurst's orders[293] regarding the reduction of the personnel in the Emperor's retinue, and the need for four people to leave Longwood.

When he returned indoors, the Emperor said to Count de Las Cases: "Did I not tell you the other day that for him to come so promptly he must have had some well-sharpened dagger to plunge into my heart? Soon they will leave no one around me: I would prefer that you all leave, than to see you tremble every instant at the constant threat of being thrown on a vessel and taken to the Cape, solely on a whim of this executioner who is always ready to interpret his restrictions in his own manner. Let him place sentries at my windows, let him feed me bread and water: my spirit is free, and I am as independent as when I commanded in Europe." The Emperor was extremely upset, pacing back and forth in his bedroom; everything in him showed his irritation had reached its peak. I was quite struck when I heard these words: I thought they were taking his officers away from him, but I soon learned that the designated people were Rousseau, Archambault, Santini, and Captain Piontkowski. This departure was not only felt by all of us, but left those who remained fearing they might be removed by a similar order. A new declaration had to be signed by each of us, and the Emperor wanted it worded in this fashion:

> *I the undersigned declare that my wish is to remain on the island of Saint Helena and to share in the restrictions imposed on the Emperor Napoleon personally.*

A few hours after having been sent to Plantation House, the grand marshal's letter and the declarations it contained were returned

---

[293]Lord Bathurst, secretary of state for the colonies since 1809, nurtured a formidable hatred for the French, the Revolution, and the Emperor. To these political reasons, one perhaps should add a personal vendetta: he accused Napoleon and his police of having assassinated one of his cousins, a secret agent sent to Vienna in early 1809 to convince the Austrian emperor to declare war on France.

Napoleon and his companions owe to him the selection of Hudson Lowe and all the pettiness, vexations, brutality, and restrictions to which they were subjected.

He corresponded with Hudson Lowe through both official and private letters. In the mail of April 15, 1816, there are two letters from Earl Bathurst: in the first beginning "Dear Sir" he invites the governor to settle the expenses of the food and the servants of Buonaparte, so they would not exceed £8,000 per year. The second bears the notation "private" and begins:

Downing Street, April 15, 1816.

My dear general, I hope you were able to greatly reduce Buonaparte's retinue, encouraging the disposition of most of his companions who must feel a need to leave Saint Helena and return home. Their residence on the island is a great addition to the expenses that, you will note through my semiofficial letter, must be reduced as much as possible. It is always possible to fear a plot by the inhabitants and possibly the commissioners, who have very little to do and could attempt some mischief. For this reason you must encourage them to seek distraction by going to the Cape for a change of scenery, and you must promise to supply them, for their courts, a detailed account of your prisoner's condition.

I remain, etc.

Bathurst

to Longwood. The Emperor forbade that anything be signed other than the declaration he had dictated himself to the grand marshal. Not only did the governor write that we had to sign the declaration as he had worded it, but he came himself to Longwood accompanied by a few officers of his staff to declare to these gentlemen and to us, whom he gathered together in the duty officer's office, that if the declaration was not signed that same day, he would issue orders that within 24 hours we should all be sent out to the Cape. There was great anguish, and the grand marshal tried every possible line of reasoning with the governor without success. The latter even thought he was being obliging by granting the request to let the Emperor choose the personnel who had to leave his service. The governor particularly wanted Count de Las Cases and Captain Piontkowski to leave the island, as he claimed that both were trying to establish illegal communications. But when the grand marshal pointed out to him that the minister's orders mentioned three servants and one officer, he agreed to let the individuals be designated by the Emperor. In the event of a refusal to sign, only the grand marshal—and this temporarily, out of consideration for the countess' pregnancy—would remain with the Emperor. I was also designated to remain, as well as a few other servants necessary for the most simple services.

The Emperor remained in his room, sad and preoccupied, pretending a calm he did not feel. For everyone, there was no doubt that the governor's words would be carried out; we therefore awaited the Emperor's decision, convinced it would in all matters be in accordance with honor and duty. When the grand marshal let us know what they had decided and the reasons for it, he told us that the title of general given the Emperor, under which we were to affix our signatures, could in no way modify our unchangeable devotion; the Emperor was, for us as for history, still the Emperor; and in view of our oppression, it was necessary to disobey his orders in order to remain with him, without thinking we were lacking in respect, and sign the declaration presented to us. Therefore we all signed except Santini, who did not want to sign except with the title of the Emperor Napoleon. As for us, we were happy to have escaped the peril threatening us, and to be free of the distressing feelings we had lived with for some days.

When the Emperor learned we had signed the declaration that was asked of us, he said nothing of our disobedience to his orders, understanding the feelings that had motivated it. What would our role have been when we arrived in Europe if, obeying his wish and refusing to accept Napoleon Bonaparte, we had been taken away from the Emperor and transported to the Cape of Good Hope, leaving him in complete isolation? We would have been criticized by everyone, and they would have said: in such a case, disobedience of the Emperor's orders was mandatory, you demonstrated a lack of courage, you are despicable people! The Emperor understood the sentiments that moved us one and all, and saw in them new proof of our devotion. However, he dictated the following note to Count de Montholon in the form of a protest:

It has come to my attention that in the conversation which took place between General Lowe and several of these gentlemen, certain things were said about my position that are not in conformity with my beliefs. I abdicated into the hands of the nation and in favor of my son; I trustfully gave myself up to England in order to live there or in America in the most complete retirement under the name of a colonel killed at my side, fully resolved to remain foreign to all political affairs of any kind.

Once I arrived on board the Northumberland, I was told I was a prisoner of war, I was being transported south of the equator, and I was to be called General Bonaparte. I made a point of wearing my title of Emperor Napoleon, by opposition to the title of General Bonaparte they wished to impose upon me.

About seven or eight months ago, Count de Montholon proposed to take care of some small problems that continually arose, by my adopting an ordinary name. The admiral saw fit to write to London about it, and matters remained there.

I am today given a name that has the advantage of not prejudging the past, but that does not agree with proper social forms. I am still ready to adopt a name that will enter into ordinary usage, and I repeat that when they decide to put an end to this cruel stay, I fully intend to remain a stranger to any form of

politics going on in the world. Such is my way of thinking, anything said other-
wise is not so.

Finally this man, Sir Hudson Lowe, whose sleep was tormented by the anticipation of the Emperor's escape and whose waking
hours were spent devising ways to torture his victim, established
restrictions that for him had become a monomania. In the midst of the
events I have just recounted, which lasted approximately two weeks,
he found the time to send Count Bertrand on October 9, the document
that follows:

*TEXT OF PROPOSED CHANGES IN THE RULES ESTABLISHED FOR THE
LONGWOOD PRISONERS.*

*Article 1. Longwood, with the road to Hutt's Gate, along the mountain
up to the signalpost near Alarm House, shall be established as the boundary.*

*Article 2. Sentries shall mark the limits which no one may cross to
approach Longwood or its garden without the governor's permission.*

*Article 3. The road to the left of Hutt's Gate that goes via Woodridge
back to Longwood, having never been frequented by General Bonaparte since
the arrival of the governor, will have its outpost largely eliminated. However,
anytime he wishes to go on horseback in that direction, by informing the officer
in time he will not encounter any obstacle.*

*Article 4. If General Bonaparte wishes to extend his travel in some
other direction, an officer from the governor's staff (if he is informed in time)
shall be ready to accompany him. If time does not permit it, then the duty officer
at Longwood will replace him. The officer watching him is ordered not to
approach him unless this is required; and never to provide surveillance except
for service reasons, that is, to watch over anything in his travels which deviates
from the established rules, and to respectfully inform him of such deviation.*

*Article 5. The regulations already in force preventing communication
with any person without the governor's permission must be strictly adhered to.
Consequently, it is required that General Bonaparte abstain from entering any
house or engaging in conversation with persons he may encounter (except to
respond to salutations and ordinary polite comments made to him), unless in the*

presence of a British officer.

Article 6. Persons who, with General Bonaparte's consent, may still receive permission to visit him, may not in spite of this permission communicate with any other person of his retinue, unless this is specifically expressed in the authorization.

Article 7. At sunset, the garden enclosure around Longwood shall be regarded as the limits. At that time, sentries shall be placed around it, but in such a way as not to bother General Bonaparte by watching him, if he wants to continue strolling in the garden. At nightfall, the sentries shall be stationed touching the house, as was done previously, and access to the house shall be forbidden until the sentries are removed the next morning from the house and garden.

Article 8. Any letter for Longwood shall be placed by the governor in a sealed envelope and sent to the duty officer to be delivered sealed to the officer in General Bonaparte's retinue to whom it is addressed, who will in this fashion be assured that no one except the governor knows of its contents.

Article 9. No letter may be written or sent, no communication of any kind may be made, except in the manner prescribed above. There can be no correspondence within the island, except for mandatory communications with the supplier; the notes containing these must be submitted open to the duty officer, who shall be in charge of delivering them.

The instructions shall take effect on the 10th of the month.

> *Hudson Lowe*
> *Saint Helena, October 9, 1816.*

The anger occasioned by reading such a document requires no comment. Was it necessary to send to a rock 600 leagues from every continent and 2,000 leagues from Europe the man who, trusting so blindly in British faith, had come to sit by the hearth of this great nation? It was under these restrictions that the Emperor had to live until the day death delivered him.

The choice of the people who were to leave Saint Helena could only fall on those whose services were the least necessary to the Emperor. They were Santini, keeper of the portfolio, Rousseau, in charge of the silver, the younger Archambault, second groom, and

Captain Piontkowski. The governor had informed them the day before they would leave for the Cape on the 17th. If this departure affected the entire colony, it did even more so those who henceforth would live far from the affections to which they had dedicated their lives. What joy would returning to Europe bring them? Would it not be poisoned by the thought of knowing the Emperor to be in the claws of the monster guarding him?

Each day Santini's fury against the governor took on a more dangerous character. His compatriot Cipriani was often forced to restrain him so he would not commit a crime. He had confided in him the idea of waiting for the governor in the woods and ridding the Emperor of that miserable man by shooting him with his rifle. Cipriani, unable to calm the man he knew well, warned the Emperor so he would reason with him about his fury.

The Emperor summoned Santini immediately and said to him: "Come, you rascal, you want to kill the governor? Don't you realize that I would be accused of having ordered you to do so! Shame on you! Committing murder! I forbid you to think about such a thing in the future: if it enters your mind again, I will have you leave the island." All the Emperor's words were spoken in Corsican. Santini replied in the same language that it was vengeance and not murder. "Well then," said the Emperor as he stood up from the settee on which he was sitting, "if it is vengeance, I forbid you to carry it out." Santini left, promising not to think about it anymore. But the Emperor told me to urge Cipriani to frequently impress on Santini that such a crime must not be committed.

Santini had served in the Corsican legion commanded by Colonel d'Ornano. He had left there to become a staff runner in the postal system. He was at Fontainebleau in that capacity when the Emperor abdicated in 1814. Presented to Grand Marshal Bertrand by General d'Ornano, he received permission to come to Elba and was employed there as keeper of the portfolio. He continued in this post during the Hundred Days, and as such came to Saint Helena. His duties became negligible, he served the meals and spent his mornings hunting. Intelligent, he was quite ingenious at making the Emperor a suit, flannel shirts, and even shoes. He would cut the Emperor's hair and reshape his hat when the need arose. All these odds and ends were not enough to keep him busy. He often spoke to Cipriani of his wish to return to Europe to inform the world, he said, of the harsh treatment the Emperor was subjected to. The Emperor was aware of Santini's frame of mind and sure of his discretion; the moment had arrived to put it to the test. He summoned him, talked to him at length of what he would say to his family, and gave him a copy written on silk of the protest dictated on August 18 to Count de Montholon, to make it known when he arrived in Europe if it succeeded in escaping the search of Sir Hudson Lowe's agents. The Emperor dismissed him, assuring him his family would take care of him.[294]

Rousseau had gone to Elba in charge of the silverware, and was in Saint Helena in that same capacity. He could easily be replaced in his duties, but his departure meant the loss of a man as devoted as the others. Such was not the case with the younger Archambault: the two brothers had been driving the Emperor's carriage, and their position was important in the stables. Additionally, the Emperor found it barbaric to separate two brothers who had devoted their existence to his service. Each of us felt the cruelty in that separation, and in order to avoid it, the grand marshal submitted the name of a certain Bernard, a servant of his own. The Emperor submitted the name of Gentilini, equally easy to replace in his service. The governor replied to those requests that Bernard was Flemish and Gentilini Italian; his instructions called for three French servants. He even added—and this comment was reported to the Emperor—that had Santini not refused to sign the declaration, he would not have accepted him among those departing, because he was Corsican. The Emperor, for whom the finest title was that of being French, smiled with pity at this impertinence that could only issue from a sick mind or a perverse soul. All attempts were fruitless, and the two brothers had to be separated.

---

[294]Santini was born in Corsica in 1790. He volunteered to serve in the Corsican riflemen in 1803, and fought the campaigns of 1804-1807 in the Grand Army. He became an army courier in 1812, and later general manager of the French postal administration. He married and had four children.

Captain Piontkowski, who was led by pure devotion to follow the Emperor to Elba and then to Saint Helena, did not spend enough time with the Emperor for his departure to be a great loss to him. All four of them were therefore ready to leave.

On October 18, before they left, the Emperor, although suffering from a lung infection, had all three of them come to his bedroom, thanked them for their good service and their devotion, and wished them happiness. All three were deeply moved and could not answer when they left, except with tears. They carried with them certificates mentioning their services, and an invitation to the princes of his family to pay them each a lifetime pension equal to one third of their salary. He kept Santini a few minutes longer. He then called for Captain Piontkowski, thanked him for the sentiments that had led him to come and share his exile, and told him that be it in France, America, or Rome, he could always use the Emperor's name as recommendation to his friends and family. He carried with him a most honorable certificate recommending him to the imperial family. All four received as a traveling allowance one year's wages or salary. Having gone on board the same day, they were subjected to a very thorough search. It was taken as far as possible with Santini and Captain Piontkowski, upon whom nothing suspicious was found. At 5 p.m. the same day they left the harbor, heading out for the Cape of Good Hope. The elder Archambault came back from town, overcome with sorrow. It was pointed out to him that his brother was far less happy than he, since to the pain of separation was added that of leaving the Emperor.

The Emperor's health was altered by all these harassments having their origin in Plantation House. Since the addition of the further restrictions, he no longer left the Longwood plateau and no longer received anyone. That was one less distraction for him; Dr. O'Meara and General Gourgaud, who rode every day on horseback, were the only people who brought him any news. Admiral Malcolm was at the Cape; before leaving the island, he had expressed to the Emperor his regrets that he was leaving him on such bad terms with the governor. But the Emperor had replied that as long as things were not returned to the earlier status, he would agree to no compromise whatsoever.

For several days the Emperor had been suffering from a chest inflammation, and he was waiting for it to subside before having a tooth pulled that he assumed to be bad. The doctor told him it was not, but that the way it was moving, there was reason to believe the root was dead. He could keep it, but it would not be of great use to him. "In that case," he replied, "if I am no longer to expect it to serve me, and as it hurts, I would just as soon have you pull it." Dr. O'Meara went to get his instrument, the Emperor sat down in an armchair, and the doctor removed the tooth with such ease that the Emperor said to him: "Is that all? At one point I thought you had missed it altogether." On seeing the tooth they greatly regretted having felt obliged to pull it, because it was not spoiled at all. A severe headache followed this extraction, but a footbath taken during the night made it disappear.

The Emperor attributed his indisposition to lack of exercise, or various other causes. Feeling unwell, he said to General Gourgaud he thought this might be attributed to the wine he was being served. As the general had himself felt the same symptoms, the Emperor asked him to have the wine analyzed and let him know the result: they found in it a coloring agent, and an abundant amount of lead oxide.

For several months young Emmanuel de Las Cases had complained from time to time of heart palpitations. The Emperor urged the father, who was worried about him, to keep a close eye on this, when suddenly the pain required a consultation. Dr. Baxter was called in to assist Dr. O'Meara, who had expressed a desire for this. Heart disease was clearly recognized by both of them; it required treatment, and its development in the climate where we lived could be much more rapid than elsewhere. The Emperor told Count de Las Cases that he did not want his son to be the victim of the awful wind at Longwood; but soon, feeling better, the young man came himself to thank the Emperor for the interest he had shown in him. The Emperor liked him very much and had grown deeply attached to the father, whose wit and manners he enjoyed. The governor knew this. It was the reason he was malicious toward him. Already, quite brutally and under pretext of illicit transports into town, he had had his servant taken away and had offered him another. But Count de Las Cases replied, with the bitterness of an irritated man, that were he to take another servant, he wanted it to be his choice and not the governor's. As soon as the Emperor had knowledge of this, he sent him Gentilini, a footman, so he would not have to suffer from this brutal act. We were far from foreseeing that the removal of the servant preceded that of the master. He was a mulatto whom the governor had already threatened with the whip, and whom he had spared only out of consideration for his master.

The Emperor was about to be dealt a blow in his habits and affections that could not be replaced; it was about to reach one of his officers and reduce to three the number of those remaining near him. It was another privation in the resources of the mind that he found in each of them. In his daily habits, he was about to feel a great void. Count de Las Cases always read the newspapers to him as soon as they arrived; speaking English better than these gentlemen, during the horseback rides the Emperor, General Gourgaud, and he himself would take, he acted as interpreter in conversations with the people they met. Along with these gentlemen he had his working hours, and his conversation with the Emperor dealt with a past these much younger gentlemen had not known. He had served as a page at the court of Louis XVI and had gone into exile.

Admiral Malcolm, returning from the Cape, hurried to send newspapers to the Emperor who as always was anxious to learn their content. Among them were a few French newspapers containing a passage about General Bertrand's condemnation to death. Count Bertrand did not worry too much about the judgment rendered against him, but it was not the same for the countess, who feared not only for her husband, but for her children's future as well. The Emperor went to see her, and offered her words of reassurance in this regard.

As always with the arrival of a ship, Dr. O'Meara had gone into town to get the news. The British newspapers were full of accounts of the festivities of the marriage of Princess Charlotte, heiress to the throne of England, to Prince Leopold of Coburg. On this occasion the Emperor told Dr. O'Meara, who was informing him of the forthcoming visit of Admiral Malcolm, that he was very happy for

Prince Leopold of Coburg that he had not named him his ADC when he had made such a request, for had he been his aide, he would not be sitting on the steps to the British throne.

The Emperor had been ill for several days. He had remained absorbed in his thoughts, not having found in the newspapers what he hoped to discover there.

Count de Las Cases, convinced that the restrictions imposed on contacts with foreigners and the island notables were proof that the British ministry feared the impression the public might get about what was taking place at Longwood, asked the Emperor for permission to inform Prince Lucien of the abominable treatment to which he was subjected. He told him how the mulatto who had been removed from his service had found a way to come back to his house at night. This young man, in whom Count de Las Cases seemed to have the greatest faith, came to beg him—as he was about to leave for London—to give him letters of recommendation so he could find a good position there. Count de Las Cases suggested to the Emperor using him to take his letter to the prince. After thinking a moment the Emperor, finding nothing very reliable about a man who, leaving Saint Helena where he had been born, arrived for the first time in a city like London, told him not to do this: it would be putting his jailer in the right if this affair were discovered. At that time, means of corresponding with the continent, with Cipriani as messenger, had been established through a tradesman on the island. News had already been given and received, and it was more prudent to use this method, for it could very well happen that, coming from Longwood, the mulatto would not be allowed to sail.

It was not the first time that Cipriani had played clever games with Hudson Lowe. As soon as the latter's name had reached Saint Helena, he immediately remembered the name of the governor of Capri, and came to tell the Emperor who Hudson Lowe was; and how he, Cipriani, attached to Saliceti, minister of police in the kingdom of Naples, had contributed to the capture of that island by managing to seduce a certain Suzarelli, one of Sir Hudson Lowe's spies, to whom they fed false reports which were then transmitted to Lowe. The governor never knew of this trick that Cipriani had told me about; it was kept secret, as can well be imagined, but I could not help laughing every time I saw him in the presence of Sir Hudson Lowe discussing the needs of the household, without the latter having the slightest idea of the active part Cipriani had played in the former expedition.[295]

The admiral had brought from the Cape a small crate of oranges that he offered the Emperor. That same day, wanting to shake off his laziness, he said, he dressed early and was chatting with Dr. O'Meara about the footraces two days before at the camp which he had watched through his spyglass, and alluded to the accident to Marquis de Montchenu's aide, who had broken his leg, when Noverraz came to announce Admiral Malcolm's visit. He dismissed the doctor who was going into town, went into the drawing room where the admiral was waiting, and led him out into the garden where they conversed for a long time. That was November 25.

When he left the admiral, the Emperor went back into the drawing room and summoned Count de Las Cases. Taking advantage of the freedom offered me, as the Emperor had not left his private apartments for several days, I was walking toward the guardhouse to go to the camp when I saw Sir Hudson Lowe, surrounded by a large staff, approaching at a gallop and heading for the house. I stepped aside to let them go by, saluting them, and they returned the salute. The governor was accompanied by Sir Thomas Reade, his ADCs Gorrequer and Pritchard,[296] two dragoons, and a gentleman in civilian clothes, whom I later learned was the police commissioner who had come from the Cape on the frigate *Adamant*.

I went on my way, concerned about what could possibly bring the governor to Longwood in such grand style. I decided to retrace my steps, worried by the thought that I might learn some unfortunate news there. Fifteen minutes had not gone by, when on entering the compound I found the same cavalcade at the place where I had just met it,

---

[295]Cipriani had in many instances been the Emperor's agent. During the Emperor's stay in Elba, he had been sent to Vienna while the congress was in session. His role, and that of Murat's agents, are brought to the attention of future researchers.

[296]Henry Huff Pritchard was not an ADC, but in charge of the telegraph service.

taking with them M. de Las Cases and heading for town. Understanding nothing of what was going on, but having seen the anguish of Count de Las Cases, I hurried in to see the Emperor who was in the drawing room. I told him of the encounter I had just had with M. de Las Cases, and the look he had thrown me that implied so much suffering in his soul; I could explain nothing, but added he could still see him. The Emperor ran to the window, and from behind the shutters was able to see his friend coming out of the guardhouse and taking the road to Hutt's Gate. He sent me to Count de Las Cases' residence but access was forbidden me, and I reported that his son was leaving to rejoin his father.

This is what had happened: the governor with Major Gorrequer had stopped at the entrance to the duty officer's quarters, while Sir Thomas Reade, the police commissioner, ADC Pritchard, and the two dragoons headed for Count de Las Cases' lodgings, which they found empty. They went in, and knowing he was with the Emperor, they sent for him through the duty officer on behalf of the governor. Saint-Denis informed him of this, and the Emperor, when authorizing him to go, said: "Come back to me soon." It was in this expectation that I found the Emperor. He summoned the grand marshal, Count de Montholon, and General Gourgaud, all three equally surprised by an abduction that had in ten minutes' time allowed the father, the son, and all the papers to be seized. The Emperor remembered Count de Las Cases' admission to him that he wished to use his mulatto to take Prince Lucien a long report on his situation. The Emperor believed he had spoken strongly enough to make him renounce this project, but Count de Las Cases, believing it would serve the Emperor that Hudson Lowe's insulting treatment be known in Europe, had written a letter to Lady Clavering recommending his servant to her, and had entrusted him with the report he had submitted to the Emperor, that his son had copied on a piece of silk. Either through some indiscretion or by treason, the governor learned of the affair and the man was thrown in prison. The governor seized the correspondence which had just served as a pretext to take away Count de Las Cases. The mulatto was later transferred to Ascension Island.

It is to be presumed in spite of the punishment inflicted on the young man that a trap had been set for Count de Las Cases by the governor, and that his servant's arrival during the night had been made easy, for the surveillance established at night would not allow anyone to believe it could be otherwise.

The Emperor left the drawing room, went back into his apartment, got undressed, and after slipping on his robe remained in his armchair, overwhelmed with painful thoughts; but soon afterwards Saint-Denis announced that the doctor had arrived from town. The Emperor replied: "Let him come in."

"Well, doctor," he said on seeing him enter, "I have just had Las Cases taken away from me."

"I know," said the doctor, "I met Sir Hudson Lowe, who came to me filled with joy, and said: 'Your friend Las Cases has been arrested, you are going to meet him.' Indeed I found him soon afterward, under escort, heading for Hutt's Gate, without my being permitted to speak to him. But in town I learned that his servant had been arrested carrying several letters."

"But, doctor, letters written to a friend in London can't contain anything other than expressions of friendship. Las Cases is incapable of having compromised me without warning me of it; they have seized papers at his home that belong to me. How could Las Cases, a man of such intelligence, make his agent of a man who can neither read nor write? The governor would have to be a great fool to allow this man from his household to leave the island. This man has betrayed him. Hudson Lowe will not fail to accuse me of having had knowledge of this project! He must have a poor opinion of my intelligence! Furthermore," said the Emperor, "it is not possible to proceed in a more ignoble manner than this Calabrian has just done. To take away from me under my very eyes a man of whom I am so fond, whose son is ill and in poor health, this is the conduct of a South Seas barbarian!"

Then, speaking to me, the Emperor asked if I had any knowledge of the diary that Count de Las Cases kept. I replied that Saint-Denis spent several hours twice a week straightening out his notes, and that he could inform him of its contents better than I. "Have him summoned," he said to me. As soon as he entered, the Emperor asked him what this diary contained. "It contains," replied Saint-Denis, "everything noteworthy that has happened since we went on board the *Bellerophon*, and several anecdotes told by Your Majesty."

"How is the governor treated in there?"

"Very poorly, but anything said of him will always be far less than what he really is."

"How is Admiral Cockburn treated?"

"Not very well, Sire."

"Does he say that I called him a shark?"

"Yes, Sire, but he adds that he is a man whose sternness equals his honesty; he also says that Your Majesty, when speaking of him, said: 'Although I do not like him, I cannot refuse him my esteem; under his uniform beats the heart of a soldier.' "

"What does he say of Sir George Bingham?"

"He is well treated, as are Colonels Wilks and Skelton; Admiral Malcolm is well treated, but if he goes through the diary, the governor will not have any cause to congratulate himself on his indiscretion."

"Does he speak of the coffee cup? Does he say that I called him a bandit and a Sicilian?"

"Yes, Sire."

"That is fine," he concluded, dismissing him, "I am not unhappy that he should know exactly what my personal opinion of him is. You have seen," said the Emperor, "with what insistence he wished to hand me Lord Bathurst's instructions personally; he could just as well have given them to Bertrand, but he was looking forward to the pleasure of plunging the dagger into my heart by giving them to me personally, because he knows that the true goal of those instructions is to get rid of the officers who are close to me. He is a true executioner. I feel such hate for this man that if my son were to come to the island and had to be presented by him, I would refuse to see him."

The Emperor asked the doctor to get on his horse and go ask the governor the reason for this arrest. A few hours later the doctor returned from Plantation House and told the Emperor the violation was flagrant, and that a letter written on silk sewn inside the lining of the servant's jacket had been seized on him.

The next day at noon, the grand marshal was sent by the Emperor to see the governor. The latter told him he regretted having to execute his government's orders, but it was not the first time M. de Las Cases had made such illegal shipments: he knew perfectly well the consequences of any infraction of the instructions, since they had been provided to him as to the other people at Longwood. He then showed him the letter written on silk, and said to him, "You see that the infraction is flagrant! He shall suffer the consequences."

"This letter," said the grand marshal, "is only a repetition of everything Montholon has written to you; there is only an infraction of the restrictions, and its only aim is to send secretly to the Emperor's brother what has already been sent officially to you." All the grand marshal could say had no effect: the governor remained unmoved in his resolution to apply the letter of his instructions to Count de Las Cases.

It was easy to understand how the Emperor was upset to see arrested a man who was so close to him, and for whom he had true affection. Almost every evening when leaving the drawing room, he would take Count de Las Cases and talk with him until he became tired. This loss was therefore deeply felt by the Emperor. Only Las Cases spoke English perfectly and translated it to his satisfaction; the Emperor owed him the English lessons that now allowed him to scan the newspapers when they reached him.

It was in the solitude of The Briars, during the daytime conversations and those of the evening wakes that almost never went past ten o'clock, that Count de Las Cases collected the material of which he composed his *Mémorial*, whose pages would number seven or eight hundred, Saint-Denis told the Emperor.

The Emperor asked the admiral through Dr. O'Meara to ensure that Count de Las Cases, if not returned to him, was well treated. The letter he wrote to his friend in London was only an expression of friendship, and assuredly there had been nothing compromising about it except for the illegal manner in which it was to reach her.

From the outset, Count de Las Cases and his son were lodged in Major Harrison's cottage located a short distance from the Longwood limits. General Gourgaud and Count de Montholon could go close enough to that house to be able to express to him through friendly gestures their regret they could not go and see him. The Emperor blamed Count de Las Cases for disobeying his orders: he was quite irritated by it, and never failed to tell Admiral Malcolm this deprived him of his regular habits, and of conversations not without charm during his captivity. A few days later, Count de Las Cases was taken further away from Longwood and transported to Rose Cottage. The furniture from his apartment at Longwood was removed to furnish the new residence where he remained until December 24, when he went into town to await his embarkation.

The Italian Campaign, on which M. de Las Cases was working under the Emperor's dictation, was quite far along. It was in his house when he was arrested, and became, along with the Longwood diary, the prey of the governor, to whose quarters it was taken. The Emperor immediately asked for it through the grand marshal; along with Count de Las Cases' papers, it had been carefully inventoried and sealed. The governor did not prevent the requested restitution, and in the presence of Count de Las Cases, it was given back to the grand marshal. The Emperor would also have liked to have Count de Las Cases' diary. But the latter expressed such a desire that it be left with him that the grand marshal did not insist. He received assurances from him that nothing in his diary could possibly hurt any of his companions in exile. The diary was sealed until the Emperor's death in 1821, at which time it was returned to Count de Las Cases. Two weeks had gone by since his removal, when the Emperor, wishing to see him return to Longwood and upset that his attempts had failed, dictated to me the following letter to be sent to him:

My dear Count Las Cases, my heart feels deeply what you are going through. Wrenched away from me two weeks ago, you have been locked up in secret without my being able to receive or give you any news, without your being able to communicate with anyone, French or British, deprived even of a servant of your choice.Your conduct on Saint Helena has been honorable and without blemish as has your life. I take pleasure in saying this to you.

Your letter to a friend in London was nothing reprehensible, you were only baring your heart within the limits of friendship. This letter is like the eight or ten others you wrote to the same person and which you sent open. The commander of this island, who lacked in delicacy by scrutinizing the expressions you entrusted to friendship, has recently reproached you these; he has threatened to send you away from the island if your letters again contained any complaint. In acting thus, he has violated the foremost duty of his position, the first article of his instructions, and the basic sentiment of honor. He has thus authorized you to seek out means to allow your feelings to reach your friends and let them know the guilty conduct of this commander. But you are without guile, and it was easy to take advantage of your trust.

They were looking for a pretext to seize your papers. A letter to your friend in London could not warrant a police visit to your home, for it contained no plot, no mystery, and was only the expression of a noble and frank heart. The illegal and precipitous conduct of this occasion bears the mark of a lowly and personal hatred.

In less civilized countries, exiles, prisoners, and even criminals are under the protection of the law and the magistrates; those entrusted with their guard are chosen either by the administration or the judicial order to watch them. But on this rock, the same man who issues the most absurd rules executes them with violence, transgresses all laws, and there is no one to restrain the excesses of his whims.

Longwood is surrounded with a veil they would like to make impenetrable, to hide criminal conduct. These precautions lead one to suspect the most odious intentions.

Through rumors cleverly disseminated, there has been an attempt to fool officers, foreigners, inhabitants of this island, and even the foreign agents which it is said are kept here by Austria and Russia. Certainly the British government is fooled in the same way, by devious and untruthful reports. Your papers—some of which they knew belonged to me—were seized without formalities, close to my apartment, with expressions of ferocious joy. I was informed of this a few moments later. I looked out the window and saw you were being taken. A large staff was gamboling around you, I thought I was seeing South Sea island savages dancing around prisoners before eating them.

Your services were necessary to me: only you read, spoke, and under-

stood English. However I urge you and if necessary I order you to request the commander of this island to send you back to the continent. He cannot refuse this, as he has no authority over you except through the voluntary act you have signed. It will be a great consolation for me to know you are on your way to more fortunate shores.

Once you arrive in Europe, whether you go to England or return to the motherland, forget the evils you have suffered here. You may boast of the loyalty you have shown me and the affection I hold for you.

If someday you see my wife and son, please embrace them; for two years I have had no news of them, directly or indirectly. For the last six months there has been a German botanist here who had seen both of them in the gardens of Schoenbrunn; a few days before his departure, the barbarians prevented him from coming to give me news of them.

However, console yourself and console my friends. My body, it is true, is within the power of the hatred of my enemies; they forget nothing that can assuage their vengeance. They are killing me with pinpricks, but providence is too just to allow this to last much longer. The unhealthiness of this devouring climate, the lack of everything that can sustain life, will shortly, I feel, put an end to this existence whose last moments shall be the shame of British character. Europe will someday point with horror at this hypocritical, evil man, whom true Englishmen will disavow as a Britisher.

As everything leads me to believe you will not be allowed to see me before your departure, please receive my embrace and the assurance of esteem and my friendship. Be happy.

> *Your affectionate*
> *Signed: Napoleon*

Once this letter had been dictated, I proceeded to copy it neatly and took it to the Emperor to have him sign it; with him was Dr. O'Meara. "Read this to me out loud and intelligibly," he said to me. When I had finished, he said: "Well doctor, what do you think?"

"I think that such a letter will be very precious to its recipient, and that it is impossible to give a higher indication of favor and a more moving declaration of friendship." The letter was placed in an envelope, sealed with the imperial seal, and taken by Count de Montholon to the duty officer to be sent to Count de Las Cases. The officer sent it to the governor, who soon thereafter sent it back to Longwood, saying he could not receive sealed letters because his instructions forbade it. The Emperor, informed of this situation by the grand marshal who was returning the letter to him, broke the seal himself, and told CountBertrand to hand it over to Captain Poppleton, who took it himself to the governor.

During all this time, and the time preceding Count de Las Cases' embarkation, the Emperor remained in his quarters much more than he was in the habit of doing. He informed the admiral, who came to see him, that he was ill and in bed. The host of The Briars, Mr. Balcombe, was more fortunate, and the Emperor received him in his robe. He was a man who had offered his services, and was disposed to continue doing so; he told me on leaving the Emperor that he found him much changed. I replied that faced with the governor's conduct it could scarcely be otherwise. The governor worried about a sequestration that did not allow the duty officer to verify the Emperor's presence at Longwood. He came to find the grand marshal, and immediately questioned him about the Emperor: he described him as being ill and quite changed. Either Hudson Lowe had considered the bad impression the removal of Count de Las Cases would create in Europe, or after reading the Emperor's letter to him, he better understood the necessity of the services Count de Las Cases had rendered the Emperor; he again declared, as he had written three days before, that he had promptly offered to return Count de Las Cases to Longwood; and the fact that he did not accept the offer made it his duty to repeat it again. The Emperor had not wanted at first to believe Count de Las Cases' refusal to accept the offer to come back to Longwood; the governor's new declaration no longer allowed any doubt of it. The Emperor first wanted to write to him, then preferred to let him do as he pleased, believing that if he left Saint Helena it was because he was certain to serve him better in Europe than he could here. The *Eurotas*, carrying on board Captain Piontkowski, Archambault, Santini, and Rousseau, arrived from the Cape and dropped anchor before sailing for England. Permission had been granted Archambault to go see his brother: the Emperor called him in, and learned from him that Captain

Piontkowski and his companions were very poorly treated on board. The Emperor's bad mood was worsened by this, and only increased his anger at seeing Count de Las Cases' affair not coming to an end.

The Emperor, having learned on the 26th that Count de Las Cases had gone into town and was preparing to embark, sent the grand marshal and General Gourgaud to see him. The decision to leave the island had been made by Count de Las Cases, who believed it was an opportunity for him to let Europe know of Sir Hudson Lowe's improper conduct. The decision was reported to the Emperor, and prompted him to send a letter to Sir Hudson Lowe through the grand marshal, asking him to allow Count de Las Cases to come to Longwood and say goodbye to him. The governor replied immediately that Count de Las Cases was free to return and remain there, but that he could not agree to his going there if he insisted on leaving.

As all attempts for the Emperor to see Count de Las Cases before his departure had been unsuccessful, and December 30, 1816, had been fixed as the day for his embarkation, the Emperor again sent the grand marshal and General Gourgaud into town. They were presented to the governor by Sir Thomas Reade and granted authorization to see Count de Las Cases in the presence of MM. Gorrequer and Wynyard, the governor's staff officers.

Count de Las Cases was happy to see them again, assured them once more he would be more useful to the Emperor in Europe than he could possibly be here, and was quoted the last words the Emperor conveyed to him: "If he leaves, that will please me; if he remains, that will please me!...."

Gorrequer and Wynyard kept themselves at a distance so they would not be uncomfortable in exchanging expressions of friendship. This allowed Count de Las Cases to give to the grand marshal the diamond necklace the Emperor had gotten from Queen Hortense when leaving Malmaison, of which he was the depository; he added a draft on London for 100,000 francs for the Emperor's needs. The sum of 400,000 francs he had previously given, along with this last sum, were reimbursed by Prince Eugène, who held some funds belonging to the Emperor.

Three days apart, two ships left Jamestown harbor: one on December 30 took Count de Las Cases and his son to the Cape; the other, having arrived a few days earlier, carrying Captain Piontkowski and his companions, sailed on January 3, 1817, for England.

When these gentlemen came back from town, they reported to the Emperor Count de Las Cases' words and handed him the diamond necklace, whose fate the Emperor had not known, having never talked of it to Count de Las Cases since he had given it to him. However, after his abduction, searches were made in his apartment in the belief that he might have hidden it in his furniture or behind some wood-work, but these were to no avail. Count de Las Cases, when he received it, had placed it around his body, and it had remained there ever since. This necklace, which the Emperor estimated was worth about 200,000 francs, is the one he bequeathed to me in his will. On returning home that evening he gave it to me, asking me to put it away in the secret compartment of his travel kit. That same day, we sadly numbered six people less in our little colony of Longwood.

That evening the Emperor went into his room to go to bed, and told me to read a few pages from *The Chinese Embassy* by Lord Mac-artney, the book on his table. After an hour's reading he was about to fall asleep and told me to retire.

For a month after Count de Las Cases had been taken from Longwood, when the Emperor went into his room he was accompa-nied by Count de Montholon or General Gourgaud, as he had previ-ously been by Count de Las Cases; he would chat with them forty-five minutes or an hour and then invite them to retire. If it so happened that neither of them went in, he would ask me to read either a serious work or a novel that he designated himself. As the obstacles he had encoun-tered in his desire to see Count de Las Cases return to Longwood were no longer the governor's fault, his agitation calmed and he accepted the separation, as his last words intended to be repeated to Count de Las Cases bear witness. To the sorrow of losing a friend was joined the aggravation caused by the governor's brutal act carried out on the per-son of one of his officers. The moment the Emperor knew the purpose of the arrest, he said to the grand marshal: "It is an act of savage brutality he will never dare execute: he will fear too much the repercussions it would have in Europe." The turn of events proved the Emperor had judged the matter perfectly. The governor had offered to allow Count de Las Cases to return to Longwood. If the Count had not, it was because he felt he would be more useful to the Emperor in Europe than he could be by remaining with him. The Emperor enjoyed Count de Las Cases' conversation very much; as he liked to live in his memories, he took pleasure in reminiscing with him about the delightful society, which in his youth, he said, lent so much charm to a fireside conversation.

Such was the end of the year 1816. One would think that after the events that just occurred, the following years would have been exempt from similar tribulations. But the Emperor's words to Count de Montholon—when the previous April it had been necessary to sign the commitment to remain on Saint Helena as long as the Emperor's captivity lasted—seemed bound to come true: "If it lasts a long time, the British may well have only the two of us to keep."

Whether Las Cases, to get away from St. Helena with his story, fabricates an incident or whether he tries to communicate with Napoleon's brother in a forbidden manner is not known. However, the incident comes to light and he and his son are sent away. Eventually, he is given back his papers, which results in the publication of his important work *Memorial of St. Helena, 1823.*

PART SIX

O'Meara's Dismissal

CHAPTER SEVENTEEN

Sadness — Quarrels between the governor and O'Meara —
The Saint Helena manuscript — The Emperor's illness —
Increased tension

J anuary 1, 1817, consummated a day of sadness for everyone; a time at which—looking back in the past—the ambassadors of all powers used to come in the name of their masters to express their friendship toward him, and behind them a pressing crowd of courtiers filled the vast drawing rooms of the Tuileries. Today, forced to seek shade under a tent erected close to his house, there being none elsewhere, he received not the caresses of a charming wife he loved, nor those of a son who represented all his hopes, but only the wishes—sterile but full of heart and soul—of a few companions in captivity.

The departure of one of these was too recent not to cast a veil of sadness over the compliments presented to him. Like the previous year, the Emperor wanted the children to come have dinner with him and receive presents. The children, through their games and the happy carelessness of their age, were able to distract his painful thoughts and bring a smile to his lips. He sent Saint-Denis to ask me for various presents he wanted to give them. The children's happiness led him to also give gifts to the parents. He sent Saint-Denis to ask me for a Chinese checkers set that he gave to Count Bertrand; a spyglass recently sent by his sister, the queen of Naples, was offered to General Gourgaud, and a silver travel kit that he had had in Egypt to Count de Montholon. Countesses Bertrand and de Montholon each received a plate from his fine Sèvres porcelain service. That of Countess Bertrand represented the passage of the Danube, whose bridges were built by the grand mar-

shal.[297] That given to Countess de Montholon showed a battle where
her husband had particularly distinguished himself, I believe it was
Austerlitz.[298]

In the morning the Emperor had received the compliments of
Count de Montholon; when he came to ask him at what time they
should present themselves, he had replied: "I am in a tomb, I do not
feel the heart for a family celebration." He retired that evening happy
with the joy he had been able to bring to those around him.

Count de Las Cases' departure was to bring about changes in
the Emperor's habits. The workload that had been divided among four
was now divided among three; these gentlemen had their working
hours, and things soon returned to usual. The Emperor continued his
conversations in the evening when he went to bed. General Gourgaud
and Count de Montholon were generally the only ones called on for
this. The grand marshal, although he lived within the Longwood
enclosure, was housed outside the moat on the location of the new
construction being built for the Emperor. At 6 p.m. a wall of sentries
separated him from us, and if the Emperor summoned him at that hour,
there was no way of getting to him other than accompanied by a British soldier. The Emperor's evenings in his private apartment were
therefore shared exclusively with the two generals who lived at Longwood; and if it happened that the Emperor, on retiring, should dismiss
both of them, he became my responsibility. The Emperor would have

---

[297]General Bertrand, commander in chief of the army corps of engineers during the
Austrian campaign in 1809, had distinguished himself by building on the Danube, on
either side of the island of Lobau, two bridges measuring 2500 feet each. Carried away
several times by burning rafts launched by the enemy, and rebuilt several times, these
bridges allowed the victory at Wagram on July 5 and 6, 1809. "It is the finest piece of
work since Roman days," the Emperor had said.

[298]During the 1805 campaign, Montholon was a captain in the general staff of the
Grand Army, working under Berthier. The duties of officers of his rank consisted primarily of copying orders and carrying them to the interested parties. This last part of
their job was often difficult and sometimes dangerous. If the order dealt with some
action on the battlefield, the staff officer was required to witness at least the beginning
of the execution of the order he brought; sometimes he took part in the attacks, either
close to the officer commanding them, or commanding a unit himself.

Napoleon works hard during the night.

me take a book he was in the process of reading, and tell me to continue reading it aloud. It happened they were called at night to work,
but in those days it was rare, as the Emperor did not want to disturb
them. He much preferred telling them when he saw them again the
next morning: "I have worked hard during the night; and you, lazy
friend, what have you done?" When you received such a greeting, you
could be sure painful thoughts had left his heart and mind. I can say
here without fear of contradiction that on this miserable rock the
Emperor always exhibited great evenness of temper, and through his
energy knew how to sustain that of others.

Suspicious as he was, the governor could not stand having the
duty officer remain more than twenty-four hours without catching

sight of the Emperor.[299] Otherwise he became anxious and arrived at Longwood at Count de Montholon's quarters with his instructions in hand, demanding to see him. Count de Montholon would reassure him about his exaggerated fears, and keep these scenes from the Emperor. Had they been reported to him, the Emperor would have remained at home, to find out just how far Lowe would press his audacity and violate his domicile. As the Emperor's apartment was on the ground floor, the duty officer, without having to approach the windows and without anyone suffering from his surveillance, during his walks around the

---

[299]The British officer assigned to Longwood was quartered in a room close to that of the doctor, and took his meals with him. He had to remain available to the Emperor if he wished to leave his domain, prevent him from going near the coast or the fortified sites, and see him at least twice a day. One or several noncommissioned officers were attached to him. The greatest deference and perfect courtesy were advised him.

Between December 10, 1815, and May 6, 1821, six officers were given that responsibility:

1. Captain T. W. Poppleton from December 1815 to July 1817. Poppleton was a clever man who knew how to remain on good terms with the inhabitants of Longwood and the governor. He was promoted to major in 1817 and died in 1827 at the age of 52. His grave in Killanin, County Galway, reads "Honored by the esteem of Napoleon, who was under his personal charge for two years in Saint Helena."

2. Captain Henry Pierce Blakeney served from July 1817 to September 1818. The captain and his wife both had a pronounced taste for hard liquor. The captain turned up one day in front of the Emperor, drunk. He died in 1823, aged 41.

3. Lieutenant Colonel Thomas Lyster replaced Blakeney for ten days in July 1818.

4. Captain George Nicholls served from September 1818 to February 1820. In his diary he mentions the difficulties he encountered during his 16 months in seeing the Emperor who sometimes remained 11 days without showing himself.

5. Captain Engelbert Lutyens served from February 1820 to April 1821. In April 1821 the dying Emperor gave Dr. Arnott a superb book to be conveyed to the 20th infantry Regiment library. The endpapers of its beautiful binding were printed with the imperial coat of arms. The captain took the book to his commanding officer, and Major Edward Jackson said "I can't really understand how an officer of the 20th believed he could convey as a present from General Bonaparte to the regiment a book in which are found the words the Emperor Napoleon." Lutyens was relieved of his duties.

6. Captain William Crokat replaced Lutyens, witnessed the death of the Emperor, was present at the autopsy, and departed on May 7 aboard the Heron to take to England the news of Napoleon's death. Crokat left a drawing of the Emperor on his deathbed.

house could spot the Emperor in one or another of the rooms he occupied.

Since the new restrictions, the Emperor no longer saw any foreigners except the admiral and Mr. Balcombe. Dr. O'Meara was the only man at Longwood who could inform him of what was occurring on the island and bring him news of Europe that had arrived recently. His importance increased for the Emperor, and his access to his private apartment thus became easier. The doctor deeply regretted, he said to me, the Emperor's decision not to receive any of the foreigners who had a permit from the governor. He thus refused a means of distraction for himself, and that of making known in Europe, through those who came to visit him, the state of disrepair of the place where he had been lodged, while the governor was living in a sumptuous mansion. This comparison was a scandal to foreigners, and it was the reason the government made such a show in the newspapers about the wooden palace shipped from London to Saint Helena.[300]

The governor was well aware of Dr. O'Meara's means of action, for he felt they went against the measures of isolation. Sir Hudson Lowe did not trust the Emperor's health bulletins; he reproached the doctor with being too eager to carry out the small errands of the French in town. The doctor had previously told me he found himself

---

[300]As soon as he arrived on the island, Hudson Lowe recognized the miserable condition of Longwood. He undertook a study for the construction of another house, and wrote to Lord Bathurst to ask for his instructions. The question was much discussed in England; there was much talk of a prefabricated wooden house, like some that had been erected on land in prisoner camps. It was also talked about in Saint Helena. Hudson Lowe suggested to the grand marshal having a long gallery (70 feet) erected, to allow the general to take walks. There was some question of purchasing Rosemary Hall.

In early 1818 the materials arrived, but where were they to be used? As the government had refused to let the building be erected in the healthy and wooded part of the island, near Plantation House, work started in 1818 a hundred yards from Longwood! The first stone was placed on October 2. The drawings submitted to Montholon did not interest the Emperor, who felt that this house, with large rooms and sheltered from the wind by a high embankment, would not be finished before his death; he only noticed a heavy gate placed in a semicircle in front of the northern terrace, intended to protect the house from cattle! The small house in which the grand marshal lived was located close to New House.

between the anvil and the hammer; the trust he inspired in the Emperor on the one hand, and on the other hand the desire the governor expressed to him in private to bring about a rapprochement between himself and Longwood, made of him a message carrier. Depending on the questions raised these became more or less violent, and ended by bringing about his dismissal from Longwood.

General Gourgaud, often on horseback, would meet island inhabitants or officers from the garrison during his outings. He was always asked with the greatest interest for news of the Emperor. Among the commissioners who had come to Saint Helena the one he met the most frequently was Count Balmain, representing Russia. Although he was courting Lady Lowe's young daughter, born of a first marriage, he did not hide from General Gourgaud that the Emperor's detention in Saint Helena was not what the Allies had intended: they had indeed left it up to England to carry out the treaty of August 2, 1815, but it was considered inhuman to nail the Emperor to this rock, in an area too small to allow him to take the exercise necessary to his health. He and his colleagues were moved by what they had learned, and Marquis de Montchenu had protested against such a state of affairs; there was therefore some reason to hope the former limits would be reestablished. When these words were repeated to the Emperor he was pleased, less by the freedom that might be restored to him than by the presence on the island of eminent men who were reproaching the governor for the way his instructions were applied.

For his part, Count de Montholon also brought back news. As he went out less on horseback, he was much more often with the Emperor, to whom he was growing close. In addition to his work hours he was in charge of correspondence, and Sir Hudson Lowe made it a busy one, so that it became an occupation and the source of long conversations between himself and the Emperor. As for the grand marshal, of whom the Emperor said: "We must love our friends even with their shortcomings," he was a friend at heart; in spite of Count Bertrand's indecision in certain circumstances, the Emperor's friendship for him was unchanged. The Emperor knew he was a man of good advice, and knew he could rely on him; he was devoted and incapable of departing from the path dictated by duty and honor. Count Bertrand was a wealthy man, surrounded by a large family of whom he took good care. He was not as close to the Emperor as his two companions, but never a day went by without his coming several hours to see him and place himself at his disposal.

Count de Las Cases' departure resulted in Count de Montholon and General Gourgaud becoming closer to each other. Their little disagreements ceased, at least in appearance, because of their common wish to provide the Emperor with means of distraction. The time was spent in friendship, work, and rides, either on horseback with the grand marshal and General Gourgaud, or in the evening with the ladies in the carriage.

The Emperor was told of a remark of the governor's, on the occasion of comments made by the commissioners, and whose content was: "I am going to see to it that he is able to ride on horseback: I do not wish him to die of a stroke, which could be very embarrassing for me and for my government. I would much prefer that he die of a lingering illness, which our doctors can easily confirm to be a natural one. A stroke would lead to too many comments. General Bonaparte cannot ride freely throughout the island; if it were only a matter of his security, a simple delegate from the East India Company would have sufficed to keep him in Saint Helena. He should consider himself fortunate that my government has sent a man as kind as I to keep him, otherwise he would be in chains, to teach him to behave better."

"In that case," the Emperor said to Dr. O'Meara, who had told him about this outburst on the part of the governor, "it is absolutely clear that if the instructions given to M. Lowe do not contain a written order to kill me, the verbal orders have been given; for if one wants to have a man die mysteriously, the first thing to do is to sequester him from any contact with society, to surround him with mystery, so that after having accustomed the world to not hearing of him, and to forgetting him, it then becomes easy to torture him and have him disappear."

The Emperor sought through work and reading to calm the agitation of his mind, which conversation always brought about in spite of himself. If a ship was in sight in the harbor, he impatiently awaited Dr. O'Meara's return to find out where it came from and what was on board. Among the brochures sent to him was one entitled *The Secret Loves of Bonaparte*. The Emperor quickly read through it, and tossing it on the carpet laughing, he said: "What a Hercules they make me out to be! There isn't a single line of truth." Miot's work on the Egyptian campaign attracted his attention. What was said in it about the poisoning of the plague victims in Jaffa is refuted in the story of the Egyptian campaign he dictated to the grand marshal. The Emperor was nevertheless quite aggravated, leading him to call that author a scoundrel. Goldsmith, in his *Secret History of Napoleon Buonaparte's Cabinet and the Court of Saint-Cloud*,[301] received the same label: "Pillet," he said, "is the work of an enemy pen, but there is some truth in it. It is a good book."

The Emperor, whose health was robust, was also stricken with dysentery. The symptoms became severe enough to frighten us, but soon went away. On that occasion he said to Dr. O'Meara: "If I had taken your medicine, I would now be done for. My chicken broth and fasting are what saved me."

Admiral Malcolm had not given up hope of reconciling the Emperor and Sir Hudson Lowe; Dr. O'Meara, in his conversation, led him to believe it was possible. And as if the governor was truly trying to take the first step, he sent for the personal use of "General Bonaparte" a small case of the highest quality Bourbon coffee. The governor begged the Emperor to accept it, knowing he complained about his supplier. Cipriani and I thought the Emperor would refuse it, and we were greatly surprised when Count de Montholon ordered it taken to the pantry.

---

[301]Lewis Goldsmith, *Secret History of Napoleon Buonaparte's Cabinet and the Court of Saint-Cloud*.

Goldsmith remained in Paris for eight years, and had run-ins with Talleyrand and particularly with Fouché. Under the pretext of directing the *Argus*, he was actually doing espionage work. His work, in the form of a lampoon, is the expression of his hatred for France, where he lived, for the men who thwarted his degrading activities, and above all, for the Emperor.

The admiral therefore came to Longwood, and trying by all possible means to open a door that had long been closed to Sir Hudson Lowe, he assured the Emperor that the governor's desire had seemed sincere; "Well then," the Emperor said, "tell him to restore things as they were in the days of Admiral Cockburn, and all will be forgotten. I have already given you such a message to take him before, and it was without result, as this one will be."

The Emperor had learned through Dr. O'Meara that the governor was worried about the effect the Emperor's letter to Count de Las Cases would have in England: he was busy making footnotes, with comments responding to the criticisms made of him.

On January 17, 1817, the grand marshal came to announce to the Emperor that Countess Bertrand had given birth to a boy (Arthur Bertrand). When the Emperor went to see her later in the day, the countess introduced the baby to him saying: "Sire, here is a Frenchman who entered Longwood without the governor's permission."

"And a fine and healthy one at that," the Emperor replied laughing. The strict night instructions had delayed the midwife's arrival by four hours.

The governor, whose mind seemed inclined toward conciliation, then came to find the grand marshal and talked to him about changes he proposed to bring about to make life more bearable for "General Bonaparte" on Saint Helena. He even showed enough goodwill to imply he would leave him free to roam throughout the island, with certain measures other than the surveillance exercised so far. The Emperor believed more in this man's duplicity than in any return to kindness toward him, and he was not mistaken. The governor wanted to precede his good intentions with a sort of memorandum justifying his acts; it purported to show that all the blame rested on Longwood and not him. The Emperor rejected this justification based on the implication that if until now there had been misunderstanding between them, his entourage was to blame for this. The memorandum was tossed in the fire, matters remained there, and the sequestration system continued to apply to Longwood. I do not believe I am mistaken in saying that since that system had been put into effect, the only foreigners the Emperor had seen were Admiral and Lady Malcolm, Captain Mansel, General Bingham, two captains from the *Newcastle* and the *Eurydice* presented by the admiral, and Mr. Balcombe and his family.[302] All these people lived on the island and the governor could not prevent their visits, which were rather rare. It was therefore in his own resources and those offered by his friends that the Emperor was forced to find his distractions.

The Emperor always waited impatiently for the arrival of a ship from Europe. When Dr. O'Meara came to announce that the *Adolphus* had just dropped anchor in Jamestown harbor, the Emperor told him to go to town and bring him back some news. When he returned in the afternoon, Dr. O'Meara brought back with him a small brochure written by Dr. Warden[303] and another published by Santini; both of these, as can be imagined, had not come through the governor's hands. The sale of the silver had caused a great commotion in England. That evening, newspapers and letters arrived. The first spoke of a long audience given by the prince regent to Admiral Cockburn on his arrival in London. The letters were those from the imperial family; all the members, on learning of the privations imposed on the Emperor and the sale of his silver in order to meet his needs, were anxious to place the remains of their fortune at his disposal, begging him to use it as if it were his own. Madame Mère, although quite elderly, asked his per-

---

[302]Captain Waughope commanded the *Eurydice*. He accompanied Sir Pulteney Malcolm and Captain Meynell, commander of the *Newcastle*, when they were received by the Emperor on January 11, 1817. The audiences granted by Napoleon were particularly numerous between January and September 1816; they became less frequent in 1817, except during the month of July, then ceased completely. Only one visit is mentioned in 1818, and one in 1819.

[303]Dr. William Warden (1777-1849) was the surgeon of the *Northumberland*. Between October 1815 and June 1816 he several times had occasion to talk to and dine with Napoleon. In his letters to his fiancée, he relates comments made by the "Great Man" during the visits he paid. At the time of his departure, the Emperor gave him a game of Chinese checkers.

Published in 1816 under the title *Letters from Saint Helena*, Warden's writings, favorable to Napoleon, met with great success, but caused their author to be stricken from the roster of naval surgeons. He was nevertheless reinstated later and became their dean.

mission to come and end her days close to him; Princess Pauline was not held back by her poor health, and requested the same permission. The Emperor could certainly expect the devotion of his family, whose glory he was; but so much heart, so much soul, so much devotion were expressed in these letters that they moved him deeply.

Dr. Warden, the doctor on board the *Northumberland*, had had the honor of knowing the Emperor during the crossing from Europe to Saint Helena. He had remained friends with Dr. O'Meara, was received by the Emperor when he left the island with his ship to return to England, and received from Count de Las Cases notes and information that he used to compose his brochure. He sent it to Dr. O'Meara, using an address agreed on between them, so the latter could show it to the Emperor. The Emperor read it with interest and spoke well of it to Dr. O'Meara, but found it had been written by a man who had misheard and misunderstood what had been said to him. This pamphlet caused the Emperor to dictate to Count de Montholon a work entitled *Letters about the Cape*.[304] This booklet, which attempted to refute the libel written regarding the Emperor, reached France secretly and was published there. Dr. O'Meara told the Emperor Dr. Warden's brochure had brought its author 50,000 francs. "That's possible," replied the Emperor, "the British do not know me; everything connected with Saint Helena and published by an eyewitness and a compatriot arouses their curiosity; they are avid for details regarding me. When Balcombe offered Marchand 50 guineas for a drawing of Longwood he had just completed, he would have made a fine speculation had Marchand accepted his offer; he would have sent it to London, had it published, and gotten a lot of money from it. All of the pamphleteers agree to make a coward out of me: they shall not succeed. These are hard blows given me by the press; never has it proved so relentless as it is in my regard. But it cannot reach me, posterity shall do justice to such dirty writings."

---

[304]The Emperor received the *Letters from Saint Helena*, examined them without attaching much importance to them, and made a few comments, which Count de Las Cases used to generate the *Lettres du Cap de Bonne-Espérance*, published in reply to those written by Dr. Warden.

As for the brochure published by Santini, the Emperor said: "The intention is good, but it is filled with pitiful nonsense mixed with lies! Where was I ever seen shooting birds for my lunch? It is completely ridiculous." He found the *Manuscript from Saint Helena* the work of a man of intelligence, but one who confused dates, placing Jena after the treaty of Tilsit.[305]

Another ship coming from Europe was again to provide distraction for the Emperor. There were newspapers, and I hoped also some letters; my expectations were not in vain, because there was one. As I expressed my joy to the Emperor, he asked me what it said and its date. It had been written on January 8 and I received it March 11: my father wrote me that the King of Rome was about to be turned over to certain men, Count Dietrichstein[306] had been named his tutor, my mother was going to leave Vienna, and they had just bought for 42,000

---

[305]The *Manuscrit venu de Sainte-Hélène d'une manière inconnue* was a 100-page booklet published in French in London in early 1817, costing 7 shillings, 6 pence.

In France, where the booklet was sought by the police, it met considerable success. In England several editions of the translation were soon exhausted. Everyone believed it to be Napoleon revealing himself, and the European liberals took it as their creed. The Emperor received the document on September 5, 1817, perhaps from the hands of Admiral Plampin, read it with curiosity, wrote some 40 notes on the subject. Marchand points out a gross error: Tilsit before Jena! There are others, for instance: the confederation of the Rhine after Jena, Bonaparte's presence in the army of the Alps, at Mount Genèvre, etc. Wellington considered these errors to be proof of authenticity. In Europe people were more skeptical; they offered theories. Certain names were suggested: Fouché, Marmont, etc., but the more enlightened minds said Benjamin Constant. At Longwood it was thought to be Madame de Staël.

The European liberals and the Emperor were right. Madame de Staël, representing liberal ideas against absolutism, remained in the background and handed her pen to a friend from Geneva, the Marquis Lullin de Chateauvieux.

[306]In his *Bemerkungen* (observations), Count de Dietrichstein relates that he took up his duties with the Emperor's son on June 30, 1815. The child was then four and a half, and since the treaty of Fontainebleau in 1814 carried the title of Prince of Parma. "Mme Marchand," writes Dietrichstein, "deserves congratulations in every respect. She has only one fault—quite excusable—and that is to talk constantly of Paris." In March 1817, when Marchand received news from his mother which coincided with the prince's birthday, Dietrichstein's text reads: "After the meal we had at the Empress', the prince said in playing, while beating on a drum, "I shall go to another country, I know very well where, but I won't say it, in another country where there was war, in France, war with the Austrians."

francs a small property in Burgundy belonging to the former prefect of Auxerre, M. de La Bergerie, who was said to have spent 100,000 francs. My father added that as soon as my mother came back to France, he intended to go shut himself up there a good part of the year. The Emperor praised M. de La Bergerie,[307] saying he was a good administrator and a learned man. "This piece of property," he added, "must be the one belonging to the former bishop of Auxerre, along the Yonne, since you are told it is about one league before town. I stopped there in my youth, the house is fine and there is much shade: I would be pleased to be there. I would have a boat so I could go out on the water."

"Sire," I said to him, "Your Majesty would not remain there very long, as the current would take you to Paris." The Emperor smiled at my comment, and thought that perhaps I had guessed rightly. The grand marshal came in to read the British papers to him; he said his father had written he should send him his son Napoleon, so he could seriously begin his education.

After the Emperor had returned to his apartment alone, I told him about an event that had just occurred in Saint Helena which he would not believe until Dr. O'Meara confirmed it the following day while he was dressing. Among the men sent to work on the new house was one called Peen, a tall man and quite husky. He was specifically in charge of the wallpapering and painting. When he left London, he told his wife to come join him by the first ship leaving for the Cape; she soon did this, boarding a ship for that destination. However along the way she forgot the purpose of her trip; once she arrived at the Cape, finding herself comfortable on board, she continued on to Bourbon Island with the ship's captain, who was heading there. On the ship's way back to Europe it stopped in Saint Helena. The captain came to find the husband, told him about his wife's misadventure, and made a deal with him by which—in exchange for the sum of 6,000 francs—

---

[307]Baron Rougier de La Bergerie had a long political career. He was prefect of the Yonne until March 1813, when he was dismissed. He was recalled during the Hundred Days and named prefect of the Nièvre. He resigned the post in May 1815 and devoted himself to agronomy and poetry.

Mrs. Peen belonged to him. The bargain having been concluded and the amount paid, a luncheon followed, attended by the wife, and—a very strange thing, I said to the Emperor laughing—heavy tears were flowing down the man's cheeks when he told me about this adventure, and he said it hurt him very much. "The tears," said the Emperor, "were certainly the result of the wine, but how is it that the military or civil authorities had not opposed such a scandalous arrangement?" The doctor replied that there existed an old English law that allowed a husband to sell his wife. This law had fallen into disuse, but had not been repealed; it was under the terms of this law that arrangement had taken place.

I had advised the doctor that the Emperor's legs appeared to me to be swollen around the ankles. The Emperor showed them to him: the swelling was noticeable, and there was even a recurrence of his dysentery, although not severe. Dr. O'Meara wanted to prescribe medication, but the Emperor would have none of it. He then advised exercise for his legs. "But," replied the Emperor, "where would you have me exercise, as my executioner has taken away from me all means of doing so?" From time to time he was taken with shivering, forcing him to go to bed, that disappeared when the sweating started. His stomach pains were quite frequent, but the application of hot towels would put an end to them. The governor was aware of this, and although he knew the lack of exercise could bring about this disorder in the Emperor's health, he changed nothing in the restrictions, continuing his system of sequestration which he found not even complete enough. One man prevented him from completely surrounding Longwood in the most profound mystery: it was Dr. O'Meara. Rumor had spread in town that the Emperor was seriously ill. The commissioners themselves were worried about it and asked Sir Hudson Lowe that reports on the Emperor's health be given to them; in fact, their instructions also recommended they be kept aware of the prisoner's health. Security measures could be taken, but they should not be pushed to the point of depriving him of the exercise necessary to his health. These comments from all, presented quite forcefully even by Marquis de

Montchenu, put the governor in an awkward position. He told them the news was false and that he was going to seek out its author.

He came to Longwood, had himself announced to the grand marshal, and told him that Dr. O'Meara said in his bulletins that "General Bonaparte" was sick when he was not, and that this rumor had spread throughout town. Everyone was trying to deceive him, and he no longer wished to be deceived by anyone. The government had sent to the island a very good doctor, Dr. Baxter, to take care of the general; if he was ill, he had to be attended by that doctor. The grand marshal answered the governor firmly: he was amazed at the doubts he expressed regarding the Emperor's health, as evidence of the illness was sufficiently visible in his physical appearance for the captain of the guard to notice it when he saw him, and he could have reported it to him. As for wanting to force the Emperor to receive another doctor than his own, he would never consent to this, and added it was improper on his part to treat this prince as he did.

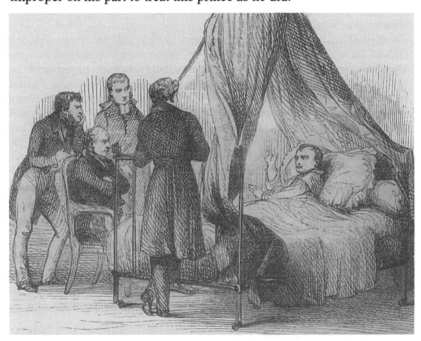

Napoleon refuses to talk to the English doctor sent by Hudson Lowe.

The Emperor approved of the grand marshal's words, and dictated to Count de Montholon in response to Lord Bathurst's speech[308]
a series of notes which, when brought to the governor's attention, led
him to return things to approximately the same state they were in at the
time of Admiral Cockburn. This communication had not yet arrived
officially at Longwood, but the Emperor had it through General Gourgaud who had met General Bingham. The Emperor said on this occasion: "He is a miserable pen pusher who caves in the moment he is
treated firmly." The commissioners had become alarmed about the
Emperor's health because General Gourgaud often encountered one of
them during his rides: not only had he told them of the Emperor's

---

[308]*Lord Bathurst's speech* as minister of the colonies, pronounced in the House of
Lords, was a reply to the *Motion made in the British Parliament by Lord Holland, to
submit documents relative to the treatment imposed on Napoleon in Saint Helena*.
Henry Richard Fox, third Lord Holland, born in 1773, was educated at Eton and
Oxford, had traveled in Spain and Italy, and in Florence met a charming woman, Lady
Webster, who became his wife in July 1797.

By tradition and by character, the nephew of William Pitt's sworn adversary was
a liberal. He had been received in Paris by the First Consul in 1801 and had been hostile to the measures taken against Napoleon by Lord Liverpool's government. On
March 18, 1817, Lord Holland made a speech full of moderation to the lords: "You are
all aware," he said, "of the opposition I expressed to the government's ministers,
regarding Napoleon's detention and exile. Although I maintain the same opinions on
this subject, my intention is not to appeal to your lordships to change this political
plan; but the complaints arriving from Saint Helena, and a note that came into my
hands which appears to have been written by General Count de Montholon, could well
mean an indelible stain on the character of the British nation." After this, the honorable lord asked that an inquest be opened, and that the ministers present to the officers
of the House of Lords the papers and the correspondence between Saint Helena and
His Majesty's governor, in order to shed some light on the treatment imposed on
Napoleon. Lord Bathurst replied with a speech that caused great emotion. He called
General Bonaparte's complaints base lies, and declared that the measures were those
taken with prisoners of war. He rejected the motion, and expressed the fear that the
noble lord, author of the motion, could not discuss with impartiality the restrictions
imposed by the bill of Parliament upon this prisoner, since, according to him, any
restriction whatever was inhuman and unjustified. Refer to the fine letter written by
Madame Mère to Lord Holland; Rome, May 1, 1817.

"Napoleon's mother cannot express any better her gratitude for the interest you
have taken in her son, than by telling you her astonishment at reading in Lord
Bathurst's reply that no one from his family had sent the minister any letters for Saint
Helena."

deplorable health, but he added he could not understand how, in their position, they could show such indifference to what was going on at Longwood, when their presence in Saint Helena was less to see to his detention than to verify that he was treated properly.

The Emperor had cured himself from this indisposition with the same regimen that had cured him before: keeping to his room, fasting, and chicken broth. He thus told General Gourgaud, who had been hit a second time by a rather severe attack of dysentery: "Do not let them drug you: those Britishers have medications that are suited to horses, but they irritate more than they relieve." And as if chicken broth were the universal remedy, he recommended it to him. The general did not follow the Emperor's advice as his symptoms required rapid and efficient remedies; they were administered to him, and he got better. Eight to ten days later his convalescence began, and he resumed his usual life, however with a great intestinal weakness.

On April 10 the China fleet arrived in Saint Helena. It was a time of festivities for the island inhabitants; they were able to purchase objects they needed and sell their goods or vegetables to the ships in the harbor at a very high price. During this short time the crews, the officers, and the passengers left much money in town and gave Jamestown an unusual degree of activity.

Aboard one of these ships was a present sent to the Emperor that could be called a debt of gratitude. Mr. Mannering, a distinguished scholar who was traveling for research in the arts and humanities, had been asked to give it to him when passing through Saint Helena. A letter accompanied the present from the honorable Mr. Elphinstone, who was thankful to the person who, on the eve of the battle of Waterloo, had brought assistance to his seriously wounded brother on the battlefield. The present consisted of a magnificent ivory chess set larger than the usual size, two large and beautiful openwork baskets, and an exquisite ivory basket filled with mother-of-pearl tokens. All of it was remarkably executed: on each piece was a crowned eagle, and the letter N capped with an imperial crown. When he arrived in Saint Helena, Mr. Mannering followed the instructions prescribed for foreigners who came to town: he handed Mr.

Elphinstone's present over to the governor, so as to have it sent on to Longwood. The governor did not know what to do with this object sent to the prisoner of Saint Helena; it had not reached him through the usual channels, and carried an imperial symbol his government did not wish to recognize. He hesitated between handing it over or sending it to Europe so that it would come back to Saint Helena. However, realizing he would appear ridiculous in the eyes of his ministers, he sent along the crates containing the objects more than a month after they arrived.

The act of humanity that had earned the Emperor this present was quite common with him; he never went through a battlefield without having his own surgeon care for friends or enemies who still seemed to be alive; and the silver wine flask carried by Roustam or Saint-Denis for his own personal use was often used to give strength to those who were exhausted. Mr. Elphinstone's brother, severely wounded the day before Waterloo, was in an almost desperate state when the Emperor, going by him, sent his surgeon to take care of him as needed. The Emperor decided to give the presents to Empress Marie-Louise and the King of Rome. Countess de Montholon, when she left Saint Helena, was to deliver them upon arriving in Europe.

At the same time a ship arrived from England, the *Baring*. A gunnery chief had taken it on himself on his arrival in Saint Helena to deliver to the Emperor a marble bust of the King of Rome, the work of a sculptor in Livorno who had added a letter to his shipment. The Emperor was immediately informed of this when the ship arrived, but eight days later the bust had not yet been sent. The governor's predicament was awkward, but his chief of staff, Sir Thomas Reade had simply suggested tossing it into the sea to solve the problem. The statement was denied, but how could one not believe it when on a previous occasion the same high ranking officer had said when speaking of the Emperor: "If I were governor, I would teach that French cur a thing or two; I would isolate him from his friends who are worth no more than he, and then I would take away his books! He is nothing but a miserable outlaw; I would treat him as such and, by God, it would be doing the king of France a great favor to get rid of him!" That fit of temper from Sir Thomas Reade had been provoked by the Emperor's refusal to receive Sir Thomas Strange, one of the superior judges in Calcutta, who had through the governor requested the honor of being presented to him. The Emperor had sent this reply: "People who have descended into the grave do not receive visits. Bertrand, make sure this judge hears my reply." Was it not strange that as the Emperor had declared he would receive no visitors unless presented by CountBertrand, the governor still brought him one? Hudson Lowe's anger was great, but that of his chief of staff exceeded all limits.

The governor put an end to his hesitations, came to see the grand marshal, and told him that a marble bust of General Bonaparte's son had been brought on the *Baring*, and that it was a mediocre piece by a Livorno sculptor. In his cover letter the sculptor admitted having been paid, but recommended himself to the generosity of General Bonaparte. The whole affair struck the governor as a speculation, and the cost of 100 louis [2,000 francs] that the artist assigned to the expected compensation, was an exorbitant and unacceptable claim. The grand marshal replied that the Emperor alone could decide that matter, and that seeing the features of his son which had been deprived him for so many years was priceless; he therefore urged the governor to send it to him that same day. The following day it arrived at Longwood. The white marble bust was quite well made, and the inscription said: Napoleon, François, Charles, Joseph, and it was decorated with the great cross of the Legion of Honor. When the Emperor received it, he remained in contemplation of this picture of his son: "How can it be," he said, "that on this rock there is a man savage enough to order this bust thrown in the ocean? He is certainly not a father. For me, this bust is worth more than millions. Put it on the table in the drawing room, so that I may see it every day." The following letter was written by the grand marshal to the gunnery chief on the *Baring*.

I have received the marble bust of young Napoleon; I have given it to his father, and it gave him the greatest satisfaction.

I regret it was not possible for you to come visit us, and give us the details which, for a father in his position, would have been of the greatest inter-

*est. From the letters you have sent me, it appears that the artist assigns the value
of £100 to his work. The Emperor has ordered me to give you a letter of credit
for £300; the excess amount is intended to indemnify you the losses he knows you
have suffered on the sale of your merchandise, as you were not able to unload it,
and for the prejudice this event has caused you, but which will entitle you to the
esteem of any honorable man.*

*Please be kind enough to convey to the people who had this kind
thought all the Emperor's thanks.*

I remain, etc.

Count Bertrand

The delay in sending these objects had irritated the Emperor
over what he called the governor's duplicity and ill will. He had Count
Bertrand write the following letter:

Governor:

*I have received the five crates you took the trouble to send me, contain-
ing a chess set, a box of tokens, and two ivory baskets, sent from Canton by Mr.
Elphinstone.*

*The Emperor was surprised to see in your letter that you believed it
your duty not to hand over these objects. You say: "If I acted in full compliance
with the established regulations, I should suspend any forwarding." In this case,
Governor, you would have done the appropriate thing by holding them back.*

*But to what does this apply? Did these objects not arrive through the
channels of the ministry? In the ministry restrictions it is specified that letters
must come through its channels, but not objects of apparel, busts, furniture, etc.
We have constantly received many objects sent to us from the Cape. In fact, Lord
Bathurst in his speech, and you yourself in letters, have always indignantly
rejected the accusation that letters coming by the post or other means, had been
sent to London to come back to this country. This cannot and could not have
authorized you to hold back objects such as busts, furniture, books, and any
other effects having no relation whatsoever to the security of the detention.*

*Would it be because there is a crown on the tokens? But there can exist
no regulation that is not brought to our attention; and there is to our knowledge
nothing to prevent us from owning an object bearing a crown. In that case it*

would also be necessary to manufacture new decks of cards, because there are crowns on the ones provided; the linen and the little silver still remaining often go to town, and they are marked with a crown.

From whom could come this ruling that you say is in force? From your government, which alone has the right to issue same, in accordance with the bill? Your ministry has declared in open Parliament that it had made no restriction, only that of taking measures of execution. In effect, you have no right to do so. The Emperor wants no favor from anyone, and wishes to owe nothing to anyone's whims, but he has the right to know the restrictions imposed upon him. Your government, the Parliament, and all nations have the same right. I therefore beg you, Sir, to communicate to us these new restrictions; if there were such restrictions, they would be in contradiction with Lord Bathurst's assertions that they may have no other goal but ensuring the security of the detention. The Emperor asks me to protest against the existence of any restriction or rule that has not been legally communicated to him prior to its execution.

I remain, etc.

Count Bertrand

The governor's response to this letter was not long in coming:

Sir,

I have received your letter of the 9th inst. Your frequent use of the title of Emperor therein and the tone in which you express your sentiments to me when employing it would give me sufficient justification for remaining silent on its contents, as being addressed to me in inadmissible form, and for referring you to my letter of August 30, 1816, to Count de Montholon. However, I will not avail myself of this reason for refusing to reply to it.

My only goal in writing to you on the 8th of this month was to prevent the impression that I tacitly recognized or approved the use of the imperial rank in the crown placed everywhere over the initial of Napoleon, found on the gifts sent by a private British subject and coming from a British factory.

If I had let them pass without comment, the conclusion would necessarily have been drawn that I saw nothing inappropriate in this. I do not know to what point this precedent could have been claimed and what complaints could have arisen had it been deviated from in the future, had I not explicitly stated my reasons in this case for allowing the objects in question to reach you.

The person who made these gifts has his own opinions. But I also have the right to exercise my judgment in not allowing them to be expressed by my intermediary. In letting the presents be delivered without other commentary than that in my letter, I went to the extreme limits of what could be exacted of me regarding General Bonaparte's wishes and expectations.

You ask me, sir, "Is it because these objects did not arrive through the channels of the ministry?" I would have considered myself fully justified in holding them back according to the general nature of my instructions, even without the decoration found on them, until I had obtained my government's express permission to deliver them, had I not made use of my discretionary power to examine them and satisfy myself they did not conceal a means of communication that could lead to a clandestine correspondence. My having sent you the letter even before the objects were debarked is sufficient proof that this was the principle I adhered to rather than awaiting instructions from England.

You note, sir, that I indignantly rejected the accusation that letters arriving through the post or by private means were returned to London to be sent again to this country. I most certainly rejected this accusation, sir, as well as the accusations to which it gave rise, because they contained no truth or justice; because I was outraged at this sentiment that finds humiliation and cause for blame in expressions of attention (because in sending family letters, I had exercised on behalf of the persons who appealed to me a discretionary power not authorized by my instructions). But I do not admit that I did not have the right and would not have been perfectly justified in returning letters to England if I found it appropriate, when they arrived by unconventional channels. Presents as well as a letter may threaten the security of the detention, and may be subject to an examination that would prevent their ever being used as objects of decoration or utility. A letter can be hidden under the squares of a chessboard or in the cover of a book as well as in the lining of a waistcoat, and I am under no obligation to trust the person sending them, whoever it may be. If I permitted the objects to be delivered to you, it was because I was convinced they were not of an objectionable nature, and you certainly have no reason, sir, to complain of the manner in which I used my discretionary authority, as much in generally consenting to the delivery of every object that arrives, as in allowing to pass other objects addressed to me whose senders left the delivery entirely up to my judg-

ment.

You observe, sir, "Is it because there is a crown on the tokens?" and you ask whether there exists a regulation forbidding you to possess an object with a crown on it.

There is certainly no explicit written regulation which forbids any object decorated with a crown being delivered to Longwood, or which forbids you to own any such thing. But in this case it is a question of the imperial crown over the initial of Napoleon, carved, gilded, engraved, and present on almost every object. His abdication, the treaty of Paris, and the acts of the British Parliament make such a regulation unnecessary.

The objects decorated with the imperial crown that are currently found at Longwood carried this mark prior to the abdication. I have never disputed your possession of them or any satisfaction they may bring you.

As for the passage where you cite Parliamentary debates, allow me to inform you that this is incorrect according to the newspapers I have seen. The newspapers themselves are not in agreement, as one speaks of regulations and another of instructions, not restrictions, as being the same without any substantial alteration to those initially stipulated.

You say, sir, "You do not have the right..."

The act of Parliament, the commission, and the instructions provided to me are, sir, my surest guides in this respect. However allow me to add that my initial instructions, which you claim to be my only guidelines, have received a wider interpretation than what their strict and literal sense would imply, relative to the degree of personal inconvenience General Bonaparte now suffers.

You add "The Emperor wishes no favors..."

I do not claim the power to do General Bonaparte a favor, much less the arrogance of subjecting him to an act of my whim. He is under no restriction my government is not aware of and which the entire world cannot know.

I will take this occasion to remind you that General Bonaparte himself, in the two conversations I have had with him, noted to me that as general officer I had to act in accordance with my instructions and do my duty as an order I was to fulfill; on another occasion, he refused to allow any direct or public inspection. How can these constraints be reconciled with the narrow limits within which you now seek to restrain the exercise of my duty?

The opinions you have presented to me coincide with my own (seeing that all exercise of my discretionary power even in the case where I try to act the most favorably only engenders new arguments). But when such opposite sentiments are expressed to me you will recognize, sir, the difficulty of reconciling them.

You say, sir, "The Emperor has asked me to protest against the existence of all restrictions..."

It is essential to my duty, each time that circumstances allow, to take into consideration all communications made to me on behalf of the person you so designate. However it would be impossible to give official notification of a measure arising from a particular circumstance before that circumstance had brought about its necessity.

The measure of which you speak was not of a nature to be communicated in advance, but it was certainly not put into effect before you had been given knowledge of it.

I remain, etc.

Hudson Lowe, Lieutenant General

CHAPTER EIGHTEEN

Admiral Plampin — Boredom — The Longwood gardens

$\mathcal{A}$ ship arriving from China on June 5 had announced that Lord Amherst, British ambassador to China, was soon to arrive in Saint Helena. Mr. Mannering was on that ship, the man who had visited Tibet and seen the Great Lama. Dr. O'Meara had talked to him in town and had told the Emperor of Mr. Mannering's desire to be presented to him. The Emperor wished very much to talk with this traveler, but wanting nothing changed in the system he had adopted of not receiving visits, he was going to deprive himself of this distraction. The grand marshal however suggested the idea of receiving Mr. Mannering at his home, where the Emperor would arrive as if by chance and find him there. The Emperor took that suggestion and talked to the great scientist. Mr. Mannering said that the Great Lama was an intelligent child, aged about seven at the time he saw him. Most of his income resulted from the beliefs of the people and the princes in that part of the world. Neither he nor his priests could marry. According to them they could, through positive signs, determine when a spirit transferred from one body to another. If the Emperor was satisfied by certain answers to his questions regarding the administrative and topographical aspects of those countries, he was less so with those given him on the subject of religion. Mr. Mannering seized that opportunity to remind the Emperor that when he was held prisoner in France after the breach of the treaty of Amiens, orders had been given to release him as soon as they learned he was traveling for research valuable to the arts and society.

When Lord Amherst arrived near the end of June, he asked to be received by the Emperor; that ambassador had failed in the mission

given him by his government by not submitting to the kowtow.[309] The
Emperor had learned of that incident in the British newspapers and
blamed the ambassador for not having submitted, saying on this occasion that an ambassador was not the sovereign regardless of what
diplomacy dictates; a king never saw his equal in the ambassador of
another king, and the latter was only entitled to be treated with the
consideration and privileges granted to high-ranking men in that state.
By refusing the ceremony of the Kowtow, he had lost for his government all the benefits he could have derived from his mission.

Lord Amherst received from the Emperor the audience that
had not been granted to Sir Hudson Lowe at his arrival on the islands.
Generals Montholon and Gourgaud remained in the parlor (which was
used as the service quarters on these occasions) with the Ambassador's
retinue, while the grand marshal introduced Lord Amherst in the draw-

---

[309]William Pitt, first Earl of Amherst, left in his diary the account of his long visit to
the Emperor. Sir Henry Ellis, secretary on Lord Amherst's mission to China, has written at the end of his book: "Bonaparte's fortune was much changed, and nevertheless I
would be lying if I said that as I was about to appear before this man so recently the
terror and astonishment of the world, I felt my usual calm. Certainly the antechamber
where I was waiting resembled scarcely that of the Tuileries, but the former Emperor,
in my estimation, could do without the decor of a palace; his actions alone sufficed to
be imposing. I did not consider him diminished by the loss of his sovereign dignity, for
his former power, his formidable armies, and his splendid court that were the envy of
hereditary monarchs barely added to the prestige of his genius, in my opinion. I felt I
was about to find myself in the presence of an intellect whose nature and extent would
be far above mine."

"Well, how is my friend the Shah?" The Emperor talked for a half hour; words
seemed to come to him as fast as ideas. "If Russia organizes Poland, she will be irre-
sistible," he said, and speaking in English: "What did you gain by making war on me?
The possession of my person and the opportunity to show yourself without generosity!
You still have your centuries-old bravado, but you shall never be a military power."
And he added: "England has fallen since it has gotten mixed up in the affairs of the
continent." Henry Ellis felt that his manners were agreeable, his attitude a remarkable
mixture of simplicity and conscious superiority. O'Meara in his *Voice from Saint Helena* and a letter from Hudson Lowe in disgrace sent in August 1822 to Lord Amherst,
as well as the ambassador's reply dated October 2, 1822 (Lowe Papers) says regarding
the conversation with Lord Amherst:

"Would you go out more than I do if outside of the presence of an officer, you
could say nothing but good morning to the people that you met?" the Emperor had
asked.

"I would do as you do, I would not leave my room," replied Lord Amherst.

ing room where the Emperor was, and remained with them. Saint-Denis and Noverraz remained at the doors to the drawing room and the verandah. If Lord Amherst's reception by the Emperor and his officers was marked by consideration for him and his retinue, they for their part were equally respectful and courteous in their manners and words.

The Emperor appeared satisfied with the audience he had just granted. He had found in Lord Amherst as much wit as knowledge. When the ambassador suggested a conciliatory mission with Hudson Lowe, he seized the opportunity to stop him after the first few words and tell him all he felt toward this man. He promised to hide nothing from the prince regent, and respectfully offered his intervention with Hudson Lowe. "It would be useless," replied the Emperor, interrupting him. "Crime, and his hatred of me, are in that man's nature; he has a need to torture me. He is like a tiger, sinking his claws into his prey whose agony he takes pleasure in prolonging. Tell the prince regent, tell the Parliament of which you are one of the principal members that I am waiting, as a favor, for the executioner's hatchet to put an end to my jailer's outrages!" The Emperor, during this audience, had his hat under his arm; it could be seen that it carried no cockade, as he had told me a few days before to take it away and set it aside.

The Emperor was about to suffer a loss that would be felt all the more because it would not be replaced. Admiral Malcolm, who so much wished to see the Emperor's position made more bearable on this miserable rock and blamed the excessive severity of the instructions given to the governor, was about to leave Saint Helena. He had often offered his services in bringing about a reconciliation between Hudson Lowe and the Emperor, without ever having succeeded. He came to ask to present his successor, Admiral Plampin,[310] who had arrived on the *Conqueror*. A few days later General Bingham asked the Emperor to allow the officers of the 53rd regiment who were leaving Saint Helena to come and take their leave of him. This regiment was being replaced by the 66th.

On July 2 Admiral Malcolm came to introduce his successor, Admiral Plampin. The Emperor had learned from Dr. O'Meara that the son of Sir Robert Wilson was on board the *Conqueror*; he told the admiral to bring him, that he would be very pleased to see the son of the man who had saved the life of one of his best friends. But the audience was short; it gave an indication of the poor relations that were to be established between the Emperor and this new admiral who was polite, cold, and not well disposed toward the Emperor.

On July 12 the Emperor received the officers corps of the 53rd. As they entered the drawing room the officers formed a semicircle, and the Emperor spoke to each of them, asking: how many campaigns, how many wounds? "I shall always learn with pleasure of any good fortune encountered by the 53rd, for whom I have only praise. You must be very sad," he said to General Bingham, "to see so many brave men leave." Captain Poppleton, the duty officer at Longwood, who had always known how to combine his surveillance duty with the attention and consideration due misfortune, received indications of personal benevolence from the Emperor. The attitude of the officers corps was that of regret on leaving Saint Helena at leaving the Emperor on this desolate piece of land. We had in the service of our household a few Englishmen belonging to the 53rd. They told us that when they left Saint Helena, the entire regiment would have liked to be able to take Napoleon with them and see him live in a fine castle in England. These sentiments did not surprise us; officers and soldiers had always shown much care and consideration toward him. Those

---

[310]Rear Admiral Robert Plampin (1762-1834), rather vulgar and of mediocre mind, was an archenemy of the French, whose language he spoke, but whom he had fought since Toulon (1793); he was full of hatred for Napoleon. His arrival caused a scandal in Saint Helena; he indeed presented to Lady Lowe as his wife a woman who was not! Reverend Boys clamored from the pulpit against the morals of this officer, but Hudson Lowe tolerated him in exchange for the promise of increased severity toward the inhabitants of Longwood. The Emperor received him on July 3, 1817, along with Captain Davie, commanding the *Conqueror*, and Secretary Elliott, presented by Sir Pulteney Malcolm. Napoleon and Plampin could not bear one another. The admiral described the Emperor in the most disrespectful terms, and the latter in turn judged him without indulgence: "that little man of some 60 years with a very unpleasant appearance. He resembles one of these vulgar Dutch sailors who are always drunk and whom I have seen in their country, seated at a table, pipe in mouth, with a piece of cheese and a bottle of gin in front of them." Admiral Plampin left the island in July 1820.

who were in the service of the household received a gratification on leaving and were replaced by Chinese.

General Gourgaud, without being bedridden, had always suffered from great intestinal weakness that never left him, and like all intestinal problems it generally made him sad. The Emperor sought to combat this through work and conversation, reminding the general of his activity on the battlefields and the glory he had acquired there. The Emperor, believing that the general might be worried about his future, one day went to talk to him about it in a fatherly way as the man was forced to stay in bed. The general was concerned about his mother, whom he loved dearly. An hour later, he received an open letter to be sent on to France. It was a pension of 12,000 francs for Mme Gourgaud, revertible to her son. General Gourgaud was not the only beneficiary of imperial munificence. General Montholon had left France hurriedly; the Emperor, learning indirectly of some financial difficulties he had left there, immediately made a certain sum available to him, so that preoccupations of this nature would not disrupt the completely devoted life he had come to offer him. I could record here many similar events, in the days of his grandeur, toward many people who, when events turned against him, abandoned him. I prefer to keep silent on the names of those who received these magnificent gifts, rather than be forced to record their ingratitude.

Among the people who were leaving, General Gourgaud found a way to pass on a letter to Prince Eugène dictated by the Emperor, along with the pension certificate for 12,000 francs that the prince was instructed to make up to Mme Gourgaud out of the funds he held for the Emperor. He used the same means to announce to his mother what the Emperor was doing for her. It was a happy day for him.

The Emperor, informed that the general had found in the 53rd the means to send a letter safely, dictated the following letter to him to be sent to Prince Eugène in Munich:

My son, I pray that you open for me a credit of 12,000 francs per month, starting in October 1817, with MM. Andrews and Parker in London.

Write to the banker that Count Bertrand will draw that sum from him every month and that he is to honor it. Here they allow me to lack the most necessary things in life. It is useless for you to write to me, as long as things remain on this footing.

After signing it, the Emperor added in his own hand:

Give news of me to my wife, my mother, and Hortense.

The officers of the 66th regiment requested the honor of being presented to the Emperor. This request was granted; the presentation was made with the same ceremony as for the 53rd. They were introduced by the grand marshal and presented by General Bingham. After the audience, the Emperor invited this high-ranking officer to dine with him. When the general invited the Emperor to take his strolls in the direction of Lady Bingham's cottage the Emperor answered that he would go there with pleasure, if it was located within the authorized limits: "See to it that it is, and I shall come and see you often."

Longwood had just experienced an existence it had not been accustomed to for some time; it soon returned to its habitual calm. The Emperor had again no other distraction in his monotonous life than the news brought back by General Gourgaud from his conversations with the Russian commissioner, or those of Dr. O'Meara with the governor; the latter were caustic and bad-tempered. The Emperor would laugh about it, and when he was told about Hudson Lowe's fits of temper, wished that he might someday die of anger.

The governor had the doctor tell the Emperor that General Bertrand's last letter was the most impertinent he had ever received, and he should remember that General Bertrand remained on the island only because he, Hudson Lowe, permitted it; if he behaved so again, he would be forced to send him immediately to the Cape. He also asked General Bonaparte to let him know who was the author of the infamous slander accusing him of having wanted to break the bust of young Napoleon, and of having prevented the gunner on the *Baring* from selling his goods. The Emperor was shaving while listening to the governor's complaints; he stopped suddenly, and turning to the doctor, said: "Tell him that it was the gunner himself who told the grand marshal that."

The doctor also told him that the governor was already worried about the effect he had had on the officers of the 66th; after the audience, the latter had not hidden their kind impression toward such great misfortune. "I have always told you," replied the Emperor, "that this man's behavior is that of the petty tyrants in Italy whose conduct is always devious and mysterious. Tell him, when he talks to you about me, that he bores me with his insinuations, and that his conduct with regard to the bust of my son is in keeping with all his actions since my arrival."

Captain Poppleton had just left us; he was replaced by Captain Blakeney of the 66th, who soon became bored with a duty requiring him to provide a surveillance that went against his character. Knowing this surveillance went as far as coming under his windows to listen to what he was saying, the Emperor had told Noverraz to make him two gardens parallel to the drawing room and the parlor, extending the entire length of the main building. They measured 60 feet in length and were as wide as the building wing, that measured 30 feet. A small wooden fence was placed around each of them, and the sentries were thus distanced that far. Pick and shovel were soon put to task in what had been only a scorched lawn, and the ground was dug deeply enough so that trees or plants to be brought there could grow easily. Trees that had been dug up with very large earth balls were carefully brought to the house. Although they were far away, they provided the Emperor with shade which he appreciated all the more as he could enjoy it in his robe, whereas previously he had to go some distance from the building in order to shade his head from the strong sun. The most remarkable of our plantings were very handsome twin lemon trees, transplanted as described above and placed facing one another. Their branches formed a high arbor, so that six people could dine underneath, and the serving was not hindered by them. The Emperor often had lunch in that shade, and sometimes even dictated there. He liked to make himself invisible to the duty captain. An arbor was built in one of the gardens; passion plants climbed over it and within a year covered it in such a way as to make it impenetrable to the rays of the sun.

These two gardens provided distraction for the Emperor, who had a small pump purchased in town and amused himself watering his flowers while Noverraz and Saint-Denis worked the pump lever. One of the gardens could be reached through the French doors in the dining room, but the one under his bedroom windows did not have any. With the Emperor's approval, Count de Montholon had one of the windows in the second room converted into a French door, allowing the Emperor to go from his apartment into either one of the two small gardens. They increased the size of his private quarters by that much, and provided him pleasures he had not imagined before, such as that of taking an interest in the development of the trees, rosebushes, or flowers before him while strolling with one or another of these gentlemen. These gardens could not have been made a few months earlier, when there was barely enough water for the Emperor's bath and for the household. Today water was not lacking, and the watering they received gave them a freshness that contrasted with the dried-out nature of everything surrounding them.

Being a faithful reporter, Dr. O'Meara reported to Longwood his conversations with the governor, and whatever they might be, he lost nothing in the esteem of the Emperor, who had always trusted him. Such was not the case when he repeated the Emperor's words at Plantation House. The governor flew into rages in which he accused Dr. O'Meara of having sold out to the French. He threatened to have him taken to the Cape bound hand and foot, if he managed to get his hands on his illegal correspondence. "Your General Bonaparte pretends to be sick and he is not. You back up his statements; his complaints against me are infamous lies. He knows it well, but it is a system to substantiate his complaints and interest Europe in his person. He should know that the truth regarding his situation is known, and that I treat him too well! Tell him so."

The Emperor reassured the doctor regarding the power the governor claimed of being able to take him away from him. "If he could do so, he would not take such great care with you. You annoy him enough through your relations with the island inhabitants and the squadron sailors for him to send you away. You may be sure that if Lord Bathurst wants Lowe to kill me, he does not want it said that he killed me with a doctor of his choice, and that the first thing his government recommended to him was not to take you away from me without my consent."

Apart from these violent outbursts that Dr. O'Meara caused at Plantation House, General Gourgaud found during his strolls men who sympathized with the Emperor's position, assuring him of a better future: among others, the Russian commissioner received from his court, to which he had written, complete censure of the harassment the Emperor was subjected to. His correspondence even urged him to go to Longwood and take whatever means necessary to make himself welcome there. This news pleased the Emperor, but nothing came of it. Count Balmain had fallen in love with Mrs. Lowe's daughter, a handsome woman to whom he proposed marriage. This alliance was about to take place, and the governor viewed with concern General Gourgaud's encounters with the man who was to become his son-in-law; they became less frequent and less communicative. The other two commissioners would have liked nothing better than to come to Longwood, but it would have meant breaking off relations with the governor. They left the responsibility for the measures to the latter, as it was not part of their instructions. Time therefore was spent in illusions conceived on one day, to be destroyed the next. The fact is that these gentlemen were not introduced, because the Emperor did not want to receive them in their official capacity.

The following August 15 on the occasion of his birthday, the Emperor received the compliments of these ladies and his officers. It was the third anniversary, which reminded us of the preceding feasts in the days of the Empire. Like the previous year, the Emperor took pleasure in giving the children presents consisting of double Italian napoleons, which he had me ask for, and he gave the ladies some chains from China.

In the early days of September races took place at the camp. The governor went there, as did the population of the island; the allied powers commissioners came there too. By using his battlefield spy-glass, the Emperor was able to see them from his quarters, but in order to get closer he went to Count Bertrand's house. Once the races had ended, the commissioners approached the perimeter gate in the hope of seeing the Emperor; Mme Stürmer, on horseback, was among them. The grand marshal and General Gourgaud went to speak with them, without either party asking to cross the gate. Without being seen, the Emperor eyed Baroness Stürmer, whom he found attractive and well seated on her horse. It was reported to the Emperor that Sir Hudson Lowe, having noticed the commissioners heading for Longwood, had gone home furious, imagining there was going to be communication between them and the Emperor, in a fortuitous manner without official presentation.

If we could have forgotten that Saint Helena owed its exist-ence to a volcano, underground fires took it upon themselves to remind us of that fact; one evening we were surprised by an earth-quake. It was 10 p.m., everyone was in bed or had gone to his quarters. The Emperor was in his bed, I was reading him a song from the Char-lemagne poem published by Prince Lucien, when suddenly violent shaking made me jump out of my chair, and lifted the Emperor in his bed. "What is that," he said to me, "an earthquake, or has the *Con-queror* blown up?" I immediately went out to seek information: I found everyone at their doors, saying it was an earthquake. I came back to tell this to the Emperor, who had not left his bed; the duration of this earthquake was between 15 and 20 seconds. That was all we needed: an earthquake, to make our stay on Saint Helena more enjoy-able! The shaking had been vertical; we learned the next day that the ships in the harbor had also felt it, and later, by ships arriving from the Cape, that it had been felt in that city. Cipriani and those who lodged above the Emperor told me they had been frightened by the noise from the roof and the partitions; Count Bertrand's and Count de Montho-lon's children were awakened by it.

The Emperor spoke one day of his admiration for the marvel-ous Nile River that, thanks to its overflowing each year, brings the necessary fertilizer to that beautiful country. He told Dr. O'Meara, who had been to Egypt, that as he was going to the pyramids with the expedition scientists he came across a caravan that had just been ransacked. The leader of the caravan came to see him and introduced his two daughters, covered with veils from head to foot. "They implored my protection," he said, "and seized my hands, which they kissed and found very attractive. This was during a halt, and my tent was set up. They went inside, I had them served sherbet, and I gave orders that searches be made at once in the tribes where the thefts had occurred. I had," continued the Emperor, "made the heads of the tribe responsible for the extortion and assassinations that took place in each of them. They hurried to return the stolen objects. The caravan resumed its way, after expressing its gratitude to me. Once in Cairo, they proclaimed that Sultan Kebir[311] was a protector of the true believers; the rumor went around that I was a friend of the prophet, and that the French were not infidels."

The doctor reminded him of the Cairo revolt, and the vigor with which it had been repressed. "Yes! without a doubt," said the Emperor, "we had every reason to fear the fanatics; the feelings of several of the sheiks were not favorable to us, among them those of Sheik Saada. This old fanatic, broken by the years and a descendant of the prophet's family, was highly revered and marched at the head of the rebels. I nevertheless had him arrested and thrown in jail, and with him some twenty of the more mutinous, whom I had put in the citadel and beheaded. As I knew the love of the people for the old sheik, I had him come before me. He was expecting a legitimate punishment; he threw himself on his knees when he came in, and admitted he was guilty. I kindly had him get up, spared his life, and requested his friendship. Kléber walked in at that instant and asked me when we were alone who that man was he had just seen kneeling before me. He was the leader of the rebellion, I said to him. "What! and you did not have him hanged?"

"No, I prefer to leave to the people this old man who can't mount a horse anymore, and cut off the heads of those who, more fit

---

[311]Kebir—Mighty Sultan—Ed.

for execution, are full of audacity." Once the rebellion had been put down, the sheiks came in great ceremony to ask pardon for the culprits. I had Sheik Saada brought in, and handed him over to them. As they seemed to expect that the others would come also, I told them the heavens had ordered that they be executed. They fell to their knees and said to me: 'They deserved it, they were truly guilty!' My clemency toward this old sheik showed in their eyes, my respect for the prophet's blood, and earned me friends among them. Had Kléber acted in the same way," the Emperor continued, "he would not have been assassinated. Having learned that this same sheik did not wish to make the payoff, instead of seeing in him an old flag they waved and seizing his advisors, he had him thrown in prison and mistreated. The people and the higher-ups were infuriated by that, and holy war was declared against him. The priests were informed of his assassin's plans by written notes he would leave each day at the mosque; one of them even asked if holy war against an infidel could please God. Receiving an affirmative answer from the priest, the assassin proceeded to carry out the crime he had been on the point of renouncing, because of the difficulty of the endeavor. When he reached Kléber, he presented him with a petition and took advantage of the moment when he was reading it to strike him down. He ran away and was found not far from there, praying, his face turned towards the east. That death meant the loss of Egypt, which Kléber's cleverness would certainly have kept for us."

We were approaching the end of 1817. A sort of status quo prevailed in the news, when a ship arriving from Europe brought newspapers and letters that were sent to Longwood. The Emperor learned with some dissatisfaction that Santini had been arrested in Vienna, and a town in Germany had been assigned him as a prison. He had already blamed his pamphlet; he also blamed a move that, although made with good intentions, could lead people to believe he had been asked to do it. This ill temper increased as a result of reports Dr. O'Meara gave to the governor which the doctor had not told him of; he was called 'General Bonaparte' in them. The Emperor demanded the doctor's word of honor that he would not give any further health bulletins without his permission, or he would no longer receive him. These annoyances occurred at a time when the Emperor was ill. He complained about his side, and about his legs being swollen. "I would have lived to the age of 80," he said to the doctor, "if the poor treatment I endure here and the abominable climate where I have been placed were not killing me sooner." The matter of the bulletins was about to renew the bitterness in relations between Longwood and Plantation House. However, Sir Hudson Lowe informed the grand marshal that he was removing the prohibition on entering the house in the valley and talking to people the Emperor and his officers might meet along their way. The Emperor had some hope that things would be returned to the way they were under Admiral Cockburn, and had him reply these last measures would change nothing to his resolve not to go out on horseback until matters had been restored to the state they were in on the governor's arrival.

Count de Las Cases, having returned from the Cape, was in the Saint Helena harbor and wrote to Count Bertrand to inform him of his return to Europe. He told him he had had unloaded two small kegs of wine from Constance for the Emperor, one red and one white, and conveyed his respects to the Emperor and his regards to his companions in exile. The Emperor called this Constance wine the Las Cases Wine.

Countess Bertrand had said to the Emperor on presenting her son to him: "Here's a Frenchman who entered Longwood without the governor's permission." Countess de Montholon, who had just given birth to a daughter, could use the same words when she presented her to him; it was her second child since she had arrived in Saint Helena. The Emperor was the godfather, as he had been for the first one. The aftermath of that pregnancy was not as fortunate as the first, but gave no hint that a year later a return to Europe was the only thing that would restore Countess de Montholon's health.

Princess Borghèse had learned that the wine given to the Emperor was no good, and had done him harm; she hurried to send a large number of cases of wine through the intermediary of Lady Holland, so that they could reach Saint Helena. She renewed the request she had previously made, to come to share and ease the Emperor's captivity. He was touched by his sister's sustained devotion, but still refused, no matter how great his affection for the princess. Lady Holland added to this shipment some boxes of delicacies which she begged the Emperor to accept.

One day Dr. O'Meara was visiting the Emperor and telling him about the difficulties the governor was causing him over the bulletins and his stern refusal to accept them with any other title than that of General Bonaparte. "I do not want this," the Emperor said, "because these bulletins go to the commissioners, and I do not want people to think I agree with this qualification. If I must lose you, I will lose you, but I shall never be forced to receive another doctor that is not of my own choosing. They insist on wanting to give me Baxter, and I do not want him." As the Emperor continued to speak, he suddenly saw the doctor collapse, fortunately in an armchair that happened to be behind him. The Emperor called out in a loud voice; I was writing in the adjoining room, entered quickly, and found him busy undoing the doctor's necktie which seemed to be bothering him. I grabbed a bottle of cologne and poured a large quantity of it on a handkerchief which the Emperor applied to his temples, while I put a bottle of smelling salts under his nose. As he regained his senses, he said to the Emperor he had been bled that morning, which had brought about this loss of consciousness. "I feared," said the Emperor, "that it was a stroke: your face became that of a dead man; I thought your soul had left you." As he was retiring, the Emperor motioned to me to accompany him.

CHAPTER NINETEEN

The Emperor's health deteriorates —
General Gourgaud's departure — False health bulletins —
The governor removes O'Meara

*M*onths went by without bringing any change in the Emperor's situation; the year 1818 was filled with events each more sad than the last. One could not avoid noticing that the Emperor's health was deteriorating visibly, and that only great moral strength allowed him to bear the difficulties of his captivity. Dr. O'Meara's refusal to comply with Sir Hudson Lowe's orders regarding the bulletins earned him an order not to go outside the Longwood compound; they claimed his visits in town and on board the ships of the squadron had no other purpose than to arrange intelligence measures to convey to England infamous lies against the governor. Sir Hudson Lowe wanted to force him to give him a full accounting of his conversations with General Bonaparte, and when the doctor reported to him what people thought of him at Longwood, he would go into violent rages. Dr. O'Meara himself insisted that the Emperor see Dr. Baxter who, he said, was a man of great talent and faultless character. "I believe all the good you say about him," replied the Emperor, "but M. Lowe wants to impose him on me, and for the sole reason that he is his friend, I shall never agree to have him near me. I could have accepted a doctor from Admiral Cockburn, who did not inspire distrust in me, but I am too ill inclined toward M. Lowe to accept one coming from him."

It was in the midst of all these annoyances that news of Prin-

cess Charlotte's death reached Longwood;[312] the Emperor was saddened by this event. As the princess had criticized his captivity on
Saint Helena, it could be hoped that once she gained the throne, she
would change or ameliorate the Emperor's situation. The Russian and
Austrian commissioners, whom these gentlemen met at times, conveyed fine words from their courts, but nothing in them constituted an
order for them to brave the governor's ill will and be presented at
Longwood, as they seemed to wish to be. The Emperor therefore
remained at the mercy of the British government, and they remained
powerless spectators to the application of the vexatious and monstrous
restrictions dictated by Lord Bathurst.

To these concerns was added the departure of General Gourgaud, whose continuous relapses weakened his health. The Emperor
had complained more than once about his irritable nature, and after
having endured these continuous annoyances, he got angry. He
advised him to request his return to Europe, because he did not wish
him to fight any longer against the destructive climate. The governor
hastened to approve his request. On January 13, the general left Longwood to go to Plantation House, accompanied by an engineering
officer, Mr. Jackson.[313] He was quartered at Bayle Cottage with this
same officer who did not leave him until they set out to sea. He waited
a month for a vessel from the East India Company to take him directly
to Europe without going by way of the Cape. His physical and mental
suffering must have been awful during this long month, having been
unable to communicate with Longwood. The Emperor did not forget
his devotion, nor the brilliant qualities of his former ADC whom he
knew to be most attached to him, and he would have liked for Generals
Montholon and Gourgaud to live as brothers. Since he could not have

---

[312]This is Charlotte Augusta, daughter of George, Prince of Wales. In 1816 she had
married Leopold of Saxe-Coburg, the future king of Belgium, and died in 1817.

[313]Basil Jackson (1795-1889), a staff lieutenant, arrived in Saint Helena at the same
time as Hudson Lowe. Under the orders of Major Emmett, he was in charge of inspecting the Longwood buildings (the old and new houses) and Bertrand's villa. Jackson
drew quite well and left many sketches. He had a conversation with the Emperor in
July 1817 and left the island in July 1819.

this, he had to regain his disturbed tranquillity by sending away the man who thwarted this desire. Their inability to get along was not based on motives of ambition, but on an equal share in the Emperor's affection, which the general quite wrongly believed he did not have.

General Gourgaud's work was going to be added to that of General Montholon; the grand marshal, farther away from the main house, would naturally be called on less often to attend to the Emperor. However the Emperor, not wishing the distractions provided by work to become tiresome, made greater use of me, either for reading during the day whether he was in his bath or not or having me write under his dictation. Very often, so as not to disturb Count de Montholon at night, he had Noverraz or Saint-Denis call me. He tried to use Saint-Denis, but he could not keep up with the Emperor; he remained in charge of straightening out his dictation, a task he performed very well as he had beautiful handwriting. Furthermore, if the Emperor wanted to have a manuscript sent to Europe, it was thus easier for it to escape the investigation of the governor and his agents.

This sad departure was followed two weeks later by a death as painful as it was regrettable for everyone in the colony. Cipriani had just died, struck down dead in two days' time; he died of awful intestinal pains, that came on him very suddenly. The Emperor truly missed him, and told me he would have accompanied him to his final resting place, had it been inside the compound. A large number of island notables and garrison officers joined the entire French colony who followed him to the cemetery at Plantation House. I alone remained with the Emperor during that sad day. General Gourgaud, who had not yet left the island, asked to join the cortege, but permission was denied him.

I had known Cipriani very well on Elba; he then had a charming young wife and two children he had brought with him. I shared his happiness and his sorrows, and our friendship from the island of Elba had only deepened on Saint Helena. Cipriani was a Corsican, and he had almost been brought up in the Emperor's household. He felt there was a mystery surrounding the death of his mother, whom he said had been found strangled in her bed. As a young man he found a protector in M. Saliceti, who was then in Italy; he became superintendent of his household, and because of his rare intelligence, was given delicate missions which he successfully carried out. He was soon involved in secret police matters, and would have reached a high position but for the death of his protector. Having acquired a good deal of money, he entered the shipping business and went to sea. The year 1815 found him in this situation, when he entered the Emperor's service on the island of Elba as butler. Cipriani was deeply attached to the Emperor, his character was strong, his heart kind, and his soul sensitive. He died of an inflammation of the lower abdomen, with the most alarming symptoms; it quickly became critical. The Emperor was quite worried, sending me constantly for news of him. On the first day he was still able to speak to me of his wife and children, whom he entrusted to the Emperor. During the night of the 25th to the 26th, the Emperor summoned Dr. O'Meara and asked if his presence would be good for Cipriani. The doctor advised him against it, saying he was still conscious enough that his love and veneration for him might bring about an emotion that would hasten his death. The following day Cipriani was no longer. He was a self-made man, had seen and retained much, and this made his conversation most interesting and lively. He was a reliable man, his feelings were republican, and he greatly admired the Girondists, of whom he had known several, and who had become his friends. May he be honored here by the memory I keep of him.

The Emperor asked me to prepare an inventory of Cipriani's belongings and papers. He told me to give these to the grand marshal, who was to send Mme Cipriani the Emperor's regrets on her husband's death, and a pension as proof of satisfaction for his good services. Cipriani had been taken to the cemetery by a Protestant priest. On this occasion, and in connection with the christening of the children of Countesses Bertrand and Montholon who had been born in Longwood, the Emperor regretted there was no priest in the establishment to attend Cipriani during his last moments and take him to his final resting place. Preoccupied by this thought, he later had Count Bertrand write to Cardinal Fesch, asking him to send a French or an Italian priest, learned, with whom he would be able to converse.

This death had caused all of us great sadness.[314]

A month after that another death occurred, touching us much less, but demonstrating with what speed one could be stricken by such inflammations of the lower abdomen. It was the death of a maid serving Countess de Montholon for her daughter, Mlle Napoléone. Like Cipriani, she was gone within a few days. That woman was British. Everyone was surprised that, being in perfect health, the young woman was taken by death so quickly.

Since he had been at Bayle Cottage, GeneralGourgaud had not been left for one minute by Lieutenant Jackson. Only the commissioners had been able to see him and offer him some company during the long month he had been away from Longwood. Before leaving, he expressed the wish to talk with the grand marshal, but the latter said he would refuse if the presence of a British officer were insisted upon. The governor in turn stood firm in those conditions. He nevertheless allowed Dr. O'Meara to see the general before he left. But as this was in the presence of Mr. Jackson, who did not leave them alone one moment, he could not pass on anything about his conversations with the commissioners and the governor himself that could have been of

---

[314]Regarding Cipriani's death, the grand marshal wrote to Cardinal Fesch on March 22, 1818:

"He died on February 27 last at 4 p.m. and was buried in the Protestant cemetery in this country. The ministers of that church paid him the same respects they would have given to one of their own religion; the death certificate states he died a member of the Apostolic and Roman church. The minister of the church of this country would have gladly attended him at the time of his death, but he would have wanted a Catholic priest; as we do not have one, he preferred not to bother with a minister of another religion. The child of one of Count de Montholon's servants had died at Longwood a few days before. A chambermaid also died a few days ago of the same illness. It is the result of the unhealthy climate.

"We feel the need for a minister of our faith. You are our bishop; we wish you to send one, a Frenchman or an Italian. Please choose a well educated man, under 40, with an even temper, and not a head filled with anti-Gallican principles." Lastly, the grand marshal sent to the cardinal: "Cipriani's wallet, a pin he generally wore, a detailed accounting of everything owed him, namely 8,287 francs or £345, and a letter of credit to settle that amount with his heirs. Knowing that you are taking care of his son and that his daughter is with Madame Mère, the Emperor is waiting to know what fortune Cipriani leaves, as he appears to have had considerable funds invested in Genoa, in order to ensure a future for his two children."

interest to the Emperor. He left on March 15, 1817, taking with him a draft for 500 louis [20,000 francs] that the grand marshal had given him.

As I have said previously, the Emperor wanted work to be a distraction and not a burden for these gentlemen. But of the four people among whom it had been divided, only two remained—and one of those was separated from him at 9 p.m. General Montholon therefore had the largest share of work to do. This is what happened: the grand marshal gave up some of his family activities to spend more time with the Emperor, but Count de Montholon—without the grand marshal losing any of the Emperor's esteem and his old friendship for him— became the man sharing his everyday habits and his affection, until the day he died. Count de Montholon became entirely the Emperor's man, and this sacrifice was even more complete when the countess' health forced her to return to Europe. If I mention the small part I played in making myself useful to the Emperor either in his work or in reading aloud to him to drive away his worries it is that I too am happy, within my modest sphere, to have contributed to easing his suffering on that awful rock, and to have deserved the honorable title of friend, which he gave me when inscribing my name in his immortal will.

The duties of butler were given to M. Pierron, the pantry chief, a discreet man who had been brought up in the Emperor's household and had followed him to the island of Elba. Like Cipriani, he went into town every week, accompanied by a soldier to whom he handed over his horse's reins on arriving. Free to move about, he went into the various stores without being followed, and like Cipriani was able to receive from or hand over to an island tradesman letters or small packages entrusted to him. Count de Montholon for his part went out riding more often than in the days of General Gourgaud; he sometimes went into town, and if he found the commissioners there, would report his discussions with them to the Emperor, which provided topics for conversation. The Emperor also found a precious resource in Countess de Montholon, who according to him combined great distinction with a firmness of character rarely encountered in her sex. Countess Bertrand, although more capricious, nevertheless helped him pass a few hours of the day, and made up for the news Dr. O'Meara could no longer bring, as he was forbidden to leave the Longwood enclosure.

Conversation, work, a few horseback or carriage rides and walks: such was the Emperor's life since General Gourgaud's departure, being that illness did not keep him at home. When Mr. Balcombe and his family came to Longwood, the pass granted by the governor stated "to see Countess Bertrand," but once they had entered, that family and particularly the young girls could not resist their natural desire to see the Emperor before leaving the island. The Emperor was kind and gracious to his guests, and wished to show his thanks for the kind hospitality he had received from them at The Briars. In giving his errands to the head of that family, he added a gift and a draft on London for 72,000 francs, and gave him a pension of 12,000 francs per year, asking him to take care of his affairs in Europe. The Emperor requested him to see his family and let them know about the shameful way he was being treated. Mr. Balcombe, without failing in his duty to his government, was able to satisfy the Emperor's wishes. The governor was informed that he had allowed himself to call on General Bonaparte without being authorized to do so, and showed much irritation. The Emperor learned with pleasure that on his arrival in England he had been named general purveyor for New Holland. As his successor in his firm on the island, he designated Mr. Hower, who had previously been introduced to the Emperor.

The matter of the health reports had come to a head; the Emperor had learned that the statements on his health given to the foreign commissioners were signed by a doctor he did not see; Dr. Baxter, the very same man whom Sir Hudson Lowe was so anxious to place near his person! Count de Montholon had ascertained this at the home of Marquis de Montchenu, and brought proof of this back to Longwood in a copy he had been allowed to take. The evidence of the false reports was well proven. The Emperor protested against such an indignity in a letter dictated to Count de Montholon to be sent to Plantation House. Three other letters, carried secretly to the commissioners the following day, informed them of the Emperor's protest over the false reports to the governor. Extremely embarrassed by this blow,

Lowe sought to explain his conduct to the grand marshal by telling him it was not health reports he was giving the commissioners, but only minutes from the head doctor on the island, based on a verbal report by Dr. O'Meara.

On learning of Dr. O'Meara's house arrest, the Emperor declared he would not accept his care until this was lifted, and not wishing his doctor to be submitted to any disciplinary action urged him to send his resignation to Plantation House. The governor did not dare take such a great responsibility on himself; he suspended the house arrest and informed the grand marshal of this decision by a formal notice. But he kept in his soul all the bitterness brought about by the matter of the health reports, in which the commissioners themselves had gotten involved and which they had considered highly irregular.

Dr. O'Meara had therefore resumed his care of the Emperor, but everyone expected an order to arrive from London forcing him to leave Longwood. He again went all around the island, into town, and on board the ships of the squadron. When he was summoned by Hudson Lowe and reported to him, it was to receive the most discourteous remarks from him. These official storms were reported to the Emperor, who replied: "You no longer have the necessary independence to take care of me; I would rather see you go than know you are treated that way. I have lived too long for them; what they want is for me to die in my bed, without any help." The Emperor at that time was kept in bed by a serious bronchial infection that had interrupted his liver treatment.

As Dr. O'Meara foresaw that any day now the governor's rage against him could result in an order to leave Longwood, he urged the Emperor to call Dr. Stokoe[315] of the *Conqueror* in for consultation. He introduced them and urged the Emperor to call on this man if he himself were forced to leave, for he felt such revulsion at seeing Dr. Baxter. However, Dr. Stokoe's visits could not please the suspicious nature of Hudson Lowe. To take a doctor from the squadron when there were so many good ones in town was in his eyes a means of establishing contact with the outside. From that point on, he subjected him to such investigations that after the second visit the doctor decided to write Admiral Plampin and declare that it was no longer possible for him to return to Longwood.

When the arrival of a ship brought several copies of the Emperor's comments on Lord Bathurst's speech and a few issues of the *Edinburgh Review*[316] mentioning Sir Hudson Lowe's conduct toward him, these were purchased at once by Sir Thomas Reade, so that they would not reach Longwood. However the butler, who went into town, got hold of them and brought them to Count de Montholon, who gave them to the Emperor. A month later Hudson Lowe learned that these publications had arrived at Longwood, and of the Emperor's pleasure in reading them. He had no doubt that Dr. O'Meara was the one who had procured them. The telegraph summoned him to Plantation House, the scene was quite violent, and irritation reached its peak;

---

[315]John Stokoe (1775-1852) was the surgeon on board the *Conqueror* that arrived in Jamestown in June 1817. He was a capable practitioner and an honest man, and became friends with O'Meara. Having expressed a great desire to see the Emperor, he was presented to him on December 10, 1817.

"In one instant," he later wrote, "my opinion of Napoleon changed; he was so different from what I had imagined; after two minutes' conversation, I was at ease with him." Stokoe received a stern reprimand from Plampin and the governor for having spoken to "the General" without permission. By 1819 O'Meara had gone, and the Emperor was without a doctor and needed care. On January 16, 1819, he was called to the Emperor's bedside: Stokoe examined him with care, and concluded in his report that he had acute hepatitis and was extremely weak. He made five calls on Napoleon, and was court-martialed for having represented "the General" as dangerously ill. Stricken from the naval rosters, Stokoe went to America and there paid a visit to Joseph Bonaparte, who had retired in Bordentown, near Philadelphia.

[316]Dr. O'Meara, in his *Napoleon in Exile*, writes on June 28, 1818: "I went into town and tried to purchase a copy of the Comments on Lord Bathurst's Speech, several copies of which I was told had arrived on the island. Captain Bunn from the ship *Mangle*, whom I asked to help me in my search, expressed his surprise at my request, adding that immediately after his arrival Sir Hudson Lowe and Sir Thomas Reade had taken five copies of that pamphlet, to send two or three of them to Longwood, so they said. He said these gentlemen had asked with much urgency an exact inventory of the books he had brought, and had taken all the modern works discussing politics, and all the copies of the *Edinburgh Review*." This did not prevent the Emperor from receiving this liberal review which strongly opposed Lord Liverpool's government, and from reading the Comments on Lord Bathurst's Speech!

Dr. O'Meara's firm and dignified replies were the drops that made the vase overflow. A few days later the threat of sending him away from the island was put into execution. A brig arrived from Europe on July 25, bringing the governor the order to have Dr. O'Meara removed from Longwood. That same day, without any concern for the condition of the Emperor, whom he knew to be ill, the governor sent the following letters to Longwood:

Plantation House, July 25, 1818

Sir,

I have the honor to inform you, so that you may bring this to the attention of Napoleon Bonaparte, that in accordance with instructions I have received from Count Bathurst dated 16 May 1818, I must forbid Mr. O'Meara any kind of services to his person, and that I have consequently given orders that he leave Longwood. On the same occasion Rear Admiral Plampin has received from the lord commissioners of the admiralty instructions concerning him, and relative to his departure from the island.

Regarding Mr. O'Meara's departure, further instructions from Count Bathurst are that I must place Dr. Baxter in charge of providing his care, as a doctor, to Napoleon Bonaparte, whenever it is required; and particularly to recommend that he should consider at all times Napoleon Bonaparte's health as the principal object of his attention. When informing Napoleon Bonaparte of this arrangement, I must not fail to inform him at the same time that should he for any reason be dissatisfied with Dr. Baxter's care as a doctor, or if he should prefer that of any person in the same profession present on the island, I am prepared to acquiesce to his desire on this point and allow the care of any doctor chosen by him, providing that he strictly conforms to the applicable regulations.

Having informed Mr. O'Meara of the order for his departure, I have given Mr. Baxter the necessary instructions. He shall consequently be ready to proceed to Longwood at the first invitation, and when the slightest wish is expressed to him. At the same time, until I can be informed of the personal wishes of Napoleon Bonaparte on this subject, I shall see to it that a medical officer remains available at

Longwood, in the event there should be a reason to call upon him suddenly.

I remain, etc....

/s/ Hudson Lowe, Lieutenant General

Sir,

Lieutenant General Hudson Lowe has asked me to inform you that, following instructions received from Count Bathurst dated May 16, 1818, he has been directed to remove you from the post that you occupy attending to General Bonaparte, and to forbid you any further communication with the inhabitants of Longwood.

Rear Admiral Plampin has received instructions from the lord commissioners of the admiralty regarding your destination when you leave this island.

You shall consequently, immediately on receiving this letter, leave Longwood, without having any other communication with the people residing there.

I remain, etc...

/s/ Edward Wynyard, Lieutenant-Colonel Secretary

Dr. O'Meara, without taking any account of the fact he had been forbidden to do so, rushed to see the Emperor and informed him of the content of the letter he had just received. The Emperor did not seem at all surprised by it, and told him he had been expecting this new outrage at any time. He spoke to him of what he should do on his arrival in Europe, and urged him to see his family and King Joseph. "You shall tell them," he said, "to give you the private and confidential letters that Emperors Alexander and Francis, the King of Prussia, and the other European sovereigns have addressed to me; you shall publish them in order to cover those sovereigns with shame, and show the world the homage they paid me when they asked favors, or begged me to leave them their thrones.[317] When I had strength and power, they solicited my protection and the honor of my alliance. Today, they crush me in my old age. By taking you away from me, doctor, the crime shall be perpetrated faster. If you learn of some slander published against me, contradict it and make sure the truth is known in Europe regarding what is going on here. Your ministers are brazen indeed," he said to him; "when the Pope was my prisoner, I would rather have had my arm cut off than sign an order to touch his doctor."

Dr. O'Meara took with him evidence of munificence equal to the Emperor's trust in him, which his conduct deserved. A small bronze statue of the Emperor, cast during the Hundred Days and which I had brought, was on the mantelpiece. The Emperor noted that he was looking at it with interest; he took it and gave it to him[318] as well as a note written in his hand: "If he sees my good Louise, I beg her to let him kiss her hand." The Emperor shook his hand, embraced him, and said goodbye to him, adding: "Be happy." As he was leaving, he called him back in and said to him: "Tell Lady Holland how grateful I am for all her kindness."

I accompanied the doctor for a few steps when he left the Emperor and told him how disastrous I considered his inopportune departure. The Emperor's health was visibly declining, and we would be without instructions to follow in the future. I then thanked him for his utmost attentive care for the colony and wished him a safe journey.

The evil deed had been done; Dr. O'Meara was taken away from the Emperor at a time when he needed him most. He was having trouble digesting, his legs were slightly swollen, and he had a pain in his side. The Emperor's indignation reached its peak: he had Count de Montholon write a letter to the governor that was taken to the duty officer to be forwarded to Plantation House:

---

[317]The Emperor's wish was only fulfilled in 1939, and then incompletely. See *Lettres personnelles des Souverains à l'Empereur Napoléon Ier*, published by Prince Napoleon and Jean Hanoteau.

In a magnificent preface, the authors established the complex history of the precious documents that came from Prince Napoleon's archives. The first volume includes letters from the sovereigns of Austria, Baden and Prussia. The second volume, dealing with Bavaria, Saxony, and Sweden, has not yet been published.

[318]Among the mementos taken from Saint Helena by Dr. O'Meara was also one of the Emperor's handkerchiefs. This handkerchief, marked with the letter N and a crown, is now exhibited in the museum at Vichy.

Longwood, July 25, 1818
Sir,

    I received your letter at 6 p.m. I cannot give it to the Emperor before tomorrow morning, because he was extremely ill today. While I translated it, I noticed that you made a mistake. You believe, because he called Dr. Stokoe in consultation, that he might receive his services as his regular doctor. I can assure you, in spite of his position, even when facing death he shall receive no care and take no remedies except from the hands of his own doctor. If he is deprived of him, he will take none from anyone, and will consider himself to have been assassinated by you.

    I remain, etc...

    /s/ Montholon

The haste with which the doctor was leaving Longwood did not allow him to give me anything other than the medication that was currently in the Emperor's room, such as mercury pills which he used very reluctantly, laxative salts, and something with which to rub his legs. On arriving in town the doctor did not forget his patient, and the day after his departure from Longwood he sent the following report to the grand marshal.

Dr. O'Meara's Report to the Grand Marshal on the Emperor's Illness

    During the last days of September symptoms developed indicating a disorder in the functioning of the liver. Prior to this period Napoleon had often experienced respiratory infections, headaches, and rheumatism, but these illnesses worsened; his legs and feet became swollen.

    His gums took on a spongy, scurvy-like appearance, and he showed signs of indigestion.

    Oct. 1, 1817. Sharp pains, warmth, a sensation of heaviness in the right abdominal region. These symptoms were accompanied by dyspepsia and constipation.

    Since this time, the illness has not left him; it has made slow but continuous progress. The pain, mild at first, has increased to the point where I fear acute hepatitis. This aggravation of the illness is the result of a severe respiratory infection.

Three molars were infected. Because of this, I believed they were in part causing the inflammation of the jaw muscles and tissues. In addition I believed they had caused the respiratory infections. I pulled them at suitable intervals, and the attacks have since been less frequent.

To combat the scurvy-like appearance of the gums, I advised vegetables and citrus. I was successful; it disappeared, recurred, and was again cleared up by the same means.

Purgatives and massage restored the legs to good health. They were again afflicted after some time, but much less severely. Laxatives, hot baths, and profuse perspiration have often lessened the pain in the abdominal area, but have never completely dispelled it. It worsened appreciably during the course of April and May, became fitful, and caused first constipation, then diarrhea, followed by copious voiding of bile and mucus. At the same time the stomach pain and flatulence were being experienced, disappearance of appetite, sensation of sluggishness, anxiety, pale face, yellowing of the whites of the eyes, strong dark urine, mental exhaustion, and headaches. The illness was not felt on the left side. The patient experienced sensations of heat in the lower right side of the abdomen, nausea from time to time, vomiting of acrid and viscous bile which worsened with the pain, almost total sleeplessness, discomfort, weakness.

The ailment in the legs returned, but less seriously than at first. Headaches, anxiety, pressure in the stomach area, high fever at nightfall, burning skin, thirst, heart pain, rapid pulse; calming, sweating toward daybreak, are all constant symptoms of the patient. The abundant sweating dissipates the fever. There is perceptible swelling on the right side of the abdomen that can be felt with external pressure. Tongue almost constantly coated, the pulse which prior to the illness was 54 to 60 beats per minute now is elevated to 98, pain over the shoulder blade. To stimulate the stomach and liver and encourage secretion of bile I administered two purgatives; relief, but of short duration. During the early days of June the results were weak and short-lived. I suggested mercury, but the patient showed an extreme loathing for it; he refused this medication in no matter what form it was disguised.

I also advised horseback riding, massaging the abdominal area each day with a brush, wearing flannel, taking hot baths, some medications, diversions, following a diet, not going out in bad weather or exposing himself to extremes of weather. He neglected the two most important elements of exercise and diversions. Finally on June 11 we overcame his repugnance and I was able to administer mercury to him. He took mercury pills and continued this treatment until the 16th. I gave them to him night and morning, and from time to time other purgatives to clear up the constipation. After six days I changed the prescription and substituted calomel, but it caused stomach pain, vomiting, diarrhea, and general anxiety; I ceased to employ it. I gave it again on the 19th, and it caused the same disorders. I returned to the first mercury preparation which I gave him three times a day, and interrupted this treatment on the 27th. The apartments are extremely humid; Napoleon had contracted a violent respiratory infection, had a high fever and extreme irritation. This medicine was administered again on July 2 and continued until the 9th, but without success. The salivary glands were still in the same condition, insomnia and irritation increased, and dizzy spells became frequent. Two years of inactivity, a murderous climate, rooms poorly ventilated, extreme ill-treatment, isolation, abandonment, everything that crushes the spirit acted in concert. Is it surprising that it is a liver dysfunction? If anything is astonishing, it is that the illness has not progressed more rapidly. This is only due to the power of the patient's spirit and the strength of a constitution that has never been weakened through debauchery, etc.

The night following Dr. O'Meara's departure had been a very bad one for the Emperor; he complained of a feverish agitation that eased toward morning and allowed him to get some sleep. During the day the grand marshal brought him Dr. O'Meara's report. He had it read to him before getting into his bath, and he took with him Count Bertrand with whom he continued talking all the time he remained in it.

The report had been left on the desk; I read it in its entirety and was frightened at what it revealed of disturbances in the Emperor's health and the consequences that could result. I found therein many instructions that, although ordered, had not always been followed, although a promise had been made to the doctor particularly for the internal ones. This rebellion against medicine could well be the cause of the Emperor's suffering, and what relief could be brought today, now that he was without a doctor? I was absorbed by the sad thoughts brought on by reading that report when the grand marshal, who had just left the Emperor, informed me he wanted to get out of his bath.

The Emperor got into bed as he frequently did, to rest a half hour and get dressed afterwards. He had been there barely ten minutes when he was seized with nausea which led to severe vomiting; it was the first time this occurred in Saint Helena. On Elba a similar nausea had occurred, but had not happened since then. Here it was not the same; the fits occurred at long intervals at first, then got closer, and when the Emperor finally took to his bed, they did not cease until his death. I was most uncomfortable about what I should give him: I carefully avoided suggesting the help of Dr. Verling, the artillery doctor who had replaced Dr. O'Meara.[319] Refusing the sugared water with a little orange flavoring that I offered him, he told me that his stomach was calming down, but his intestines were quite disturbed. He summoned Count de Montholon, with whom he spent several hours.

For a long time the Emperor had complained of pain in his side and a sharp pain in his right shoulder that he had me massage with cologne, which I then dried by rubbing my hand rapidly on the skin. He did the same for his side: first he would rub it with a soft brush, then I poured a little cologne in the hollow of his hand, which he applied and rubbed himself on the pain he was feeling. All this was only a makeshift procedure, where strong remedies were required; I ventured one day to tell the Emperor I had prepared pills that the doctor had left me, as well as what was needed to rub his legs. "As for that," he said, "fine; but as for everything that must enter my stomach, you can toss it into the fire."

---

[319]James Roche Verling, MD (1787-1858), surgeon in the royal artillery at Saint Helena, arrived on the *Northumberland*. He was a learned man, courteous, witty, and his medical experience was acknowledged; he spoke French and Italian. Unfortunately the Emperor never called on him because the governor had sent him to Longwood without prior notice, trying to impose him.

Verling had been able to see Napoleon from a distance and declared he was struck by his beaten eyes, his complexion that was yellowish and leaden, and other obvious signs of chronic disease.

Having seen the Emperor several times on the *Northumberland*, Verling noticed a great change in his condition.

Dr. O'Meara's report on the Emperor's health was sent to Rome. Madame Mère and Cardinal Fesch submitted it for evaluation to the best doctors, who wrote up a report. It arrived in Saint Helena ten months later, at more advanced stages of the illness than those that had prompted the report submitted to their examination. The Emperor nevertheless saw in this his mother's anxiousness to bring to his suffering the only remedies she was allowed to offer him, that is a consultation that tackled the disease at its source and indicated means of easing it, if not curing it. It was signed by Dr. Machielli, Madame Mère's doctor, and some professors at the university, Jean-Baptiste Bomba, Pierre Lapi, Dominique Morichini, and Joseph Sisco,[320] all doctors with very good reputations. Trust cannot be commanded; the Emperor liked to talk with his doctor about his art or any other subject, if he was a man capable of understanding him, but he felt a great revulsion for any medication. He would fight disease through fasting when he felt sick, and used to say that man ate much more than he needed to survive. He often said to his doctor: "I am a spoiled child, I have never needed any of you. My constitution was made of steel, and it took the abominable climate where they have thrown me in order to destroy it." A few days before leaving Longwood, Dr. O'Meara urged the Emperor to take some chatnam salts. He could not make up his mind, for fear of inducing vomiting. I offered it to him diluted in the required amount of water; before he swallowed it, he told me to bring him a silver basin, fully expecting to throw it up as soon as he had swallowed it. This did not happen, but this aversion made him feel ill at ease all day, and that evening when the doctor returned from town, the Emperor said to him: "Doctor, your medication is fit for horses, but not for a gentleman."

I remember that same evening the doctor told him a discussion had arisen in town between officers of the garrison on the question of whether Ney had spoken in good faith, when he promised the king he

---

[320]Dr. Sisco (1742-1830) was born in Bastia but moved to Rome, where he became a very famous surgeon and professor of clinical anatomy and surgery, and finally chief professor of medicine and surgery on the Roman faculty.

was taking his army corps to fight against his return from the island of Elba. "Ney acted in good faith," said the Emperor, "in his promise to Louis XVIII when leaving him; but the enthusiasm of the population he saw along the way, and that of his army, made him hesitant. Bertrand's letter giving him an order to move his troops, and the certainty of being received by me as on the day after the Moskova, made up his mind, and awakened affection and patriotism in him. He came to see me in Auxerre where I had spent the night, and we embraced like two brothers. His death is a vengeance on the part of the Bourbons, who saw fit to take out on him, rather than themselves, the shame of their flight."

The Emperor's health, left to itself after Dr. O'Meara's departure, far from improving, was getting worse. He would calm the frequent ailments he felt by drinking hot lemonade, and ease his headaches with frequent footbaths. If his stomach got swollen, he would take chicken broth. Only his legs were subjected to the rubdown treatment prescribed by Dr. O'Meara: his feet were always cold and could never get warm, either in bed or when he was stretched out on his settee, except through the application of hot towels. He would also put some of these on his side and his stomach when he felt "pale," as he called it. This suffering ceased the moment he was in the bath; that is why he took one every day and enjoyed remaining there for two hours, allowing a trickle of hot water into the bath to maintain a constant temperature. His decline was obvious; the grand marshal and Count de Montholon urged the Emperor not to remain any longer without a doctor, and suggested the one who had replaced Dr. O'Meara, Dr. Verling. For several months he had taken care of Countess de Montholon for a liver problem that had appeared following her last pregnancy, and which seemed to resist the treatment she was following. Countess Bertrand considered herself and her children well cared for, but the Emperor flatly refused. This refusal was not aimed at the doctor, but at the governor, who with this doctor would have had a man of his own choosing. The Emperor considered Dr. Verling a perfectly honest man, he had spoken with him several times on the *Northumberland*, either at the table when he was invited

there, or during his strolls on deck. He preferred to let nature take care
of saving him, or killing him. If I took the liberty of telling him he was
spending too much time at work and not enough taking exercise, he
would look at me smiling and reply: "I am a dead man, my son; they
begrudge me the very air I breathe. It is up to me to find, through
work, a few flowers to cast on the path leading me to my grave. Don't
I go into my gardens from time to time? In my carriage? What more do
you wish? I know very well that a good ride on horseback for seven or
eight leagues would do me good and restore the equilibrium that is no
longer mine; but how can I do this on a rock where there is not even
enough room to reach a full gallop!"

The governor had ceased to insist on having Dr. Baxter admitted. Because of the frequent strolls the Emperor took from his bedroom to his garden, the captain of the guard was sufficiently informed
of the presence of his prisoner at Longwood and of the decline of his
health through the little exercise he took. The governor decided to
extend the boundaries of Longwood, and the last weeks of 1818 were
exempt from the harassment suffered during the preceding period.

By a ship arriving from Europe, the Emperor learned, thanks
to a communication from the governor to the grand marshal, that Lord
Bathurst announced the departure from Italy of two priests, a doctor, a
butler, and a cook, sent by Cardinal Fesch to Saint Helena to serve at
Longwood. The Emperor and all of us were filled with joy. The
Emperor was thus going to receive the medical help of which he had
been deprived and some food for his mind, if the priests and the doctor
were learned men, as there was reason to believe. The cook would also
be very welcome, as the one who had replaced Lepage was quite bad.

That same ship brought newspapers with insignificant news;
but during the evening two letters were sent to the grand marshal, who
brought them to the Emperor. One was from Count de Las Cases and
the other from General Gourgaud: both encouraged the Emperor to
continue living and brought some hope. From London General Gourgaud wrote the following letter to Empress Marie-Louise:

Madame,

If Your Majesty will kindly remember the conversation I had with her in 1814 at Grosbois, when—seeing her unfortunately for the last time, I told her everything the Emperor had undergone at Fontainebleau—I hope she will forgive me for the sad duty I am fulfilling at this time by informing her that the Emperor Napoleon is dying in the greatest torment and the longest agony. Yes, Madame, the man united to you by divine and human laws through the most sacred bonds, the man you have seen receive the homages of almost all the sovereigns in Europe, the man over whose fate I saw you shed so many tears when he was leaving you, is dying the most cruel death, captive on a rock in the middle of the oceans, 2,000 leagues from those dearest to him, alone, friendless, without relatives, without news of his wife and son, and without any consolation.

Since my departure from that fatal rock, I had hoped to be able to come and tell you of his suffering, certain of all that your generous soul could attempt; my hope has been disappointed. I have learned that no individual who could remind you of the Emperor, describe his situation, tell you the truth, could possibly approach you—in a word, that you were in the middle of your court which serves as a prison. The Emperor had suspected it; during his moments of anguish, when to offer him some consolation we spoke to him of you, he often replied: "You can be sure that if the Empress does nothing to alleviate my suffering, it is that she is kept surrounded by spies who prevent her from knowing anything of the suffering I am subjected to, for Marie-Louise is virtue itself."

Deprived of the pleasure of coming to see you, I have tried since my arrival here to send you some news. It is only now that a reliable opportunity has been offered me, and I hasten to take advantage of it to send you this letter, full of hope and trust in the generosity of your character and the kindness of your heart. The Emperor's suffering may still last a long time; there is still time to save him, and the moment seems well chosen. The sovereigns are about to gather at the congress of Aix-la-Chapelle. Passions seem to have calmed, Napoleon is no longer to be feared, he is so miserable that noble souls can only take an interest in his fate. Under such circumstances, I beg Your Majesty to reflect on the effect such a grand step on your part would produce in going yourself to this congress, soliciting the end of the Emperor's suffering, begging your august father to join his efforts to yours to obtain that Napoleon be entrusted to him, if politics does not yet allow him to be freed. Even if such an attempt did not fully succeed, the Emperor's fate could be greatly improved. What consolation he would feel to see you acting thus! And you, Madame, how happy you would be: what praise and blessings would be yours through such conduct, dictated to you by religion, honor, duty, a conduct which only your greatest enemies could advise you not to undertake. It will be said: The European sovereigns, after having vanquished the Great Napoleon, abandoned him in the hands of his most cruel enemies. They were allowing him to die of the longest and most barbaric suffering, the duration of his agony forced him to ask that his executioners be quicker, he appeared to have been forgotten, without help, but Marie-Louise remained, and life was restored to him.

Ah! Madame, in the name of everything that is dearest to you, your reputation, your duty, your future, do everything you can to save the Emperor. The memory of Marie-Thérèse orders you to do so.

Forgive me, Madame, for speaking to you in this fashion: I allow myself to be carried away by the feelings I have for you. I would like to see you first among all women.

May Your Majesty remember that during a trip to Amsterdam where I had remained ill, I was about to die for lack of care when Your Majesty, having been informed of this, sent me her own doctor with orders to attend to me with all of the resources of the art. You have saved my life, Madame, that memory shall never fade from my heart, and I feel I can best express my thanks by having the courage to write this letter to you.

I remain, etc....
/s/ General Gourgaud.
London, August 25, 1818

This letter, filled with deep love for the Emperor, full of heart-felt and noble feelings, was only brought to my knowledge on my return to France; I have placed it here at the time when it must have arrived in Saint Helena. It should serve to counter the indiscreet conversations in which Walter Scott spoke out against the general during his month's captivity in Saint Helena and on his arrival in Europe.[321]

---

[321]Marchand refers to Walter Scott's book *Vie de Napoléon Bonaparte, Empereur des Français*. In the last chapters the author violently attacks General Gourgaud, and accuses him of having made very serious declarations to Sir Hudson Lowe and his entourage prior to leaving Saint Helena, and also to various British officials when he arrived in London.

However, General Gourgaud is wrong in stating in his letter, when speaking of the Emperor, that he was left in Saint Helena "alone, without friends, without relatives." Without relatives, yes, but without friends, no! It is impossible to doubt the great admiration, deep respect, and sincere friendship of Count Bertrand for the Emperor, as well as that of Count de Montholon, whose attentions were those of a son.

Top: Lord Bathurst
Bottom: Metternich

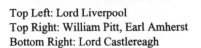
Top Left: Lord Liverpool
Top Right: William Pitt, Earl Amherst
Bottom Right: Lord Castlereagh

Top Left: Admiral Keith
Top Right: Captain William Crokat
Bottom Left: Sir Thomas Reade
Bottom Right: Duke of Wellington

Top Left: Major Gideon Gorrequer
Top Right: Denzil Ibbetson

Top Left: Dr. Francis Burton
Top Right: Dr. Thomas
Shortt
Bottom Left: Dr. Archibald

Top: Dr. Barry O'Meara
Bottom: Dr. Stokoe

Top: Dr. Alexander Baxter
Bottom: Dr. James Verling

Louis XVIII

Top Left:
  King Charles X
Top Right:
  Emperor of
  Austria
Bottom Left:
  King of Rome

Top: Alexander I
Bottom: Talleyrand

Top Left: Duchess d'Angoulême
Top Right: Madame Georges
Bottom Left: Madame de Staël

Top Left: Marshall Ney   Top Right: Caulaincourt
Bottom Left: Kléber   Bottom Right: General Saliceti

Top: Napoleon on St. Helena.

Bottom: On the *Northumberland.*

Napoleon on St. Helena.

Napoleon on St. Helena.

Top: Napoleon on St. Helena

Bottom: On the *Northumberland*

PART SEVEN

Final Struggles

CHAPTER TWENTY

Dr. Stokoe — I become ill — The Emperor's kindness toward me —
Countess deMontholon's departure —
New conflicts and correspondence with the governor

We had reached the last months of 1818. Nature had come to the Emperor's aid, and allowed us to believe that his health was improving, but this was only in appearance. He had found distractions in work and his small gardens. The ladies had each offered the consolations the Emperor could expect from them out of friendship, when the final days of December brought back the symptoms Dr. O'Meara had attempted to combat previously. The Emperor was taking no precautions against the weather: he would withdraw his legs from the flannel sack in which he kept them part of the morning to warm his feet, slip on silk stockings, small buckled shoes, a pair of white cloth trousers, then go outside and let himself be taken unaware by the coolness of the evening. Having thus remained outside too late, he caught a cold that at first was only an irritation, but soon became a serious infection causing nausea, vomiting, chills, and fever. The ailment in his legs recurred, and I brought him some relief with rubdowns; but as for the cold, the Emperor fought it only with the totally insufficient use of his licorice. The Emperor had been suffering this way for only a few days when January 1, 1819 arrived. He was not able, as he had been the preceding years, to have a "family" luncheon as he called it, but he did not want the children to miss out because of that. He asked me for some gold coins, and gave this to them for their New Year's presents.

The grand marshal and Count de Montholon thought the Emperor was sufficiently ill to urge him to be attended by Dr. Stokoe from the *Conqueror*, as he did not want the help of Dr. Verling, the doctor imposed on Longwood by Hudson Lowe. The Emperor reminded the grand marshal of the bitter correspondence he had had with the governor during the preceding visits, and said it would only renew them to call on him. However, after much insistence, the Emperor on January 10 allowed the grand marshal to call for that doctor. On the 17th, as he had no news and the Emperor's condition was getting worse, the grand marshal wrote again insisting that he come as soon as possible, because the Emperor's situation was worsening each day.

It was only on the 19th that the doctor arrived, apologizing for all the difficulties he had had in coming to Longwood, and declaring that judging from all the obstacles placed in his way today in coming to visit his patient, he was almost sure that similar permission would not be granted him the following day. Brought to the Emperor's bedside, he examined him at length, saw his legs, and found the symptoms already described by Dr. O'Meara. He suggested bloodletting, and prescribed a few pills each day and leg rubdowns. Fearing he would not be admitted to see his patient any more, he wrote the grand marshal a letter in which he indicated a diet to follow, and in view of the seriousness of the illness, urged the famous patient to use Dr. Verling, if he was not called to the honor of bringing his own ministrations. The grand marshal proposed that he replace Dr. O'Meara at the Emperor's bedside under the conditions stipulated by the governor, and Dr. Stokoe said he would accept those conditions if the governor and his admiral did not object to it.

Informed by the grand marshal of Dr. Stokoe's decision, the Emperor dictated the following note to Count de Montholon, to be sent to Plantation House:

Dr. Stokoe must remain at Longwood if he is to continue the treatment interrupted since Dr. O'Meara's departure, that is for the past six months. This has considerably aggravated the hepatitis, the first symptoms of which were noticed some sixteen months ago. The Emperor's entire state of health is in disarray: it is necessary that Dr. Stokoe see the patient several times a day.

The attack the day before yesterday is the fifth one in the last six months; all occur at night. Count Bertrand and Count de Montholon were with the patient, without the help of any professional; never had the attacks been as serious as that of the other night, and for a moment they despaired of the Emperor's life. Count Bertrand offered to summon Dr. Verling, but the patient refused. That very offer altered his appearance, and increased his illness at that moment; Count Bertrand therefore called at 2 a.m. for Dr. Stokoe, who arrived at 6 a.m. The duty officer is not authorized to write to town; they had to request the governor's permission, which doubled the travel time, and the doctor arrived too late. Fortunately the patient's strong constitution overcame the attack. Thus we have confirmation of what was stated in Count de Montholon's letter addressed to the governor on July 26 last, when Dr. O'Meara, who had been removed from Longwood, was still in town: "Even in the last throes of death, the Emperor shall receive care and medication only from the hands of his own doctor; if he is deprived of him, he will receive no one, and will consider himself to have been assassinated by you."

When Dr. Stokoe arrived, he went to see General Bertrand. The latter proposed that he replace Dr. O'Meara, and showed him the seven articles sent to the governor. He accepted, and was then shown in to the patient; the governor could not prevent this transaction, either directly or indirectly, without revealing his position.

Thus the treatment of the disease which has been interrupted for six months is again suspended until the arrival of the French doctor. The hepatitis will do even more damage during this last period, and should it finally become incurable, who will have killed the Emperor? What has happened in the last six months causes us to fear he may have one attack a month, and if he calls for Dr. Stokoe, he will arrive too late. Should the patient someday die of this, who will have killed him? The world and history answer that question loudly!
Longwood, January 19, 1819

The governor replied to this letter, which was not signed, as follows:

No communication relative to Napoleon Bonaparte can be received, if it does not bear his signature or that of one of his officers, who, in that case, must clearly state he is writing and signing by his order.

When the paper attached hereto has been thus signed, it will be replied to.
Plantation House, January 19, 1819

Dr. Stokoe was authorized to come on the 20th and 21st, but he did not reappear on the 22nd. During those two days, reports on the Emperor's health were given to the governor by this doctor, who was subjected each time to an interrogation on what had been said or done in his presence in the patient's bedroom. The governor told him he did not believe any of this alleged illness, that he was only trying to fool him, and that it was nothing but a play to support Dr. O'Meara's statement regarding General Bonaparte's illness. Admiral Plampin declared he needed the doctor's services on board. Several months later he was sent to London to appear before an admiralty board. I am told he was accused of having been bribed by Napoleon's money, and was demoted.

The bloodletting that had been performed had a beneficial effect: the headaches disappeared, the cheltelham—although the Emperor took it very reluctantly—brought him great relief. He again took the mercury pills he had given up since Dr. O'Meara's departure, the rubdowns restored circulation to his legs, and little by little his strong constitution overpowered the illness and allowed him to resume the work which frequent illness had interrupted.

The Emperor had barely gotten better and was beginning to recover his strength, when I myself became gravely ill, without any warning. I was busy drawing a few sketches for the ladies' embroidery at their request, when I was seized with awful intestinal pain that forced me to go to bed. The attack was as violent as it was sudden; I summoned Dr. Verling, who found I had a rapid pulse, but no fever. He put off the bloodletting until the following day in case the temperature went up, and gave me some medication to calm me. I remained in bed three weeks.

Informed by Saint-Denis that I was in bed, and of the suffering that had put me there, the Emperor—although he was ill himself—had the extreme kindness to come up to my bedroom accompanied by the grand marshal. The room was located under the roof, just above his own, separated from the burning rays of the tropical sun only by lathing and some slates. The heat was excessive in spite of the door and windows being open. "He cannot remain here," the Emperor said to the grand marshal, "you must have a bed placed in my library." I begged the Emperor not to do this, thinking of the disruption my moving into that room would cause. The next morning I was settled there, and I remained there for the duration of my illness. When he went from his bedroom to the drawing room, the Emperor never failed to stop at the library door to ask how I felt.

Dr. Verling deplored that the Emperor's appearances did not occur while he was visiting me, regretting that the Emperor refused to be taken care of by him. He knew the Emperor's repugnance was not for himself, but for the governor's wanting to impose a doctor on him. He did not know that when the Emperor was about to go into the drawing room, the door to the dining room—which was between the bedroom and the library—was locked, so that he would not find himself on the Emperor's path.

The pills he gave me to take were mercury pills; they soon loosened my teeth and caused blisters in my mouth. He then said he had the disease under control. When I started my convalescence, I was ordered to take baths. The Emperor heard this, and as there was no other bathtub at Longwood except his own, he told me to use it. I thanked him, saying that Dr. Verling was going to send a wooden tub from the town hospital. I mention these details only because they indicate the Emperor's kindness.

When I resumed my duties with the Emperor, I looked very much like Lazarus. "You have been affected," he said to me; "these British doctors are used to treating horses with chicken broth; you would have recovered from this without the help of what they call heroic medicines." I also learned with some pleasure that being accustomed to my care, he had felt deprived of it during my illness. "Saint-Denis and Noverraz also offered care, even devotion," he said of them, "but they don't know my habits as Marchand does."

The way I had been stricken recalled the illness leading to Cipriani's death. At the beginning, everyone was quite worried; expressions of interest were shown me by Countesses Montholon and Bertrand, who were kind enough to ask how I was. My strength slowly returned. Until then, I had always slept across the Emperor's bedroom door, in the room adjoining his. Starting from that time, he did not want me to do so anymore, fearing I might have a relapse. If he happened to need me, he had one of the valets send for me. During the day, he believed the way to entertain me was to occupy me as he had previously done when he did not have one of these gentlemen at hand, by having me write under his dictation or having me read to him.

The Emperor had not acquired in Saint Helena this portliness that many people took pleasure in ascribing to him. He was as he had been during the Hundred Days; suffering often caused shadows under his eyes, but his gaze had lost nothing of the penetrating character for which it was known. His face was quite pale, and his flesh had lost its hair. He said he felt like his side was being cut, as if a razor blade was stuck into him. No matter what annoyances the governor seemed to want to overwhelm his existence with, his courage never failed: on the contrary, he appeared to stiffen against the harassment visited on him every day by the governor. The strength of his constitution, along with his occupations and his ordinary strolls, seemed to have overpowered illness. He was worried about Countess de Montholon's health; she was suffering seriously from her liver. If she did not go riding in his carriage, he never failed to go every day to see her, and it was the same for Countess Bertrand if she was ill. Never did either of those ladies find him indifferent.

The Emperor busied himself commenting on the campaigns of Turenne, Frederick, Hannibal, and Marlborough, which he dictated to Count de Montholon. He dictated to me some comments on Caesar's campaigns, and made notes on Rogniat,[322] the Abbé de Pradt,[323] and

---

[322]Joseph Rogniat, born in 1776, a graduate of the engineering school in Metz in 1794, had a brilliant military career, became a general in 1809, and served at Waterloo. He was an engineering inspector, a peer of France, a member of the science academy, and wrote many technical and political books. His *Considérations sur l'art de la guerre*, published in 1816, is filled with attacks against Napoleon.

[323]The Abbé de Pradt owed his fortune to Duroc, to whom he was related. He became chaplain to the Emperor, bishop of Poitiers, archbishop of Malines, and ambassador to Warsaw. Sent back to his diocese for having disobeyed the Emperor's orders, de Pradt then became one of his staunchest adversaries. He wrote a great deal about the Spanish revolution, the American revolution, and the colonies, and his *Histoire de l'ambassade dans le Grand Duché de Varsovie en 1812* defends his position.

Jomini. He took up field fortifications with the grand marshal, dictated portions of it to me, and had me make drawings. In one of the shipments of books sent to him by Lady Holland[324] were two small volumes entitled *Souvenirs de madame Durand*.[325] I had known that lady when she was in the service of Empress Marie-Louise; she had the title of first lady-in-waiting: they numbered six at that time. My curiosity was aroused, and while the Emperor was devouring the books I had set on the table near the settee where he was sitting, I glanced at the two books. That evening when he went to bed, I reviewed them for him, telling him this lady claimed the Emperor never went near Empress Marie-Louise without asking if her dress was made of very fine linen, because linen reminded him of a woman he had dearly loved who always wore it. "What nonsense!" he replied, "I liked fine linen because I wished to favor the city of Saint-Quentin." The next day when I picked up that book along with those scattered across the rug, I found written in pencil in the Emperor's hand, particularly in the margin of the first volume's pages, comments such as "false! absurd! nonsense!" I must say that, with the exception of certain passages deserving the Emperor's disapproval, the balance was written with good intention, and that it suffered perhaps from ignorance but not ill will.

Many notes were written in the margins of the Emperor's cor-

---

[324]Lady Holland was a very attractive woman, with great wit and charm. Of American origin, Elizabeth Vassall first married Sir Godfrey Webster and later Lord Holland. Like her husband, Lady Holland admired the Emperor; she encouraged Lord Holland when, in March 1817, he made a speech in Parliament that created quite a stir, as he requested the government to change its policies regarding Napoleon. Lady Holland sent the prisoners a few treats, and many books. In 1845, the year of her death, Lady Holland gave the British Museum the gold box decorated with an antique cameo that Napoleon had bequeathed her on his deathbed with this note: "Emperor Napoleon to Lady Holland, as a token of appreciation and esteem."

[325]Madame Durand was the widow of General Durand, an old soldier who died in 1807. She was one of the Empress' ladies-in-waiting. She wrote her *Mémoires sur Napoléon, l'Impératrice Marie-Louise et la Cour des Tuileries avec notes critiques faites par le prisonnier de Sainte-Hélène...* Indeed Napoleon had that book in his hands and made a number of often derogatory marginal notes.

respondence published by the bookseller Panckoucke,[326] and on M.
Fleury de Chaboulon's book; the Emperor read with pleasure the refutation of Rogniat's work by Colonel Marbot.[327] He said of that book:
"It is written by a young man, but that is how one should write, and
confound the detractors of the glory of France." This book earned its
author a mention in the Emperor's will for 100,000 francs, and the recommendation that he write about the campaigns from 1793 to 1815.
"To write otherwise than Marbot does in his refutation of Rogniat,"
the Emperor said, "is to stain one's uniform." When a satirical tract
came to his attention, he read it, and often laughed at the silly things
said about him. If someone happened to be present, he would read out
loud the passage that had provoked his laughter and say, "What nonsense is fed to the public! What do you want! One must sell! Time will
do justice to all that!" If on the contrary the book was well written,
even if it said something against him, he said with the same honesty:
"It has good in it," or "It's a good work."

The newspapers related the city of Rennes' refusal to accept a

---

[326]The first edition of the *Correspondance inédite officielle et confidentielle de
Napoléon Bonaparte*, published in 1819 by Panckoucke, consists of seven volumes,
and was known to the Emperor. It includes two volumes on Italy, two on Egypt, two
on Venice; the last one contains various letters. The copy that was part of the Saint
Helena library is now in the Bibliothèque Nationale. The paperbound books, enclosed
in a green leather case, belonged to Marchand, who gave them to French Premier
Thiers. The half-title page of Volume II reads: "This correspondence, since its arrival
at Longwood, remained constantly on Emperor Napoleon's desk, and was only
removed from there after his death. Some of the notes written by the Emperor in pencil
were inked in by Count de Montholon. Marchand, Paris, June 16, 1840." This was
twenty-one days before the departure of the *Belle-Poule* for Saint Helena. "The minister who joins in the noble and generous thinking of the king, by returning the
Emperor's ashes to France, is entitled to his inheritance," Marchand wrote to M.
Thiers in his cover letter.

[327]*Remarques critiques sur l'ouvrage de M. le lieutenant général Rogniat sur l'art de
la guerre*, by Colonel Marbot, September 1820. Marbot is the author of *Mémoires*
published in 1891, in which he violently protests against General Rogniat's attacks on
the soldier who led the revolutionary and imperial epic.

statue of Moreau[328] that the government had intended for one of the squares in that town. "This," he said, "is how ministers lead sovereigns into making mistakes. It would hurt the inhabitants of Rennes' national pride to send them the statue of a man killed in the ranks of the enemy."

The Emperor reminisced about what during his childhood had provided the background for good manners. "The fireside chat is a lost art in France," he said; "there are no more of these witty and spirited conversations that made for such pleasant evenings. The family spirit is being lost, and with it the respect of the young for the elderly." The grand marshal told him that the arrival of his library had changed nothing in his dictation, and that the facts as well as the dates had been in agreement with the research he had done. The Emperor replied, "It is because my memory comes from the heart, and it keeps a faithful record of everything that is dear to it."

His relaxation through light reading included: *Paul et Virginie*, *Don Quixote*, *Manon Lescaut*, and the novels of Ms. de Cottin,[329] Mme de Souza,[330] Mme de Staël, and Charles XII, whose body was like his head, he said, made of iron.

---

[328]In 1816, at the time when a monument in memory of Pichegru was being erected in Arbois, there was talk of erecting a statue of Moreau in one of the squares of Morlaix, his birthplace. This project was abandoned for lack of public interest.

[329]Marie Ristaud (1770-1807) had married a banker from Bordeaux, M. Cottin, and was widowed at age 20. She filled her solitude by writing novels in which she bared her "sensitive soul." The profits she derived from the sale of her books went to the poor.

[330]Mme de Souza was one of the more attractive women of her time; she had a fine mind and a romantic character. At the time of the Bastille, she was 28, had a husband, Count de Flahaut, and a 4-year-old son whose father was the Abbé de Périgord—Talleyrand.

In 1793 Flahaut was guillotined and his wife went into exile. In 1802 the attractive widow married a Portuguese writer, his country's minister in Paris, M. de Souza-Botelho. She took to writing, and painted the society of her period with taste, elegance, and sincerity. In 1813 her son Charles was ADC to the Emperor, and the father of a son born of a passing fancy of Queen Hortense: he was the future Duke of Morny, who was brought up by his grandmother. Mme de Souza died in 1836.

The Emperor's health appeared to be better; I told him so one day and expressed the happiness we all felt over this. He came close to me, took me by the ear, and said: "Don't believe it, my son, I haven't long to live. It is right here," he said, showing me the area of his liver; "this is only a moment of rest granted me by nature; the illness will again gain the upper hand and do me in." I was saddened by the Emperor's words, without however believing in his prediction. In any case, this welcome peace, often disturbed by the governor, was soon to be even more so by a departure deeply affecting the Emperor: Countess de Montholon was seriously ill, and Dr. Verling had declared that the climate would prevent her recovery. Her departure was decided following a consultation that was submitted to the Emperor. This departure would deprive the Emperor of a person whom he valued, and his social life was to be completely disrupted. Through her wit, to which the Emperor had become pleasantly accustomed, she provided some distraction to his work, and the time he spent with her played a large part in his daily routine. Her children, through their games, broke up the monotony of Longwood; a great void was to follow, for him and for the colony. The Emperor had always been grateful to her for having remained pent up with her husband and child in a single room in order to be near him when we arrived at Longwood, hence his affection for this lady.

This departure worried Count de Montholon, who saw his wife leaving alone with three children and a nurse, without even being sure where she would land. Her maid remained on the island to marry Noverraz. The Emperor did not want this marriage to take place, as he did not find it in the interest of a man whom he wished well, and it was to deprive Countess de Montholon of her maid during such a long voyage. Madame de Montholon had insisted that the Emperor keep M. de Montholon with him and begged him not to oppose the fortunate offer made to her servant, Joséphine, to remain in Saint Helena and marry Noverraz.[331]

On the eve of the departure, the Emperor again spoke to Count de Montholon of his wish that he not let his wife leave alone, and that he accompany the countess. "Sire," replied the general, "Madame de

Montholon does not want to add to her regrets at leaving Your Majesty that of depriving him of the services I may be able to offer him here. Her decision is made, and so is mine. I am remaining with Your Majesty."

"Then see to it that she lacks nothing on board the ship on which she is to go." Orders were given to M. Pierron, the butler, for provisions of all kinds to be placed on board, and this in addition to the price agreed on for her transport to Europe; letters of credit for a sum of 200,000 francs and a 20,000 franc pension were given to her before she left Longwood.

The day chosen for the departure having arrived, the Emperor went into the drawing room to receive Madame de Montholon and her children. He thanked her for the sacrifice she was making in letting her husband remain with him, and gave her a rich gold box with his portrait surrounded by very large diamonds, assuring her of his wishes for her happiness and that of her family. He gave her various instructions for Europe and his family which the countess received in tears. The poor children shared their mother's sorrow; it soon became such a sad scene that the Emperor, too moved himself, did not wish to prolong it. He embraced them one after another and went back into his apartment. "These tears hurt me," he said to me, "and poor Montholon appears overwhelmed with sorrow; I did not want that sacrifice, but both of them wanted it. He is going to find a great void when he comes home this evening. So that he will be less lonely, I believe you should take a room in his lodging." The Emperor had undressed to bathe, and as he

---

[331]The marriage of Noverraz and Joséphine Brulé took place on Sunday, July 12, 1819, in Countess de Montholon's parlor: there was a great feast. "The bride, Marchand's friend Esther, and Mlle Odile were all three inseparable," wrote Montholon; "a great many toasts were drunk to the future of the couple." Life indeed was starting well for them; they had put aside 20,000 francs in savings. However the Emperor was not in favor of this union. He nevertheless hired Joséphine as a laundry woman, and gave her the wages she had been receiving from Madame de Montholon. As she was quite capable, Joséphine also worked for Countess Bertrand. The Emperor had been right: the Noverraz couple separated, and the "Helvetica Bear" died without issue in his little white house in Lausanne, called *La Violette*, on January 12, 1849, at the same hour as his master.

was coming out of his room to get into his bath, the carriage was leaving. Without being seen, by raising a corner of the curtains he could see Mme de Montholon's last look at the house where so much glory and grandeur remained connected, mixed with memories of friendship. It was also a final goodbye.[332] Count de Montholon was accompanying his wife and his children on horseback to town. He had received permission to go on board the ship on which she was sailing, and to remain there until it hoisted its sails, so that he came back to Longwood very late and did not see the Emperor that evening.

The Emperor got into his bath, feeling the impact of that departure. "Montholon," he said to me, "feels he cannot leave me for another two years. You shall return to Europe, you will see your families again; your friends will surround you, and will want to know every last detail of my existence on this miserable rock. You will enjoy the consideration given to men of valor. Montholon will find his wife and his children, you shall find your mother, and I will be dead, abandoned in this sad solitary place."

My soul was stirred by the departure that had just taken place, for the memory of my family had come into my mind. The Emperor's words brought my thoughts fully back to him. The calm with which he spoke of his forthcoming end, and his belief that he would remain alone, alone on this rock after his death, moved me so much that he noticed my emotion. "When death comes," he said to me, "is it not a blessing for me? I shall do nothing to hasten it, but I shall not grasp at straws in order to live. Until then, Montholon will make my days more bearable. He knows my habits, and he has become quite necessary to me. What is happening with Montholon will soon happen with Bertrand; the poor grand marshal's wife is often ill, is she not? She has difficulty adapting to our existence, she is used to being surrounded and often looks back at the past. Her children are growing up, their education will one day require that she return to Europe."

---

[332]Madame de Montholon left Saint Helena on July 2, 1819, on board the *Lady Campbell*.

The Emperor had remained silent, and I was thinking about what abandonment he would be reduced to when Saint-Denis announced the grand marshal. The Emperor, ceasing his daydreaming, said theatrically: "He has delayed a long time, let him enter! Well, Sir Grand Marshal," the Emperor said to him, "how is Madame Bertrand?"

"Sire, like everyone else, moved by the departure of Montholon's wife." I left them, as I usually did when the person he had summoned arrived. Countess Bertrand herself was ill and in bed.

Having dismissed the grand marshal, the Emperor got out of his bath, went to bed for a short time, then dressed and dined alone. That evening he donned a coat and told me to accompany him to the end of the garden where he wanted to take a walk. As I was going out without a hat, he told me to go get it because it was damp. As I walked next to him, he enumerated some of Count Bertrand's fine qualities, among others: "Bertrand is a true man of honor!" When we arrived at the end of the garden, he sent me for news of Countess Bertrand; I came back to tell him she was quite ill. The Emperor was about to enter her house when he noticed they were posting the sentries. Night had fallen. As we returned to the dining room, two rats scattered between his legs, almost making him trip. "What is that?" he said.

"It was two rats," replied Noverraz, "who came in through the open door and ran away when Your Majesty approached." Alone at Longwood, I had to spend the evening with the Emperor: it was the first time I had accompanied the Emperor on one of his walks. It was also the first evening I spent entirely with him. It was easy for me because he went to bed early, and the evening was spent reading the tragedy of Mohammed. The Emperor, seeing at 9 p.m. that Count de Montholon had not returned, told me to take away his covered lamp and go to bed.

At the beginning of our stay there were rats throughout the house, from attic to ground floor. For a long time, except for a few of them who still remained in the attic, they had all taken refuge in and kept close to the pantry. They came out at night through holes they had made and were so thick on the floor it appeared black. They climbed the walls up to a certain height, and then jumped sometimes success-fully onto pieces of meat suspended from the ceiling on iron hooks. In order to avoid being poisoned by food mixed with arsenic that would kill them in their holes, large baited rat traps were set up which were made of very strong wire and well anchored to the ground. Every morning eight to ten rats were caught; and furious at being unable to get out of the trap they had entered, they fought amongst themselves. The rat trap was then brought to the middle of the lawn where the sta-ble dogs were all waiting. As soon as a rat came out, a dog would catch it, break its back, and leave it dead on the ground. The rats, desperately defending themselves, occasionally bit the dogs, which would return resolving to be more careful the next time.

Countess de Montholon's departure had taken place on a very fine day; the evening was also pleasant. But around 9 p.m. a heavy rain started falling, and continued part of the night. Count de Montholon was in the rain all the way from Jamestown to Longwood and was soaked to the bone. He went to bed feeling uneasy: he had a bout of fever during the night, spat out some blood, complained of a pain in his side, and was kept in bed the following day with rheumatism in his knee. These numerous complications kept him in bed for several weeks. Besides the visits the Emperor made, sitting next to his bed, I was sent for news of him in the morning, and again during the day. The grand marshal's wife, whom he also visited, was beginning to go out, and she took some rides through the woods of Longwood with the Emperor in his carriage. One day I had gone to her house on behalf of the Emperor, and on my return reported to him about the health of this lady, who thanked the Emperor and said she was feeling very well. "Well, Bertrand!" he replied, "I told you two weeks ago—when you told me of your fears concerning your wife—that she would recover from it, because her disease was a known one, and that I would die because mine was unknown. You seemed to disbelieve what I was saying to you, but you can be sure I have not long to live."

The Emperor had taken ill again, as he had several months before, and for two or three days had not been seen. Since Count de Montholon was in bed, the grand marshal gave more of his time to the

Emperor during the day, and came in the evening after his dinner if he asked for him. Otherwise the Emperor worked alone, or called me to read to him while he was in bed.

So the Emperor was sick again, and without the help of a doctor. The duty captain reported to Plantation House that he had not been able to see the Emperor for two days. While I was sick, on a similar occasion, the governor had first insisted, then threatened, so the duty officer would be admitted to see the Emperor every day. A correspondence then took place between Longwood and Plantation House; the firmness with which the Emperor refused the new outrage they wanted to impose on him led to Sir Hudson Lowe's not daring to push matters all the way to the end. He did not even dare to refuse the request that Dr. Stokoe take care of the Emperor, but he ordered such visits to take place in the presence of an island doctor. To put an end to the requested visits by this doctor, he had Admiral Plampin declare he needed Dr. Stokoe for the service of his squadron, and—as I have already said—in a short time the doctor left Saint Helena harbor to return to England.

The Emperor was therefore again threatened with a violation of his domicile, and General Montholon was still sick, when Captain Nicholls presented himself at Longwood with a sealed package addressed to Napoleon Bonaparte. He was told that the Emperor had a greater need of help than of things likely to irritate and hurt him; as the Emperor was bedridden, he could not take this letter, because of the offensive form in which it was presented. The officer was no more fortunate in his attempt with the grand marshal, who told him that when the communication was made in the normal manner, he would bring it to the Emperor's cognizance when his health allowed it. This took place on August 10, 1819. The Emperor, informed of this new attempt, had the grand marshal write Sir Hudson Lowe the following:

Governor:

Captain Nicholls presented himself at my door with a sealed package addressed to Napoleon Bonaparte. He wished me to give this to the Emperor. I replied to him that the prince, being in bed and very ill, needed the assistance of a doctor, and not things likely to irritate him and that he considered insulting. He knew very well that the Emperor had refused that method of correspondence, and that for the past four years, a protocol had been established which he was departing from. Count de Montholon protested in his letter of April 11. He told you very clearly that to write in this way was the same as writing in Chinese or Hebrew. In fact, Count de Montholon has sent back all the packages you addressed to him in this manner. As you sent them back again and forced the captain to hand them over, he kept them to avoid a vexatious fight, but as you know, he took them in to the Emperor who immediately threw them into the fire, because he saw your intended insult. Thus, for the past few months, he is unaware of everything you have attempted to tell him. If the captain presents your package for the third time, I shall take it, but I declare that it will be treated the same as the others. Is not the Emperor's situation deplorable enough? Why do you wish to aggravate it even more by raising obstacles that custom had made smooth? One of your officers asked the Emperor's valet to be shown in, but his health did not allow him to receive anyone other than a doctor, either Dr. O'Meara or Dr. Stokoe, or any other doctor he chooses under the same conditions as those accepted by Dr. Stokoe. Without this, he would consider him a police officer, and not a medical officer.

As Count de Montholon is seriously ill, should you wish to communicate with me in the usual manner, I will seize a moment when the Emperor's health allows me to bring it to his awareness.

If there is a remission in the Emperor's illness, it is possible to see him. When he is bedridden, the most appropriate way to see him is that proposed by the government: to let him take a doctor who will be in charge only of medical duties, as he had agreed to take Dr. Stokoe.

I remain, etc.

Signed: Count Bertrand

This letter having been given to the grand marshal, the Emperor had it sent to Hudson Lowe with the following note:

I will take no notice of the contents of this package, any more than I have taken notice of the contents of two or three other similar ones that were forced on Count de Montholon in spite of my written protests:

1. Because I may not receive direct correspondence;

2. Because the form is offensive;

3. Because any means of response is unavailable;

4. Because for four years there has been a protocol which I cannot violate.

For two years I have been suffering from chronic liver disease, an illness endemic to this country. For the last year I have been without a doctor because Dr. O'Meara and Dr. Stokoe were intentionally sent away. For some days I have been in the grip of an attack, abandoned and unable to receive any medical relief. However, as if this illness were not noxious enough in the climate of this country and the unhealthy location I inhabit, you have taken this moment to redouble offensive conduct, insults, abuse, in short all possible assaults. What! In the four years peace has reigned in Europe, British vengeance is not yet satisfied? What cowardice!

Napoleon

Here are the reasons that gave rise to this correspondence and that which you will read farther on:

Captain Nicholls, having failed with Count de Montholon and the grand marshal in his attempt to deliver the governor's sealed package to the Emperor, had returned to Plantation House to report on his mission. The following day Sir Hudson Lowe sent Colonel Wynyard of his staff to give the package to the Emperor personally. This senior officer went to the duty officer's, and as he knew no other entrance than that to the parlor, went to knock at that door. But since the Emperor was no longer receiving visitors, no one went in this room except to open the door if he decided to pass that way. Colonel Wynyard knocked for some time without getting any response until I happened to be passing by this way outside the house. I asked what he wanted, explaining why there had been no answer to his knock.

He said to me, "I am carrying a message from the governor to General Bonaparte, be so good as to announce me." This situation had not come up since the Emperor had been at Longwood, but I knew what had happened the previous day and supposed that they were attempting a direct insult. I answered, "Monsieur le Colonel, if you have a message to transmit, you must address yourself to General Montholon or the grand marshal according to established practice, so that it may reach the Emperor."

"One of them is ill," he said to me, "and the other is not at home. My orders are that you announce me to His Excellency or that you take charge of my message for him. Do so," he said with much insistence, "and you will avoid unpleasant consequences for the general."

"I know my duty too well to do that, no matter what may result from it," I answered.

"I will await your response at the captain of the guard's."

"Colonel," I said, "my decision is already made. The Emperor is ill, and I will not speak to him of a proceeding that can only be displeasing to him."

I made as if to continue my walk and at once went to the Emperor, whom I had left at his desk. He was still there and humming a tune, as he sometimes did when in better health, and cried, "Who goes there?" He was in a good mood! I approached him, and without looking at me he said, "What is it, my son?" I told him how I had found Colonel Wynyard at the parlor door and my conversation with him. "That is fine," he said, "let him do it, he won't have the audacity to force my door." The Emperor returned to his work for a time; then as he had slept little during the night, he got into bed and told me to continue reading *Gil Blas*, which was on the table, to him. I left his bedroom only when I saw he was asleep.

During this time, the captain of the guard had come several times to ask for me. He had been answered that I was with the Emperor. He had insisted on having me informed that Colonel Wynyard was in his quarters awaiting my response. Noverraz, who was on duty, had refused, saying there was no precedent to do things that way. The two of them were at that point in their conversation when I came out of the Emperor's room. Captain Blakeney approached me and told me of Colonel Wynyard's desire to speak to me before returning to Plantation House. The colonel reproached me for the impolite manner in which he had been received when he appeared with a message from the governor. I answered that this impoliteness was not at all intentional, and I believed I had sufficiently explained the reasons to leave no need to justify myself further.

"Will you, or will you not, give this letter to General Bonaparte?" he said, handing it to me.

"No, sir," I said.

"Well then, I will report your refusal to the governor." He mounted his horse and rode away at a gallop, followed by his aide. Leaving Captain Blakeney's quarters, I went to see Count de Montholon, who was still in bed. I asked about his health and told him what had just happened. "He tried to intimidate you," he said to me. "They will not dare violate the Emperor's residence. You did well not to accept this communication. What a difference in times and events: only a few years ago at the time of August 15, the ambassadors of the kings of Europe were at his feet, offering the homage of their masters. Today he is insulted and they want to violate his residence!"

When the Emperor awoke I told him of how I had been called to the duty captain's, my refusal to comply with his demands, the bad temper he had demonstrated and, if I had correctly understood his final words on leaving, his intention to gain entrance by force.

The Emperor sent Saint-Denis to find the grand marshal and spoke with him a long time. He gave orders to Noverraz to barricade all the doors with strong bars hammered into the wall at each end and to place planks across the French door to the garden, to offer resistance. By midnight, all this closing-off had been done. Not a single door could be opened to enter the Emperor's apartment except by the use of force. The valuable objects were taken to the grand marshal's, as well as a will the Emperor kept locked inside a drawer of his desk. He told Saint-Denis to load his pistols and rifles, which gave him twelve shots. These preparations made, the Emperor went to bed with his firearms in the bedroom and his sword within reach, his mind made up to use them on the first person who appeared. Saint-Denis slept in the dining room, defending this room's communicating door to the bedroom. Noverraz, in the inside hall, prevented anyone approaching from this side, and I in the bathroom across the door leading to the Emperor's bedroom, all three having weapons nearby. The night passed quietly. At 9 a.m. the next day the captain of the guard came to knock at the outer door, the same one where I had found Colonel Wynyard the previous day. Seeing that no one answered, he came to find me and told me the governor had ordered him to see the general. He added that had I taken the message the governor had sent yesterday, I could have avoided all the resulting trouble. "My conduct," I answered, "had the Emperor's approval, and it is no more my duty to announce you today than it was yesterday to transmit your message." No matter how he insisted on being announced, I refused. He left. But I informed the Emperor of the duty captain's latest attempt.

At noon, Colonel Harrison[333]came to Longwood. He had me summoned to the guard captain's quarters and told me it was the governor's direct order that I transmit the message he gave me to the general. "It is neither to Count Bertrand nor to Count de Montholon I am to address myself but to you, sir, whose refusal may entail serious consequences."

"Colonel," I said to him, "having never served as intermediary between the governor and the Emperor, I cannot do so without being authorized. To do so would be lacking in my duty and in the respect I owe the Emperor's wishes. No matter how serious the results of my refusal, I absolutely refuse to accept it."

"Well then! If this is how it is, we will obtain by force what we ask of your good will." The two of them went to the outer door, where they were going to strike. I returned to the Emperor whom I found seated on his couch occupied in reading. I told him of the latest attempt and my refusal to comply with it. We heard renewed blows from the outer door. Tired of this, they returned to the dining room where Noverraz was and attempted to enter. Meeting with resistance,

---

[333]Arriving in October 1815, Charles Harrison, captain of the 53rd infantry regiment, was named brigadier major at the time of his corps' departure and remained in Saint Helena until the Emperor's death. He attended the autopsy with three other British officers: Commissary Ibbetson, and Lieutenants Mathias and Hutchins of the artillery.

they withdrew, threatening to report this to the governor. Major Harrison left for Plantation House.

Count Bertrand came to spend several hours of the afternoon with the Emperor, as the countess was feeling much better. Through his shutters the Emperor saw her walking with her children and had her summoned. He sent me for news of General Montholon and I told him what had just taken place and our defense measures. "Tell the Emperor," he said to me, "that I deeply regret being kept in bed when such insults are perpetrated against his person and his residence."

That evening I stayed alone with the Emperor. He went to bed and asked me to read to him, which happened regularly every evening since General Montholon had taken to his bed. The Emperor could not sleep, got up, and told me to retire. As I was preparing to leave he called me back and said to me, giving me a small medal case M. Denon[334] had struck for him which Lady Holland had sent: "It will remind you of the day they wanted to violate my lodging." I expressed to the Emperor how happy I was to have such a precious gift and how the words accompanying it would remain engraved in my memory. The central medal showed the Emperor seated on the rock of Saint Helena, elbow on knee, his head supported by his right hand. A kneeling genie offers him a pen, inviting him to write the history of his reign, which his widespread fame carries to the four corners of the earth. On the opposite side is the bust of the Emperor, with "Napoleon at Saint Helena" engraved underneath. Two smaller medals accompany this one: on one are the statues of Memnon, and on the back: "They will always speak for him." On the other is the bust of Baron Vivant Denon, and on the back: "And he too lived during the Great Century!" This kindness of M. Denon's pleased the Emperor very much.

The following day at noon the governor came with his staff and three dragoons. They entered Longwood at a gallop and dis-

---

[334]Dominique Vivant, Baron Denon (1747-1825) was embassy secretary in Saint Petersburg and Naples and the artist of innumerable engravings. Napoleon made him director of the imperial museums.

mounted at the captain of the guard's. I informed the Emperor, who told me to stay with him so that I would not be forced to see the governor if he asked for me, and to tell Saint-Denis to remain in the drawing room and Noverraz in the bathroom. Followed by his staff, the governor walked beneath the Emperor's windows, but all the shutters were closed. I thought for a moment he was going to present himself at the outer door, but he turned left and walked toward the new house. Half an hour later he called for his horses and left at a gallop as he had come. The Emperor had been able to observe his strategy without being seen. So went this little scene, which I had believed for a moment was going to end like that of Charles XII at Bender.

The duty captain continued to knock at the outer door for several days. He would stay there a few seconds, then coming inside would ask me to present him to the Emperor, which I refused each time. This refusal could not last long without being anything but a farce. Colonel Harrison, followed by another officer and two aides, came to Longwood and asked to see me. Fearing a trap or an abduction, I went in to warn the Emperor. He was talking with the grand marshal and at first did not think I should enter, then, changing his mind, told me to go ahead. It was to tell me that the duty officer had orders from the governor to present himself each day at General Bonaparte's door in order to see him, and to arrest anyone on the spot who stood in his way to be deported. This was evidently intended for me, but he added, "I am in charge of informing each of General Bonaparte's servants of the governor's will, please send them in to me."

"Colonel," I said to him, "I was able to hear your message as I was taken unaware, but do not count on me to send you anyone if it is not first authorized by the grand marshal." I left him to go to the Emperor, to whom I repeated what had been said to me, and the order given me to send each member of his staff to receive the same message. "Tell each of them that I forbid them to go." Colonel Harrison had to return to Plantation House having only partially fulfilled his mission. But the next day, the following memorandum and note were sent to Count de Montholon:

I the undersigned, Lieutenant General and Governor of Saint Helena, have the honor of informing Napoleon Bonaparte that I have received various reports from the duty officer at Longwood, establishing his continued inability to view the person of Napoleon Bonaparte daily. Although he is said to be indisposed, he has refused to receive Dr. Arnott,[335] principal physician on the island of Saint Helena, or Dr. Verling, the doctor assigned to Longwood, or any other British medical officer who, in conformity with the rules established in Lord Bathurst's instructions of November 30, 1818, could provide assurance morning and evening that he is indisposed and currently at Longwood. In consequence, the undersigned finds it unfortunately necessary to inform Napoleon Bonaparte that in accordance with the instructions in Count Bathurst's letter of November 6, 1818, he has granted the duty officer whatever means he finds it necessary to use to remove all obstacles he may find opposed to his obtaining daily access to a place where Napoleon Bonaparte may be seen.

In the event of any opposition being made or resistance or attempted resistance offered by one of the persons of Napoleon Bonaparte's suite while he is executing the above-mentioned orders, the duty officer has also been authorized to immediately remove from Longwood the person or persons making such opposition or offering such resistance, and this person or persons will be held responsible for all consequences which may result from their actions.

Additionally, the undersigned has observed through the duty officer's reports that in spite of the respectful manner with which he is charged with fulfilling his duties by the instructions given him August 11, 1819, of which he has sent a copy, as well as other communications to Napoleon Bonaparte on August

---

[335] Archibald Arnott, born April 18, 1771, in Scotland, had studied medicine in Edinburgh. Assistant in the 11th dragoons, then surgeon of the 20th infantry, he had served in Holland, Egypt, and Spain. He arrived in Saint Helena with his regiment at the beginning of April 1819. He attempted, with devotion and respect, to relieve the illustrious patient's suffering. A certain liking was eventually established between the patient and his doctor, which Hudson Lowe did not fail to hold against Arnott.

From May 1, 1821, Arnott settled in the library and did not leave the Emperor until his death, sending the governor short notes written in pencil:

"He is dying."

"He is worse."

And at 5:49 p.m. on May 5: "He has this moment expired." We owe to Dr. Arnott a fine sketch of Napoleon on his deathbed, prior to the autopsy which he attended.

Arnott died July 6, 1855, at the age of 84.

11 and 23, 1819, he had found that the doors of Napoleon Bonaparte's residence were closed to him, and he experienced continually renewed difficulty in assuring himself that the person of Napoleon Bonaparte was indeed at Longwood and in making known his desire to be presented to him. In consequence, he has authorized the duty officer on days when he has not seen Napoleon Bonaparte before 10 a.m. to go to the hall or outer apartment of his residence and to that part of his house where his retinue is likely to be, and if he does not find a person who will take a message to Napoleon Bonaparte and inform him of his wish to be admitted to see him, to act on his own to procure means of admission while following, insofar as possible, the procedures established in the instructions sent to him April 11, 1819, without recourse to any means of force until it proves impossible for him to be admitted otherwise.

> *Hudson Lowe, Lieutenant General*
> *Jamestown castle, August 29, 1819*

At the time when this letter arrived at Longwood, the governor could have had no further doubt of the Emperor's presence in Saint Helena because, feeling better and wishing to obtain news of Count de Montholon personally, the Emperor had put on a coat, and with him leaning on my arm we passed behind the house, thinking we would not be seen by the duty officer. The opposite happened: the first person we met before arriving at Count de Montholon's was this same officer, who was able to reassure Sir Hudson Lowe on his fears of escape, and also tell him how physically changed the Emperor was.

To the governor's letter was attached the following note signed by Sir Thomas Reade:

Memorandum for the information of the persons in the retinue of, or who live near, Napoleon Bonaparte at Longwood.

The duty officer at Longwood having made his report to the governor on the absolute impossibility he has experienced for some days of obtaining a distinct view of Napoleon Bonaparte's person, and no response having been made to the proposals communicated to Napoleon Bonaparte on March 21, 1819 to admit the duty officer to his presence, the governor finds it indispensable, following the instructions he has received to this effect from the British govern-

ment, to order the duty officer to take the appropriate and necessary measures in order to daily assure himself through his personal observation of Napoleon Bonaparte's current presence at Longwood.

At the same time the governor orders that it be declared to the officers and other persons in the suite of, or who live near, Napoleon Bonaparte, and it is hereby declared to these persons that if he has had recourse to this measure already amply justified, it is because Napoleon Bonaparte refuses to admit the duty officer to his presence or, if he is ill, to receive a British medical officer who could give assurance each morning and evening that he is ill and currently at Longwood.

After this declaration anyone who dares attempt any resistance whatsoever will not only be irrevocably removed from Longwood, but will expose himself to all risks and dangers that may result, as well as all the consequences of such an action.

Reade, Lieutenant Colonel
By order of his Excellency the Governor,
Saint Helena, August 19, 1819

This letter and this note had no sooner come to the Emperor's attention than the following declaration was dictated to Count de Montholon by the Emperor to be given to the duty officer if, as for some days past, he again presented himself to make his visit.

The day before yesterday you came to my home three times in the space of two hours. Yesterday, three times, without my being able to understand your intention. It appears that you wish to violate the Emperor's apartments, hitherto respected, and which are under the protection of the laws of the people and the specific acts of your government. I replied to you that only the prince regent and the privy council can make legal restrictions, and that the prince regent and the members of the privy council have known for the past four years that between enduring shameful treatment and death, there can be no doubt over the Emperor's choice. They have ordered nothing, at least that has been communicated to us, that changes the state of affairs and the established practices of four years. Alone, ill, deprived of all communication with the universe, even with the British officers and inhabitants of this rock, he bares his throat to his murderers' sword; there is no need to seek any pretext.

I have asked you to communicate the acts of the prince regent or the

*privy council or even the instructions by virtue of which you act since the 11th of
the month. You have not communicated any of these acts to me.*

*I told you that as the Emperor does not recognize any duty officer, you
have not spoken to him, he has not seen you nor the officers who preceded you in
your post for four years. The declaration of August 16 answers all this, I append
it again here. Since that time, the health of this prince has become much worse,
and he needs more than ever the assistance of his doctor whom he demands.*

*All the attempts made via servants are unworthy; they are useless
because they are rejected by our manners and our customs.*

*I repeat to you what I told you two weeks ago, that the Emperor prefers
the refuge of the grave to suffering ignominious treatment. He can know no
restriction in the terms of your law if it does not come from the prince regent or
the privy council. He has sacrificed all, abandoned all, and he is reduced to the
most miserable life to satisfy the hatred of his enemies. If their vengeance has not
yet abated, let them strike a single blow: it would be a kindness, because it would
put an end to an agony that has lasted since August 11 and which you seem to
take pleasure in prolonging.*

> *General Count de Montholon*
> *Longwood, August 31, 1819*

This letter served to have Captain Blakeney removed shortly
afterward. In accepting the position of duty officer at Longwood, he
had understood that he was being offered a post of honor. The role he
had been obliged to play went against his nature; he asked to be
removed and was replaced by another captain of the 66th. A few outings by the Emperor either on foot or in his carriage put an end to the
offensive correspondence from Plantation House and the daily visits
by the duty officer.

CHAPTER TWENTY-ONE

New arrivals — Fathers Buonavita and Vignali — Dr. Antommarchi —
The Emperor's dictations — Thoughts on suicide — Gardening —
Details regarding the Emperor's dress

$\mathcal{A}$ ll the time that Count de Montholon's illness lasted, the grand marshal came twice a day to see the Emperor. As soon as her convalescence began, Countess Bertrand also came. All three of them, after an outing on foot or by carriage through the woods of Longwood, would go get news of Count de Montholon.

I had the honor of sharing some of these walks with the Emperor. Not wanting to disturb the grand marshal or Count de Montholon, who was not yet fully recovered, he took me with him several times in the morning on the path through Deadwood. One day when he found he was tired, he sent me to notify the stables so they would bring his carriage, and I accompanied him on several trips he took. Another time, it was on a Sunday, the workmen were not at the house under construction. This residence was already sufficiently advanced that its layout was recognizable, and we went there. He found the interior layout poor: my room, he said, was too far away from his own; he showed me where doors could be cut to facilitate serving. He found the rooms large and airy, and went down into the service quarters, not suspecting that the stones on which he walked would serve to build his tomb. He nourished the hope that this visit would not be known to Plantation House, but he was wrong: the governor was informed of it.

Once Count de Montholon's health returned, these privileges no longer fell to me and rightfully reverted to Count de Montholon, whose every moment was given over to the Emperor, with an abnegation and a devotion that came to an end only with His Majesty's death.

The governor, based on the instructions he passed on, could have applied his Longwood rules to Count de Montholon and the grand marshal, because of several letters written to him and signed by these gentlemen. He never dared do this for fear of the repercussions in Europe, and also because these gentlemen's signatures only covered the reproaches the Emperor was addressing to him.

Things had reached that point when, on September 21, the grand marshal came to inform the Emperor of a ship's arrival from Europe, carrying on board two priests, Fathers Buonavita and Vignali,[336] a surgeon, Antommarchi,[337] the butler Coursot,[338] and the cook

---

[336]The priests sent to Longwood by Cardinal Fesch were Corsican, largely uninteresting, and of no resource to the Emperor, who nonetheless was acquainted with them.

Father Antonio Buonavita had been Madame Mère's chaplain on the island of Elba. He was a saintly man who spoke haltingly due to a stroke suffered in 1810. He spoke Italian and Spanish, but little French. He trembled chronically: he was 67 and a troubled life spent in Mexico and the United States for more than 40 years had worn him down. In July 1815 following Napoleon's second abdication, Madame Mère had sent him to London with orders to await the deposed Emperor there and act as his chaplain during his stay in England. The departure of the *Northumberland* for Saint Helena had forced him to return to Rome where Princess Borghèse welcomed him in her chapel.

As for Angelo Vignali, he was 30 years old. Short, stocky, swarthy, and a bit wild-looking, he was intelligent, had studied at Saint-Sulpice and dabbled in medicine. The Emperor had known him for a time on Elba, where he had gone in 1814.

Both priests wore ecclesiastic garb only at Longwood, as British law forbade it on His British Majesty's territory.

[337]François Antommarchi was born in Corsica in 1789. Many books were written about him offering contradictory theories, one of which even implied that perhaps he was not a doctor.

[338]Jacques Coursot worked for Madame Mère prior to leaving for Saint Helena. He served there with devotion, quietly, without joining in any intrigue. He was present at the last minutes of the Emperor's life and at the autopsy, came back to France in 1821, and returned to Rome. In 1840 Coursot returned to Saint Helena with his comrades to retrieve the Emperor's ashes, then moved back to Paris where he died in May 1856.

Coursot brought back a few mementos from Saint Helena, among them the picture of Christ that was placed on Sundays in the dining room at Longwood, at the time when mass was said, a lock of the Emperor's hair, his last beard shavings, and a piece of tendon that Antommarchi had secretly stolen from the British after the autopsy.

Chandelier[339] who had been sent from Rome by Cardinal Fesch for his service. The governor had them come to Plantation House to dine, and surrounded them with attentions, believing he could extract from them what he wanted before they arrived at Longwood.

Informed of this contact with a man who lacked every courtesy, to the point of keeping close to him those who could have given him news of his family, the Emperor became so angry that he put off receiving them until the following day, and asked the grand marshal to see each of them, as if the grand marshal's passage between him and the governor could wash away the impurity stemming from the contact they had had with Hudson Lowe.

Among the arrivals, whom we received with joy for the Emperor's sake and for our own, was Father Buonavita, whom I had known on the island of Elba as Madame Mère's chaplain. After so many misfortunes, we saw each other again with strong and deeply felt emotion. According to what the grand marshal told him about the personnel sent to him, the Emperor, while taking into account the devotion which he appreciated, appeared to be little satisfied. The doctor was unknown to him; of the two priests, the younger had studied medicine, and the older, whom he had known with Madame Mère, could offer him few conversational resources; it was however what they should have concentrated on. Learned men such as doctors and priests could have been a great fortune for him; he would have discussed theology with the priests and all kinds of other subjects with a doctor who had knowledge of more than his own art. "They send me," he said to

---

[339]Napoleon had lost his cook Lepage in May 1818: he had returned to England. He was replaced by Pierron, then by Laroche—lent by Ambassador Amherst—but Laroche went back to England and Pierron resumed his duties. In September 1819, Jacques Chandelier arrived. He had worked for Princess Pauline. When he went to England, Chandelier visited Laroche, who informed him of the poor state of the kitchen. Chandelier brought an entire set of cooking utensils, an ice machine, tin to re-tin the pans, and the parts for a German oven. In Saint Helena he was an excellent cook; complaining about the scrawny poultry, he started raising chickens and turkeys. He would prepare fish that resembled sea bass, small cakes, banana desserts marinated in rum, and at the Emperor's request, a soldier's soup. Unfortunately he was not able to use the ice machine.

the grand marshal, "a man already broken by the years, and whose entire life was spent in Paraguay; what kind of resource can that be for me? I am surprised they did not ask France to send me a doctor from one of my armies: Larrey would have been glad to attend me. They should have chosen a man whom I could trust. Instead, they send me a young surgeon and a priest who dabbles in medicine! They couldn't have done anything more stupid! I certainly recognize Cardinal Fesch's hand in all this. I am a great enough lord, it seems to me, that they could have given 30 to 40,000 francs a year to a man who would come to offer me his services."

Although the Emperor was then complaining of the pain in his side, no one could foresee that eighteen months later one of these priests, Father Vignali, would walk before his coffin and bless his grave.

As I have already said, the Emperor did not receive them the day of their arrival. He summoned Chandelier and Coursot. The first was Princess Pauline's cook in Rome and had been sent by that princess. Coursot had served Madame Mère. They came in together. The Emperor asked each of them several questions about his family and Madame Mère's health: What was her house in Rome like? Did she receive foreigners? What was the cardinal doing? Coursot answered all those questions, saying among other things that Madame's generosity was never refused to French military personnel who solicited her help in getting to America. Her Imperial Highness bore with courage and resignation the pain of knowing the Emperor to be in Saint Helena, and she never sat down at the table without saying: "If only I could send this supper to my son!" All that she owned was certainly at the Emperor's disposal. "And the cardinal, what is he doing?" asked the Emperor.

"Sire, His Eminence keeps Madame company, and leaves her only to go look at his paintings."

"Is his gallery attractive?"

"It is said to be very valuable, and he intends it to go to Your Majesty." When he interrogated Chandelier, the Emperor asked him what Princess Pauline was doing. "Sire," Chandelier replied, "Her

Highness receives many people, and she never speaks of Your Majesty without her eyes filling with tears. She would very much like to receive permission to come stay with the Emperor, she has instructed me tell you this. Lord Douglas,[340] who was with her when I had the honor of seeing her before my departure, told her that we would perhaps not find Your Majesty here. I can see that he was giving Her Imperial Highness false hopes, when he said in front of me: 'I can assure you that they will no longer find the Emperor in Saint Helena.'
"

"That's fine," the Emperor said to them, telling them to leave. "They seemed to be good people," the Emperor said after they left. "Put them down for 2,500 francs in wages; tell Pierron to get them each settled in their duties."

Night had tempered the previous day's bad mood. All that Count Bertrand and Count de Montholon had said about the priests and the doctor did not dispel the irritation he had felt on learning of their visit to Plantation House. The next morning the Emperor summoned them, the priests first. Father Buonavita and Father Vignali knelt when they neared the bed in which the Emperor was lying and kissed his hand. The Emperor told them to sit down, asked them questions about his family, and then talked with them for some time. To everything he was told about Madame's love for him, he replied that his mother had always loved him very much, he and Princess Pauline had been the spoiled children of the family, and in the great crises where she had found herself, Madame had always shown a superhuman courage and strength of character. He talked to Father Buonavita of his age, his health, the dangers of his voyage, and his fear that the intemperate climate might be harmful for him. He asked a few ques-

---

[340]The Marquis of Douglas and Anglesea was among the tasteful foreigners who came to the Villa Borghèse in Rome. The Duke of Blacas, ambassador for the king of France, kept a close eye on this fine house; he could nevertheless not prevent the great English lord from coming daily to visit Princess Pauline. She admitted the wealthy lord to her dressing ceremony, where he handed pins to the chambermaid. "In the evening, when he serves as my footstool," wrote the beautiful Pauline, "I think with a certain joy that I have one of the greatest lords of Great Britain under my feet."

tions of Father Vignali about his stay at the Saint-Sulpice seminary and on the island of Elba, spoke to him of Corsica where he was born, and asked him a few questions regarding his practice of medicine. He told Father Buonavita he wanted mass to be given the following Sunday in his drawing room; they should arrange this between the two of them, everyone would attend. He dismissed them both, expressing again his thanks for their coming to share his exile. The two priests were happy with the fine reception they had just received; joy showed on their faces.

When Dr. Antommarchi was shown in, he questioned him about his family, Corsica where he had also been born, and his studies. He appeared satisfied by his replies and his knowledge, but he found him a little young and presumptuous. The grand marshal was asked to tell Father Vignali that at Longwood he would only be concerned with priestly duties. In dismissing the doctor, he said to him: "I place Father Buonavita in your care, I fear that the cardinal has sent this good old man here, only to have him buried here. He is a respectable man who should be well cared for."

All these people took up their duties. The doctor received wages of 9,000 francs, Father Buonavita 6,000, and Father Vignali 3,000, which the Emperor told me to pay them. As that sum was not entirely necessary to them, he told me to give each of the priests 250 francs a month for his needs by withholding 500 francs from Count de Montholon out of the 2,000 francs previously allocated him when the countess was still at Longwood, and to take 250 francs out of the house expenses for the doctor. Each had a Chinese man to serve him, and a common table for the three of them. The doctor had Dr. O'Meara's former lodgings, Father Buonavita had those occupied by General Gourgaud; and Father Vignali had those of the captain of the guard, who was given other accommodations at Count de Montholon's.

The following Sunday mass was celebrated in the drawing room, and the entire household attended. The Emperor left everyone free to practice his religion, but it would have made a bad impression to appear irreligious. The Emperor was concerned with the priests' well-being, but saw little of them as they were a meager resource in the way of conversation. They brought with them a case of books; the commented gospel brought by Father Buonavita and a Bible already in the library were the only religious works at Longwood. It is not true, as M. de Beautern stated in his book *Napoleon's Religious Conversations in Saint Helena*, that the Emperor found intellectual nourishment in these two books, which he claimed were constantly on his table. The Emperor recognized the beauty of the gospel, he sometimes read passages from it, and said that in Egypt one could cover the entire country with gospel in hand, but those works remained in the library. In Saint Helena the Emperor read all kinds of books, even the *New Heloise*, in which he left some notations in his own handwriting. With the Emperor's approval, the grand marshal entrusted the religious education of his children to Father Vignali, who later celebrated mass at the marshal's wife's residence for herself and her family.

During his first calls, Dr. Antommarchi carefully examined the Emperor's health. He gathered from the grand marshal, Count de Montholon, and myself the information that would allow him to make no mistakes in the application of remedies he wished to prescribe. Like his predecessors, he recommended exercise, rubbing the legs—which caused the swelling to decrease, making it easier for him to walk—and rides on horseback and by carriage.

Count de Montholon, now fully recovered, gave all his time to the Emperor. When he came to see him for the first time, the Emperor told him that now that he was alone, his table was his, and that in the future he would dine with him. "There," he said indicating me, "is my nurse since you have been in bed. He has served me both as secretary and reader; he reads perfectly and without tiring me, which I appreciate a great deal." It is true that since General Gourgaud's departure, the Emperor, aside from having me read aloud to him frequently, often kept me near him to write under his dictation. I had managed a sort of shorthand that allowed me to follow him and to reread back, if he wished, the dictation he had just made. Those dictations, copied over, were reread and corrected by him, then given to Saint-Denis to be copied and kept in manuscript form. It was particularly during the time when Count de Montholon remained in bed that I became of more use to the Emperor. His time was divided between Count and Countess Bertrand, and in their absence I was with him. Finding me more often at his side, he dictated to me *the Summary of Caesar's campaigns*,[341] saying to me one day on that occasion: "You will be able to tell your children that you wrote this work under my dictation." Often at night the Emperor had me awakened by the duty valet in order to write, for since my illness he no longer wanted me to sleep near him, although it disrupted his habits.

The first time I wrote under the Emperor's dictation in Saint Helena, I asked him to repeat himself: "Continue," he replied. After that I carefully avoided doing so. There were always a dozen well-sharpened pencils on the Emperor's desk and I used them, thus saving all the time I would have taken to dip my pen in the inkwell, had I used one. He dictated with such clarity and flow that one could see no other thought entered his mind to disturb the work he was doing. The Emperor had an astonishing memory; he used to say on this subject that he knew better than the war or naval offices what the personnel and equipment of the regiments or squadrons were. When he went back to bed at night after a few hours' dictation he would tell me to go and put his notes in order for his awakening. If it should happen this was not done, he would approach me, say I was lazy, and put his hand on my ear. This was a sign of approval, of which everyone was jealous; for him it was a sign of satisfaction with the man who was thus touched, and helped to relieve the monotony of our existence. I have already said, and I repeat it again, the Emperor was kind, mirthful, playful in his own quarters; he possessed all the qualities that caused devotion in men. Among the dictations made after some readings is

---

[341] *Précis des guerres de César par Napoléon, écrit par M. Marchand à l'île Sainte-Hélène, sous la dictée de l'Empereur* (Paris, 1836). "The nature of my service," Marchand writes in the preface, "kept me constantly with the Emperor, who called upon me either to read to him or to write under his dictation. It is thus that the notes on Caesar's commentaries were dictated entirely and almost constantly during long periods of insomnia, during which he said work brought some relief to his suffering, and cast a few flowers on the path leading him to the grave."

the one that follows. It was a first draft that the Emperor never saw again, and I show it here only as a sort of literary relaxation on this miserable rock.

Thoughts on suicide:

Does a man have the right to kill himself?—Yes, if his death harms no one and if life is an evil for him.

When is life an evil for man?—When it offers him only suffering and sorrow. But as suffering and sorrow change each moment, there is no time in life when a man has the right to kill himself. That time could arrive only at the very moment of his death, as only then would he have proof that his life was nothing but a web of evil and suffering. There is no man who has not wanted to kill himself several times in his life, yielding to the moral afflictions of his soul, but who a few days later would have regretted it because of changes in his feelings and circumstances. The man who would have killed himself on Monday will want to live on Saturday, and yet you can only kill yourself once. Man's life is made up of the past, the present, and the future, or at least the present and the future. But if it is evil only in the present, he sacrifices the future: the ills of one day do not authorize him to sacrifice his life to come. Only the man whose life is bad and who can be certain—which is impossible—that it will always be so, and will change in neither position nor will, either through changes in circumstance or situation or through habit and the passage of time—which still is impossible— would have the right to kill himself. The man who, succumbing to the weight of present evils, takes his life, commits an injustice toward himself, obeying through despair and weakness a momentary fantasy to which he sacrifices future existence. The comparison with a gangrened arm severed to save the body is not valid: when the surgeon amputates the arm, he is certain that it would kill the body: it is not a feeling but a certainty. Whereas when life's sufferings lead a man to kill himself, not only does he put an end to his sufferings, but he also destroys the future. A man may never regret having had an arm cut off, but if he could know it, he would almost always regret having taken his life.

It was with such literary diversions that the Emperor passed the boredom of his long exile on the rock of Saint Helena.

The year 1819 had gone by with alternating spells of good and bad health for the Emperor. He had gotten in the habit of strolling in one or the other of his small gardens whose upkeep was the responsibility of Noverraz. They were located under his windows and surrounded by a small wooden fence, and either in his robe in the morning, or dressed in the afternoon, he could enter them straight from his apartment. The duty officer found this advantageous to more easily verify the Emperor's presence at Longwood without his surveillance bothering the Emperor, and thus reassure the governor, whose mind was always fixated on attempted escape. That year he even granted larger boundaries to allow His Majesty to exercise on horseback, but the Emperor only took advantage of this to reconnoiter the terrain in which he could ride with solely his staff.

On January 1, 1820, the Emperor received, as in the preceding years, the wishes of the grand marshal and his family, those of Count de Montholon, the priests, and Dr. Antommarchi. They were all invited to dinner, including the children, who on such occasions he would always reward with a few gold napoleons bearing his profile.

The announcement of ships coming from Europe was always a moment of happiness for him because of the news he could receive from France. It was the same for the colony: newspapers were read with great interest. One day Count de Montholon on looking through them said to the Emperor that they were about to demolish the fountain on the Place Royale to erect a statue of Louis XIII. "They only know how to do stupid things," replied the Emperor. "Why destroy an object of public utility to put such an insignificant king there?" Another article reproached him for having had the weakness to surround himself with nobility. "Marmont and Fouché were not nobles," he said. "Talleyrand had not gone into exile; I entrusted my destiny to the former by sending him to Paris, and he went there only to consummate my ruin."

A few days later he commented, "My actions and events answer all the libelous statements made against me. I am innocent of the ordinary crimes of dynasty heads. I have nothing to fear from posterity, history will perhaps even accuse me of having been too good.

Montholon, my son," he said to the general, grabbing him by the ear, "I can present myself with confidence before God's judgment seat."

The Emperor's way of thinking was that one should die in the religion in which one had been born: that of one's forefathers. He said there was a destiny we must all obey.

For some time, the Emperor had spoken of enlarging the gardens under his windows. He felt the need to protect himself from the winds with an elevated grass berm. Not only did he see in this a means of distraction for himself and the colony, but he also found in it the advantage of further separating the house from the line of sentries placed there every evening at 9 p.m. Once the measurements had been taken and decided, everyone had to participate in the work. The Emperor thus engaged in exercise beneficial to his health. It was also, he said to me, a means of facilitating Count de Montholon's convalescence and of providing shade around a house that had none. He also believed that, in walking, he would find a way to escape the observation of the guard captain. Count de Montholon did not guess what sentiment motivated the Emperor: he agreed with His Majesty's idea only because he saw it as a means of improving his obviously declining health.

The butler, M. Pierron, was sent to town to buy wheelbarrows, pickaxes, shovels, and all the gardening tools suitable to clear and plant a fairly large area of land. Each had his own tools: the Emperor himself had his rake and spade, which he used as a walking stick or to lean on when he watched the work. It began with the lawn berm on the southern side, which rose to nine feet in height, with a base nine feet wide and running eighty feet in length. Sir Hudson Lowe saw in that berm only what he was told, a shelter against the wind, and did not oppose it. But when he saw that the fence around the little gardens had been moved out that same distance, and that the night sentries were thus moved away from the house, he feared for the security of the detention. He mentioned this, but nevertheless did not dare take it upon himself to oppose what the Emperor had just undertaken, and so the Emperor gained that much more freedom around his house.

The Emperor and Count de Montholon supervised the work. Every morning at daybreak, the colony was awakened by the duty valet. Often a stone thrown against my shutters by the Emperor would announce that the time for work had arrived. Mine consisted mainly of tracing the layout under the direction of the Emperor. If I took a spade, it was more to rectify than to dig, which led His Majesty to call me "the monitor." The Emperor had adopted for dress a nankeen jacket like a farmer's and a pair of trousers of the same fabric, with red slippers and a wide-brimmed straw hat to protect him from the sun, with the shirt collar over that of the jacket. So as to be less recognizable, he had ordered Saint-Denis and Noverraz to dress the same way. By his presence, the Emperor spurred on each one to work. The doctor and the priests were also called on, as well as the Chinese. Everyone worked in proportion to his strength. Count Bertrand never arrived before eight o'clock, to chat while strolling with the Emperor; Count de Montholon was there at the same time as His Majesty. It sometimes happened that the Emperor placed a shovel in their hands, but it was not used as it was in Noverraz's hands. "Gentlemen," he said, "you are incapable of earning a shilling a day." The Emperor himself wanted to use a pickax, but soon abandoned this as an instrument poorly suited to his hands. The planning of the gardens gave the Emperor healthy exercise: this outdoor conversation for several hours did him good, and made him tackle lunch with an appetite, a sensation we all generally felt at ten o'clock. Then it got too hot, and everyone went inside.

When the walls were built, he had a wooden fence enclose all the part facing the camp, where he did not have to fear the wind, which he said parched him and made him irritable. It was to prevent animals from coming into the planted area he intended to make there. These gardens were considered interior gardens, and moved the line of sentries posed at night to 80 feet from the house, instead of 40 feet.

When the work was started, the governor came to Longwood and offered everything we might desire, even soldiers, if this were judged necessary. Count de Montholon thanked the captain of the guard who made this offer, and said that the Emperor was quite satisfied with what he had around him and needed no one. The Longwood personnel was increased by four Chinese for the care of the gardens and to continue the work during our absence in the course of the day. The Emperor told me to give them each 30 shillings a month, and in addition to that they received their government wages and food. Only the cook had been exempted from the morning work to attend to the preparation of the Emperor's lunch: this was served at ten o'clock in one of the small gardens, in the shade of his little orange grove, while waiting for our new plantings to provide shade in the larger gardens. Count de Montholon was regularly present at this luncheon. Count Bertrand, if he remained until that time, was also invited. The priests and the doctor in turn were invited occasionally, but rarely. The luncheon was a soup, a vegetable, and a meat dish, then coffee which he had poured over sugar. The meat dish consisted of chicken or a leg of mutton, or a grilled rack of lamb.

The Emperor ate with appetite and his health seemed to be satisfactory, although he continued to complain about his side. The Emperor liked to extend the conversation at the table; it was generally the time he chose to tell stories of his youth, and it was a pleasure to listen to him because he spoke well and without ever searching for his words that seemed to flow naturally. Saint-Denis and Noverraz served him; some of these anecdotes were reported to me by them.

He talked about Egypt, and told how after arriving in Cairo, he had sent his son Eugène to present his regards to Mourad Bey's wife, who remained locked up with the women in her harem. She was touched by the gracious manners of the young Frenchman and the general's politeness toward her. She had him served sherbet and gave him a very valuable ring. "I sent her a message," the Emperor said, "that she was free to remain in Cairo or to go and join her husband. When Mourad Bey was informed of my consideration to his wife, he sent me his thanks."

Another time he related how on his return from Syria he wished to have news of Europe, and sent one of his officers aboard the Turkish flagship to deal with the prisoners, fully thinking he would be stopped by Sidney Smith; that officer informed him of the loss of Italy. It was after reading the newspapers sent to him that he gave orders to

Admiral Ganteaume to prepare the frigate *Muiron*; it was ordered to proceed to a given rendezvous, where he got on board and returned to France, after leaving instructions for Kléber. This return trip had been told so many diverse ways that I was charmed to hear it told so simply by the Emperor himself.[342]

The Emperor said one day, while glancing through *The Miracles of Jesus Christ*, that Jesus should have done his miracles not in some isolated spot in Syria and only in front of a few men whose good faith could be suspect, but in a city like Rome in view of the entire population.

Leaving the table following lunch, the Emperor returned to his bedroom followed by Count de Montholon. If he dismissed him, he would get into bed and have me read to him until he fell asleep. Between two and three o'clock he took his bath and conversed with one or the other of these gentlemen. If the doctor had been called, the Emperor talked with him about medicine and about the anatomical work of Mascagne, whose plates he continued to trace in Saint Helena. When the Emperor got out of his bathtub, two very hot sheets were ready. One would be thrown over him and he would wrap it around himself and go from the bathroom into his bedroom, where a bright fire was prepared; the second sheet was placed on his shoulders, and this way he was well dried. If the Emperor was feeling well, he would dress immediately. He would put on silk stockings and buckled shoes, then don a pair of white cloth trousers and remain stripped from the waist up to do his beard; but in Saint Helena he shaved only every other day. All the details of his preparations were seen to with great care. His teeth had remained very fine and quite shiny, although he had not had any opiate for a long time, and had to content himself with a

---

[342]Boudin de Tromelin, a Breton officer who had gone into exile, was taken with Sidney Smith in 1796 and locked up in the temple under a false name, then freed. He had followed the commodore to the Orient, who after quite a lively escape, commanded the *Tigre* in 1799, before Alexandria. It was Tromelin who in July provided the newspapers that revealed to Bonaparte the state of affairs in France. In his memoirs, Tromelin recounts how the commander in chief of the army of the Orient escaped the Anglo-Turkish cruise ships.

little brandy mixed with water. After having run a brush over his head and combed his hair, he had his shoulders and body brushed, insisting that we press hard on the liver side while brushing briskly as well as on the right shoulder where he felt some pain. He then had cologne poured in his hand, and would rub his side and chest with it, and put some under his arms, after having washed his face in a larger silver basin containing water mixed with cologne. For his hands and nails he used a lemon. When all this washing was done, he completed his dress as I have already described in the chapter on the Hundred Days, and went into the drawing room. While on bivouac, in his tent, these details of dress were carried out just as in the palace of Saint-Cloud or the Tuileries. If the Emperor did not feel well, instead of dressing he would get into bed to induce sweating, which always did him good. In Saint Helena the Emperor wore only civilian clothes, carrying the badge of the Legion of Honor; his head was covered with the uniform hat so well known to all of Europe. His Majesty dressed in white every day; he liked to be very neat in his appearance, but took no precautions or care not to get dirty. He liked to feel at ease in his clothing, and did not want anyone to change its shape. He hated having pimples in his mouth, and to avoid them, once he had finished dressing he would apply a handkerchief soaked in cologne to his lips. All the Emperor's linen was marked with an "N" capped by an imperial crown; even on his silk stockings, a crown was placed over the embroidered corner of the stocking.

One day when Count Bertrand was present while he was dressing, the Emperor, while brushing his body as I described above, asked him if he didn't do the same thing. "No, Sire," replied the grand marshal.

"You are mistaken, Bertrand, it prevents many diseases."

"Sire, I have reached the age of nearly fifty without using it, and I am none the worse for it."

"Well, rubbing my liver is good for me; you don't believe it?" asked the Emperor. And as the grand marshal was smiling while looking at him: "You don't believe that I am ill, you are like your wife who does not want to believe it either!"

"Sire, Your Majesty will allow me to say that he does not appear to be in bad health."

"You dare to argue, Bertrand!" Taking the grand marshal by the throat and pinning him against the wall he said: "Your money or your life!—Aristocrat!" he said, releasing him.

"Your Majesty will permit me to say that all his strength does not seem to have left him, for he was certainly holding me very tightly."

"Without being tall, I never failed to be quite strong," said the Emperor. "I remember when I was in military school we minor nobles would have fights with the sons of great noblemen, and I always came out victorious!" Knowing the very liberal ideas of the grand marshal, the Emperor called him "aristocrat!"

CHAPTER TWENTY-TWO

*A*s long as the work on the gardens lasted, the Emperor would come out at 4 p.m. and head for the Chinese workers. One day, one of them was digging close to a tall yew tree and cutting some large roots, which I believed would injure the tree. I pointed this out to the Emperor, who replied: "If a fine table is served behind you, and you are hungry and allowed to sit down, you will certainly find a way to turn around to satisfy your appetite. It will be the same for this tree: it will take from its remaining roots on the other side the substance that has been withdrawn from it."

A small pump had been purchased and mounted on wheels; it could be transported easily to all points of the garden. Saint-Denis or Noverraz would work the pump lever, and the Emperor amused himself by using the hose in those areas that seemed to him to be suffering from drought. In his gardens, he waited for dinnertime while walking with Count de Montholon. On leaving the table, weather permitting, he would get into his carriage and invite Count and Countess Bertrand to join him. But more often he went alone with Count de Montholon, and had himself taken on his way back to see Countess Bertrand, who was often ill, and spent a few hours with her. The work at Longwood had caused quite a commotion in town.

Among the visitors who came to see the gardens was Lady Lowe's daughter, a young and attractive person. She was curious not only to see the gardens, but also to catch a glimpse of the Emperor, whom she did not know. Fate would have it that having entered the compound, she was met by Count de Montholon, to whom she expressed the desire that drew her to Longwood. The Emperor's repugnance for the governor did not extend to his family. Count de Montholon promptly offered her his arm and took her around the various paths in the garden, but a providential coincidence served her even better: she found herself face to face with the Emperor under a long bower covered with passion leaves where he was strolling. Her first reaction was that of great embarrassment, but it soon ceased before the gracious way in which the Emperor received her. Sweets were served to her, and he offered her a rose as a memento of her pilgrimage. That young lady had been born of Lady Lowe's first marriage. Her mother was herself a very attractive woman, and would have asked nothing better than to be introduced at Longwood and have the honor of receiving the Emperor in her home; but the unending harassment by her husband was always an obstacle to that wish.

The priests had brought with them two trunks: one contained church vestments and ornaments of great beauty, presents from Cardinal Fesch; the other, newspapers and books that would have been of little interest, had the Emperor's correspondence published by Panckoucke not been among them. When he opened the first of the trunks, the Emperor said: "This is of the domain of Saint Peter, send it to Buonavita. As for the second, it belongs to me." The eight volumes of his correspondence in particular caught his attention, and were gradually covered by notes written in his hand; the other books interested him very little, for he said to me: "The cardinal could have spared a few thousand francs and sent me some good works." However after pulling them out one by one, I reached the bottom and found a handsome portfolio of green leather, holding the portrait of the King of Rome and that of Prince Eugène's son, sent by the prince. The Emperor smiled with great pleasure at the sight of this miniature of his son. His eyes moistened: "Poor child," he said, "what a destiny!" Then, handing it to me: "Here," he said, "place it open on my desk, so that I may see it every day." I had taken from the Elysée a portrait of the King of Rome as a child, painted by Isabey, and on that same day the Emperor gave it to me.[343]

Since the arrival of the priests, mass was said in the drawing room. The Emperor decided that the dining room, which he no longer used, would be converted into a chapel and his drawing room would serve as a dining room. Up until then, a table served to hold the divine office, and nothing enhanced its appearance. We all went to work, and the transformation was complete. Noverraz, aided by a Chinese carpenter, built an altar with two steps that were easily removable after the service. M. Pierron, who was quite a handyman, built a very fine gold and white tabernacle in which to place the ciborium and the blessed sacrament. Red satin was purchased to stretch across the back wall and six feet around. On the side, a drapery held back by two gilt curtain hooks kept this material away from the ceiling. Green velvet covered the altar steps and extended like a carpet under the feet of the Emperor's prayer bench; a crowned "N" one foot tall decorated the middle, and other smaller ones were located at each corner of the same carpet. We had no braiding to add crowns, which we wanted. If the imperial dignity was forgotten by the British government every day, it was not by us, for all the Emperor's prestige existed as if he were still on his throne. I mentioned this to Count de Montholon, who remembered the remnants of a uniform he had worn as an aide to the prince of Neufchâtel; on it we found not only the braiding we were lacking for our crowns, but the means of adding a large cross to the base of the altar, which was covered by cloth decorated with a broad edging of antique lace. Two silver candelabra with six branches were placed on either side of the tabernacle, itself crowned by a black cross with a very fine silver Christ. Two china vases, decorated with flowers on Sundays, were set on a platform overlooking the altar, and in line with the candelabra. All this work was completed between Monday and Saturday without the help of outsiders. Strong arms and willingness

---

[343]There was in the Emperor's study at Longwood a small portrait of the King of Rome painted by Isabey. The child was shown wearing the uniform of the national guard, kneeling with hands joined; the caption read as follows: "I pray God for my father and for France." This painting has a replica, also engraved by Bouillon, but in it the child wears ordinary clothes.

were lacking in no one, when it was a matter of serving the Emperor and showing him our zeal and devotion. The following Sunday we were able to enjoy the Emperor's surprise, for His Majesty had no knowledge of the preparations made to properly decorate the room he had just assigned as a chapel. Everything was prepared for the hour of noon. The only door allowing light into this room was closed, and it was lit by the candles in the candelabra and two lamps with frosted globes set on tables on either side of the altar.

Father Buonavita, who was saying mass, had arrived wearing his finest vestments; Father Vignali assisted him, and Count Bertrand's oldest son was to serve mass. Count and Countess Bertrand, along with their other children and servants, had arrived. I went to inform the Emperor, who was in his apartments with Count de Montholon, that the priest was at the altar. A few moments later the door leading from his bedroom to the chapel opened, and the Emperor came and took his place between the armchair and the prayer bench set for him ahead of everyone. The grand marshal, Countess Bertrand, her children, and General de Montholon were behind him, and behind them the household servants. As daylight did not enter through any opening it gave a mysterious air to the religious ceremony. After having greeted the Emperor, the priests started mass, which was heard reverently. When it was over the Emperor went into the drawing room and then the garden, followed by the people in his retinue. A half hour later, everything had been removed from the dining room, and was put back in place only the following Sunday.

As long as the Emperor's health allowed it, things continued this way. But when his health declined, he only listened to mass from his bed, with the door between his bedroom and the chapel open. He authorized the grand marshal to have Father Vignali say mass at his home, and if the governor did not object, to invite the Irish officers and soldiers of the camp who were deprived of Catholic services to come and attend mass there. However, this never occurred.

The Emperor had added to the already beautiful chapel ornaments an alb decorated with lace, and altar cloths decorated the same way. Father Buonavita had albs made of coarse cloth, and wished to have finer ones. He talked to me about it and asked if I couldn't tell the Emperor that they had been damaged by rats during the voyage. "If you want to have such a lie on your conscience," I said to him laughing, "I shall do it."

"No," he said, "but the sin would not be a very large one." That same evening I mentioned it to the Emperor, who laughed heartily over the good father's trick and told me to have some made for him out of fine linen.

When he came in, the Emperor expressed to me his satisfaction at the surprise we had prepared for him. Count de Montholon told me he had been moved when he was told that everything had been done without the help of outsiders. The Emperor had a religious soul, his profession of faith made as he was dying: "I die in the Roman Catholic and Apostolic church in which I was born more than fifty years ago" bears witness to his feelings on this matter. I cannot say however that these feelings were more pronounced in Saint Helena than in Paris or on the island of Elba. When he entered the chapel, he would go to his place, cross himself, and kneel on his prayer bench. At the moment of elevation, he would bow without affectation. The Emperor's religious sentiments went back to his childhood, and were the result of his early education; they were deep in his heart, and later his genius made use of them as a means of government. He said he believed that those people who liked mystery should look for it in the sound morals of religion rather than in Lenormand or Cagliostro. But his religious habits did not go beyond mass; he neglected to practice any others, and only refrained from eating meat on Good Friday. The proof of this sentiment, which he kept even at the peak of his glory, is in the words the Emperor spoke to Countess de Montesquiou when he entrusted his son to her: "Madame, I entrust you with the destinies of France: make my son a good Frenchman and a good Christian, one cannot be without the other." As a few courtiers present smiled at this instruction, he said to them: "Yes, gentlemen, religion is to me the basis of morality and good manners."

The ease with which the chapel had been created gave the Emperor the idea of changing the wall coverings in his two bedrooms, the nankeen material being dirty and rotted by the humidity. Count de Montholon suggested using white muslin, and having several spares made allowed him to always have clean material. The Emperor preferred silk, but I mentioned to him the difficulty we had experienced in getting the small quantity needed for the back of the chapel, and that it would be impossible to find the necessary number of rolls to cover the walls of his room. On the contrary, striped or plain muslin from India could easily be purchased. The Emperor was in a good mood and said to me: "Well, I can see you don't want silk. Give me the height and dimensions of the room, so that I may calculate the expense." I gave him the measurements. He made approximate calculations, and gave me a free hand to arrange his two bedrooms one after the other.

The Emperor was firmly opposed to having Englishmen come into his home to clean the furniture and the walls, so I told him that among ourselves, helped by a Chinese, we needed no one. With a pocket knife the Emperor had made a large opening in the wall covering, to take a look at the walls, which were quite dirty and in poor condition. The next day everyone demonstrated his zeal: the nankeen covering stretched on the frame was removed, and white paper was pasted onto the walls of the bedroom. A Chinese man whitewashed the ceiling while others cleaned and waxed the furniture that had been taken outside. Once the measurements were taken, a quantity of striped muslin was purchased. Noverraz' wife, helped by a woman from the camp, cut and attached the lengths of material to one another. Next she made a hem in the top and bottom of each piece and, as these sections together were much wider than the wall, they could be stretched on ropes to achieve a ribbed look much more graceful than if they had simply been stretched flat. A small gathered drapery eight inches high, made of the same material, helped to hide the upper seam, while the one at the bottom rested on the baseboard. Count de Montholon had a rug brought from town to replace the one that had not been changed for the past four years. I had some green silk bought in town to make new curtains for the Emperor's two little field beds, and in place of the brass on the bedposts and the crown, we substituted the silver eagles from the broken silverware: they fitted perfectly, and produced a very fine effect. The portraits of the Empress and the King of Rome were put back in place. Eight days had been sufficient to achieve the metamorphosis we had projected. The grand marshal wanted to contribute to it by sending a small gilt-brass clock and a small bust of the King of Rome as a child, and these objects were placed on the mantelpiece. Our plans would have been disrupted had everything not been put back in place on the same day; it was necessary that the Emperor be able to take possession of the room that evening and sleep there. Count de Montholon understood the wish I expressed, and saw to it that the Emperor remained in the drawing room a few hours beyond his usual time. As busily as we worked during the day, we finished only at 7 p.m. The Emperor was kind enough to come back into his room only at that time. Two wafers of Houbigant were burning in the incense burner; as for a long time he had been content with sugar or vinegar as perfume, his sense of smell was pleasantly surprised when he entered, and he thought it was aloe wood. I told him it was two wafers from six boxes that had arrived in town. Pierron had brought them back, knowing that I had been asking for these whenever a new ship arrived from Europe. The room, so freshly decorated, smelling so good, and so well lit by the covered light made the Emperor smile and say: "It is no longer a bedroom, it is the boudoir of a young mistress!" He had not yet noticed his bed; when he saw the eagles replacing the brass balls, he turned to me and took my ear, smiling, with the smile that expressed so well his soul's feelings: "This," he said, "is the crowning touch; the idea is all the better as it works so well; what do you think of it, Montholon?"

The freshness of this room was in such contrast with the one preceding it that the Emperor said to me: "It is absolutely necessary that my other room be arranged like this one." A few days later, a similar transformation took place in the other room, still without the help of outsiders, which increased its worth in the Emperor's eyes. All these various projects begun in October 1819 were finished in December of the same year.

In Saint Helena the Emperor had two small camp beds; at night he would go from one to the other, passing from one bedroom to the next. He had told me several times that if he fell ill, these beds would be too narrow. Count de Montholon had one in gilt brass that he had purchased in town, and he offered it to me to put in the second bedroom. It was taking a great risk to do it without the approval of the Emperor, who did not like changes. It even meant the risk of losing the precious reward that we hoped for from him: a sign of his satisfaction. Green curtains were purchased for this bed. In the Emperor's linen supply I had various laces, including one from Alençon; I had the quilt trimmed with it, as well as the pillowcases. This bed was in fact to be nothing but a showbed. That room had no mirror and I had one requested in town, but there were none. Mr. Darling, who was in charge of the furniture for the new house, learned about this and immediately sent me one four feet high by three-and-a-half feet wide that was intended for the new house. We placed it on top of the dresser, for in that bedroom there was no mantelpiece. Two small bookcases were also sent to me and served to furnish that room. When it was completed the Emperor came in, and appeared as satisfied as he had previously been. However as he was getting into bed he said to me: "I do not want Montholon to be deprived of his bed, we will have to give it back to him." It was replaced by the second camp bed, as the Emperor had tried it out and found he was very uncomfortable in it. "All this lace," he said to me the next morning, "is only good for the marshal's wife." As the two bedrooms were approximately the same size, I had a third set of wall coverings made, which allowed a change every two months in one of the two rooms which was easily accomplished in two hours. The Emperor wanted to know how much it was going to cost for what he called "so many fine things." The labor, I said to him, was provided by Noverraz' wife who refused to set a price on her work. "I do not want that, but as she does not do anything, put her in charge of the household linen with 1,200 francs a year, and pay her for the first month." When at the end of December 1819 I presented the Emperor with the accounting for the month which included the expenses for the chapel, the two bedrooms, and the gardens, which came all together to 1,200 francs, he said to me laughing: "Well! master treasurer, how much are you making on this amount? because something always remains stuck to the hands of a financier." He then went on to talk about the dishonesty of cashiers. He cited a well-known name, a man who had his trust, and took care of his cash supply: "He lost both for some nonsense," the Emperor said, "30 or 40,000 francs. He wanted to insist I had given it to him, but I have an excellent memory. I said to him: I will give away a million, but I do not want one penny stolen from me. Bring me back your accounts." And he added: "I have always forced thieves to return what they stole, every time I caught them."

The Emperor demanded that receipts be given in support of all expenses shown on the books, but he never looked at them. I received 12,000 francs a month, drawn on Count Bertrand's funds in England which he had made available to the Emperor. It was Mr. Hetson, the government commissioner, who had the job of giving them to me on my receipt. These funds were distributed in the following manner:

	per month	per year
The Grand Marshal	*2,000*	*24,000*
General de Montholon	*2,000*	*24,000*
(After his family departed Montholon received only 1,500 francs)		
Supplementary household expenses	*3,500*	*42,000*
Wages for household employees	*1,500*	*18,000*
(This sum represented only an advance against wages)		
For the Emperor's dress	*1,000*	*12,000*
Priests and doctor:		
Father Buonavita	*250*	
Father Vignali	*250*	
Dr. Antommarchi	*250*	

These sums were only advances against their salaries. The 500 francs for the priests were taken from Count de Montholon's account, after the departure of the countess, so that he only received 1,500 francs per month. The 250 francs for the doctor were taken from funds intended for the supplementary expenses of the household.

When I had a considerable sum of money in my cash box, I would change it into gold, either Spanish pieces of four or Indian rupees. I would inform the Emperor of this, and place them in what was called the reserve cash box, to which I had a key. That cash box kept under the Emperor's desk contained 300,000 francs when he passed away, and mine had 25,590 francs.

The Emperor said one day that after the loss of his fleet at Alexandria, he had to find a way to conciliate the sheiks and impress the fanatical population. "I was informed of the embezzlement committed by the treasurers of the great mosque of Djemil el Azhar.[344] I went there one day," he said, "and I was accompanied by the sheiks; I showed my astonishment that the prophet's temple was so poorly maintained. I called for the treasurers and asked them to bring in their books. On examination it was easy to see the infractions that had been pointed out to me, without their being able to say anything in their defense. I chased away the biggest culprits, calling them unworthy of working there, and urged those who remained to have the mosque better maintained in the future. The sheiks, before whom this scene took place, fell on their knees and expressed their admiration, crying out: *Schala! schala!*[345] I did the same for the Coptic Christians, in whose hands part of the financial administration was already placed: since the arrival of the French in Egypt, they permitted some thefts, believing they were sufficiently protected by the presence of our weapons. I knew there were many complaints against them, and I had irrefutable proof of their embezzling. I had several of them thrown in prison, and

---

[344]Djemil el Azhar, the great mosque of Cairo. At the beginning of his stay, Bonaparte showed much concern for the sheiks and the muftis, particularly those of the great mosque, which he called the Sorbonne of El Azhar. He even asked them to translate the *Koran* into French. However, on October 21, 1798, an insurrection broke out; in less than 20 minutes the batteries from the citadel crushed the barricades that had been erected around the mosque, which was immediately occupied. The sheiks were put to death.

[345]Inch' Allah!... By the grace of God.

chased away others, keeping only the small number among them whose accounts showed they were honest. This severity in my administration made a good impression, it calmed the fanatics and earned me the trust of the sheiks, even Sheik Saada, whose feelings were not at all favorable toward us."

The Emperor related that one day when he was leaving for Egypt, Empress Joséphine asked him to take along a dwarf who had been in her service, and whom she said he could trust. "I soon did so, and he appeared worthy of her words, until I left Egypt to go to Syria. I left him in Cairo with all of my belongings, but a short time after that, rumors spread that we all had been defeated and killed. That rascal, certain that I would not come back, got the idea of selling my wine cellar full of excellent wines. He was quite disappointed when he saw me again, and even more so when, in his presence, my butler told me I had only a few bottles of wine left. I asked him what he had done with it, and he admitted that believing me dead, he had sold it to make some money. I was so angry that I wanted to hang him, but I only threw him out."

"Sire," said the grand marshal who had witnessed all of this, "I remember that very well, and we drank some fine wine from the commanding general's cellar at the house of a high-ranking officer, who was not boasting about how he had procured it."

In December the gardens and the planting were completed. In order to have shade near the house, we did not hesitate, even at the risk of seeing them die, to move some old trees with mounds of earth requiring the strength of twenty men. We had already attempted this successfully with the lemon trees that provided such good shelter for the Emperor in the small garden; we tried this with oaks which in this latitude—or at least at Longwood—did not grow very tall, but spread their branches out like apple trees in France. We transplanted several that did well, and one was called "the Emperor's oak tree"; it was placed along a path near the house. If he did not have lunch inside, the Emperor asked to be served under his oak tree which, with the natural arrangement of its branches, created shade above him. Peach trees were also transplanted, and they grew very well. Twenty years later when I was called on to go retrieve the Emperor's ashes in Saint Helena, I found no trace of the gardens; everything had disappeared. Only the oak tree was standing, but had not grown; the great stone basin was still there, in a state of ruin, along with a piece of the grass berm.

One day, the Emperor wanted to have the noisy company of Countess Bertrand's children at lunch. Saint-Denis told me the luncheon had gone very well, but that towards the end they started throwing bread balls at each other. The Emperor had taken the youngest on his knees, and was kissing and teasing him as he was pulling at his ears. This scene that took place under the orange trees reminded me of the way the Emperor acted with his son. When Madame de Montesquiou brought him to his luncheon, the Emperor would take him on his knees and have him taste his reddened water—although he was still being breast-fed—or he would place to his lips a little gravy or sauce that he found at hand. Countess de Montesquiou complained about this mixture: the Emperor would burst out laughing, and the royal child shared in his father's laughter. The Empress, who was present at these scenes, was also amused, but would not have known how to initiate them, either out of shyness or out of fear of hurting her son. One did not find the spontaneous signs of affection that mothers have for their children in her; she was even ill at ease carrying him, and that gave birth to the rumor she did not like her son. My mother always told me the opposite: she had much affection for the King of Rome. It is true that she seldom took him in her arms, but if she did not show all her affection for him, it was because he was always accompanied by Madame de Montesquiou. She had been made to feel uncomfortable around this lady to whom she did not always do justice, while the Emperor knew how to demonstrate his trust in her. The qualities of generosity and sensitivity do honor to the heart and soul of this princess, who could not be faulted for anything during her stay in France. My mother has always told me that her first reaction was always excellent, but bad influences spoiled everything. It is deplorable that later on, as Marie-Thérèse's granddaughter, she did not know how to remain Hector's widow.

For a long time, Longwood had no other water than that brought in barrels pulled on a cart by the Chinese servants. Great works had been undertaken by the governor to build an enormous reservoir at Diana's Peak; when this work was completed, conduits brought water not only to Longwood, but also to the camp. For some time, a trickle of water had been flowing through the conduits to the reservoir raised several feet above ground, from which we could distribute water to all the areas in the garden where irrigation was difficult. The Emperor conceived the idea of setting up basins and bringing water there by conduit; the gardens were on a slight incline, and it was easy to channel the overflow from one basin to another. The Emperor indicated the shape he wanted to give to the first one, placed at the highest elevation, its width, its depth, as well as the dimensions of the two others to be placed beneath it.

The first one was 14 feet in diameter by 2 1/2 feet deep. The second was an enormous vat 12 feet in diameter and 4 feet deep, and the third, another vat 6 feet in diameter by 4 feet deep. These two vats alone cost 1,800 francs; the one made of masonry, semicircular in shape and lined with lead, cost 1,000 francs. A very large aviary built in Chinese style was placed at the side of that basin, which was connected to the one in the middle by a canal dug in the lawn. The bottom was a piece of wood a foot wide, sunk two inches deep, in which the overflow would pass from the first basin into the second. This second basin was likewise connected to the third by a similar canal; and when needed the latter would conduct the water through wooden gutters to the vegetable garden, located in a lower place. All the earth from these basins had been placed in a circular mass at the end of the garden, at the height of the verandah. It was given a cylindrical shape and arranged in terraces to form an amphitheater. Each tier was planted with grass to hold back the earth, and flowers and rosebushes could be planted there. The whole thing had a fine appearance, but this mass of earth interrupted the view of the vegetable garden.

One morning the Emperor had us take our pickaxes and shovels, had some beams and boards brought, and said he wanted to cut a hole through that mass of earth in order to make a small grotto there.

He first had us dig between the second and third basins a trench 4 feet deep, 8 feet long and 4 feet wide. It thus reached the level of the vegetable garden, which he now could enter by going through the grotto. The most difficult part was to cut through the earth that had been brought in without its crumbling; by means of beams and boards, it was kept in place and the hole was made. This trench, as I have said, started at the middle basin that was uncovered in this part, and continued to the third basin, by going through the grotto. Stairs located close to the large basin allowed one to enter the trench and pass this way into the vegetable garden. A wooden spout at the bottom of the center basin allowed the water to flow into the large wooden gutter that went through the grotto and into barrels placed to make watering easier. I give all these details because they amused the Emperor very much, and show that we were all disposed to do whatever would make His Majesty forget his sufferings and his captivity.

The grotto was circular in shape; small doors with windows were put in, the wooden interior was painted with oil paints, and the Emperor often came to sit there. Fish were placed in the basins, but several died. With a lead pipe coming from the main reservoir, we created a small fountain in the center basin. Chandelier, the head cook, had been put in charge of that use, and had succeeded perfectly. It was only put in use when the Emperor went out. All these details will appear futile, but they show, on the part of those who shared the Emperor's captivity, their desire to ease the bitterness. A smile of satisfaction from the Emperor was the only reward they sought.

The Emperor did not seem interested in new modifications. The paths were finished everywhere, the flower beds had been established, and the various patches had been seeded. Already the Emperor saw with pleasure peas and string beans sprouting from the ground, when one morning, going out of his apartment in his bathrobe, he noticed five or six hens scratching in his vegetable patches. He had instructed me to tell those who owned chickens to keep them shut away, because he had already noticed a few of them wandering through his garden. The order had been promptly executed, but the chickens had escaped the surveillance of the cook who was raising and selling them to the household supplier. Maddened by the damage he was witnessing, the Emperor immediately came back in, called Saint-Denis and asked him for his shotguns, took one and went outside saying: "That is too impertinent!" Saint-Denis and I followed the Emperor. The poor chickens continued doing their damage, not suspecting that lead was about to put an end to it. They were close together. Aim was taken, three fell with one shot, the others flew away, and a fourth was hit with the second shot on the wall where it was perched. "Pick up my game," he said to Saint-Denis, "take it to the kitchen, and have a fine soup made for me with it." Then turning to me: "I forbid you to pay for them," he said, "no matter who the owner is!" It so happened they belonged to the cook, who was careful not to complain, and found a way to lose nothing by offering a good chicken broth! A shot fired so close to the house had brought everyone outside; those who owned hens were considered to have been warned, and no more chickens were seen.

They were the first shots the Emperor had fired for a long time, and made him regret the absence of game that did not allow him the exercise of hunting. There were some turtledoves, but they went from one valley to another and it was necessary to cover a lot of ground to follow them. One day when some landed not far from him, he sent for his shotgun, but they had already disappeared before it arrived.

A few days later a goat and some kids belonging to Archambault were grazing on the lawn some fifty or sixty paces from the house. The mother was tied up, and the young ones were jumping around her. They were doing no harm, but the Emperor wanted to prove his skill; he had Saint-Denis load his shotgun with ammunition, aimed at one of the kids, and broke its shoulder. The mother and the second kid lifted their heads, not knowing where the shot came from. The Emperor was about to aim at the second one when he said: "He is still conscious, the shot is too easy, carry the wounded one to the kitchen!" For several weeks he had Archambault buy a few young kids, which he rarely missed from some distance. On this occasion the Emperor said to General Montholon that in his youth he was always complaining about the numerous goats in Corsica that caused much damage to the property, and particularly to the young trees they would attack. "I was always in favor of destroying them, and I had tremendous arguments with my old uncle the archdeacon, who owned many of them. One day when he had reached the peak of his furor, he accused me of being an upstart."

One afternoon when he was strolling with the Emperor before dinner, Count de Montholon came to fetch one of the Emperor's shotguns and had Saint-Denis follow him with the other. It was to shoot a small suckling pig that had wandered away from a drove led by its mother. He was too far away to suppose the young animal would have anything to fear. "Montholon, my son," said the Emperor, who handed him the shotgun, "I am going to offer you a roast worthy of Ulysses for your dinner!" He aimed and shot the pig dead. The animal was immediately prepared and appeared at the dinner table; it had been shot right through the head. The last shot fired by the Emperor was at an ox belonging to the East India Company that had entered the compound from the vegetable garden and was eating everything in it. It had already happened that these animals had spoiled everything while roaming, and complaints had been made to the captain. The Emperor saw nothing better to do with the ox than he had done with the chickens: the ox was turned so as to receive the shot between its two horns. He aimed and the animal fell dead. It was a plow ox belonging to the company; its loss served as an example, and oxen and chicken no longer appeared. The youngest of Countess Bertrand's children, Arthur, had come to fetch the shotgun with Count de Montholon: he was so frightened at seeing this enormous animal fall under the impact of the shot that he threw himself between the Emperor's legs, not wanting to turn his head toward the ox. The Emperor often referred to that child's fright, and when he saw him would say: "Well, Arthur, what about the ox?"

The soil in the gardens did not always respond to the effort expended there. The caterpillars were devastating, and would cause much damage in a single night. Vegetables nevertheless grew in the garden and ended up on the Emperor's table, and he never failed to ask if they came from his garden. Generally speaking, they were affected by the dryness of the climate, the drought and also the iron content of the ground in which they grew. The peas were hard as were the string beans, the cauliflower would not form properly, while cabbage did rather well, but what came from town was not any better. The peach trees we had transplanted bore fruit that same year; the Emperor ate some of them as well as a few strawberries. The strawberry plants were covered with flowers but bore very little fruit. The Emperor sometimes entertained himself counting the number of beans in a row to see what would be yielded.

We had finally succeeded in arranging some shade for the Emperor close to the house. A bower forty feet long was covered in three months' time with passion leaves, and became impenetrable to the rays of the sun. The vegetation is luxurious in this climate, where excessive heat during the day is replaced during the night by abundant dew.

Once the gardens were completed, we kept only two Chinese servants out of the four that had been hired at the beginning of the work. The Emperor sometimes amused himself watching them work, and as he had noticed that his presence would prompt them to work harder than usual, he one day asked that a bottle of wine be given to them. Instead of handing it over as a present from the Emperor, the man who brought it threw it on the ground saying: "Hey, Chinamen!" The Emperor was present and expressed his dissatisfaction to the man who had behaved like this: "It takes away the value of an object to give it with as little consideration as you did."

Among the Chinese, there was one on the island who sculpted with great taste and was a carpenter by trade. The Emperor expressed the wish that M. de Montholon have him build a Chinese kiosk in a corner of the garden which he himself designated, in the corner and at the same height as the berm, so that he could see the ocean from that point and retire there from time to time. When it was built, it was decorated inside with white muslin and was furnished with a Chinese armchair, some stools, and a small table. From there the Emperor could see the ocean and part of the panorama surrounding Longwood. He went there a few times, then never returned again. When the grand marshal asked him why he did not make more use of his kiosk, he answered: "I have to climb up, and I no longer can do that! I had it built only to distract Montholon."

One day as the Emperor was returning to his apartment to go to bed, Count de Montholon was present, and the Emperor asked me to tell him the story of the Englishwoman who wished so much to see him at the Elysée after his return from Waterloo, and had fixed a meeting place in Saint-Philippe-du-Roule. I told him the story as can be seen in the chapter on the Hundred Days. "Well, Montholon, what do you think of that?"

"But, Sire, I believe she was quite wrong, if it was a love affair, not to come and pursue it here. No doubt you are now a widower, Sire, and Your Majesty will allow me to tell him that I am not thinking of myself!"

"Ah! my son," the Emperor replied, "when you are past fifty and in my state of health, it is no longer worth the trouble." The first thing the Emperor looked at in a woman were her hands and feet; if both were unattractive, he would say: "She has rogue swatters." He said on this subject that Empress Marie-Louise was beautifully made, that she had charming hands and feet: "When I went to meet her, it was the first thing that struck me. She was fresh as a rose and without any coquetry; she differed in that respect from Joséphine, who had much."

On learning of the Duke of Berry's assassination, the Emperor blamed that prince for having gone to the opera for a purpose as futile as the one that took him there, but "there is a destiny one cannot escape," he said. When the French newspapers later announced the birth of the Duchess of Berry's baby, the Emperor said to Count de Montholon: "Read this report, and tell me if you could possibly write one more stupid, or more inclined to give the impression that the child is not his? How can such a high-ranking princess find herself abandoned to the point of having no one with her, when she can expect to give birth any moment? When the Empress was ready to give birth, the Duchess of Montebello remained nine days without leaving the

Tuileries. When the first labor pains were felt, it was 7 p.m. Dubois came down from the room where he was staying, and the Empress spent the entire night in pain, having with her the Duchess of Montebello, Countess de Luçay, and Countess de Montesquiou, who was to be governess. The Empress' ladies-in-waiting, the nurse, Corvisart, Bourdier were there, my entire family was in the adjoining drawing room, and I went constantly back and forth between Marie-Louise and Madame, who was also there. As the night passed and I saw no sign that she was ready to give birth, I got into my bath at 5 a.m., leaving Dubois with her, along with her ladies and her household staff." We know the Empress was so tired she fell asleep, but soon new labor pains awakened her, and increased without bringing on the final crisis required by nature. Dubois sent to notify the Emperor the birth was going to be difficult and dangerous. The Emperor got out of his bath to go encourage Marie-Louise by his presence, and told Dubois, who didn't think he could save both mother and child, to think only of the mother and to treat her as a woman from the rue Saint-Denis. He entered the Empress' bedroom, kissed her tenderly, and urged her to be courageous and patient. Corvisart, Bourdier and Yvan came in at that moment and held Marie-Louise, as the baby was presenting himself feet first. They had to use forceps to bring out the head; that labor lasted 26 minutes and was most painful. The Emperor could not take it anymore and went to sit in an adjoining dressing room to await the results. He was given news every minute. The child was finally born, but gave no signs of life for five minutes. The Emperor ran to Marie-Louise, whom he again held in his arms, and had Cambacérès enter, who in his position of Arch-Chancellor was required to verify the birth and sex of the child. Berthier was also there and also came in. All of the Emperor's attention was directed toward the Empress, and he believed his child was dead. Then he heard a cry that announced the contrary. He ran to embrace him and brought him to the Empress, who felt far too weak to share his happiness. "Well," said the Emperor, "in spite of all the people surrounding her, the rumor circulated that the Empress had given birth to a daughter for whom a boy had been substituted. Other people said the child was stillborn, or that she had never been pregnant—the most absurd rumors. What will they say about the delivery of the Duchess of Berry, when that of Marie-Louise, which occurred among thirty people, was suspect?—This one took place without any important person of the court, such as the Duke of Orléans or others!"

Among his snuffboxes, the Emperor had a portrait of Empress Joséphine which he did not consider a good likeness. Countess Bertrand had one decorated with pearls that this princess had given her: it had been painted by Saint and was a very good likeness. The Emperor asked her for it and told me to make a copy. I thought this was a joke and protested, but the Emperor was serious. I showed much good intention, if I was lacking in talent; I had learned a little how to draw figures, landscapes, and architecture; I painted a little, but regardless, I was not capable of undertaking the copy of a portrait by Saint! I took a gamble and set to work, and luck helped me beyond my greatest hopes: when I showed it to him, the Emperor found it a very good likeness. He had me frame it and then hung it on one side of his mantelpiece, where it remained until his death.

Whenever Countess Bertrand came to inspect the progress of our work, as soon as the Emperor saw her he never failed to go and greet her, offer her his arm, walk her about, and pick her a rose, if he spotted one that was sufficiently beautiful and worthy of being offered to her. During one of these visits, the Emperor told me to bring him the remaining snuffbox decorated with his portrait. It was surrounded by very handsome diamonds and was identical to the one he had given Countess de Montholon before she left Longwood. The Emperor was in the billiard room, and I presented the snuffbox on a gilt tray. He took it, opened the leather box that held it, and said: "Here, Madame, I am giving it to you at a very sad time, but it will be a token of my esteem and my friendship." The countess thanked the Emperor with a grace that showed how flattered she was by the present he had given her and how much she appreciated it. No one was more gracious than that lady when she wished to be. To a great deal of distinction, she added a charming appearance, and often revealed a foot that was very handsome, as were those of all her children. At that time the Emperor was in fairly good health. I am pleased to be able to record a few moments spent beguiling his captivity: during one of these mornings as he was having lunch under his oak tree in the company of Count de Montholon, he amused himself watching the grand marshal's children playing in the distance and had them called over. A city resident had come to Longwood riding a small pony, and Arthur, the youngest of the children, having seen it, asked the Emperor to buy it for him. As he spoke only English, the Emperor told him in that tongue: "Come at noon." But as was his habit, he went back inside, leaving the children to continue their games, got undressed, and soon fell asleep. I was leaving the Emperor's bedroom quietly when the fort cannon announced the hour of noon, and in the bathroom I found young Arthur fighting with Noverraz to enter the Emperor's bedroom. I feared my refusal would make him cry and awaken His Majesty: I therefore made him understand that the Emperor was sleeping, and if he agreed to be good, I would let him enter and wait for His Majesty to awaken. "Yes," he answered; I took him by the hand, he went near the bed where the Emperor was resting, saw he was sleeping, then sat on the rug and stayed with me almost an hour, playing alone and noiselessly. When the Emperor awoke, he was quite surprised to find him there: "There you are, Arthur, what do you want, my boy?"

"You tell me gun fire." I was not aware of the promise made to him.

"What does he say?" the Emperor asked.

"He is telling Your Majesty that he told him to come back when the gun went off."

"Take him to Montholon, to find out what he wants." At that very moment, Count de Montholon was announced at the Emperor's bedroom; he learned that during lunch he had told the child to come at noon, and he would buy him the little pony. "Gun fire" was the cannon announcing that hour, and he came to claim the promise made to him. "Indeed! What a memory," said the Emperor, "is the horse still there?" Count de Montholon, who had discussed the price with the owner, assured him it was. "But," said the Emperor, caressing the child and embracing him, "do you have any money?"

"Yes, I have two dollars."

"That is not enough."

"Papa give you everything!"

"But Papa Bertrand has no money."

"I have plenty gold."

"Will you be good?"

"Yes."

"How much does he want for this horse?" the Emperor asked General Montholon.

"Fifty louis [1000 francs], Sire."

"Give this big boy 1,200 francs," the Emperor said to me. I went upstairs to get the money that was locked up in a bag. The child was four years old, and on seeing me arrive, he held out his pinafore to catch the money. "You won't be able to carry it."

"Yes, yes." I put the money gently in his pinafore to test his strength. He turned rapidly and, accompanied by Count de Montholon, he went to purchase the horse he wished to buy. Riding his horse, and held up by Count de Montholon, he came back almost immediately to the Emperor's door, to thank His Majesty. Later on, having fallen from the horse, he no longer wanted it and switched back to his burro, a much quieter mount and more responsive to his wishes. The horse was given to Napoleon Bertrand, the eldest of the children, who sometimes accompanied the Emperor when his mother rode in the carriage with him.

The Emperor was very fond of children, and there was nothing he wouldn't do to please them. Never did Count Bertrand or Count de Montholon's children leave him without taking with them some memento of his affection and munificence. He had some jewelry bought in town to give to them, and very much enjoyed watching their pleasure.

The Emperor one day told Count de Montholon to bring in his little Napoleone, today Countess Lapérouse. He was in his bed when the child was brought and asked me to bring him a few gold chains from China. He spread them out in front of her, believing that she would not know the difference between the prettiest and the less pretty; but to his great surprise, after having looked at them one after the other, she chose the prettiest!

The Emperor did not limit his generosity to the children: the parents also received their share. On New Year's Day, the Emperor gave the children double napoleons, and the ladies each received a plate from his Sèvres porcelain service, representing some historical scene. Countess Bertrand received one which depicted the passage of the Danube, whose bridges had brought the general fame. The gentlemen were not forgotten either; they received several presents from the Emperor. Count de Las Cases received a small campaign travel kit and a pair of spurs worn by the Emperor; Count de Montholon, his travel kit from the Egyptian campaign; General Gourgaud, a cross of the Legion of Honor; and the grand marshal, a gold watch. "Here, Bertrand," said the Emperor, "it was striking 2 a.m. at Rivoli, when I gave Joubert the order to attack."

We had brought from Paris a very fine Sèvres porcelain service for the Emperor's use. Each dozen was enclosed in lined leather cases; a magnificent set of twenty-four cups and accessories were enclosed in a similar case, and two vases from the same manufacturer. The Emperor only used this to make presents. Each piece represented some view of a battlefield or a major city. One day while looking at them with Count de Montholon, the Emperor paused in front of the one representing the city of Ajaccio at the moment the frigate *Muiron* was dropping anchor in the harbor. General Bonaparte was on board returning from Egypt. "There you are, Montholon, here's my house," he said, "I am sure that rowboat next to the frigate is my wet nurse's; the poor woman was one of the first to come and see me. The town was under the control of a few gang leaders who were very much disappointed when I arrived; complete confusion prevailed, the municipality accused the parliament, the parliament accused the magistrates; nevertheless everyone wanted to see the famous Napoleon! The entire population lined the shore, and the garrison, quite spontaneously, had placed itself under arms and formed a double row up to my house. The health service assembled under the presidency of a certain Barberi, one of my former comrades, was opposed to our landing. Barberi himself came to express his regrets, and crossing the line of boats that already surrounded us, he came on board to congratulate me on my victories and return. Those who accompanied him followed, so that communication was established without my intervention. There was in fact no danger, as none of us had any disease. As I was anxious to go ashore, I accepted the offer made to me, and few citizens have been received with greater enthusiasm than I was by my compatriots. I passed the garrison in review; the poor men were very badly dressed, for they had not received any pay for seven or eight months. I took 40,000 francs from my mother's holdings to bring their pay up to date."[346]

I have already related that when you were with the Emperor, you could leave only when he dismissed you. If in the evening he retired to his bed and did not feel like sleeping, he had the light carried into the adjoining room, and would continue the conversation in semi-darkness. One evening I was in his room, and he fell asleep without having told me to retire. For fear of disturbing him I remained sitting in one of the corners waiting for him to awake. I was deep in my thoughts about the destiny that had called me to live near the greatest man of the century while my mother was in Vienna with his son, when I heard a few brief words that I did not understand. The Emperor seemed to me to be having a nightmare that I ended by making a little noise. He rang his bell to call Saint-Denis, who was on duty and sleeping in the adjoining room. I immediately responded to his call; he inquired whether he had been sleeping for a long time, and I told him for approximately an hour and a half. "Give me my covered lamp and my bathrobe, and go to bed, for it is late." It was 11 p.m. The next

---

[346]Bonaparte's stay in Corsica on returning from his expedition to Egypt was particularly eventful. His landing was opposed for health reasons. The quarantine was lifted only due to the intervention of Jean Barberi, a personal friend of Bonaparte, who took a boat and came himself to find the general on board the *Muiron*. Bonaparte stayed in his father's house, which had been restored the previous year by his mother and Joseph, and settled in the alcove bedroom on the third floor. The general opened up the prisons, fired the central administration, and welcomed many friends, and in particular, Madeleine and Jean Jérôme Levie who, in 1793, had offered the Bonaparte family a friendly shelter from the pursuit of the Paolists.

morning, knowing the Emperor had only gone back to bed at 3 a.m., I only went into his bedroom at 7 a.m. to open the shutters without drawing the blinds. This was the way he wanted it, because full daylight hurt his eyes. I stood in front of his bed awaiting his orders. He was looking at me as if preoccupied by something other than the object he was staring at. Suddenly he told me he had dreamt of Empress Marie-Louise and his son, whom she was holding by the hand. It was a new experience for me to hear the Emperor mention a dream. "She was as fresh," he said to me, "as when I saw her in Compiègne; I took her in my arms, but no matter how hard I tried to keep her, I felt her escape me; and when I wanted to hold her again, everything had disappeared and I was awakened."

"Your awakening must have been cruel, Sire, but I witnessed Your Majesty's dream; I even thought from the agitation I heard that you were ill, and I was about to awaken you when you called Saint-Denis."

"Ah," he said, jumping out of his bed and taking me by the throat, "it is you, miserable wretch, who are the reason I could not remain any longer with my wife and my son! What does your crime deserve? Confess."

"May heaven grant me the power to place both of them in Your Majesty's arms, to atone for the error, and obtain my forgiveness."

"It is enough for me to bear the burden of my misery alone without having them for witnesses," he replied, letting me go.

Saint-Denis, whom the Emperor was very fond of, had married a young Englishwoman who was most charming, as sweet as she was kind and pretty.[347] She had been sent from London to educate

---

[347]In June 1818, Lady Jerningham sent a maid from London to Countess Bertrand, Mary Hall. This attractive blonde created quite a stir at Longwood: the happy winner was Saint-Denis, who married her in October 1819.

Mlle Hortense Bertrand, today Mme Thayer.[348] The Emperor was opposed to this marriage, which was a love match for Saint-Denis, without monetary advantages, and which was going to deprive Countess Bertrand of her daughter's governess. He asked that six months go by before their wedding take place, believing that time would allow Saint-Denis to reconsider. But that time had arrived, and his feelings remained the same. Father Buonavita blessed the marriage, but was strongly reprimanded by the Emperor for having celebrated it without telling him about it. Once it was over, the Emperor never mentioned it again; Saint-Denis found in Miss Hall a charming wife, and a kind and excellent mother for his children. At the time I am speaking of, Mme Saint-Denis had just given birth to a daughter who promised to be pretty, and in fact did become so; Count de Montholon and Countess Bertrand held her over the baptismal font. That day the Emperor came out of his apartment, went to sit down in his robe under his oak tree to have lunch there; when the meal was over, he said to Saint-Denis: "Call Marchand, and bring me your daughter." The weather was calm and mild; Saint-Denis presented the child to the Emperor, who looked at her kindly and complimented the father. Saint-Denis was naturally very happy about the interest shown in his daughter; he predicted great happiness for her future. "Go," the Emperor said to me, "bring the prettiest of my Chinese chains." I hurried there and returned, handing it to him. The Emperor took it and placed it on the child, saying: "May you be as happy as you promise to be pretty." The Emperor showed great kindness toward all of us; he knew that our care was not limited to obeying his wishes, but also anticipating them. This chain had been previously attached to one of the Emperor's watches, and he had taken it off to replace it with a chain made of Empress Marie-Louise's braided hair.

---

[348]Mme Amédée Thayer, born Hortense Bertrand, daughter of the general and Fanny Dillon, his wife. In 1828 Hortense married Amédée Thayer, born in Orléans of an American father and an English mother. A distinguished lawyer and musician, M. Thayer was a Protestant; his Catholic bride converted him shortly before his death. A number of memories of Saint Helena were collected by Mme Thayer, who was eleven years old when the Emperor died, yet remembered him very well.

PART EIGHT

Deliverance

CHAPTER TWENTY-THREE

Plans for Countess Bertrand's departure — The Emperor's suffering
increases — Complaints against Dr. Antommarchi — The Emperor's
lack of energy — Departure of Fr. Buonavita and Gentilini —
The illness worsens — Will and codicils

On New Year's Day 1820, General Montholon, the grand marshal, his children, the priests, and the doctor came to present their respects to the Emperor, who had them all stay for lunch. The first six months of that year passed relatively well. Work was still being accomplished, although periods of illness came to interrupt it. It was not the same in the months that followed, when all that can be recorded was a visible deterioration in the Emperor's health, a long illness, and finally death. During the last months of that period, there was some discussion of Count and Countess Bertrand's departure for Europe. The Countess' health worsened in this abominable climate, but she said what dictated her return more than anything was the education of her sons and daughter: until then it had been entrusted to a British sergeant to teach them to write, to Father Vignali for their religious education, and whatever else to Miss Hall, who had married Saint-Denis. This could not possibly represent the education she would have chosen to give them. The grand marshal decided to speak to the Emperor of it, and to request not for himself, but for his wife permission to take her children to France or England, so they could receive the education that had become mandatory. The Emperor, while offering objections to this request, agreed to it only when he saw that Countess Bertrand's mind was made up. He only expressed the desire that it take place at a time he himself would decide, and that the grand marshal accompany his wife and children. The grand marshal then requested a leave of absence for nine months to accompany his family to Europe, as the Emperor had advised him. He would settle them in London, arrange his personal affairs, and then come back to devote himself entirely to the Emperor. For anyone who has known the grand marshal, there can be no doubt that decision was dictated by his duty as a father, and by his sincere attachment and devotion to the Emperor.

At that time, Count de Las Cases and his son, General Gourgaud, and Countess de Montholon along with her children had all gone back to Europe. If the grand marshal left Longwood with his wife, four children, and the servants, who all brought a certain animation to the colony, an immense void would ensue for the Emperor. He would remain alone with Count de Montholon, whose self-sacrifice was as exemplary as his devotion, but who was not invulnerable to an illness that might keep him in bed. In that case the Emperor would be left on his own. His Majesty did not speak of this departure plan which obviously displeased him, but which everyone talked about. In the months that followed, it led to some coolness, less with the grand marshal perhaps than with the countess. Sometimes capricious, Countess Bertrand was gracious and very attractive; her quick and keen mind made her conversation pleasant and amusing, even during the moments of bad temper when her mouth sometimes allowed words to escape that belied her heart, which was true. A few hours with her allowed the Emperor to pass the time his health no longer allowed him to spend on work. She did not believe the Emperor was ill to the extent that his days were in danger and Dr. Antommarchi, who shared that opinion, supported her in the belief that the grand marshal could take her to Europe and return to Saint Helena where he would see the Emperor again.

For his part, His Majesty was preparing himself for this isolation by seeing the countess less often. He saw he had been mistaken about an affection he thought he had acquired; he did not complain of it, but his heart was wounded by it. One day while the Emperor was in his bath, he talked to me about the forthcoming departure of Countess Bertrand. "It is I," he said, "who advised Bertrand to accompany his wife to Europe, both to take care of his personal affairs and to organize the expenditures of his wife, who by her lack of care would soon spend all his children's fortune." I pointed out to him the emptiness that would result for him. "Am I not already accustomed to it?" he replied. "The marshal's wife does not spoil me." "It is true, Sire, but the grand marshal is always available to Your Majesty, and this house that is so often visited by the grand marshal and his family is going to become a desert. Your Majesty will no longer be able to look toward the camp without feeling sad."

"But what can I do? I am not forcing her to leave; Bertrand himself does not see that if I let him take his wife to Europe, he will not find me here when he returns. I have only one means of keeping him close to me: it is to do for Madame Bertrand what I am doing for Madame de Montholon."

"Sire," I said, "I deeply share the grand marshal's feeling. I believe that he can go to Europe and find Your Majesty on his return, but between now and then I see a great deal of loneliness for Your Majesty following that departure. Your habit of summoning one or the other of these gentlemen shall be upset, and through Count Bertrand's departure, you will be deprived of a resource which is that much greater, in that if he were to remain alone at Longwood, he would spend all his time with Your Majesty, as does Count de Montholon since his family's departure."

I had reached that point when Saint-Denis announced the grand marshal, whom I left alone with the Emperor. On the desk in his bedroom I saw written in pencil the following names in the form of a list: Duke of Vicenza (Caulaincourt), Rovigo (Savary), Ségur, Montesquiou, Daru, Drouot, Turenne, Arnaud, Denon. I since learned it would have been pleasant for the Emperor to have one of these men close to him to replace the grand marshal, should he leave Saint Helena. Destiny had decided otherwise, and the words spoken previously by the Emperor were to come true: "The name of Bertrand is linked to mine, and as long as I live, he shall live."

The man who had the most difficulty adjusting to the monotonous life at Longwood was Dr. Antommarchi. He had been seriously ill, but had recovered quickly. For distraction, the Emperor had urged him to take horseback rides around the island, and walks, going to the camp to visit those who were ill and become familiar with the diseases there. These errands gave him a certain amount of independence in the use of his time. The Emperor paid no attention to his walks into town or elsewhere as long as he felt well, but they earned him strong criticism when His Majesty's health required his care.

I have said that the Emperor no longer worked, his strength was waning, and even the wind caused him pain. The doctor felt it was necessary to place vesicatories on both his arms. The Emperor refused: "Don't you think," he said, "that M. Lowe is torturing me enough without your wanting to share in it?" His Majesty's trust in him was not yet established, and it was necessary for Count de Montholon and the grand marshal to talk to him about the excellent result Dr. Antommarchi's proposal might have before he would agree to it. Thus, one morning, he offered his two arms, but his repugnance was evident. The doctor placed one on each arm. However these vesicatories had no shape, that is instead of being round or oval they were simply square. The Emperor expressed his surprise when they were applied, and complained that the spots had not been shaven. Remaining in bed, he was bothered by them all day, which put him in a bad mood. He told Count de Montholon to go take a walk around the camp, and requested that I read to him. He had difficulty using his arms for dinner, and this made his mood even worse. He had called for the doctor several times, but each time was told he had not returned from town. The grand marshal came; he complained of being badly cared for and of having both arms encumbered so he could not move. On returning to Longwood the doctor was shown in, and asked the Emperor how he felt after the application of the vesicatories. "I don't know," the Emperor answered brusquely; "leave me alone. You place vesicatories that have no shape, you do not shave the place before applying them: this would not be done to the poorest man in a hospital; it seems to me that you could have left one of my arms free, without affecting both arms! That is no way to tie up a poor man." The doctor wanted to reply. "Go away," he said, "you are an ignoramus, and I a greater one for having let you do this." When the vesicatories were removed, they had some result and brought his appetite back; after a few weeks of bandages, they dried up by themselves.

For the past fifteen months, the creation of the gardens had provided the Emperor with daily occupation and exercise for his body and legs; but now, with the bad weather, his health declined. Father Buonavita gave the doctor a serious enough scare that the Emperor invited the clergyman to return to Europe. Gentilini, head boatman on the island of Elba, had asked to follow the Emperor's household to Paris as a footman, and was in Saint Helena in this capacity. But he was suffering from a chest ailment to such a point that the Emperor decided he should return to Elba, his homeland. Both of these men put off their departure, which only took place the following year.

The Emperor's days were spent partly inside his apartment which he kept closed part of the day. If he went out it was to get into his carriage, or to stroll through the garden, sit there, and spend an hour in the company of Count de Montholon or the grand marshal. Countess Bertrand herself was ill and rarely came, while her young Arthur was also ill and being treated for a liver ailment. The Emperor's lethargic state increased daily; if he came back from a stroll, the air had been bad for him; he would go into the billiard room and have everything shut tightly. Count Bertrand and Count de Montholon relieved each other, and in their absence I remained with him. His appetite had disappeared, nothing appealed to his sense of taste. He would eat only roast, and was served the crispiest part; he would extract the juice without being able to swallow the meat. His bouillon tasted good only if it was reduced to juice, which was bad for his digestion; he received the doctor without telling him any of what he felt. The latter did not hide the seriousness of the Emperor's condition; he told Count de Montholon and the grand marshal, assuring them that should the Emperor continue in this way, he would not live more than three months: it was necessary to apply a cautery as soon as possible. These gentlemen insisted with so much perseverance that they convinced His Majesty to have one placed on his left arm. At first this cautery seemed to have the effect the doctor expected; after a few days his appetite returned a little, and the spasmodic sighs that had

Because Dr. O'Meara refuses to report in detail to Sir Hudson Lowe on Napoleon's health, he is sent away from St. Helena. Here Napoleon says farewell to Dr. O'Meara who eventually writes *A Voice From St. Helena, 1822.*

The Emperor becomes very ill. Marchand sits up with him. Napoleon thinks he has been poisoned. Recent works suggest that may have been the case. See Weider, *Assassination at St. Helena Revisited.*

been frequent decreased. One day he felt he had been poorly bandaged and called for the doctor during the afternoon, but Saint-Denis came to say he had gone into town. "He could at least," said the Emperor, "let us know when he goes there, so I am not left alone in my current state of health." His Majesty waited another hour, then, aggravated by the pain he felt, told me he wanted to change the bandage himself. All his flannel shirts had been opened, and it was easy to reach the wound by removing his robe and rolling up his shirt sleeve. I had watched this bandage changed every day and was sure I could do it myself. I prepared everything that was necessary, and assisted by Count de Montholon who held the Emperor's arm, I removed the bandage and took away the patch that had become quite saturated. I washed the wound by placing a small silver basin under the arm, applied a fresh patch, then a small piece of cloth folded in four, a bandage, and the strap holding everything together. The Emperor felt relieved. I noticed that the wound, instead of being red, was purple in color. The Emperor was pleased with the experiment that had just been performed, and to have been able to do it without the doctor: "In the future," he said to me, "you shall change my bandage, I no longer want him to touch me." And I continued bandaging him myself every day, until the last days of his life when this cautery dried up completely.

At that time the governor had us informed that the ship from India which was to take the grand marshal and his family was in the Saint Helena harbor; but the grand marshal had decided against this departure, unwilling to leave the Emperor in his current state of health. After remaining a few days in the harbor, the ship set out for Europe.

We thus reached the year 1821, which the Emperor would see begin, but alas, would not see end. As in the previous years, he received everyone's respects. That morning when I entered his room, he was in bed. "Well," he said to me, when his shutters were open, "what are you giving me as a present?"

"Sire," I said to him, "the hope of seeing Your Majesty get well very soon and leave a climate so bad for his health."

"It won't be long, my son, my end is near, I cannot go on much longer." I hurried to tell him that was not the way I meant my wish. "It shall be," he replied as he got out of bed with difficulty, "as the heavens wish."

Dr. Antommarchi lacked the assiduous attention to which the Emperor had always been accustomed from those who were around him. On several occasions he had brought well-deserved criticism on himself through the aggravation he caused the Emperor, who did not find him at hand when he called for him. A certain awkwardness in his service led him to believe he did not have His Majesty's trust, and he asked to be sent back to Europe. The Emperor answered that as he could not give him his full trust, he authorized him to ask the British officer commanding in Saint Helena if it was possible for him to take the same ship as Father Buonavita, who was returning to Europe, in order to help this kind, old man during the crossing. Chandelier, the cook, who was riddled with rheumatism, was waiting for another cook to come and replace him so he could also go back to Europe. These departures, which everyone talked about, brought a certain sadness to the rest of the colony. At the same time the Emperor had letters written to Europe saying that he would gladly accept the care of MM. Corvisart, Larrey, Desgenettes, or Percy.[349] Once his anger had passed, the grand marshal and General Montholon interceded with the Emperor, so that he would see the doctor again, who was asking to leave the island only because he feared if he did not have the Emperor's trust that he would compromise this man's health for which he was held responsible in the eyes of the entire world. The Emperor forgave him, and he resumed his duties.

The Emperor dressed infrequently now. He had told Count de Montholon to force him to go out, but in spite of repeated pleas the general did not always succeed in overcoming the Emperor's reluctance to expose himself to the southeasterly wind, which he said harmed him and irritated his nervous system. His walks and carriage

---

[349]Corvisart (1755-1821) was chief doctor for the Emperor and both Empresses; Larrey (1766-1842) was chief surgeon of the imperial guard. Desgenettes (1762-1837) had been chief doctor for the Egyptian army at the age of 36. Baron Percy (1754-1825) was considered the father of military surgery and was the creator and organizer of mobile ambulances.

rides became more and more rare, and he always came home and threw himself on his settee looking exhausted. His feet were always cold, and the only way to warm them was with hot towels, which he preferred to hot water bottles or anything else. During the previous six months, this condition had gotten steadily worse, when on March 17 the Emperor took to his bed and almost never left it again. That same day Father Buonavita was leaving Jamestown to return to Europe: the morning of his departure he came to say goodbye to the Emperor, whom he had not seen for several weeks. The Emperor had heard mass from his bed, by opening the door connecting his bedroom to the chapel. As this kind, elderly man walked with difficulty, when he approached the bed and knelt to kiss the Emperor's hand, he was invited to get up and be seated. I assisted by approaching and offering my arm for him to lean on. The Emperor talked to him about what he was to say to his mother and his family when he arrived in Rome. Father Buonavita was deeply moved by the Emperor's calm and resignation; he was also astonished at the ravages of his features, to the point where he could no longer hold back his tears as he was leaving the room. "My dear friend," he said to me, "the Emperor is much changed; I am going to inform his family that if he is not removed from here as soon as possible, he is done for." After I had accompanied him a few steps outside, I turned away after I had embraced and wished him a safe voyage. Two weeks later Gentilini, who had not wanted to take advantage of the ship leaving with Father Buonavita, left for Europe alone. The Emperor gave him a letter of recommendation addressed to his family for a pension of 1,200 francs; he had with him a draft for the sum of 16,000 francs, the product of his savings and wages. As he did not want to take that money with him, he handed the sum over to me to place in the account of the Emperor, who then requested that the cardinal pay it to the man on his arrival. We were too worried about the Emperor's health for these two departures to have the same effect as the preceding ones, for the Emperor's habits were not changed very much by them. Prior to all this, the Emperor had learned of the death of Princess Elisa. That news saddened him, and he told Count de Montholon who was with him: "Well, my son, it's my turn next." And as the general was trying to distract the Emperor from such depressing thoughts, he added: "It is in vain that you try to give me hope. I feel it, I am no longer the proud Napoleon; soon the sovereigns will no longer have to fear my escape from this rock."

I have related that the Emperor had urged Count de Montholon to use force to get him to go out. On the morning of March 17, the count came as usual to try and convince the Emperor to get into his carriage; the doctor was present and also insisted. The Emperor was in bed, resisting their wishes: "I feel so poorly when I come home," he said, "and I am so well in bed! Well, Montholon, as you insist, see if the carriage is there." The general came back immediately to say it was there, and that there was almost no wind. The Emperor ate a little jelly I had offered him, put on a pair of trousers, some slippers, a necktie, a green overcoat, and a round hat, and he went out leaning on Count de Montholon's arm. Once he reached the carriage he was unable to get into it. He came back inside feeling an icy chill through his whole body and went directly to bed. I covered him with a second blanket, while Saint-Denis and Noverraz heated towels that I wrapped around his feet, changing them often. "You are bringing me back to life," he said; "I fear I am about to have a relapse: it will save me or kill me." As he was complaining about his stomach, I applied hot towels there too. He felt better and managed to perspire a little, after which he dismissed the doctor and told Count de Montholon, "My son, go and have lunch, I know that I am going to sleep." When these gentlemen had departed, I was asked to read to him about the campaigns of Dumouriez.

During the day, Count Bertrand came at his usual time, and the Emperor conversed with him about that general's operations. The sweating had been so abundant that several times the Emperor felt the need to change his underclothes. Feeling better, he wanted to go out to his oak tree to sit down while they aired out his room. He could not remain outside for too long, and he returned to his bed, supported by Noverraz and Count de Montholon, just as a new attack was occurring. He sent for the doctor, who had not yet returned from town where he had accompanied Father Buonavita. When he showed up, the crisis had already passed; the Emperor, annoyed that he had not been there when he had his relapse, refused to see him. I spent the night close to the Emperor, but in the adjoining room; the night was quiet.

The following day, the 18th, Count Bertrand, informed of the new chills that had seized the Emperor, came at nine o'clock to inquire about him. That hour was unusual for him: the Emperor was astonished, and had me answer he was feeling fine. He ate a biscuit, and drank a little Malaga wine, and as he was getting ready to go into the garden, he called for Count de Montholon. On reaching his bench he vomited everything he had swallowed, but nevertheless insisted on staying there until he was forced to go back in. The Emperor's features were very drawn; as on the previous day, he was forced to get into bed and was only able to warm his feet and body by using hot towels. The doctor was immediately called in: he talked about medication to be taken; the Emperor did not want any. Count de Montholon kept him company until Count Bertrand arrived. After the grand marshal's departure, the Emperor had me resume reading about the campaigns of Dumouriez.

On the 19th, the Emperor was again seized with fever, "which crept up on him like a snake," he said. He had me cover him with several blankets and tried unsuccessfully to sleep. He summoned Count de Montholon, who spent part of the morning with him, and he called for the doctor, who again was not at home. When the grand marshal arrived, the Emperor expressed his dissatisfaction with the doctor who had not yet seen him during a crisis. He told Count de Montholon to go get some fresh air, which he must have needed.

On the 20th, the Emperor's condition remained the same. The night had been calm, and that morning he wanted to take a short walk outside. He spotted a peach that appeared ripe and ate it with a great deal of sugar, but it made him ill, and he threw it up a few moments later. When he came in he said, "Poor me!" The day was spent conversing with one or the other of these gentlemen, but that evening the fever increased. He had the covered lamp put in the adjoining room to draw away the mosquitoes that were bothering him, and had the mosquito netting lowered, but they got inside. He got up so that I could chase them away, and then went back to bed and called for Count de Montholon; in the afternoon Count Bertrand came to spend a few hours with him.

On the 21st, an emetic was offered the Emperor, who refused any kind of medication. The doctor explained the results to be expected from it; General Bertrand and Count de Montholon joined him, and the following day he decided to take it. Countess Bertrand came to inquire about the Emperor's health: he asked me to express his gratitude as well as his regret that he could not receive her. She told me how worried she was, for the doctor had told her the Emperor's situation was most serious, and that symptoms of gastritis were evident.

On the 22nd, the Emperor yielded to the wishes of these gentlemen and took the emetic that was administered to him in two doses taken some time apart; the result was drastic. Count de Montholon and the doctor were present. Some phlegm came up after repeated efforts, and sleep overcame him in the afternoon. I lowered the mosquito netting, and the stuffiness got him out of bed: he settled in his armchair where he spent part of the evening in the dark, with the covered lamp placed in the adjoining room.

On the 23rd, after having his cautery bandaged, the Emperor felt the need to shave and brush his teeth. Once these cleansings were completed, he felt refreshed. In the morning he agreed to again take the emetic, but his stomach convulsions were so severe he would have no more of it. Once Count Bertrand and Montholon had departed, I remained alone with him. He fell asleep while I was reading to him. When he awoke he ate a little soup and jelly, his only food since he took to his bed. During the night he had perspired and changed his flannel undershirt several times. He asked me for a small bottle and some licorice, poured a small quantity, and told me to fill it with water, adding that in the future he wished to have no other beverage but that. He then forbade me to offer him any liquid he had not authorized.

On the 24th, he showed Count de Montholon the beverage that he proposed to take: "If it doesn't do me any good," he said to him, "it will do me no harm." The doctor, who was present, smiled at the

Emperor's words, but declared that his stomach needed an emetic, which he must suggest to His Majesty. "Why don't you go jump in the lake," said the Emperor, "and take the emetic yourself!" That same day the doctor told the Emperor that Noverraz had gone to bed with a very severe liver attack, and that he had just attended to him. The Emperor feared that his illness might be quite long and, as I had not fully recovered from my own, that I would have a relapse because of fatigue. I had indeed spent the nights from the 18th to the 24th, attending him, assisted by Saint-Denis or Noverraz, who slept in the adjoining room. Count de Montholon, to whose care the Emperor was accustomed during the day, offered his services for the night. The Emperor decided he would remain with him from 9 p.m. to 2 a.m., and that at that time I would come and resume my service with him. So in addition to the hours he spent with the Emperor during the day, Count de Montholon took on this night duty. The grand marshal came regularly at 3 p.m. and left at 6 p.m., and I took advantage of his presence in the Emperor's bedroom to have dinner. The Emperor told him of the new arrangement he had just made. Count Bertrand immediately offered his services, and the Emperor replied: "Montholon's services are sufficient, I am used to his taking care of me; if that were not sufficient I would accept yours." Countess Bertrand came to inquire about the Emperor, who asked me to thank her.

On the 25th and 26th, wet towels were applied several times to the Emperor's stomach; the doctor told me of his concern, and said that the illness was progressing rapidly from day to day, because he refused the help that could be offered him. "I see only one way," he said to me: "and that is to put an emetic in his adopted beverage, and in those that may be offered to him, without letting him know about it." He whispered his proposal to me in the bedroom of the Emperor, who was sleeping at the time. I answered that I would absolutely not give the Emperor beverages with emetics in them, because I had received orders regarding this very matter, and the Emperor would not at all appreciate being treated this way. "Consult General Montholon and the grand marshal," I added, "but for myself, I refuse to have any part

in it." The conversation came to an end, and he never mentioned it to
me again.

The following day, the 27th, the doctor came as he usually did
at 8 a.m., and entered after having been announced. The Emperor told
him his night had not been bad, and that General Montholon had
helped him change his flannel shirt several times. The doctor took
advantage of his good mood to tell him that he should put more trust in
medicine. "That's all very well," said the Emperor, "you work like
blind men, and medicine kills more men than it saves." The day went
by; he alternated between his bed and his armchair in the adjoining
room, conversing with Count de Montholon and then Count Bertrand,
who replaced him. A table holding several decanters filled with cool
drinks stood in front of him, but he had not drunk anything all day
long.

When he saw Count Bertrand, the Emperor asked him: "Well,
Sir Grand Marshal, how do you feel?"

"Perfectly well, Sire. I wish the same could be said for Your
Majesty; how do you find these drinks with emetics in them? Are they
doing you good?" The Emperor knew nothing about the proposal that
had been made to me, and as he felt sick to his stomach, he immediately called me; I was in the adjoining room. A sudden anger showed
on his face, in contrast with my calmness. "Since when, sir, do you
allow yourself to poison me by putting beverages with emetics in them
on my table? Didn't I tell you not to offer me anything without my
authorization? Did I not forbid you? Is this the way you justify my
trust in you? You knew it! Get out!" I was speechless: never had the
Emperor spoken to me in that way, but his anger was misplaced.
"Sire," I said to him, "I can assure Your Majesty that as far as I know,
there is no emetic in these drinks. It is true that yesterday, in Your
Majesty's bedroom, the doctor talked to me about the need to put an
emetic in the drinks that would be served to you, without telling you
about it; but I thought I had dissuaded him by telling him he could not
allow an act of this nature toward Your Majesty. As for myself, I
refused to allow any to come into this room. If the doctor has followed

through on his idea, I was not informed of it, and it must have taken place in the pantry."

"Have Antommarchi called in."

Fortunately he was not at home; I had received the brunt of his outburst, and that evening he came in for his share. He tried to excuse himself by telling the Emperor that continuing to refuse the help offered him was endangering his life. "Well, sir, do I owe you an account? Do you not believe that for me death would be a blessing from heaven? I do not fear it, I will do nothing to hasten it, but I will not grasp at straws to survive." He dismissed him curtly and went two days without seeing him. This incident had put the Emperor in a bad mood the rest of the day. He had me throw all the drinks that were on his table out the window and said with some irritation: "I certainly hope no one has taken the liberty of adding anything to my licorice."

During the day I had bandaged his arm: the flesh was pale and the patch not very wet. As I have mentioned, soups and jellies were almost the only food the Emperor had taken since keeping to his room. The governor worried that the duty officer no longer saw the Emperor and insisted that he see a British doctor.

The days of the 28th and 29th were much like the preceding ones. The shutters were drawn, the Emperor went often at night and during the day from his bed to his settee or armchair. He had the door to his garden opened and told Count Bertrand to go find him a flower. He brought back a pansy that the Emperor placed on his table. The grand marshal and Count de Montholon pleaded the doctor's case, describing how worried he was; a great responsibility lay on his shoulders. He had but one thought; to bring some relief to the Emperor's suffering, and he would be content if the Emperor were to allow him to bring in a doctor likely to inspire a trust he could not. "That's fine, tell him I shall see him tomorrow." The Emperor did see him the following day and uttered: "Doctor, I am a dead man."

"If Your Majesty refuses all help!" The doctor came up to the bed, felt his pulse, placed his hands on his stomach, found it bloated, and told him he would advise the use of pills that would cause this condition to disappear. "Doctor," the Emperor said to him laughing, "you are a great, ignorant man, my friend; you know that Hippocrates said yes, and Galen said no. In this situation, this is the best medicine:" and he showed him a small bottle filled with licorice water, which he preferred to all the various drinks placed on his table.

The grand marshal and General Montholon, as I have said, had already talked to the Emperor about the doctor's wish to bring in another physician. During the night Count de Montholon discussed it with him. But the Emperor had been opposed to this action, and told me after these gentlemen had left: "What use is there in bringing in another doctor; will he know my illness any better? If Corvisart or Larrey were here, I would trust them and have some hope; but these ignorant people know nothing about my ailment. A good ride on horseback, that is what I need! Find a book and read me something."

Count de Montholon told me on leaving the Emperor that he had talked to him during the night of the need to have Dr. Arnott and Dr. Antommarchi come together, and that he was less reluctant than he had been the previous day. If the Emperor were to mention it to me, I was to praise the idea, because having him come was all the more urgent as the Emperor had not been seen by the duty officer for more than two weeks, and the governor had ordered the latter to find a way to see the "general" to obtain news.

The duty officer indeed showed the order he had received from the governor. Count de Montholon explained to him that given the Emperor's state of health, violating his domicile was a murderous act, and furthermore, he would be received by His Majesty with a pistol in his hand. He immediately wrote to the governor to wait until the next day so he could talk to the Emperor about it. That reprieve lasted several days, and was used to prepare the Emperor to receive Dr. Arnott. For some time the Emperor had been saying: "This Calabrian of a governor is leaving us alone. What does this mean? He probably knows that I am ill through the Chinese." He did not suspect that, at that very moment, he was ordering his domicile to be violated, by ordering the Captain of the Guard to enter the Emperor's quarters! The latter, certain that Napoleon was ill as was being said, and upset by the mission he had been given, said he would rather submit his resignation than carry out such orders; a few days later he was replaced by Captain Crokat. Count de Montholon managed to make the governor understand they were urging the Emperor to see a British doctor in addition to Antommarchi. He asked him to wait until they had convinced him, which could not take very long. The governor could then be reassured that the Emperor was much closer to dying than escaping from him, which he seemed to fear.

CHAPTER TWENTY-FOUR

Dr. Arnott — The Emperor dictates his last wishes —
The Emperor weakens — Conversations with Dr. Arnott —
The Emperor's final requests

On April 1, due to our repeated requests and feeling his strength abandoning him from day to day, the Emperor agreed to receive Dr. Arnott. "Your British doctor," he said to Count Bertrand, "will go report my condition to that executioner. It will give him far too much pleasure to learn of my agony; but afterwards, what more can he do if I agree to see this doctor? Well! It is more for the satisfaction of the people around me than for my own, for I expect to gain nothing from his opinions! Well, Bertrand, tell him to come to your house; let him consult with Antommarchi, explain to him the progress of my illness, and then bring him to me."

The grand marshal immediately summoned Dr. Arnott, who, after being informed of the Emperor's illness, replied that in order to assess the illness he had to see the patient. That same evening at 9 p.m. he was shown into the Emperor's bedroom, which was barely lit by the covered lamp placed in the adjoining room. I lifted the mosquito netting from the bed, and he approached. After taking his pulse and feeling his stomach, the doctor said that he would go find out more about the ailment by speaking with Dr. Antommarchi and asked for permission to come back the next morning at 9 a.m.

The Emperor asked daily for news of Noverraz, who had been bed-ridden for several days, and whose severe illness had overcome his strength. "As soon as he is better," said the Emperor, "I want him to return to Europe. It is the second attack of this kind, and I don't want that good man to die a victim of this awful climate." Count Bertrand knew that Saint-Denis slept in the room adjoining that of the

Emperor every night, and again offered his services to the Emperor, who thanked him, saying: "You have plenty to do with your wife and your children; Montholon's care is enough. I have arranged so that he and Marchand can take care of me without getting too tired." Although Countess Bertrand received news of the Emperor at least once a day, she still came in person to inquire. I never failed to tell the Emperor, who had me thank her and express his regret that his attire did not allow him to receive her. I was sure the Emperor was making the lady feel his displeasure that she had expressed her intention to return to Europe.

The next day, April 2, Dr. Arnott arrived at 9 o'clock accompanied by Count Bertrand; the Emperor allowed him to be followed by Dr. Antommarchi. The Emperor was half reclining and received him graciously, saying that it was because of the esteem he enjoyed in his regiment that he had agreed to see him, and on his promise not to report his condition to the governor. The Emperor's face, always noble and handsome, nevertheless showed the signs of long suffering. A beard of several days added even more to the paleness of his complexion, and his eyes so full of expression showed the calmness of perfect resignation. After having asked several questions concerning the abdominal organs, the entry of food and its exit through the pylorus, the Emperor said to him: "I have an acute pain here that seems to cut me like a razor. Do you think it might be the pylorus that is affected? My father died of this disease at the age of 35; could it not be hereditary?" Dr. Arnott approached, felt his abdomen again and told him it was an inflammation of the stomach and the pylorus did not seem to be affected. The liver was not involved at all, the pain he felt in his intestines came from the air that had entered them; and if he did not refuse medication, all that would disappear. He prescribed poultices and some potions to be taken every hour. The grand marshal translated the doctor's words: "Tell him that I have never suffered from my stomach, that occasionally I have cramps, but that all my life my digestion has been excellent." Pulling his covers back over himself, the Emperor talked to him of Egypt and of Abercromby's expedi-

tion,[350] in which the doctor had participated. In dismissing him he
said: "Doctor, we will discuss this again: in the future, I will expect
you at four o'clock with the grand marshal," to whom he addressed,
"that hour shall become that of my dinner." These visits were afterwards a distraction for the Emperor and provided a diversion from his
suffering. He would keep the two doctors a half hour to forty-five
minutes, dismiss them, and keep the grand marshal with him until 6 or
7 p.m. It was also the time chosen by Count deMontholon to go get
some fresh air and have dinner; he would return between 9 and 10
o'clock and remain with the Emperor until 2 or 3 in the morning, and I
relieved him at that time. He said of Dr. Arnott that he appeared to be
a good man.

That same evening as I was relieving the grand marshal, I told
the Emperor that we could see a comet. "Ah," he said to me, "my
death shall be marked, as was Caesar's." Struck by the Emperor's
words, I hastened to say that it did not threaten us with such a catastrophe! It was showing the course toward France: "Ah, my son! I no
longer have any hope of seeing Paris again." Those words were said
with so much conviction that they hurt me. Count de Montholon confirmed the existence of the comet, but forbade Dr. Antommarchi to
mention it during his evening visit.

The following day the grand marshal arrived a few moments
before 4 o'clock. He told the Emperor of the imminent arrival of two
cooks who had left England to replace Chandelier, whose condition
had gotten even worse. One was named Perrusset and the other Chandelier, the latter being a cousin of the man he was coming to replace.
At that moment, the doctors arrived and were shown in.

Dr. Arnott told the Emperor that the new house was completed, and its apartments were large and airy: he would be better there
than in his bedroom, which was much too small. "Doctor," replied the
Emperor, "it is too late; I informed your governor when he submitted

---

[350]General Ralph Abercromby (1734-1801) was a Scotsman of great reputation. He
had been sent in 1801 to reconquer Egypt from the French; he landed at Aboukir on
March 8, and was mortally wounded on the 21st at the battle of Canopus.

the plans for the house to me, that it would take five years to build, and by then I would need a grave; you can see they are offering me the keys, and I am finished!" Dr. Antommarchi pointed out that such a move could lead to serious complications, and that if the Emperor lacked ventilation in his bedroom, he should be moved into the drawing room. Leaving His Majesty and examining the vomit that contained black matter, Dr. Arnott concluded there was ulceration of the stomach. He informed the grand marshal, and Count de Montholon wrote several prescriptions, but the Emperor remained as defiant to medicine from him as he had been with Dr. Antommarchi.

Several days passed without Dr. Arnott's care and attentions bringing about any improvement in the Emperor's health. At night, perspiration forced him to change his flannel undershirt five or six times; during the day, his restlessness was not as considerable, due to the distraction he got from conversation or reading. One evening after Count Bertrand had departed, I remained alone with him; he talked to me about Princess Pauline and her little house in San Martino on the island of Elba, his hermitage at the Madonna, and the cool shade that made a visit there so pleasant. Then he told me to read him a chapter on Syria which had been recopied by Saint-Denis, but written so small that it was difficult to read it back to him.

During each visit, the doctor always offered pills or other medication; the Emperor would reply that he did not see any objection to that, change the conversation, and always manage not to take anything. One day while Dr. Arnott was taking his pulse, he asked the Emperor how he felt. "Not well, doctor, I am about to return to the earth a remnant of life that seems so important for the kings to have." And as the doctor insisted on his taking medication, the Emperor replied: "Always medication? Well, Doctor, we'll take some! What diseases are there in your hospitals?" Then getting out of bed, he donned his bathrobe and went to sit in front of a table on which his dinner had been served. He had the doctor taste some of the dishes and offered him a glass of claret. There was a small piece of Savoie cake on his table: he cut it in four parts and gave one to the grand marshal, one to Dr. Arnott, the third to Dr. Antommarchi, and the fourth to me.

Two days earlier, the Emperor had wanted to shave: everything had been prepared for the procedure, but it had been postponed. "I should be less lazy," he said, "because I feel refreshed when it is done. It is your fault," he said taking me by the ear, "if I do not shave. You must force me in the future. Poor me," he uttered, looking at himself in the mirror. A few days later, he did not feel well and was very thirsty; I offered him some barley water that was on his table. "I certainly hope," he remarked looking at me, "that no one has dared introduce something into my beverages?"

"Sire," I said, "the lesson was too harsh for anyone to try again." The Emperor was obviously annoyed. At dinner he took a little jelly; he was offered some tonic wine, but replied to Dr. Arnott that he would see.

The night of April 7 had been troubled. Count de Montholon told me when I relieved him at 3 a.m. that he had changed the Emperor's flannel undershirt three times. So much sweating decreased his strength; however, he felt better in the morning and wanted to shave, but fearing that his strength would betray him, he sat in an armchair. Since the days of the Consulate, no one had touched the Emperor's face. Finding it inconvenient to have someone shave him, he had gotten into the habit of shaving himself with both hands. After staring at himself for a few moments in the mirror, he turned his tender eyes toward me and making a grimace, said to me: "I certainly don't look very well, my son: call Saint-Denis to hold this mirror." After several tries, he managed a complete wash. He slipped on a bathrobe, remained seated in his armchair, glanced at a few newspapers, had the window opened, and asked for Count de Montholon, whom he had sent out to get some fresh air. Saint-Denis came to tell him that General Montholon was not at home. "The weather is nice," he said to me, "he must have gone to camp to bring me news." A few moments later the general arrived.

At 4 p.m. the Emperor took a little jelly with his soup. I have said that the grand marshal translated the Emperor's words to the doctor, and vice versa. "Your satirists," he said to Dr. Arnott, "have completely twisted the facts: they accuse me of having poisoned my soldiers, when I gave my own horses to transport them. The pharmacist whom you mention in your fable, who died in Egypt because I refused to let him come back to France, was a miserable man, dismissed from the army for commandeering some of the drugs from his pharmacy and selling them for his own profit; there are witnesses who can testify to this.[351] A few sick people who were unable to be moved remained in the hospital: I left my ADC Lavalette there until their death, which came to pass the following day." Dr. Arnott had brought some tonic wine in concentrated form, and the Emperor had me taste it. I found it bitter, but not disagreeable. He consented to take some, and said that he would start using it the next day. Dr. Arnott found his pulse stronger, which offered us a little hope.

On April 9 and 10, I proposed the tonic wine concentrate. Several times he rebuffed me and told me to take it instead; it would do him just as much good that way. The shutters in the two bedrooms remained closed all day. The Emperor's side was hurting him, and he got some relief from the application of hot towels. Count de Montholon remained with him, and did not leave him until the grand marshal arrived, followed by the doctors. The Emperor put his hand to his side and told Dr. Arnott: "Here doctor, it's the liver!" Dr. Arnott assured him it was not so, but the Emperor remained convinced of it. He asked Dr. Antommarchi how Noverraz was. "He is not out of danger," said the doctor, "but I think I have mastered the illness." During the evening the Emperor complained of feeling nauseated. At 6 p.m. I relieved the grand marshal; at 9 p.m., Count de Montholon replaced me. The Emperor did not delude himself about his condition: during the day he had spoken to Count de Montholon about the arrangements in his will, and asked him in front of me if two million would be enough to buy back his family property in Burgundy. Did the Emperor

---

[351]This is probably Jean François Royer, chief pharmacist of the army of the orient in 1798, and during the expedition to Syria.

For professional errors and infractions against discipline, he was dismissed at the end of the Egyptian campaign and left in that country, where he was murdered in 1804. The Emperor refers here to the accusation made against him regarding the plague victims in Jaffa.

intend to write another will? I knew there was one that I carried to Count Bertrand during that evening. He complained that bullets had spared him, only to leave him helpless and without the care his condition required. The Emperor was less restless during the night of the 11th; the doctor attributed this to a sedative the Emperor had taken on Count de Montholon's insistence.

On April 13, His Majesty continued to dictate; Count de Montholon remained locked behind closed doors with the Emperor, who dictated his last wishes to him until 3 o'clock. When the doctors were shown in, he asked Dr. Arnott if one could die from weakness: "I have eaten so little in the last two days, and my stomach barely keeps down what I put into it: a little jelly is my only food." Twice he vomited, and this interrupted his dictation to Count de Montholon for a few moments. In the evening the Emperor took a little soup, but vomited it up immediately.

On the 14th, he took advantage of a moment of calm to continue to dictate to Count de Montholon, with whom he remained shut away in the room. At 4 o'clock Count Bertrand arrived with the doctors; a few ink stains on the sheets demonstrated that the Emperor had been busy writing. He said nothing about it, but spoke of his weakness. Dr. Arnott took his pulse counting the beats on my watch, a present from the Emperor. He insisted that the next day the Emperor take some pills he habitually brought with him.

The Emperor stopped talking about his health, and spoke to him about the Abercromby expedition; as usual, the grand marshal translated what the Emperor was saying. "You can't imagine," he said, "an expedition more poorly conceived whose execution could be any more successful! Masters of the sea, you went ashore without horses for your artillery or your cavalry. Had Menou followed the plan of my Aboukir battle, you would have been defeated, and had Lannes had 2,000 more men with him, he would have completely overwhelmed you during the lateral march you made in front of him. The loss of my fleet at Aboukir had vast consequences for France's destiny; had it not been for that, I would have reached the goal I had to make her master of the world! Menou was a good man and a good administrator, but a bad general; had I given the command to Lannes, who burned with zeal, your expedition would have failed. Reynier was an excellent general, but too cool; had Kléber lived, Egypt would have been retained by France." After dismissing the doctors, he remained alone with Count Bertrand until 6 o'clock. When I relieved him at 2 a.m., Count de Montholon told me the Emperor continued weakening from day to day, and Dr. Arnott thought him very ill.

On the morning of the 15th, the Emperor shaved and was refreshed by some light washings. He went back to bed and called for Dr. Antommarchi, who found his pulse good and advised him to take the previous day's pills. As His Majesty agreed with great reluctance, I suggested placing them between two noodles in a soup they had just brought him: I offered them to him in a soup spoon with a little bouillon. "My stomach," he said, "turns just at the thought of taking them. You take them," and they immediately found their way into my stomach. "Let's see," he said, "they don't seem to bother you." I wrapped some more pills and offered them in the same manner; then he made up his mind to take them, and fearing he would throw up, he grabbed a silver basin in his left hand. After taking them he said that he had not felt them and for me to offer them the same way in the future. Nevertheless, he did vomit that morning.

That same day the Emperor had me draw up inventories of the silverware, his Sèvres porcelain, his wardrobe, and other belongings. He continued to work with Count de Montholon until 3 o'clock; at 4, the grand marshal and the doctors were shown in. The Emperor got out of bed, leaned on Count Bertrand's arm, went to his armchair, and ate very little of what was served him. He talked to Dr. Arnott about the camp, asked if the regiment had a good library, discussed the generals who commanded the British armies, and praised Marlborough. The Emperor proposed to write commentaries on that general's campaigns, as he had done for Caesar, Turenne, Frederick, and Hannibal. He asked Dr. Arnott if the regimental library had a copy of Marlborough's campaigns; the doctor replied that he was not sure. "Well, I want to make a gift of it to your regiment." The Emperor had me take the book from his library: it was a very fine copy with illustrations, and beautifully bound. "Here, Doctor," he said, taking it from my hands, "I like brave men from all nations." At that moment, Dr. Antommarchi laughed; the Emperor shot him a disapproving look, which made him realize how inappropriate his laughter was. "Put it in your regimental library. If I have agreed to see you, doctor, it is to satisfy the people around me, and because you are a man of honor, esteemed by the officers of your regiment." The grand marshal, who had translated the Emperor's words into English, expressed Dr. Arnott's gratitude in French. The doctor was visibly moved, and realized the value of the words accompanying the gift. "The jailer of Saint Helena," the Emperor continued, "to put me on bad terms with the 66th did not hesitate to slander me by saying I did not like redcoats; you can enlighten them, and tell them this is untrue. I am," he said, "going to write to the prince regent and your ministers: they have wanted my death, which they are about to obtain having assassinated me with pinpricks. I wish for my ashes to rest in France. Your government will oppose this, but I predict the monument it erects for me will be to its shame, and that John Bull will emerge from my ashes to overthrow the British oligarchy. Posterity shall avenge me for the executioner assigned to keep me, and your ministers shall die a violent death." The doctor, who could see death closing in on the Emperor, was full of admiration for his spirit that would not be subdued.

Having dismissed the doctors, he kept Count Bertrand with him. That same evening, we learned the governor had prevented the volumes from leaving Longwood, but the officers, informed of the Emperor's courtesy, sent their thanks; and after his death, they demanded that the governor give them the books.

When I returned to Europe, I was amazed to read in Dr. Antommarchi's book, page 94 of the second volume on Saint Helena, that the Emperor, after praising Marlborough and giving the general's campaigns as a present to Dr. Arnott for his regiment, joked about Marlborough and sang the first verse of the song written about him.

That the author, who was present when the gift was made, was unable to repress a moment of mirth caused by a song with which he was rocked to sleep as a child—so he said—I do not contest. But he was wrong in reporting a false anecdote that casts ridicule on the honorable reasons for the 20th regiment receiving the Emperor's gracious gift. He would have done better to keep quiet, for I certainly would not have revealed the severe and disapproving look his laughter earned him.

Dr. Antommarchi had a frivolous character, but was not a bad man. His humor, inclined toward mockery, led to a few admonitions from the Emperor. The latter questioned the doctor's ability, and if he appeared satisfied after chatting with him on his arrival in Saint Helena, it was more in order to inspire trust among those who surrounded him than through any personal conviction.

It only took me a few days after Dr. Antommarchi arrived to judge, if not his knowledge, at least his character. Having never in his life approached an eminent and powerful personage like the Emperor, he was ignorant of the ground on which he trod. When he arrived, he had discussed the Emperor's health with me frequently, and every morning he talked to me to learn of the night's events. I thus attempted to warn him about what might give the Emperor a bad opinion of him. "Be more serious when with the Emperor," I told him, "when you answer the questions asked of you; and when speaking of Count de Montholon and the grand marshal, refrain from saying Bertrand and Montholon; the Emperor speaks to them that way, but you must not allow yourself to do so." He thanked me and took my advice; perhaps he even believed I had been asked by the Emperor to say this to him, which was not the case. The priests, for their part, were very respectful and never failed to use the title of Count or Excellency when speaking to either one.

On April 16, the Emperor's feet could be kept warm at night only with hot towels. When Dr. Antommarchi was announced, he strongly reprimanded him for his flippancy and the impropriety of his behavior the previous day. The doctor tried to excuse himself through the memory prompted by a song with which he had been rocked to sleep as a child; when he dismissed him, he asked him to summon Count de Montholon. He remained with him until 3 o'clock. I only entered the room during that time to hold his head when he vomited twice in succession and to wrap his feet in hot towels. The Emperor told me to give him some of the Las Cases wine. I took the liberty of expressing my fears about the reaction this might cause. Count de Montholon urged him not to continue dictating his last wishes, assuring the Emperor he had all the time he needed to worry about bequests, also adding he thought the wine might do him harm. The Emperor insisted on having some, dipped a biscuit in it, resumed writing, and said to Count de Montholon: "My son, it is time that I finish this, I feel it." Sitting up in bed, the Emperor held a board with one hand and wrote with the other without support; standing next to the bed, Count de Montholon held an inkwell.

When the grand marshal arrived with the doctors, the Emperor revealed nothing of what he had been doing, but nausea seized him, and he told Dr. Antommarchi that to give him strength, he had taken some Constance wine with a biscuit. The doctor replied that was like throwing oil on a fire. He then asked Dr. Antommarchi what his chances were; he replied that they were good, and that his condition was not desperate. "Doctor, you are not telling the truth," replied the Emperor. "You are wrong in trying to hide my condition from me, I know what it is. Have you heard of Corvisart, of Larrey? More of the latter than the former? What consideration Larrey had for his patients, both in Egypt or during our desert crossing, and in Europe! He was always seen going from one end of the column to the other, to tender his care; what a man! What a brave and noble man was Larrey! I developed an esteem for him that was never disappointed; if the army should erect a column to gratitude, it owes the original to Larrey."

If we were fortunate enough to hear the Emperor's last words, let us not forget, when faithfully reporting them, to make known those in honor of the virtuous man who deserved them so well. In another instance, when expressing his dissatisfaction to Dr. Antommarchi because he was never at home when we went to find him, he said, "If Larrey were here, he would not leave my room, and he would sleep at the foot of my bed as Montholon and Marchand do."

The Emperor continued to query the doctor, asking about British army dress; how the sick were tended to in camp; if, after a battle, the British experienced more casualties than the French. Dr. Arnott replied that French doctors were very knowledgeable, but he believed the losses were greater on our side. The Emperor seemed to believe the opposite and thought that a properly executed amputation saved men who otherwise would have been lost to the country. "That," he said, "was Larrey's opinion. Your infantry acquitted themselves well at Waterloo, and did better than your cavalry. You would have good soldiers if you knew how to inspire a love of glory in them, but your punishments of rope lashes only turns them into brutes. The French soldier, who is capable of great understanding and judgment, wants someone to speak to his soul. It is impossible for a soldier who has just received several dozen lashes to then want to distinguish himself in front of his comrades. I have been told," said the Emperor, "that the British soldier is so little interested in reaching officers' rank that during the Spanish war, where losses were high, they disliked seeing the noncommissioned officers become officers, because they were not gentlemen."

Countess Bertrand, who had not come for several days, appeared after the doctors had left to inquire about the Emperor's health. I informed His Majesty, who had remained alone with the grand marshal; the Emperor told me to thank her. When Dr. Antommarchi left, he expressed a hope not shared by Dr. Arnott, and Drs. Shortt and Mitchell[352] were called in consultation during the day at Count de Montholon's house.

On the 17th and 18th the Emperor spent several hours alone with Count de Montholon. Tired of his licorice water, he tried a little of the refreshments placed on his side table, such as lemonade, raspberry water, and barley water. Count Bertrand arrived a few minutes before the doctors. When they came in, the Emperor, sitting in his armchair, said to me in a tone indicating great weakness: "Open that

---

[352]Drs. Thomas Shortt, Charles Mitchell, Matthew Livingstone, and Francis Burton were called in consultation on Thursday, May 3, 1821, by Drs. Antommarchi and Arnott. None of the four saw the Emperor, and the conference took place in the French surgeon's room. They issued totally diverging and inconclusive diagnoses. Only Livingstone was present for part of the autopsy.

door to the garden, my son, that I may breathe God's air. Bertrand," he said to the grand marshal, "go get me a rose. Air is such a sweet thing," he said, looking up. Then taking the rose offered him, he said looking at Dr. Arnott: "It is not enough to be surrounded by them, we want to enjoy them even more by bringing them near, just as the lungs never dilate enough to breathe in air that is pure and scented. We like to bring a rose close to better enjoy its fragrance. What do you think, doctor? We aren't spoiled much here."

The grand marshal immediately translated the Emperor's words, to which the doctor replied: "The air in Saint Helena is not bad, it is entertainment and exercise that you are lacking."

"You mean a grave, doctor, and that won't take long; your government shall be satisfied." The Emperor was already so weakened, his physical strength so diminished, that it was impossible to doubt he was telling the truth. He ate a light soup for dinner with a little jelly, and had great difficulty shaving the next morning. During the day, I gave Count de Montholon the inventories he had asked me for. "The night was as restless as all the previous ones," Count de Montholon said as he left the Emperor.

On April 17, as Count de Montholon had arrived much earlier than usual, he told him to continue reading about Hannibal's campaigns. Drs. Arnott and Antommarchi arrived at 4 p.m.; the Emperor got out of bed to sit in his armchair, leaning on Count Bertrand to reach it. He ate very little of what was offered him for dinner, and Dr. Arnott urged him to eat some more. "What's the use," the Emperor replied, "since my stomach will not keep it down? You will only know exactly what my illness is when you open me up."

That morning, the Emperor had talked to Count de Montholon about our return to Europe. He reviewed the provisions on hand, and those likely to be put on board to serve during our crossing: even the sheep kept in the stables were not overlooked. The Emperor spoke of all those details with a calm that belongs only to a spirit as strong as his. That evening after the grand marshal left, the Emperor told me to place the covered lamp at the head of his bed, so that he would not be bothered, and to continue reading to him about Hannibal's campaigns.

At 9 o'clock, Count de Montholon arrived; I left him alone with the Emperor and left Saint-Denis asleep in the adjoining room. Since he had been bed-ridden, the Emperor listened to mass from his bed. The night of the 19th was difficult, he was unable to rest; the following day showed the effects of this agitation that finally subsided in the afternoon.[353] Having dismissed Count de Montholon, the Emperor sent me to look for Homer, and told Count Bertrand to read him a song from it: "He depicts so well the image of the watches and councils I often held on the eve of battles, that I always enjoy hearing it." At 4 o'clock he took some meat jelly, and had it tasted by Dr. Arnott, who found it to be good. He did not feel any nausea during the day because, he reasoned, he had not moved around.

This improvement lasted part of the night and into the morning. The weather was fine, and the Emperor urged Count de Montholon to get some fresh air and find out news. As I remained alone with him, standing at the foot of his bed, he told me that he was naming me, jointly with Counts de Montholon and Bertrand, as the executors of his will. My surprise was as great as the honor bestowed on me; I stammered that I would remain worthy of the trust and the position to

---

[353]Marchand's note: M. de Beauterne, in his book entitled *Conversations religieuses de Napoléon à Sainte-Hélène*, says that on the 20th, after mass, the Emperor made a confession and was given the sacrament, and that this event related by M. de Norvins, was confirmed by me.

I never said any such thing to M. de Beauterne, as it never occurred to the best of my knowledge. The Emperor could have called in Father Vignali that same day, although he rarely did so, but had he had him shown in for this religious act, I would not have forgotten it; nothing to this day has indicated to me he intended to fulfill this duty M. de Beauterne speaks of. Nor did I tell him, as he claims, that General Bertrand, leaving the Emperor one day, shrugged his shoulders while murmuring the word Capuchin.

M. de Beauterne attempts to tarnish the honorable character of Count Bertrand by representing him as a man who filled the Emperor's last moments with bitterness, when, on the contrary, this great officer remained as he had been all his life: full of attachment, respect, and devotion.

The author attributes to the Emperor thoughts which are not his own, and a way of speaking which is not his; he makes him Christian to his liking and not as we knew him in Paris, Elba, and Saint Helena.

M. de Beauterne either was misinformed or poorly reported what was said to him. This he did in what he relates, which concerns me.

which he promoted me, and my emotion was very deep. "I have left with the grand marshal," he said, "a will to be opened by him after my death; tell him to give it to you, and bring it to me." I left the Emperor. When I made this request of the grand marshal on His Majesty's behalf, he appeared surprised; but he went to get it in his desk, and handed it to me without anything betraying the thought that the Emperor might be making new arrangements. The Emperor took the envelope, unsealed it, read through the pages of the document, and tore it in two, telling me to put it in the fire. These were beautiful pages to keep, written in the Emperor's own hands! I held them in my hand, but the Emperor wanted them destroyed! Such as they were handed to me, they were thrown into the fire, where they were soon consumed by the flames, without my knowing anything of what they had said. General de Montholon told me he had found them in the Emperor's papers written in pencil, and I remembered these provisions very well when he mentioned them to me. The diamond necklace the Emperor gave me in one of his codicils was at that point divided between Countess Bertrand and her daughter, and Countess de Montholon and her daughters.

During the afternoon, Count Bertrand came as usual. The doctors arrived after him; the Emperor got out of bed and, supported by the grand marshal's arm, went to sit in his armchair to have dinner, but he took very little of what was served. He talked to Dr. Arnott about the shameful treatment he received from the British government, and told the grand marshal to translate his words.

I came to sit at the hearth of the British people, requesting honest hospitality, and against all rights on earth, I was answered with irons. I certainly would have been received better by Alexander, by Emperor Francis, even by the King of Prussia; those princes would have been more generous. But it was England's part to lead the kings, and to give the world the unheard-of spectacle of four great powers all intent on harming one single man. It is your ministry that has chosen this awful rock where the life of a European is consumed in a few years, in order to finish mine through assassination. How have I been treated in the time I have been here? There are no indignities they did not take pleasure in heaping on me! The simplest communications with my family have been denied me; they have allowed no news of my wife nor my son to reach me; as a residence, I have been given the least habitable place, where the murderous climate of the tropics is felt the most; I have had to lock myself up inside four walls in an unhealthy atmosphere, I who used to travel on horseback throughout all of Europe. That, doctor, is the hospitality I have received from your government; I am being slowly assassinated with great precision, with premeditation, and the infamous Hudson Lowe is the executioner of your ministers' high works. You shall end up like the proud republic of Venice, and I, dying on this awful rock, I bequeath the shame of my death to the ruling house of England.

The Emperor was admirable in his short but spirited speech which, accurately reproduced sentence by sentence by Count Bertrand, deeply moved the doctor. He answered nothing to the accusations he recognized to be true, but his face showed his disapproval of his governor's conduct. After some conversation, the Emperor dismissed the two doctors and kept Count Bertrand with him until 7 p.m. Night had fallen an hour before the grand marshal left.

I went into the Emperor's room; the covered lamp was in the room adjoining the one he occupied. I was quietly approaching the bed, when he told me to bring him the diamond necklace that Queen Hortense had given him when he left Malmaison. I went to get it in the travel kit, where it was carefully locked up along with the receipts for the amounts deposited with M. Laffitte. I brought it to the Emperor who told me, as he handed it to me: "Kind Hortense gave it to me believing I might need it. I estimate its value at 200,000 francs; hide it around your body, I give it to you. I do not know what condition my affairs in Europe are in, it is the only object of value of which I can dispose. It shall allow you to await the fate that I am planning for you in my will and my codicils; you shall have a title[354] and I shall write to the Empress for her to give you a decoration from her states. Marry honorably, make your choice among the families of officers or soldiers of my old guard. There are many of these brave soldiers who are not happy; a better fate would have been theirs if not for France's reversals of fortune. Posterity shall recognize what I would have done for them, had circumstances been otherwise."

He was tired and kept quiet a short while, then resumed: "Once you have returned to France, you shall arrange to go and see the Empress and my son. When he has reached his fifteenth year, you shall give him the objects of which I make you depositary, and you shall encourage him to take back his name of Napoleon." I assured the Emperor I would not fail to follow any of his instructions, and that his wishes were sacred to me. I promised him as much as my emotion allowed me to—as I was choking—that the fortune and honors he was bestowing on me would be shared with a girl whose father had spilled his blood for the motherland and the Emperor's glory.

I could not bring myself to wear the necklace on my body as the Emperor had told me to do; I put it back in the travel kit where it was. I can even say that such a valuable gift bothered me for a time, in caring for the Emperor; my readiness and eagerness until then could not have been brought under suspicion, and I feared for a moment that I would show too much eagerness, and this would be attributed to the great destiny the Emperor intended for me. It was certainly very

---

[354]Marchand's note: On my return to France, many people gave me the title of count, others that of baron. The imperial family wrote to me using either one, and I was given the first as a result of the Emperor's will, which ends with these words: "I appoint Counts de Montholon, Bertrand, and Marchand as my executors." In 1840, as I was about to leave Saint Helena, we had to sign the certificate accepting the Emperor's body from the governor of the island. The grand marshal took me aside and said to me, "Marchand, you can assume the title the Emperor bestowed on you in his will." I then reported to Count Bertrand the words of the Emperor, when he gave me Queen Hortense's necklace, but when I returned to Europe I had not raised this question in view of governments which might refuse its consecration. Under some circumstances, I had used the title of the Emperor's executor, and I proposed to use that again on this occasion: "That one," he replied, "certainly is worth many others; do as you wish." That is the one I used.

stupid, but it was a fear I felt, and that I only overcame through being aware of it.

As I had told the Emperor that his improvement seemed to have lasted the whole day, he replied: "I am a little quieter, but not better; it is a moment of respite. Had my illness been taken care of in time, they might perhaps have been able to cure me; my end is near. Nature wanted to give me a good day in order to settle my affairs. I told Montholon to have you purchase a property close to his in Burgundy; you shall be happy there, the inhabitants are good people whom I have always found to be patriots." Count de Montholon, who was coming to take up his watch over the Emperor, was announced.

CHAPTER TWENTY-FIVE

The Emperor's religious arrangements — Bequests and instructions —
Last care — Countess Bertrand's visit —
Father Vignali with the Emperor — The Emperor's agony and death

*O*n the 21st, the Emperor felt less well than the previous day. He sent Count de Montholon, who had spent several hours with him, to get some fresh air and summoned the doctor, and then Father Vignali. He told the former that shaving had tired him, and his strength was abandoning him; then turning to Father Vignali, he said: "Do you know what a mortuary chamber is?"

"Yes, Sire."

"Have you ever served in one?"

"Never, Sire."

"Well, you will serve in mine when I am in the throes of death. You shall have an altar erected in the adjoining room, expose the holy sacrament there, and recite the prayers of the dying. I was born in the Catholic religion; I wish to fulfill the duties it imposes, and receive the assistance it administers." This scene was quite moving; the Emperor was about to continue when, turning to Dr. Antommarchi standing at the foot of the bed, he thought he noticed some trace of amusement on his face. Offended by what he called a lack of heart, he said to him: "Your foolishness tires me, sir; I can forgive your frivolity and your lack of good manners, but a lack of heart, never! Leave!" Then he said to the priest, "When I am dead, I shall be placed in the funeral chapel: you shall celebrate mass and not cease praying until I am placed in the ground." The Emperor fell silent. The priest and I remained under the impact of the scene that had just taken place, when the Emperor banished the stillness. He talked to the priest about Corsica, Ponte Nuovo, and Rostino, telling him he should build a house there. The Emperor took pleasure in describing a happy, peaceful life for his future there, implying he would grant him the means to realize the dreams he had just spoken of. Moved by the Emperor's affectionate kindness, Father Vignali knelt and seized the Emperor's hand that was lying on the side of the bed. He pressed it to his lips and arose again, his eyes full of tears. After the Emperor had dismissed him, he told me: "That poor Vignali's heart is stricken with sorrow, seeing me in my condition; I like his character, it is that of a Corsican child. As for that imbecile, he is hardly worth my concern. Has anyone ever been cared for worse than I by him?" I did not reply, but I thought the Emperor would not continue to be angry; that his habitual spirit of generosity which led him to forgive would not falter in the case of Dr. Antommarchi. I was not mistaken.

Father Vignali attending the Emperor in his last moments.

The Emperor's conversation with Father Vignali, although it was the first one I heard of this nature, did not surprise me. With the same calm with which he had just tended to his mundane affairs, the Emperor, feeling his last hour approaching, wanted as a Christian to also put things in order for eternity. I had heard the Emperor proclaim the existence of God and say that religious feeling was such a consolation that it was of great benefit to possess it.[355]

On the 22nd, the Emperor agreed to take a sedative administered by Dr. Arnott, who came alone. The Emperor said he had a fever, and placing his hand on his stomach said: "It is there, doctor, nothing goes through anymore, the pylorus is affected, I feel it." The little food he ate was vomited during the evening. The grand marshal, who remained alone with him, spoke of Dr. Antommarchi's regret that the Emperor held such reprehensible feelings toward him. He felt the Emperor's state of health should not allow him to worry about such things. "What am I to do," the Emperor said: "he may not possess a

---

[355]Marchand's note: M. de Beauterne has taken the text of this conversation between the Emperor and Father Vignali and built a fable out of it. Describing it to me as something that had been said to him, M. de Beauterne told me that Count Bertrand had been opposed to having the altar set up for mass, and that in the days ensuing this conversation, it resulted in an estrangement between him and the Emperor brought on by differences of religious opinion expressed in heated terms.

I told him I knew nothing of the argument he described between the Emperor and Count Bertrand. During the Emperor's illness, Count Bertrand came regularly from 4 to 6 p.m., and I had seen no evidence of the furious scene he told me of. In any case, a number of days later, at the moment they were arranging to set up the altar, Count Bertrand asked me for what purpose it was being erected. I told him I did not know; he then told me he was going to see Count de Montholon, and the altar was only put up after the Emperor's death.

I said to M. de Beauterne that if the Emperor's intention had been for mass to be said every morning from the 21st on as he was telling me, I would have known of it, as would Saint-Denis, and the Emperor was not a man to yield to the grand marshal on this point any more than on any other. The Emperor did not speak to me of it; when we set up the altar, we were going beyond his intentions. What is certain is that the altar we had begun to set up was not finished, and I perceived no sign of the slightest estrangement between the Emperor and Count Bertrand. Neither of them spoke to me of this incident, and I myself did not think to ask what had brought about the unfinished preparations, as this matter seemed so trivial. M. de Beauterne took no notice of what I told him and preferred to speak for the Emperor in describing a scene that never took place.

bad soul, but he is an imbecile." No doubt during the night Count de Montholon and the grand marshal pleaded in his favor, as he received the order to return for the next day's visit along with Dr. Arnott.

The Emperor had signed all the inventories shown him, yet there remained the inventory of the snuffboxes to be done. He asked me to bring the case containing them, and dictated the listing to me in the absence of Count de Montholon. He put aside one decorated with a very fine cameo for Lady Holland; this box had been given to him by Pius VI after the treaty of Tolentino. He wrote on a card: Napoleon to Lady Holland, as a token of esteem and affection. He asked Count de Montholon to give it to her, expressing his gratefulness to her for the care she and her husband had shown him. He also took out one intended for Dr. Arnott and told Count de Montholon to add 12,000 francs in gold to it. This box had originally been intended for the minister who had accompanied Cipriani to his final resting place; it was adorned with a crest. The Emperor, while telling me to have an N engraved on it, made one with the tip of his scissors instead. "Sire," I said, "when its origin is known, this one will be far more precious than any with other engravings." At the Emperor's death, it was given to Dr. Arnott by Count de Montholon.

Once that inventory was completed, the Emperor asked me what items remained with Count de Turenne; I went up to my room, found the inventory, and gave it to him. He made arrangements for these things, as can be seen on inventories 1, 2, and 3. He also told me what I was to do with his hair that would be cut after his death: "You shall give each of my family members a locket with some of my hair, a bracelet for the Empress, and a watch chain for my son." That day was certainly one of the most tiring for the Emperor during his long illness, and one of the saddest for us, because of the rapidly developing symptoms announcing his imminent end. The morning had been spent writing his codicils: although he was extremely tired, he had me sit next to his bed so he could dictate the official instructions for his executors; instructions I recopied, and which he signed on the 26th after reading them over.

During this work he was seized with vomiting spells, forcing him to suspend his dictation for a few minutes each time. But everything I said to urge him to cease this work that brought about such serious consequences was unable to deter him: "I am tired indeed," he said, "but little time remains for me, and I must finish; give me a bit of the Las Cases Constance wine." I dared remind him of the effect it had produced a few days ago: "Bah," he said, "a drop could not possibly do me harm, and"—shrugging his shoulders—"all of them know nothing about it, everything is lacking in this country, what do you want me to wait for? I wish to do nothing to shorten my days, but I certainly will do nothing to extend them. Take this," he said, handing me the little glass in which the Constance was, "it's like a razor blade cutting into me as it slides down." After such a long dictation, he still wanted to personally close the three boxes containing his snuffboxes whose inventory he had dictated, and in which some other objects were placed. He wrapped them up with ribbons, sealed them with his crest, and handed me the keys, making me their trustee.

The Constance wine did not take long to induce vomiting, but this did not prevent him from continuing his work until the grand marshal and the doctors were announced. When they came in, the room contained torn papers and sealed boxes wrapped in blue ribbons. "I have written too much," he said to Dr. Arnott, "I am tired, and my abdomen is cramped." He took little food, dismissed the doctors after a moment, and kept Count Bertrand with him. Countess Bertrand came to inquire about the Emperor's health as she had not seen him since he had taken ill; she let me see all the anguish she felt over this. I spoke of it to the Emperor, who replied that one day when he was shaved, he would receive her.

The same day, the Emperor told Count Bertrand he wished to be buried along the banks of the Seine; otherwise on an island at the junction of the Rhône and the Saône near Lyon; or finally in Corsica, in the cathedral where his ancestors were buried, because he would still be in France there. "But," he said, "the British government will have anticipated my death. In the event instructions have been given that my body not leave the island—which I doubt—have me buried under the shade of the willows where I have rested at times when I went to see you at Hutt's Gate, near the fountain where they go for my water every day." These words, spoken with so much calm and resignation, implied the possibility of abandonment on this accursed rock, which wrenched the soul. He also said that he had restored religion in France, that in his palaces as in Saint Helena he had attended mass on Sunday, and that he wanted his last days to be in accordance with the balance of his life. Father Vignali would say mass and recite the forty-hour prayers, and when he did so, he was to be left alone with him. That evening, his stomach was not able to keep down what he had eaten during the day.

Nature had sustained the Emperor's energy enough to allow him to settle his affairs. On April 26, he felt calmer and wanted to use that day to finish them entirely. During the four o'clock visit the preceding day, Dr. Arnott took his pulse and stated that it was rather weak. Afterwards, he offered his arm to Dr. Antommarchi, which he had not done for several days, and gave each of them a piece of biscuit. He offered some claret to Dr. Arnott and dismissed them saying: "I will see you tomorrow."

On the 27th, the Emperor shaved in bed, and I hoped he would summon Countess Bertrand. He said that he felt refreshed, but thought he looked very unwell. He was in a good mood of sorts, chatted with Count de Montholon, and seemed satisfied with what he had accomplished in the previous days. He called for Dr. Antommarchi and acted friendly toward him, which delighted me. During the prior visits, having had the opportunity to note the regret on his face, he asked him if Dr. Arnott would be satisfied with the sum of 12,000 francs for the care he had given him. "You shall be pleased with what I do for you," and a moment later he added, "I shall leave you 100,000 francs and if you so desire, I shall write you a recommendation to the Empress." Before retiring, the doctor expressed his profound appreciation to the Emperor.

During the day, hot towels were applied to his feet to bring back the warmth they lacked. At four o'clock he received the doctors' visit, told Count de Montholon to come back at 8, and said the same to the grand marshal when he left at 6. The Emperor had eaten almost nothing and had gone back to bed after the doctors departed. At 8:30, the Emperor went from his bed to his armchair, leaning heavily on myself and Saint-Denis. He had the carafes removed from his table and told me to place his covered lamp, writing kit, and some paper there. Various sealed packages were on the dresser, and he told me to give them to him and to request the presence of Count de Montholon and Father Vignali. The grand marshal soon arrived; the Emperor, showing him the packages on his table, told him to draw up a statement, and to place our signatures and seals under his own, on each of the codicils and the will, as he had done himself. It read as follows:

Saint Helena, April 27, 1821
Statement establishing the existence of the Emperor's will and codicils.

On this day, April 27, 1821, at 9 p.m. we, Count Bertrand, grand marshal of the Emperor Napoleon, in execution of his orders, had presented to us his various wills, codicils, and instructions, in the care of M. Marchand. These number nine separate envelopes or packages, all having approximately the same shape but different thicknesses, folded in one of the four corners, three of them attached together with a red ribbon. All packages bear the Emperor's signature, and are sealed with his crest and bear the signatures of Count Bertrand, Count de Montholon, M. Marchand, and Father Vignali. After we were shown three mahogany chests locked with a key, wrapped with green ribbons, and sealed with the imperial coat of arms and those of the four people designated above, namely Count Bertrand, Count de Montholon, M. Marchand, and Father Vignali, we have read the notes written in the Emperor Napoleon's own hand, and we have transcribed them as follows:

On an envelope bearing no number is written: This is my will, written in my own hand. Signed: Napoleon.

On envelope No. 1 it is written: This is a codicil to my will, written entirely in my own hand. Signed: Napoleon.

On envelope No. 2 is written: This is a second codicil to my will, written entirely in my own hand. Signed: Napoleon.

On an envelope with no number is written: This is a third codicil to my will, written entirely in my own hand, signed, and sealed with my crest, to be opened the same day and immediately after the opening of my will. Signed: Napoleon.

On envelope No. 5 is written: This is my codicil or statement of my last wishes, whose execution I entrust to my very beloved wife Empress Marie-Louise. Signed: Napoleon.

On envelope No. 6 is written: This is my codicil or statement of my last wishes, whose execution I entrust to my son Eugène Napoleon; it is written entirely in my own hand. Signed: Napoleon.

On an envelope with no number is written: This is a set of instructions for my executors; Montholon, Bertrand, and Marchand. I have written a will and seven codicils, of which Marchand is the trustee. Signed: Napoleon.

On the orders of the Emperor Napoleon, we, Count Bertrand, his grand marshal, have drawn up the present draft to serve as inventory and minutes.

Executed in the Emperor's bedroom at Longwood, on the day and date stated above.

Signed: Count Bertrand

When this statement was completed, he dismissed these gentlemen a few minutes later and kept only Father Vignali with him. Shortly afterwards he came out; I went into the Emperor's room and found him in bed. He handed me his will, his codicils, and the draft drawn on M. Laffitte, instructing me to hand all this after his death only to Count de Montholon, in the presence of Count Bertrand and Father Vignali. I locked everything in the travel kit, where the necklace the Emperor had given me was, and I remained with him until Count de Montholon arrived, which on this day was only at 11 o'clock. On seeing him, the Emperor said: "Well, my son, wouldn't it be a shame not to die after having settled my affairs so well?"

"Sire, only Your Majesty could have such a thought," replied the general. I retired in order to leave him alone with the Emperor. The Emperor had ordered me to take to Count de Montholon's house that evening his manuscripts and the box containing what he called his reserve, which he had disposed of in one of his codicils; to Count Bertrand's house, the weapons; and to my quarters the travel kit, as well as the three mahogany cases holding his snuffboxes. After such a busy day, with so much effort being expended, the night was bound to be a restless one, and it was indeed. The Emperor tried to sleep, but to no avail.

The 28th began badly; his strength was failing before our eyes, and his feet had become permanently cold. A great number of hot towels restored a little warmth; the Emperor asked Saint-Denis, who brought them to me, how his child was. "You must be very tired from sitting up with me so much, my boy; how is Noverraz today? He has really been afflicted by his illness." We replied that he was feeling better and his convalescence was about to begin.

The previous day the doctors and Count Bertrand had insisted that the Emperor change rooms, saying his two bedrooms were not ventilated enough. The Emperor disliked change that upset his habits, however he agreed. Dr. Antommarchi reminded the Emperor that he had promised to take the drawing room as his bedroom: "I am willing, is everything ready?" he said, looking at me.

"Yes, Sire," I said. A small camp bed had been placed between the two drawing room windows, a folding screen in front of the door, and a small table by the bedside. The Emperor who, the preceding day, had already felt very weak when he made his way from his bed to his armchair, became even more tired moving from his bedroom to the drawing room. He got out of bed, put on his bathrobe and slippers, and when he was standing, said: "Poor me, my legs can no longer hold me up." We offered to carry him, but he refused. Supported by Count de Montholon and myself, he reached the drawing room with great difficulty and climbed into bed. During that trip, leaning heavily on Count de Montholon, he said to him: "My son, I have no strength left, I am now destitute." As soon as he got into bed, we wrapped his feet in hot towels. We then placed a second camp bed in the corner of the drawing room, near the door connecting with the billiard room, on the same side as the fireplace. The other one, between the two windows and facing the fireplace, is the one in which the Emperor died.

The night of April 28 to 29, the Emperor was unable to sleep; he attributed the insomnia to his apartment change. When I entered his room at 3 o'clock, I found Count de Montholon writing under his dictation, and I was about to retire when he told me to stay: "Montholon, my son, go and rest, you have need of it, I am going to continue with Marchand." I took M. de Montholon's place, and the Emperor told me to entitle his dictation *Second Reflection*. For an hour and a half he dictated at great length on the subject of organizing the national guard in order to defend the territory of France, whose welfare and grandeur were always on his mind. When he finished, he told me to rewrite this neatly and attach it to the one he had dictated to Count de Montholon, who remained standing by his bed. He said to me: "I was so weak yesterday and so well today that I feel strong enough to go horseback riding."

I opened the shutters when daylight arrived. Since he had changed beds during the night, and the sunlight hurt his eyes, he asked to move again; which he did with great difficulty, leaning on Saint-Denis and myself. Nature had just granted him a last effort; the two dictations were his swan song. It is regrettable they have been lost.

Count de Montholon returned around 11 o'clock. The Emperor complained of a little weakness, but he still wanted to add an eighth codicil to his will. His strength soon left him after a few lines. "Poor Napoleon," he said, and unable to remain sitting up in bed, he rested his head on the pillow. The unfinished codicil is worded in this way:

With a sick body but a sane mind, I am writing in my own hand this eighth codicil to my will:

1. I name as my executors MM. Bertrand, Montholon, and Marchand, and Las Cases or his son, my treasurer.

2. I beg Marie-Louise to take in her service Antommarchi and to pay him a pension of 6,000 francs, which I bequeath to him.

The Emperor, feeling a little better after this moment of weakness, said to General de Montholon: "My son, go and get some fresh air, you need it." Before he left, the general took me aside and handed me two drafts of letters the Emperor had had him prepare: one for M.

Laffitte, and the other for M. de La Bouillerie. He asked me to copy them, so that on my return he could present them for the Emperor's signature. He feared that if he did not sign them today, he perhaps would not be able to do it tomorrow. The Emperor had fallen asleep, and leaving Saint-Denis with him, I went into the library to copy the following two letters.

M. Laffitte,

I gave you in 1815, at the time I was leaving Paris, a sum of close to six million, for which you gave me a duplicate receipt. I am assigning Count de Montholon to present the other receipt to you, so that you may hand over said sum to him, after my death, with interest in the amount of 5 percent, dating from July 1, 1815; after subtracting the payments you have made based on orders received from me. I wish for the liquidation of my account to be carried out by mutual agreement between you, Count de Montholon, Count Bertrand, and M. Marchand, and once this liquidation has been completed, I hereby give you full and complete release for said sum.

I also gave you a box containing my medals, and I entreat you to give these to Count de Montholon.

As this letter has no other purpose, I pray to God, M. Laffitte, to keep you in his holy care.

Longwood, island of Saint Helena, April 25, 1821

Napoleon.

Here is the other:

Baron de La Bouillerie, treasurer of my private estate, I request that you provide an accounting and the amount to Count de Montholon, after my death, whom I am charging with the execution of my will.

As this letter has no other purpose, I pray to God, Baron de La Bouillerie, to keep you in his holy care.

Longwood, April 25, 1821

Napoleon.

While writing these letters, I was surprised by the title of "Monsieur" given to me in one of them, as Count de Montholon who had drawn them up knew very well that the Emperor honored me with the title of count through the dispositions of his will, because he had talked to me about it himself before the Emperor had. At this final moment, when death was on the verge of taking away everything that was great and eminently kind toward me, vanity could not take possession of my soul. When he returned, I handed Count de Montholon the two letters he had given me to copy without comment, except that I had dated them April 25 as they were, although it was the 29th.

If I am dwelling on these two letters, it is because Count de Montholon, in the two volumes he published on Saint Helena—where his memory is often at fault—says that the two letters were dictated to me by the Emperor, which is not the case.[356] These letters were the work of Count de Montholon: the word "Monsieur," either in the will or in the codicils, does not precede my name, and that is so true that

---

[356]Marchand's note: This is not the only error in those memoirs:

1. Count de Montholon erroneously states that after the sale of the silverware the Emperor was forced to eat from earthenware plates. It suffices to look at inventories B and C to see all the silverware that remained at Longwood, and the Sèvres porcelain as well.

2. No one ever saw M. de Las Cases in the oriental costume that drew so much praise from the Emperor, he states, which certainly would never have escaped anyone's attention, had it really existed.

3. His memory is also at fault in saying I was in bed the whole time the Emperor was sick. All one has to do is read Saint-Denis' notes at the end of the book to know that we both took care of the Emperor.

4. The scene where the Emperor collapses on himself when getting out of bed and rolls over on the rug is a flight of imagination; and to have Archambault intervene in this case is another event that was never known to Saint-Denis or to myself.

No one besides ourselves took care of the Emperor. Archambault went like all the household servants on the morning of the 5th, to be present as the Emperor was dying. All of them would no doubt have offered to take care of the Emperor at this last moment, but there was no need to do so. The Emperor did not say and could not have said: "I can trust that one." The degree of faith the Emperor had in each of his servants is shown in his will.

A few weeks before his death, Count de Montholon talked to me about a new edition he wished to publish, and asked me to rectify the mistakes that had slipped into the first edition. I intended to satisfy his wish, but death struck too suddenly for that to be done.

the eighth codicil which is later than the Emperor's letters says: "I name as my executors MM. Bertrand, Montholon, and Marchand, and Las Cases or his son as my treasurer." When that book appeared, I complained about several errors and in particular this one. Count de Montholon replied that as those letters were in my handwriting, he had believed they had been dictated to me by the Emperor.

In the afternoon the doctors came, accompanied by the grand marshal. The Emperor talked to these gentlemen about his insomnia, which he said had been put to good advantage by dictating to each of us for two hours. "I felt so strong," he said, looking at Dr. Arnott; "why am I no longer? I am exhausted." The doctor, to whom these words were translated by the grand marshal, replied that it was the result of the overexertion of four hours' work. That same evening the Emperor talked a great deal, and his speech seemed to me somewhat difficult at times. Between 8 and 9 p.m., concerned with the dispositions of his will that had occupied his morning and full of tender solicitude for his son, although Dr. Antommarchi and I were close to his bed without any light, he told me to get some paper in order to write. I replied that I had some without actually having taken any, believing that his mind was not quite there. However, after some time went by, he asked me again if I had paper: I replied that I did and grabbed a playing card[357] and a pencil that were at hand. He dictated to me the following lines that I have kept written on that same playing card:

I bequeath to my son my house in Ajaccio and its dependent buildings, two houses with gardens near the salt works, all my property in the territory of Ajaccio, which should yield him an income of 50,000 pounds.

"I bequeath to my son..." he stopped there and said to me: "I am very tired, we shall continue tomorrow." Along with his memory, the life of this great man dwindled every day. I had heard of the Emperor's properties in Corsica, and never had they been evaluated at

---

[357]This card still exists and is in the possession of M. Tainé in Paris.

such a sum. That evening's delirium recurred often until May 5th, the day when so much genius disappeared from the earth.

The following day, the 30th, there was talk of placing a vesicatory on his stomach, because the cautery I bandaged every day since the Emperor kept to his room was no longer producing anything, and the flesh was quite purple. Dr. Antommarchi had his bed brought into the library to be nearby to care for the illustrious patient. During the day, the latter instructed him when the time came to make a careful examination of his stomach, in order to save his son from a disease that had led his own father and himself into the grave. Count de Montholon, who had remained with the Emperor part of the day distracting him with conversation, retired when Count Bertrand and the doctors arrived. The Emperor was withdrawn, little inclined to talk, and did not join in the conversation as he usually did. These gentlemen withdrew, leaving the grand marshal alone with the Emperor, whose eyes remained closed. On opening them he spotted Count Bertrand, and spoke a few words to him, among them: "...You are sad, Bertrand, what's the matter?" The grand marshal replied with one of those looks that revealed how much his heart was moved and saddened. I retired, so as not to disturb him in what he had to say to the Emperor, who at the time was asking him for news of the countess. That lady had remained without seeing His Majesty until then: she had talked to me about it, and I therefore knew how distressed she was. The grand marshal suffered greatly himself; he no doubt talked to the Emperor about it, as when he came out, he told me with a cry of satisfaction the Emperor had told him to bring his wife and children.

During the evening, he learned that Pierron had gone into town. He summoned him and asked if he had found some good oranges, and if they came from the Cape or from Rio de Janeiro. He also asked him if people in town were talking about his illness, and Pierron replied he was the first one who had mentioned it in the shops he had visited. "What," he said, "they don't know in town that I am ill? Hudson Lowe and Baxter are hiding this from the inhabitants?" Then dismissing him a few moments later, he said to him: "That is fine, you have pleased me, I want you to be happy after my death." During the day the Emperor's eyes often focused on the small oil portrait of the King of Rome. During the night he had the hiccups.

The first of May at 11 a.m., Countess Bertrand was shown in to the Emperor's bedside. After having her sit down and asking how she was, he said to her: "Well, Madame, you too have been ill. You are now well. Your illness was a known one, mine is not, and I am dying. How are your children? You should have brought Hortense to me."

"Sire," replied the countess, "they are all well. Your Majesty has accustomed them to so much kindness that they feel a great privation not seeing you anymore, and they came with me every day to inquire about Your Majesty's health."

"I know it, Marchand told me. Thank you." The Emperor talked to her a few minutes more and told her to come back and see him. Countess Bertrand retired so as not to further tire the Emperor. Her emotion was then fully revealed, her eyes filled with tears. I accompanied her out to the garden, and she said to me: "What a change has occurred in the Emperor since the last time I saw him! Those emaciated features, that long beard hurt me to see; the Emperor was very cruel in refusing to receive me. I am very pleased for this return of friendship. But I would be even happier if he had accepted my care."

After that Countess Bertrand came every day to spend a few moments by the Emperor's bedside, and he continued to be kind to her. The Emperor's speech had become much shorter these last two days, and Drs. Arnott and Antommarchi were sleeping in the library. Count de Montholon and Count Bertrand remained alternately in the Emperor's bedroom.

The 2nd was quieter: the Emperor often cast his eyes on the portrait of his son, he accepted the care of his generals alternately, and often dozed. Having remained until midnight with Bertrand, we were relieved by Count de Montholon and Saint-Denis; I threw myself fully clothed on a mattress in the dining room. The Emperor who in spite of his weakness had always wanted to get up for the slightest need, wanted to get out of bed: Count de Montholon and Saint-Denis approached. Having remained standing for an instant, his legs gave way under the weight of his body, and the Emperor would have fallen if both of them had not held him up. After he was back in bed, such great weakness followed that for a moment they thought life was about to escape him. Dr. Antommarchi suddenly arrived and brought him back to life.

Count and Countess Bertrand spent the entire day of the 3rd at Longwood, and even dined there. The Emperor did not want anything but sugared water with a little wine; every time I offered him some, he said, looking at me with satisfaction: "That's good, that's very good." The vesicatory he agreed to have placed on his chest produced very little results, and the cautery was completely dry and no longer needed bandaging.

That same day the governor expressed the desire that a consultation take place between Drs. Antommarchi and Arnott and Drs. Shortt and Mitchell. The grand marshal spoke of it to the Emperor, presenting it as a wish of Dr. Arnott's, and he replied he saw nothing wrong with it. These gentlemen assembled in an adjoining room and deliberated in the presence of Count Bertrand and Count de Montholon. The grand marshal came to report on this consultation: the outcome was that the small of his back should be rubbed with cologne mixed with plain water, because it was getting sore. He should take a tranquilizing potion that was supposed to do him good. "That's fine," he said to the grand marshal, "we'll see." Then when Count Bertrand was outside, he said, looking at me and making a face: "What great results from science! What a consultation! To rub the back with cologne water! Very well! As for the rest, I want no part of it."

When Noverraz learned of the Emperor's condition, and that he might die without his having seen him, he got out of the bed where he himself had been for a whole month. Pale, wasted from illness, he walked unsteadily to the Emperor's bed. When the latter noticed him, he said: "You are much changed, my boy, are you better now?"

"Yes, Sire."

"I am very pleased to know you are out of danger: do not tire yourself by remaining on your feet, go get some rest." Noverraz felt weak; distressed by the condition in which he had seen the Emperor, he barely had time to reach the next room, where he fainted. When he recovered, he said to me: "I can't tell you what I felt when I looked at the Emperor, but it seemed to me that as he spoke he was drawing me to him and telling me to follow him." Abundant tears relieved his heart, so deeply moved by the spectacle he had just witnessed.

That same day around 2 o'clock, I was alone with the Emperor when Saint-Denis quietly came to tell me Father Vignali wanted to talk to me. I went to see him. "The Emperor," he said, "has asked me through Count de Montholon to come and see him, but I need to be alone with him." The priest was in civilian clothes, and held something inside his coat he was trying to hide. I did not attempt to guess at what it was, knowing that he had come to perform a religious act; my heart tightened painfully at the thought that all hope was lost. I left Father Vignali alone with the Emperor, remaining by the door to prevent any-one who came from entering. The grand marshal approached me and asked what the Emperor was doing; I told him Father Vignali had asked me to be shown in and had requested to remain alone with him, and that I thought he was currently performing a religious act to which the Emperor wanted no witnesses. "I am going to see Montholon," he said, "inform me as soon as Vignali comes out." About a half hour later, the priest came out and said to me: "The Emperor has just received last rites, the condition of his stomach does not permit any other sacrament."[358]

I went back into the Emperor's room, and found him with his eyes closed and his arm stretched out along the edge of his bed. I knelt by his side and brought my lips to his hand, without his eyes opening. Saint-Denis had done the same previously without the Emperor opening his eyes then either. I remained alone, standing before the Emperor's bed holding back my sobs, but allowing my tears to flow freely. Saint-Denis came to inform me that Dr. Arnott was there; I went out to greet him. Understanding my grief which he attributed to the Emperor's desperate condition, he shook my hand affectionately.

---

[358]Marchand's note: This religious act, taking place without any witnesses, is the only one I know of. It was known in the household through Father Vignali's revelation.

Approaching the Emperor's bed, I softly announced Dr. Arnott and showed only a calm face, when my heart was so cruelly torn. I immediately moved aside to give free rein to my tears, which still flow today for the man who so richly deserved our sorrow and our devotion. The grand marshal arrived soon afterwards. The Emperor talked to the doctor about the result of the consultation, which he found to be quite insignificant, and told me to give him something to drink. I remained alone with him after these gentlemen left; he did not talk to me about the religious act he had just fulfilled.

As a result of this consultation, I was called on to give the Emperor some calomel. I told the grand marshal and Count de Montholon, who talked to me about it, that the Emperor had positively told me he wanted no beverage or potion that was not approved by him, and that they should remember the Emperor's anger at Dr. Antommarchi in a similar circumstance. "Yes, no doubt," the grand marshal said to me with his usual kindness, "but this is a last resource we are attempting. The Emperor is lost, we must not have reason to reproach ourselves for not having done everything humanly possible to save him." Encouraged by these last words of the grand marshal, I diluted the powder in some water with a little sugar, and when the Emperor asked me for something to drink, I presented it to him as sugar water. He opened his mouth and swallowed with difficulty, and even tried, without success, to spit it all out. Then turning toward me, he said, in a tone of reproach so affectionate and so difficult to describe: "You too are deceiving me?" Seeing the look he gave me, in which was expressed so much pain at being deceived, the grand marshal, who was present when he said it, was moved and said to me with deep feeling: "There is so much friendship in that reproach!" It was true, and I was shattered for having just broken the promise I had made to him not to give him anything without his permission. The Emperor was certainly very ill, but he was still conscious of what he was saying, and I would have been miserable indeed if those words had been the last he spoke to me. They had hurt me so much I feared that perhaps he would no longer want to accept anything from me. Then a half hour later he asked me for something to drink, and trustingly took from me the reddened sugar water that I offered him. "That's good, that's very good," he said after drinking it. I confess that only then did I feel better about what I had done, because he no longer remembered it himself.

The Emperor's feet were constantly wrapped in hot towels to restore warmth, and Count Bertrand and Count de Montholon watched over him all night. The marshal's wife came for a moment to see the Emperor, and spent the day in the library where a table had been set up for dinner. The few French servants who did not have access to the Emperor's bedroom waited anxiously for news that Saint-Denis or I gave them when we came out.

On May 4, the Emperor refused all help offered to him. He continued to drink water and wine with sugar, or sugar water flavored with orange blossoms: these were the only drinks that appeared to please him. Each time I served them to him, he answered me with these words: "That is very good, my boy." He often vomited what he took, the retching became more frequent. He made an effort to get up. Dr. Antommarchi tried to prevent him from doing so, but he pushed him away, appeared very upset by the attempt to constrain him, and demanded to be left alone. During the day, hiccups set in and lasted late into the evening. From time to time Count de Montholon offered him something to drink. Around 10 o'clock, he seemed to be asleep under the mosquito netting that had been lowered. I remained close to his bed watching his every move, while the two doctors, Count de Montholon, and the grand marshal spoke softly among themselves next to the fireplace. The Emperor made an effort to vomit: I immediately raised the mosquito netting to offer him a small silver basin into which he vomited a blackish liquid, after which his head fell back onto the pillow. The hiccups that had appeared at intervals became much more frequent, and delirium set in; the Emperor pronounced a lot of inarticulate words that were translated "France,... my son,... The army..." One can conclude with absolute certainty that his last preoccupation, his last thoughts, were for France, his son, and the army. These were the last words we were to hear. This condition continued until four o'clock in the morning, and the vesicatories applied to his legs had no effect.

The Emperor's grave.

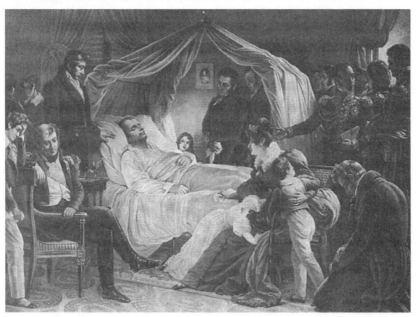

Three months before his 52nd birthday, Napoleon dies surrounded by his friends on May 5, 1821.

At 4 a.m. calm followed this agitation. It was the calm of courage and resignation; the Emperor's eyes remained fixed, his mouth drawn. A few drops of sugar water introduced by Count de Montholon strengthened his pulse, a sigh escaped his noble chest, hope reawakened in us, but alas! it was only the flight of his soul escaping its mortal shell to rise toward eternity.

At 6 o'clock the shutters were opened, and the grand marshal had Countess Bertrand informed of the Emperor's condition. She arrived at 7 o'clock, and an armchair was moved to the foot of the bed, where she sat all day. The French personnel in the Emperor's service whose duties did not give them access to the interior came in at 8 o'clock.[359] They restrained the pain closing in on them; their souls chilled by the silence of a dead man's room, they joined us around the bed. Noverraz, although quite weak, still wanted to be present for the Emperor's last breath. Our eyes were fixed on that august head, leaving it only to look into Dr. Antommarchi's eyes to see if there remained any hope. It was in vain, merciless death was amongst us. From time to time, using a sponge dampened with a little sugar water, Count de Montholon quenched the thirst of the Emperor, who no longer had the strength to swallow any other way. His motionless lips were thus refreshed; what did not enter was wiped away by Count de Montholon with a fine linen handkerchief.

At 5:50 p.m. the retreat gun was heard, and the sun disappeared in a flash of light. It was also the moment when the great man who dominated the world with his genius was about to wrap himself in his immortal glory. Dr. Antommarchi's anxiety intensified; the hand that had led victory, and the pulse of which he was counting, became ice-cold. Dr. Arnott, eyes on his watch, counted the intervals from one sigh to the next, fifteen seconds, then thirty, then a minute went by. We stood still in anticipation, but in vain.

The Emperor was no more!

---

[359]Marchand's note: They were MM. Pierron, Coursot, Archambault, Chandelier, Mmes Saint-Denis and Noverraz, Thierry in the service of the grand marshal, MM. Saint-Denis and Noverraz.

The eyes suddenly opened; Dr. Antommarchi, who was near the Emperor's head, following the last pulse on his neck, closed them immediately. The lips were colorless, the mouth slightly contracted; in that state, his face was calm and serene, a soft impression became noticeable. At that moment, our sobs burst out all the stronger as they had been suppressed. The grand marshal approached the bed, knelt down, and kissed the Emperor's hand. Count de Montholon and all those present, with the same religious respect, approached and placed a kiss on the hand that had acted so kind to all, and which death had just turned to ice.

Countess Bertrand called for her children, so they too could kiss the hand that for the past six years had lavished so many caresses on them. The scene of mourning before them did not permit their young hearts to withstand such strong emotion; the oldest one fainted, and they had to be taken away from this grief-stricken place. Mme Saint-Denis also wanted her little girl, barely a year old, to press her lips on the hand that had already shown goodness to her, predicting her happiness. I took her in my arms, and kneeling down, brought the Emperor's hand close to her, so her lips could touch it without causing undue fear.

Captain Crokat, accompanied by Dr. Arnott who had gone to inform him of the Emperor's death, came in to verify the time. His step revealed the turmoil of his soul; he withdrew respectfully, and appeared to apologize for his obligation to fulfill that task. Shortly afterwards, two British doctors came in and respectfully approached the victim. They returned to verify Dr. Arnott's report to Sir Hudson Lowe.

Thus perished the Emperor Napoleon, bequeathing the shame of his death to the ruling house of England, leaving to posterity the duty of avenging the assassin assigned to guard him. He had been surrounded by friends and a few faithful, devoted servants, but exiled far from the objects of affection a man yearns for most during his last moments: a mother, a wife, and a son.

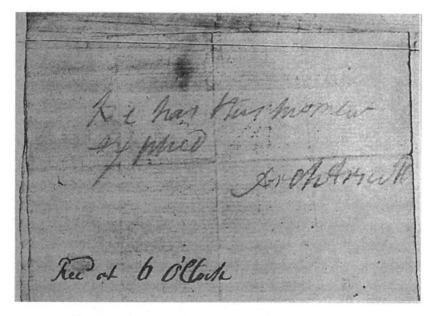

Dr. Arnott informs Sir Hudson Lowe that Napoleon is dead. By 6 p.m., Sir Hudson Lowe is informed.

PART NINE

Last Respects

CHAPTER TWENTY-SIX

*Death certificate — Funeral preparations and autopsy — Arrange-
ment of funeral chapel — Minutes of autopsy and placement in casket
— Inventories*

A chin strap was placed by Dr. Antommarchi under the
Emperor's chin to prevent the mouth from opening. As we
had to wait until midnight to wash the Emperor's body and place him
on another bed, we left Father Vignali, Saint-Denis, Pierron, and
Noverraz to watch over the body, and at the grand marshal's request,
we gathered in the billiard room to draw up the death certificate. It was
there that, in accordance with the Emperor's request and in the presence of Count de Montholon and Father Vignali, I handed Count Bertrand the will, the codicils, and M. Laffitte's receipt which the
Emperor had told me to give him after his death.

We read the two codicils that were to be opened immediately
after death: one pertained to the bonuses the Emperor was granting
from his personal funds to all the people in his household, and to the
alms he was distributing to the poor in Saint Helena.

April 15, 1821, Longwood
Codicil N. 1.

*1. I wish for my ashes to rest along the banks of the Seine, amid the
French people I have loved so much.*

*2. I bequeath to Counts Bertrand, Montholon, and Marchand the
money, jewelry, silverware, porcelain, furniture, books, weapons, and generally
all that belongs to me in Saint Helena.*

*This codicil, written entirely in my own hand, is signed and sealed with
my crest.*

Signed: Napoleon

Count de Montholon then told us he had been ordered by the Emperor to open, immediately after his death and in our presence, a codicil dated last April 16, which read:

This is a second codicil to my will, written entirely in my own hand.—Napoleon.

Here it is:

April 16, 1821, Longwood
Codicil N. 2.
This is a second codicil to my will. By my first codicil on this date, I settled everything belonging to me in Saint Helena on Counts Bertrand, Montholon, and Marchand; it is a formality to dispense with the British. My wish is that my belongings are to be disposed of as follows:

1. You will find 300,000 francs in gold and silver, from which 50,000 francs shall be kept back to pay what is owed my servants. The rest shall be distributed as follows: 50,000 francs to Bertrand—50,000 francs to Montholon—50,000 francs to Marchand—15,000 francs to Saint-Denis—15,000 francs to Noverraz—15,000 francs to Pierron—15,000 francs to Vignali—10,000 francs to Archambault—10,000 francs to Coursot—5,000 francs to Chandelier. The surplus shall be given as a bonus to the British doctor, the Chinese servants, and as charity to the parish.

2. I bequeath my diamond necklace to Marchand.

3. I bequeath to my son all the objects I used personally, in accordance with the attached list.

4. The balance of my belongings shall be divided between Bertrand, Montholon, and Marchand, and I forbid that anything used on my body be sold.

5. I bequeath to Madame, my very kind and very dear mother the busts, frames, and small paintings that are in my rooms and the sixteen silver eagles that she will distribute among my brothers, sisters, and nephews. I assign to Coursot the task of taking these to her in Rome, as well as the chains and necklaces from China that Marchand will give him for Pauline.

6. All the settlements contained in this codicil are independent of those in my will.

7. My will shall be opened in Europe in the presence of all the people who have signed the envelope.

 8. I name as my executors Counts Montholon, Bertrand, and Marchand.

 This codicil, written entirely in my own hand, is signed and sealed with
my crest.

 Signed: Napoleon

 Montholon, Bertrand, Marchand, Vignali

After this reading, Count de Montholon read to us a letter the
Emperor had dictated to him on April 25 to be sent to the governor
after his death. It bears witness to the energetic resignation of his soul
as he went to the grave. Here it is:

Governor:

 I have the honor of informing you that the Emperor Napoleon died
on_____, following a long and painful illness. He has authorized me, if you so
desire, to inform you of his last wishes. Please let me know what arrangements
have been dictated by your government for the return of his body to Europe, as
well as that of the people in his retinue.

I remain etc....

 Signed: Count de Montholon

In reply to this letter, the governor informed us the next day,
May 6, at 5 p.m., that since 1820 he had been ordered not to allow the
mortal remains of General Bonaparte to leave the island, but that he
did not care where they were placed. That choice was in our hands. As
a result of these arrangements, against which we could only protest
and invoke the respect owed the dead man's last wishes, we selected
the Torbett spring.

 When the Emperor went to see the grand marshal while he
was living at Hutt's Gate, he went with some difficulty down the valley in front of that house, and reached a small plateau from where he
could see the ocean. A spring of pure and cool water at the foot of
three willows quenched his thirst and gave him shade. He found the
water very refreshing and said to Count Bertrand when he left the
place: "Bertrand, if after my death my body remains in the hands of

my enemies, place it here." Once back at Longwood, he asked that we go every day and fetch water for him from this spring. A Chinese was given that job, and the Emperor then drank only that water which he had found so pure and which was brought to him in two large silver flasks used in the field. So His Majesty had been to this place only once, but he had retained a fond memory of it, as the serenity had consoled him; as a result, that spot was chosen as his burial place, on the advice of Count Bertrand. That same evening we attended to the preparation of his death certificate as well as the following statements.

Death Certificate of the Emperor:

Failing the presence of the imperial family's official registrars designated by the senatus consulta to that effect, I Count Bertrand, grand marshal of the Emperor Napoleon, as civil officer of his household, have written the present document in order to verify that on this day, May 5, 1821, at 5:45 p.m., the Emperor Napoleon died in his quarters at Longwood, island of Saint Helena, following a long and painful illness, in the rites of the Roman, Apostolic, and Catholic faith, in the presence of we the undersigned and of all the members of His Majesty's household serving at Longwood.
Longwood, island of Saint Helena, May 5, 1821.

Signed: Count Bertrand, Count de Montholon

Statement verifying the presentation of the will and codicils to Count de Montholon and the opening of the second codicil, on this day May 5, 1821, at Longwood, island of Saint Helena:

We the undersigned, Count Bertrand, Count de Montholon, Father Vignali, and Louis Marchand, have gathered in accordance with the Emperor Napoleon's orders, immediately after his death;

M. Marchand declared to us that he held and had been assigned by the Emperor to present the following to Count de Montholon, which he did in our presence:

1. Nine envelopes or packages sealed with the imperial crest and our own, as described in the minutes of last April 27;

2. One package sealed with the imperial crest;

3. Two receipts;

4. Two papers torn into several pieces;

5. One diamond necklace.

M. Marchand also told us that he was holding three mahogany chests listed in the aforementioned minutes of last April 27, and approximately 6,000 francs in white silver, in accordance with his books.

Count de Montholon declared that he was holding:

1. Nearly 100,000 francs in gold;

2. Two gold snuffboxes, one adorned with an antique cameo; that he had in his hand an unsigned paper labeled 8th codicil, written in part by the Emperor and in part under his dictation, after delirium set in.

Count Bertrand declared that he was in possession of the Emperor's weapons.

In accordance with our instructions, we proceeded immediately with the opening of codicil No. 2, and in execution of its instructions, we presented the aforementioned diamond necklace to M. Marchand, subject to his returning it to us should later codicils specify another disposition.

We have placed our seals on the keys to the chests, after which we prepared and signed this statement on the date indicated above.

Signed: Count Bertrand, Count de Montholon, Vignali, Marchand

Having thus attended to the immediate matters, we waited for the hour of midnight assigned by the doctors to remove the Emperor from his bed. Noverraz, Saint-Denis, Pierron, and I fulfilled that reverent duty assisted by the doctors, in the presence of Count Bertrand, Count de Montholon, and Father Vignali. How heartfelt were our thoughts on seeing the inanimate body of the man who had commanded Europe, stretched on a camp bed, dead in exile.

After cleansing his body by washing it with cologne mixed with plain water, Noverraz, in spite of his weak condition, shaved him (a part of the shavings are today in my reliquary). Once this respectful duty was completed, we put a shirt on him and placed him on the second field bed made up in white for this purpose. This replaced the one from which we had taken him, and the doctor put back the chin support that we had removed. In this state, the Emperor's face looked as it did when he was Consul; his slightly drawn mouth gave his face an air of satisfaction, and he appeared no older than thirty. The calmness of his face appeared more like sleep than death. Had we taken an imprint of his face at that moment, it would have been far better than the one taken two days later: the character of the face was then aged as a result of the sagging of the flesh, which at this time was taut. We then brought close to the bed two small tables on which we placed candelabras bearing lighted candles used in the chapel. Father Vignali placed a silver crucifix on the Emperor's chest, and after removing all the unnecessary items from that room, we withdrew. The Emperor was left in the care of the priest who did not leave the body until it was buried. Pierron and Dr. Arnott[360]awaited to prepare the mortuary chapel the following day.[361]

I had barely retired for an hour when Count de Montholon had me informed that the governor, his staff, and the French commissioner would come to Longwood at 6 a.m. Hudson Lowe arrived at 7 a.m.: he had with him his staff, Rear Admiral Lambert, General Coffin,[362] and Marquis de Montchenu along with his ADC M. Gors, a few naval officers, and a few island doctors and surgeons. The purpose of the visit was to verify to both himself and the French commissioner that the Emperor was truly dead. All was prepared for this reception: the gentlemen entered through the parlor and were shown into the drawing room, now the Emperor's bedroom, where a deathly silence prevailed. Father Vignali was praying next to the bed, and Pierron, Saint-Denis, Noverraz, and I were at each corner. After having greeted the gover-

---

[360]In the Lowe Papers, the governor states Dr. Arnott watched over the body during the night of May 5.

[361]Marchand's note: The following days, watch was kept over the Emperor's body night and day by Saint-Denis, Noverraz, Pierron, Coursot, Archambault, and Chandelier in turn.

[362]Rear Admiral Robert Lambert (1772-1836) commanded the Saint Helena station from July 1820 to September 1821. He asked for an interview with the Emperor, but was not received. He has left some interesting but unpublished letters on Saint Helena.
Brigadier General John Pine Coffin had commanded the Saint Helena troops since August 1820.

nor, Count de Montholon and Count Bertrand invited him to approach the bed where the Emperor's mortal remains rested. Followed by Marquis de Montchenu and those accompanying him, he approached slowly and said to the marquis, referring to the Emperor: "Do you recognize him?" The marquis first nodded, then said: "Yes, I recognize him." After a few moments of religious contemplation, they withdrew. I noticed that in speaking of the Emperor, he had abstained from using the name 'general.' I must say that when leaving, they all bowed with deep respect. I was told that the governor while leaving said to Count de Montholon that his government was changing its position, the ministry had informed him that the time was near when he could have been set free, and had finally ended: "He is dead, it is all over, tomorrow we shall pay our last respects to him." He offered Dr. Antommarchi the services of a doctor who was adept at plaster casts, to help him take the Emperor's; the doctor replied that he needed only plaster and not help for this process.

At 2 p.m. we proceeded with the autopsy. A table covered with a sheet had been prepared in the billiard room. The doctors took the body and placed it on the table, in the presence of the executors and MM. Saint-Denis and Pierron whom Count de Montholon showed in. This painful undertaking was begun, carried out by Dr. Antommarchi with the help of Drs. Thomas Shortt, Arnott, Mitchell, Matthew Livingstone, and several others. Sir Thomas Reade, accompanied by a few staff officers, was also present.

When the anatomical observations the Emperor had suggested—in order to protect his son from the disease of which he believed he was dying—had been made, Dr. Antommarchi wanted to examine the brain, saying that that particular organ of the Emperor was of great interest. Count de Montholon and the grand marshal were opposed to this, stating that the Emperor's body was here to enlighten science in the ways he himself had designated, but that they were not to pursue the mutilation of his body any further. The interests of science were forced to submit to this strongly expressed will. The heart was then removed and placed in a silver vessel filled with wine spirits, in accordance with the Emperor's wish, to be sent to Empress Marie-Louise. The governor objected, saying that the stomach would be sent to England by itself; a heated argument ensued. Count de Montholon and Count Bertrand objected to this profanation. Like the heart, it too was placed in a silver vase filled with wine spirits, and the two sealed vases were to be enclosed in the casket. The inside of the body was wiped and washed with an aromatic fluid. As Sir Hudson Lowe had declared his government opposed to any kind of embalming, needle stitching by Dr. Antommarchi restored everything to its original state.

Prior to dressing him, Dr. Antommarchi, now alone, asked me to help him take the Emperor's measurements, and be kind enough to write them down for him. Here are the results of his observations:

1. The Emperor has grown considerably thinner, and is not now one quarter of what he was before my arrival.

2. The face and body are pale but without distortion, unlike a corpse. The face is handsome, and with eyes closed he appears more to be asleep than dead. His lips are slightly pinched in a sardonic smile.

3. The body reveals a cautery wound on the left arm, a scar on the head, one on the left ring finger, and a deep one on the left thigh.

4. The overall height from the top of the head to the heels is 5 feet, 2 inches, 4 lines.[363]

5. His reach, stretching between the tips of his middle fingers, is 5 feet 2 inches.

6. From the pubic symphysis to the top of the head, 2 feet, 7 inches, 4 lines. [2 feet 7 1/3 inches]

7. From the pubis to the heel bone, 2 feet 7 inches.

8. From the top of the head to the chin, 7 inches 6 lines. [7 1/2 inches]

9. The head is 20 inches 6 lines[364] *in circumference, the hair is sparse and light chestnut.*

---

[363] 5 feet 6 3/8 inches in US measurements. He wasn't short by the standards of the day, but appeared so when standing among marshals and officers of the imperial guard, all very tall (Murat, Mortier, Lannes, Ney, etc.).

[364] 21.85 inches in US measurements.

10. The neck is short but normal, the chest broad and well shaped.

11. The hands and feet are a little small, but handsome and well shaped.[365]

Saint-Denis and I proceeded to dress the Emperor in the complete uniform of the mounted chasseurs of the imperial guard: a white shirt, a white muslin tie with a black silk collar over top, tied in back with a buckle, white silk stockings, white trousers and a jacket of the same material, the green uniform with red trim of the chasseurs of the guard, with the decorations of the Legion of Honor, the Iron Cross, the Reunion, the star and sash of the Legion of Honor, riding boots, and his hat with the tricolor cockade.

Thus attired, at 4 p.m. the Emperor was carried to his former bedroom, which had just been draped in black and turned into a mortuary chapel. The field bed in which he died had been prepared. We spread over it the blue cloak the Emperor had worn at Marengo and placed his body on it. An altar in accordance with the instructions given to Father Vignali was set up at the head of the bed, the priest was praying there, and the stained portions of the sheet covering the table on which the autopsy took place were divided up.[366]

When the doctors withdrew after the autopsy, they found Countess Bertrand in the drawing room. She asked one of them if it would not be possible to find some plaster suitable to take an imprint of the Emperor's face and save it for his family and posterity. Dr. Burton said there was some gypsum suitable for this on the island; he was going into town and would procure some for her.

During the morning of the 6th, we had been busy obtaining all the black cloth available, either in the company store or at the merchants', to drape the entire room; we had also managed to find enough purple velvet to make a mortuary cloth. The fact of such a consider-

---

[365]Marchand's note: These are the observations he made, and I did not see him apply the cranial measurement system he mentions on page 139 of his second volume.

[366]Marchand's note: One of these fragments is today in my reliquary.

able purchase revealed to the town the Emperor's illness and his death, which was not known to the inhabitants. The interest they did not dare show while he was alive, for fear of the governor, was evident after his death in the religious care everyone took to come pay their last respects and bless his body, and some cried over his excessive misfortunes. The officers and men of the various units, those of the 20th and 66th regiments, had requested the honor of filing past the Emperor's mortal remains; we were waiting for everything to be prepared to open the doors to them.

As I have said, the Emperor in his full uniform of the chasseurs of the imperial guard, with his hat on his head for a crown, was on one of his camp beds, an old witness to his glory and the deep thoughts that had occupied him on the eve of battles, while his pall was the cloak he had worn at Marengo. On his forehead one could read the names of kings vanquished and forgiven by him, a crucifix was placed on his chest, a silver eagle held up the white curtains pulled back at each corner by four eagles. On a small table near the bed, in silver vases, were the heart and stomach that were to be enclosed in his casket with the Emperor; at the head of the bed at the altar, the priest in a surplice prayed. At the four corners of the bed stood Saint-Denis, Noverraz, Pierron, and I in mourning. Count de Montholon and the grand marshal stood between the altar and the bed, the other servants between the door and the window, to allow room for the people who were going to file past. Dr. Arnott had been assigned not to leave the Emperor's body until it was interred, and to keep watch over the two vases containing the heart and stomach, to safeguard against substitutions.

When the doors opened, Captain Crokat, the duty officer at Longwood, took charge of organizing the procession himself, to avoid any confusion and to urge forward those who would have liked to remain longer in contemplation. The superior officers, regular officers, and noncommissioned officers came in first, and then the soldiers and many detachments from the naval squadron. The deepest emotion was visible on all faces; some of the noncommissioned officers had children which they brought along, and one of them, stopping before the

Emperor, said to his son: "Take a good look at Napoleon, he is the greatest man in the world." These bursts of generosity and affection were natural; they were the result of restrained high admiration that now overflowed without fear. This procession took place without confusion and in a religious silence. At that moment, events certainly did not favor Hudson Lowe. By their presence, all seemed to repudiate the part they had played in bringing to an end such a fine life, sustained by admirable resignation on this miserable rock.

That same evening Captain Crokat, the duty officer at Longwood, left aboard the *Acheron* to take the news of the Emperor's death as well as the minutes of the autopsy to England.

On the morning of the next day, May 7, the officers and soldiers who had not had the honor of filing past the Emperor were admitted, as well as the more important island inhabitants, men and women. Miss Mason admired the Emperor's hand lying on the bed, touched it, and went away with tears filling her eyes. Many people also came with the intention of seeing the man they had heard of without knowing him, but they were stopped at the first Longwood gate.

The Emperor had asked that his hair be given to the members of his family. Prior to making a plaster cast, it was shaved and placed under seal by Count de Montholon, who entrusted it to me.

Dr. Burton had procured the necessary plaster. Dr. Antommarchi, helped by him and by Archambault, who held up the Emperor's head, made the cast in our presence. It turned out well. It showed the face of that moment, and not that of six hours after his death; freshly shaven, the face of the Consul. The doctors who had witnessed the autopsy had the inconceivable pretension not only of drawing up the minutes of what Dr. Antommarchi had done, but also of giving it to him to sign. He rightly refused, stating that as he had performed the autopsy, it was up to him to sign it, and that he would give them a copy if they wished; but they refused. Here are the minutes we drew up that day, and the report given us by Dr. Antommarchi regarding the Emperor's autopsy.

Minutes covering the autopsy performed on the Emperor's body:

On this day, May 6, 1821, at Longwood, island of Saint Helena, at 7 a.m., the garrison general staff had the honor of filing past the camp bed on which the body of the Emperor Napoleon was laid out.

At 2 p.m., in accordance with our instructions, Dr. Antommarchi, his regular doctor, aided by several medical officers, proceeded to open the body in our presence. It was recognized, as is evident from the attached report, that death resulted from a cancerous growth in the stomach. The heart was placed in a silver vase to be given to Empress Marie-Louise, in accordance with the Emperor's orders. As the stomach had been set aside by the medical personnel to verify the disease, it was placed on our orders in a silver box to be included in the casket.

At 4 p.m. the body of the Emperor, dressed in the uniform of the chasseurs of his guard, was put back on a camp bed and exposed in a mortuary chapel. The officers corps and the principal island inhabitants had the honor of filing past him.

At 5 p.m. that same evening, the governor of the island notified us he had orders to have the Emperor Napoleon buried in Saint Helena, regardless of any other wishes he had expressed, and that the heart was to be enclosed in the casket.

After protesting as much as we could against these arrangements, we designated the Torbett fountain as the most suitable place on the island for the burial.

Having done so, we have signed these minutes, on the date stated above.

Signed: Count de Montholon, Count Bertrand, Marchand

Report prepared by Dr. Antommarchi in charge of opening the Emperor's body.

I the undersigned, François Antommarchi, the Emperor Napoleon's regular surgeon, in execution of orders given me by Count Bertrand and Count de Montholon, proceeded to open the Emperor Napoleon's body.

After opening the cavities of the thorax and abdomen, I observed the following:

1. The convex exterior face of the lung adhered in several places to the facing intercostal pleura.

2. There were approximately 3 ounces of lymphatic fluid in the left costal pleura sac.

3. There were approximately 8 ounces of the same lymphatic fluid in the right costal pleura sac.

4. The lungs were in normal condition.

5. The heart was in good condition, surrounded by the pericardium, and *covered with a little fat.*

6. The stomach, intestines, liver, spleen, and greater omentum were in their normal place.

7. The convex upper face of the left lobe of the liver adhered to the facing concave surface of the diaphragm.

8. The convex lower face of said lobe adhered strongly to the anterior face and to the small curvature of the stomach, as well as to the lesser omentum.

9. After carefully parting said adhesions, with the scalpel and with the hand, I observed that the adherence of the concave face of the left liver-lobe formed a hole about 3 lines [1/4 inch] in diameter in the anterior stomach face, next to its right extremity.

10. After opening the stomach along its greater curvature, I observed it was partially filled with a blackish liquid with an acrid and disagreeable odor.

11. After removing said liquid, I observed a widespread cancerous ulcer *located in the upper part of the internal face of the stomach, extending from the esophageal orifice to approximately one inch from the pylorus.*

12. On the edge of this ulcer, toward the pylorus, I recognized the hole described above (item 9) caused by the ulcerated corrosion of the stomach walls.

13. The ulcerated portions of the stomach were considerably swollen and hardened.

14. Between the ulcer and the pylorus, next to the ulcer, I observed a swelling and a cancerous hardness a few lines wide surrounding the right extremity of the stomach.

15. The liver was bloated and larger than normal.

16. All the intestines were in good condition, but filled with gas.

Signed: François Antommarchi

On May 6 the casket that was to hold the Emperor arrived, and we placed him in it. The heart, which according to the Emperor's orders Dr. Antommarchi was to give to the Empress, was placed in the casket along with the stomach. These two silver vases filled with wine spirits were hermetically closed and soldered by a British plumber, and entrusted to Dr. Arnott's keeping. He felt he had fulfilled his assignment only when they were put in the casket.

The Emperor, placed in a tin casket lined with white quilted satin, could not have his hat on his head for lack of space. The head had to rest on a pillow of the same material, and the hat was placed on his legs. Various coins bearing the Emperor's effigy and a few pieces of silver listed on the minutes shown below were added. The same man who had soldered the vases carefully soldered this first casket. It was placed inside another mahogany casket, which in turn was placed inside a third leaden shell that was also soldered. Finally, it was set within a fourth mahogany casket, which was sealed with silver-headed iron screws. The casket was put back on the camp bed, covered with a purple, velvet pall on which we spread the Marengo cloak. Candles were kept lit on the altar near the casket, on which a crucifix was placed. Holy water and a sprinkler were placed next to it. Dr. Arnott continued his watch and Father Vignali his prayers while two servants constantly remained with the casket; one at the foot and the other at the head. The doors were opened to all those who came from the various parts of the island to sprinkle holy water on the Emperor's casket. That evening we drew up the following minutes:

Burial Minutes

On this day, May 7, 1821, at Longwood, island of Saint Helena, the body of the Emperor Napoleon, wearing the uniform of the chasseurs of his guard, was placed by us the undersigned inside a tin casket lined with white satin, with a pillow and ticking of the same material. We also placed in it the heart, enclosed in a silver vase topped with the imperial eagle, and the box containing the stomach. In addition, a silver vase with the imperial crest, a silver place setting, a silver plate, six double French gold napoleons, four single gold napoleons, one double silver napoleon, one single silver napoleon, a half-franc napoleon, and two double Italian gold napoleons.

This tin casket, having been soldered in our presence, was placed inside another made of lead which after also being soldered, was enclosed in a third mahogany casket.[367]

The casket was placed on the camp bed in the mortuary chapel and cov-

---

[367]Marchand contradicts himself. Were there three or four coffins? The exhumation minutes confirm the four-coffin version.

*ered with a purple, velvet pall on which we spread the cloak that the Emperor
had worn throughout all his campaigns since the battle of Marengo.*

*Having done so, we have drawn up and signed these minutes on the
date stated above.*

Signed: Count de Montholon, Count Bertrand, Marchand

The Emperor was in his casket, but we could not proceed with
the burial. The work had started only on the morning of the 7th, and no
matter how quickly it went, it could not be completed before the morning of the 9th. It was necessary to dig a hole eleven feet long by ten
wide and eight deep, and to create a two foot thick masonry bottom
with a surrounding wall 18 inches thick to restrain the earth; at the bottom of this was to be the tomb in which the casket would be placed.
The bottom, sides, and top consisted of four slabs five inches thick, six
feet long by three wide. At the head and foot were two smaller slabs.
Measurements were taken so that even with the passage of centuries
moisture could not reach the mahogany casket that was itself to rest on
two pieces of wood. All this work was perfectly planned and rapidly
accomplished; the slabs came from the new house, where they would
have become the kitchen floor.

The Emperor in his casket.

Count Bertrand and Count de Montholon felt it was appropriate to spend the day of the 8th[368] writing minutes, providing an inventory[369] of the chests and that of the payments made in compliance with the second codicil, as found below.

They also asked me to draw up a general inventory of the Emperor's belongings in Saint Helena, as can be seen on the following pages, and we placed our signatures at the bottom of this.

---

[368]Marchand's note: Inventory of the contents of the chests

On this day, May 8, 1821, at Longwood, on the island of Saint Helena, we the undersigned, executors of the Emperor Napoleon, did inventory the contents of the chests and determined they contained:

1. In Count de Montholon's possession, in accordance with the notes written by the Emperor in his own hand:

In gold, at the Saint Helena exchange rate:

1,072 quadruples at 96	102,720
8,818 napoleons at 21.6	190,472
Coins from China and India	6,930
	300,122
In a purse, various coins	632
In British Banknotes	576
Total	301,833

2. In M. Marchand's possession, in accordance with his accounts register, and also at the Saint Helena exchange rate, the sum of 22,086 shillings, or in francs: 26,503

Overall total on hand   327,833

Executed and signed on the above date.
Count de Montholon, Count Bertrand, Marchand

On the same day, the following minutes were established:
Minutes of payments made in compliance with the 2nd codicil.

[369]On this day, May 8, 1821, at Longwood, on the island of Saint Helena, we the undersigned, executors of the Emperor Napoleon, in execution of the provisions contained in His Majesty's second codicil, dated April 16 last, have established the present list of payments to be made from the funds found in His Majesty's reserve funds, representing the sum of 301,330, Saint Helena exchange rate, and have made said payments as follows:

1. Reserves for wages due last April 1, in francs	47,285
to wit: Dr. Antommarchi (payments for 1st quarter)	1,500
MM. Marchand	25,232
Saint-Denis	7,800
Noverraz	9,053
Pierron	3,400
Coursot	150
Chandelier	150
	<u>45,785</u>
Total payments	47,285

2. Bonuses subject to 3% withholding specified in His Majesty's will or codicils, for which he has given verbal instructions: 235,000

	Sums shown in second codicil	Sums paid out less 3% withholding
Count Bertrand	50,000	48,500
Count de Montholon	50,000	48,500
MM. Marchand	50,000	48,500
Saint-Denis	15,000	14,550
Noverraz	15,000	14,550
Pierron	15,000	14,550
Vignali	15,000	14,550
Archambault	10,000	9,700
Coursot	10,000	9,700
Chandelier	<u>5,000</u>	<u>4,850</u>
3% witholding to be turned over to the treasurer		<u>7,050</u>
Total payments		235,000

3. Bonus to Dr. Arnott, British surgeon called upon to attend His Majesty	13,960
Bonus to Dr. Antommarchi	6,000
	18,960
Bonuses to Chinese personnel	<u>85</u>
Total payments	301,330

The undersigned, in execution of the provisions of the above-mentioned codicil, have given to M. Marchand, who hereby recognizes having received it, the diamond necklace shown on the inventory of May 8.

Executed and signed on the above date.   Count de Montholon, Count Bertrand, Marchand

Inventory of the belongings of His Majesty the Emperor Napoleon in the Longwood house, island of Saint Helena, on His Majesty's death, May 5, 1821.

The Emperor's weapons.

The small sword he wore at Austerlitz
The saber he wore at Aboukir
A dagger
A box of pistols from Versailles
A hunting knife
Three shotguns

His Majesty's decorations.

Two small crosses of the Legion of Honor
Two crosses of the Reunion
Two small crosses of the Iron Cross
One large cross of the Legion of Honor

His Majesty's seals.

Two seals bearing the imperial crest
Snuffbox decorated with five medals
from the Middle Ages
Gold box: cameo, portrait of Madame Mére
Gold perfume box: portrait of the queen
of Naples
Gold box: portraits of Joséphine, Louis,
Hortense, and Eugène
Snuffbox: view of Laeken castle
Snuffbox: Paul I
Snuffbox: map of Vienna
Snuffbox: two portraits of King Joseph's
daughters
Snuffbox: mosaic landscape
Snuffbox: Charlemagne
Snuffbox: battle of Marengo

Gold snuffbox: portrait of King
Joseph
Persian box decorated with diamonds
Box: Frederick the Great at Potsdam
Snuffbox: head of Alexander, gold
medal
Lava box decorated with medals
The King of Rome praying God for
his father
Snuffbox: Empress Marie-Louise

Sacred vases.

One gilt chalice
Two gilt cruets
One small crucifix on an ebony cross

His Majesty's boxes.

Chest No. 1

The wisdom of Scipion
The King of Rome as a child
Empress Joséphine, decorated with
fine pearls
Oval snuffbox, four silver medals:
Regulus, Sylla, Pompei, J. Caesar
Oval gold box: the king and queen of
Westphalia
Ivory toothpick box: portrait of
Madame Mére
One Fontainebleau hunt
One gold box with ivory landscape
Snuffbox: three antique medals

Candy box: portrait of Madame Mére
Snuffbox covered with agate
Gold snuffbox: antique cameo, head
of Alexander
Gold snuffbox: Augustus and Livy
Snuffbox in Viennese stone: cameo
of the Emperor
Snuffbox: portrait of Turenne

Chest no. 2

Twelve gold boxes with imperial crest
One small spyglass
One machine box with portrait
One ivory box

Chest no. 3

Snuffbox decorated with four silver medals
Snuffbox decorated with two silver medals
Snuffbox decorated with three silver medals
Two Legion of Honor sashes
One pair of gold shoe buckles
One gold collar buckle
One small pair of gold garter buckles
One tortoise shell candy box
One large silver watch (Frederick the
Great's alarm clock)
Two boxes of red leather, one holding a
smooth gold box, the other a box with
an antique cameo

His Majesty's silverware.

96 flat plates with palmettos
17 soup plates
96 flat field plates
23 soup plates

Snuffbox: Milan Federation
6 serving platters
20 dessert platters
2 serving platters
3 oval balls
2 soup tureens with lids
2 gravy boats without platters
18 bottle servers
8 salt cellars
2 mustard holders
2 oil cruets
1 bowl with cover
34 knives
93 spoons
82 forks
47 coffee spoons
8 serving spoons
2 soup ladles
12 cream pots with lids and bottoms
15 cups
1 chafing dish
2 wine buckets
1 tray
3 brandy flasks
4 coffee pots
1 milk pitcher
2 sugar bowls
2 chocolate pots
1 sugar tong
1 fish server
2 silver bottles
4 table candelabras

His Majesty's giltware.

28 forks

6 oval platters

29 knives

32 coffee spoons

6 dessert serving spoons

2 sugar spoons

1 punch ladle

8 salt spoons

1 mustard spoon

2 coffee pots

1 chocolate pot

2 pitchers

His Majesty's porcelain.

54 Sèvres porcelain dessert plates

8 compote dishes

4 table settings

12 soup plates

6 flat plates

2 ice cream dishes

21 coffee cups

20 saucers

All this service shows views

of cities and battlefields

His Majesty's maps.

Maps of France by Capitaine

Swabia; small map

Switzerland; small map

Russia; post map

Austrian empire

Scotland; 2 parts

United States; small map by Lapie

Ottoman empire

Italy; general map

Ferrara

Chaussard

Bohemia

Tyrol

Moravia

Serbia and Bosnia

Scotland; 4 parts

France; war depot.

Saxony

Moldavia

Sylvia

United States by Lapie

Santo Domingo

Morée

Prussia state

Adriatic Sea

Switzerland; large map

Spain

France, incomplete; by Capitaine

Bavaria

Holland

Russia, by Lapie

Kingdom of Italy

Spain and Portugal

Serbia and Bosnia

Scotland

French empire

British isles

Syria

United States

New York

Pennsylvania

Jamaica

Virginia

Boston

Italy; d'Albe
Ireland
North America
Atlantic Ocean
South America

Miscellaneous belongings.
1 chess game
1 small lorgnette
1 small spyglass
1 small gilt clock
3 large spyglasses, 2 of them copper
2 small Chinese tables
2 thermometers
3 saddles with bridles and snaffles
3 muslin curtains
1 brass bed
2 iron field beds, complete
2 garden chairs
2 portraits
1 tapestry
1 picture of Christ for the chapel
5 small framed portraits
1 portrait of Empress Joséphine
2 small marble busts
2 pieces of gold cloth from
Constantinople

His Majesty's wardrobe.
47 Dutch linen shirts
63 handkerchiefs
15 towels
21 flannel undershirts
4 black collars
14 pairs of linen sheets

9 sets of nightclothes
10 pairs of socks
19 madras scarves
37 pairs of silk stockings
4 civilian suits
2 uniforms of grenadier of the guard
1 of chasseur of the guard
1 of the national guard
2 gray overcoats and 1 green
1 embroidered coat, that of Marengo
1 sable coat
3 charivaris
(blue, yellow, and red)
2 pairs of pants of blue cloth
3 pairs of pants and 2 jackets of
nankeen
11 quilted vests and 11 pairs of pants
of nankeen
19 pairs of white pants and 10 jackets
15 pairs of gloves
3 uniform hats, 1 round hat, and 1
straw hat
1 pair of spurs and 1 pair of garter
buckles
1 pair of gold shoe buckles; one collar
buckle
4 pairs of boots, 4 pairs of shoes and
slippers
2 pairs of suspenders, 10 undershorts

Toilet articles.
1 toilet kit with its components
2 gold watches, with a chain made of
the Empress' hair
1 razor box, 1 gilt incense burner

1 washbasin with its pitcher, all silver	*2 bidets, one silver, the other*
8 bathrobes	*silver-plated*
2 night tables, with their silver utensils	*3 body brushes*

His Majesty's books.

Books brought from France	*588 volumes*
Books sent from England, and pamphlets	*1,226 volumes*
Total	*1,814 volumes*

Cash.

The toiletry case, in the care of his first valet, in accordance with the cash register balance and in standard currency, contains 22,086 shillings, worth 26,503 francs at the island exchange rate. Count de Montholon is holding 301,330 francs.

Objects left in Paris with Count de Turenne, inventory provided by M. Marchand.

The Sobieski saber
The Legion of Honor necklace
The gilt sword
The Consular dagger
The Golden Fleece necklace
A Henry IV headdress and cap
A small steel travel kit, a silver nightlight
A gilt candlestick
His Majesty's lace, a small medal case
An embroidered coat, 2 small Turkish rugs, 1 antique hilt
A gold kit that remained with the dentist.

We certify the preceding inventory to be accurate, and have drawn up and signed same, to serve as inventory for the Emperor Napoleon's estate.

Executed in the Longwood house, on the island of Saint Helena, May 8, 1821
Count Bertrand, Count de Montholon, Marchand

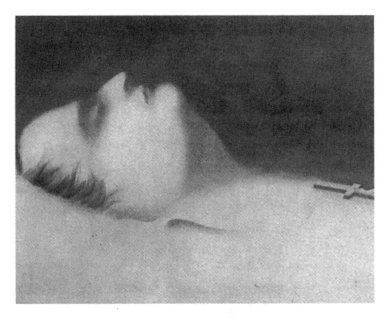

The Emperor is dead. From the oil painting by Denzil Ibbetson.

CHAPTER TWENTY-SEVEN

The Emperor's funeral — Sorrow at Longwood —
New inventories — Departure from Saint Helena — Return trip

*O*n the 9th at 10 a.m., Father Vignali celebrated mass and the funeral office, which we attended. The governor informed us that at daybreak the garrison in mourning would come under arms, and the procession would begin at 11 a.m. The governor arrived at the stated time along with the rear admiral, followed by all the civil and military land and naval officials.

At 11 a.m., twelve grenadiers came to retrieve the casket, placed it on their shoulders with some difficulty, and carried it to the large garden path where the hearse was waiting. They placed it on the carriage, the grand marshal rested the sword on the cloak covering the casket (it was Count Bertrand's sword), and the procession got under way in the following order:

Father Vignali, in religious garb, walked at the head, and next to him was young Henry Bertrand carrying a silver container of holy water with its sprinkler; Drs. Arnott and Antommarchi followed them.

The hearse was pulled by four horses led by four grooms in mourning, escorted by twelve grenadiers without weapons walking on either side, who, when we reached the valley, were to carry the casket by hand, as the road was not passable for carriages. The corners of the pall were carried by Count de Montholon, Count Bertrand, young Napoleon [Bertrand], and myself. Behind the hearse came the Emperor's horse, led by Archambault, and the Emperor's household in full mourning. Countess Bertrand with her daughter Mlle Hortense and her son Arthur followed in a carriage hitched to two horses led by hand by her servants. Then came Marquis de Montchenu on horseback, the governor, and the rear admiral, followed by a large staff from all services, either on foot or on horseback; lastly the town notables joined the procession. We left Longwood in that order, the guards were under arms, and the troops of the garrison, about 2,000 men, lined the hill to the left of the road. They stretched as far as Hutt's Gate, where the artillery was located and the gunners by their pieces were ready to fire. During the march, the flagship and the forts fired every minute, and the bands from each branch played as the procession passed them; the somber tunes added to the sadness of the ceremony.

When the procession had gone by, the troops fell in behind and accompanied it, lining up along the road and atop the hill crest overlooking the valley. The Protestant minister of the island followed the procession as a private individual. When we arrived at Hutt's Gate, Lady Lowe and her daughter were standing by the road with their servants; they were all in mourning, and they followed the casket after it passed. When we reached the place on the side of the mountain where the new road had been built, everyone dismounted. The grenadiers took the casket on their shoulders and carried it to the grave site. The casket was set down on two pieces of timber placed across the open grave that had been sheathed in black; a trestle and ropes had been prepared to lower it. This was the place where, even after his death, the Emperor's ashes were to remain captive. Our emotion was deep and intense. Amidst a deeply religious silence, Father Vignali came forward, the casket was uncovered, he recited the traditional prayers, and blessed the tomb. The governor then asked if the grand marshal wished to say something; at his negative reply, the body was lowered into the grave, feet toward the Orient and head toward the Occident. The artillery then fired three salvos of 15 rounds each; the scene was overwhelming in its sorrow and grief.

When the religious ceremony ended, an enormous stone that was to cover the tomb was lifted using a ring embedded in it. There the mortal remains of the Emperor were to lie, locked up for centuries. The stone rose and came down slowly, hiding the casket from our eyes. The ring was removed and the whole surface was covered with a layer of Roman cement. This masonry, whose stones were to be connected by pieces of iron, was to rise one foot, then be covered with earth up to ground level. When I returned there the next day, three slabs resting on bondstones covered the opening.

Once the burial was over, a crowd of people ran to the willows to strip off branches that were already becoming the object of veneration; the governor immediately had them distanced, in order to preserve the willows that would have been immediately stripped by those who wished to have a memento of this sad ceremony. Was this eagerness not a protest on the part of the islanders against the governor's behavior toward the Emperor? A temporary barricade was erected around the grave, guarded by two sentries, and a guard post was established there with twelve men commanded by an officer. Before returning to Longwood, the governor allowed us to take a branch from the willows that were henceforth to shade the Emperor's body.

We returned to Longwood, hearts heavy with sadness, and it was then that our loss struck home. The house had become a desert; we walked through the rooms filled with emptiness. The soul that used to animate them, the object of all our affection, was no longer there; our whole existence was altered. Several times in the short period we remained after the Emperor's death, either by night or by day, I awoke with a start, thinking I heard his voice calling me. Or if I left the house, I was stopped by the thought the Emperor might have need of me. His presence was still among us; it appeared at the most unexpected moments. The sound of his voice reached our ears and struck at our hearts with mortal anguish, when coming out of a sort of dream we would say: "He is no longer there!"

On returning to Longwood, Count de Montholon wrote the following minutes:

Affidavit of Burial:

On this day, May 9, 1821, at Longwood, on the island of Saint Helena, last respects were paid to the Emperor Napoleon.

At 10 in the morning, Father Vignali celebrated mass and the funeral office.

At 11, the garrison under arms lined the road. The procession left

Longwood, and the corners of the pall were carried by Count Bertrand, Count de Montholon, Napoleon Bertrand and Marchand. Countess Bertrand and the Emperor's entire household surrounded the hearse, followed by the general staff and the entire garrison in turn.

At noon, the Emperor's chaplain blessed the tomb constructed at the Torbett fountain and finished the prayers. The casket was then lowered, to the accompaniment of artillery salvos from the forts and the naval squadron.

The vault was closed and sealed with masonry in our presence; an honor guard was placed there.

After which, we have drawn up and signed these minutes on the date stated above.

Signed: Count de Montholon, Count Bertrand, Marchand

On May 11, the governor sent men to Longwood to inventory the furniture belonging to the government. There were some pieces that had been used by the Emperor, and that we would have treasured taking with us, but the orders received by the inventory-takers were precise, and we did not insist on having these objects, nor did we point them out so as to turn them into trophies. On the evening of the 11th, Count de Montholon informed me that the governor would come the following day to inventory the Emperor's belongings. He thought that it would be good to have them carefully laid out in the drawing room so that the governor might inventory them himself or have it done by others. The Emperor's belongings were sacred relics to us; it was important that when exhibiting them to the eyes of the foreigners accompanying the governor that they inspire reverence, and not give the impression of a secondhand clothing sale. Dim lighting was arranged, and Saint-Denis and I brought in everything that had belonged to the Emperor. All was displayed so that as one entered, the mere sight of it would elicit respect.

Sir Hudson Lowe came in the morning, accompanied by his staff, Marquis de Montchenu, his ADC M. Gors, and a few other people. He examined each object in turn, read codicil no. 1, as well as the attached inventories, and asked that the seals affixed to the three mahogany chests be broken. Once the seals were broken, I opened the chests. He examined each of the snuffboxes with care, his comments revealing his knowledge of painting, cameos, and medals. After about an hour of examination, he declared that we could proceed with the provisional execution of the deceased's will, as he could not authorize its final execution without referring the matter to his government. These remnants of a past glory were inspected with empathy and admiration by all. After his departure, I reclosed the chests, the drawing room doors were locked, and Count de Montholon wrote the following statement:

Statement regarding the inventory by the governor
and the opening in his presence of codicil no. 1.

On this day, May 12, 1821, at Longwood, island of Saint Helena, the governor of the island came to Longwood to proceed with the examination and inventory of the Emperor Napoleon's clothing and other property in Saint Helena. We the undersigned, in accordance with our instructions, did open in his presence codicil no. 1 as well as the attached inventories.

Having read said papers, he had broken in our presence the seals affixed to the three mahogany chests mentioned in the minutes of April 27 that contained the items listed in the enclosed inventories numbered 1, 2, and 3.

He declared to us that he could not authorize the final execution of the codicil provisions mentioned to him and had to refer same to his government, but that we could proceed with the provisional execution of same.

After which, we have drawn up and signed this statement on the above date.

Signed: Count de Montholon, Count Bertrand, Marchand

Statement regarding the division of the belongings.

On this day, May 14, 1821, at Longwood, island of Saint Helena, in accordance with the instructions contained in codicil no. 2, we proceeded to divide the Emperor Napoleon's belongings and books and placed in crates two of the items that he left to princes and princesses of his family.

After which, we have drawn up and signed these minutes, on the above date.

Signed: Montholon, Bertrand, Marchand

In order to divide the remaining belongings amongst ourselves, approximately equal shares either of books or other belongings were made, and we drew lots. Each took his share and arranged to transport it to Europe in crates. We were to set sail for France on the 27th. In this apportionment, there was a complete uniform of grenadier of the guard, which included the decoration of the Legion of Honor, his colonel's epaulets, a uniform hat, and riding boots; it could not be separated. The grand marshal and Count de Montholon in their scrupulousness said it had to be drawn by lots, and I became its heir. The manuscripts were at Count de Montholon's, and once we arrived in Europe, they were to be published in both a general edition and another large, special edition dedicated to the King of Rome. The Emperor had designated this task to his executors in his will. General Count Bertrand took those regarding Egypt, which the Emperor had dictated to him; Count de Montholon took Italy, and on his arrival to France, gave General Gourgaud the Consulate. It did not occur to me to make any claim; but later, while in France, I asked Count de Montholon for the section the Emperor had dictated to me, the *Short History of Caesar's Campaigns*. He replied that he did not have it; I then asked Count Bertrand, who gave it to me.

All that remained was to attend to the disbursement of the wages and salaries of the people who made up the Emperor's household during April and May of 1821, and the expenditures made. This led to the following statement:

Statement of the disbursement of wages and salaries of the people in the Emperor's household at Longwood, for the months of April and May 1821, and various other expenses. [370]

On this day, May 16, 1821, at Longwood, island of Saint Helena, the undersigned executors of the Emperor Napoleon's will did determine the payments to be made on behalf of the estate out of the funds present in His Majesty's private cash box, amounting to 25,590 francs, as follows:

---

[370]Editor's Note: Marchand's arithmetic is in error.

1.	*Wages and salaries for April 1821*	*7,333*
	Count Bertrand	*2,000*
	Count de Montholon	*2,000*
	Father Vignali	*500*
	Antommarchi, surgeon	*750*
		4,750
	MM. Marchand	*666*
	Saint-Denis	*333*
	Noverraz	*333*
	Pierron	*400*
	Archambault	*150*
	Coursot	*200*
	Chandelier	*200*
	Joséphine (Noverraz' wife)	*50*
	M. Richard	*150*
		2,583
	Total:	*14,666*

2. Arrears to Dr. Antommarchi, from October 1, 1819, to January 1, 1821, or 15 months at 500 francs, to be paid to his family in Rome, in accordance with a letter written in 1819 by Count Bertrand to Cardinal Fesch, with no acknowledgment received since that date.   *7,500*

3.	*Another expenditure (which I can no longer find)*	*3,423*
	Total amount	*25,590*

Executed and signed the above date:

Count de Montholon, Count Bertrand, Marchand

The governor had informed Count de Montholon and the grand marshal that accommodations were being made on board the storeship *Camel* for our return to Europe, but the departure could not take place before the end of the month. Every day we made a pilgrimage to the Emperor's grave, where we were permitted to enter the enclosure. Then, back at the house we busied ourselves preparing our belongings for our return voyage to Europe.

Prior to leaving the island, the grand marshal and the governor were exchanging correspondence, and one had challenged the other to a duel. Admiral Lambert offered his services to settle the feud between them. The mediation was accepted, and the disagreement was settled to the satisfaction of both parties.

On the 26th, the governor advised that we set sail the following afternoon. The entire day was spent transporting the baggage we were taking on carts. A deep sadness permeated this activity; we were leaving the Emperor alone in this land of exile, and the bitterness of such a sorrowful thought prevented us from imagining our joy at being reunited with our families and motherland; ours became, for six years, where the Emperor had been banished.

On the day of departure, I went to the Emperor's grave. I stood after kneeling by the tomb, giving free reign to my tears. One last time I kissed the cold stone that covered everything that had been so great to me, and yet so miserably unhappy. I picked a pansy and placed it in my wallet. I cast one last look, penetrating all the way down to the Emperor, got back on my horse, and rode toward town. I discovered that the grand marshal, his family, and Count de Montholon had gone to Government House at the governor's invitation. We were waiting in town to board, which took place at 4 p.m.

The ship was unpleasant and extremely cluttered; and as it was used to carry supplies, was more sturdy than elegant. A noticeable lack of cleanliness dominated. I was shown a small cabin into which I settled, and could not complain about my fate, as others were far worse off. It had been a fine day, we weighed anchor on the evening of the 27th. I got up from the bunk, where I rested with a headache, in order to salute Saint Helena one last time. I wished to assure my benefactor I was leaving behind that my thoughts would be with him each day. All night there was an infernal racket as they secured the crates that cluttered the deck and storage area. They had packed in two hundred soldiers, some of whom had wives and children. Everyone settled in as best he could for the first night, then everyone found his place, and the deck was cleared in order to allow maneuvering the sails and to provide room to stroll about.

As we sailed past Ascension Island and crossed the equator, a light, reassuring breeze descended on us; the air had been so stifling, packed in as we were. They scented the ship from time to time with vinegar. A few cases of dysentery occurred, but those taken sick were attended to, and during the crossing we lost only one mother and her

Full military honors were ordered once Napoleon had died. A long procession followed the casket to the Valley of the Geraniums.

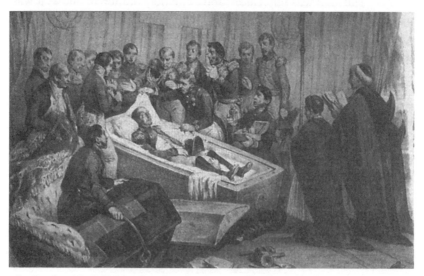

On October 15, 1840, Napoleon's casket is opened by those who have come to take his remains back to France. They find him intact looking as if he sleeps. According to recent studies, it is claimed that the arsenic that was administered to Napoleon, given to him over a long period of time, acted as a preservative. See Weider, *Assassination at St. Helena Revisited*.

child. That woman had come on board on the verge of giving birth: a few days after our departure labor pains started, and she delivered a boy. She already had one child, and you can imagine the poor woman's situation, being as her labor was so difficult. Countess Bertrand, as kind as she was charitable, told her she would give her the milk she was receiving every day for her coffee, and sent her the linen she lacked. Three weeks later the child died, and the mother followed him to the grave soon after: the sea had to provide for both. Before dying, she had requested to be put in a coffin; not in a cloth, as is done at sea. The day of the ceremony was announced by the ringing of a bell, as is done in a village. Everyone came up on deck where the coffin lay covered with a flag. The captain began reciting the prayers, all present removed their hats, and afterwards they allowed the coffin to slide into the sea. It dived, then suddenly came back to the surface, floating on one side with the body on the other! To sink the coffin they had placed a cannonball or two at the poor woman's feet; but no one had thought that, falling from the height of the rail to the sea, the weight of the cannonballs would break through one end of the coffin. As the wind was quite strong, we were soon far from that disturbing sight.

Another accident befell us a few days later: the regiment's cobbler had fallen asleep on the rail and fallen overboard. As the wind was blowing with considerable force, we were soon far away from him. We immediately brought the ship to and put a rowboat into the water. Fortunately, the man swam quite well, and we managed to save him; the captain had him served some hot wine. During the crossing we managed to catch several dolphins of various sizes, which replaced the meat that was beginning to run short. In those days we didn't have on board ship, as we currently do, canned food, allowing passengers to live well during long crossings. The water on board was extremely awful; Countess Bertrand had brought a large quantity with her and was kind enough to share it with me, along with some porter. The countess had fallen very ill before we were struck by a storm in the Bay of Biscay. The sky darkened, the wind blew wildly, and the sea became so rough that the only horizon we had was the wave that lifted us and then dropped us into the abyss. It took us unaware: the crates that were not tied down flew in every direction, and we spent the whole night that way. I lost the Constance wine I was bringing back, but the losses which mattered the most were the glass the Emperor had used during his illness, which broke in my trunk, and our willow cuttings that died from being drenched in seawater.

Africa was behind us. On July 25, in accordance with the Emperor's wishes, Count de Montholon gathered us together in his cabin and proceeded to open the wills, codicils, and instructions in our presence. The following statement was prepared:

On this day, July 25, 1821, in European waters, at the latitude of Paris and 160 leagues from the French coast, we the undersigned, the executors of the Emperor Napoleon, in accordance with our instructions and in the presence of Father Vignali, have opened the wills, codicils, and instructions referred to in the minutes of last April 27.

At sea, on the date indicated above:

Count de Montholon, Count Bertrand, Vignali, Marchand

TESTAMENT OF THE EMPEROR NAPOLEON

Napoleon,

On this day, April 15, 1821, at Longwood, on the island of Saint Helena.

This is my testament or document of my last wishes:

I.

1. I die a member of the Roman and Apostolic religion in which I was born over fifty years ago.

2. I wish for my ashes to rest along the banks of the Seine, amid the French people I have loved so much.

3. I have never had anything but praise for my very dear wife Marie-Louise; to the last moment I hold the most tender feelings for her and beg her to protect my son from the perils still threatening his childhood.

4. I urge my son never to forget that he was born a French prince, and never to allow himself to become an instrument in the hands of the triumvirate oppressing the peoples of Europe. He must never fight or harm France in any way; he must adopt my motto: all for the people of France.

5. I am dying prematurely, assassinated by the British oligarchy and its executioner; the British people will soon avenge me.

6. The two unfortunate outcomes of the invasions of France, when she still held such great resources, were due to the treason of Marmont, Augereau, Talleyrand, and La Fayette. I forgive them: may French posterity forgive them as I do!

7. I thank my kind and most excellent mother, the cardinal, my siblings Joseph, Lucien, Jérôme, Pauline, Caroline, Hortense, Catherine, Eugène for the concern they kept for me. I forgive Louis for his libelous publication of 1820: it is full of untrue assertions and falsified documents.

8. I disavow the manuscript of Saint Helena, and other works under the titles of maxims, statements, etc. that people have taken to publishing in the past six years; these are not the rules that guided my life. I had the Duke of Enghien arrested and sentenced because it was necessary for the safety, interest, and honor of the French people, when the Count d'Artois, by his own admission, employed sixty assassins in Paris. In similar circumstances, I would do the same.

II.

1. I leave to my son the boxes, decorations, and other objects such as silverware, camp bed, weapons, saddles, spurs, chapel vases, books, linen for my personal use, in accordance with the inventory given in Appendix (A). I wish for this modest bequest to be dear to him, capturing for him the memory of a father of whom the world will speak to him.

2. I leave to Lady Holland the antique cameo that Pope Pius VI gave me in Tolentino.

3. I leave to Count de Montholon two million francs, as proof of my satisfaction for the filial care he took of me for the past six years, and to indemnify him for the losses his stay on Saint Helena caused him.

4. I leave to Count Bertrand 500,000 francs.

5. I leave to Marchand, my first valet, 400,000 francs. The services he rendered me were those of a friend. I wish for him to marry the widow, sister, or daughter of an officer or soldier of my old guard.

6. Idem, to Saint-Denis, 100,000 francs.

7. Idem, to Novare (Noverraz), 100,000 francs.

8. Idem, to Pierron, 100,000 francs.

9. Idem, to Archambault, 50,000 francs.

10. Idem, to Coursot, 25,000 francs.

11. Idem, to Chandelier, 25,000 francs.

12. Idem, to Father Vignali, 100,000 francs. I wish for him to build his house near Ponte Nuovo di Rostino.

13. Idem, to Count Las Cases, 100,000 francs.

14. Idem, to Count Lavalette, 100,000 francs.

15. Idem, to Chief Surgeon Larrey, 100,000 francs. He is the most virtuous man I have ever known.

16. Idem, to General Brayer, 100,000 francs.

17. Idem, to General Lefebvre-Desnouettes,[371] 100,000 francs.

18. Idem, to General Drouot, 100,000 francs.

19. Idem, to General Cambronne, 100,000 francs.

20. Idem, to the children of General Mouton-Duvernet,[372] 100,000 francs.

21. Idem, to the good La Bédoyère's children, 100,000 francs.

22. Idem, to the children of General Girard,[373] killed at Ligny, 100,000 francs.

23. Idem, to General Chartrand's[374] children, 100,000 francs.

---

[371]Former colonel in the mounted chasseurs of the imperial guard, one of the great cavalrymen of the Empire. As a reward for his valor and fidelity, in 1805 he was given one of the Emperor's cousins in marriage.

[372]A general in the imperial guard, he joined the Emperor after the return from Elba, served as a deputy, and after Waterloo proposed the nomination by acclamation of Napoleon II. He was sentenced to death and shot in Lyon in 1816.

[373]He commanded the vanguard of the "sacred battalions" during the Belgian campaign of 1815. Mortally wounded at Ligny in June 1815, he was named Duke of Ligny by the Emperor, but died ten days later.

[374]He commanded a brigade in the Barrois division at Waterloo. Exiled during the second Restoration, he returned to Paris, conspired, was arrested, sentenced to death, and shot in Lille in May 1816.

24. Idem, to the virtuous General Travot's[375] children, 100,000 francs.

25. Idem, to General Lallemand the elder,[376] 100,000 francs.

26. Idem, to Count Réal, 100,000 francs.

27. Idem, to Costalde Bastelica,[377] in Corsica, 100,000 francs.

28. Idem, to General Clauzel,[378] 100,000 francs.

29. Idem, to Baron de Méneval, 100,000 francs.

30. Idem, to Arnault,[379] the author of Marius, 100,000 francs.

31. Idem, to Colonel Marbot,[380] 100,000 francs. I urge him to continue to write for the defense of the French army's glory, confounding slanderers and apostates.

32. Idem, to Baron Bignon,[381] 100,000 francs. I urge him to write the history of French diplomacy from 1792 to 1815.

---

[375]Retired by the Restoration, he conspired, was arrested, and sentenced to death in January 1816. The sentence was commuted to 20 years' detention at the Ham fort, where he went insane. He was eventually pardoned, and died in 1836 at the age of 70.

[376]General Lallemand, the elder of two brothers, both generals in the imperial guard, had followed the Emperor on board the *Bellerophon*, but was not allowed to accompany him to Saint Helena. Sentenced to death by the Restoration, imprisoned in Malta, he left for America, where he founded a French settlement in Texas in 1817. Having fallen on hard times, he was reinstated in 1830 and died in Paris in 1839.

[377]Notable Corsican family.

[378]General Clauzel commanded the army of the Pyrénées that marched against the Duchess of Angoulême during the Hundred Days. After Waterloo, he sought refuge in America, was sentenced to death in absentia, and amnestied in 1820. He returned to service in 1830, headed the army of Africa, replacing Bourmont, and was made a marshal in 1831. He died in 1842.

[379]Antoine Arnault had written, at the age of 25, the popular tragedy *Marius à Minturnes*.

[380]Author of *Mémoires*.

[381]Baron Bignon, minister of foreign relations during the Hundred Days, wrote *Histoire de France depuis le 18 Brumaire jusqu'en 1812*, on which he worked until his death in 1841.

33. Idem, to Poggi de Talavo,[382] 100,000 francs.

34. Idem, to Surgeon Emery,[383] 100,000 francs.

35. Those sums are to be taken from the 6 million that I invested when leaving Paris in 1815, and from the interest at 5% since July, 1815. The accounts shall be settled with the banker by Counts de Montholon, Bertrand, and Marchand.

36. All that this investment has produced above the sum of 5.6 million, distributed above, shall be distributed in bonuses to those wounded at Waterloo, and to the officers and soldiers of the Elban battalion, based on a list drawn up by Montholon, Bertrand, Drouot, Cambronne, and Surgeon Larrey.

37. These bequests, in the event of death, shall be paid out to the widows and children, and failing this, shall return to the overall sum.

III.

I.—As my private property belongs to me, and no French law I know of has deprived me of it, an accounting will be requested of Baron de La Bouillerie,

---

[382]A Corsican, he became Napoleon's chief of intelligence.

[383]The story of Dr. Emery is one of the clandestine, historical elements of the Hundred Days. As military surgeon, Emery had participated in all the campaigns of the Empire. Having joined the Second Unmounted Chasseurs of the guard in 1811, he was surgeon to the Elban battalion and served at Waterloo with his former regiment.

When he debarked at Golfe Juan with Napoleon on March 1, 1815, Emery had known for five months that the Emperor would take the route over the mountains and go through Grenoble, where all would be ready to receive him (see Book One, note 215). A native of Isère made liaison between Napoleon and Dumoulin when the latter came to Elba. Through the intermediary of Genoese merchants, Emery received messages hidden in bundles of gloves.

After the landing, going on ahead of the Emperor, he "put to sleep" the prefect of Digne, secretary general of Gap, got horses given to him in Laffrey by General Mouton-Duvernet who would pay for this complicity with his life, and arrived in Grenoble where he informed Dumoulin of Napoleon's landing.

Later, tracked down, arrested, imprisoned, and finally released in 1816, Emery married a charming young woman named Pauline Blanchet from a family of stationers in Rives. Her sister-in-law, the beautiful Madeleine Augustin-Blanchet, had served Napoleon at the Hôtel de la Poste on March 9, 1815, while disguised as a servant. Emery died at the age of 35 in Grand Lemps, where he had been born. His moss-grown grave can be seen in the cemetery there.

Emery's devotion explains the imperial bequest equally as large as those of Larrey and Percy. The surgeon's daughter received 55,000 according to the distribution made in 1826 by the banker Laffitte. At the time of the distributions of 1854 and 1895 the bequest became void, as Mme Emery and her daughter were dead.

who is its treasurer. It must amount to over 200 million francs, to wit:

1. A portfolio containing the savings I made over 14 years on my civil list, which amounted to more than 12 million per year if I remember correctly.

2. The yield from that portfolio.

3. The furniture from my palaces in Rome, Florence, and Turin. All that furniture was purchased with income from my civil list.

4. The liquidation of my estates in the kingdom of Italy, such as money, silverware, jewelry, furniture, stables; accounts will be provided by Prince Eugène and the crown superintendent Campagnoni.

Napoleon

II.—Second sheet.

I bequeath my private estates: half to the remaining officers and soldiers of the French army who fought from 1792 to 1815 for the glory and independence of the nation. The distribution shall be prorated according to active salaries; half to the towns and countryside of Alsace, Lorraine, Franche-Comté, Burgundy, Ile-de-France, Champagne, Forez, Dauphiné that suffered from one or the other invasion. Out of this sum, one million shall be kept for the city of Brienne, and one million for that of Méry.[384]

I name Counts de Montholon, Bertrand, and Marchand my executors. This will is entirely written in my own hand, signed, and sealed with my crest.

(seal)

Napoleon

---

[384]Méry-sur-Seine, department of the Aube. During the 1814 campaign, the Méry bridge was bitterly fought over, destroyed, and rebuilt several times, and the village was completely burned down.

Inventory (A) attached to my will

I.

Longwood, Saint Helena, April 15, 1821

    1. The sacred vases that were used in my chapel at Longwood.

    2. I ask Father Vignali to keep these and give them to my son when he reaches the age of 16.

II.

    1. My weapons, to wit: the sword I wore at Austerlitz; the Sobieski saber, my dagger, my small sword, my hunting knife, my two pairs of Versailles pistols.

    2. The gold travel kit I used on the morning of Ulm, Austerlitz, Iena, Eylau, Friedland, the island of Lobau, the Moskowa, and Montmirail; for this reason, I wish it to be precious to my son (it has been in Count Bertrand's possession since 1814).

    3. I ask Count Bertrand to care for and keep these objects, and give them to my son when he reaches the age of 16.

III.

    1. Three small mahogany chests, containing, in the first: 33 snuffboxes or candy-boxes; in the second: 12 boxes with imperial crests, two small spyglasses and four boxes found on Louis XVIII's table at the Tuileries, on March 20, 1815; in the third: three snuffboxes decorated with silver medals used by the Emperor, and various toilet articles listed in inventories I, II, and III.

    2. The camp beds I used throughout all my campaigns.

    3. My battlefield spyglass.

    4. My toilet kit, one of each of my uniforms, a dozen shirts, and one complete set of each of my clothes, and generally all that served me while washing and dressing.

    5. My washbasin.

    6. A small clock that is in my bedroom at Longwood.

    7. My two watches and the chain made of the Empress' hair.

    8. I ask Marchand, my first valet, to keep these objects and give them to my son when he reaches the age of 16.

IV.

1. *My medal case.*

2. *My silverware and the Sèvres porcelain I used in Saint Helena (Inventories B & C).*

3. *I ask Count de Montholon to keep these objects and give them to my son when he reaches the age of 16.*

V.

1. *My three saddles and bridles, and the spurs I used in Saint Helena.*

2. *My five shotguns.*

3. *I ask my runner Noverraz to keep these objects and give them to my son when he reaches the age of 16.*

VI.

1. *400 volumes chosen from my library among those I used most.*

2. *I ask Saint-Denis to keep them and give them to my son when he reaches the age of 16.*

Napoleon

Inventory (A)

1. *None of the things I used personally are to be sold; the balance is to be divided between my executors and my brothers.*

2. *Marchand shall keep my hair, and have it made into a small bracelet with a gold lock, to be sent to Empress Marie-Louise, my mother, and each of my brothers, sisters, nephews, and nieces, the cardinal, and a larger one to my son.*

3. *Marchand shall send a pair of my gold shoe buckles to Prince Joseph.*

4. *A small pair of gold garter buckles to Prince Lucien.*

5. *A gold collar buckle to Prince Jérôme.*

Inventory (A)

Inventory of items that Marchand shall keep to give to my son:

1. My silver toilet kit, on my table, with all its utensils, razors, etc.

2. The alarm clock I took from Frederick II at Potsdam (in box no. 3).

3. My two watches, one with a chain made of the Empress' hair, and a chain of mine for the other. Marchand shall have it made in Paris.

4. My two seals (one of France, in box no. 3).

5. The small gold clock now in my bedroom.

6. My washbasin, pitcher, and stand.

7. The night tables I used in France, and my gilt bidet.

8. My two iron beds, mattresses, and blankets, if they can be preserved.

9. My three silver flasks, used to hold brandy during my campaigns.

10. My French spyglass.

11. My spurs, 2 pairs.

12. Three mahogany chests, no. 1, 2 and 3, holding my snuffboxes and other items.

13. One gilt incense burner.

Household and personal linen:

6 shirts

6 handkerchiefs

6 neckties

6 towels

6 pairs of silk stockings

4 black collars

6 pairs of socks

2 pairs of linen sheets

2 pillow cases

2 bathrobes

2 sets of nightwear

1 pair of suspenders

4 trousers and jackets of white cloth

6 kerchiefs

6 flannel undershirts

4 undershorts

6 pairs of gaiters

1 small box filled with my tobacco

Napoleon

1 gold collar buckle

1 pair of gold garter buckles

1 pair of gold shoe buckles

(the last 3 items contained in chest no. 3)

Clothing:

1 chasseur's uniform

1 grenadier's uniform

1 national guard uniform

2 hats

1 gray overcoat

1 green overcoat

1 blue overcoat (the one I had at Marengo)

1 sable coat, green

2 pairs of shoes

2 pairs of boots

1 pair of slippers

6 belts

Inventory (B)

Inventory of items I left with Count de Turenne:

the Sobieski saber
(It was mistakenly listed in inventory A.
This is the saber the Emperor wore
at Aboukir which is now in
Count Bertrand's keeping.)
the great collar of the Legion of Honor
1 gilt sword
1 Consular dagger
1 steel sword
1 velvet belt

the collar of the Golden Fleece
1 small steel toilet kit
1 silver night-light
1 antique saber hilt
1 Henry IV hat
the Emperor's lace
1 small medal case
2 Turkish rugs
2 embroidered crimson velvet coats
with jackets and trousers

1. *I leave to my son the Sobieski saber.*
Idem, the necklace of the Legion of Honor.
Idem, the gilt sword.
Idem, the Consular dagger.
Idem, the steel sword.
Idem, the necklace of the Golden Fleece.
Idem, the Henry IV hat and cap.
Idem, the gold tooth kit that remained with the dentist.

2. *I leave the following to Empress Marie-Louise: my lace.*
to Madame Mère: the silver night-light.
to the cardinal: the small steel travel kit.
to Prince Eugène: the gilt candlestick.
to Princess Pauline: the small medal case.
to the Queen of Naples: a small Turkish rug.
to Queen Hortense: a small Turkish rug.
to Prince Jérôme: the antique saber hilt.
to Prince Joseph: an embroidered coat with jacket and trousers.
to Prince Lucien: an embroidered coat with jacket and trousers.
Napoleon

Longwood, April 24, 1821

> *This is my codicil or statement of my last wishes.*

> *From the funds in gold remitted to Empress Marie-Louise, my dear and beloved wife, in Orléans in 1814, two million remain to me, which I am disbursing by the present codicil to reward my most faithful servants, whom I recommend to the protection of my beloved Marie-Louise:*

> *1. I request the Empress to have restored to Count Bertrand the 30,000 francs' income he owns on the Duchy of Parma and Mount Napoleon in Milan, as well as the arrears.*

> *2. I request the same for the Duke of Istria (Bessières), Duroc's daughter, and other servants who have always remained faithful and are dear to me; she knows them.*

> *3. From the 2 million mentioned above, I bequeath 300,000 francs to Count Bertrand, out of which he shall deposit 100,000 francs in the treasurer's account, to be used, in accordance with my instructions, for bequests of conscience.*

> *4. I bequeath 200,000 francs to Count de Montholon, out of which he shall deposit 100,000 francs in the treasurer's account, for the same use as above.*

> *5. Idem, 200,000 francs to Count de Las Cases, out of which he shall deposit 100,000 francs in the treasurer's account, for the same use as above.*

> *6. Idem, 100,000 francs to Marchand, out of which he shall deposit 50,000 francs in the account, to be used as above.*

> *7. To the mayor of Ajaccio at the beginning of the Revolution, Jean-Jérôme Levi, or his widow, children, or grandchildren, 100,000 francs.*

> *8. To Duroc's daughter, 100,000 francs.*

> *9. To the son of Bessières, Duke of Istria, 100,000 francs.*

> *10. To General Drouot, 100,000 francs.*

> *11. To Count de Lavalette, 100,000 francs.*

> *12. Idem, 100,000 francs, as follows:*

> *25,000 francs toPierron, my butler.*

> *25,000 francs to Noverraz, my runner.*

> *25,000 francs to Saint-Denis, the keeper of my books.*

> *25,000 francs to Santini, my former usher.*

13. Idem, 100,000 francs, as follows:

40,000 francs to Planat,[385] *my ADC.*

20,000 francs to Hébert, former concierge at Rambouillet, who was part *of my household in Egypt.*

20,000 francs to Lavigne, former concierge in one of my stables, and my groom in Egypt.

20,000 francs to Jeannet Dervieux, a groom in my stables who served me in Egypt.

14. 200,000 francs shall be paid out in alms to the inhabitants of Brienne-le-Château who suffered most.

15. The remaining 300,000 francs shall be distributed to the officers and soldiers of my guard battalion in Elba still living, or their widows and children, prorated as a function of their pay, and in accordance with a roster to be drawn up by my executors; the amputees or severely wounded shall receive double; the list shall be made by Larrey and Emery.

This codicil is written entirely in my own hand, signed, and sealed with my crest.

Napoleon

Longwood, April 24, 1821

This is my codicil or statement of my last wishes.

From the liquidation of my civil list in Italy, on such items as money, jewelry, silverware, linen, furniture, stables, of which the viceroy is the depository and which belong to me, I have available 2 million that I bequeath to my most faithful servants. I hope that without need of any other reason my son Eugène Napoleon shall faithfully fulfill these bequests; he cannot forget the 40 million I have given him, either in Italy or through the distribution of his mother's estate.

---

[385]Planat de la Faye, the Emperor's ADC, wanted to follow him to Saint Helena, and Napoleon would have liked to have had him. When Las Cases returned to Europe, he informed Planat of the Emperor's wish. This loyal officer wrote several times to Cardinal Fesch, but received no answer. In July 1820, Fesch refused; in July 1821, Fesch finally aquiesced, but tried to discourage Planat from going. What was happening in Rome? Napoleon was already dead.

1. From this 2 million, I leave Count Bertrand 300,000 francs, out of which he shall deposit 100,000 francs in the treasurer's account, to be used in accordance with my instructions for bequests of conscience.

2. To Count de Montholon, 200,000 francs, out of which he shall deposit 100,000 francs in the account, to be used as above.

3. To Count de Las Cases, 200,000 francs, out of which he shall deposit 100,000 francs in the account, to be used as above.

4. To Marchand, 100,000 francs, out of which he shall deposit 50,000 francs in the account, to be used as above.

5. To Count de Lavalette, 100,000 francs.

6. To General Hogendorp,[386] a Dutchman, my ADC, a refugee in Brazil, 100,000 francs.

7. To my ADC Corbineau,[387] 50,000 francs.

8. To my ADC Caffarelli,[388] 50,000 francs.

9. To my ADC Dejean, 50,000 francs.

10. To Percy, chief surgeon at Waterloo, 50,000 francs.

---

[386]Count Hogendorp, a Dutchman serving in the French army, rejoined the Emperor after his return from Elba, fought at Waterloo, and asked to follow him to Saint Helena. He sought refuge in Rio de Janeiro, where he lived in abject poverty. He died shortly after Napoleon, in October 1822.

[387]General Jean-Baptiste Corbineau, brother of General Claude Corbineau, killed at Eylau. The former was with the Emperor on the eve of Brienne in 1814.

[388]General Caffarelli du Falga accompanied the Empress to Vienna in 1814, joined the Emperor for the Hundred Days, and sat in the house of peers in 1832. In 1840, he was part of the commission overseeing the return of the Emperor's ashes; he died in 1849. His wife was politically active against Napoleon, who cherished an unrequited passion for her, and yet she was the only one to visit him at Malmaison in 1815, before he left for Rochefort.

On learning of Napoleon's death, Countess Caffarelli wrote: "It is finished then, the life of this astonishing man who filled the universe with his genius, his glory, and his misfortunes. How strange the human heart is! I no longer see in him the despot against whom I so often rebelled; I see in him the being who spread the glory of the name 'Frenchman' from one end of Europe to the other. I see in him the benefactor, the friend who forgave me so many wrongs against him, wrongs that a kindly sovereign could have punished by prison or exile and still would have been considered indulgent... I have often felt a sort of shame at being seen as one of his favorites. Today I experience a kind of pride in it. I have thus earned the right to mourn him, the right to keep silent over his faults and to make known all the good he has done."

11. 50,000 francs, divided thus:

10,000 francs to Pierron, my butler.

10,000 francs to Saint-Denis, my first runner.

10,000 francs to Noverraz.

10,000 francs to Coursot, my pantry chief.

10,000 francs to Archambault, my groom.

12. To Baron Méneval, 50,000 francs.

13. To the Duke of Istria, son of Bessières, 50,000 francs.

14. To Duroc's daughter, 50,000 francs.

15. To La Bédoyère's children, 50,000 francs.

16. To Mouton-Duvernet's children, 50,000 francs.

17. To the children of the brave and virtuous Travot, 50,000 francs.

18. To Chartrand's children, 50,000 francs.

19. To General Cambronne, 50,000 francs.

20. To General Lefebvre-Desnouettes, 50,000 francs.

21. 100,000 francs to be distributed among the banished wandering through foreign countries, French, Italians, Dutch, Spaniards, or those from the Rhine departments, upon orders of my executors.

22. 200,000 francs to be distributed among the amputees or severely wounded at Ligny, Waterloo, if still alive, based on lists prepared by my executors, joined by Cambronne, Larrey, Percy, and Emery; double will be given to the guard, quadruple to those of Elba.

This codicil is written entirely in my own hand, signed, and sealed with my crest.

Napoleon

Longwood, April 24, 1821
This is a third codicil to my will.

1. Among the crown jewels handed over in 1814, there were some 5 or 600,000 francs' worth that were not part of them, and belonged to me personally; they shall be incorporated in order to pay out my bequests.

2. I had with the banker Torlonia in Rome 2 to 300,000 francs in letters of exchange, the proceeds of my income from the island of Elba since 1815. M. de La Perusse [Peyrusse], although he was no longer my treasurer and had no authority, drew upon that money; he shall be made to return it.[389]

 3. I leave to the Duke of Istria 300,000 francs, only 100,000 of which carry over to his widow, if the duke is dead at the time of distribution. If this presents no inconvenience, I wish for the duke to marry Duroc's daughter.

 4. I leave to the Duchess of Frioul, Duroc's daughter, 200,000 francs. Should she die before the distribution, nothing shall revert to her mother.

 5. I leave to General Rigaud,[390] *who was banished, 100,000 francs.*

 6. I leave to Boinod,[391] *commissioner of supplies, 100,000 francs.*

 7. I leave to the children of General Letort,[392] *killed in the 1815 campaign, 100,000 francs.*

 8. These 800,000 francs in bequests shall be added after item 36 of my will, which would bring to a total of 6.4 million francs the sums I bequeath through my will, excluding the settlements made in my second codicil.

 This is written in my own hand, signed, and sealed with my crest.

 Napoleon

 (seal) (On the back of the page.)

---

[389]Marchand's note: The Emperor is mistaken here: the grand marshal declared that in 1819 these drafts had been challenged and judged worthless as a result of political events, and that M. Peyrusse's accounts were perfectly in order during the Hundred Days.

[390]General Rigaud was severely wounded many times; he served in 1814 and 1815, ordered the arrest of the Duke of Bellune (Victor), and hid Lefebvre-Desnouettes. Sentenced to death in absentia in 1816, he fled to the United States and died in New Orleans in 1820.

[391]This was an old friend of the Emperor's, who joined him in Elba [see Marchand's earlier memoirs covering Elba]. He was inspector of the guard during the Hundred Days, attending to their demobilization under the second Restoration. Forced into retirement in 1817, he went back on active duty in 1830, and was again retired in 1832; his legacy from the Emperor came to only 53,000 francs. He died in 1842, and was considered a model of honesty and loyalty.

[392]General Letort was one of the great cavalryman of the Empire, wounded many times, and highly decorated. He was mortally wounded near Gilly on June 15, 1815, and died two days later.

This is the third codicil to my will, written entirely in my own hand, signed, and sealed with my crest. To be opened the same day and immediately after the opening of my will.

Napoleon

Longwood, April 24, 1821
This is a fourth codicil to my will.

With the arrangements previously made, we have not fulfilled all our obligations, which has prompted us to write this fourth codicil:

1. We leave to the son or grandson of Baron Dutheil, lieutenant general of the artillery, former lord of Saint-André, who commanded the Auxonne school prior to the Revolution, the sum of 100,000 francs, as a token of our gratitude for the care this good general showed us when we were under his command as lieutenant and captain.

2. Idem, to the son or grandson of General Dugommier, commander in chief of the Toulon army, the sum of 100,000 francs. Under his command, we led that siege and commanded the artillery. It is in remembrance of the signs of esteem, affection, and friendship this brave, intrepid general showed us.

3. Idem, we leave 100,000 francs to the son or grandson of Gasparin, a convention deputy, representing the people in the Toulon army, for having protected and approved by his authority our plan that led to the capture of that city, contrary to that sent by the Committee for Public Safety. Gasparin protected us from persecutions due to the ignorance of the general staff commanding the army before the arrival of my friend Dugommier.

4. We leave 100,000 francs to the widow, son, or grandson of our ADC Muiron, killed beside us at Arcole, covering us with his body.

5. Idem, we leave 10,000 francs to noncommissioned officer Cantillon,[393] who was tried for planning to murder Lord Wellington, but found innocent of the charge. Cantillon had as much right to murder that oligarch as the latter

---

[393]In February 1818, Wellington was returning to his home in Paris when a shot was heard; a bullet missed the coachman. A Bonapartist pamphlet quipped:...The imbecile fired too high; he thought he was aiming at a great man... The duke was urged to leave Paris, but he refused. The police soon arrested Cantillon and brought him to trial, but he was acquitted the following year, in spite of strong presumptions.

had to send me to perish on the rock of Saint Helena. Wellington, who had suggested murder, justified it as being in Great Britain's interest. Had Cantillon actually murdered the lord, he would have been covered and justified by the same motives, France's interests, in getting rid of a general who had violated the capitulation of Paris, and because of that was responsible for the blood of the martyrs Ney, La Bédoyère, etc., etc., and for the crime of robbing the museums, against the terms of the treaty.

6. This 400,000[394] francs shall be added to the 6.4 million we have already distributed, and will bring our bequests to 6.8 million francs; these 410,000 francs are to be considered part of our will, article 35, and handled just as the other bequests, in all respects.

7. The 900,000 pounds sterling we gave to Count and Countess de Montholon, if they have been paid out, must be deducted from the bequests we made to them in our will; if they have not been paid, our notes shall be canceled.

8. In view of our will's bequest to Count de Montholon, the 20,000 franc pension to his wife is canceled; Count de Montholon is to pay it to her.

9. As the management of such an estate until its entire distribution will require office expenses, errands, missions, consultations, and pleadings before tribunals, we intend that our executors retain 3% of all the bequests, on either the 6.8 million francs, the sums listed in the codicils, or the 200 million francs of the private estates.

10. If the sums yielded by these deductions are not sufficient to cover the expenses, these shall be covered at the expense of the three executors and the treasurer, each in proportion to the bequests made to them in our will and codicils.

11. If the sums yielded by these deductions exceed the expenses, the remainder shall be divided among our three executors and the treasurer, in proportion to their respective bequests.

12. We name as treasurer Count de Las Cases, or failing that, his son, or failing that, General Drouot.

This codicil is written entirely in my own hand, signed, and sealed with my crest.

Napoleon

---

[394]The figure should read 410,000 francs.

First letter: to M. Laffitte

M. Laffitte, I gave you in 1815, at the time of my departure from Paris, a sum of almost 6 million, for which you gave me a duplicate receipt. I have canceled one of these, and ask Count de Montholon to present the other to you, so that after my death you can give him said sum, with interest at 5%, dating from July 1, 1815, after subtracting the payments you have been asked to make based on instructions from me.

I wish for the settlement of your account to be made in agreement among yourself, Count de Montholon, Count Bertrand, and M. Marchand, and once this has been done, I hereby give you full and absolute release for said sum. I also gave you a box containing my medals, and I request that you give this to Count de Montholon.

As this letter has no other purpose, I pray to God, M. Laffitte, that he keep you in his holy care.

Longwood, Saint Helena island, April 25, 1821

    Napoleon

Second letter: to Baron de La Bouillerie

Baron de La Bouillerie, treasurer of my private estate, I request that you remit the accountings and the corresponding amounts, after my death, to Count de Montholon, whom I have named executor of my will.

As this letter has no other purpose, I pray to God, Baron de La Bouillerie, that he keep you in his holy care.

Longwood, Saint Helena island, April 25, 1821

    Napoleon

Apart from these arrangements, one regarding General Gourgaud instructed Prince Eugène to capitalize an amount to pay this general the 10,000-franc pension the Emperor had left his mother when he left Paris. That settlement was made as a token of his gratitude for General Gourgaud's devotion and the services he had rendered the

Emperor for ten years as first ADC, whether on the battlefields of Germany, Russia, Spain, and France, or in Saint Helena.

Count de Montholon told us the Emperor had left an unfinished codicil; it was dated April 27, 1821, and began this way:

> *With a sick body but a sane mind, I have written in my own hand this eighth codicil to my will:*

> *1. I name as my executors Montholon, Bertrand, and Marchand, and as my treasurer, Las Cases or his son.*
>
> *2. I pray my beloved Marie-Louise to take into her service my surgeon Antommarchi, to whom I bequeath a lifetime pension of 6,000 francs, that she shall pay to him...*

The Emperor had gone no further; the distributions that followed were to Countess Bertrand and Countess de Montholon, under the Emperor's dictation.

CHAPTER TWENTY-EIGHT

My gratitude toward the Emperor — Landing in England —
Accountings and minutes — Return to France —
Visits and formalities — My wedding

When the reading of all these documents containing the Emperor's last thoughts of love, attachment, and gratitude was completed, we parted, each filled with the various impressions they had generated within us. Mine was of deep gratitude and admiration. We took with us the immortal dictation of the Emperor, who had created a monument to his literary glory, and we had just become aware of a monument no less great to his heart.

If in the first we could find the greatest leader and the greatest man of the century, the other showed the Emperor who had so often been labeled insensitive as the best son, father, husband, friend, and the least forgetful of services rendered. How touching those precious tokens of his memory are; in the details he joins to the bequests to Baron Dutheil, General Dugommier, Gasparin, Muiron, and those of a lower rank: d'Hubert, de Lavigne, de Dervieux, three of his servants in Egypt! And at what time of his life was the Emperor creating this monument of his heart's sensitivity? While he was suffering from acute pain and nausea that forced him to interrupt what he was writing with such clarity, precision, order, and calculation. The many codicils, as well as his will, were all written in his own hand; as he almost always dictated, he was little used to writing.

Of the Emperor's arrangements, I only knew of the inventories and instructions he had dictated to me. All the provisions we had just learned about had been made only in the company of Count de Montholon, and I was unaware of any of them. The Emperor had indeed told me to choose as a wife the daughter of an officer or soldier of his old guard,[395] but I did not know the extent of his munificence toward me. What I placed far above all else was the Emperor's accompanying testimony: "The services he rendered me were those of a friend." Those words filled my soul; they were more dear to me than all the rest. I felt lifted toward him, and I promised myself never in my life to do anything that would lower me from the high position where the Emperor's kindness had just placed me in society and for posterity.

We continued under way with a stiff wind, and our crossing was long but fortunate. Below the tropics we had encountered calm, but a few days later in the Bay of Biscay, we were struck by rough weather that lasted twenty-four hours, after which we soon caught sight of the coast of England. The first land we espied was the Isle of Wight, then we arrived in Portsmouth and the Spithead harbor where we dropped anchor on July 31 after 65 days of a difficult crossing, having only two sheep left on board.

We had also seen the coast of France. I did not feel my heart pound at its sight, as it should have: the thought that we were returning to the motherland alone, without the Emperor whose body had remained in the hands of his enemies, embittered any happiness I might have felt. The officer carrying the Saint Helena governor's dispatches went ashore and immediately left for London. As for us, we had to remain on board; our arrival coincided with an outing the king of England was taking aboard a yacht so magnificent that gold was shining everywhere. On all sides, the forts and the vessels fired artillery salvos; our modest *Camel* also took part. The king's yacht approached us, and then the whole squadron sailed by only a short distance away. We saw three people disembark, climb into a rowboat, and come aboard to inquire on the king's behalf about Countess Bertrand's health. They talked for about half an hour with Count Bertrand and Count de Montholon, then departed, doubtless satisfied with all the details they had learned about the Emperor's death, which they reported to their sovereign.

---

[395]Marchand's note: I did not know that instruction had been written down.

The third day after our arrival, we debarked at Portsmouth; the population was curious to see men faithful in adversity. There was visible interest in the multitude of people gathered at our landing place; we were all moved by the feelings of a population that disapproved of the crime committed by its government against the person of the Emperor Napoleon. Countess Bertrand, surrounded by her four charming children, was in particular the target of benevolent curiosity. Count de Montholon, the grand marshal, and his family left the next day for London. I was left in charge of supervising the unloading of everything we brought back from Saint Helena, and sending it all to London where we expected to await instructions from the French government.

Seals were placed on all the trunks. Everywhere I went, at the mere mention that I had come from Saint Helena, people promptly acceded to my requests, and were eager for all sorts of details about the Emperor's captivity. This same curiosity was evident in London, where I arrived on August 8. The grand marshal and Count de Montholon were housed in Leicester Square, and I went to see them the day after my arrival. They told me that they had gone to the French embassy to see about obtaining our passports, and these were delivered to us on August 16. I then asked these gentlemen to go over my accounting, which led to the following minutes:

On this day, August 18, 1821, in London, the undersigned, Emperor Napoleon's executors, have established and approved these minutes of the expenses incurred by the estate from May 5th last until today. Such expenses, in accordance with the attached supporting documents, amounting to 40,184 francs, to wit:

1. Burial expenses:	*3,932*
20 gold napoleons placed in casket	*432*
Silver coins with the Emperor's profile	*3*
Velvet cloth for casket	*113*
70 lengths of black cloth to drape mortuary chapel	*3,024*
Payment to workmen	*144*
Clothing for grooms driving the hearse	*216*
Total	*3,932*

2. Two invoices in arrears covering burial expenses
for Cipriani, the butler   *1,392*

3. Payment to the British servants   *600*
Payment to the grooms   *500*
Payment to the Chinese   *563*
                                                             1,663

4. Dr. Antommarchi's travel expenses back to Florence
                                                             3,000

5. Reimbursement of expenses in arrears on His Majesty's
account, for General Gourgaud   *2,400*

6. Food supplies placed on board ship for the crossing,
transportation of baggage on unloading in London   *2,206*
Expenses for the estate, May 5 to 16, per accounting   *25,590*
Expenses for the estate, May 16 to August 18   *14,594*
Total expenses for the estate, May 5 to August 18   *40,184*

The above sum was covered by the following funds:
1. Cash on hand as of May 5, per inventory   *26,503*
2. Cash advanced by Count Bertrand   *2,400*
3. Cash advanced by Count de Montholon   *4,231*
4. Cash advanced by Marchand   *7,050*
                                                             13,681
Total advanced   *40,184*

The undersigned have verified the accuracy of the above mentioned expenses incurred for the Emperor Napoleon's estate since May 5, date of His Majesty's death, to this day, August 18, 1821, such expenses totaling 40,184 francs at the Saint Helena exchange rate.

Bertrand, Montholon, Marchand

Up until then, minutes had certified the expenditures or money paid out in accordance with the Emperor's orders. This same day Count de Montholon drew up the following minutes consolidating the previous ones: [396]

Minutes of the liquidation of expenses of the Emperor Napoleon's

---

[396]Editor's Note: Marchand's arithmetic is in error.

estate from May 5 to August 18, 1821.

On this day, August 18, 1821, in London, the undersigned, the Emperor Napoleon's executors, have drawn up and approved the present list of expenses incurred by the estate from May 5 last until today. The combined payments, in accordance with the attached supporting documents, amount to 341,478 francs, as follows:

May 17, 1821:

Payment to Dr. Arnott	*13,960*
Coins with the Emperor's profile placed in casket	*435*
Velvet cloth for casket	*113*
70 lengths of black cloth to drape mortuary chapel	*3,168*
Mourning clothes for British servants	*216*
Lighting of mortuary chapel	*602*
Butler's memo - expenses from May 1 to May 5	*1,027*
Arrears - expenses on the Emperor's private funds	*3,010*
Subtotal:	*22,531*

Amounts withheld from servants' wages as ordered by the Emperor:

Marchand	*25,232*
Saint-Denis	*7,800*
Pierron	*9,053*
Coursot	*150*
Chandelier	*150*
Archambault	*150*
Subtotal:	*45,785*

Regular wages for April	*7,705*
Regular wages for May	*7,705*
Payment to the British servants	*1,663*
Dr. Antommarchi's bill	*18,060*
Arrears covering burial expenses for Cipriani, the butler	*1,392*
Reimbursement charged for General Gourgaud	*2,400*

Payments in execution of codicil no. 2, dated April 16, 1821:

Count Bertrand	*48,500*
Count de Montholon	*48,500*
M.Marchand	*48,500*
Saint-Denis	*14,550*
Noverraz	*14,550*

Pierron	*14,550*
Vignali	*14,550*
Archambault	*9,700*
Coursot	*9,700*
Chandelier	*4,850*
Subtotal:	*82,450*

To the British soldiers carrying the casket	*2,000*
Food supplies placed on board the Camel for the crossing	*2,286*
Grand total:	*341,478*

The above sum was covered with the following funds:

In the Emperor's cash box:

Cash on hand with M. Marchand	*26,503*
Cash on hand with Count de Montholon	*301,330*
Total:	*327,833*

Cash advanced by executors:	
by Count Bertrand	*2,400*
by Count de Montholon	*4,195*
by Marchand	*7,050*
Total:	*13,644*
Total paid out:	*341,478*

The undersigned have verified the accuracy of the above mentioned expenses and resources, which balance, and have signed these minutes on the above date in Count Bertrand's house on Leicester Square, London.

Signed: Bertrand, Montholon, Marchand

During the ten days I was in London, I spent my time visiting the most curious and largest establishments worthy of being seen in this grand capital and its surroundings. My national pride had been wounded to find in the street stores a luxury I had seen at home only at the Palais-Royal; but I was six years behind the progress achieved in France, and when I arrived in Paris, I noticed we had not fallen behind, compared to our neighbors: luxury had also reached our stores. I therefore had nothing left to do in London, where Count Bertrand and Count de Montholon were detained by their political position. I went to see them on the morning of my departure, August 19, to inquire about any errands they might have, as well as Countess Bertrand. They gave me verbal messages for a few friends, and letters to M. Laffitte and Count de Turenne.

I then left London for Dover, and was in Calais the next day. My trunks and crates were taken to customs to be inspected. I had apprehensions about such an inspection, not because I was violating any laws, but for fear that the Emperor's belongings, which for me were sacred relics, would not be treated with the respect I felt for them. They knew I was arriving from Saint Helena, and several employees or others were impatiently waiting for the arrival of their supervisor, who was to preside over the inspection. He finally arrived, and told me to open a trunk he pointed out: it was in fact the one containing the clothing. The large circle of people drew closer around us and all were able to see, in the open trunk, the Emperor's hat with the tricolor cockade, laying on a uniform of the chasseurs of the imperial guard, where the decoration of the Legion of Honor could be seen. Two employees were about to investigate, when the supervisor said: "Don't touch a thing, close it. Sir," he said to me, "those are things that must be allowed to rest in peace. You have nothing in your crates that might be liable to duties? Nor these gentlemen?" he added, addressing Saint-Denis, Pierron, and Noverraz. We answered we did not, and that was the extent of the inspection we were subjected to. I had avoided the great inconvenience of unpacking, and was moved by the respect the sight of the Emperor's belongings had inspired. I set out that same evening, and on the evening of the 22nd I was in Paris in the midst of a family gladdened to see me again, while I was happy to see there was no one missing.

The day after my arrival, I carried out the errands I had been given. I went to M. Laffitte's to inform him of the forthcoming arrival of Count de Montholon and Count Bertrand, and gave him a copy of the Emperor's letter to him. He asked me many pressing questions regarding the Emperor's captivity and death, which I answered to his satisfaction. He offered me his house, invited me to his evening receptions, and asked me to dinner the following day. I thanked him for his kindness and hearty welcome, saying that my father and mother were in their country house near Auxerre, and that I was leaving to join them there.

Immediately afterwards I went to see Count de Turenne, whom I informed of the Emperor's arrangements regarding the objects he had left with him in 1815. He was deeply moved by all I told him about the Emperor's captivity and his death filled with resignation. As I was leaving, he said: "But there is a rumor that the Emperor made you a count; I hold it on good authority that the king (this was Louis XVIII) is prepared to grant you that title if you ask him."

"Count," I said to him, "I do not believe I can ask for a title given by the Emperor from a sovereign who, in Saint Helena, kept a commissioner to ensure His Majesty's detention. I am sufficiently honored that the Emperor wrote in his will that my services had been those of a friend." I left him to go see General Gourgaud. On the 25th, I was on my way to Burgundy, and on the 26th, my parents' arms opened to greet me. Many tears had accompanied our separation at Rambouillet in 1815; they had spilled then from excessive sorrow, but those shed seven years later came from their joy at holding me in their arms again.

I had been enjoying this pleasant family life for barely a month—not without thinking of our dear Emperor, the frequent subject of our conversation—when I received a letter from Count de Montholon announcing his arrival in Paris and inviting me to meet him there, as matters dealing with the estate required my presence. He informed me of Dr. Burton's claim to the ownership of the plaster cast molded in Saint Helena; the matter had gone to court. Count Bertrand and Count de Montholon intervened and stated that this plaster cast of the Emperor did not belong to Dr. Antommarchi, but was intended for Madame Mère, and was not to be the object of speculation. Dr. Burton's claim was voided by that declaration, and authorization was given for it to leave England and reach its destination. I also learned that, in accordance with our instructions, a request had been made of the British government to allow the Emperor's remains to be returned to France, to rest in peace where he himself had asked: along the banks of the Seine, amid the French people he had loved so much. Should the

French government refuse this, we were to request that a grave be opened for him in Ajaccio, near that of his ancestors; the following correspondence resulted:

To Lord Liverpool, President of the British Council

    Milord, as executors of the Emperor Napoleon's last wishes, we beseech you to submit to the king the request we have the honor of addressing to him.

    We remain, etc...

    Signed: Count de Montholon, Count Bertrand

    London, September 21, 1821

To the King of England

    Sire, we are fulfilling a religious duty imposed upon us by the Emperor Napoleon's last wishes: we request his ashes. Your ministers, Sire, know of his desire to rest amid the French people he loved so much. The provisions of his will were communicated to the governor of Saint Helena, but that officer—without regard for our request—had him buried in that land of exile. His mother, listening only to her sorrow, begs you, Sire, for her son's ashes, and the feeble consolation of being able to shed her tears on his grave. If, when on the throne, he was the world's arbiter, and on his rock was still the terror of his enemies, in death his glory alone must survive him.

    We remain, etc...

    Signed: Count de Montholon, Count Bertrand

    London, September 21, 1821

The British ambassador to Count de Montholon

    The British ambassador has the honor of informing Count de Montholon that having received from his government orders to communicate information to him and General Bertrand, he shall expect him tomorrow Friday at 12:30, hoping that he would care to come, if that hour is suitable.

    The British ambassador sends Count de Montholon his highest regards.

Paris, December 2, 1821

    This communication was a verbal declaration that the British government did not consider itself the depository of the Emperor's ashes, and that it would return them to France as soon as the French government expressed such a desire. As a result of this declaration, formalities were immediately initiated with the French ministry, but to no avail. Only in 1822, the Duke of Montmorency, then minister, allowed the following letter to be submitted to King Louis XVIII.

> *Sire, prior to returning to the motherland, we had been directed to request permission from the king of England to bring back to the banks of the Seine the Emperor Napoleon's ashes, currently resting in a land of exile.*
>
> *The execution of such a wish rests with Your Majesty: the British government has told us this. Please, Sire, at least allow the same marble in Ajaccio to cover the son beside the father, in ground hallowed by the faith in which he was born and lived.*[397]
>
> *Sire, we have raised our voices to Your Majesty in order to fulfill a holy mission. We shall await your royal decision in silence, but we felt that no consideration could free us from a commitment consecrated by the religion of the grave.*
>
> *We have the honor of submitting to the king the homage of our deepest respect.*
>
> *Signed: Count de Montholon, Count Bertrand, Marchand*
> *Paris, May 4, 1822*

This request was unsuccessful. It fell to the prince raised to power after the Revolution of 1830 to satisfy public opinion by sending his son, the Prince de Joinville, to Saint Helena to retrieve the Emperor's ashes and bring them back triumphantly across the seas to the glorious shadow of the Austerlitz flag.

I had barely returned to Paris when I received visits from many of the Emperor's friends who came to express their sympathy, inviting me to come to see them: the Dukes of Vicenza (Caulaincourt),

---

[397]Napoleon's father, Charles de Buonaparte, died in Montpellier in 1785. First buried in the Cordelier vault in that city, he was moved in 1804 to the church crypt in Saint-Leu Taverny, and finally to the imperial chapel in Ajaccio, where his wife was ultimately buried.

Bassano (Maret), Padua (Arrighi); Countess Regnault de Saint-Jean d'Angély; de Cambacérès, de Rambuteau, de Montesquiou, Turenne. They all showed me great friendship that I cultivated, and for which I will remain forever grateful.

The Emperor had asked me to have his hair made into a bracelet for the Empress and a watch chain for his son. The operation was difficult; as the hair was short, it had to be placed end to end, and I had these assembled at home to ensure there would be no substitution. I also had gold lockets made in which I placed the Emperor's hair, and sent them to all the members of the imperial family: Madame Mère, his brothers, sisters, brothers-in-law, nephews, and nieces, as well as Cardinal Fesch. This wish had been expressed to me by the Emperor. The most flattering letters were sent back to me, bearing witness to the feelings that dictated them and honoring the hearts that wrote them; perhaps I shall include these at the end of this book.

The settlement of the estate was painfully slow, in spite of all Count de Montholon's efforts to remove the obstacles preventing its end. One last, sacred wish was left for me to fulfill; that of marrying a widow, sister, or daughter of an officer or soldier of the imperial guard. Count and Countess de Montholon, who have always demonstrated their kindness to me, said that they had found a charming young person for me who perfectly fulfilled the Emperor's wish, and would, they believed, "also be the choice of your own heart. Brought up in hardship, she is connected to a great German family on her mother's side; through her father, she brings you one of the most honorable names in the army: that of General Brayer; he heads the generals listed by the Emperor in his will. Does this suit you?" Countess de Montholon asked. "Madame," I said, "women are in a better position than men to judge what might suit us. As you have the goodness to take an interest in this marriage, it is because you have looked at it from all viewpoints, and you are almost certain that in ensuring Mlle de Brayer's happiness, you will also ensure mine. I now have but one fear; that of not pleasing her. The family knows me, you say, and she knows mine: I am too honored by this union not to accept it. Kindly assure Countess de Brayer that my life shall be entirely devoted to making her daughter happy."

This offer was made to me on July 15, 1823. On November 15, four months later, marriage was celebrated in the church of Notre-Dame-de-Lorette, in the faubourg Montmartre. It was filled with people, including many distinguished ones: the crowd was eager to see a marriage celebrated under the Emperor's auspices, the result of a wish he expressed on his deathbed in Saint Helena. Among the generals and high-ranking officers attending were: the Duke of Trévise (Mortier), Generals Montholon, Gourgaud, Ornano, Merlin, Meunier, Saint-Clair, who were all official witnesses. The organ had stopped playing, a graceful and pretty young girl, 17 years old, knelt on a prayer stool before the main altar, wrapped from head to toe in a lace veil, a rich present from Empress Marie-Louise. She waited quietly for the arrival of the venerable parish priest who was to bless her union. When he appeared, she rose to listen to a speech as simple as it was touching on the new duties imposed on her by marriage. That young lady, my dear Malvina, was Mathilde: she was your mother, this was my wedding being celebrated. I fervently promised the Lord, at the foot of his altar, to bring happiness to the angel of kindness and virtue whose destiny was entrusted to me.

Many years have passed since that time; if you were not here, my child, to remind me of the time so quickly gone, I would wonder how it passed, so perfectly and cloudless has my happiness remained.

Many times I have satisfied your wish to know the Emperor by answering your questions regarding this great man. It is in order to better teach you—and later, your children—what he meant to me that I leave you these recollections. It is to better show you the man who was the arbiter of kings, as great in adversity as on his throne when he commanded Europe; and to tell you of his resignation as he was dying on the rock of Saint Helena—kept there by the hatred of kings—dreaming of this beautiful France whose destiny he had abdicated, and giving his last breath for her, his son, and the army.

October 18, 1842
Marchand

The *Belle Poule* is sent from France under the command of the King's son to bring back Napoleon's remains.

Removing the Emperor's casket at Cherbourg to be taken to Paris.

The *Belle Poule*.

Belle Poule embarkation.

The funeral cortege of Napoleon in the Place de la Concorde December 15, 1840.

Napoleon's remains rest at the Invalides in Paris.

Although the building in Paris in which Louis-Joseph Marchand lived for many years at Number 5 Place du Palais-Bourbon has disappeared, its original facade remains.

The quarters of the Marchand family had this view of the Palais-Bourbon.

Appendix One

Proctor Jones

For some reason neither Marchand nor his editors included the British doctor's report of the autopsy. We include this documentation.

Sir Thomas Reade's report:

"St. Helena,
6th May, 1821

Sir,

Agreeable to your request, I proceeded to Longwood this morning, in order to attend at the opening of the body of General Bonaparte. Upon my arrival there I mentioned to Count Montholon that it was your desire that I should be present on the occasion, and also that I should be accompanied by Brigade-Major Harrison and the orderly officer. Count Montholon offered no objection whatever, but on the contrary said he thought it highly expedient and proper that some officer on the part of the Governor should attend. I accordingly proceeded with Brigade-Major Harrison and the orderly officer to the room where the body lay. There were present on the occasion Count Bertrand, Count Montholon, Signor Vignali, Marchand, Pierron and Ali (St. Denis), Dr. Shortt, Dr. Mitchell, Dr. Arnott, 20th Regiment, Dr. Burton, 66th Regiment, Mr. Henry, Assistant Surgeon 66th Regiment, Mr. Rutledge, Assistant Surgeon 20th Regiment, and (a part of the time) Mr. Livingstone, Surgeon in the East India Company's service. Professor Antommarchi was the operator.

During the first part of the operation nothing appeared to arrest the attention of the medical gentlemen except the extraordinary quantity of fat which covered almost every part of the interior, under the chest, but particularly about the heart, which was literally enveloped in fat.

Upon opening the lower part of the body where the liver lay, they found the stomach had adhered to the left side of the liver, in consequence of the stomach being very much diseased. The medical gentlemen immediately and unani-

mously expressed their conviction 'that the diseased state of the stomach was the sole cause of his death.' The stomach was taken out and exhibited to me. Two-thirds of it appeared in a horrible state covered with cancerous substances, and at a short distance from the pylorus there was a hole sufficient to admit a little finger through it.

The liver was afterwards examined. The moment the operator took it out Dr. Shortt instantly observed 'it was enlarged.' All the other medical gentlemen differed with him in this opinion, particularly Dr. Burton, who combated Dr. Shortt's opinion very earnestly. Dr. Henry was equally divided with Dr. Burton. Dr. Arnott said there was nothing extraordinary in the appearance of the liver, it might be a large one, but certainly not larger than the liver of any man of the same age as General Bonaparte. Dr. Mitchell said he saw nothing extraordinary, and Mr. Rutledge said it certainly was not enlarged. Notwithstanding all these observations, Dr. Shortt still persisted in saying 'it was enlarged.' This struck me so forcibly that I stepped forward and observed to the medical officers generally, that it appeared to me very important that they should all be prepared to give a decided and prompt opinion as to the real state of the liver, and I recommended a very careful re-examination of it. Dr. Shortt made no more observations, but all the other gentlemen reiterated their first opinion to me. At this moment the liver was in the hand of the operator, and upon my appearing desirous to see it close, he immediately took his knife and cut it open from one end to the other, observing to me, "It is good, perfectly sound, and nothing extraordinary in it." He observed at the same time that he thought it was a large liver. This opinion, however, did not appear to have been made in the manner as Dr. Shortt had expressed, viz. 'that the liver was enlarged.' There is a large difference between 'a large liver' and 'a liver being enlarged.' I made this observation to Dr. Burton and Dr. Arnott, who coincided.

After this I desired Dr. Shortt would give directions for the body being sewed up, and I requested it might be done previous to my leaving the room. Dr. Shortt desired Professor Antommarchi to do so. The Professor turned to Count Montholon and said something which I did not hear. The Count, however, came to me and took me aside. He said it was the particular wish of General Bonaparte that his heart should be preserved in order to its being sent to his wife, Maria Louisa. I informed Count Montholon that I had not received any particular directions upon the subject, and consequently I conceived it would be *proper to return the heart again into the body. He was, however, so exceedingly earnest in his request and pressed me so very hard, that I consented to leave the heart separate from the body until a reference could be made to you. It was accordingly put in a small silver cup and given in charge to Assistant Surgeon Rutledge, of the 20th Regiment, to whom I gave the most pointed orders that he was not to allow it out of sight until your directions should be received as to the disposal of it.*

Counts Bertrand and Montholon made no observation whatever upon the liver. The whole of the stomach was described and shown to them, and the medical gentlemen having told them 'that the diseased part of the stomach was the sole cause,' they expressed themselves perfectly satisfied.

I have the honour, etc.,

T. Reade

His Excellency

Lt.-General Sir Hudson Lowe, etc. etc. etc. "

The report of the British doctors:

"Longwood, St. Helena,
May 6, 1821

Report of appearances on dissection of the body of Napoleon Bonaparte.

On a superficial view the body appeared very fat, which state was confirmed by the first incision down its centre, where the fat was upwards of one inch thick over the sternum, and one inch and a half over the abdomen. On cutting through the cartilages of the thorax a trifling adhesion of the left pleura was found to the pleura costalis. About three ounces of reddish fluid were contained in the left cavity, and nearly eight ounces in the right.

The lungs were quite sound.

The pericardium was natural, and contained about an ounce of fluid.

The heart was of natural size, but thickly covered with fat. The auricles and ventricles exhibited nothing extraordinary, except that the muscular parts appeared rather paler than natural.

Upon opening the abdomen the omentum was found remarkably fat, and on exposing the stomach that viscus was found the seat of extensive disease, strong adhesions connected the whole superior surface, particularly about the pyloric extremity, to the concave surface of the left lobe of the liver, and on separating these an ulcer which penetrated the coats of the stomach was discovered one inch from the pylorus, sufficient to allow the passage of the little finger. The internal surface of the stomach to nearly its whole extent was a mass of cancerous disease or schirrous portions advancing to cancer; this was particularly noticed near the pylorus. The cardiac extremity for a small space near the termination of the esophagus was the only part appearing in a healthy state; the stomach was found nearly filled with a large quantity of fluid resembling coffee grounds.

The convex surface of the left lobe of the liver adhered to the diaphragm, and the liver was perhaps a little larger than natural. With the exception of the adhesions occasioned by the disease in the stomach no unhealthy appearance presented itself in the liver. The remainder of the abdominal viscera were in a healthy state. A slight peculiarity in the formation of the left kidney was observed.

Thomas Shortt, M.D., PHY. & P.M.O.
Arch. Arnott, M.D., Surgeon 20 Regt.
Charles Mitchell, M.D., Surgeon of H.M.S. Vigo.
Francis Burton, M.D., Surgeon 66 Regiment. "

Antommarchi, *The Last Moments of Napoleon*, 1825:

The spleen and liver were indurated, enlarged, and distended with blood. The texture of the liver, which was of a brownish red colour, did not, however, exhibit any remarkable alteration in structure. The gall bladder was filled and distended with very thick and clotted bile. The liver, which was affected by chronic hepatitis, closely adhered by its convex surface to the diaphragm; the adhesions occupied the whole extent of that organ, and were strong, cellular, and ancient...

The concave surface of the left lobe adhered closely and strongly to the corresponding part of the stomach; at every part of contact the lobe was sensible, thickened, swelled and hardened.

Appendix Two

Ben Weider, CM, Ph.D.

This extraordinary book was the "time bomb" that exposed the almost perfect crime.

All historians are in agreement that Marchand was an honourable and honest man. (See the preface for Jean Toulard's remarks.)

Scientific tests made by the Harwell Nuclear Research Laboratory of London, England and of the FBI, proved without a doubt what Marchand reported was indeed symptoms of arsenical poisoning and this poisoning was confirmed through nuclear science.

In a letter from the FBI signed by Roger M. Martz, Unit Chief Chemistry and Toxicology, who conducted nuclear tests on Napoleon's hair, he states: "The amount of arsenic present in the submitted hairs is consistent with arsenic poisoning."

It is well known that cancer is a wasting disease and if you will refer to the medical report made by Sir Thomas Reade on page 765, he confirms that Napoleon died fat. Furthermore, the Marquis Henri de Montchenu, who was appointed by Louis XVIII to represent France at St. Helena during the exile, also confirms this. Montchenu reported the day after Napoleon's death that "of the five doctors present at the autopsy, not one knows the exact cause of his death."

To ignore what Marchand wrote is to ignore history. The arsenical intoxication symptoms of Napoleon's illness as reported by Marchand was confirmed by nuclear science.

Bibliography

Henry Lachouque

INVENTORY OF THE LOWE PAPERS IN LONDON

Volumes 20115 à 20133.—Quatre-vingt volumes contenant des copies de la correspondance officielle de Hudson Lowe avec le gouvernement britannique, des officiers et autres personnalités de l'Ille.

Notes relatant les six conversations entre l'Empereur et le Gouverneur.

Notes sur la Garde de l'Empereur, 1816-1821.

Volumes 20135 à 20140.—Six volumes de lettres du "secretary of war " et autres personnalités officielles. 1816 à 1826.

Volume 20141. Correspondence de H. Lowe avec Las Cases, Bertrand, Gourgaud. 1816-1818.

Volumes 20142 à 20144.—Trois volumes. Conversations entre le Gouverneur, Napoléon, les officiers d'ordonnance, d'autres personnes. 1816-1821.

Volume 20145.—Correspondance entre H. Lowe et O'Meara et entra Gorrequer et O'Meara.

Volume 20146.—Notes relatives aux conversations entre H. Lowe et O'Meara. Lettres de O'Meara à Finlaison, conservateur des archives de l'amirauté. Rapport de O'Meara sur la maladie de l'Empereur et observations du Dr. Baxter.

Volumes 20147 à 20150.—Copies des lettres a écrites par H. Lowe aux Foreign Stations et à quelques habitants de l'Ille.

Volumes 20151 à 20153.—Correspondence entre H. Lowe et les commissaires étrangers.

Volume 20154.—Salaires des officiers et employés civils.

Volume 20155. Copies des dépositions des personnes soupçonnées d'entretenir des correspondances clandestines avec Napoléon. 1816-1819.

Volume 20156.—Bulletins de santé rédigés par Baxter et O'Meara.

Volume 20157.—Informations concernant la dernière maladie de l'Empereur (communications du Dr. Arnott).

Volume 20158.—Lettres ou documents concernant Longwood.

Volume 20159.—Instructions aux officiers commandant les gardes de Longwood.

Volume 20160.—Correspondance entre l'amiral Malcolm et Jos. Luson au sujet des traités passés even le Cap.

Volume 20161.—Liste des bateaux qui ont fait escale à Sainte Hélène de 1816 à 1821.

Volumes 20199 à 20202.—Lettres officielles de lord Bathurst, de sir Henry Goulburn, sous-secrétaire aux Colonies de 1812 à 1826 et de sir Henry Bunbury. 1816 à 1823.

Volume 20203.—Correspondance privée et officielle de H. Lowe et de Gorrequer avec les commissaires étrangers.

Volume 20204.—Soixante-treize lettres se rapportant à l'Empereur et à sa suite.

Volume 20205.—Lettres des amiraux Malcolm, Plampin et Lambert à H. Lowe, relatives à Sainte-Hélène.

Volume 20206.—Lettres originales de sir George Bingham et du général Pierre Coffin à H. Lowe, concernant les affaires de Sainte-Hélène.

Volume 20207.—Lettres des sir Thomas Reade et du major G. Gorrequer à H. Lowe.

Volume 20208.—Lettres des officiers d'ordonnance stationnés à Longwood. Poppleton, Blakeney, Lyster à H. Lowe et major Gorrequer.

Volume 20209.—Lettres du capitaine Nicholls, officier d'ordonnance à Longwood, adressées à H. Lowe.

Volume 20210.—Journal du, capitaine Nicholls.

Volume20211.—Lettres du capitaine Lutyens officier d'ordonnance à Longwood, publiées en1919.

Volume20212.—Les rapports hebdomadaires du capitaine Nicholls.

Volume 20213,—Lettres des Révérends, Boys et Vernon à H. Lowe,Reade et Gorrequer.

Volume 20214.—Lettres de Reade à Gorrequer Lettres de Baxter, O'Meara, Verling, Antommarchi, Arnott à Gorrequer et à H. Lowe.

Rapport officiel de l'autopsie de Napoléon singé par les cinq médecins anglais; le Rapport du Dr. Henry; critique du Dr. Antommarchi par Ruthledge.

Volume 20215.—Extraits de conversations entre H. Lowe et différentes personnalités.

Volume 20216 et 20217.—Lettres d'OMeara à Jos. Finlaison.

Volume 20218.- Documents relatant les griefs d'O'Meara contre le Gouverneur.

Volumes 20223 à 20240.—Documents, lettres, papiers relatifs aux officiers résidant à Sainte-Hélène, au mobilier de Longwood, aux affaires de Cap, etc.

PUBLICATIONS

ANONYME, *Carnet d'un voyageur ou recueil de notes curieuses sur la vie, les occupations, les habitudes de Buonaparte à Longwood.*

ABELL (Mrs. Lucia, Élisabeth), *Napoléon à Sainte-Hélène.*

ADVIELLE (Victor), *la Bibliothèque de Napoléon à Sainte-Hélène.*

LE MAMELUK ALI (Saint-Denis), *Souvenirs.*

ANTOMMARCHI (Dr.), *Mémoires.*—*Derniers moments de Napoléon.*

AUBRY (Octave), *Sainte-Hélène.*

COMTE DE BALMAIN, *Mission de Sainte-Hélène.* 1817. Correspondance officielle.

BARTHE, *Réfutation de la relation officielle du capitaine Maitland.*

BERTRAND (général), *Cahiers de Sainte-Hélène présentés et annotés* par Paul Fleuriot de Langle. Janvier 1821, mai 1821 et 1816-1817.

BORJANE (Henry), *Napoléon à bord du* Northumberland.

CABANÉS (Dr.), *Au chevet de l'Empereur.*

CAHUET (Albéric), *Après la mort de l'Empereur.*

-*Napoléon délivré.*

CHAPLIN (Arnold), *A Saint-Helena Who's who.*

CHERFILS (Christian), *Bonaparte et l'Islam.*

ESPITALIER (Albert), *Antommarchi était-il médecin?*

—*Le Chirurgien Emery et le gantier Dumoulin.*

—*Un missionnaire de Sainte-Hélène: le chef d'escadron Piontkowski.*

FIRMIN DIDOT, *la Captivité de Sainte-Hélène*, d'après les rapports inédits du marques de Montchenu.

FLEURIOT DE LANGLE (Paul), *Napoléon et son geôlier.*

FRÉMEAUX (Paul), *les Derniers jours de l'Empereur.*

—*Napoléon prisonnier.*

—*Dans le chambre de Napoléon mourant.*

GANIÈRE (Paul), *Corvisart.*

GONNARD (Philippe), *les Origines de la légende napoléonienne; l'œvre historique de Napoléon à Sainte-Hélène.*

GOURGAUD (le général baron), *Journal inédit.*

GRASSET-MOREI, *les Bonaparte à Montpellier.*

HAUTERIVE (Ernest D'), *Sainte-Hélène.*

—*Les Femmes à Sainte-Hélène.*

—*Dernières conversations de Sainte-Hélène, etc.*

HUDSON LOWE (Mémorial de), 1830.

ISOLA (Maria Dell'), *Sainte-Hélène, Pauline et le Vatican.* (Revue de l'Institut Napoléon, 4ᵉ trimestre 1939.)

JACKSON (lieutenant-colonel Basil), *Waterloo et Sainte-Hélène* par R.C. Seaton. M.A. traduit de l'anglais par Em. Brouwet.

LAS CASES (comte De), *le Mémorial de Sainte-Hélène* par Marcel Dunant de l'Institut.

MALCOLM (lady), *Journal.* Traduction de Mme Léon Raynal. (Revue de Études napoléoniennes 1931, II, 2-3-4-5.

MASSELIN (capitaine), *Sainte-Hélène.*

MASSON (Frédéric), *Napoléon à Sainte-Héléne.*

—*Autour de Sainte-Héléne.*

MANGUIN (Georges), *le Napoléon de Sainte-Hélène*

MONTHOLON (comtesse De), *Souvenirs de Sainte-Hélène.*

MONTHOLON (général De), les *Souffrances de Napoléon.*

—*Lettres du comte et de la comtesse de Montholon.*

—*Récits de la captivité de l'empereur Napoléon à Saint-Hélène.*

O'MEARA (Barry), *Relation des énvénements arrivés àSainte-Héléne postéurieurement à la nomination d'Hudson Lowe.*

—*Napoléon en exil.*

PARDEE (M.A.), *Sainte-Hélène.*

PARISOT, *Relation du capitaine Maitland, ex-commandant du Bellérophon.*

—*Recueil de pièces authentiques sur le captif de Sainte-Hélène.*

ROSEBERRY (lord), *Napoléon. La dernière phase.*

SAINT-CÈRE et H. SCHLITTER, *Napoléon à Sainte-Hélène.*

—*Rapports officiels du baron Stürmer, commissaire du gouvernement autrichien.*

SENTINI (sic) (Mr.), *Napoléon à Sainte-Hélène.*

SANTINI (Noël), *Sainte-Hélène. Le Tombeau de l'Empereur.*

—*De Sainte-Hélène aux Invalides.*

VIEL CASTEL (L. De), *Sir Hudson Lowe et la Captivité de Sainte-Hélène.*

One can easily say that the news of the death of the Emperor, heard in Paris at the start of July 1821, went virtually unnoticed and left the public indifferent.

One relies on the hundred of brochures for or against Napoleon published during the months of July, August, and September 1821. Often anonymous or signed by initial, not revealing the editor's names and carrying only: "On sale at the bookstores."

"It's raining brochures on Paris, since one learned of the death of Napoleon," cried Contant Taillard. "They cover the boutiques of Paris Royal."

Here are some of the titles:

GOUJON (Alexandre, ancien capitain d'artillerie), *Pensées d'un soldat sur la sépulture de Napoléon.*

BERTON (général), *Lettre au baron Mounier, derecteur général de la police, sur la mort de Napoléon.*

PIQUOT (L.), *Encore un mot sur Napoléon.*

E. F., *Sentiments d'un citoyen sur les cancers héréditaires.*

MORGAS (lady), *Encore une victime.*

ANONYME, *Pensées de braves sur les hauts faits de Napoléon.*

SANS-GÊNE, *les Dix-neuf cancer.*

UN BONHOMME DE LETTRES, *les Coliques et les cancers.*

UN AMI DE LA PATRIE, *Il n'est pas mort.*

ANONYME, *Napoléon et la reine d'Angleterre au bord du Styx.*

GRAND (P.), *le Cri de la France.*

A.M., *Un patriote, aux braves.*

M.P**. A., *le Coucher du soleil du 5 mai 1821.*

M.B., *l'Ombre de Napoléon au Conseil des ministres.*

Index

WRITTEN BY DR. KYLE O. EIDAHL

Also available from Greenhill Books

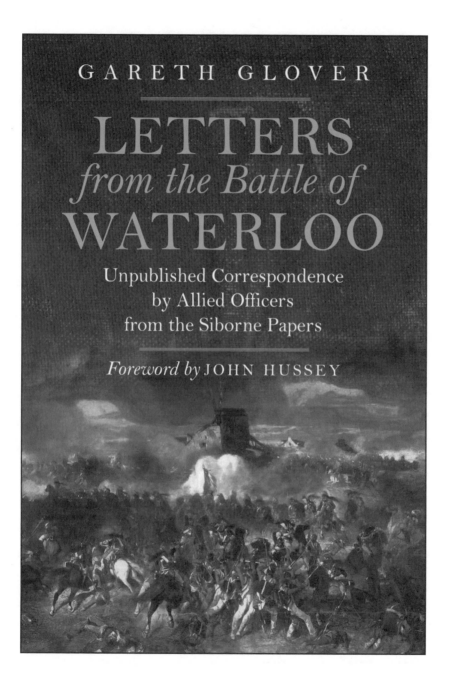

GARETH GLOVER

LETTERS
from the Battle of
WATERLOO

Unpublished Correspondence
by Allied Officers
from the Siborne Papers

Foreword by JOHN HUSSEY

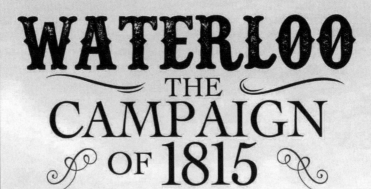

WATERLOO

THE CAMPAIGN

OF 1815

VOLUME I

FROM ELBA TO LIGNY
AND QUATRE BRAS

JOHN HUSSEY
FOREWORD BY HEW STRACHAN

'It will be decades before this book is superseded as the best account
of those extraordinary events of 1815.' ANDREW ROBERTS

WATERLOO

~ THE ~
CAMPAIGN
~ OF 1815 ~

VOLUME 2

FROM WATERLOO TO THE
RESTORATION OF PEACE IN EUROPE

JOHN HUSSEY
FOREWORD BY MUNGO MELVIN

SUNDAY, 18TH JUNE 1815

NAPOLEON VICTORIOUS

An Alternative History of the Battle of Waterloo

The Battle of Waterloo

YOU Sons of Britain list awhile,
To deeds of valiant ame,
Brave Wellington has added one,
More laurel to his name.

CHORUS.

His mighty arm with Blucher join'd
Has made proud Boney yield;
And after a long fierce raging fight
To fly the crimson field,
Brave Wellington, &c,

At more by ten, the British force,
Began the dreadful fight;
Continued with most vengeful heat,
By both till darksome night.
Brave Wellington, &c.

Three hundred captive cannons show,
Our Victory's complete.
While Boney's Eagle crouching low.
Now kiss our Regent's feet,
Brave Wellington, &c,

For our brave men who nobly died,
Let Pity's tear be shed,
Relieve their hapless widow's wants
And give their orphan bread,
Brave Wellington &c,

PETER G. TSOURAS

JOHN H. GILL

WITH EAGLES
TO GLORY

NAPOLEON AND
HIS GERMAN ALLIES IN
THE 1809 CAMPAIGN